(126)

are writ down before them with Chalk *on a* Table. 6.
 	
   Some fit at a Table, and write : 7.
he mendeth 8.
their Faults.
 	
   *Some ftand and rehearfe things committed to memory.*9.
 	
   Some talk together, 10.
and behave themfelves wantonly, and carelefly ;
thefe are chaftifed with a Ferrula, 11.
and a Rod. 12.
	præ___
	in t___
	
	   Quidam fedent ad menfam, & fcribunt : 7.
	ipfe corrigit 8.
	Mendas
	
	   Quidam ftant, & recitant memoriæ mandata. 9.
	
	   Quidam confabulantur, 10
	ac gerunt fe petulantes,
	& negligentes
	hi caftigantur *Ferula* (baculo) 11.
	& *Virga.* 12.

The Study.	XCVIII.	*Mufeum.*

The Study 1. *is a place where a* Student 2. *apart from Men,*	*Mufeum* 1. eft locus ubi ftudiofus, 2. fecretis ab hominibus, fitteth

Johann Amos Comenius from Orbis Sensualium Pictus (1658)

Prologue to TEACHING

READINGS AND SOURCE MATERIALS WITH TEXT

MARJORIE B. SMILEY
Hunter College

JOHN S. DIEKHOFF
Western Reserve University

New York • OXFORD UNIVERSITY PRESS • *1959*

© 1959 BY OXFORD UNIVERSITY PRESS, INC.

Library of Congress Catalogue Card Number: 59-10032

Second Printing, 1960

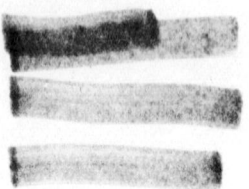

PRINTED IN THE UNITED STATES OF AMERICA

Preface

Prologue to Teaching began when the editors took part in a revision of the curriculum in teacher education at Hunter College of the City of New York. Dissatisfied with attempts to introduce prospective teachers to the social and ethical dimensions of education through textbook accounts of the history and philosophy of education, we undertook to identify major issues which have confronted teachers now and in the past. These issues—the role and character of the teacher, who should be educated, the aims of education, and the relation of the school to other educative agencies such as the family and the church—provided the substance of the introductory course in the new curriculum and became the basis of this collection of readings. The intent of *Prologue to Teaching* is to bring the student face to face with different, indeed conflicting, views on these questions, and by discussion foster his professional orientation.

Although these readings were designed for a first course, they should be equally appropriate for a culminating course in a teacher education program. At whatever point it is used, the book provides varied and vital material for study and for classroom discussion. The introductory essays preceding each of the four sections highlight some questions for discussion. Other questions will undoubtedly grow out of the special interests of the instructor and the students.

Prologue to Teaching makes no attempt to provide a systematic overview of the history of education. In general, the readings are arranged thematically, and within this framework chronologically. Where chronology is ignored, it is to bring side by side materials that bear directly on one another. Each of the four major divisions is a unit in itself. The four parts may be read in any order; in practice different instructors using the experimental edition of the book have followed different sequences with equally good results.

Some texts reprinted are modernized. They are identified in the bibliographical notes. For the most part original spelling and punctuation have been retained, even though they are sometimes internally inconsistent.

ACKNOWLEDGMENTS

We owe thanks to many people. The Department of Education of Hunter College and the Division of Teacher Education of the Municipal Colleges of the City of New York have encouraged and supported the project. Mrs. Maud Cole, librarian in the Rare Book Division of the New York Public Library, was extremely helpful in the search for old textbooks from which facsimile pages were prepared. Arthur Goldzweig, assistant librarian at Hunter College, located and verified numerous original texts. Florence Christman, secretary of the Office of Institutional Research at Hunter College, has been a continuous help in the preparation of the manuscript and the securing of permissions. Mrs. Mary Houston Davis of Finch College has shown a sustaining interest in the selection of readings and in discussions of the text. Mrs. John S. Diekhoff has been a helpful critic, particularly in editorial matters. Colleagues and students at Hunter College have suggested revisions of the experimental edition of the readings—revisions that have improved the book.

Finally, we wish to thank the individuals, organizations, and publishers whose permission to use materials has made *Prologue to Teaching* possible: Mortimer J. Adler, Henry Steele Commager, C. H. Dobinson, Margaret Mead, George L. Miller, Joseph Ratner, Harold Rugg; The American Institute of Architects, The American Academy of Political and Social Science, The American Legion, The Board of Education of the City of New York, The Fund for the Advancement of Education, The Journal of General Education, the National Education Association, the National Congress of Parents and Teachers, the Progressive Education Association, the Russell Sage Foundation, the Society for Cultural Relations with the USSR (London), Science Research Associates, the State of Florida Department of Education, the Yale-Fairfield Study; The Catholic University of America Press, The University of Chicago Press, the University of Illinois Press, New York University Press; American Book Company, Charles H. Kerr & Company, Doubleday & Company, E. P. Dutton & Company, Follett Publishing Company, Harcourt, Brace and Company, Harper & Brothers, Henry Holt and Company, The John Day Company, John Wiley & Sons, J. B. Lippincott Company, The Macmillan Company, McGraw-Hill Book Company, William Morrow & Company, W. W. Norton & Company, Rand McNally & Company, Random House, and Simon and Schuster.

M. B. S.
J. S. D.

Contents

INTRODUCTION—WHAT'S PAST IS PROLOGUE, xiii

Part 1

THE VOCATION OF TEACHING, 3
Readings:

THE TEACHER AS A PERSON

Quintilian	*The Teacher*	40
Thomas Fuller	*The Good Schoolmaster*	42
Johann Heinrich Pestalozzi	*Their Hands Were in Mine*	45
Samuel Read Hall	*Requisite Qualifications of Teachers*	47
Louis Henry Sullivan	*The Taskmaster*	50
B. P. Yesipov and N. K. Goncharov	*The Authority of the Teacher*	56
Karl Menninger	*Love Against Hate*	57
Herbert A. Thelen	*The Picture in Our Minds*	60

HIS PROFESSIONAL FUNCTIONS

Tasks of a Teacher		65
Jean-Baptiste de la Salle	*Things to Which the Teachers Must Attend*	67
Clyde Milton Hill	*Teachers' Activities in Grade One*	68
Nathaniel Cantor	*Function of the Teacher*	72
NEA Code of Ethics		79

HIS SOCIAL AND ECONOMIC STATUS

Plato	*The Gadfly*	84
A New Jersey Schoolmaster's Oath, 1777		86
A Protest Against Oaths by the Society Called Quakers, 1779		87

Contents

The Feinberg Decision, 1952		89
Frederic W. Terrien	Who Thinks What About Educators?	96
Beardsley Ruml and Sidney O. Tickton	Teaching Salaries Then and Now	110

HIS EDUCATION AND CERTIFICATION

William A. Alcott	They Wrote Me a Certificate	113
Henry Barnard	The First State Normal School	115
William James	Talks to Teachers on Psychology	117
W. Earl Armstrong and T. M. Stinnett	Minimum Requirements for Lowest Regular Teaching Certificates	122

Part 2

SCHOOLING FOR ALL, 127

Readings:

BEGINNINGS IN THE EAST

A Massachusetts Bay Law of 1642	154
A Grant of Land for Schools, Dedham, Massachusetts, 1643	155
The Old Deluder, Satan—a Massachusetts Bay Law of 1647	155

BEGINNINGS IN THE SOUTH

The Will of Benjamin Syms, 1634	157
The Legislature Confirms the Will, 1642	158
Propagating the Xtian Knowledge	158
Prohibition Against Teaching Slaves in South Carolina to Write, 1740	159

AMERICAN STATESMEN ON EDUCATION

Thomas Jefferson	To Diffuse Knowledge More Generally	160
Benjamin Franklin	To Qualify Those Restored to Freedom	163
	A Petition of the Left Hand	164
George Washington	The Time Is Come	165
De Witt Clinton	No Privileged Orders	166

EARLY LEGISLATION AFTER THE UNION

Early Constitutional Provisions	174
Georgia Makes Aliens of Those Who Study Abroad, 1785	175
First Constitution of Indiana, 1816	175

Contents vii

The Debate on Public Education in the 1830's

Public Education and Pauperism	177
Equality Only in Custody?	180
The Mechanic Must Labor	182
Why Should the Propertied Classes Pay?	182
Gross Injustice in Some of Our Manufactories Exposed	184

The Education of Negroes in Boston Before the Civil War

Resolution of Boston Negroes Against Segregated Schools	185
Report on the Smith School	186

Toward Universal Schooling

First Morrill (Land-Grant) Act, 1862		188
School Committee Report for the City of Framingham, Massachusetts		189
L. Van Bokkelen	Compulsory Education	190
The Kalamazoo Decision, 1874		196
Effects of the Compulsory Education Act in New York City		202
Ben R. Lindsey	Child Reform Through Education for a Trade	203
The Oregon Decision, 1921		204
W. L. Warner, Havighurst, and Loeb	The Sorting Machine	207
The Desegregation Decision, 1954		213
Herold C. Hunt	Education for All, Do We Mean It?	218
Rockefeller Report	Excellence in a Democracy	223

Part 3

THE PURPOSES OF EDUCATION, 227

Readings:

Formulations and Discussions

Harold Benjamin	Saber-Tooth Curriculum	254
Aristotle on Education		261
Plutarch	Lycurgus of Sparta	265
John Amos Comenius	Instruction for the Present and the Future Life	269
Benjamin Franklin	Proposals Relating to the Education of Youth in Pennsylvania	273
Johann Heinrich Pestalozzi	Education for the Different Classes	281

Contents

Friedrich Froebel	The Education of Man	282
Horace Mann	The Business of the Schoolroom Is the Interests of Society	284
Herbert Spencer	What Knowledge Is Most Worth?	294
Booker T. Washington	Cast Down Your Bucket Where You Are!	305
Commission on the Reorganization of Secondary Education, NEA	Cardinal Principles of Secondary Education	307
The Nebraska Decision		313
Pope Pius XI	Encyclical Letter on Christian Education of Youth	316
John Dewey	Aims in Education	320
Boyd H. Bode	The Concept of Needs in Education	328
Educational Policies Commission, National Education Assn.	The Purposes of Education in American Democracy	332
B. P. Yesipov and N. K. Goncharov	Character Education	334
Mortimer J. Adler	Labor, Leisure, and Liberal Education	336
Nolan C. Kearney	Elementary School Objectives—"Primary Period"	342
Arthur E. Bestor	The School and the Practical Needs of Youth	346
Report of the Committee for the White House Conference on Education		350

Illustrations

Arthur I. Gates	The Curriculum (1932)	357

The Language Arts

S. A. Mitchell	English: The Leading Language (1868)	359
Lou LaBrant et al.	Languages of the World (1956)	360
Lindley Murray	Address to Young Students (1825)	363
Lou LaBrant et al.	The Term Begins (1956)	364
Johann Amos Comenius	The First Pictured Alphabet for Children (1700)	366
The New England Primer	A Primer for Piety	367
Campbell and Dunn	A Logical Beginning (1864)	368
Bailey and Horrocks	Beginning with the Child's Experience	369

Contents

THE SOCIAL STUDIES

Jean Jacques Rousseau	*How Emile Learns Geography* (1762)	370
Nathaniel Dwight	*Geography of the World* (1807)	373
Jedidiah Morse	*That Useful Science, Geography* (1804)	376
J. E. Worcester	*The Science of History* (1834)	378
Emma Willard	*Causes of the Revolutionary War* (1851)	381
R. W. Cordier and E. B. Robert	*The Stamp Tax* (1954)	383
Mrs. M. B. Moore	*This Sad War* (1864)	385
	Old Aunt Ann (1864)	386
Noah Webster	*Story of the Treatment of African Slaves* (1790)	386
Charles F. Horne	*Asiatic Immigration First Brought a New Problem* (1925)	388
McGuffey's *New Eclectic Primer*	*American Education Comes to Japan* (1871)	389
Harold Rugg	*Why Do Our Laws Forbid the Immigration of Laborers from China and Japan . . . ?* (1926)	390
National Education Association, Educational Policies Commission	*Students Discuss the Constitutional Rights of Those Who Oppose Democracy* (1940)	391
To the Teachers of Modern History in the USSR (1958)		393

MATHEMATICS AND SCIENCE

Plato	*Socrates Elicits a Geometric Theorem from a Slave Boy*	395
Charles DeGarmo	*The Number Three* (1892)	399
Edward Brooks	*Arithmetical Language* (1877)	400
Clifford B. Upton	*Seeing and Counting* (1958)	401
Victor C. Smith and Barbara Henderson	*Studying Science in Fifth Grade* (1956)	402
Howard E. Wilson et al.	*Early Man* (1954)	402
Fred Turner and Sara de Keni	*Comparison of Science Topics in Schools in Florida and the Soviet Union* (1958)	406

EDUCATION FOR LIFE ADJUSTMENT

Noah Webster	*Adjustment to an Agricultural Economy* (1790)	408

Contents

Benjamin Rush	*Exercises Subservient to Future Employments* (1790)	409
Alta McIntire et al.	*Third Grade Clothing Projects for Public and Parochial School Children* (1957)	410
Board of Education, City of New York	*Adjusting to a New Culture* (1958)	412
E. Montaissoff	*Topics for Rural Elementary Grades, USSR* (1953)	413
Adolescents Study Themselves (1958)		413

EDUCATION IN MORAL AND SPIRITUAL VALUES

City of New York, Report of Superintendent of Schools	*"To Beget a Love of Order and Propriety"* (1855)	414
Mrs. M. B. Moore	*The Face* (1864)	415
Richard M. Smith	*The Honest Indian* (1864)	416
National Education Association, Educational Policies Commission	*Sanctions* (1951)	417
Soviet of People's Commissars of the RSFSR	*Rules for School Children* (1943)	420
Baltimore County, Maryland	*The American Pupil's Creed* (1958)	421

STUDENT EVALUATION

An Eighth Grader Writes a Letter of Self-Evaluation (1958)		422
Wantagh Schools, Long Island	*Reporting Pupil Diligence at Home and at School* (1918)	423
William M. Stewart School, University of Utah	*Evaluating Pupil Growth* (1958)	424

Part 4

THE SCHOOL IN CONTEXT, 427
Readings:

GROWING UP IN TWO CULTURES

Margaret Mead	*Growing Up in New Guinea*	466
Geoffrey Gorer	*The All-American Child*	480

EDUCATION AND THE FAMILY

Marcus Aurelius Antoninus	*From These I Learned*	492
Martin Luther	*Letter to the Mayors and Aldermen of All the Cities of Germany*	494

Contents   xi

Johann Heinrich Pestalozzi	*Home! Thou School of Morals and of the State!*	496
	Christopher and Alice	497
C. Kegan Paul	*Who Is the Proper Judge?*	499
William Oland Bourne	*An Address*	501
Karl Marx and Frederick Engels	*Manifesto of the Communist Party*	504
U.S. Office of Education	*Preschool Education in Russia*	505

RELIGION AND EDUCATION

Rules of a School in St. Augustine, Florida, 1786		507
John Dewey	*The Schools and Religions*	509
Pope Pius XI	*Encyclical Letter on Christian Education of Youth*	518
The Released Time Decision, 1952		530

COMMUNICATIONS AND EDUCATION

Plato	*On the Stories Children Hear*	535
David Riesman et al.	*Storytellers as Tutors*	537

EDUCATION AND THE SOCIAL ORDER

Alexis de Tocqueville	*Of the Use Which the Americans Make of Public Associations in Civil Life*	556
William H. Whyte, Jr.	*The Organization Man and His Schools*	558
Willard Waller	*The School and the Community*	565
C. H. Dobinson	*English and Russian Education Contrasted*	567
Henry Steele Commager	*The Conscience of Society*	576

Are you he who would assume a place to teach or be a poet here in the States?

The place is august, the terms obdurate.

Who would teach here may well prepare himself body and mind,

He may well survey, ponder, arm, fortify, harden, make lithe himself,

He shall surely be question'd beforehand by me with many and stern questions.

Who are you indeed who would talk or sing to America?

Have you studied out the land, its idioms and men?

Have you learn'd the physiology, phrenology, politics, geography, pride, freedom, friendship of the land? its substratums and objects?

Have you consider'd the organic compact of the first day of the first year of Independence, sign'd by the Commissioners, ratified by the States, and read by Washington at the head of the Army?

Have you possess'd yourself of the Federal Constitution?

Do you see who have left all feudal processes and poems behind them, and assumed the poems and processes of Democracy?

Are you faithful to things? do you teach what the land and sea, the bodies of men, womanhood, amativeness, heroic angers, teach?

Have you sped through fleeting customs, popularities?

Can you hold your hand against all seductions, follies, whirls, fierce contentions? are you very strong? are you really of the whole People?

Are you not of some coterie? some school or mere religion?

Are you done with reviews and criticisms of life? animating now to life itself?

Have you vivified yourself from the maternity of these States?

Have you too the old ever-fresh forbearance and impartiality?

Do you hold like love for those hardening into maturity? for the last-born? little and big? and for the errant?

WALT WHITMAN,
By Blue Ontario's Shore

Introduction—What's Past Is Prologue

The five- or six-year-old entering a classroom for the first time, the newly appointed teacher assembling roll book and teaching materials for his first lesson, and the student starting his first course in a program that will qualify him to teach are all encountering situations that have the excitement of the new and unexplored. For the child, the teacher, and the student, nothing exactly like this experience has ever happened. These are moments when the sense of here, now, in this time, in this place is vividly present. But in each instance the present is what it is because of what has gone before. The school itself, the child's free—and compelled—attendance, the character of the textbooks, the very existence of a special program for the prospective teacher, all these have their roots in a past which has helped to shape them.

The value of historical perspective. The man or woman who is seriously considering a career of teaching has usually been much interested in current educational practices and questions. He has probably noticed more and thought more than the average layman about the quality of teaching to which he has himself been exposed, the curriculum he has passed through, and the debates in the press and on the air dealing with education. Part of the prospective teacher's development from a more than usually interested layman to a person of professional competence, however, is learning to view these matters in historical perspective. The layman often views a particular educational practice as a peculiarly modern phenomenon; his criticisms may be distorted by the half light emanating from sentimentalized notions of "the good old days." One of the obligations of the teacher is to bring to discussions of educational questions the temperance derived from more extensive and more accurate knowledge of their origins and history.

What aims and what subjects ought to have priority in education is a question much discussed today. Critics of utilitarianism and vocationalism in modern high school and college curricula sometimes attack this emphasis as the result of recent maneuvers foisted on an unwilling public by professional educators. In fact, utility as a criterion in determining the aims and content of education is anything but a recent innovation. Usefulness in preparing the young to discharge their civic obligations, both in war and in peace, has been a justification for including in the curriculum gymnastics, history, hygiene, foreign languages, and physics, depending on the educational setting: fifth-century Athens, colonial America, nineteenth-century England, or the U.S.S.R. The chief liberal arts subjects in today's colleges constituted in the medieval university a curriculum essentially professional in intent. Most subjects can be, and many have been taught for liberal and for vocational purposes. Vocational subjects and utilitarian aims have long had widespread public support.

The inclusion of new and highly technical subjects like typing in the modern curriculum will not surprise those who know something of the amount of time and the degree of importance given to penmanship in an earlier period. To those who are informed about the changes in the United States high school population over the past three-quarters of a century, statistics showing a decline in the proportion of high school students enrolled in science courses have a very different meaning than to those who see only this year's figures.

Of course, whether a particular educational aim or practice is of ancient or recent origin does not determine its merit and does not justify its adoption or rejection. Neither Benjamin Franklin's advocacy of education for trade—and his probable enthusiasm for instruction in typing had such a machine been in use in his time—nor Aristotle's cautions against subverting education to slavish ends, decides today's educational priorities for us. But today's debate is illuminated and sharpened when those who participate in it have some knowledge of past as well as of present arguments and conditions. Decisions made in such perspective may be wise rather than merely expedient.

For the teacher, acquaintance with the origins and developments of the educational system in which he teaches, and with the growth of the teaching profession in scholarship as well as in size gives him a sense of participating in an endeavor serious and of a certain magnitude. Having gained such a background of our educational enterprise, the teacher may be the more impelled to work for its continuing improvement. The layman is likely to take public education from kindergarten through college for granted. The student of history knows something of the bitter opposition and litigation, something of the long struggle of the American people to make education free and to extend it through the university.

Introduction—What's Past Is Prologue

The plan of the book. This collection of readings includes earlier counterparts of a number of contemporary educational practices, legislation, and opinion. But it is not, despite the editors' belief in the value of historical perspective, a history of education. In the main it is not even chronological in its organization. The readings have been selected to develop and illustrate four topics, each of which has been of perennial concern in the field of education: the character, tasks and education of the teacher; the extent and justifications of state-supported education; the purposes of education; the relation of education to the social order and to other agencies of society. Among these readings there are historic documents such as laws, contracts, and judicial decisions. There are examples of lesson plans and pages from children's school books. There is a report of a poll of public opinion of teachers and there are tables of teachers' average salaries. The greater part of the readings, however, are "opinion pieces" chosen to present a wide range of views on these four topics. The observant reader will conclude that the editors had other purposes than that of providing a background in educational history.

They think it desirable for students of education, as of any subject, to become familiar with primary materials. Too often prospective teachers read about Plato or Pestalozzi, Horace Mann or John Dewey but do not read anything written by these writers themselves. Even in a brief excerpt something of the flavor of a man's thinking can be captured. No description of the Socratic method gives the sense of the process as well as does a reading of even a portion of the *Dialogues*. The strength and also the weakness of the method are more evident to one who follows the series of questions by which Socrates endeavors to lead Meno's untutored slave to "recall" the Pythagorean theorem than to one who has only read accounts of the process.

Any outline history of education will report the influence of men like Pestalozzi and Horace Mann on the methods and organization of modern education. But it is through reading the work of these men themselves that the reader catches something of the deeply felt enthusiasm and dedication that gave their beliefs such potency. The teacher who espouses and the teacher who rejects the methods attributed to Dewey should know these recommendations as they were formulated by the man himself rather than through the interpretations and frequent misinterpretations of his followers. Teachers will hear that Dewey (following in the tradition of Fuller, Rousseau, and Pestalozzi) held that children's interests and readiness are central in the teaching-learning process. They should know through first-hand familiarity with his writing in what context this principle was defended and how Dewey related it to his concern for organized subject matter. Of course, these selections do no more than introduce the reader to these and other writers on education; the interested student will wish to supplement this beginning by more extended reading.

Each of the four sets of readings that comprise the core of the book is preceded by an introductory essay. These, too, exemplify a fundamental concern of the editors. Each of these essays undertakes to raise a series of questions relevant to its topic. Each calls on the reader for a somewhat different kind of participation. The first, "The Vocation of Teaching," asks the reader to make personal applications of what he reads: to ask himself, "How do I see myself as a teacher?" "What satisfactions and what limitations will I find in teaching?" "How can I best prepare myself to teach?"

The second essay, "Schooling for All," and its accompanying readings make a quite different demand upon the reader. Here he is asked first to look chronologically at the growth of the system of universal, free, compulsory education that is a distinctive feature of the American way of life. He is called upon for a kind of historical imagination to fill out from the clues presented in the readings a picture of the schooling of earlier days. He is introduced to some evidences of the political, economic, and humanitarian forces that were engaged in what some historians have termed a national controversy second in intensity and significance only to the controversy over slavery. He is asked to consider thoughtfully current criticisms of the educational system: that even today education is not really "universal," that too many are educated too long, that the intellectually gifted are not adequately served.

"The Purposes of Education" brings the reader to what many conceive to be the central debate in education. To what end are schools established, teachers educated, and children compelled to learn? The reader will find that the educational enterprise has been at various times justified as essential to the welfare of the state, as a means of bringing men to an understanding of God, and as a way of realizing man's fullest potentialities. The reader will discover that each of these positions is not merely a historic one, but that all still have their advocates. He will begin to sense what subsequent more systematic study of philosophies of education may clarify: that each of these ends stems from distinctive ideas of the nature of man, the sources of knowledge and the learning process, and the qualities of the good life. As subject and as prospective agent the reader is asked to weigh alternative educational purposes and to begin to consider priorities among them.

In the last section of the book, "The School in Context," the reader is asked to turn from his close-up views of education and to look at the school from the viewpoint of the social scientists. The readings in this section serve as reminders that formal schooling is only one phase of the complicated process by which the young are prepared to live in society and that

Introduction—What's Past Is Prologue

the results of this process differ fundamentally in different cultures. Here also, the reader is faced with a series of questions and problems. What limits on the school are set by the interests and educational effects of other agencies of society? To what extent do the prerogatives of the family and the church have priority over those of the state or the school? Is conflict among these agencies inevitable in a pluralistic, secularized society? Is the modern school undertaking more than it should? Can the school change the social order, or is it inescapably its creature?

Learning is inquiring. These four essays and the accompanying readings repeatedly confront the reader with questions. Furthermore, the questions posed are not those that can be answered on the basis of facts alone. In most instances they are questions for which there are no definitive, universally accepted answers. Even after all the facts pertaining to these questions are in, the answers to them will be made in the light of the inquirer's governing values. Systematic surveys may, for example, convincingly demonstrate that a sizable proportion of young people capable of further education drop out of high school for economic reasons. But the facts themselves do not dictate the answer to the question: how much schooling should be provided at public expense? There is a serious shortage of high school teachers of science and mathematics. The U.S.S.R., according to the 1957 Office of Education report, solves this problem by assigning the necessary number of university graduates to teaching posts. Is this a "good" answer? is it an acceptable answer for us? Even if there were conclusive evidence linking inaccurate knowledge of sex and unwholesome attitudes toward it with physical and psychological ills, the decision to include or ban sex education in schools could not be made on this evidence alone. In brief, the questions and problems posed throughout this book are not primarily matters of fact but matters of judgment. And necessarily so, because education, a social phenomenon, is essentially a moral enterprise. Replete with alternatives, it requires all who are concerned in it to make value judgments. Often these judgments are made without due recognition of possible alternatives or on the basis of unexamined predilections. One of the purposes of this book is to call attention to alternatives and to encourage responsible consideration of them. The reader at the beginning of his study of education may feel ill-equipped to decide among these alternatives, but the making of tentative choices and their continuous re-examination are a necessary part of his professional development.

The selection, trial, and re-evaluation of alternative solutions to problems are, according to Dewey, essential phases of thinking in any subject. Without inquiry, without some degree of doubt or uncertainty, decisions may be made, but they are made on the basis of habit, accident, or the dictates of authority. This is true whether he is thinking through to a solution of a mathematical problem, selecting appropriate language to communicate his ideas, choosing a political position, or determining educational policies and practices.

But inquiry is not generated merely by the posing of questions. The inquirer must be actively concerned with the questions; he must feel genuine doubt or uncertainty as to the answers. Though this book raises many questions, the reader who comes to them convinced that he, or indeed that anyone, has the "right" answers will be unlikely to engage in inquiry. He must in some instances willingly suspend prior beliefs so as to look afresh at some things he has taken for granted. Even so, not all the questions posed will actively engage every reader; the editors hope that their queries are central enough and have sufficient range so that some will challenge each reader. They hope the readings themselves will engender additional inquiries.

Finally, it is important that the reader's inquiry lead him to examine actual and potential consequences of the various alternatives presented. An idea has not been fully grasped as long as it is considered without reference to what may or must follow from it in thought or in action. At first glance, differences between conceptions of man that highlight his rational or his social nature may seem "merely" theoretical. Similarly, arguments as to whether freedom is first of all the absence of restraints, or the ability to control negative impulses, or the possession of the power to will may seem no more than philosophical quibbles. But these ideas make a difference in action. In education they underlie different practices with respect to classroom discipline, curriculum design, and the role of the teacher.

In the end, the quality and character of all the teacher does is conditioned by the clarity and integrity of his inquiry into these and other fundamental questions. At this point in his professional development the reader's task is to acquaint himself with past and present alternatives and, face to face with these, to examine, question, and apply. At this point in his personal history he may profitably recall

> . . . what's past is prologue, what to come
> In yours and my discharge.

Part 1

The Vocation of Teaching

Contents of Part 1

The Vocation of Teaching

THE TEACHER AS A PERSON

HIS PROFESSIONAL FUNCTIONS

HIS SOCIAL AND ECONOMIC STATUS

HIS EDUCATION AND CERTIFICATION

The Vocation of Teaching

The subject of education is many-faceted. In order to think about it at all it is necessary to consider educational aims and their effects on teaching method and curriculum, to know as much as possible about the character of the school population, to understand how the educational system is organized, financed, and controlled. But important as are clearly defined educational aims, sufficient and well-planned schools, laboratories, and books, all these are only as good as the teacher using them.

In recent years much publicity has been given to the teacher shortage, much attention paid to plans for securing more teachers. There are today more than a million men and women teaching in the public and private elementary and secondary schools of the United States. Within the next decade an additional half a million teachers will be needed, and this figure does not include the approximately 10 per cent of the existing teaching force that must be recruited each year to replace teachers who retire, take other jobs, or assume family responsibilities. The recruitment and preparation of teachers, then, take place on a mass scale. But they take place also on a personal, intimate scale as individual men and women ponder, prepare, and commit themselves to the vocation of teaching.

A decision to teach is a major decision for the individual. The preparation is long and demanding, the responsibilities extensive and complex. "Who would teach," Walt Whitman admonished, "may well prepare himself," and Whitman's long catechism might still serve to alert the prospective teacher to some of the questions he should ask himself. Probably the reader who is contemplating a career as a teacher has already asked many questions of his own. What specifically does the teacher do? What is the teacher's distinctive role? Can it be learned? And if it can be, how? What does the teacher need to know? How are teachers regarded? What do they earn? What are the limitations and satisfactions characteristic of the vocation of teaching?

THE ROLE OF THE TEACHER

Like other people, the teacher has many roles—some by virtue of being a human being, some by virtue of being a citizen, a member of a family, and some by virtue of being a teacher. The role of the teacher is also a multiple role: it would be better to speak of the roles of a teacher. The teacher is part nursemaid (in some grades at least), part judge, part parent, part manager and accountant, part friend, part policeman, part counselor, part instructor, part expert, part learner. Just as he is never merely teacher, so he is never merely any one of these parts of a teacher.

The teacher's roles of instructor, judge, parent, learner are the activities in which he engages as a consequence of his being a teacher. In his role as instructor he writes and solves arithmetic problems on the blackboard, writes comments on pupils' papers to show them where they are in error, guides the primary schoolchild's hand as he makes his first letters, asks questions and answers children's questions or tells them where they may find answers. In earlier times the instructional role was the teacher's chief, sometimes his sole, professional obligation. The man or woman who plans to teach because of an enthusiasm for a subject sometimes fails to realize the many other roles expected of teachers today. Unprepared for these additional demands, the beginning teacher may be disappointed in his choice of career.

Of course the expectation that teachers do other things besides impart knowledge and awaken an appetite for learning is not entirely new. Perhaps the most universal expectation is that the teacher act as preceptor and model for the character development of his charges. Sometimes this role has been defined as the teaching of manners and speech appropriate to the student's station; sometimes as the development of attitudes of reverence and devotion to God or loyalty to the state; training in good sportsmanship, honesty, and co-operation has sometimes been viewed as a function of the teacher of equal or greater consequence than his teaching of subjects.

In the role of moral arbiter the classroom teacher commends children for playing or working together in a friendly manner; arranges contests between class teams according to his intent to encourage children to conform, co-operate, or compete. He punishes the boy or girl who is unruly; or, if he wishes to avoid the role of judge, sends the offender to the principal, expecting him to undertake the disciplinary function.

As the family, church, and other agencies in many communities have in recent years suffered from disruption or diminution of influence, the teacher is often expected to serve in what seem to be an endlessly increasing number of capacities. Comenius and Pestalozzi, recognizing the child's need for mothering in his earliest learning, recommended that mothers act as teachers. Rousseau thought only a father should teach his son; this plan failing, the tutor should teach as a father. Teachers of children in nursery schools and kindergartens have always expected to serve in a mother's role. Even older boys and girls, especially if deprived by broken homes of parental love and guidance, need such attention. Should it come from the teacher? Is the parental role an appropriate role for teachers of children of all ages? Is it possible to specify an age at which the teacher should cease to act *in loco parentis?*

The sex of the teacher obviously determines the psychological role to some extent. In the United States only one of six elementary school teachers is a man; high school teachers include about the same number of men as women. In European countries teachers, even elementary teachers, are more often men. Partly because the teacher's role with younger children in the United States has been thought to call for certain maternal attributes, men have been disinclined to prepare for teaching at this level. (The fact that until recently elementary school teachers had lower salaries and less prestige than their colleagues in secondary schools was a deterrent, too.) Some sociologists believe that one of the reasons for the traditional American preference for the unmarried woman teacher was the fact that she represented a psychological position part way between the child's mother and the unrelated adult. Today it is customary for women teachers to continue to teach after marriage, and increasing numbers of men are teaching in elementary schools. Sociologists and psychologists who consider that American children and American culture are too much dominated by women approve the entrance of men into elementary school teaching. They believe that young children, the boys especially, should have opportunities to develop under the guidance of men and women teachers. A recent survey of male elementary school teachers reports that they find few disadvantages and many satisfactions in teaching at this level.[1]

Nathaniel Cantor questions the soundness of expecting teachers to serve in an ever-increasing number of roles. Parental and counselor roles especially, he believes, may make demands beyond the teacher's professional competence. Not the child's need, Cantor suggests, but the special competence of the teacher should be the criterion for extending or limiting his roles.

Cantor, however, represents a minority view. Although a great many

[1] Dorothy Rogers, "A Study of the Reactions of Forty Men to Teaching in the Elementary School," *The Journal of Educational Sociology* 27:24-35, September 1953.

specialized educational positions have developed in the past hundred years, many authorities on education still agree with Horace Mann, who urged teachers to be school missionaries, selling the public on the need for financial support for decent school buildings, talking with and educating parents, checking on the reasons for absenteeism, and accepting as a special and welcome task the reformation of delinquents. ". . . cannot the teacher," he asks, "like a prosecuting attorney, or a policeman, exhaust the knowledge of all professional books, learn new languages, watch his pupils in the streets as with the eyes of Argus, follow them to their pestiferous homes, court hardships by day and vigils by night, so that at length he may bring back to the fold of the Savior every lamb that has been intrusted to his care. . . ."

Several of the activities Mann urged on teachers in 1839 are now commonly accepted responsibilities of school principals or superintendents. Today there are, at least in large or well-supported school systems, school social workers, attendance officers, counselors, psychologists, and many other educational specialists. Nevertheless there is much to be said in favor of the teacher's functioning as counselor for his students. Advocates of this view point out that only the classroom teacher sees and works daily with the child. And in poor or understaffed schools, the teacher is likely to find that if children need special help, there is no one but the classroom teacher to meet these needs. How can he refuse? On the other hand, how many roles, how many functions can he undertake without seriously impairing his effectiveness in some?

THE TEACHER'S TASKS

School teachers in earlier times were correctly described as "keeping" school. Instruction took only a part of days filled with sharpening pens, sweeping the floor, tending the stove, and shoveling snow. Teachers' contracts no longer require them to dig graves, as did the 1682 contract with a school master in Flatbush reprinted in the readings. But every teacher still is expected to maintain a hygienic classroom—opening and closing windows, raising and lowering shades to regulate temperature and light. He erases or sees that students erase blackboards. The elementary school teacher especially may be judged by principal and parents on the neatness and attractiveness of his classroom—on well-planned bulletin board displays and colorful and appropriate seasonal decorations. Every teacher is responsible for student accounting: absences, tardiness, behavior and health records, as well as marks for daily work, tests, term grades, and report cards are recorded for each student.

In 1929 Charters identified literally a thousand and one activities of teachers. A more recent survey of Connecticut elementary school teachers' days, included in these readings, reports activities before and after school as well as during school hours. These multiple activities are grouped in twelve major functions "dominating the profession."

Some critics think too much is expected of the teacher. They are especially critical of using teachers to perform activities which they think could be done as well by less highly educated persons. At a time when there are not enough teachers to meet the needs of an expanding school population, the idea of using teachers' aides seems to have much to commend it. Over a quarter million dollars was invested in the Bay City-Central Michigan pilot study of the practicality of utilizing teacher aides to relieve elementary school teachers of "time-consuming, energy-wasting, non-professional tasks or chores" so that they might concentrate on the instructional phases of teaching and so that each regular teacher might instruct twice as many children as he could otherwise deal with. The idea of using non-professional aides is not new. Rabbi Chuyya in the third century used students as aides.

> I go to a place and instruct five children in the Five Books of Moses and six children in the Six Orders of the Mishnah; then I tell them, "By the time of my return, teach each other the Pentateuch and the Mishnah."

The modern development of mass education was given impetus in England and the United States by the Lancastrian system of teacher aides. This system was hailed enthusiastically by DeWitt Clinton and was adapted for the first "free school for the education of poor children" in New York City in 1806. Lancaster, a benevolent and ingenious Quaker, established a charity school in London in 1798 which utilized what Clinton described as:

> ... in education, what the neat finished machines for abridging labor and expense are in the mechanic arts. ... It arrives at its object with the least possible expense. Its distinguishing characters are economy, facility, and expedition, and its peculiar improvements are cheapness, activity, order, and emulation.

But we are unlikely to share Clinton's enthusiasm over the sight of "one great assembly of a thousand children under the eye of a single teacher" learning their letters by rote from youthful student monitors supervising "companies" of children. By the middle of the nineteenth century the Lancastrian system had come into disrepute and school men were beginning their efforts to provide more individualized education for children in small groups. Teacher organizations during the past century have endeavored to establish standards of class size as a criterion of effective education.

The Bay City experiment, of course, contemplates nothing like such mass companies of children under each teacher, and proposes to use adults, not children, as aides. But teachers and educational psychologists have questioned the soundness of the teacher aide plan not only on grounds of pupil-teacher quotas. Their chief objection has been to the separation of certain roles and functions of the teacher from others. The teacher's performance in the instructional role itself is dependent, they believe, on relationships with children that are based on the teacher's performance of some of the nursemaid and student accounting functions that the Bay City study assumes to be "non-professional chores." Preliminary evaluation of the project indicates equivalent academic achievement for children in teacher aide classes and control classes. Many teachers in the experiment are not persuaded by this evidence. They believe that although the plan may help to solve emergency shortages of teachers, it does not give children the kind of close relationship with the teacher they believe desirable.

In any case, each teacher should expect to develop versatility. The ability to function in the various roles and acceptance of the multiple tasks appropriate to a particular teaching level and situation are important characteristics of successful teachers.

THE TEACHER KNOWS HIS SUBJECT

The peripheral tasks of the teacher differ in different societies and according to the age of those he is teaching. But the teacher has always been expected to see to it that learners acquired certain knowledge prescribed by the culture. His methods may vary: he may intone the verses of the Koran and listen to his scholars repeat the verses after him; he may, like Socrates, ask questions which he does not expect his students to answer correctly but which set the stage for his own dissertations; he may, like the Kwakiutl chief or the modern teacher of shop subjects, demonstrate the technique of sharpening a javelin or of machine turning of chair legs. Whatever the subject, the teacher's competence in it, whether gained from long experience or from special study, is taken for granted. Prescriptions from Quintilian to Dewey expect of the teacher not only knowledge of his subject but enthusiasm for it: "in the art of teaching, it is what is taught that counts; not the teacher."

His knowledge of his subject is an essential source of authority for the teacher. Lacking mastery of what he professes, the teacher is driven to rely solely on his authority as a person. In a democratic society this is a questionable alternative because it may lead the teacher to manipulate students in order to maintain control rather than to liberate them to learn. It is the difference between directions given "because I said so," and those justified "because you can see this is a good way to do this problem." Authority based on subject mastery is not, of course, the same as dogmatism. Quite the contrary: the teacher who is the better informed is less sure that he—or anyone—has the final answers than his less well-grounded colleagues. The authority and confidence that result from sound knowledge of one's subject are well worth seeking even though they are in the fullest sense unattainable goals. The good teacher, like Chaucer's clerk, must "gladly lerne" for the duration of his professional career.

In simpler, more stable societies, the teacher can more easily achieve relatively complete command of the knowledge or skills he teaches. In certain cultures there is only one way to make a canoe; there is only one cosmogony and a man may hope to master it in a lifetime. Even as late as the eighteenth century the Encyclopedists could hope that exceptional men might encompass all the sciences. But the twentieth century has seen a revolutionary expansion and reorientation of scholarship. A recent Nobel Prize-winning scientist has declared it almost impossible for a scientist to complete a book in his field before it is out-dated by new advances in knowledge. New discoveries in old disciplines like archaeology do more than add to the factual knowledge in the field; they challenge fundamental theories—of the process of human evolution or of the relationship of Judaeo-Christian doctrines. In the course of the first half of the twentieth century, fields that had just begun to be delineated at the end of the nineteenth century have developed into systematic and increasingly popular disciplines: psychology and sociology are two of the most striking instances of this development. A growing number of interdisciplinary fields of study, of which child development is an instance, demonstrate that the movement toward specialization characteristic of the late nineteenth century has been paralleled by a return to and reformulation of the broad scholarly ideals of the eighteenth.

These developments are of more than academic interest to the teacher. They have substantially increased the difficulty of the teacher's task. They have increased both the length and scope of the academic preparation expected of teachers at all levels. This is true even of school systems where junior and senior high school curricula have remained strictly departmentalized. Even in such schools the movement toward the correlation and integration of two or more fields has had its effect. English-social studies core programs, a still growing trend, general science, general language, call for competence in more than a single subject. Even if the high school teacher teaches only traditional subjects like English or history, he will find that these subjects include topics not included in his own high school or college courses. The Seattle, Washington, program for social studies in the twelfth grade provides electives in contemporary problems, problems of the Far East, and Latin America, which include current American foreign policies and the resources and internal problems of nations rising to prominence today. The English–Speech–Language Arts program for senior high schools in New York City calls upon the teacher for units of work that develop concepts of semantics, the psychology of communication, and an understanding of the structure of language that go far beyond his probable pre-service preparation. Teachers of mathematics are urged to acquaint students with the fundamentals of automatic computation; science teachers can hardly claim literacy without knowledge of fission and the debate on the effects of strontium 90.

As the number of subjects in the high school curriculum has multiplied, teachers frequently find that they are expected to teach at least one other subject than that in which they have had their major preparation. The 1956 National Education Association study of teacher supply and demand shows that, in most of the twenty-nine states included, teachers are assigned to teach classes in one or more subjects in addition to that in which they have received their major preparation. For example, of 2294 new English teachers in 1955, 291 were assigned classes in a foreign language and 562 were assigned social studies classes, with smaller numbers given classes in commercial subjects, mathematics, general science, and music in addition to their major teaching assignments in their field. New mathematics teachers, 1168 in number, were given classes in general science (280), in social studies (103) and in smaller numbers were assigned classes in English, chemistry, biology, physics, and industrial arts.

The academic competence of elementary school teachers is similarly challenged. No longer is the elementary school teacher's knowledge adequate if he is well grounded in reading, writing, simple arithmetic, and some facts of United States history. Almost without exception he is expected to have some knowledge of physical and biological sciences including hygiene, of music, art, and community study methods. What is expected of today's elementary school teacher makes him a counterpart of the eighteenth-century Encyclopedists in range if not in depth of knowledge. He is expected to be able to answer affirmatively the questions posed by Walt Whitman in his poetic address to "those who would assume a place to teach":

> Have you studied out the land, its idioms and men?
> Have you learn'd the physiology, phrenology, politics,
>   geography, pride, freedom, friendship of the land?
>   its substratums and objects?

Moreover, the modern elementary school teacher is not only expected to know much more than the three R's, he is also expected to have his learning so completely in command that he can bring it to bear on the spontaneous interests and queries of children. The elementary curriculum today of course calls for systematic instruction in reading and arithmetic, but it is designed also to incorporate units of work that arise out of children's curiosity about current events and new developments in the world of science. The teacher whose own academic background is impoverished, the teacher who does not keep abreast of the changing world will be unable to capitalize on children's emerging intellectual interests.

The popularization of new knowledge through mass media in general and television in particular brings children in their earliest school years acquaintance with new technological discoveries and with the names and appearances of people in distant lands, sometimes even before their teachers have heard of these things. Not infrequently the elementary school teacher will encounter in her classes eight-year-old "experts" on jet propulsion who will not only ask her questions she cannot answer, but who will also tell her things she has not heard before and does not understand.

Learned societies and professional teachers' associations, recognizing the teacher's problem in keeping abreast of new knowledge, have recently established institutes and workshops offering refresher courses for teachers in service and advisory centers preparing teaching materials embodying newer developments in their fields of knowledge. The Service Center for Teachers of History is one such enterprise, established by the American Historical Association with the aid of a grant from the Ford Foundation. It is concerned with "the growing gap between the teachers in the schools and the experts working on the frontiers of historical knowledge." Under ordinary circumstances new knowledge in this as in other fields does not find its way into the schools for a generation.

Most analyses of the professional activities of the teacher have started with his function as a disseminator and expositor of knowledge. Teachers today must add to these professional roles, as master teachers have instinctively done, that of learner. The teacher's awareness and acceptance of this role are essential both in the interests of his subject and as part of his obligation to the children he teaches. Moreover, his acceptance of his role as learner is important to the teacher's own sense of security. The teacher who teaches all he knows is likely to feel himself continually on the edge of a precipice. Certainly he is unlikely to feel free to urge his more able students to extend their inquiries. Whether or not teachers have formulated their recognition of these demands, summer session and university extension enrollment figures and travel statistics show teachers as a group to be confirmed seekers after knowledge. Through continuously deepening and broadening his knowledge and intellectual enthusiasms, the teacher at once reinforces his authority and confidence in the classroom and insures against what some have considered one of the occupational hazards of the profession—the narrowing and deadening effects of continuous repetition of identical content at relatively immature levels.

As the various fields of knowledge have grown in scope, complexity, and interrelatedness, the definition of the teacher's task as that of presenting, explaining, and testing students' acquisition of basic facts and fundamental principles has begun to undergo modifications. Increasingly teachers are held accountable less for imparting some particular set of facts and more and more for teaching sound procedures of inquiry. Current school syllabi are less likely to list a specified number of words that fourth graders should be able to spell than to require that children at this stage learn how to use an abridged or simplified dictionary and spell correctly the words they use. Similarly, the teacher is expected rather to teach junior high school boys and girls how to use an atlas and how to look up facts in an almanac than to drill them on the names of capitals and the natural resources of countries. Thus the teacher's competence in his subject depends not only upon his greater accumulation of facts but also upon the mastery of the intellectual skills peculiar to his field. Simultaneously he will try to give children confidence in their mastery of facts and skills and a sense of intellectual humility—attitudes which he can communicate only if they are his.

Are the teacher's sole functions those inherent in his role as an imparter of knowledge? Are his interest and competence in his subject the only requirements for his fulfillment of this role? The teacher who lacks enthusiasm for and mastery of his subject will be unlikely to find satisfaction in his teaching. But the teacher whose eyes are turned always and only on his subject may fail to communicate his enthusiasm to his students, especially if they are beginners in learning. The teacher must continuously keep his students in sight if he is to lead them to share his enthusiasm. Those who turn to teaching because they see no other way to make a living out of their learning are likely to be disappointed in their profession. An exclusive interest in his subject may even lead a teacher to view the children he teaches as a means of perpetuating his subject. It is to correct this misconception of teaching that many writers on education have called attention to the necessity of "teaching the child." Pestalozzi endeavored to discriminate between teachers whose concern was only with their subject and those who taught a subject *to children*. The first type of teacher he criticized for having "a form of instruction to which he subjects the child." The second type of teacher, he noted, starts with the child and subjects the course of instruction to the child. This position actually makes explicit what outstanding teachers have always sensed: that knowledge of children and their capacities is as necessary to successful teaching as is mastery of subject. "Lacking this knowledge we sometimes spoil all," Montaigne warned.

The Vocation of Teaching

THE TEACHER UNDERSTANDS CHILDREN

Educators from Quintilian on have recognized the importance of adapting subject and approach to the child's capacity, but this kind of knowledge and skill was apparently thought to be instinctive with the gifted teacher. "A skilled teacher will know," Quintilian declared, "how to adapt his work to the capacity of the child's mind." There are some who still think this kind of insight is native and who therefore question the necessity for formal study of the nature and capacities of children and of methods for teaching them. Perhaps the single most important influence in the shaping of modern education, however, was the development of child study and pedagogy as essential knowledge for teachers.

The meaning of individual differences and developmental stages in human growth for teaching became a major concern of educators during the Renaissance. From Vitorino da Feltre onward the great teachers and educational theorists who set the direction of modern education in the Western world turned their attention to study of child nature and of methods of stimulating learning among children of different abilities and at different ages. Fenelon, Locke, Erasmus, Montaigne, Luther, Comenius, Rousseau, Pestalozzi, Froebel, and Herbart, some of whose writings for teachers are included in this book, all wrote not only of what should be taught but also of how children learned. During the Renaissance also two great Catholic teaching orders, the Jesuits and the Christian Brothers, developed a systematic pedagogy, outlined in the *Ratio Studiorum* and in de la Salle's *Conduct of the Schools*. These manuals contained explicit methodological directives for teaching.

Many of the basic concepts in what later came to be called child study, educational psychology, and pedagogy or methods appeared in the educational writings of these reformers. The importance of interest in motivating learning, the developmental character of the individual's capacities, the influence of emotion and teacher-pupil relationships on learning, the desirability of pupil activity, the utilization of visual aids in teaching, and the systematization of a teaching-learning sequence all were explicitly formulated during the period from the fourteenth to the eighteenth centuries. In some instances these formulations were vague and some, like the principles of faculty psychology, were later discredited. But many were surprisingly similar to modern formulations in educational psychology and methods. What is chiefly significant is that during this period there was laid down a large body of knowledge that teachers were expected to possess.

Not until late in the nineteenth century was there another intensive development of knowledge about human growth and learning. During the last century, however, knowledge in these fields has been refined and extended through experimental and analytical studies. Beginning with Darwin the whole question of the influence of environment and nurture on the development of personality and intelligence has been studied by biologists, psychologists, sociologists, and cultural anthropologists. The significance of early childhood experiences within the family and of later interpersonal relationships in shaping the individual, documented in the case studies of Freud, Horney, and Sullivan, re-emphasized the need for teachers to understand the dynamics of personality. Cottrell, Thorndike, and Binet and Piaget extended the knowledge of the dynamics of learning and developed objective techniques for measuring intelligence and learning. All these fields are now generally considered important to the teacher.

In his instructional role the teacher depends on knowledge of this kind to devise ways of stimulating children's intellectual curiosity and to set achievement goals appropriate to children's intellectual ability and developmental level. The teacher who has assimilated basic principles of child development, learning, and measurement knows that he should plan graded experiences for children to prepare them for their first steps in reading. He understands that language development tends to progress from listening and speaking to writing and reading, that the teaching of complex sentence structure should wait upon the child's readiness to conceive of complex ideas. Though the teacher should probably have studied formal grammar himself, he will realize that children will best learn verb tenses when they have developed an interest in time relationships. He will exploit children's spontaneous curiosity about why water solidifies in cold weather and why jet planes boom when they drop from one altitude to another to teach what he has learned in more formally organized courses. He will not be surprised to find that a very bright five-year-old's letters are less well formed than those of an average seven-year-old, whose small-muscle coordination is further developed. He will recognize and act upon information from standardized tests to plan the work for individual children and groups of children so that it is difficult enough to be challenging but not so difficult as to be discouraging.

John Dewey, who pioneered in applying the new knowledge of children and their learning to curriculum and classroom procedures, summarizes its significance for the teacher as follows:

> Teaching may be compared to selling commodities. No one can sell unless someone buys. We should ridicule a merchant who said that he had sold a great many goods although no one had bought any. But perhaps there are teachers who think they have done a good day's teaching irrespective of what pupils have learned. There is the same exact equation between teaching and learning that there is between selling and buying.

... The more a teacher is aware of the past experience of students, of their hopes, desires, chief interests, the better will he understand the forces at work that need to be directed and utilized for the formation of reflective habits.[2]

Knowledge of the emotional needs of growing children and adolescents will make it possible for the teacher to perform her roles as parent, counselor, friend, intelligently rather than sentimentally. The informed teacher knows the importance of responding to children warmly but not possessively, of striking an appropriate balance between freedom and control.

TEACHER EDUCATION

Recognition that teachers needed knowledge of child development and of the psychology of learning fostered the professionalization of teaching. The professions have traditionally been characterized by a special form of education, generally more extended than that received by other members of their society, as well as by an acceptance of obligations beyond those of personal achievement and self-aggrandizement.

Teacher education as professional education is relatively recent; it is predominantly a development of the late nineteenth century. No aspect of education is currently more widely questioned or more violently attacked. The popular press as well as professional literature on education are crowded with questions about the education of teachers. Is teaching a science or an art? If it is an art, how can it be taught? Is not a good liberal education sufficient preparation for teaching? What should be the content of professional courses for teachers? Should professional education be incorporated into undergraduate programs or should it be deferred until the novice is actually teaching and offered then as graduate education? Which institution, the liberal arts college, the teachers college, or the employing school system should bear the major responsibility for educating teachers?

The medieval universities at Bologna, Paris, and Oxford offered studies in the arts and prepared for the learned professions of theology, law, and medicine; graduates of these universities also became teachers in the advanced secondary schools of the period, and in the universities themselves. A special advantage of the original university degrees was that they conferred the right to teach; they constituted a form of licensing. The titles of the degrees themselves indicated this purpose: the degree of doctor stemmed from *docere,* to teach; the master's degree was honored in the title, schoolmaster. The university preparation of teachers at this time did not, however, differ from that received by other university scholars. It included nothing that would today be considered professional content for teachers.

[2] John Dewey, *How We Think,* rev. ed. (Boston, D. C. Heath and Company, 1933), pp. 35-6.

Some critics of present-day teacher education are of the opinion that the bachelor's degree should in itself confer the right to teach, at least in the lower schools.

If the state of knowledge, the population of the schools, and the pace of social change had remained what they were in the Middle Ages, it is entirely possible that teacher education would not have developed as a special form of higher education.

As long as education was a prerogative of a wealthy minority, few teachers were needed; as long as the dull, the uninterested, and those from impoverished cultural backgrounds were not required to remain in school, teachers were not required to demonstrate a wide repertory of teaching skills. The onus of failure to learn was on the student, not on the teacher. Nevertheless, even during the period when education was for a small elite only, some men recognized that learned men did not always make good teachers. Elyot, Montaigne, and Fuller deplored poor teaching in their time and recommended methods they thought would prove more effective. The good teacher, Fuller maintained, "studies his scholars' natures as carefully as they their books" and is "methodical" in his teaching. But though some books on pedagogy appeared during the sixteenth and seventeenth centuries, professional schools for teachers were a later development. In its broad outlines professionalized teacher education followed the development of universal education, which demanded an army of teachers skillful enough to teach even those children once considered uneducable.

The first training school for teachers grew out of the concern of religious orders to provide religious instruction for the poor. St. Jean Baptiste de la Salle founded a training school at Rheims (1685) to prepare the Christian Brothers to teach working-class children. The professional content of the Brothers' preparation is typified by the pedagogic precepts, chiefly relating to classroom management, in de la Salle's *Conduct of the Schools*. Essentially the Christian Brothers learned to teach by teaching under supervision in the charity schools.

During the seventeenth and eighteenth centuries humanitarian impulses toward more widespread education were reinforced by the Protestant desire that every man learn to read his Bible and by the political and economic revolutions that made increasing demands on the common man as citizen and worker. As the new national states made provisions for primary education for the common people, the demand for teachers increased and governments began to support their training. In the last half of the eighteenth century, Prussia began to subsidize teacher training schools. These seminaries were not institutions of higher learning as we know them. They provided an opportunity for able primary school graduates to review primary school subjects and to advance a little beyond this level. As in de la Salle's school, the professional aspect of the teacher's education centered on his apprentice teaching in the orphanage or model schools attached to these seminaries.

The Prussian seminaries, which incorporated the precepts of Pestalozzi and Froebel early in the nineteenth century, were enthusiastically reported in this country by visitors like Stowe, Cousin, and Horace Mann. They set the pattern for the normal schools of the United States. Massachusetts, which had pioneered in legislation for universal schooling, made the first provision for a state-supported normal school in 1839. By the end of the nineteenth century, state normal schools were the principal source of elementary school teachers in the United States. Students entered at graduation from elementary school, or with some high school education, and pursued a course of study that was academically comparable to that of present-day secondary schools. Teacher education still labors under the stigma of these early conditions. It is still often judged a sub-collegiate type of education and deprecated as attracting less able students than are attracted by liberal arts colleges. The professional content in these schools gradually expanded from a curriculum limited to educational methods, originally called pedagogics or didactics, based on the principles of Pestalozzi and Herbart, and practice teaching. Subsequently, courses in the history and philosophy of education were added, and eventually systematic study of educational psychology was included. These subjects, often under different titles, still constitute the core of professional curricula for teachers, and are reflected in state certification requirements.

During the period when the normal schools were evolving as one source of professionally prepared teachers, private academies and high schools were also engaged in preparing teachers for the common schools. Even before the establishment of the first state normal school in Massachusetts, New York State voted (1834) to subsidize private academies to train teachers. The academies tended to give less time to professional courses than did the normal schools; they did not provide the review of elementary subjects in which many teacher candidates were deficient. In time they gave way to the normal schools and to higher institutions of learning as sources of professionally trained teachers.

When the movement toward universal compulsory education in the United States expanded to include some high school education for all youth, the demand for high school teachers began to approximate the early demand for elementary school teachers. Obviously preparation adequate for elementary teachers was not suitable for secondary school teachers. Two approaches to the education of secondary school teachers were made beginning at the turn of the century: the extension of the normal schools to four-year teachers colleges and the enlistment of liberal arts colleges and universities in this task.

The controversy between protagonists of liberal and professional education for teachers was evident immediately. Although the University of Michigan established a chair in education, probably the first of its kind, in 1879, and New York University and Columbia University incorporated colleges of education in the last decade of the century, universities generally were not at first hospitable to this development. At the 1889 meeting of the New England Association of Colleges and Preparatory Schools the question of whether the colleges should undertake to prepare teachers was a major topic of debate. The presidents of Harvard and Yale were reluctant to have the liberal arts colleges accept this function and advocated an extension of the normal schools for the purpose. President Eliot of Harvard reported that his faculty had "but slight interest or confidence in what is ordinarily called pedagogy." Presidents and professors in many liberal arts colleges today are of the same opinion. Many are bitterly critical of teachers colleges and schools of education; few seem to recognize that the growth of these professional institutions was fostered by the disinclination of liberal arts colleges to assume responsibility for teacher education. At present most teachers are educated in liberal arts colleges and universities. A recent survey of the preparation of teachers shows that only 17 per cent of all teachers graduated in 1955 were educated in teachers colleges; 83 per cent were prepared in liberal arts colleges and universities.[3]

Current opposition to teacher education centers on many of the criticisms originally directed against it: teachers who are well prepared in what they teach do not need courses in how to teach; there is no definitive science of pedagogy; much of what is included in the professional curriculum—notably history of education, philosophy of education, and educational psychology—can be taught in regular courses of history, philosophy, and psychology; even though teachers might profit from some professional courses, there are far too many required in most teacher education programs; and, finally, the content of courses in education is thin and repetitious and the standards of achievement demanded are low.

Those who defend the value of professional education for teachers point out that schools and colleges afford innumerable examples of scholars who fail as teachers because they lack understanding of how people learn and are innocent of skills in presenting subject matter. They hold that regular courses in history, philosophy, and psychology give little or no attention to educational matters. They contend that courses in liberal disciplines are also sometimes thin and repetitious and that students may emerge from

[3] National Education Association, Research Division, "The 1956 Teacher Supply and Demand Report," *The Journal of Teacher Education* 7:33-79, March 1956.

these courses with deplorable standards of rhetoric, logic, and appreciation.

Little is to be gained by the mutual ridicule, intemperance, and vituperation that characterize this debate. Some of the generalizations made by professors of liberal arts are based on evidence these writers would consider totally inadequate in their own disciplines. Their criticisms are sometimes couched in language as unbecoming to scholarly discourse as the educational jargon which is the subject of their derision. On the other hand, professors of education, forced into a defensive position, are sometimes tempted to defend indefensible practices. Frequently they have failed lamentably to communicate their intentions. To the extent that the argument is conducted at the level of a contest of vested interests rather than at the level of intellectual inquiry, its effect is illiberal and destructive. Those who are genuinely concerned with the improvement of teacher education will wish to examine the bases of these criticisms and the arguments of the proponents of professional teacher education and of liberal education alike. With good faith professors of liberal arts and of education can find substantial areas of agreement and can collaborate in reassessing teacher education and trying out new curriculum designs. In recent years the American Council on Education and other interested groups have sponsored a number of conferences to consider the present status of liberal and professional education of teachers. Reports from these conferences show that there are important areas of agreement among professors of education and professors in the liberal arts. The present state of agreement in principle between these groups includes such points as these:

1. The responsibility for the preparation of high school teachers should not be the prerogative of any single type of higher institution, but should be shared by various kinds of schools, colleges, and universities.
2. Professors of liberal arts subjects and professors of education should work together with teacher licensing agencies in determining requirements and standards.
3. All high school teachers should have a strong background in the humanities, social sciences, and natural sciences.
4. Teacher education programs should include study of philosophy, history, and sociology as these relate to education.
5. Graduate schools should review their offerings to assure that appropriate courses in the subjects taught in secondary schools are available for teachers.

Undoubtedly a major concern of all those interested in the education of teachers is the proportion of liberal and professional studies in teacher education curricula. In general the proportion of professional work in liberal arts colleges that prepare teachers is about one-fourth of the total curriculum for elementary teachers and somewhat less than one-fifth of the total for secondary teachers. Teachers colleges tend to require more work in professional subjects, though even in these institutions the proportion is less than many critics assume. In a study of the curricula for elementary teachers in sixty-eight state teachers colleges the minimum required non-professional courses constituted 40 per cent of the total program; the average teachers college curriculum for elementary teachers required half of the student's work to be in non-professional courses.[4]

Whether the teacher has been educated in a teachers college or in a liberal arts college and whatever the proportion of liberal and professional studies in his curriculum, he is likely to continue his education after he becomes a regular teacher. Short-term institutes for teachers were inaugurated in this country by Henry Barnard in the mid-nineteenth century. In-service courses offered by school systems, special workshops, and graduate courses in subject matter fields and in professional subjects are contemporary provisions testifying to teachers' inveterate appetite for study. As members of a profession they generally accept an obligation to continue learning for the duration of their professional careers.

THE CERTIFICATION OF TEACHERS

Certification is another aspect of the professionalization of teaching. Certification as a means of controlling the teacher's loyalty to church or state antedated interest in the amount and character of the teacher's education by centuries. The degrees granted by the medieval universities licensing recipients to teach were issued under the authority of the chancellor of the cathedral in the university town and testified to the religious orthodoxy as well as to the learning of the candidate. The Society for the Propagation of the Gospel in Foreign Parts, which was active in supporting schools in colonial America in the early eighteenth century, required that the schoolmasters "bring certificates" of the following particulars:

1. his age
2. his condition of life whether single or mary'd
3. his temper
4. his prudence
5. his learning
6. his sober and pious conversation
7. his zeal and Xtian Religion and diligence in his calling
8. his affection to the present government

[4] Leonard H. Clark, "The Curriculum for Elementary Teachers in Sixty-eight State Teachers Colleges," *The Journal of Teacher Education* 6:115, June 1955.

The Vocation of Teaching

    9. his conformity to the doctrine and discipline of the Church of England [5]

Specifications concerning the teacher's religious and political beliefs tend to appear during periods when established beliefs are under attack and following the establishment of new religions or political systems. This was the case in the seventeenth century in England; it throws light on the efforts to legislate teachers' loyalty at the time of the First World War and more recently as a response to alarm over the communist threat to the American way of life.[6]

The contribution of certification requirements to the professionalization of teaching, however, rests chiefly upon its influence on the education of teachers. Critics of teacher education are equally critical of state certification practices, which they consider require inadequate preparation in academic subjects and excessive preparation in professional courses. The charge is made that certification requirements are established by "educationists" who are joined in a "conspiracy" to advance professional education over liberal education. In fact, education is almost unique among the professions in that the control of licensing is not wholly or chiefly in the hands of members of the profession. Attorneys, physicians, nurses, dentists, architects, and accountants are licensed in most states through boards composed largely or wholly of attorneys, physicians, nurses, dentists, architects, and accountants. In only four states must the boards controlling certification of teachers be composed entirely or in part of teachers. The teaching profession has generally accepted and endorsed public control of educational policy, though professional organizations, like other interested groups, have participated in and endeavored to influence public decisions and legislation relating to education.

The chief contribution of state certification in the United States has unquestionably been in raising the over-all educational requirements for teachers. During the early period of the development of universal education the teacher shortage was too acute to make certification practicable; any teacher was better than none. State certification of teachers began toward the end of the nineteenth century; in the first decade of the twentieth century, elementary school teachers were typically certified, if at all, on the basis of high school graduation. During the second quarter of this century a majority of states set certification standards that included four years of

---

[5] Quoted in E. W. Knight and C. L. Hall, *Readings in American Educational History* (New York, Appleton-Century-Crofts, 1951), p. 28.

[6] In 1957, thirty-one states required United States citizenship for certification of teachers; twenty-nine states required oaths of loyalty or allegiance.

college for elementary and secondary school teachers. Four states now require a fifth or graduate year of study for high school teachers.

PROFESSIONAL ASSOCIATIONS FOR TEACHERS

When Horace Mann in 1839, the year of the founding of the first state normal school, called on teachers in every town to form "an association for mutual improvement," he drew attention to another important phase in the development of teaching as a profession. The faculties of medieval universities had constituted a kind of professional guild banded together, sometimes with their students, to control the conditions under which instruction was offered. But teachers of elementary and high schools in the early years of public education in the United States hardly constituted a profession. Leading educators like Horace Mann and Henry Barnard thought that teachers and teaching would gain from associations that would encourage discussions of educational policy and practice. The first organizations of teachers in this country were local affiliations in cities like Boston and New York City. Within a few years of Mann's statement in his *Common Journal* the first state associations of teachers were formed in Alabama, Rhode Island, and New York. From 1840 to 1900 the number of state teachers associations grew to forty-six, and membership in them by 1955 to almost 90 per cent of the teaching force.

Ten presidents of state teachers organizations came together at Philadelphia in 1857 to form the National Teachers Association (for men only), which became the National Education Association in 1870. The National Education Association is today the largest professional organization in the world, with well over half a million members and more than a million affiliated members. Through its various committees and commissions the NEA has exerted a major influence in elementary and secondary curricula, methods of instruction, teacher certification, and teacher salaries and tenure provisions. NEA conferences are attended yearly by thousands of teachers and administrators; NEA publications are read by an even larger audience. The extent of NEA influence on American education is held by some critics to be excessive, and to have placed education in the hands of a professional oligarchy dominated by administrators. On the other hand, the NEA has to its credit many significant contributions to education generally and to the professionalization of teaching in particular.

One of the marks of commitment to teaching as a profession is participation in appropriate professional organizations. Unlike the man whose work is only a means of livelihood, whose interest in it is confined to his working hours, the members of a profession are continuously concerned with appraising and improving it and with formulating its obligations to society. The beginning teacher will wish to study the policies and activities of professional associations in his field. In most instances he will find one or more that can contribute to his professional growth.

Though membership in teachers associations and learned societies is generally recognized to be desirable, opinion on membership in teachers unions is sharply divided. Unions are based upon the concept of a necessary conflict of interest between employer and employee. This concept is not generally accepted by teachers as applicable to their relationship with their employers, who are the public. Some teachers think their status as government employees limits their freedom to strike and hence see little practical value in union membership. The American Federation of Teachers, the principal teachers union in the United States, has explicitly renounced the use of the strike as an instrument of settling disputes between teachers and school boards.

Some states have passed legislation regarding union membership of public employees: Alabama opposes this practice; New Jersey guarantees it. Most teachers, of course, are employees of municipalities and local school boards. Municipalities also vary in their willingness to allow public employees to be unionized. Courts have tended to uphold school boards which forbade teachers to form or join unions. Nevertheless, there are locals of the American Federation of Teachers, affiliated with the AFL-CIO in three-fourths of the United States cities with populations of 100,000 or more. But membership in this and in local non-affiliated unions has made relatively slight appeal to teachers; membership in the AFT in 1955 was less than 8 per cent of that in the NEA for the same year.

During the period of the most rapid growth of the AFT, in 1918 and 1919, the NEA and a number of college teachers engaged in a campaign against unionization as "unprofessional" and undignified. As is indicated in the poll of public opinion included in these readings, sentiment on the unionization of teachers is divided, among laymen as well as among teachers themselves. In this survey, acceptance of union activities for teachers decreased with the amount of education of respondents, though more than two-thirds of those questioned believed teachers were justified in unionizing. Teachers' opinions are probably very similar to those of this 1947 sample of Connecticut voters.

THE TEACHER AND SOCIETY

Although teachers are now expected to have a lengthy and specialized education and to dedicate themselves to service to society, they are frequently not accorded the status commonly given clergymen, physicians, and lawyers. Different cultures and other eras have viewed teachers with varying degrees of approbation, awe, or contempt. For the most part, however, the teacher seems to have occupied a peculiarly ambiguous position.

In ancient China the teacher was revered. According to Confucius, he should not be subject even to the king; at the same time he was considered outside the basic clan relationships of the society. Though honored for his learning, he was likely to have achieved his position after failing to achieve the more exalted status of a government official. In Greece the teacher of the very young was a servant or slave; Plutarch complained that slaves assigned as companions to children were often the least able in the household. But Greece also produced Socrates and other teachers not greatly inferior to him, recognized even by contemporaries as distinguished, if sometimes dangerous, public figures.

Although teachers are regarded differently in different societies and at different times, it may be that ambivalent attitudes towards them are to a degree inherent in their social role in any culture. Teachers, like other professionals, find themselves inescapably on the fringes of the accustomed patterns of their society. Once teaching has become a specialized vocation its practitioners, like other professionals, are inevitably separated from the daily rounds of doing and producing by which most members of a society earn their living. As long as education is in the hands of the family or is an avocational activity of the tailor or the cobbler, the act of teaching does not separate the teacher from his fellow men. Once it becomes specialized and professionalized, however, the teacher becomes a man apart from other men. His daily intercourse is with children, not with other men. No longer is his first concern the sowing and reaping of a crop, the harvesting of the produce of the sea. In cultures that prize active striving and the conquest of material obstacles, it is easy to regard the teacher as not merely out of the mainstream of life but as unequal to it.

This view of the teacher has been a characteristic one in America, where the challenge of transforming a wilderness into a new world conferred the prizes of wealth and status on the makers and doers. Those who neither plowed nor produced were likely to be considered of little consequence in practical affairs. The gulf between men of action and men whose life is that of books was recognized and deplored by Emerson in 1837; it describes as well a current attitude typified by such terms as "egghead," "brain," and "highbrow."

"There goes in the world," Emerson remarked, "a notion that the scholar should be a recluse, a valetudinarian,—as unfit for any handiwork or public labor as a penknife for an axe. The so-called 'practical men' sneer at speculative men, as if, because they speculate or *see,* they could do nothing." Though the elementary or secondary school teacher may not think of himself—or be thought of—as a scholar, he may be similarly viewed by "practical men."

There is another characteristic of the American temperament that is particularly relevant to a discussion of the teacher's status and prestige. As observers from other cultures have noted, the American people typically reject figures of authority. More than a century apart, Tocqueville and Geoffrey Gorer observed that in America authority over things was considered worth striving for, but that to seek authority over people was suspect. Walt Whitman's advice to the States, "Resist much; obey little," might stand equally well as an unspoken motto of American youth. The American teacher, like every teacher, necessarily occupies a position of authority even in the most democratically organized classroom. Unlike teachers in many other cultures he must find a way to operate within a climate inimical to authority. The nation's origin in a revolt against the authority of the mother country, and the American political system of checks and balances tend to reinforce in subtle but deeply ingrained ways the American disposition to resist authority. Accustomed to playing one parent against the other and neighboring parents against their own, children come to school predisposed to play one teacher's requirements against another's and parents' and teachers' expectations against each other. Successful teachers in America are likely to have developed a particular kind of authority: one based on "the rules of the game," in which the teacher does not exercise authority as a person but rather as a delegate or representative of the school. The American teacher cannot rely on the kind of conformity among his colleagues that is recommended in the excerpt from a text for teachers in the U.S.S.R. which is included among these readings.

American children do not usually choose authority figures as heroes. Comparison of German and American older adolescents' choices in studies made at the end of World War II, of "the greatest men (or women) in history" show a marked difference in this respect. The first ten on the American list included Christ, Columbus, Edison, and Ben Franklin in addition to American presidents and generals; the German list had only heads of state and military conquerors. Perhaps their basic rejection of authority figures is one of the reasons why American children tend to name figures from the theater and sports world as adults they would like to be like, and why they rarely name teachers in this connection.

The teacher's separateness from the mainstream of his society tends to be increased by his employment status as a civil servant. Public school teachers, who comprise the majority in the profession, are bound by special regulations as civil servants and have special benefits not enjoyed by other workers. In some countries, as in Germany, civil servant status is highly prized and teachers share the prestige accorded judges and other civic officials. In the United States the subservient rather than the official aspect of civil service is often emphasized.

As civil servants, teachers work outside the typical risk economy of

Western civilization. They are less immediately affected by changes in economic cycles than is the average man. With rare exceptions they enjoy a degree of security from which they may view political and economic crises with some detachment. But while such detachment may enable the individual to view social changes with equanimity and objectivity, it is unlikely to endear him to those for whom these changes may have serious personal consequences.

The teacher's social distance from others in the community is further widened by his education. Most teachers are educated significantly beyond the average man. Their tastes, even their vocabulary, as well as their ideas are likely to differ markedly from those of other citizens, including the parents of most of the children they teach. Their detachment and their education encourage teachers to view their environment critically. Even in relatively static societies where the teacher's social function is to prepare the young for a future that is in essence a reproduction of the present, he is charged with reproducing an idealized present. Though the young squire in Chaucer's *Canterbury Tales* might fill his days with dalliance, he was probably expected to realize all that was best in his father's tradition of "trouthe and honour, fredom and curteisye." Always the teacher has been accountable for teaching his charges what was aspired to rather than what was practiced, whether in virtue or in penmanship. Such a task is likely to call out the critic in the teacher.

The teacher's obligation to prepare succeeding generations for a future different from the present makes him an agent of change. Today's teacher is asked to prepare his students not merely to do better the things their fathers did, but to do things their fathers have never done. That the teacher must be critical of and educate to change the nutrition and agronomy of a backward rural economy may be taken for granted. But what is he to teach in the universe of changing domestic and international politics? Shall he present, advocate, or deplore the ideal of national sovereignty or that of the United Nations? Shall he praise children for emulating the thrift of their grandfathers or for accepting current economic policies to "buy now"?

Though teachers in the United States have not entered actively into politics and are not as a group significantly different in their political affiliations or economic views from the general population, they are frequently judged to be committed to social change. And to some extent this seems an inescapable commitment, though it need not be antithetical to dominant trends in a changing society. Where different generations and different interests compete for the loyalty of the next generation, however, the teacher, who can hardly be equally committed to all the values of a changing and heterogeneous society, is easily suspected of disloyalty to some.

Efforts to legislate the teacher's loyalty through certification and conditions of employment have been characteristic especially of periods of rapid or radical change. Efforts to formulate and insure academic freedom as essential to the performance of the teacher's task have been almost as frequent. The right, indeed the obligation, of the teacher to question and to criticize existing practices and beliefs was affirmed by the prophets of the Old Testament as well as by Socrates. In the United States the teacher shares with all citizens the privilege of freedom of speech; many believe, however, that as a teacher he has special obligations that should curtail his exercise of this right.

With respect to loyalty also the American situation is a special one. In countries with a relatively long established and homogeneous population loyalty may be taken for granted; this would seem to be the case in England, where, even during wartime, loyalty was more likely to be assumed than in the United States. In America, with its large numbers of foreign-born citizens, the tendency has been to consider loyalty less a birthright than an achievement. The fact that loyalty is for so many a matter of choice—a choice that might not be made—perhaps explains why it has periodically occasioned so much concern.

What is critical in any discussion of loyalty as an aspect of the teacher's relationship to society is the question: loyalty to what? To the immediate community or to some larger community? To the traditions of this time, this state, or to the national community? To a party or to a democratic way of life? To a nation, a denomination, or mankind? For the teacher there is the further complication, pointed out by Justice Minton in the majority decision in the Adler case, that the teacher speaks to a captive audience of unformed and highly suggestible minds unprepared to enter equally into controversy. Perhaps the recommendation made in a recent article on academic freedom in the journal of a professional organization of university teachers is also applicable to those who would teach younger students.

> There is one loyalty oath that every man in the teaching profession is compelled to take, and the penalty for its violation is not the legal penalty of treason, but the damnation of his immortal soul. He may not take this oath before a notary public, but if he doesn't swear it on the altar of God, he is no teacher, but a quack. Its terms are simple. They are: "In speaking to this class I swear to tell the truth, the whole truth and nothing but the truth, so help me God." [7]

If the teacher's loyalty to existing economic and political systems is a major problem in his relationship to society, it is by no means the only

[7] Gerald W. Johnson, "A Journalistic View of Academic Freedom," *AAUP Bulletin,* Summer 1956, p. 268.

one. This problem is unlikely to impinge on the daily life of the teacher; only rarely does it become critical for any single teacher. A sense of separateness and distance, however, may be a daily experience for many teachers. Governmental agencies or other organized groups may be interested in the social ideas and loyalty of teachers generally, but what the individual teacher is more likely to feel are the attitudes of the parents of his students. A consequence of the teacher's function as an agent of social change is that he may be perceived as the person responsible for weaning children away from the beliefs and customs of their parents. Especially in first generation homes the child's retort to parental demands or instructions may often be, "but teacher says . . ." And what teacher says, whether it be the approved method of subtraction or modern views of hygiene, is likely to lead parents raised in other cultures and other classes to feel rejected and discarded. Although the teacher may seek to provide a link between the generations, he may be perceived as the one who breaks it.

The teacher's separation from the community stems not only from his commitment to change but also from his own social mobility. In most communities women who enter teaching do so in part because it is a way of improving their position in life. Desirous of leaving behind them their own less advantaged backgrounds, they may be very critical of the many children in their classes who are not equally ambitious, able, or hopeful of improving themselves. Teachers' extended education and the fact that their interest in professional advancement takes them away from their home towns, often divorce them from their families, class, and community. The teacher's mobility is not only upward from one social class to another; it is a geographic mobility also. Since communities differ greatly in the salaries paid to teachers, many teachers move from one community, even from one region of the country to another, in search of higher income. In a recent survey of the job placement of beginning teachers it was found that nearly two-thirds were not teaching in their home communities.[8] And it is probable that many more experienced teachers make additional moves in the course of their professional careers. For these reasons the teacher is often quite literally a stranger in the community. If he is to find personal happiness and be professionally effective despite his status as an "outsider," the teacher will need to learn to understand and take account of values and behavior different from his own.

The teacher's position in society, his status, is evidenced by a variety of outward and visible signs. Titles, special privileges, and monetary compensation are the most usual forms of recognizing status. In Germany the teacher at each rank in the school system is designated by a special title

[8] *First-year Teachers in 1954-55.* National Education Association Research Bulletin, 34:1-24, February 1956.

by which he is addressed not only by his students and colleagues but also by the butcher, the baker, and the postman. To all who have dealings with him he is Herr Studienrat, Herr Oberstudienrat, Herr Studiendirektor, Herr Doktor Oberstudiendirektor, as he advances in his profession. Even the teacher's wife is addressed by his titles, as, of course, are the wives of all other German officials. The rules for Russian school children require boys to bow respectfully to their teachers when they meet them on the street; European children generally rise when the teacher enters the classroom; European teachers as a matter of course are given precedence in corridors, dining rooms, and assemblies. Of course, these tokens of respect are not always paid. Mrs. Squeers warned Nicholas Nickleby upon his arrival at Dotheboys Hall that he would have to demand, perhaps even fight for, the respect due him.

> . . . mind *you* take care, young man, and get the first wash. The teacher ought always to have it; but they get the better of him if they can.

Society may recognize the special status of teachers, as of other special groups, by granting special privileges. At various periods in Europe teachers were exempted from taxes or from military service. A limited tax reduction is among the proposals recently advanced in this country as one means of inducing men and women to enter teaching and to remain in the profession. Teachers in most communities in the United States are excused from jury duty. Very recently some communities, aware of the relatively low level of prestige accorded American teachers, have inaugurated a "Teacher Recognition Day." Teachers have often indicated that lack of prestige was a more serious cause for dissatisfaction than meager salaries. They may welcome such expressions of public regard; or they may think such tokens indicate general lack of regard rather than genuine respect.

Although it is possible to speak separately of status and income, the two are related. In Western cultures especially the price paid for a man's services is an index to his status. The discrepancy between expressions of the importance of teachers' contributions to society and what society was willing to pay for them has been chronic. This discrepancy has been rationalized as a peculiar distinction. "There are," Rousseau declared, "employments so noble that we cannot fulfill them for money without showing ourselves unworthy to fulfill them. Such an employment is that of a soldier; such a one is that of a teacher."

The economic status of teachers depends on their availability and the demand for them. Throughout the colonial period in America some teachers began their teaching as indentured servants. An advertisement as late as 1786 offers:

Men and Women Servants [9]
Just Arrived

In the ship *Paca,* Robert Caulfield, Master, in five Weeks from Belfast and Cork, a number of healthy Men and Women SERVANTS.

Among them are several valuable tradesmen, viz.

Carpenters, shoemakers, Coopers, Blacksmiths, staymakers, Bookbinders, Clothiers, Diers, Butchers, Schoolmasters, Millwrights, and Labourers.

Their indentures are to be disposed of by the subscribers,
Brown, and Maris,
William Wilson

Baltimore, May 29, 1786

Teachers during this period were paid by parents who could afford to pay for their children's education on the basis of the number of days the child attended school. Sometimes teachers were paid partly in goods; in rural areas part of the teacher's compensation was in board and room with various families in the community. Public or philanthropic funds were used, often haphazardly and sporadically, to pay teachers of charity schools. Even after schooling became free to all the children in a community, teachers were paid only subsistence wages. For this reason teaching remained for many years a stepping-stone occupation rather than a career, especially for men. Although teachers today are much more likely to persist in their profession than in earlier times, because of better salaries and benefits and the commitment established through a longer preparation, many still leave teaching for higher paying occupations. Whitman's editorials in the Brooklyn *Daily Eagle* in 1848 deploring the low salaries paid to New York City teachers and their consequent flight from the profession might have been written today. The recent unprecedented demand for teachers, occasioned by the disproportionate increase in the birth rate since World War II has probably done more to raise teacher salaries than any other single factor. Though teachers' salaries are still low in comparison with those in occupations requiring comparable preparation, and have not kept pace with rising costs of living, the national average salary for teachers rose from about $2000 to about $4000 in the decade from 1946-56.

Salaries and conditions of employment, like living conditions and costs, differ markedly in different communities, but the trend in recent years has been toward greater equalization. Salary differentiation based on sex or on race is no longer common practice. Professional teachers associations have played a major part in the trend toward better salaries for all teachers, tenure, or continuing contract provisions, and a single salary schedule for

[9] *Maryland Gazette or Baltimore Advertiser,* May 30, June 6 and 13, 1786.

elementary and secondary school teachers. At the present time the National Commission on Teacher Education and Professional Standards of the N.E.A. estimates that more than 80 per cent of the nation's public school teachers are now employed in systems having tenure provisions. More than 90 per cent of the urban school districts in the United States pay elementary and secondary school teachers with comparable preparation the same salaries.

Although the development of equitable salary scales has obvious advantages in attracting and holding individuals to a teaching career, some critics of this system fear that it tends also to favor mediocrity. It may be argued that a system that does not recognize exceptional competence by higher salaries discourages the most able teachers. On the other hand, merit systems, in which teachers are accorded salary increments not on the basis of years of service but on demonstrable excellence have proven extremely difficult to administer. In large school systems the size of the teaching staff makes it almost impossible to observe and reach conclusions about individual teachers. Since merit systems depend on the recommendations of the teacher's supervisors, they may lead to biased and preferential decisions. What is perhaps the chief obstacle to merit systems is the fact that there are such wide differences of opinion on what constitutes outstanding performance in teaching. The man who works with things may be judged by the quantity of his output, by the speed and economy of his operation; his product may be weighed, measured, put to the test of demand in a public market. Reasonable men can agree on the best mousetrap and the best machine for a particular purpose. But the teacher's product, if it can be called this, is his small contribution to the development of a human being. Even to raise the problem is to suggest its difficulties.

Nevertheless current efforts to attract the master teacher and to reward him financially without promoting him out of teaching into higher paid administrative positions have reopened the question of merit compensation. A study by Coen reports 248 school districts, employing nearly half of the nation's public school teachers, use some form of merit ratings. Ninety per cent of the teachers in the 71 districts he studied were reported to favor it.[10]

THE TEACHER AS A PERSON

The teacher must have a sound general education and must be well-informed about what he plans to teach. He must understand children and how they learn. His chances of finding himself as a professional person will be enhanced by a knowledge of the social functions and limitations of the teacher in a particular society. Beyond these things, perhaps of greater

[10] Alban Wasson Coen, II, "An Analysis of Successful Merit Rating Programs," *Phi Delta Kappan 39:394-7,* June 1958.

importance than any one of them, is the teacher's character and personality.

Some writers set a level of propriety and ethical excellence for the teacher that is almost out of reach. Increasingly, however, writers and public opinion alike have come to think of teachers as people, too. Only twenty years ago a teacher's contract in a small town in North Carolina could require of the teacher promises like these:

> I promise to abstain from all dancing, immodest dressing, and any other conduct unbecoming a teacher and a lady.
>
> I promise not to go out with any young man except in so far as it may be necessary to stimulate Sunday School work.
>
> I promise not to fall in love, to become engaged or secretly married.
>
> I promise to remain in the dormitory or on the school grounds when not actively engaged in school or church work elsewhere.[11]

Today teachers are expected to exemplify generally recognized social virtues, but not to adhere to standards that would be considered unreasonable for other adults.

But expectations of this kind are by no means those truly critical in discussions of the personal qualities that fit men and women for teaching. Probably the single most important quality sought in the teacher is the character of his relationship to his students. Sometimes, as with Pestalozzi, the teacher is asked to be "everything" to his students; sometimes, as in Cantor's view, he is warned against personal involvement. Repeatedly the teacher is admonished to be loving but to avoid intimacy. Is it possible to define the qualities in his relationships with children that are of primary importance?

To begin with, no one should undertake to teach who does not like children and like to be with them. A teacher will spend six hours a day, five days a week, forty weeks of the year with children. Enthusiasm for his subject will not compensate the man or woman who finds the company of children boring or irritating. Sometimes the prospective teacher, thinking of the children he will teach, imagines them all made in an idealized image and is disappointed to find that real classrooms hold many children quite unlike this image. Whitman's query to those "who would assume a place to teach" may well be pondered by the prospective teacher. "Do you," he asked, "hold like love for those hardening into maturity? for the last-born? little and big? and for the errant?"

---

[11] The actual wording of a teacher's contract in a small North Carolina town, quoted in *Social Frontier* 2:158, February 1936.

Of course teachers, like parents, can love children in ways that restrict rather than liberate. As the selection by Menninger points out, teachers whose love for children stems from their own need to be loved are likely to make unreasonable emotional demands upon their students. The teacher must be prepared to give love to children; he should not expect a like return from them. The teacher who is gratified to see the children he teaches make some progress in learning and in character without expecting to be thanked or remembered is likely to find most satisfactions and fewest frustrations in teaching—and is most likely to be remembered in the end.

People choose to teach for all kinds of reasons—often for reasons not apparent even to themselves. The wish to improve one's socio-economic position has already been cited as one motive. Wattenberg and Havighurst conclude, on the basis of their studies, that individuals from different socio-economic backgrounds are motivated to teach for different reasons.[12] From less advantaged groups teaching seems to draw upward striving individuals, whereas intensely ambitious young people from upper class families are less likely to be attracted to teaching. Middle class boys and girls who look forward to teaching are often those with strong social interests who enjoy associating with groups, whereas those from slum backgrounds who are drawn to teaching are often those boys and girls who are relatively isolated from their peers.

Symonds's analysis of the autobiographies of fifty women teachers reveals a variety of unconscious emotional motives underlying overt reasons of earning a living or following a family tradition.[13] In some instances it seemed that the choice of teaching stemmed from a wish to relive an unsatisfactory childhood, the need to gain the approval of elders, the need to overcome childhood feelings of inferiority, or the need to dominate others. Sometimes there seemed to be an impulse toward self-denial and self-sacrifice. What is important in considering motives, however, is how they are expressed in the teacher's relationships with children. Symonds concludes that personal needs leading to teaching as a vocation should not be used as criteria for selecting or rejecting teacher candidates. It is precisely those whose needs can be met through teaching who are likely to find it genuinely rewarding—provided they are able to find ways of meeting their own needs which are not detrimental to children. An important safeguard is the individual's understanding and accepting his own needs.

The ability to deal with others with understanding and to accept them for themselves depends upon self-understanding and self-acceptance. Erich

[12] William Wattenberg and Robert J. Havighurst, "The American Teacher, Then and Now," in *The Teacher's Role in American Society*, L. J. Stiles, Ed. (New York, Harper and Brothers, 1957).

[13] Percival M. Symonds, "Personality Adjustment of Women Teachers," *American Journal of Orthopsychiatry* 11:14-21, 1941.

Fromm speaks for many psychologists when he points out that the Golden Rule, "Love thy neighbor as thyself," does not imply that love of self is reprehensible. It is so only when it sets self-interest before or against the interests of others. The individual who rejects his own needs will find it difficult to accept children's needs. The teacher who cannot forgive his own weaknesses and errors, will not easily forgive children theirs. He will need to learn to be patient with his own efforts if he is to be patient with the slow processes by which children learn and grow.

What Fromm describes as the "productive character" and Horney as the "nurturant personality" epitomize much that has been written about the personal qualities desired of teachers. The behavior of the productive, nurturant person toward others is characterized in Fromm's terms by *care, responsibility, respect,* and *knowledge*. These qualities are common to the love of the teacher for his students, of the mother for her children, of friends and of lovers. The teacher whose love for his students is productive feels responsible for their growth and development and is willing to exert himself to that end. Does this imply, as Pestalozzi held, that the teacher should be all things to his students? On the contrary, may not care and responsibility be sometimes best expressed by sharing them? Even the mother, who of necessity begins by being all things to her child, will, if her love is genuinely nurturant, recognize that the child's best interests require that she relinquish total care and responsibility. From Cantor's point of view the teacher who enlists the care of specially competent people in the child's behalf is showing not less but more responsibility and love than the teacher who assumes the total task himself.

In addition to care and responsibility a productive relationship demands respect and knowledge. The teacher demonstrates these qualities by his efforts to see each child as he is and not in terms of his own wishes for the child or of abstractions, even scientifically valid abstractions, of what children are like generally.

Since the teacher often finds himself the target of hostilities engendered in children by unhappy home experiences or the scapegoat for parental anxieties about their children, he must develop a large tolerance for these projections. One of the hardest things for beginning teachers to learn is to accept, without retaliating, children's expressions of hostility, which may often come not from the classroom situation at all but from other frustrations in the child's life.

There are successful teachers who like and demand a highly organized classroom, who are most comfortable with a very detailed course of study, and who prefer a system of classroom regulations clearly spelled out. Other teachers, equally effective, prefer to work in a more permissive atmosphere and to develop teaching and learning plans and rules of behavior as they go along. The school system in the United States includes both these styles of teaching and organization, often within the same school. Most children can accommodate to either of these patterns and to many other variations. Nevertheless, some degree of flexibility and spontaneity is probably a necessary quality for successful teaching. A teacher may teach the third grade for the major portion of his teaching career; but each class of eight-year-olds will differ from its predecessors. Though a curriculum may change but little over the years, neighborhoods and the children are continuously changing. In most school systems today curricula are changing too. It is a safe if broad generalization to say that one unchanging rule for teachers is that no procedure works in all situations. Each new day makes some new demands on the teacher that can be met only if he is willing and able to improvise.

Teaching calls for social sensitivity and spontaneity to meet the fluctuating needs of groups of children. It also requires the teacher to establish and maintain certain values and standards so that children may have a sense of stability and confidence in their situation. Child psychologists agree that children need limits as well as freedom if they are to realize their potentialities.

The teacher's liking for children must not only extend to all kinds of children but must also include a liking for children in groups. There are some individuals who have all the qualities so far described who do not like working with groups of children, though they may work well with one or a few children at a time. The classroom teacher, however, should be the kind of person who finds groups of children stimulating and who is able to stimulate children in groups. To some extent this quality seems to include a gift for projecting himself as well as his subject in the classroom. Like the good counselor the good teacher needs to know how to listen to others; it may be that one of the traits differentiating the teacher and the counselor is the teacher's impulse to communicate, to tell, to show how.

Perhaps it is fortunate that relatively little is known about the attributes of effective teachers. Present knowledge suggests that effective teachers are to be found among a wide variety of personalities, that they relate to children in many different ways. One of the challenges to the beginning teacher, a challenge which only he can meet, is to discover the style of teaching that best suits his individual gifts. The selection by Thelen in this section of the readings suggests some widely held images of the teacher; the reader doubtless can supply others. A major task in the development of the professional person is the harmonious coming together of the individual's self-image and his image of the teacher he hopes to be.

The choice of teaching involves all of the problems suggested in this discussion, and others as well. It calls for self-examination and for long-range planning, for a considered view of one's social role and for a quality of human relationships not easy to attain, for enthusiasm, humor, and patience. The good teacher could almost always better himself by seeking his livelihood in other vocations; the poor teacher will be unlikely to experience the compensating rewards of teaching. Perhaps the complexities and fascination of teaching can best be described by a distinguished teacher of many years' experience.

> No one can teach English with completeness. It requires more knowledge, wisdom, and sympathy than any one man or woman can possess. It requires more reading, more writing, more study than the hours of the day allow. It results, as does all teaching, in defeats, in regrets, and in disappointments. But it results also in achievement, and adds to the very knowledge, wisdom, and sympathy it requires. It deals with the intimate matters of the mind, and so terrifies the thoughtful and sensitive teacher. There are a thousand reasons why you should not begin to teach English, and if you have begun, why you should leave for other fields; there are a thousand reasons, but there are a thousand and one why you should begin and why those of us who have begun would not stop.[14]

WHAT DOES THE READER DO?

The selections on *The Vocation of Teaching* are intended to move the reader to think critically about himself as a teacher. They may confirm and strengthen a decision to teach. They may help to define such a decision with reference to a preferred level of teaching through their presentation of the distinctive expectations and satisfactions of teaching young children or older boys and girls. Teaching, these selections show, is more than a way of earning a living, though it is that too. Like all professions, it is a way of life. By examining this way of life the reader can begin his participation in a peculiarly human activity. Through these and other readings, and through observation and discussion, teachers and prospective teachers can imagine themselves fulfilling the various roles and obligations and meeting some of the problems and issues of a life of teaching.

If the reader decides that teaching is not for him, that its rewards are not those likely to be most important to him, or that its limitations outweigh its rewards, he will have profited nonetheless from thoughtful consideration of what it means to be a teacher. As citizen and parent he may have a livelier and more intelligent understanding of teachers and teaching and, as he reads and considers the other sections of this book, of the other aspects of education which are of public as well as professional interest.

[14] Lou La Brant, *We Teach English* (New York, Harcourt, Brace and Company, 1951), p. 312.

The Vocation of Teaching

This introductory essay has indicated some of the important and recurring questions about the teacher and teaching that should be used as a framework for reading the selections. These selections present a range of viewpoints on the primary and secondary roles of the teacher, on desirable and undesirable personal qualities of teachers, and on the teacher's relationships and obligations to parents and to the state. Some of these selections are about individual teachers remembered, as Moses Woolson was, by a pupil; some, like the selection from Pestalozzi, are autobiographical accounts of teaching experiences; still others are sociological or psychological inquiries of teachers' professional activities or satisfactions or of public opinion about teachers. These views of teachers and teaching are intended to prompt further inquiries. Information about other teachers and different ways of teaching is genuinely enlightening only as the reader makes personal application of these facts and ideas. The thoughtful reader will begin to establish his own criteria for the social and professional attributes of a good teacher, even though he may never wholly meet them.

Whether the reader's first concern is teaching children or teaching a subject, he will need to think about how these seemingly contradictory interests may be reconciled. Putting himself in the place of the social scientist, he will ask himself if the degree of intimacy between teacher and child should supplement, imitate, or counterbalance the relationship between children and their parents. Many societies, including earlier periods in American society and numerous primitive cultures, make rather sharp differences in the teacher-child relationship before and after puberty. These instances provide a perspective from which to view the current trend toward extending the parental, counseling functions of the teacher into the secondary school years. This is an issue that is important as it affects the individual's choice of the level, and perhaps the kind of school, at which he prefers to teach. Beyond this, teachers as citizens as well as in their professional roles have a part in determining this and other educational practices and for this reason should have clearly defined ideas about them.

The early and continuing recognition of the personal and scholarly qualities desired of teachers will provide the prospective teacher with a background against which his own preparation may be planned. To what extent are modern certification requirements, though couched in very different terms, consonant with those ideals of character, learning, and sympathy affirmed by educational spokesmen of earlier periods and other countries? Quintilian's description of the ideal orator, "a good man, skilled in speaking," is implicit in much of the current controversy on the professional education of the teacher. What is implied by a similar definition of the good teacher? Nearly two thousand years later John Dewey declared, "There is truth in the saying that education must first be human and only after that professional." Does the fact that general human qualities are given priority over professional competence imply that general education should precede professional education in time?

Is it reasonable to suggest, as many writers have, and as popular opinion seems still to expect, that teachers be models of deportment, virtue, and loyalty? And if it is reasonable, is it possible? Is the teacher first a citizen and secondarily a teacher? Or as a teacher is he a special kind of citizen? Should the teacher conform to and represent the values and mores of the community in which he teaches? Of the national community? To realize that this problem is more than theoretical the reader has only to visualize the dilemma of many teachers in communities sharply divided on the question of racial segregation.

This and other questions relating to the professional tasks and social obligations of the teachers are, of course, integrally related to variant aims of education and should be considered in the light of the readings in that section. Dewey saw the teacher as "a social servant set apart for the maintenance of proper social order and the security of the right social growth." The teacher has been implicitly or explicitly conceived as a servant of society by exponents of social systems as different as those of Sparta, pre-revolutionary France, National Socialism, and the U.S.S.R. Dewey's description of the teacher as social servant, however, must be seen in the light of his view of education as "the fundamental method of social progress and reform." The teacher Dewey envisioned was a critic as well as a servant of the state; though he was the servant of the state, he was not the slave.

The reader will need continuously to look for the connotations, the underlying and accompanying assumptions that make the same words mean very different things. The search for similarities and continuities is an important step in reading and thinking about any subject. But it is a first step only. The sophisticated reader learns to look with equal care for dissimilarities and change.

Not only the aims of education but the clientele of the schools, the sources and quality of the control of education, and the division of educational functions among the school, the family, the church, and other social agencies all affect what the teacher is expected to do and be and what he can do and be. If children of retarded mental ability or children with serious emotional disturbances or physical handicaps are enabled or required to attend school, will the teacher need special knowledge and skills? Teachers in parochial schools and in publicly supported schools may have different duties; do they have different loyalties? By what alternative means may teachers influence educational policies and practices? Should they act through professional organizations like the National Education Association, or through civic organizations like the Citizens Committee for Better Schools, or through local Parent-Teacher Associations—or through all of these? How will the teacher compromise his professional concern for raising teachers' salaries with his equally legitimate interest as taxpayer?

An important part, then, of the reader's task is to read and consider the selections in each section of this book in connection with relevant selections and issues raised in the other sections and in additional readings. This kind of careful reading is necessary to an understanding of any complex subject; in reading about education, which is permeated by many preconceptions and unrecognized biases, it is essential. Everyone is inclined to come to the study of education, having been its subject, thinking there is little he does not know. One of the purposes of this book is to suggest that there is much to know about education—and few answers ready made.

The Teacher as a Person

THE TEACHER *

Let the teacher, first of all, assume the attitude of the father toward his pupils. He stands in the place of the parents who have entrusted their children to him. He must have no personal vices, and must not tolerate them in others. He must be austere, but not gloomy; genial, but not dissipated. Otherwise he runs the risk of incurring hatred or contempt. His speech must be constantly concerned with what is honorable and good. He must warn frequently, that he may seldom have to chastise. He must not lose his temper, but neither must he disregard the necessity for correcting faults. He must be simple in his teaching, able to endure labor, steadfast, never unreasonable. He must have a ready answer, for those who ask questions, and must draw out those who fail to ask them. In praising the recitations of his pupils, he must not be too sparing or too diffuse; for in the one case the pupils will grow tired of their work, and in the other they will become self-satisfied. In correcting mistakes he must never be harsh or abusive. Many pupils who have the best of intentions are led to abandon their plans for further study, because certain teachers act as though they hated their students.

The teacher ought to be a good speaker himself, and in his daily speech he should present an example to the pupils. Though they can learn much from reading, the living voice furnishes a more perfect inspiration—par-

---

* Quintilian, *Quintilian on Education, Selections from the Institutes of Oratory*, Edited by Herman Harrell Horne . . . newly translated by Catherine Ruth Smith (New York: New York University, 1936), pp. 145-8. (First century A.D.)

The Teacher as a Person

ticularly the voice of their teacher, whom they should both love and reverence. We imitate most easily the persons of those of whom we are fond. . . .

The father who is selecting a teacher for his son must make sure that the instructor's moral character is above reproach. All the other qualities which the teacher should possess, and should use for the benefit of his young charges, will be utterly useless if he is lacking in this one point. . . .

There are those who feel that, when a boy is ready to commence his studies in rhetoric, it is a mistake to place him with a man who is eminent in that profession. They prefer to keep the boy back for a time, and to have him guided by teachers of less importance. The mediocre instructor, they say, is the proper person to handle the early part of the boy's education; for such a teacher is easy to understand and imitate, and besides, he is not too conceited to undertake the task of elementary teaching.

It should not require much persuasion, however, to convince my readers how much better it is to have the very best instructor at the beginning, and how hard it is to eradicate faults that have become fixed. . . .

People who advocate the retention of inferior teachers at this state of the boy's education fall into a double error. It is all very well to say that such teachers are sufficient for the time being: this might be true if the work of an inadequate teacher were merely less in amount, and not also inferior in quality. But the other difficulty is a more serious one. It is that the skilful orator frequently does not care to devote himself to the details of elementary instruction. Sometimes he is bored by this preliminary work, and sometimes he is actually incapable of performing it.

But the man who will not devote himself to such work is unworthy of being counted a teacher. The most excellent of orators can certainly engage in this work, if he wishes to do so. . . .

Someone may raise the objection that there is a type of eloquence which is obviously over the heads of undeveloped pupils. I would be the first to admit this. But the eloquent speaker who is also a skilled teacher will know how to adapt his work to the capacity of the pupil's mind. So a champion walker, taking a little boy out for an airing, would give him his hand and moderate his pace, and not go so fast that the toddler could not follow him.

Besides, it is true that things are often easier and clearer to understand when they are spoken by a very learned man. The first virtue of eloquence is clearness. But the less talent a man has, the more he will try to lift himself up and spread himself out, as short people walk on tiptoe, and weaklings often become bullies. . . . Similarly, the worse a teacher is, the harder he will be to understand. . . .

THE GOOD SCHOOLMASTER *

There is scarce any profession in the commonwealth more necessary, which is so slightly performed. The reasons whereof I conceive to be these: First, young scholars make this calling their refuge, yea, perchance before they have taken any degree in the university, commence schoolmasters in the country, as if nothing else were required to set up this profession but only a rod and a ferula. Secondly, others who are able, use it only as a passage to better preferment, to patch the rents in their present fortune, till they can provide a new one, and betake themselves to some more gainful calling. Thirdly, they are disheartened from doing their best with the miserable reward which in some places they receive, being masters to the children and slaves to their parents. Fourthly, being grown rich, they grow negligent, and scorn to touch the school, but by the proxy of an usher. But see how well our schoolmaster behaves himself.

His genius inclines him with delight in his profession. Some men had as lief be schoolboys as schoolmasters, to be tied to the school as Cooper's Dictionary and Scapula's Lexicon are chained to the desk therein; and though great scholars, and skilful in other arts, are bunglers in this: but God of his goodness hath fitted several men for several callings, that the necessity of Church and State, in all conditions, may be provided for. So that he who beholds the fabric thereof may say, God hewed out this stone, and appointed it to lie in this very place; for it would fit none other so well, and here it doth most excellent. And thus God mouldeth some for a schoolmaster's life, undertaking it with desire and delight, and discharging it with dexterity and happy success.

He studieth his scholars' natures as carefully as they their books; and ranks their dispositions into several forms. And though it may seem difficult for him in a great school to descend to all particulars, yet experienced schoolmasters may quickly make a grammar of boys' natures, and reduce them all, saving some few exceptions, to these general rules.

1. Those that are ingenious and industrious. The conjunction of two such planets in a youth presage much good unto him. To such a lad a frown may be a whipping, and a whipping a death; yea, where their master whips them once, shame whips them all the week after. Such natures he useth with all gentleness.

2. Those that are ingenious and idle. These think with the hare in the fable, that running with snails (so they count the rest of their schoolfellows) they shall come soon enough to the post, though sleeping a good

---

* Thomas Fuller, *The Holy and Profane States* (Boston, Little, Brown, 1864), pp. 104-10. (First published in 1642.)

The Teacher as a Person

while before their starting. Oh, a good rod would finely take them napping.

3. Those that are dull and diligent. Wines the stronger they be the more lees they have when they are new. Many boys are muddy-headed till they be clarified with age, and such afterwards prove the best. Bristol diamonds are both bright, and squared and pointed by nature, and yet are soft and worthless; whereas orient ones in India are rough and rugged naturally. Hard, rugged, and dull natures of youth acquit themselves afterwards the jewels of the country, and therefore their dullness at first is to be borne with, if they be diligent. That schoolmaster deserves to be beaten himself who beats nature in a boy for a fault. And I question whether all the whipping in the world can make their parts, which are naturally sluggish, rise one minute before the hour nature hath appointed.

4. Those that are invincibly dull and negligent also. Correction may reform the latter, not amend the former. All the whetting in the world can never set a razor's edge on that which hath no steel in it. Such boys he consigneth over to other professions. Shipwrights and boatmakers will choose those crooked pieces of timber which other carpenters refuse. Those may make excellent merchants and mechanics which will not serve for scholars.

He is able, diligent, and methodical in his teaching; not leading them rather in a circle than forwards. He minces his precepts for children to swallow, hanging clogs on the nimbleness of his own soul, that his scholars may go along with him.

He is and will be known to be an absolute monarch in his school. If cockering mothers proffer him money to purchase their sons an exemption from his rod, (to live as it were in a peculiar, out of their master's jurisdiction), with disdain he refuseth it, and scorns the late custom in some places, of commuting whipping into money, and ransoming boys from the rod at a set price. If he hath a stubborn youth, correction-proof, he debaseth not his authority by contesting with him, but fairly, if he can, puts him away before his obstinacy hath infected others.

He is moderate in inflicting deserved correction. Many a schoolmaster better answereth the name paidotribes than paidogogos, rather tearing his scholars' flesh with whipping, than giving them good education. No wonder if his scholars hate the Muses, being presented unto them in the shapes of fiends and furies. Junius complains *de insolenti carnificina* (harsh brutality) of his schoolmaster, by whom *conscindebatur flagris septies aut octies in dies singulos* (he was scourged seven or eight times a day). Yea, hear the lamentable verses of poor Tusser, in his own Life:

> From Paul's I went, to Eton sent,
> To learn straightways the Latin phrase,

> Where fifty-three stripes given to me
>   At once I had.
> For fault but small, or none at all,
> It came to pass thus beat I was;
> See, Udal,[1] see the mercy of thee
>   To me, poor lad.

Such an Orbilius mars more scholars than he makes: their tyranny hath caused many tongues to stammer, which spake plain by nature, and whose stuttering at first was nothing else but fears quavering on their speech at their master's presence; and whose mauling them about their heads hath dulled those who in quickness exceeded their master.

He makes his school free to him who sues to him *in forma pauperis*. And surely learning is the greatest alms that can be given. But he is a beast who, because the poor scholar cannot pay him his wages, pays the scholar in his whipping. Rather are diligent lads to be encouraged with all excitements to learning. This minds me of what I have heard concerning Mr. Bust, that worthy late schoolmaster of Eton, who would never suffer any wandering begging scholar such as justly the statute hath ranked in the forefront of rogues to come into his school, but would thrust him out with earnestness, (however privately charitable unto him) lest his schoolboys should be disheartened from their books by seeing some scholars, after their studying in the university, preferred to beggary.

He spoils not a good school to make thereof a bad college, therein to teach his scholars logic. For, besides that logic may have an action of trespass against grammar for encroaching on her liberties, syllogisms are solecisms taught in the school, and oftentimes they are forced afterwards in the university to unlearn the fumbling skill they had before.

Out of his school he is no whit pedantical in carriage or discourse; contenting himself to be rich in Latin, though he doth not jingle with it in every company wherein he comes.

To conclude, let this amongst other motives make schoolmasters careful in their place, that the eminencies of their scholars have commended the memories of their schoolmasters to posterity, who otherwise in obscurity had altogether been forgotten. Who had ever heard of R. Bond, in Lancashire, but for the breeding of learned Ascham his scholar? or of Hartgrave, in Brundley school, in the same county but because he was the first did teach worthy Dr. Whitaker? Nor do I honor the memory of Mulcaster for anything so much as for his scholar, that gulf of learning, Bishop Andrews. This made the Athenians, the day before the great feast of Theseus their founder, to sacrifice a ram to the memory of Conidas his schoolmaster that first instructed him.

---

[1] Nich. Udal, Schoolmaster of Eton in the reign of King Henry the Eighth.

THEIR HANDS WERE IN MINE *

... I wanted to prove by my experiment that if public education is to have any real value, it must imitate the methods which make the merit of domestic education; for it is my opinion that if public education does not take into consideration the circumstances of family life, and everything else that bears on a man's general education, it can only lead to an artificial and methodical dwarfing of humanity.

In any good education, the mother must be able to judge daily, nay hourly, from the child's eyes, lips, and face, of the slightest change in his soul. The power of the educator, too, must be that of a father, quickened by the general circumstances of domestic life.

Such was the foundation upon which I built. I determined that there should not be a minute in the day when my children should not be aware from my face and my lips that my heart was theirs, that their happiness was my happiness, and their pleasures my pleasures.

Man readily accepts what is good, and the child readily listens to it; but it is not for you that he wants it, master and educator, but for himself. The good to which you would lead him must not depend on your capricious humor or passion; it must be a good which is good in itself and by the nature of things, and which the child can recognize as good. He must feel the necessity of your will in things which concern his comfort before he can be expected to obey it.

Whenever he does anything gladly, anything that brings him honor, anything that helps to realize any of his great hopes, or stimulates his powers, and enables him to say with truth, *I can,* then he is exercising his will.

The will, however, can not be stimulated by mere words; its action must depend upon those feelings and powers which are the result of general culture. Words alone can not give us a knowledge of things; they are only useful for giving expression to what we have in our mind.

The first thing to be done was to win the confidence and affection of the children. I was sure that if I succeeded in doing that, all the rest would follow of itself. Think for a moment of the prejudices of the people, and even of the children, and you will understand the difficulties with which I had to contend. ...

And yet, however painful this want of help and support was to me, it was favorable to the success of my undertaking, for it compelled me to be always everything for my children. I was alone with them from morning

---

* Pestalozzi, Letter on his work at Stanz, 1799, in Roger de Guimps, *Pestalozzi, His Life and Work,* International Education Series, Vol. XIV (New York, D. Appleton, 1890), pp. 152-4, 156, 157, 161.

till night. It was my hand that supplied all their wants, both of body and soul. All needful help, consolation, and instruction they received direct from me. Their hands were in mine, my eyes were fixed on theirs.

We wept and smiled together. They forgot the world and Stanz; they only knew that they were with me and I with them. We shared our food and drink. I had neither family, friends, nor servants; nothing but them. I was with them in sickness and in health, and when they slept. I was the last to go to bed, and the first to get up. In the bedroom I prayed with them, and, at their own request, taught them till they fell asleep. . . .

This is how it was that these children gradually became so attached to me, some indeed so deeply that they contradicted their parents and friends when they heard evil things said about me. They felt that I was being treated unfairly, and loved me, I think, the more for it. But of what avail is it for the young nestlings to love their mother, when the bird of prey that is bent on destroying them is constantly hovering near? . . .

For most of them study was something entirely new. As soon as they found that they could learn, their zeal was indefatigable, and in a few weeks children who had never before opened a book, and could hardly repeat a *Pater Noster* or an *Ave,* would study the whole day long with the keenest interest. Even after supper, when I used to say to them, "Children, will you go to bed or learn something?" they would generally answer, especially in the first month or two, "Learn something." It is true that afterwards, when they had to get up very early, it was not quite the same.

But this first eagerness did much towards starting the establishment on the right lines, and making the studies the success they ultimately were, a success, indeed, which far surpassed my expectations. And yet the difficulties in the way of introducing a well-ordered system of studies were at that time almost insurmountable. . . .

My one aim was to make their new life in common, and their new powers, awaken a feeling of brotherhood amongst the children, and make them affectionate, just and considerate. I reached this end without much difficulty. Amongst these seventy wild beggar-children there soon existed such peace, friendship, and cordial relations as are rare even between actual brothers and sisters.

The principle to which I endeavored to conform all my conduct was as follows: Endeavor, first, to broaden your children's sympathies, and, by satisfying their daily needs, to bring love and kindness into such unceasing contact with their impressions and their activity, that these sentiments may be engrafted in their hearts; then try to give them such judgment and tact as will enable them to make a wise, sure, and abundant use of these virtues in the circle which surrounds them. In the last place, do not hesitate to touch on the difficult questions of good and evil, and the words connected with them. And you must do this especially in connection with the ordinary events of every day, upon which your whole teaching in these matters must be founded, so that the children may be reminded of their own feelings, and supplied, as it were, with solid facts upon which to base their conception of the beauty and justice of the moral life. . . .

. . . the pedagogical principle which says that we must win the hearts and minds of our children by words alone, without having recourse to corporal punishment, is certainly good, and applicable under favorable conditions and circumstances; but with children of such widely different ages as mine, children for the most part beggars, and all full of deeply-rooted faults, a certain amount of corporal punishment was inevitable, especially as I was anxious to arrive surely, speedily, and by the simplest means, at gaining an influence over them all, for the sake of putting them all in the right road. I was compelled to punish them, but it would be a mistake to suppose that I thereby, in any way, lost the confidence of my pupils. . . .

REQUISITE QUALIFICATIONS OF TEACHERS *

Having adverted in the preceding lecture, to certain existing evils, unfriendly to the character and usefulness of common schools, I shall, in this, call your attention to the *requisite qualifications of an instructer*. The subject is one of high importance. It is not every one of those, even, who possesses the requisite literary attainments, who is qualified to assume the direction of a school. Many entirely fail of usefulness, though possessed of highly cultivated minds. Other ingredients enter into the composition of a good school master. Among these *common sense* is the first. This is a qualification exceedingly important, as in teaching school one has constant occasion for its exercise. Many, by no means deficient in intellect, are not persons of common sense. I mean by the term, that faculty by which things are seen as they are. It implies judgment and discrimination, and a proper sense of propriety in regard to the common affairs of life. It leads us to form judicious plans of action, and to be governed by our circumstances, in such a way as men in general will approve. It is the exercise of reason, uninfluenced by passion or prejudice. It is in man nearly what instinct is in brutes. It is very different from genius or talent, as they are commonly defined, but is better than either. It never blazes forth with the splendour of noon, but shines with a constant and useful light.

2. *Uniformity of temper* is another important trait in the character of an

* Samuel Read Hall, *Lectures on School-Keeping,* 2nd ed. (Boston, Richardson, Lord and Holbrook, 1830), pp. 30-33.

instructer. Where this is wanting, it is hardly possible to govern or teach with success. He, whose temper is constantly varying, can never be uniform in his estimation of things around him. Objects change in their appearance as passions change. What appears right in any given hour may seem wrong in the next. What appears desirable to-day, may be held with aversion to-morrow. An uneven temper, in any situation of life, subjects one to many inconveniences. But when placed in a situation where his every action is observed, and where his authority must be in constant exercise, the man who labours under this malady is especially unfortunate. It is impossible for him to gain and preserve respect among his pupils. No one who comes under the rule of a person of uneven temper, can know what to expect or how to act.

3. A capacity to *understand and discriminate character,* is highly important in him who engages in school-keeping. The dispositions of children are so various, the treatment and government of parents so dissimilar, that the most diversified modes of governing and teaching need to be employed. The instructer who is not able to discriminate, but considers all alike, and treats all alike, does injury to many. The least expression of disapprobation to one, is often more than the severest reproof to another; a word of encouragement will be sufficient to excite attention in some, while another will require to be urged, by every motive that can be placed before him. All the varying shades of disposition and capacity should be quickly learned by the instructer, that he may benefit all and do injustice to none. Without this, well meant efforts may prove hurtful, because ill-directed, and the desired object may be defeated, by the very means used to obtain it.

4. It is desirable that teachers should possess much *decision of character.* In every situation of life this trait is important, but in none more so than in that of which I am treating. The little world, by which he is surrounded, is the miniature of the older community. Children have their aversions and partialities, their hopes and fears, their plans, schemes, propensities and desires. These are often in collision with each other, and not unfrequently in collision with the laws of the school, and in opposition to their own best interest. Amidst all these, the instructer should be able to pursue a uniform course. He ought not to be easily swayed from what he considers right. If he be easily led from his purpose, or induced to vary from established rules, his school must become a scene of disorder. Without decision, the teacher loses the confidence and respect of his pupils. I would not say, that, if convinced of having committed an error, or of having given a wrong judgment, you should persist in the wrong. But I would say, that it should be known as one of your first principles in school-keeping, that what is required must be complied with in every case, unless cause can be shown why the rule ought, in a given instance, to be dispensed with. There should *then* be a

frank confession of error. In a word, without decision of purpose in a teacher, his scholars can never be brought under that discipline, which is requisite for his own ease and convenience, or for their improvement in knowledge.

5. A schoolmaster ought to be *affectionate.* The human heart is so constituted, that it cannot resist the influence of kindness. When affectionate intercourse is the offspring of those kind feelings which arise from true benevolence, it will have an influence on all around. It leads to ease in behaviour, and genuine politeness of manners. It is especially desirable in those who are surrounded by the young. Affectionate parents usually see their children exhibit similar feelings. Instructers, who cultivate this state of temper, will generally excite the same in their scholars. No object is more important than to gain the love and good will of those whom they are to teach. In no way is this more easily accomplished than by a kind interest manifested in their welfare; an interest which is exhibited by actions as well as words. This cannot fail of being attended with desirable results.

6. A just *moral discernment,* is of pre-eminent importance in the character of an instructer. Unless governed by a consideration of his moral obligation, he is but poorly qualified to discharge the duties which devolve upon him, when placed at the head of a school. He is himself, a moral agent, and accountable to himself, to his employers, to his country and to his God, for the faithful discharge of duty. If he have no moral sensibility, no fear of disobeying the laws of God, no regard for the institutions of our holy religion, how can he be expected to lead his pupils in the way that they should go? The cultivation of virtuous propensities is more important to children than even their intellectual culture. The *virtuous* man, though illiterate, will be happy, while the learned, if *vicious,* must be miserable in proportion to his attainments. The remark of the ancient philosopher, that "boys ought to be taught that which they will most need to practise when they come to be men," is most true. To cultivate virtuous habits, and awaken virtuous principles;—to excite a sense of duty to God, and of dependence on Him, should be the first objects of the teacher. If he permits his scholars to indulge in vicious habits—if he regard nothing as sin, but that which is a transgression of the laws of the school, if he suffer lying, profaneness, or other crimes, to pass unnoticed and unpunished, he is doing an injury for which he can in no way make amends. An instructer without moral feeling, not only brings ruin to the children placed under his care, but does injury to their parents, to the neighbourhood, to the town, and, doubtless, to other generations. The moral character of instructers should be considered a subject of very high importance; and let every one, who knows himself to be immoral, renounce at once the thought of such an employment, while he continues to disregard the laws of God, and the

happiness of his fellow men. Genuine piety is highly desirable in every one entrusted with the care and instruction of the young; but morality, at least, should be *required,* in every candidate for that important trust.

THE TASKMASTER *

The English and Latin High Schools, in those days, were housed in a single building, rather old and dingy, on the south side of Bedford Street; a partition wall separating them, a single roof covering them. The street front was of granite, the side walls of brick. There were brick-paved yards for the recess half-hour with overflow to the street and a nearby bakery. It was a barn-like, repellent structure fronting on a lane as narrow as the prevailing New England mind of its day.

Louis passed the examinations and his name was entered in the year book 1870-71.

He was among those—about forty in all—assigned to a room on the second floor, presided over by a "master" named Moses Woolson. This room was dingy rather than gloomy. The individual desks were in rows facing north, the light came from windows in the west and south walls. The master's platform and desk were at the west wall; on the opposite wall was a long blackboard. The entrance door was at the north, and in the southwest corner were two large glass-paneled cabinets, one containing a collection of minerals, the other carefully prepared specimens of wood from all parts of the world.

The new class was assembled and seated by a monitor, while the master sat at his desk picking his right ear. Louis felt as one entering upon a new adventure, the outcome of which he could not forecast, but surmised would be momentous.

Seated at last, Louis glanced at the master, whose appearance and make-up suggested, in a measure, a farmer of the hardy, spare, weatherbeaten, penurious, successful type—apparently a man of forty or under. When silence had settled over the mob, the master rose and began an harangue to his raw recruits; indeed he plunged into it without a word of welcome. He was a man above medium height, very scant beard, shocky hair; his movements were panther-like, his features, in action, were set as with authority and pugnacity, like those of a first mate taking on a fresh crew.

He was tense, and did not swagger—a man of passion. He said, in substance: "Boys, you don't know me, but you soon will. The discipline here

* Louis Henry Sullivan, *The Autobiography of an Idea* (New York, Press of the American Institute of Architects, 1924), pp. 157-69.

will be rigid. You have come here to learn and I'll see that you do. I will not only do my share but I will make you do yours. You are here under my care; no other man shall interfere with you. I rule here—I am master here—as you will soon discover. You are here as wards in my charge; I accept that charge as sacred; I accept the responsibility involved as a high, exacting duty I owe to myself and equally to you. I will give to you all that I have; you shall give to me all that you have. But mark you: The first rule of discipline shall be SILENCE. Not a desk-top shall be raised, not a book touched, no shuffling of feet, no whispering, no sloppy movements, no rustling. I do not use the rod, I believe it the instrument of barbarous minds and weak wills, but I will shake the daylight out of any boy who transgresses, after one warning. The second rule shall be STRICT ATTENTION. You are here to *learn,* to *think,* to *concentrate* on the matter in hand, to hold your minds steady. The third rule shall cover ALERTNESS. You shall be awake all the time—body and brain; you shall cultivate promptness, speed, nimbleness, dexterity of mind. The fourth rule: You shall learn to LISTEN; to *listen* in *silence* with the whole mind, not part of it; to listen with your *whole heart;* not part of it, for sound listening is a basis for sound thinking; sympathetic listening is a basis for sympathetic, worth-while, thinking; accurate listening is a basis of accurate thinking. Finally you are to learn to OBSERVE, to REFLECT, to DISCRIMINATE. But this subject is of such high importance, so much above your present understanding, that I will not comment upon it now; it is not to be approached without due preparation. I shall not start with you with a jerk, but tighten the lines bit by bit until I have you firmly in hand at the most spirited pace you can go." As he said this last saying, a dangerous smile went back and forth over his grim set face. As to the rest, he outlined the curriculum and his plan of procedure for the coming school year. He stressed matters of hygiene; and stated that a raised hand would always have attention. Lessons were then marked off in the various books—all were to be "home lessons"—and the class was dismissed for the day.

Louis was amazed, thunderstruck, dumbfounded, overjoyed! He had caught and weighed every word as it fell from the lips of the master; to each thrilling word he had vibrated in open-eyed, amazed response. He knew now that through the years his thoughts, his emotions, his dreams, his feelings, his romances, his visions, had been formless and chaotic; now in this man's utterances, they were voiced in explosive condensation, in a flash they became defined, living, real. A pathway had been shown him, a wholly novel plan revealed that he grasped as a banner in his hand, as homeward bound he cried within, *"At last a Man!"*

Louis felt the hour of freedom was at hand. He saw, with inward glowing, that true freedom could come only through discipline of power, and he

translated the master's word of discipline into its true intent: SELF DISCI-
PLINE OF SELF POWER. His eager life was to condense now in a focusing
of powers: What had the words meant—"silence," "attention," "promptness," "speed," "accurate," "observe," "reflect," "discriminate," but powers
of his own, obscurely mingled, un-coordinated, and thus far, vain to create?
Now, in the master's plan, which he saw as a ground plan, he beheld that
for which, in the darkness of broad daylight, he had yearned so desperately
in vain; that for which, as it were with empty, outstretched hands, he had
grasped, vaguely groping; as one seeing through a film, that for which he
had hungered with an aching heart as empty as his hands. He had not
known, surely, what it was he wished to find, but when the master breathed
the words that Louis felt to be inspired: "You are here as wards in my
charge; I accept that charge as sacred; I accept the responsibility involved
as a high exacting duty I owe to myself and equally to you. I will give to
you all that I have, you shall give me all that you have,"—a veil was
parted, as it were by magic, and behold! there stood forth not alone man
but a TEACHER of the young.

As it has but little import in this story, we shall pass over the breaking-in
period of Moses Woolson's class, and begin an exposition of Moses Woolson's plan and method, and Louis's responses thereto at that period the
master himself had forecast as "when I have you firmly in hand at the most
spirited pace you can go." Suffice it to say that with great skill in intensive
training he had brought them to this point within three months.

The ground work of his plan was set forth in his opening address; and
is now to be revealed in its workings in detail.

The studies on which Louis set the highest value were Algebra, Geometry,
English Literature, Botany, Mineralogy, and French language. All these
subjects were to him revelations. Algebra had startled him; for, through its
portal, he entered an unsuspected world of symbols. To him the symbol
X flashed at once as a key to the unknown but ascertainable. Standing
alone, he viewed this X in surprise as a mystic spirit in a land of enchantment, opening vistas so deep he could not see the end, and his vivid imagination saw at once that this X expanded in its latent power, might prove
the key to turn a lock in a door within a wall which shut out the truth he
was seeking—the truth which might dissolve for him, the mystery that lay
behind appearances. For this X, he saw, was manipulated by means of
things unknown.

Thus he saw far ahead; looking toward the time when he would be
mature. Geometry delighted him because of its nicety, its exactitude of relationships, its weird surprises—all like fairy tales, fairy tales which could
be proved, and then you said: Q.E.D. He began to see what was meant by
a theorem, a postulate, a problem, and that *proof* was a reasoned process

The Teacher as a Person   53

based on certain facts or assertions. It was well for him, at the time, that he did not perceive the Euclidian *rigidity,* in the sense that he had noted the fluency of Algebra. As to Botany, had he not always seen trees and shrubs and vines and flowers of the field, the orchard and the garden?

Now he was learning their true story, their most secret intimacies, and the organization of their world. He loved them all the more for this. Mineralogy was new and revealing, the common stones had begun as it were, to talk to him in their own words. Concerning French he was ardent, for he had France in view. English literature opened to him the great world of words, of ordered speech, the marvelous vehicle whereby were conveyed every human thought and feeling from mind to mind, from heart to heart, from soul to soul, from imagination to imagination, from thought to thought; and to his ever widening view, it soon arose before him as a vast treasure house wherein was stored, in huge accumulation, a record of the thoughts, the deeds, the hopes, the joys, the sorrows, and the triumphs, of mankind.

Moses Woolson was not a deep thinker, nor was Moses Woolson erudite or scholarly, or polished in manners, or sedate. Rather was he a blend of wild man and of poet. But of a surety he had the art of teaching at his fingers tips and his plan of procedure was scientific to a degree, so far beyond the pedagogic attainments of his day that he stood unique, and was cordially hated by his craft as lambs might fear and hate a wolf. Today men would speak of such a man as a "human dynamo," a man ninety-nine per cent "efficient." His one weakness was a temper he all too often let escape him, but his high strung, nervous make-up may be averred in part extenuation, for this very make-up was the source of his accomplishment and power; he surely gave in abundance, with overflowing hands, all that he had of the best to give.

His plan of procedure was simple in idea, and therefore possible of high elaboration in the steady course of its unfolding into action and results. For convenience it may be divided into three daily phases seemingly consecutive, but really interblended; first came severe memory drill, particularly in geometry, algebra, French grammar and in exact English; this work first done at home, and tested out next day in the school room. Second, (first, next day) a period of recitation in which memory discipline and every aspect of alertness were carried at high tension. At the end of this period came the customary half-hour recess for fresh air and easing up. After recess came nature study with open book. Chief among them Gray's School and Field Book of Botany—Louis's playground; then came a closing lecture by the Master.

Thus it may be said, there was a period of high tension, followed by a period of reduced tension, and this in turn by a closing period of semi- or complete relaxation, as the master reeled off in easy, entertaining talk, one of his delightful lectures. It was in the nature studies, and in these closing lectures, particularly those in which he dwelt upon the great out-of-doors, and upon the glories of English literature, that the deep enthusiasms of the man's nature came forth undisguised and unrestrained, rising often to the heights of impassioned eloquence, and beauteous awakening imagery. These lectures, or rather, informal talks covered a wide range of subjects, most of them lying beyond the boundaries of the school curriculum.

Thus, in a sense, Moses Woolson's school room partook of the nature of a university—quite impressively so when Professor Asa Gray of Harvard came occasionally to talk botany to the boys. He did this out of regard for Moses Woolson's love of the science. The unfailing peroration of these lectures—every one of them, was an exhortation in favor of "Woman's Rights," as the movement was called at the time; for Moses Woolson was a sincere and ardent champion of womankind. On this topic he spoke in true nobility of spirit.

But the talks that gripped Louis the hardest were those on English literature. Here the master was completely at his ease. Here, indeed, he revelled, as it were, in the careful analysis and lucid exposition of every phase of his subject, copious in quotation, delightfully critical in taking apart a passage, a single line, explaining the value of each word in respect of action, rhythm, color, quality, texture, fitness, then putting these elements together in a renewed recital of the passage which now became a living, moving utterance. Impartial in judgment, fertile in illustration and expedient, clear in statement, he opened to view a new world, a new land of enchantment.

One day, to Louis's amazement, he announced that the best existing history of English literature was written by a Frenchman, one Hyppolite Taine by name. This phenomenon he explained by stating that the fine French mind possessed a quality and power of detachment unknown to the English; that Monsieur Taine further possessed that spiritual aspect of sympathy, that vision, which enabled him to view, to enter freely and to comprehend a work of art regardless yet regardful of its origin in time or place; and he rounded an antithesis of French and English culture in such wise as to arouse Louis's keenest attention, for the word *culture* had hitherto possessed no significance for him; it was merely a word! Now his thoughts, his whole being, floated o'er the sea to distant France, whereupon he arose from his seat and asked Moses Woolson what culture really meant, and was told it signified the genius of a people, of a race. And what was meant by the *genius* of a people? It signified their innate qualities and powers of heart and mind; that therefore their culture was their own expression of their inmost selves, as individuals, as a people, as a race. Louis was magnificently bewildered by this high concentration. He seemed to be in a flood of light which hid everything from view; he made some sheepish rejoinder, whereupon Moses Woolson saw his own mistake.

He came down from his high perch to which he had climbed unwittingly, for it was dead against his theory and practice to talk above the heads of his boys. He thereupon diluted the prior statement with a simply worded illustration, and Louis was glad to find his own feet still on the ground. Then Louis put the two aspects of the statement side by side, again, and "culture" became for him a living word—a sheer veil through which, at first, he could but dimly see; but living word and sheer living veil had come from without to abide with him. It seemed indeed as though Moses Woolson had passed on to him a wand of enchantment which he must learn to use to unveil the face of things. Thus Louis dreamed.

By the end of the school year Moses Woolson, through genius as a teacher, had turned a crudely promising boy into, so to speak, a mental athlete. He had brought order out of disorder, definition out of what was vague, superb alertness out of mere boyish ardor; had nurtured and concentrated all that was best in the boy; had made him consciously courageous and independent; had focused his powers of thought, feeling and action; had confirmed Louis's love of the great out-of-doors, as a source of inspiration; and had climaxed all by parting a great veil which opened to the view of this same boy, the wonderland of Poetry.

Thus with great skill he made of Louis a compacted personality ready to act on his own initiative, in an intelligent purposeful way. Louis had the same capacity to absorb, and to value discipline, that Moses Woolson had to impart it, and Louis was not a brilliant or showy scholar. He stood well up in his class and that was enough. His purpose was not to give out, but to receive, to acquire. He was adept in the art of listening and was therefore rather silent of mood. His object was to get every ounce of treasure out of Moses Woolson. And yet for Moses Woolson, the master and the man, he felt neither love nor affection, and it is quite likely that the master felt much the same toward him. What he felt toward the man was a vast admiration, he felt the power and the vigor of his intense and prodigal personality. It is scarcely likely that the master really knew, to the full extent, what he was doing for this boy, but Louis knew it; and there came gradually over him a cumulative reciprocity which, at the end, when he had fully realized the nature of the gift burst forth into a sense of obligation and of gratitude so heartfelt, so profound, that it has remained with him in constancy throughout the years.

THE AUTHORITY OF THE TEACHER [*]

Significance of authority of the teacher. The higher the authority of the teacher the better will his demands be fulfilled. A conviction has great power for children simply because it is uttered by some adult close to him. A teacher clothed with authority easily obtains obedience from his pupils. But whence comes authority? How is it created?

If the child feels that the teacher treats him with concern and is sensitive to his needs and interests, his affairs, his joys and sorrows; if the child receives aid and care from the teacher; if he learns that the teacher insists on obedience—all these things strengthen the authority of the teacher in the eyes of the child.

But the most important condition tending to establish the *moral* authority of the teacher over children is the setting of a worthy example in his relations to work and people and in the entire conduct of his life.

However, while using his authority and leaning upon it, the teacher must at the same time strive to develop in children independence in their moral judgments. Let it be said that what the adult tells them must become a conviction of their own which will guide them in life and which they will defend in the presence of others.

Occasionally teachers seek to build their authority on false foundations. Thus, for example, some assume that if the child fears them and trembles before them, standing in terror of their wrath and of severe punishment for every fault, then he will always be obedient. Such authority, holding children in a state of perpetual fear, A. S. Makarenko calls the authority of suppression. It evokes lies and cowardice and cultivates cruelty in children. "Out of oppressed and suppressed children come either slushy, good-for-nothing people, or hard and stubborn people, who throughout their entire lives seek revenge for childhood frustration."

On the other hand, some teachers strive to build their authority on excessive kindness: in their relations with children they practice compliance and unnecessary and at times even decided softness. By such means they hope to evoke in their pupils love and gratitude. In reality children soon sense their weakness and not only cease to obey them, but even begin to order them around.

True authority is founded on the making of reasonable demands on the child, combined with respect for his personality, devotion to his in-

[*] B. P. Yesipov and N. K. Goncharov, *I Want To Be Like Stalin* from the Russian text on Pedagogy. Translated by George S. Counts and Nucia P. Lodge, with an introduction by George S. Counts (New York, The John Day Company, 1947), pp. 46-9. Copyright 1947 by The John Day Company.

terests, ability to help him, clarity and firmness of educational purposes, and worthiness of personal example.

Necessity of consistency in educational work. It is extremely injurious to the pupil for a teacher to make certain demands and then to forget them, or even to contradict them through his own actions. Such a teacher is inconsistent. He gives an assignment to children. He warns them: "Beware, I shall check strictly." And then he does not check at all. He perpetually threatens his pupils for the slightest violation of order, but fails to carry a single threat into action. He promises to do something interesting and then forgets his promise. Naturally such a person does not inspire children with respect and deference. It is imperative that every teacher permit no contradiction between word and deed; it is imperative that he be *consistent*. . . .

Consistency must be observed by all adults who share in the rearing of the young. The several teachers of a given child should not contradict each other, but rather should follow a single line. As his teachers change, provision should be made for an orderly and consistent sequence of influences. When a child passes with age from certain teachers to others, he suffers injury if he encounters an entirely different treatment, if, for example, mildness changes sharply to severity, or if firmness changes to weakening softness. It is injurious also if the child experiences a duality or even a trinity of educative influences, if, for example, the elders in the family say one thing to him and the teacher tells him something else, if one teacher follows one line and his comrade in work another.

LOVE AGAINST HATE [*]

One teacher faces her schoolroom in the morning with some such attitude as this: "Here are twenty students, the offspring of twenty taxpayers who have hired me to tell these children that $6 \times 6 = 36$. They could find it out for themselves in time, but they will never get to long division and the computation of interest rates if I do not hurry them up and make them take this for a guaranteed fact right now and remember it forever. They may not see why $6 \times 6 = 36$, and I don't know why it is myself; they may not see why they have to learn it and I can't make it seem very reasonable to them, so I will just tell them they *have* to learn it. They haven't anything else to do; they won't have the courage to defy me and refuse to believe it; I am bigger than they are, and I am the teacher, and so I can make them say it and if I make them say it often enough it will

---

[*] From *Love Against Hate* by Karl Menninger. Copyright 1942 by Karl Menninger and Jeanetta Lyle Menninger. Reprinted by permission of Harcourt, Brace and Company, Inc., pp. 248-51, 253, 255.

stick. Later they will be grateful to me. Maybe, in the meantime, their parents will consider me a good teacher and not complain to the principal."

In addition, of course, this same teacher may be chafing at the necessity of teaching the third grade when she would like to teach the eighth grade, resenting the obstreperousness of certain of the children, brooding over the principal's reproaches of yesterday, worrying over the impossibility of doing justice to so large a class as she has been given, etc. But these things I ignore for the moment, because I want to concentrate on the teaching philosophy.

Another teacher might face her class with some such attitude as this: "These children love me. They think I know lots more than I do. I tell them that 6×6 is the same as 3 tens plus a 6, called "thirty-six" by agreement, and I must tell them that this is one of those conveniences that people have agreed upon in order to save time. I will show them that they could count this up for themselves every time if they liked, and I will do it for them once, to show them how one *does* save time by remembering it instead of having to count it up. I will show them how much fun multiplication is, and I can tell them how 6 is one of the numbers that always show themselves again when they are multiplied by themselves. I will tell them how the numeral came to assume its present form. I will show them how much easier it is to multiply with an Arabic 6 than with a Roman VI. I will make 6 have a personality for them different from the personality of 7 or 3. I realize that the personality of 6, 7, 3, and all other numbers I tell them about will be reflections of my own personality. And because they love me and because they want so much to please me, they will be interested in my numbers, and in all that I tell them, and they won't have to *try* to remember anything. They will remember it automatically, just as they will remember me. Then, later, when someone tells them that $6 \times 6 = 40$ or that one can spend money and still have it, they will not be impressed or misled. They will remember, not that Miss Jones made them learn the multiplication table, but that there was a Miss Jones once who knew them and loved them, and knew the world too and loved it—and showed them the 6's in the world and what the 6's do to one another."

Some will insist that this is merely a difference in skill or intuition in teaching. And with this I should not quarrel, because intuitive skill in teaching depends upon the intuitive recognition of the child's need for love, and I am sure some teachers have it in spite of their training and in spite of oppressive systems. . . .

The greatest difficulty hampering the successful application of the psychiatric concept of education is the problem of personnel. It has been pointed out many times of late that a significant proportion of teachers are either mentally ill or suffering from serious emotional maladjustments. How can such a teacher inspire or bestow love? Many others have so meager a background of experience in life that they lack adequate grasp of reality or any possibilities for either insight or genuine affection. To the extent that they attain any influence with their students, they often foster prejudice, superstition, emotionalized attitudes, and, worst of all, fears and withdrawal. The drab, colorless, empty lives of many teachers, lacking in esthetic sensitivity or cultural background, not only fail to stimulate latent capacities in students, but indeed discourage the expression of those capacities in students who show them spontaneously. Other teachers reveal their emotional pathology in the form of moodiness, sulkiness, sarcasm, hypercriticalness, bullying, and domination. Many teachers are best remembered by their children for the hate-charged atmosphere of their schoolrooms.

Still other teachers suffer from pronounced neurotic conflicts—inferiority feelings, racial prejudices, hypochondriasis, depression, feelings of being discriminated against. Such afflictions make them sources of psychic contagion and induce them to use the teaching situation as a means of obtaining relief. The effect of such teachers upon children is incalculable.[1] And yet all these things are deemed of no consequence if only the intellectual qualifications of the teacher are to be considered important in education. It is only if one accepts the thesis that the process of learning depends upon the stimulation of love by the teacher that the full importance of a normal personality appears. One might almost say that a teacher, by very virtue of her role of teacher, must be not only a normal but a supernormal person. She must be able to give large quantities of love, regardless of the preliminary attitudes or the direct personal responses of the children. *That her pupils will love her in return is secondary; if it becomes primary, her usefulness as a teacher is handicapped.* For this reason we must add to the categories of unsuitable teachers three more:

1. The teacher whose personal need for love is so great or is to such a degree unsatisfied that she seeks it in a direct expression of the children's love. This attitude encourages love situations rather than sublimations. For the teacher must constantly live as if to say "I love you; I will show you this by my genuine attitude and by the patience and honesty and vividness with which I communicate to you the information you are scheduled to receive. That you love me in return I will infer from the extent to which you accept my teaching." It is the art of teaching to obtain love in this sublimated form instead of through a direct expression.

2. Teachers who have a conscious or unconscious resentment toward children in general, or toward certain children in particular, or toward

---

[1] Some of the phrases in the above passages are taken from Daniel Prescott, *Emotion and the Educative Process* (American Council on Education, 1938), pp. 265-6.

their administrative officers, or toward the need of having to earn a living at all—such teachers by inflicting their hostilities upon the children will not only retard their pupils' acquisition of knowledge, but will arouse in them patterns of retaliatory hostility which will subsequently be inflicted upon other people.

3. The teacher whose neurotic guilt feelings are so dominant that teaching for her is a kind of penance, an absolution from guilt. The result of such teaching is the infusion of compulsive attitudes toward the subject matter in the child, and even a turning from it.

To summarize all we have said about personnel in education: *What the teacher is, is more important than what she teaches.* . . .

THE PICTURE IN OUR MINDS *

As one watches different classrooms, he notes that each teacher has a style of his own. He is quite consistent in the way he operates: the amount of challenge to the class, the depth or superficiality of his comments, the feelings about his job. It is as if he had a model in mind and operated consistently to make the classroom conform to this model; it represents the teacher's idea of what the classroom should be like. When the classroom situation deviates from this image, the teacher then tries to rectify matters by taking action: making more of an explanation, reassigning working partners, bringing in a personal experience to increase interest, stopping talking so that the students have a chance, and so on. The teacher's model summarizes for him the principles of learning; his action is taken to maintain the model, using principles of educational method as his guide.

Let us look at a number of models which teachers have used.

Model 1: Socratic Discussion

The image is of a wise, somewhat crusty philosopher getting into arguments with more naive people. The issues discussed are known to both Socrates and the other party, and both have adequate factual knowledge for the discussion. Socrates shows the other up by pointing to inconsistencies in his logic. The arguments are primarily to clarify concepts and values.

As applied to classrooms, this type of discussion is an aid to the assimilation of ideas. *After* the children have learned some facts and had some experiences together, the teacher-Socrates can challenge the class

* Herbert A. Thelen, *Dynamics of Groups at Work* (Chicago, University of Chicago Press, 1954), pp. 36-41.

The Teacher as a Person

and test their conclusions. The teacher has a central role, and the discussion has much of the emotionality of argumentation.

Model 2: THE TOWN MEETING

The image is of a group of citizens whose lives are interdependent meeting together to decide on courses of action required to solve problems. These problems are objectively defined in terms of acts of God, services needed, demands to be met. The group draws on the experiences, feelings, and thoughts of each other, and the method is co-operative. The leader is a moderator rather than an expert. The most appropriate action is decided by vote of the majority.

As applied to classrooms, this type of discussion best fits teacher-class planning of activity, in which the task is to decide how to organize to carry out specified learning activities. Some differences between class and town hall, however, are that the neighbors immediately recognize the problem to be solved as important, whereas the students do not; the action to be selected makes a financial or status or other difference to all the citizens, whereas there are fewer "real" consequences for the students; the citizens are competent to testify because they have all experienced the problem, whereas the students do not have such backing of relevant experience; the moderator is simply looking for the most complete consensus he can get, whereas the teacher must also give information and the results of his past experience.

Model 3: APPRENTICESHIP

The image is of a young person's life being "taken over" by an older one. The apprentice learns a trade, how to behave in the social-class level of his chosen occupation, how to be a parent in the family, and so on. The master is teacher, father, friend, colleague, and boss. Psychologically, the apprentice identifies himself with and imitates the master: he is there to learn how to be like the master and to live like him.

Some of the dynamics of apprenticeship apply in the classroom. The student does identify himself with the teacher, and he learns many attitudes in imitation of the teacher. And many teachers, basically, attempt to make the student over into their own image (as they perceive it). Much of the master's warmth and concern for the welfare of the apprentice is appropriate for the teacher also. In many universities today, training for the Ph.D. has considerable resemblance to apprenticeship experience.

Model 4: BOSS-EMPLOYEE, OR ARMY MODEL

The image here is of a person who has higher status and also the power to reward or punish, telling others what to do and how to do it, then seeing that it gets done, and, finally, evaluating how good a job he thinks it is. It is not necessary that the relationship be harsh or unfriendly, but it is necessary that there be considerable acceptance of many kinds of dependency by the subordinate. The rather small minority of people who thrive best as dependents may be quite creative in this situation.

This is probably the most prevalent model of the classroom, although there is wide variation in the extent to which the model is "softened up" by procedures for taking account of what the students feel about the teacher's demands. In other words, the teacher has to modify the image in the direction of more attention to pupil motivation and interest. This image is realistic for skill learnings like typing in which the requirement is to practice objectively described behaviors until a clearly defined level of performance is reached. It is also realistic with respect to a class working on a project involving physical work laid out according to plan.

Model 5: THE BUSINESS DEAL

The image is of one person with money (or some other inducement) making a bargain for the services of someone else. Thus one might pay a cabinetmaker to build him a chair. He would discuss specifications for the object, be available for making some decisions as the work progressed, and would finally decide whether to accept or reject the object.

This is essentially the "contract plan," in which the teacher makes the best deal he can with each individual workman (student) and consults with him as the work proceeds. The advantage of this model is that the child assumes a high degree of responsibility and the contract can be written to fit reasonable expectations of him. The disadvantages are that the teacher has to supervise a wide variety of different jobs, and the social factor and possibilities of learning better through working together are either denied or ignored.

Model 6: THE GOOD OLD TEAM

The image is of a group of players listening to the coach between quarters of the football game. This is followed by inspired playing which defeats the opposing team. The coach's objective is to get better playing, and almost any devices of persuasion or threats or promises that will produce high-level performance are accepted as legitimate.

This is an unrealistic model for the classroom, although its use is sometimes encouraged. The coach is working for a quick spurt rather than for long-range effects; there has to be an "enemy" team to compete with; the product to be evaluated is a score run-up by the group, rather than individual achievement; the team players are required to submerge all but very limited aspects of their individuality as completely as possible; and finally, the team is primarily an instrument for expressing the will of the coach. Few of these characteristics can really be found in the teacher-pupil relationship.

Model 7: THE GUIDED TOUR

The image here is of a group of interested children following closely behind a mature guide as he leads them through the jungle, brewery, courthouse, or wherever. From time to time he calls their attention to objects he wants to tell them about, and he gives them information, stories, and opinions. He also answers questions. He maintains order and sees to it that the number of children who arrive home equals the number who set out in the morning. He may or may not plan with them certain questions or major categories of information the field trip is supposed to answer.

The acceptance by the teacher of the fact that he has been "over the field" before and has much to tell should be realistic. His personal enthusiasm and ability to "let the class see for itself" help motivate the children and arouse their interest. The experience of learning names for objects is a rather small intellectual task, and usually is inadequate to absorb the class's energies. The guided tour (e.g., survey course) is a quick way to cultural ornamentation but the "knowledge" learned may be unrelated to possibilities of personal use. . . .

Models like the above help the teacher define the working relationship between himself and his class. They serve to clarify the role of the teacher: his power, his concerns, his style of teaching. The roles of the students are not differentiated in these models—all the students are expected to behave alike in ways which enable the teacher to enforce *his* role.

The view of teaching implied by the existence of these models is realistic, but it is also inadequate. It is realistic in recognizing that the only behavior under the direct control of the teacher is his own; and the teacher, by virtue of the authority of his position, age, and professional competence has the power to determine his behavior pretty much apart from consideration of student needs. The models also realistically recognize that the roles possible to the students depend upon the role that the teacher chooses to play. In effect, the freedom of students is with respect to whatever functions the teacher does not pre-empt for himself. These two basic principles provide us with clues for understanding how the teacher consciously and by design alters the activities in the classroom.

The inadequacy of the models becomes apparent with the realization that they only illuminate half the problem of method. The models make clear what is expected of teacher and students once the teacher's role is decided. They do not, however, give any basis for determining the appropriate role of the teacher, and they start from the needs of the teacher rather than from an analysis of the requirements of learning situations. Effective thinking about the design and control of educative activity must begin with the question "What sort of participatory role must students have, to learn what they need to learn and are supposed to learn?" Only after this question has been answered quite apart from any consideration of the teacher's needs can we begin to see the sort of role the teacher must play if student experience is to be educative. The most significant quality of a good teacher is that he is able to meet his own needs through playing the roles required to make activities educative for students.

His Professional Functions

TASKS OF A TEACHER, A COLONIAL CONTRACT *

ARTICLES OF AGREEMENT
with
Johannes van Eckkelen
Accepted Schoolmaster and Chorister of Flatbush
(Contract to Teach School in Flatbush, New York, 1682)

School Service.—I. The School shall begin at eight o'clock, and go out at eleven; and in the afternoon shall begin at one o'clock and end at four. The bell shall be rung when the school commences.

II. When the school begins, one of the children shall read the morning prayer, as it stands in the catechism, and close with the prayer before dinner; in the afternoon it shall begin with the prayer after dinner, and end with the evening prayer. The evening school shall begin with the Lord's prayer, and close by singing a psalm.

III. He shall instruct the children on every Wednesday and Saturday, in the common prayers, and the questions and answers in the catechism, to enable them to repeat them the better on Sunday before the afternoon service, or on Monday, when they shall be catechised before the congregation. Upon all such occasions, the schoolmaster shall be present and shall

---

* Daniel J. Pratt, *Annals of Public Education in the State of New York from 1626 to 1746* (Albany, The Argus Co., 1872), pp. 65-7.

require the children to be friendly in their appearance and encourage them to answer freely and distinctly.

IV. He shall be required to keep his school nine months in succession, from September to June, in each year, in case it should be concluded upon to retain his services for a year or more, or without limitation; and he shall be required to be regulated by these articles, and to perform the same duties which his predecessor, Jan Thibaud, above named, was required to perform. In every particular therefore, he shall be required to keep school, according to this seven months agreement, and shall always be present himself.

Church Service.—I. He shall keep the church clean, and ring the bell three times before the people assemble to attend the preaching and catechism. Also before the sermon is commenced, he shall read a chapter out of the Holy Scriptures, and that, between the second and third ringing of the bell. After the third ringing he shall read the ten commandments, and the twelve articles of our faith, and then take the lead in singing. In the afternoon after the third ringing of the bell, he shall read a short chapter, or one of the Psalms of David, as the congregation are assembling; and before divine service commences, shall introduce it, by the singing of a Psalm or Hymn.

II. When the minister shall preach at Brooklyn, or New-Utrecht, he shall be required to read twice before the congregation, from the book commonly used for that purpose. In the afternoon he shall also read a sermon on the explanation of the catechism, according to the usage and practice approved of by the minister. The children as usual, shall recite their questions and answers out of the catechism, on Sunday, and he shall instruct them therein. He, as chorister, shall not be required to perform these duties, whenever divine service shall be performed in Flatlands, as it would be unsuitable, and prevent many from attending there.

III. For the administration of Holy Baptism, he shall provide a basin with water, for which he shall be entitled to receive from the parents, or witnesses, twelve styvers. He shall, at the expense of the church, provide bread and wine, for the celebration of the Holy Supper; He shall be in duty bound promptly to furnish the minister with the name of the child to be baptized, and with the names of the parents and witnesses. And he shall also serve as messenger for the consistory.

IV. He shall give the funeral invitations, dig the grave, and toll the bell, for which service he shall receive for a person of fifteen years and upwards, twelve guilders, and for one under that age, eight guilders. If he should be required to give invitations beyond the limits of the town, he shall be entitled to three additional guilders, for the invitation of every

His Professional Functions

other town, and if he should be required to cross the river, and go to New York, he shall receive four guilders.

School Money.—He shall receive from those who attend the day school, for a speller or reader, three guilders a quarter, and for a writer four guilders. From those who attend evening school, for a speller or reader, four guilders, and for a writer, six guilders shall be given.

Salary.—In addition to the above, his salary shall consist of four hundred guilders, in grain, valued in Seewant, to be delivered at Brooklyn Ferry, and for his services from October to May, as above stated, a sum of two hundred and thirty-four guilders, in the same kind, with the dwelling-house, barn, pasture lot and meadows, to the school appertaining. The same to take effect from the first day of October, instant.

Done and agreed upon in Consistory, under the inspection of the Honorable Constable and Overseers, the 8th, of October, 1682.

Constable and Overseers	The Consistory
Cornelius Barrian.	Casparus van Zuren, Minister.
Rynier Aertsen.	Adriaen Reyerse.
Jan Remsen.	Cornelius Barent Vandwyck.

I agree to the above articles, and promise to perform them according to the best of my ability.

Johannes van Eckkelen.

THINGS TO WHICH THE TEACHERS MUST ATTEND *

The teachers should take care that the pupils bring with them every day their breakfast and lunch, and, without obliging them to do so, a little basket will be placed in an appointed place in the classroom, into which the children, when they are so piously inclined, may put what bread they have left over to be distributed among those of them who are poor. The teacher will see that they do not give away any of their bread unless they have enough left for themselves. Those who have bread to give will raise their hands, showing at the same time the piece of bread which they have to give, and a pupil who has been appointed to receive these alms will go to get them. At the end of the meal, the teachers will distribute the bread to the poorest and will exhort them to pray to God for their benefactors.

The teachers will also take care that the pupils do not throw either nuts

---

* Jean-Baptiste de la Salle, *The Conduct of the Schools,* trans. F. de la Fontainerie (New York, McGraw-Hill Book Company, 1935), pp. 55-6. (Original, *Conduite des écoles,* Avignon, 1720)

68   *The Vocation of Teaching*

or shells on the floor: he will oblige them to put them into their pockets or into their bags.

They must be made to understand that it is desired that they eat in school in order to teach them to eat with propriety, with decorum, and in a polite manner and to invoke God before and after eating.

The teachers will see that the pupils do not play during breakfast and lunch but that they be very attentive to the exercises that are being done in school during this time; and in order to discover whether they are exact in the performance of this duty, they will, from time to time, make one of them repeat what has been said, excepting those who are occupied in writing.

The pupils will not be permitted to give anything whatsoever one to another—not even any part of their breakfast—nor to exchange it.

The teachers will see, in so far as possible, that the pupils finish breakfast by half past eight o'clock.

TEACHERS' ACTIVITIES IN GRADE ONE *

DESCRIPTION OF ACTIVITIES IN GRADE ONE

(Time data based on reports of fifteen teachers for in-session activities, of four teachers for out-of-session activities.)

Before school. Arrange for filmstrip machine; assistant principal came in to check on some book replacements; put mural up on bulletin board; meeting on salaries; put out clay and puzzles for people who complete work early; put work on board; make a chart; faculty meeting; pull up shades; check fish bowl; select word and phrase cards for reading groups; review plans for day; place materials to be used in morning session on table; review preprimer program of Ginn series; clean up following P.T.A. discussion meeting of previous evening; open blinds; open windows; water plants; get cards for reading out of box and in card holder; discuss books with another teacher.

Entering. Help children with boots and rubbers; direct hanging of clothing; children put clothing in closets; stand at boys' lavatory and cloakroom entrance to see children behave properly; let children in; children go to own places; teacher goes out to playground to bring in line.

----
* Clyde Millton Hill, editor, *Yale-Fairfield Study of Elementary Teaching; a cooperative project conducted by Yale University and the Fairfield, Connecticut, Public Schools and financed by a grant from the Fund for the Advancement of Education; report for 1954-1955;* prepared by Constance M. Burns, Claude A. Eggersten, Clyde M. Hill, John J. Howell, Louis E. Raths, J. Warren Tilton (New Haven, Connecticut, February 1956), pp. 207-11.

Opening. Flag salute led by child, guided by teacher; morning prayer; health inspection; sing "America"; supervise children putting flowers in vase; child holds flag; taking and writing of attendance; change of seats; new child (leader) picked by child leader for previous week; children show various objects; teacher helps them express ideas about them; child gives weather report, including information on day, month, year, etc.; guiding discussion of film "Grey Squirrel" seen previous afternoon; teacher asks for news of the day; children tell of things that happened night before or something they heard on radio or saw on television; children show wolf costumes (for Red Riding Hood ballet); teacher praises them and displays to group.

Collect money. Collect hot lunch and milk money writing each child's name on form; change seating; collect Red Cross money; give pins; collect card-party money.

Reading. Correct workbooks; explain next lesson; review words; write sentences on board; teach and explain word "said." Children draw various objects as instructed and number them; discuss picture story in books with children; ask leading questions, encouraging children to tell picture story as they saw it; exercise in matching same words with big letters and little letters; write on board heading for children's work folders; explain what is to be done and how; help individual children get right position on folders; direct vocabulary exercises and games; introduce groups to "Big Red Book"; oral reading and related activities; children listen to explanation, answer questions, read with teacher, teacher explains coloring of like objects in each row; children follow as directions are explained; reread pre-primer story; children take parts of story people; introduce new words by writing sentence containing them on board; talk about new story from picture on title page; discuss pictures on each page; children "frame" words, match words and phrases; show "surprise chart" prepared previous evening, which children read, children correct mistakes in workbook, have children read seatwork on board; talk about making interesting pictures; use own ideas; children read sentences on board and locate pictures to match them in book; teacher directs rereading, emphasizing reading with expression; directs game in phonics: letter *h;* children locate "funny" sentences; children identify words that rhyme; teacher puts sentences on board; children match words and build same sentence in card holder; play guessing game with rhyming words; teacher helps children compose story on "My Baby," one boy in room has a baby brother; check to see if each child understands and is following directions carefully; children tell back what they are going to do; each child takes a turn reading a page orally; each child reads page silently after discussing picture and then is called on for oral reading; flash cards: first reading all together, then taking turns; "Big Red Book": each child reads a line, then a page; teacher puts short story on board to introduce new words; one group on reading readiness in "Games to Play" seeing likenesses; drill on color words; teacher prepares for showing filmstrip.

Lavatory. Children go to lavatory; wash hands; filing; get drink; new leaders for boys and girls chosen by last week's leaders.

Recess and physical education. Supervise playground; direct games; ask children to choose favorite indoor game; direct indoor games; children play relay races; free play on jungle gym, bars, and slides; play squirrels in trees; play bean bags; play jump rope, punch ball, others catch ball; assemble costumes and get ready to go to another room to practice program of three dances to be given in first grade assembly; teacher directs rehearsal of three dances; children give criticism for bettering it.

Lunch and rest. Teacher goes downstairs for coffee; let two "best resters" take charge; encourage quiet resting; play Brahms' Lullaby on record player; children choose "best resters" to be in charge next time; children say grace, eat snacks; teacher teaches courtesy; teacher calls milk list; instruct children; read story; children listen; children drink milk and take out cartons; small discussion groups on work; teacher corrects papers; teacher checks music books for Thanksgiving songs.

Arithmetic. Flash cards at children for number recognition; write number problems on board; numbers and music combined; count with children; certain numbers sing chosen songs, children count, sing and play out "Ten Little Indians"; work with sticks, paper, blocks, and objects; review *one* to *eight;* teacher introduces word "pair" and explains meaning; children make pairs of various objects on blackboard; check themselves to see what things on bodies are in pairs, clothing, etc.; children do written exercise on completing pairs.

Noon period. Eat lunch; playground duty; bring children in for hot lunch; cold lunch duty; walkers go home; put up easel paintings; work on Y-F study; work on children's individual folders; supervise getting food, eating, cleaning up; put work on board for afternoon; get records, materials ready; correct papers, preview filmstrips; discard one; lend book to another teacher.

Penmanship. Pass out paper; form letters on blackboard; assist different children; draw lines and print on board; remind of standards of good writing; on lines drawn on board direct one letter at a time calling attention to formation one or two spaces high, etc.; put little turkey seals on top of

His Professional Functions

papers well done, teacher writes "Big Book" on the board: children watch and work from board, write and correct own mistakes; children name letters used.

Social studies, language. Story hour: read story of Dumbo to children; lead discussion of good breakfast foods; discussion on pets; story: teacher reads *Pinocchio;* children listen and relax; discussion: children explain pictures on "Tour Riding" to class: language noticed; teacher writes children's suggestions on board.

Health and safety. Unexpected assembly on safety; take children to hall, seat them, and watch safety movie; lead discussion on care of teeth; discuss safety at home; children cut out magazine pictures and teacher places them on chart; discuss and do paper on dogs; teacher shows and narrates filmstrip on visit to doctor; children tell various medical experiences and answer questions on use of medical instruments, need for sterilizing, what are some internal parts of body.

Art. Tell children about Pilgrims and describe their clothing; help draw picture; help children make hand turkeys; free coloring; show papers to group and comment favorably on well-made pictures, original ideas, improvement in individual work; children evaluate and give constructive criticism; draw Pilgrim on board; teacher demonstrates; art teacher took over class after it settled down, not expected; directed lesson; previously doing safety at home with magazines and scissors, (art teacher) directed art lesson Thanksgiving and turkeys.

Music. Lead children in singing the songs; play tone games; exchange groups with another teacher who teaches dancing; practice in tone matching; teacher introduces "Yellow Bird," children listen and repeat, review song learned previously; children use rhythm instruments to a march.

Clean-up and dismissal. Children straighten desks, chairs, games, etc.; evaluation of day's activities led by teacher; get ready for dismissal; pass out P.T.A. family list notes; child passes wastebasket, quietest; teacher hands out notices; remind children of stamp day Tuesday; children chosen to close windows, pull shades, put out light; first child in each row collects pictures; get church people (released for religious instruction) ready to leave by 2:30; children pick up papers and clean desks.

After school. Talk with parent; cut out pictures for dental chart we are making; erase blackboards; dust ledges; straighten out room and desk; hang up some of the pictures of Pilgrims which children had drawn; bus duty; worked with three children who remained after school for extra help, one with reading, two with numbers; complete form on materials required for next year; check workbooks; mark three sets of papers for each child; fill in register; listen to records to be used later in week; read teacher's manual on reading; finish correcting papers; mimeograph work for following day; make up before-school work which was not realized essential when done previously; work on Y-F report; operate rexograph; notes to three parents; check Red Cross money; try to get extra desk and chair for new pupil; eight bus children stay after dismissal until 3:30; work on Y-F study with interruptions from children; take children to bus line in front hall; wash boards, easel, counter tops; supervise children; put morning work on boards; remind children about lunch and milk money; check A-V catalogue and order and return films; put out paint and prepare easel for tomorrow; correct papers.

FUNCTION OF THE TEACHER *

... The teacher's function is to create the most favorable conditions for the teaching-learning process. Although, in the last analysis, the pupils must learn in their own ways, the teacher cannot escape the professional responsibility of guiding the process within limits which control her, just as pupils must learn within limits over which they have no control.

The function of the teacher is to help the pupils face problems and reach decisions. Which problems? Any problem which relates to the responsibilities entrusted to her by the school administration is relevant. A geometry teacher does not, ordinarily, act as a school nurse. An arts and crafts teacher is usually not competent to act as a social-science instructor. The school nurse is not responsible for English literature. The English teacher cannot undertake a case worker's function. In a "core curriculum" or in a nursery school or in the very early grades the teacher's obligations may involve several functions. These teachers therefore, are professionally responsible for more than one activity.

The point is that the teacher must have delegated tasks which define the limits of her operation. She has to be anchored somewhere to protect *her* against the limitless demands of pupils and, at the same time, to safeguard the *pupils*. Otherwise, the pupils would be confused, not realizing what is expected, what their part in the teaching-learning process is. The teaching-learning process must be structured so that the confusion is narrowed and the respective obligations and responsibilities of teacher and pupils are understood.

* Nathaniel Freeman Cantor, *Teaching-Learning Process* (New York, Dryden Press, 1953), pp. 123-41. Reprinted by permission of Henry Holt and Company, copyright 1953.

The teacher is the professional person representing the school, which offers a specific service through the teacher. The teacher does not carry all of the responsibility for what happens in her class, nor does she permit the pupils to carry the entire responsibility. The teacher's job is to perform professionally in her role. Her concern should be with the movement and direction of the class as it deals with the specific service she offers.

The teacher structures the classroom activity. She helps the pupils to clarify what they think they want and discuss what the school thinks she should offer and what, together, they might accomplish in that area. Suppose some of the pupils indicate they don't want any part of her offer or any part of the school? They want nothing, they assert.

A professional teacher can certainly understand this reaction and accept it, sometimes even sympathize with it. The teacher who has thought through and accepted the functional approach presented here is not disturbed by this kind of response. She simply makes clear that for a definite period of time they will all be together. Her job is to help them in a certain area, and their responsibility is to use that help to accomplish the purpose or purposes which bring them together. There is little any of them can do about changing the requirements they have to meet or the situation they are in. She will try to do her job well and wonders what, if anything, the pupils will do about their part. That, of course, is up to them.

The foregoing situation has been somewhat exaggerated in order to clarify the meaning of structure and function. The teacher has the responsibility to make clear, in the beginning, the purpose which brings all of them together, to inquire patiently about the kind of help the pupils think they want for the attainment of the purpose. None of this exploration should be mechanically and rigidly controlled. There can be *wide latitude* in exploration, modification, and redirection, so long as all of this occurs within the limits which structure the specific class. In brief, the pupils' wishes and suggestions and needs as *they* express them should certainly be genuinely considered so long as they do not call for the kind of help or service the teacher is not authorized to give. On the other hand, the teacher must indicate what her responsibilities are. Between these two limits— namely the pupils' wishes and needs in the specific area and the teacher's service—movement and growth can occur.

What takes place between teacher and pupil provides the dynamic conditions which can be used by the pupil in his own way. Learning which is significant in the life of the student takes place when the help offered by the teacher, elucidating the meanings of the data, is accepted by the student as an aid toward making the meanings his own.

Let us try to make clear the meanings and implications of the "limited functions" of the teacher. We start by relating an experience in which we participated.

A meeting of the parents and teacher of the sixth-grade pupils was arranged to discuss the work of the children. The teacher described the progress of the children in arithmetic and indicated some of the difficulties. There was some discussion. The teacher inquired whether any of the parents had any further questions. There were none. She then proceeded to tell the parents that they were not providing their children with proper lunches. She had observed that there was too much bread and not enough fruit or vegetables. Did anyone have any comments?

A mother of one of the pupils was restrained by her husband from asking the *arithmetic* teacher whether in her judgment there was enough starch in the pupils' blouses. The parents, as a group, expressed indignation after the meeting adjourned. Who was she to tell them how to feed their children? Someone suggested to the irate parents that her criticism may have been prompted by her interest in the development of the whole child. "Next thing," remarked a parent, "she will be ready to practice medicine for our children!"

One can view this incident sympathetically and conclude that the teacher was sincerely interested in the physical welfare of her pupils. The question is, however, whether it was her business, her province or function, to raise the question of pupil diet.

Before discussing the question of the teacher's focus (which will be answered by the following excerpts), let us present the substance of an exciting discussion carried on by one of the teacher groups which involves a similar point.

> MABEL: I have a little girl in my class who is sexually fully developed. I noticed that all through the hour, while we read our English assignment, she was reading a magazine slipped in behind her reader. I watched for an opportunity and discovered that she was interested in certain diagrams involving the sexual organs of both male and female. I spoke to her, knowing that she was not doing satisfactory work either in my class or in other classes. I asked her if I couldn't help her in understanding some of that material. She seemed very frightened and said, "Please don't tell my Mummy about this." I said, "What seems to be the trouble, dear?" She said, "My Mummy would break my neck if she knew I was reading this stuff. She hollered at me and she said she'd punish me if she caught me reading it. Please, please, don't tell her." The child was ten years old. She would talk to children about friends in her neighborhood who were coming home with babies. That's the one thing she seemed to be interested in. She was a terribly, terribly disturbed child. I knew there was a problem

that needed attention. I went to the supervisor and asked her what was I to do. The supervisor didn't seem to be interested. She said, "I don't think we ought to get into this. This is not a matter for the classroom." So I said, "Well, it is certainly a matter for someone." And she said, "Well, if you want to, go see the principal." The next day I went to see the principal and I told him about the fact that this little girl needed attention, and that I would like to go with her to her mother. The principal replied to me, "We don't want any more neighborhood troubles and complaining parents on our hands. You had better let the whole thing alone." Well, I feel very guilty about this. I feel something should be done, I can just see this little girl failing her classes and becoming neurotic and I don't think she ought to be left alone. Somebody has got to give her help. It's gotten so that I no longer enjoy my dinner and I can't sleep nights because I worry about this kid. I simply don't know what to do.

INSTRUCTOR: Mabel, what is the issue in this story, from the point of view of your function and responsibility as an English teacher?

MABEL: I want to know what my job is in regard to that child. She's getting very peculiar and perverted notions about sex and it's interfering with her classroom work. She needs help. Now, how can I give her help?

Mabel, a sympathetic and sincere teacher, wants to help the child and feels frustrated and guilty because she cannot. The instructor tried to help her come to grips with the problem by asking her what her function is as an English teacher. Mabel does not answer the question because she does not, as yet, understand it. Instead she replies, "I want to know what my job is in regard to that child. . . . She needs help. Now, how can I give her help?" The answer is that she can help the child only by focusing on the areas for which she is responsible—namely, teaching English—and in special problems referring the child to other school resources, if available, for help.

Neither Mabel nor the other students would, at this point, understand the answer if it were given. In the following discussion, the teacher, carrying out his responsibility, focuses on this one issue, Mabel's limited responsibility as a teacher of English. The teacher keeps this issue central and guides the discussion accordingly.

HARRY: It seems to me that you should be interested in the whole child and deal with the whole situation smoothly and not bring in outside complaints. Why don't you go and talk to the mother about these matters?

MABEL: The mother will not talk to anybody. The school called her once and she refused to come to the school, and she refuses to see anybody.

HARRY: I think it would be wrong for you to refer this child to a guidance bureau. She wanted to talk with you about it and you have her confidence, and I think it's your job to help the child.
MABEL: But how?
HARRY: Is the mother a problem, too?
MABEL: I'm sure she is.
INSTRUCTOR: Is that properly a problem for the Children's Guidance Bureau of the city? Or do you feel, Mabel, that you are competent to do a case-work job with that mother?
MABEL: Of course not.
HARRY: It seems to me someone in her own school set-up must share that problem with her. I guess it's not only Mabel's problem.
INSTRUCTOR: Mabel tells us that when she talked with the supervisor the supervisor said the mother is a stumbling block and we can't do anything about it. Then Mabel tells us she went to the principal and the principal doesn't want to make the next move. Now what does Mabel do? Is she professionally competent to deal with this kind of a case? She has failed to enlist the aid of her own superiors; they do nothing. Now what is Mabel's responsibility? Is Mabel justified in refusing to accept the responsibility because of her unpreparedness to do that kind of work?
HARRY: What about the child?
HELEN: I think the child is just unfortunate. There is nothing Mabel can do about it.
INSTRUCTOR: I see most of you do not like my question and Helen's answer, and I can understand your feeling. Now would you please tell me what other answer you can give? Suppose the child had a bad cold and no physician wanted to take the case and the school authorities, for whatever reason, did not want to report it. What would Mabel's obligation be?
JOHN: Mabel's job is to report that case to the school nurse, or to the principal, and the principal would be the one to refer the child to proper medical attention.
INSTRUCTOR: And if the principal or nurse, for whatever reason, does not report it, now what does Mabel do?
HARRY: I guess she can't do anything.
INSTRUCTOR: Mabel, do you feel you have the right, professionally, to go beyond your superiors?
MABEL: Definitely no.
INSTRUCTOR: Now, your superiors do nothing about it. What's your position?
MABEL: I guess I can't do anything about it—though I must confess I feel guilty about it. I've still got to meet that child every day, and her problem is there with me in the classroom.
HARRY: You can by-pass your principal. It might mean, of course, that

His Professional Functions 77

you'll lose your job, but you can do it. You can go to a social agency and tell them about the case.

INSTRUCTOR: Then Mabel may properly be suspended for insubordination?

HARRY: What comes first, Mabel's job or the welfare of the child?

INSTRUCTOR: I thought we had said that her duty as a teacher was fulfilled by her reporting this to her superiors. Maybe you mean, Harry, her duty as a citizen, not as a teacher?

NED: There is more than duty involved here. There is fellow sympathy, regard for a child, and I think that Mabel as one human being relating to another should do something for that child.

INSTRUCTOR: You mean not as a teacher, but as a human being?

HARRY: I think a teacher could use a great deal of ingenuity in finding ways of showing the child her affection and interest. And giving her some help in that way and doing that as a teacher.

NED: I'd like to say that this situation, not just this particular situation, but situations like it, arise many, many times in our school. We find ourselves in conflict between our jobs as teachers, and our feelings as human beings.

Harry and Mabel still feel that the teacher has the obligation to help. Harry thinks it is "Mabel's duty as a teacher" to help, even if it means the loss of her job for insubordination. The incongruity of losing one's job for performing one's duty doesn't occur to Harry. His question, "What comes first, Mabel's job or the welfare of the child?" reveals how far away he is (as are many other teachers) from distinguishing one's professional function from responsibility for the over-all "welfare" of a child.

Ned is close to the distinction when he states, "We find ourselves in conflict between our jobs as teachers and our feelings as human beings."

INSTRUCTOR: Suppose Mabel or any one of you had to deal not with this one case but with a dozen such cases each week. Would you soon stop being a classroom teacher and become a social worker or psychiatric interviewer? This child is very much disturbed emotionally. Now, what is the function of the teacher?

MABEL: I'm not a therapist; I tried to do the best I could to refer it to the proper authorities; and there is nothing more I can do.

HARRY: I can see that you take on so many different kinds of activity that you become frustrated and cease to do a job in the classroom and are torn in a thousand different directions.

Mabel and Harry have reached the point where an explanation of the teacher's function will clarify what they are now feeling.

INSTRUCTOR: The issue is what are the limits of Mabel's job. It is difficult for the average teacher to see that she must operate within the limits of her professional capacities and function. If you do, you are protected against that which you may not do, either because of your responsibility as a teacher or because of your lack of competence. Isn't the problem one of the teacher's protecting herself against feeling guilty by understanding her function and not being disturbed by the fact that she cannot do what her function doesn't call for? Isn't she protected by operating within her limits?

MABEL: I must add here that certainly after this discussion I don't feel quite so guilty as I formerly felt. I can't tell you how relieved I am.

INSTRUCTOR: I wonder if some of you, for the first time, aren't becoming aware of a concept of the limits of the teacher, and whether you don't see how helpful an awareness of limits is. You can see that this concept of the whole child has not been too carefully examined, as it is usually expressed. You can see, can you not, that no teacher can be directly responsible for the whole child. Your responsibility is met by doing the limited job you are competent to perform. Now, when you have done that, maybe the child will do something, with the help you offered him, in other areas of his experience.

NED: As a matter of fact, there is a law which states that if a teacher, for example, removes a sliver from a child's hand and an infection sets in, the school authority will not protect the teacher against a suit.

INSTRUCTOR: The legal reason for that, may I add, supports our analysis of limited function. The teacher, in helping the child with the sliver, is acting in his capacity as a private citizen, not as a teacher. He is acting outside his official function as a teacher and may be liable in a negligence suit.

HARRY: When I say we are to consider the whole child, that involves the cooperation of parents, school authorities, physicians, and community agencies. The teacher alone is not responsible for the whole child but it means all community agencies, school and otherwise.

MABEL: I think the teacher has to know enough about the community resources to know when to make a referral, where to make it, and to whom to make it. And if she does that, I think she has fulfilled her obligation toward the child as a teacher of a particular class.

The teacher who is able to accept the views on limited function expressed in this chapter is likely to save a great deal of energy and avoid a good deal of frustration. Each one of us is engaged to discharge specific duties. Our professional responsibility is to carry out our delegated tasks, not to become martyrs or to perform miracles. Sufficient unto the task are the difficulties thereof.

Functioning within prescribed limits is the surest way of structuring the specific educational services and meeting the specific problems of pupils. What the *pupil* does to and with the specific experience will have its effects on him, however restricted or extensive. The teacher has a limited function, which the whole child reacts to in whatever way he does.

The teacher keeps the general goal of education, the development of the whole child, in the background, but she focuses upon her own specialty. Personality is shaped not in a vacuum but in contexts made up of specific situations. Habits, attitudes, and feelings are acquired as one is exposed to and works through specific problems. No one person, whether parent, teacher, physician, friend, music instructor or minister, can possibly be competent or wise or skilled enough to guide a child in every direction.

One doesn't learn generally; one always learns within specific situations characterized by limits and focus. What the individual does to and with any experience cannot be accurately predicted in advance. What the pupil will learn from any *given,* limited experience and apply to *other* areas of knowledge and action lies beyond the control of the teacher, although she should always be aware of the possible implications.

The belief current in some educational circles that we teach the "whole child" is half true and half false. In a mediate sense, the teacher is concerned with the development of the personality of the child. In practice, however, the teacher must confine herself to the limitations of time and place, and to her own skills or tools—that is, she must function within limited, clearly defined objectives. This is the *specific* goal of education. The general and specific goals cannot be separated, but they should be distinguished. The child *learns* as a whole, but the teacher focuses within the limited area of her responsibility.

One final word of caution. Children are not in the classroom so that teachers can perform a function. Teachers are performing in a way calculated to help children to develop. Slavish adherence to rigid function can become a stupid ritual. The question is "Who can best meet the specific needs of pupils?" The answer is "The person who is professionally qualified to deal with the specific needs." There may be times, places, and events which call for a teacher's assuming responsibilities for which she was not prepared. Generally, however, both teacher and pupils will be protected as well as helped by defining limits and remaining within them.

NEA CODE OF ETHICS [*]

We, the members of the National Education Association of the United States, hold these truths to be self-evident—

—that the primary purpose of education in the United States is to develop citizens who will safeguard, strengthen, and improve the democracy obtained thru a representative government;

[*] "New NEA Code of Ethics," *NEA Journal,* XLI, September 1952, pp. 371-2.

—that the achievement of effective democracy in all aspects of American life and the maintenance of our national ideals depend upon making acceptable educational opportunities available to all;

—that the quality of education reflects the ideals, motives, preparation, and conduct of the members of the teaching profession;

—that whoever chooses teaching as a career assumes the obligation to conduct himself in accordance with the ideals of the profession.

As a guide for the teaching profession, the members of the National Education Association have adopted this code of professional ethics. Since all teachers should be members of a united profession, the basic principles herein enumerated apply to all persons engaged in the professional aspects of education—elementary, secondary, and collegiate.

FIRST PRINCIPLE

The primary obligation of the teaching profession is to guide children, youth, and adults in the pursuit of knowledge and skills, to prepare them in the ways of democracy, and to help them to become happy, useful, self-supporting citizens. The ultimate strength of the nation lies in the social responsibility, economic competence, and moral strength of the individual American.

In fulfilling the obligations of this first principle the teacher will—

[1] Deal justly and impartially with students regardless of their physical, mental, emotional, political, economic, social, racial, or religious characteristics.

[2] Recognize the differences among students and seek to meet their individual needs.

[3] Encourage students to formulate and work for high individual goals in the development of their physical, intellectual, creative, and spiritual endowments.

[4] Aid students to develop an understanding and appreciation not only of the opportunities and benefits of American democracy but also of their obligations to it.

[5] Respect the right of every student to have confidential information about himself withheld except when its release is to authorized agencies or is required by law.

[6] Accept no remuneration for tutoring except in accordance with approved policies of the governing board.

SECOND PRINCIPLE

The members of the teaching profession share with parents the task of shaping each student's purposes and acts toward socially acceptable ends.

His Professional Functions

The effectiveness of many methods of teaching is dependent upon cooperative relationships with the home.

In fulfilling the obligations of this second principle the teacher will—

[1] Respect the basic responsibility of parents for their children.

[2] Seek to establish friendly and cooperative relationships with the home.

[3] Help to increase the student's confidence in his own home and avoid disparaging remarks which might undermine that confidence.

[4] Provide parents with information that will serve the best interests of their children, and be discreet with information received from parents.

[5] Keep parents informed about the progress of their children as interpreted in terms of the purposes of the school.

THIRD PRINCIPLE

The teaching profession occupies a position of public trust involving not only the individual teacher's personal conduct, but also the interaction of the school and the community. Education is most effective when these many relationships operate in a friendly, cooperative, and constructive manner.

In fulfilling the obligations of this third principle the teacher will—

[1] Adhere to any reasonable pattern of behavior accepted by the community for professional persons.

[2] Perform the duties of citizenship, and participate in community activities with due consideration for his obligations to his students, his family, and himself.

[3] Discuss controversial issues from an objective point of view, thereby keeping his class free from partisan opinions.

[4] Recognize that the public schools belong to the people of the community, encourage lay participation in shaping the purposes of the school, and strive to keep the public informed of the educational program which is being provided.

[5] Respect the community in which he is employed and be loyal to the school system, community, state, and nation.

[6] Work to improve education in the community and to strengthen the community's moral, spiritual, and intellectual life.

FOURTH PRINCIPLE

The members of the teaching profession have inescapable obligations with respect to employment. These obligations are nearly always shared employer-employee responsibilities based upon mutual respect and good faith.

In fulfilling the obligations of this fourth principle the teacher will—

[1] Conduct professional business thru the proper channels.

[2] Refrain from discussing confidential and official information with unauthorized persons.

[3] Apply for employment on the basis of competence only, and avoid asking for a specific position known to be filled by another teacher.

[4] Seek employment in a professional manner, avoiding such practices as the indiscriminate distribution of applications.

[5] Refuse to accept a position when the vacancy has been created thru unprofessional activity or pending controversy over professional policy or the application of unjust personnel practices and procedures.

[6] Adhere to the conditions of a contract until service thereunder has been performed, the contract has been terminated by mutual consent, or the contract has otherwise been legally terminated.

[7] Give and expect due notice before a change of position is to be made.

[8] Be fair in all recommendations that are given concerning the work of other teachers.

[9] Accept no compensation from producers of instructional supplies when one's recommendations affect the local purchase or use of such teaching aids.

[10] Engage in no gainful employment, outside of his contract, where the employment affects adversely his professional status or impairs his standing with students, associates, and the community.

[11] Cooperate in the development of school policies and assume one's professional obligations thereby incurred.

[12] Accept one's obligation to the employing board for maintaining a professional level of service.

Fifth Principle

The teaching profession is distinguished from many other occupations by the uniqueness and quality of the professional relationships among all teachers. Community support and respect are influenced by the standards of teachers and their attitudes toward teaching and other teachers.

In fulfilling the obligations of this fifth principle the teacher will—

[1] Deal with other members of the profession in the same manner as he himself wishes to be treated.

[2] Stand by other teachers who have acted on his behalf and at his request.

[3] Speak constructively of other teachers, but report honestly to responsible persons in matters involving the welfare of students, the school system, and the profession.

[4] Maintain active membership in professional organizations and, thru participation, strive to attain the objectives that justify such organized groups.

[5] Seek to make professional growth continuous by such procedures as study, research, travel, conferences, and attendance at professional meetings.

[6] Make the teaching profession so attractive in ideals and practices that sincere and able young people will want to enter it.

His Social and Economic Status

THE GADFLY *

I will begin at the beginning, and ask what is the accusation which has given rise to the slander of me, and in fact has encouraged Meletus to prefer this charge against me. Well, what do the slanderers say? They shall be my prosecutors, and I will sum up their words in an affidavit: 'Socrates is an evil-doer, and a curious person, who searches into things under the earth and in heaven, and he makes the worse appear the better cause; and he teaches the aforesaid doctrines to others.' . . .

. . . if you say to me, Socrates, this time we will not mind Anytus, and you shall be let off, but upon one condition, that you are not to enquire and speculate in this way any more, and that if you are caught doing so again you shall die;—if this was the condition on which you let me go, I should reply: Men of Athens, I honour and love you; but I shall obey God rather than you, and while I have life and strength I shall never cease from the practice and teaching of philosophy, exhorting any one whom I meet and saying to him after my manner: You, my friend,—a citizen of the great and mighty and wise city of Athens,—are you not ashamed of heaping up the greatest amount of money and honour and reputation, and caring so little about wisdom and truth and the greatest improvement of the soul, which you never regard or heed at all? And if the person with whom I am arguing, says: Yes, but I do care; then I do not leave him or let him go at once; but I proceed to interrogate and examine and cross-examine him,

* Plato, *The Apology*. William Chase Greene (ed.), *The Dialogues of Plato, Selections from Translation of Benjamin Jowett* (New York, Boni and Liveright, 1935), pp. 4-6, 9-13, 15-19. (Fourth century B.C.)

and if I think that he has no virtue in him, but only says that he has, I reproach him with undervaluing the greater, and overvaluing the less. And I shall repeat the same words to every one whom I meet, young and old, citizen and alien, but especially to the citizens, inasmuch as they are my brethren. For know that this is the command of God; and I believe that no greater good has ever happened in the state than my service to the God. For I do nothing but go about persuading you all, old and young alike, not to take thought for your persons or your properties, but first and chiefly to care about the greatest improvement of the soul. I tell you that virtue is not given by money, but that from virtue comes money and every other good of man, public as well as private. This is my teaching, and if the doctrine which corrupts the youth, I am a mischievous person. But if any one says that this is not my teaching, he is speaking an untruth. Wherefore, O men of Athens, I say to you, do as Anytus bids or not as Anytus bids, and either acquit me or not; but whichever you do, understand that I shall never alter my ways, not even if I have to die many times. . . .

And now, Athenians, I am not going to argue for my own sake, as you may think, but for yours, that you may not sin against the God by condemning me, who am his gift to you. For if you kill me you will not easily find a successor to me, who, if I may use such a ludicrous figure of speech, am a sort of gadfly, given to the state by God; and the state is a great and noble steed who is tardy in his motions owing to his very size, and requires to be stirred into life. I am that gadfly which God has attached to the state, and all day long and in all places am always fastening upon you, arousing and persuading and reproaching you. You will not easily find another like me, and therefore I would advise you to spare me. I dare say that you may feel out of temper (like a person who is suddenly awakened from sleep), and you think that you might easily strike me dead as Anytus advises, and then you would sleep on for the remainder of your lives, unless God in his care of you sent you another gadfly. When I say that I am given to you by God, the proof of my mission is this:—if I had been like other men, I should not have neglected all my own concerns or patiently seen the neglect of them during all these years, and have been doing yours, coming to you individually like a father or elder brother, exhorting you to regard virtue; such conduct, I say, would be unlike human nature. If I had gained anything, or if my exhortations had been paid, there would have been some sense in my doing so; but now, as you will perceive, not even the impudence of my accusers dares to say that I have ever exacted or sought pay of any one; of that they have no witness. And I have a sufficient witness to the truth of what I say—my poverty.

Some one may wonder why I go about in private giving advice and busying myself with the concerns of others, but do not venture to come forward in public and advise the state. I will tell you why. You have heard me speak at sundry times and in divers places of an oracle or sign which comes to me, and is the divinity which Meletus ridicules in the indictment. This sign, which is a kind of voice, first began to come to me when I was a child; it always forbids but never commands me to do anything which I am going to do. This is what deters me from being a politician. And rightly, as I think. For I am certain, O men of Athens, that if I had engaged in politics, I should have perished long ago, and done no good either to you or to myself. And do not be offended at my telling you the truth: for the truth is, that no man who goes to war with you or any other multitude, honestly striving against the many lawless and unrighteous deeds which are done in a state, will save his life; he who will fight for the right, if he would live even for a brief space, must have a private station and not a public one. . . .

A NEW JERSEY SCHOOLMASTER'S OATH, 1777 *

. . . And whereas it is of the last Moment to a free and independent State, that the rising Generation should be early instructed in the Principles of publick Virtue, and duly impressed with the amiable Ideas of Liberty and Patriotism, and at the same Time inspired with the keenest Abhorrence of despotick and arbitrary Power: AND WHEREAS publick Teachers and Instructors may be greatly instrumental in tincturing the youthful Mind with such Impressions, either in Favour of a just and equal Administration, or of a slavish Submission to lawless Rule, as in their riper Years are not easily obliterated, and are, for that Reason, important Objects of legislative Attention, BE IT THEREFORE ENACTED *by the Authority aforesaid,* That every Schoolmaster or Usher in this State, who shall not, within two Months after the Publication of this Act, take and subscribe the said Oaths, or, if one of the People called *Quakers,* the Affirmations of Abjuration and Allegiance, before some proper Officer herein after mentioned, shall, for every Week after the Expiration of the said two Months that he continues to keep School, or teach as an Usher, until he shall take and subscribe the said Oaths or Affirmations, forfeit the Sum of *Six Pounds;* to be recovered by Action of Debt or otherwise, before any Justice of the Peace, with Costs

---

* New Jersey, Statutes, *Acts of the Council and General Assembly of the State of New Jersey from the Establishment of the present Government, and Declaration of Independence to the end of the first Sitting of the eighth Session, on the 24th Day of December, 1783* . . . (Trenton, Isaac Collins, Printer to the State of New Jersey, 1884), pp. 28, 29.

of Suit, by any Person who will sue for the same; and applied one Half to the Use of the Person who shall sue for the same, and the other Half to be paid to the Overseer of the Poor, for the Use of the Poor of the District where the Offence was committed.

A PROTEST AGAINST OATHS BY THE SOCIETY CALLED QUAKERS, 1779 *

To the General Assembly of Pennsylvania: The memorial and address of the religious Society called Quakers respectfully sheweth:

That divers laws have been lately enacted which are very injurious in their nature, oppressive in the manner of execution, and greatly affect us in our religious and civil liberties and privileges, particularly a law passed by the last Assembly entitled "A further supplement to the test laws of this State," in the operation whereof the present and succeeding generations are materialiy interested. We therefore apprehend it a duty owing to ourselves and our posterity to lay before you the grievances to which we are subjected by these laws.

Our predecessors on their early settlement in this part of America, being piously concerned for the posterity of the colony and the real wellfare of their posterity, among other salutory institutions promoted at their own expence the establishment of schools for the instruction of their Youth in useful and necessary learning and their education in piety and virtue, the practice of which forms the most sure basis for perpetuating the enjoyment of Christian liberty and essential happiness.

By the voluntary contributions by the members of our religious Society, schools were set up in which not only their children were taught but their liberality hath been extended to poor children of other religious denominations generally, great numbers of whom have partaken thereof; and these schools have been in like manner continued and maintained for a long course of years.

Duty to Almighty God made known in the consciences of men and confirmed by the holy Scriptures is an invariable rule which should govern their judgment and actions. He is the only Lord and Sovereign of Conscience, and to him we are accountable for our conduct, as by him all men are to be finally judged. By conscience we mean the apprehension and persuasion a man has of his duty to God and the liberty of conscience we plead for is a free open profession and unmolested exercise of that duty,

* Isaac Sharpless, *A Quaker Experiment in Government; History of Quaker Government in Pennsylvania, 1682-1783* (Philadelphia, Ferris & Leach, 1902), II, pp. 184-7.

such a conscience as under the influence of divine grace keeps within the bounds of morality in all the affairs of human life and teacheth to live soberly righteously and godly in the world.

As a religious Society, we have ever held forth the Gospel dispensation was introduced for completing the happiness of mankind by taking away the occasion of strife contention and bloodshed and therefore we all conscientiously restrained from promoting or joining in wars and fightings: and when laws have been made to enforce our compliance contrary to the convictions of our consciences, we have thought it our duty patiently to suffer though we have often been grievously oppressed. Principle we hold in this respect requires us to be a peaceable people and through the various changes and revolutions which have occurred since our religious Society has existed, we have never been concerned in promoting or abetting any combinations insurrections or parties to endanger the public peace or by violence to oppose the authority of government apprehending it our duty quietly to admit and peaceably to demeanor ourselves under every government which Divine Providence in his unerring wisdom may permit to be placed over us; so that no government can have just occasion for entertaining fears or jealousies of disturbance or danger from us. But if any professing with us deviate from this peaceable principle into a contrary conduct and foment discords, feuds or animosities, giving just occasion of uneasiness and disquiet, we think it our duty, to declare against their proceeding.

By the same divine principle, we are restrained from complying with the injunctions and requisitions made on us of tests and declarations of fidelity to either party who are engaged in actual war lest we contradict by our conduct the profession of our faith.

It is obvious that in these days of depravity, as in former times, because of oaths the land mourns and the multiplying the use of them and such solemn engagements renders them familiar, debases the mind of the people and adds to the number of those gross evils already lamentably prevalent which have drawn down the chastisement of heaven on our guilty country.

We are not actuated by political or party motives; we are real friends to our country, who wish its prosperity and think a solicitude for the enjoyments of our equitable rights, and that invaluable privilege, Liberty of Conscience, free from coercion, cannot be justly deemed unreasonable. Many of us and other industrious inhabitants being exposed to heavy penalties and sufferings, which are abundantly encreased by the rigour of mistaken and unreasonable men under the sanction of law, whereby many are allready reduced to great straits and threatened with total ruin, the effects of whose imprisonment must at length be very sensibly felt by the community at large through the decline of cultivation and the necessary employments.

We have been much abused and villified by many anonymous publications and our conduct greatly perverted and misrepresented by groundless reports and the errors of individuals charged upon us as a body in order to render us odious to the people and prepossess the minds of persons in power against us; being conscious of our innocence and "submitting our cause to the Lord who judgeth righteously" we have preferred patience in bearing the reproach to public contest, not doubting that as the minds of the people become more settled and composed, our peaceable demeanor would manifest the injustice we suffered, and being persuaded that on a cool dispassionate hearing we should be able to invalidate or remove the mistaken suggestions and reports prevailing to our prejudice.

The matters we have now freely laid before you are serious and important, which we wish you to consider wisely as men and religiously as Christians manifesting yourselves friends to true liberty and enemies to persecution, by repealing the several penal laws affecting tender consciences and restoring to us our equitable rights that the means of education and instruction of our youth which we conceive to be our reasonable and religious duty, may not be obstructed and that the oppressed may be relieved. In your consideration whereof, we sincerely desire that you may seek for and be directed by that supreme "wisdom which is pure, peaceable, gentle and easy to be entreated, full of mercy and good fruits" and are your real friends.

Signed on behalf of a meeting of the Representatives of the said people held in Philadelphia the 4th day of the 11th mo 1779.

JOHN DRINKER, CLERK

THE FEINBERG DECISION, 1952 *

(Mr. Justice Minton delivered the opinion of the Court.)

The preamble of the Feinberg Law, § 1, makes elaborate findings that members of subversive groups, particularly of the Communist Party and its affiliated organizations, have been infiltrating into public employment in the public schools of the State; that this has occurred and continues notwithstanding the existence of protective statutes designed to prevent the appointment to or retention in employment in public office, and particularly in the public schools, of members of any organizations which teach or advocate that the government of the United States or of any state or political subdivision thereof shall be overthrown by force or violence or by any other unlawful means. As a result, propaganda can be disseminated among

* *Adler et al.* v. *Board of Education of the City of New York,* 342 U.S. (1952).

the children by those who teach them and to whom they look for guidance, authority, and leadership. The Legislature further found that the members of such groups use their positions to advocate and teach their doctrines, and are frequently bound by oath, agreement, pledge, or understanding to follow, advocate and teach a prescribed party line or group dogma or doctrine without regard to truth or free inquiry. This propaganda, the Legislature declared, is sufficiently subtle to escape detection in the classroom; thus, the menace of such infiltration into the classroom is difficult to measure. Finally, to protect the children from such influence, it was thought essential that the laws prohibiting members of such groups, such as the Communist Party or its affiliated organizations, from obtaining or retaining employment in the public schools be rigorously enforced. It is the purpose of the Feinberg Law to provide for the disqualification and removal of superintendents of schools, teachers, and employees in the public schools in any city or school district of the State who advocate the overthrow of the Government by unlawful means or who are members of organizations which have a like purpose.

Section 3022 of the Education Law, added by the Feinberg Law, provides that the Board of Regents, which has charge of the public school system in the State of New York, shall, after full notice and hearing, make a listing of organizations which it finds advocate, advise, teach, or embrace the doctrine that the government should be overthrown by force or violence or any other unlawful means, and that such listing may be amended and revised from time to time.

It will be observed that the listings are made only after full notice and hearing. In addition, the Court of Appeals construed the statute in conjunction with Article 78 of the New York Civil Practice Act, Gilbert-Bliss' N. Y. Civ. Prac., Vol. 6B, so as to provide listed organizations a right of review.

The Board of Regents is further authorized to provide in rules and regulations, and has so provided, that membership in any listed organization, after notice and hearing, "shall constitute prima facie evidence for disqualification for appointment to or retention in any office or position in the school system"; but before one who is an employee or seeks employment is severed from or denied employment, he likewise must be given a full hearing with the privilege of being represented by counsel and the right to judicial review. It is § 12-a of the Civil Service Law, as implemented by the Feinberg Law as above indicated, that is under attack here.

It is first argued that the Feinberg Law and the rules promulgated thereunder constitute an abridgment of the freedom of speech and assembly of persons employed or seeking employment in the public schools of the State of New York.

It is clear that such persons have the right under our law to assemble, speak, think and believe as they will. *Communications Assn.* v. *Douds,* 339 U.S. 382. It is equally clear that they have no right to work for the State in the school system on their own terms. *United Public Workers* v. *Mitchell,* 330 U.S. 75. They may work for the school system upon the reasonable terms laid down by the proper authorities of New York. If they do not choose to work on such terms, they are at liberty to retain their beliefs and associations and go elsewhere. Has the State thus deprived them of any right to free speech or assembly? We think not. Such persons are or may be denied, under the statutes in question, the privilege of working for the school system of the State of New York because, first, of their advocacy of the overthrow of the government by force or violence, or, secondly, by unexplained membership in an organization found by the school authorities, after notice and hearing, to teach and advocate the overthrow of the government by force or violence, and known by such persons to have such purpose.

The constitutionality of the first proposition is not questioned here. *Gitlow* v. *New York,* 268 U.S. 652, 667-672, construing § 161 of the New York Penal Law.

As to the second, it is rather subtly suggested that we should not follow our recent decision in *Garner* v. *Los Angeles Board,* 341 U.S. 716. We there said:

> We think that a municipal employer is not disabled because it is an agency of the State from inquiring of its employees as to matters that may prove relevant to their fitness and suitability for the public service. Past conduct may well relate to present fitness; past loyalty may have a reasonable relationship to present and future trust. Both are commonly inquired into in determining fitness for both high and low positions in private industry and are not less relevant in public employment. 341 U.S., at p. 720.

We adhere to that case. A teacher works in a sensitive area in a schoolroom. There he shapes the attitude of young minds towards the society in which they live. In this, the state has a vital concern. It must preserve the integrity of the schools. That the school authorities have the right and the duty to screen the officials, teachers, and employees as to their fitness to maintain the integrity of the schools as a part of ordered society, cannot be doubted. One's associates, past and present, as well as one's conduct, may properly be considered in determining fitness and loyalty. From time immemorial, one's reputation has been determined in part by the company he keeps. In the employment of officials and teachers of the school system, the state may very properly inquire into the company they keep, and we know of no rule, constitutional or otherwise, that prevents the state, when determining the fitness and loyalty of such persons, from considering the organizations and persons with whom they associate.

If, under the procedure set up in the New York law, a person is found to be unfit and is disqualified from employment in the public school system because of membership in a listed organization, he is not thereby denied the right of free speech and assembly. His freedom of choice between membership in the organization and employment in the school system might be limited, but not his freedom of speech or assembly, except in the remote sense that limitation is inherent in every choice. Certainly such limitation is not one the state may not make in the exercise of its police power to protect the schools from pollution and thereby to defend its own existence.

It is next argued by appellants that the provision in § 3022 directing the Board of Regents to provide in rules and regulations that membership in any organization listed by the Board after notice and hearing, with provision for review in accordance with the statute, shall constitute prima facie evidence of disqualification, denies due process, because the fact found bears no relation to the fact presumed. In other words, from the fact found that the organization was one that advocated the overthrow of government by unlawful means and that the person employed or to be employed was a member of the organization and knew of its purpose, to presume that such member is disqualified for employment is so unreasonable as to be a denial of due process of law. We do not agree.

> The law of evidence is full of presumptions either of fact or law. The former are, of course, disputable, and the strength of any inference of one fact from proof of another depends upon the generality of the experience upon which it is founded. . . .
>
> Legislation providing that proof of one fact shall constitute *prima facie* evidence of the main fact in issue is but to enact a rule of evidence, and quite within the general power of government. Statutes, National and state, dealing with such methods of proof in both civil and criminal cases abound, and the decisions upholding them are numerous. *Mobile, J. & K. C. R. Co.* v. *Turnipseed,* 219 U.S. 35, at p. 42.

Membership in a listed organization found to be within the statute and known by the member to be within the statute is a legislative finding that the member by his membership supports the thing the organization stands for, namely, the overthrow of government by unlawful means. We cannot say that such a finding is contrary to fact or that "generality of experience" points to a different conclusion. Disqualification follows therefore as a reasonable presumption from such membership and support. Nor is there here a problem of procedural due process. The presumption is not conclusive but arises only in a hearing where the person against whom it may arise has full opportunity to rebut it. The holding of the Court of Appeals below is significant in this regard:

> The statute also makes it clear that . . . proof of such membership "shall constitute prima facie evidence of disqualification" for such employment. But, as was said in *Potts* v. *Pardee* (220 N. Y. 431, 433): "The presumption growing out of a *prima facie* case . . . remains only so long as there is no substantial evidence to the contrary. When that is offered the presumption disappears, and unless met by further proof there is nothing to justify a finding based solely upon it." Thus the phrase *"prima facie* evidence of disqualification," as used in the statute, imports a hearing at which one who seeks appointment to or retention in a public school position shall be afforded an opportunity to present substantial evidence contrary to the presumption sanctioned by the *prima facie* evidence for which subdivision 2 of section 3022 makes provision. Once such contrary evidence has been received, however, the official who made the order of ineligibility has thereafter the burden of sustaining the validity of that order by a fair preponderance of the evidence. (Civil Service Law, § 12-a, subd. [d].) Should an order of ineligibility then issue, the party aggrieved thereby may avail himself of the provisions for review prescribed by the section of the statute last cited above. In that view there here arises no question of procedural due process. 301 N. Y. 476, at p. 494, 95 N. E. 2d 806, at 814-815.

Where, as here, the relation between the fact found and the presumption is clear and direct and is not conclusive, the requirements of due process are satisfied.

Without raising in the complaint or in the proceedings in the lower courts the question of the constitutionality of § 3021 of the Education Law of New York, appellants urge here for the first time that this section is unconstitutionally vague. The question is not before us. We will not pass upon the constitutionality of a state statute before the state courts have had an opportunity to do so. *Asbury Hospital* v. *Cass County,* 326 U.S. 207, 213-216; *Alabama State Federation of Labor* v. *McAdory,* 325 U.S. 450, 460-462; *Plymouth Coal Co.* v. *Pennsylvania,* 232 U.S. 531, 546.

It is also suggested that the use of the word "subversive" is vague and indefinite. But the word is first used in § 1 of the Feinberg Law, which is the preamble to the Act, and not in a definite part thereof. When used in subdivision 2 of § 3022, the word has a very definite meaning, namely, an organization that teaches and advocates the overthrow of government by force or violence.

We find no constitutional infirmity in § 12-a of the Civil Service Law of New York or in the Feinberg Law which implemented it, and the judgment is *Affirmed.*

Mr. Justice Douglas, with whom MR. JUSTICE BLACK concurs, dissenting.[1]

I have not been able to accept the recent doctrine that a citizen who enters the public service can be forced to sacrifice his civil rights. I cannot for example find in our constitutional scheme the power of a state to place its employees in the category of second-class citizens by denying them freedom of thought and expression. The Constitution guarantees freedom of thought and expression to everyone in our society. All are entitled to it; and none needs it more than the teacher.

The public school is in most respects the cradle of our democracy. The increasing role of the public school is seized upon by proponents of the type of legislation represented by New York's Feinberg law as proof of the importance and need for keeping the school free of "subversive influences." But that is to misconceive the effect of this type of legislation. Indeed the impact of this kind of censorship on the public school system illustrates the high purpose of the First Amendment in freeing speech and thought from censorship.

The present law proceeds on a principle repugnant to our society—guilt by association. A teacher is disqualified because of her membership in an organization found to be "subversive." The finding as to the "subversive" character of the organization is made in a proceeding to which the teacher is not a party and in which it is not clear that she may even be heard. To be sure, she may have a hearing when charges of disloyalty are leveled against her. But in that hearing the finding as to the "subversive" character of the organization apparently may not be reopened in order to allow her to show the truth of the matter. The irrebuttable charge that the organization is "subversive" therefore hangs as an ominous cloud over her own hearing. The mere fact of membership in the organization raises a prima facie case of her own guilt. She may, it is said, show her innocence. But innocence in this case turns on knowledge; and when the witch hunt is on, one who must rely on ignorance leans on a feeble reed.

The very threat of such a procedure is certain to raise havoc with academic freedom. Youthful indiscretions, mistaken causes, misguided enthusiasms—all long forgotten—become the ghosts of a harrowing present. Any organization committed to a liberal cause, any group organized to revolt against an hysterical trend, any committee launched to sponsor an unpopular program becomes suspect. These are the organizations into which Communists often infiltrate. Their presence infects the whole, even though the project was not conceived in sin. A teacher caught in that mesh is almost certain to stand condemned. Fearing condemnation, she will tend to shrink

[1] Mr. Justice Frankfurter also dissented in a separate opinion. Editors' note.

His Social and Economic Status

from any association that stirs controversy. In that manner freedom of expression will be stifled.

But that is only part of it. Once a teacher's connection with a listed organization is shown, her views become subject to scrutiny to determine whether her membership in the organization is innocent or, if she was formerly a member, whether she has *bona fide* abandoned her membership.

The law inevitably turns the school system into a spying project. Regular loyalty reports on the teachers must be made out. The principals become detectives; the students, the parents, the community become informers. Ears are cocked for tell-tale signs of disloyalty. The prejudices of the community come into play in searching out the disloyal. This is not the usual type of supervision which checks a teacher's competency; it is a system which searches for hidden meanings in a teacher's utterances.

What was the significance of the reference of the art teacher to socialism? Why was the history teacher so openly hostile to Franco Spain? Who heard overtones of revolution in the English teacher's discussion of the Grapes of Wrath? What was behind the praise of Soviet progress in metallurgy in the chemistry class? Was it not "subversive" for the teacher to cast doubt on the wisdom of the venture in Korea?

What happens under this law is typical of what happens in a police state. Teachers are under constant surveillance; their pasts are combed for signs of disloyalty; their utterances are watched for clues to dangerous thoughts. A pall is cast over the classrooms. There can be no real academic freedom in that environment. Where suspicion fills the air and holds scholars in line for fear of their jobs, there can be no exercise of the free intellect. Supineness and dogmatism take the place of inquiry. A "party line"—as dangerous as the "party line" of the Communists—lays hold. It is the "party line" of the orthodox view, of the conventional thought, of the accepted approach. A problem can no longer be pursued with impunity to its edges. Fear stalks the classroom. The teacher is no longer a stimulant to adventurous thinking; she becomes instead a pipe line for safe and sound information. A deadening dogma takes the place of free inquiry. Instruction tends to become sterile; pursuit of knowledge is discouraged; discussion often leaves off where it should begin.

This, I think, is what happens when a censor looks over a teacher's shoulder. This system of spying and surveillance with its accompanying reports and trials cannot go hand in hand with academic freedom. It produces standardized thought, not the pursuit of truth. Yet it was the pursuit of truth which the First Amendment was designed to protect. A system which directly or inevitably has that effect is alien to our system and should be struck down. Its survival is a real threat to our way of life. We need be bold and adventuresome in our thinking to survive. A school system producing students trained as robots threatens to rob a generation of the versatility that has been perhaps our greatest distinction. The Framers knew the danger of dogmatism; they also knew the strength that comes when the mind is free, when ideas may be pursued wherever they lead. We forget these teachings of the First Amendment when we sustain this law.

Of course the school systems of the country need not become cells for Communist activities; and the classrooms need not become forums for propagandizing the Marxist creed. But the guilt of the teacher should turn on overt acts. So long as she is a law-abiding citizen, so long as her performance within the public school system meets professional standards, her private life, her political philosophy, her social creed should not be the cause of reprisals against her.

WHO THINKS WHAT ABOUT EDUCATORS? *

The object of this study was to assess the status of educators and of education, largely at the secondary level, from the opinions of a representative sample of the people of a small American community. The data are from a survey of public opinion conducted by the author and a staff of interviewers during the spring and summer of 1948 in New London, Connecticut. The present paper will treat of the status of educators. The findings about education will be analyzed in a subsequent paper.

METHODS

The universe for the survey was the 1947 voters list of New London, comprising 12,770 persons. Of a total population of 30,456 (1940 Census), those twenty-one years old or over numbered 20,668. The sample was a random 5 per cent, 639 persons, who were interviewed in their homes or places of business by means of a lengthy schedule.

The schedule contained a series of key questions relating to the status of educators—for example, the professional level of teachers. The summary statement of replies to each question is broken down and analyzed with reference to sex, age group, nativity, parenthood, religion, occupation, education, and income. By such analysis we discover that opinions on educators are significantly related to the selected characteristics of New London's voting population.

For convenience, the questions concerning the status of educators are divided into four generalized groups. The first is heterogeneous, pertaining to a variety of attitudes toward teachers. The second group is broadly re-

* Frederic W. Terrien, "Who Thinks What About Educators?," *American Journal of Sociology*, LIX (September 1953), pp. 150-58.

lated to the community activities of teachers; the third treats of their professional status; and the fourth, of their financial condition.

Attitudes Toward Teachers: A. THE FRIENDS OF TEACHERS

The first question in this group was: "Are there any grade or high-school teachers among your particular group of friends?" The percentage distribution of the replies was as follows: Yes, 45.9 per cent; No, 53.5 per cent; No answer, 0.6 per cent.

Females showed a higher affirmative response than did males—a result which might have been anticipated, since the great majority of American public school teachers are female. Unlike sex, age was not found to be related to the replies. The third factor, nativity, showed a significant difference in the opinions of persons of native and of foreign birth. Parenthood and religion were not significantly related to friendship with teachers. Occupation, however, was related. Persons in the general category of clerks have friends who are teachers significantly more often than do those in the immediately adjacent occupational categories. A test of the significance of the difference between replies of clerks and those of proprietors and of service workers showed, at the 5 per cent level of confidence, that teachers are more likely to be friends of the clerks. The more advanced the individual's education, the more likely he was to have teachers as friends. No significant relationship was found between income level and friendship with teachers.

The next question was closely related to the first: "If there are no teachers among your friends, would you welcome any as members of your group?" Since this question applied properly only to those who replied negatively to the first, no correlations were run. Less than 1 per cent answered that they would *not* welcome teachers as members of their group. The replies of these few persons generally indicated a lack of common bond with teachers: "No, we have nothing in common"; "No, they are probably not my type."

B. MINORITY GROUP DISCRIMINATIONS

The second subgroup of questions under the general heading "Varied Attitudes" contained three items aimed at discovering the degree to which there was discrimination against teachers from minority groups. The first question read, "Should teachers coming from minority groups be employed (in the schools of New London)?" The replies were: Yes, 85.6 per cent; No, 12.4 per cent; No answer, 2.0 per cent. Males, significantly more than females, answered this question in the affirmative, as did Jews significantly more than Protestants and Catholics combined. A negative response was given significantly more often by the native-born than by the foreign-born ($P = 0.02$).

The next two questions, concerning which minority representatives should *not* be hired and why, yielded no further correlations but served to isolate the direction of prejudice. Of the 12.4 per cent who thought that teachers coming from minority groups should not be hired, nearly all specified Negroes. One or two persons in each instance voiced sentiments against Orientals, Italians, Catholics, Jews, and Communists. The objection to minority-group members—aside from the usual stereotyped statements of their "inferiority"—was principally rooted in an unwillingness to have their children taught by Negroes.

C. THE SEX OF TEACHERS

The next subgroup of questions concerned opinions on the sex of teachers. The first of two questions read, "Do you prefer men or women teachers at the high-school level?" The answers were distributed thus: Men teachers, 16.1 per cent; Women teachers, 2.2 per cent; No preference, 77.3 per cent; No answer, 4.4 per cent. Men replied in favor of men significantly more often than did women. The foreign-born were more pro-male than the native-born ($P = 0.03$), the Catholics than the Jews, and skilled laborers more than all other occupational groups.

D. THE CONDUCT EXPECTED OF TEACHERS

Most studies conclude that persons in education feel that the general public expects an especially high standard of conduct from teachers. A pair of questions in this survey checked on the item. The first question was phrased thus: "Should the standards of conduct for teachers differ from those of other good citizens?" The replies were: Yes, 16.3 per cent; No, 83.3 per cent; No answer, 0.4 per cent. The older the interviewee, the more likely he was to feel that the standard of conduct of teachers should differ from that of other good citizens ($P = 0.001$). Foreign-born respondents held this opinion significantly more than did native-born respondents.

The second question asked of those who thought teachers' standards of conduct should differ, the reasons for their belief. The replies were about evenly split between those who thought that teachers should teach good behavior by example and those who thought that they should be "more moral."

Opinions Concerning the Community Activities of Teachers

The second of the major groups of questions covered three topics: community activities, unionization, and political activities.

A. Community Activities

The first question read, "Do the high-school teachers of New London join in the activities of the community, such as the League of Women Voters, Rotary, Kiwanis, church groups, Red Cross, athletic groups, and the like?" The distribution of the answers was: Yes, 61.2 per cent; No, 8.9 per cent; No answer, 29.9 per cent.

The next query read, "In your opinion, *should* teachers join in community activities?" This was answered thus: Yes, 92.0 per cent; No, 2.2 per cent; No answer, 5.8 per cent.

Finally, the respondents were asked, "If you know any teachers personally, what specific organizations are they in?" The fact that several organizations were named in the first question may have had considerable effect; on the other hand, the named activities may have been an accurate reflection of the popular conception of the interests of teachers. Of the total of 639 interviewees, 106, or 16.5 per cent, named some community activities in which they believed the teachers engaged. Those cited four or more times, with the percentages of times cited by the 106 interviewees are given in Table 1.

Table 1

	Per Cent
Rotary *	26.4
Red Cross	24.5
Church activities	22.6
League of Women Voters	18.9
Kiwanis *	8.5
"Y" activities	7.5
Elks *	7.5
Masons	6.6
Scouts	5.7
Zanta	5.7
American Association of University Women	3.8
Athletic activities or groups	3.8
Community Chest	3.8
USO	3.8

* The women's auxiliary was included.

The large "No answer" category on the first and second questions probably reflects a fact demonstrated by the first question in the survey itself—namely, that a majority of the interviewees did not have friends who were teachers. Hence, for just over half the respondents replies were based on general observation only. No significant correlations were obtainable for these questions.

B. Union Activities

The matter of the unionization of teachers is one which generated strong popular feelings during the depression of the 1930's and again during the immediate postwar years. It is one, further, on which teachers themselves are sharply divided. Because of its recurrent importance, the item was taken up on this survey. The first of two questions dealing with it was, "Do you think that teachers are justified in unionizing?" Replies were distributed as follows: Yes, 68.9 per cent; No, 26.4 per cent; No answer, 4.7 per cent.

Males replied significantly more often in the affirmative than did females ($P = 0.05$). Laboring groups, as one would expect, when their combined opinions were contrasted with those of the combined professional and proprietor groups, proved themselves more in support of unionization. The older respondents were less likely than the younger to support teacher unionization, and this "conservative" opinion was shared by childless persons ($P = 0.05$), and by Protestants as opposed to Catholics. The greater the individual's education, the less likely he was to feel that teachers have the right to unionize.

Respondents who commented extensively on the unionization of teachers were chiefly concerned with the possibility that the "right to organize" would mean association with the big labor unions. Apparently a teachers' union for protection and adequate pay found support, but a union as a powerbuilding organization did not. In the ideology of most unions, the strike is the logical ultimate step in the achievement of goals. That this should not apply in the case of teachers' unions, however, seemed to be the opinion of most respondents. To the question "Do you think teachers are justified in striking?" the replies were as follows: Yes, 32.9 per cent; No, 62.4 per cent; No answer, 4.7 per cent. On this second question, males supported their original standing favoring unionization, and again laboring groups, as contrasted to the combined professionals and proprietors, were more convinced of the justice of strikes. Older respondents proved less likely than the younger to feel that the strike, like unionization itself, was justified ($P = 0.001$), and in the same way the upper-income group, as compared with the combined lower-income groups, significantly opposed the use of the strike ($P = 0.05$).

Comments on this aspect of teacher activities were numerous. Many interviewees felt that a strike was unwise and should be resorted to only in extreme cases. Most objectors to striking appeared to regard the strike as, in effect, against the students and, in addition, as actually impossible because of the official nature of the teachers' position. Illogically, a number of interviewees protested that teachers should be paid enough so that they would not *have* to strike. The most notable *non sequitur* was that of one respondent who said, "Well, it all depends on what the child has done."

C. POLITICAL ACTIVITIES

Like union membership, political activity among teachers has engendered warm debate. To the question "May teachers be active politically if they so desire?" replies were: Yes, 80.1 per cent; No, 17.8 per cent; No answer, 2.1 per cent. Females significantly more than males replied in the affirmative, but no other correlation was found between opinions and the various socio-economic conditions. The comments, while numerous, were confined almost entirely to qualifying the majority position with the stricture that the political activities of the teachers should not cut down the time devoted to their work or their objectivity.

Opinions Concerning the Professional Status of Teachers

The third group of questions undertook to discover in several ways how the people of the community compared teachers with persons in other occupations.

A. PROFESSIONALISM

The first question read, "Do you consider high-school teaching to be one of the professions?" The affirmative replies reached near-unanimity: Yes, 96.7 per cent; No, 2.0 per cent; No answer, 1.3 per cent.

B. JOB COMPARISONS

The next three questions approached the matter of status by means of comparisons. All questions were designed to be shown to, rather than asked of, the interviewee. They were:

Which of these occupations is about on the same social level as high-school teaching?

1. Factory worker
2. Pharmacist
3. Plumber
4. Executive of large business
5. Policeman
6. Waiter
7. Doctor
8. Shoe clerk
9. Laborer
10. Proprietor of a small business
11. Shop foreman
12. University professor

(number)_____

In the processing of the replies, the occupations were grouped in virtually the same general categories as were the occupations of the interviewees themselves, the exception being the lumping of all "labor" occupations under one heading. A great many of the respondents listed more than one job from the choices, but in such cases most of these clustered in one general category or another; the predominating category, therefore, was selected as characterizing the response of the interviewee. So processed, the

TABLE 2

	Per Cent
Choices predominantly in:	
Professional category	44.3
Proprietor category	21.9
Clerical category	0
Service category	3.6
Labor category	5.0
Disparate choices without pattern	5.6
Choices predominantly in both professional and proprietor categories	9.9
No answer	9.7

replies in Table 2 appear in terms of that percentage of the interviewees who marked one or another general category of occupations as being on the same level as high-school teaching. When the first five items in the table were analyzed, it was found that the older the respondent was, the more likely he was to compare teachers with professionals ($P = 0.05$). Foreign-born persons significantly supported the stand that teachers were "professional" ($P = 0.05$), while native-born interviewees tended to select jobs from the list which were in the proprietor category ($P = 0.02$). More childless persons than those with children made up that small percentage of persons who held that jobs in the labor category were comparable to teaching. Almost all who refused to comment explained that they held that all people and all occupations are on the same social level.

Further enlightenment on the comparative position of teaching was sought by asking the interviewees, "In the matter of *salary,* where do you think the high-school teacher *should* stand on this list (about equal to what number)?" The replies, when processed in the same manner, as were those for the preceding question, showed considerable variance therefrom (Table 3). In the surprisingly large percentage of respondents who felt that teachers' salaries should be comparable with those of persons in the labor category, males were significantly better represented than were females ($P = 0.02$). Reflecting their replies on the preceding query, foreign-born persons were more convinced that the salaries of teachers should be comparable with those of persons in the professional category, while native-born interviewees felt that they should be comparable with the proprietor category ($P = 0.05$). When the replies were analyzed according to occupation and education, it was found that the higher the interviewee's occupation fell on the census gradient or the more his years of schooling, the more likely he was to believe that teachers' salaries should approximate those in both the

TABLE 3

	Per Cent
Choices predominantly in:	
Professional category	32.1
Proprietor category	21.8
Clerical category	0.8
Service category	7.5
Labor category	11.3
Disparate choices without pattern	4.7
Choices predominantly in both professional and proprietor categories	3.3
No answer	18.5

professional and the proprietor categories, as contrasted with those prevailing in other categories (by occupation, $P = 0.01$; by education, $P = 0.05$).

Finally, a clarification of teacher status in terms of other occupations was sought in a question phrased thus: "In the matter of *importance to the community* where do you put high-school teachers on this list (about equal to that of what number)?" Once again, a marked shift of emphasis may be noted in the replies (Table 4). Females, significantly more than males,

TABLE 4

	Per Cent
Choices predominantly in:	
Professional category	51.6
Proprietor category	12.8
Clerical category	0
Service category	11.4
Labor category	3.6
Disparate choices without pattern	5.6
Choices predominantly in both professional and proprietor categories	2.8
No answer	12.2

believed that teaching was comparable in importance to professional occupations, while in that small percentage of persons who compared the importance of teaching to that of jobs in the labor category, males predominated. Again, the native-born, more than the foreign-born, compared the importance of teaching with that of positions in the proprietor category. In the sizable percentage of interviewees who equated teaching to the service and labor categories, professionals and proprietors were significantly less represented than were persons in the laboring groups ($P = 0.02$). The job most often selected by the latter for comparison was that of "policeman." Most of the comments attested to a widespread public belief in the importance of teachers—a number placing them above any other occupational group.

The Financial Status of Teachers

The fourth and last group of questions concerning educators was on their financial status. The questions were divided into two groups: the first was made up of four queries on salaries, and the second was a single question whereon the respondent was asked to comment generally.

A. TEACHERS' SALARIES

It should be remembered that the field work for this report was completed in the early summer of 1948. The first question was, "What is your estimate of the average yearly salary of teachers in the high schools of New London?" The replies were distributed as in Table 5. The correlations

TABLE 5

	Per Cent
$1,799 and less	3.9
1,800-1,999	3.0
2,000-2,249	12.4
2,250-2,399	2.8
2,400	4.4
2,401-2,749	17.4
2,750-2,999	5.9
3,000-3,249	14.4
3,250-3,499	1.6
3,500 and up	5.9
No answer	28.3

between responses to this question and various socio-economic factors proved particularly interesting. It was discovered, first, that the "higher" the occupational level of the respondent, the higher was his estimate of teachers' salaries ($P = 0.05$). Next, it was found that the greater the individual's education, the higher was his estimate of the teachers' salaries, and, finally, that the higher the respondent's income level, the higher was his estimate of these salaries ($P = 0.001$).

The interviewees were next asked: "Do you feel that the teachers are, in general, underpaid, overpaid, or fairly well paid?" The replies fell as

His Social and Economic Status

follows: Underpaid, 60.6 per cent; Overpaid, 0.9 per cent; Fairly well paid, 32.4 per cent; No answer, 6.1 per cent. The first correlation which proved significant was that Jews, more than Catholics and Protestants, believed that the teachers were underpaid. Reflecting the results of the previous question, it was found that the greater the respondent's education ($P = 0.05$) and the higher his income ($P = 0.02$), the more likely he was to believe that the teachers were underpaid.

Table 6

	Per Cent
$1,799 and less	3.8
1,800-1,999	4.5
2,000-2,249	13.9
2,250-2,399	5.0
2,400	6.7
2,401-2,749	19.6
2,750-2,999	3.4
3,000-3,249	16.3
3,250-3,499	0.6
3,500 and up	9.7
No answer	16.5

The next question was: "What would you consider a good starting salary for a high-school teacher?" The replies, distributed on the same scale as the previous question, ranged as shown in Table 6. The single significant correlation paralleled one found on the previous questions: the higher the respondent's income, the higher his estimate of the proper starting salary for teachers.

The final question in this group read, "What would you consider a good top salary to be paid, say, after fifteen years' teaching?" The replies for

Table 7

	Per Cent
$3,499 and less	22.2
3,500-3,999	15.0
4,000	11.4
4,001-4,499	2.5
4,500-4,999	8.5
5,000-5,499	12.4
5,500 and up	6.6
No answer	21.4

this question quite naturally required a different scaling than did those for the preceding salary items. They were distributed as in Table 7. Once again, occupation, education, and income proved to be significant. The higher the interviewee was placed on the occupational continuum, the greater his education, and the higher his income ($P = 0.05$), the higher was the top salary which he believed suitable for teachers.

B. GENERAL STATEMENTS

In order to elicit the respondents' general opinions concerning teachers and their status, an open question was included: "How do you account for the present difficulties of primary and high-school teachers in the United States?"

The replies were first grouped by the predominant reason (Table 8). Whether or not the interviewees reached in this survey had an accurate appreciation of the historical background of teaching in this country, they evidenced a fair knowledge of prevailing conditions. The following comments are necessarily selected, and hence unrepresentative from a statistical standpoint; they demonstrate, however, the more perceptive range of opinion tapped by the survey.

TABLE 8

	Per Cent
Teachers are underpaid	51.2
General economic conditions in the country are accountable	5.5
The public is uninterested in education	2.5
Teachers lack prestige	2.3
Administrative policies in education are faulty	1.9
There are too few teachers	1.4
No answer	35.2

"About 350,000 teachers," said one interviewee, "have left the profession since 1941. Financially they are at a low level, and they have low prestige. The competition with other more lucrative positions and those with more prestige pull people away from teaching. There is a poor attitude in the community toward a teacher. Many girls take it up as a stop-gap until they get married." Said another: "The teachers are underpaid; possibly it is because they are not regarded with as much consideration as they should be in the community, whether personally or politically." A third said: "The community looks upon teachers as outsiders and won't give them a chance to become active in the community. It regards them as a class apart." Others stated: "Youngsters have lost respect for their teachers within the last few decades, since much of the discipline has been taken out of the schools and out of the hands of the teachers"; "The world is upside down"; "Heartaches go along with teaching; the teachers can get better jobs." One respondent was particularly explicit: "I attribute their difficulties to three things: first, the unwillingness of the average person to pay for the cost of good education; second, the lack of public recognition of the importance of education; and, third, control of education by political groups." Another remarked: "Teachers are underpaid because they haven't given enough effort to fighting for themselves, for adequate compensation." Others said: "Teachers are afraid to take part in controversies; they are at the mercy of school boards"; "This is a time of lowered morale —a lag between material and spiritual achievements."

Summaries by Socio-Economic Factors

It remains to reassemble the material according to the characteristics of the people holding the opinions. This section of the report summarizes opinions of teacher status in eight categories. Statistically significant correlations were found in all categories.

A. SEX

Males interviewed in this study differed from females, in that they were more likely

1. To favor the employment of teachers from minority groups
2. To favor the hiring of men teachers
3. To feel that teachers are justified in unionizing and in striking
4. To be among those who felt that the teachers were comparable to persons in the occupational category of laborer, with reference to the pay they should receive and their importance to the community

The males differed from the females, in that they were less likely

5. To have teachers as friends
6. To feel that teachers should be free to be active politically
7. To compare teachers to professionals as to their importance to the community

B. AGE GROUP

The older the respondents, the more likely they were

1. To feel that the standards of conduct for teachers should differ from those of other good citizens

2. To compare teachers to professionals in social level and the less likely they were

3. To feel that teachers are justified in unionizing and in striking

C. NATIVITY

The native-born differed from the foreign-born in that they were more likely

1. To have teachers as friends
2. To oppose the hiring of teachers from minority groups
3. To believe that teachers were comparable to proprietors in social level, salary, and importance to the community

The foreign-born were more likely

4. To believe that the standards of conduct for teachers should differ
5. To prefer men to women for teaching positions
6. To feel that teachers were comparable to professionals with reference to social level and salary

D. POSSESSION OF CHILDREN

Childless interviewees differed from those who had children, in that they were more likely

1. To feel that teachers are not justified in unionizing
2. To be among the few who felt that teachers were comparable to laborers in social level

E. RELIGION

Protestant interviewees differed from Catholic interviewees, in that they were more likely

1. To feel that teachers are not justified in unionizing
2. To believe that teachers should be comparable to professionals with reference to salaries

Catholics differed from Jews, in that they were more likely

3. To prefer men as teachers

Jews differed from Protestants, in that they were more likely

4. To believe that teachers should be comparable to proprietors with reference to salaries

Jews differed from Protestants and Catholics, in that they were more likely

5. To believe that teachers from minority groups should be employed
6. To believe that teachers were underpaid

F. OCCUPATION

It was discovered that the higher the place of the respondent in the occupational hierarchy,

1. The higher was likely to be his estimate of the teachers' current salaries and of suitable top salaries to be paid after fifteen years of experience
2. The more likely he was to believe that teachers' salaries should be comparable to those of both professionals and proprietors

Respondents in the two laboring groups differed from those in the professional and proprietor groups, in that they were more likely

3. To feel that teachers are justified in unionizing and in striking
4. To feel that teachers were comparable to laborers and service workers with reference to their importance to the community

G. EDUCATION

The greater the education of the interviewee, the more likely he was

1. To have friends who were teachers
2. To believe that teachers' salaries should be comparable to those of both professionals and proprietors
3. To believe that the teachers were underpaid

The greater the education of the interviewee,

4. The higher was his estimate of the teachers' current salaries, and also of suitable top salaries

and the less likely he was to

5. Feel that teachers are justified in unionizing

H. INCOME LEVEL

The higher the income level of the interviewee,

1. The higher was likely to be his estimate of the current salaries, of a good starting salary, and also of a suitable top salary for the teachers
2. The more likely he was to feel that the teachers were underpaid

The upper-income group, as contrasted to the two lower-income groups, was

3. More likely to feel that teachers are not justified in striking

TEACHING SALARIES THEN AND NOW *

I—Analysis for the 50 Year Period 1904-1953 as a Whole

Conclusion: Wages and salaries rose in all parts of the American economy during the 50 year period 1904-1953. Relatively, salaries in the field of education rose less than salaries in other occupations and industries, with the result that the economic position of people in education has deteriorated over the years, after allowing for income and social security taxes and changes in the cost of living.

1. During the 50 years 1904-1953 wages and salaries increased in all industries and occupations. "Real" wages rose too except at the top of the income scale in the field of education. The figures are compared in Table A, p. 111.

II—Analysis of Trends in Industry and Education

(a) 1904-1933   (b) 1933-1947   (c) 1947-1953

Conclusion:

(a) Between 1904 and 1933, the "real" purchasing power of the salaries and wages of most people in industry and education rose substantially, but the rise in the field of education was less, generally, than in industry and the rate of increase was slower.

(b) Between 1933 and 1947, the real purchasing power of a great many people in industry rose further—in some cases a great deal further—but in the field of education, the real purchasing power of people in all types of teaching declined.

(c) Between 1947 and 1953, real purchasing power rose throughout the economy. Many people in the field of education obtained increases comparable to those provided in industry, and teachers in small cities and towns obtained even greater increases. On the other hand, the purchasing power of the salaries of junior members of university faculties increased less, proportionately, than wages in industry.

* Beardsley Ruml and Sidney G. Tickton, *Teaching Salaries Then and Now, Bulletin No. 1* (New York, The Fund for the Advancement of Education, 1955), pp. 31-40.

TABLE A

COMPARISON OF WAGES AND SALARIES IN VARIOUS OCCUPATIONS AND INDUSTRIES 1904 AND 1953

Position	1953 Actual Salary (Average)	1904 Actual Salary (Average)	1953 Salary Deflated to "Real" Purchasing Power	50 Year Change in "Real" Purchasing Power
Education Position				
Presidents, large universities	$16,500	$4,300	$4,196	− 2%
Professors, large universities	7,000	2,000	1,956	− 2%
Associate professors, large universities	5,600	1,500	1,596	+ 6%
Assistant professors, large universities	4,600	1,300	1,338	+ 3%
Instructors, large universities	3,700	800	1,106	+ 38%
Principals, big city high schools	9,156	3,552	2,497	− 30%
Principals, small city high schools	6,523	1,931	1,833	− 5%
Teachers, big city high schools	5,526	1,597	1,577	− 1%
Teachers, small city high schools	4,292	918	1,259	+ 37%
Teachers, big city elementary schools	4,817	873	1,394	+ 60%
Teachers, small city elementary schools	3,682	547	1,102	+101%
Teachers, small town elementary schools	3,190	446	977	+119%
Railroad Position				
Executive officials, large railroads	11,592	2,803	3,109	+ 11%
Railroad engineers	7,352	1,313	2,063	+ 57%
Railroad conductors	6,676	1,116	1,873	+ 68%
Railroad firemen	6,180	736	1,745	+137%
Railroad switchtenders	4,697	583	1,363	+134%
Railroad clerks	3,984	615	1,180	+ 92%
Industry Position				
Workers in automobile manufacturing	4,947	594	1,428	+140%
Workers in bituminous coal mining	4,198	470	1,235	+163%
Workers in electrical machinery manufacturing	4,133	527	1,218	+131%
Workers in stone, clay and glass manufacturing	3,956	527	1,172	+122%
Workers in furniture manufacturing	3,570	452	1,073	+137%
Telephone operators	3,224	468	986	+111%
Workers in tobacco manufacturing	2,709	413	856	+107%

1. During the thirty years 1904-1933, wages and salaries rose throughout the American economy. "Real" wages rose too, the percentages of increase frequently running above 40% for industrial occupations. . . .

2. . . . Until after World War II, people in industry fared much better than those in the field of education. When the purchasing power of industrial wages in the economy went up, for example (1904-1933), the purchasing power of salaries in the field of education did not rise proportionately. And when the purchasing power of most wages in industry went up again (1933-1947), the purchasing power of salaries in the education field actually declined.

3. In the postwar period, the relative performance of salaries and wages for people in industry and education varied. People in some categories of teaching (for example, junior members of university faculties) obtained smaller increases in purchasing power than people in industry. On the other hand, elementary school teachers in small cities and towns obtained greater increases than people in industry. But this was not enough to make up for the lag in the previous four decades.

4. The failure of purchasing power of university faculty and other teaching salaries to keep pace with industrial salaries has been the subject of considerable comment during the past fifty years and there has been a wide variety of explanations. One suggestion has been that low salaries in the teaching field have been due, in part at least, to an oversupply of teachers and potential teachers. Carrying this point of view to its logical conclusion, proportionate increases in teaching salaries and purchasing power will occur only when a shortage of teachers develops (except, of course, for depression periods). These increases could happen locally in particular geographic areas (as well as for the whole country) and may explain, in part, the better showing of teachers' salaries in small cities and towns since the end of the war. During the war, teachers moved out of these cities and towns as opportunities expanded elsewhere, or shifted to occupations in other fields of activity. This reduced the supply of teachers in many areas to a level below that needed to handle the growing student load. The situation has had to be corrected during the past few years by the payment of larger salaries, net, after changes in purchasing power.

His Education and Certification

THEY WROTE ME A CERTIFICATE *

The next thing for me to do, was to be examined by the Board of School Visitors. . . .

The parson was to commence. How many sounds has B? was the first question. Though B is called a mute, and is one of the more difficult letters for the embarrassed or diffident person to enunciate, and though I did not expect they would begin thus, yet I soon recollected what I had so often repeated at school; and faintly articulated; B has but one sound as in *bite*.

How many sounds has C? The reply to this question was more ready than the former; for having once broken the ice, and that successfully, all now seemed to go on very smoothly. I could have repeated the "Introduction to the Spelling Book," as it is called, in which they were then examining me, from beginning to end without a failure. There was, indeed, a little trouble, when questions were asked promiscuously, but such an event did not often occur.

I was also required to spell. In this exercise, as I have already observed, I was pretty correct. I could not only spell all the common words of the spelling book, but also recollect them if they were separated from their companions. And although I now dislike this method of teaching to spell, believing it to involve a great waste of valuable time, yet it certainly made *me* a speller. I do not remember the time when there were more than half a dozen words in common use which I spelt wrong, even in writing.

But I was required to repeat the rules of common arithmetic, and to read and write. The rules of arithmetic, I had at my tongue's end, and I believe I understood their import. . . .

* William A. Alcott, *Confessions of a Schoolmaster* (Andover, Newman and Saxton, 1839), pp. 21, 23-7, 28.

As to writing, my hand was too unsteady, just at that time, to permit me to write well. As the committee, however, perceived my embarrassment, and as some of them were already acquainted with the character of my handwriting, I found no difficulty, I learned afterward that they made the requirement as a mere formality.

My deficiency in regard to reading was most obvious. I read too loud, and too fast; as well as in a tone of voice altogether different from that of common conversation. This habit I had acquired, during my first years at school, in reading in books whose language I did not understand; and to the meaning of which none of my teachers ever furnished me with a clue. Besides I did not articulate well.

This branch, however,—strange as it may appear to some—the Committee did not deem an important part of their examination. They had embraced the opinion,—very common in the world, as I have since found—that a teacher who cannot read well himself can teach others to read well. They seemed wholly to overlook the force of example in this matter, and the fact that children learn to read chiefly by imitating others. I do not say that they learn *to pronounce the words when they see them in a book,* in this way; but I do not regard that as worthy of the name of reading.

It has already been observed that Grammar and Geography were not taught in the school which I had engaged to teach. And as they were not taught, the committee were not accustomed to examine the candidate in regard to them. They had adopted the fashionable idea that it is unnecessary for a teacher to understand any other branches except those which he teaches. . . .

There was one more reason, I confess, why they adopted such a principle of examination. Not one in three—probably not one in six—of the individuals who presented themselves for examination as candidates for the teaching of our schools in those days, knew anything of grammar or geography; and some were mere blockheads in arithmetic. Had those branches been required therefore, the districts would have been deprived of their teachers. . . .

Shall the teacher retire, said Dr. Physic, while we consult together? That is quite unnecessary, said the parson. Captain, said he, you are the youngest, what do you say to giving the candidate a certificate? Aye, or Nay? Aye; said the Captain. Aye, said the Doctor, in his turn. And I say aye, too, said the parson. So saying, they wrote me a certificate. . . .

Was this the whole of the examination? perhaps some inquisitive reader may ask. I have related the substance of it; not always the very words. Nor have I related all the minutiae of the conversation. What I have told is the truth; only I have not been particular to give the whole truth in every instance.

"Was nothing then said to you about the management and discipline of a school?" Not a word, that I remember. All the examinations I had ever been acquainted with at that time, seemed to be based on the opinion that if a person understood a science or thing himself, he could teach it well to others. As to governing a school, I believe I have already mentioned that the erroneous opinion prevailed, that this was a "gift"; or rather as some seemed to regard it, a matter of mere haphazard.

THE FIRST STATE NORMAL SCHOOL *

The State Normal Schools, of which there are three in Massachusetts, are designed for those *only* who purpose to teach, and especially for those who purpose to teach in the common schools. The school at West Newton is for females.

It was opened at Lexington, July 3rd, 1839, with the examination of three pupils, who were all that presented themselves as candidates. At the close of the first term it numbered twelve pupils.

The school continued at Lexington five years. In May, 1844, having by far outgrown its accommodations, it was removed to West Newton, where the liberality of the Hon. Josiah Quincy, Jr., of Boston, had provided for it by the purchase of a building, formerly used as a private academy, which he generously gave to the Institution.

The whole number of graduates is 423, nearly all of whom have engaged in teaching, the most of them in the public schools of this state.

CONDITIONS OF ENTRANCE.—1. The applicant must be at least sixteen years old.

2. She must make an *explicit declaration of her intention to become a Teacher*.

3. She must produce a certificate of good PHYSICAL, INTELLECTUAL, and MORAL CHARACTER, from some responsible person. It is exceedingly desirable that this condition be strictly complied with on the part of those who present candidates.

4. She must pass a satisfactory examination in the common branches, viz.:—Reading, spelling and defining, arithmetic, grammar, writing and geography.

5. She must give a pledge to remain in the school at least *four consecutive terms,* and to observe faithfully all the regulations of the Institution, as long as she is a member of it.

6. All candidates for admission must be at the school-room on the morning of the day which precedes that on which the term commences, at half-past eight o'clock. None will be admitted after the *day of examination*.

* Henry Barnard, *Normal Schools and Other Institutions, Agencies, and Means Designed for the Professional Education of Teachers* (Hartford, Case, Tiffany & Co., 1851), I. pp. 59-61.

7. Each pupil, at entrance, must be supplied with slate and pencil, blank book, Bible, Worcester's Comprehensive Dictionary, and Morse's Geography. Many of the other books used will be furnished from the library of the school.

STUDIES.—The course of study in each of the State Normal Schools begins with a review of the studies pursued in the Common Schools, viz.:— Reading, writing, orthography, English grammar, mental and written arithmetic, geography and physiology.

The attention of pupils is directed, 1st, to a thorough review of elementary studies; 2d, to those branches of knowledge which may be considered as an expansion of the above-named elementary studies, or collateral to them; to the art of teaching and its modes.

The advanced studies are equally proportioned, according to the following distribution, into three departments, viz.:—1. The mathematical, including algebra through quadratic equations; geometry, to an amount equal to three books in Euclid; bookkeeping and surveying. 2. The philosophical, including natural philosophy, astronomy, moral and intellectual philosophy, natural history, particularly that of our own country, and so much of chemistry as relates to the atmosphere, the waters, and the growth of plants and animals. 3. The literary, including the critical study of the English language, both in its structure and history, with an outline of the history of English literature; the history of the United States, with such a survey of general history as may be a suitable preparative for it; and historical geography, ancient and mediaeval, so far as is necessary to understand general history, from the earliest time to the period of the French Revolution.

"The art of teaching and its modes," includes instruction as to philosophy of teaching and discipline, as drawn from the nature and condition of the juvenile mind; the history of the progress of the art, and the application of it to our system of education; and as much exercise in teaching under constant supervision, toward the close of the course, as the circumstances and interests of the Model schools may allow.

Members of the higher classes give teaching exercises before the whole school, several each week. Members of the senior class spend three weeks, each, in the public grammar school of District No. 7, which is connected with the institution as its Model department.

Pupils who have had considerable experience in teaching, and are otherwise qualified for it, will be allowed to enter existing classes.

Pupils who may desire to study the Latin and French languages, and to prepare themselves to instruct in those branches usually taught in High Schools, can have an opportunity to do so, by giving a pledge to remain in the school for a term of three years, provided the number is sufficient to warrant the forming of a class.

EXAMINATIONS.—The school is visited and examined by the Visiting Committee of the Board of Education, at the close of each term; and a public examination is held whenever a class graduates. The school is open to visitors at all times.

LIBRARY AND APPARATUS.—A well-selected library, consisting mostly of works on education, belongs to the school, and also a well-assorted Apparatus, for the illustration of principles in natural philosophy, chemistry, mathematics, &c. &c.

TUITION.—For those who purpose to teach in the public schools of the state, tuition is free; for such as intend to teach elsewhere, it is $10 per term, payable at entrance, and such can not be admitted to the exclusion of those first mentioned. At the beginning of each term, each pupil pays to the Principal $1.50, to meet incidental expenses.

BOARD.—Board may be had in good families at from $2 to $2.50 per week, including washing and fuel. Some of the pupils take rooms and board themselves at a lower rate. The whole annual expense is about $100.

TALKS TO TEACHERS ON PSYCHOLOGY *

In the general activity and uprising of ideal interests which every one with an eye for fact can discern all about us in American life, there is perhaps no more promising feature than the fermentation which for a dozen years or more has been going on among the teachers. In whatever sphere of education their functions may lie, there is to be seen among them a really inspiring amount of searching of the heart about the highest concerns of their profession. The renovation of nations begins always at the top, among the reflective members of the State, and spreads slowly outward and downward. The teachers of this country, one may say, have its future in their hands. The earnestness which they at present show in striving to enlighten and strengthen themselves is an index of the nation's probabilities of advance in all ideal directions. The outward organization of education which we have in our United States is perhaps, on the whole, the best organization that exists in any country. The State school systems give a diversity and flexibility, an opportunity for experiment and keenness of competition, nowhere else to be found on such an important scale. The independence of so many of the colleges and universities; the give and take of students and instructors between them all; their emulation, and their happy organic relations to the lower schools; the traditions of instruction in them, evolved from the older American recitation-method (and so avoiding on the one hand the pure lecture-system prevalent in Germany and

* William James, *Talks to Teachers on Psychology* (New York, Henry Holt & Co., 1902), pp. 3-14.

Scotland, which considers too little the individual student, and yet not involving the sacrifice of the instructor to the individual student, which the English tutorial system would seem too often to entail,)—all these things (to say nothing of that coeducation of the sexes in whose benefits so many of us heartily believe), all these things, I say, are most happy features of our scholastic life, and from them the most sanguine auguries may be drawn.

Having so favorable an organization, all we need is to impregnate it with geniuses, to get superior men and women working more and more abundantly in it and for it and at it, and in a generation or two America may well lead the education of the world. I must say that I look forward with no little confidence to the day when that shall be an accomplished fact.

No one has profited more by the fermentation of which I speak, in pedagogical circles, than we psychologists. The desire of the schoolteachers for a completer professional training, and their aspiration toward the 'professional' spirit in their work, have led them more and more to turn to us for light on fundamental principles. And in these few hours which we are to spend together you look to me, I am sure, for information concerning the mind's operations, which may enable you to labor more easily and effectively in the several schoolrooms over which you preside.

Far be it from me to disclaim for psychology all title to such hopes. Psychology ought certainly to give the teacher radical help. And yet I confess that, acquainted as I am with the height of some of your expectations, I feel a little anxious lest, at the end of these simple talks of mine, not a few of you may experience some disappointment at the net results. In other words, I am not sure that you may not be indulging fancies that are just a shade exaggerated. That would not be altogether astonishing, for we have been having something like a 'boom' in psychology in this country. Laboratories and professorships have been founded, and reviews established. The air has been full of rumors. The editors of educational journals and the arrangers of conventions have had to show themselves enterprising and on a level with the novelties of the day. Some of the professors have not been unwilling to co-operate, and I am not sure even that the publishers have been entirely inert. 'The new psychology' has thus become a term to conjure up portentous ideas withal; and you teachers, docile and receptive and aspiring as many of you are, have been plunged in an atmosphere of vague talk about our science, which to a great extent has been more mystifying than enlightening. Altogether it does seem as if there were a certain fatality of mystification laid upon the teachers of our day. The matter of their profession, compact enough in itself, has to be frothed up for them in journals and institutes, till its outlines often threaten to be lost in a kind of vast uncertainty. Where the disciples are not independent and critical-minded enough (and I think that, if you teachers in the earlier grades have any defect—the slightest touch of a defect in the world—it is that you are a mite too docile), we are pretty sure to miss accuracy and balance and measure in those who get a license to lay down the law to them from above.

As regards this subject of psychology, now, I wish at the very threshold to do what I can to dispel the mystification. So I say at once that in my humble opinion there *is* no 'new psychology' worthy of the name. There is nothing but the old psychology which began in Locke's time, plus a little physiology of the brain and senses and theory of evolution, and a few refinements of introspective detail, for the most part without adaptation to the teacher's use. It is only the fundamental conceptions of psychology which are of real value to the teacher; and they, apart from the aforesaid theory of evolution, are very far from being new. I trust that you will see better what I mean by this at the end of all these talks.

I say moreover that you make a great, a very great mistake, if you think that psychology, being the science of the mind's laws, is something from which you can deduce definite programmes and schemes and methods of instruction for immediate schoolroom use. Psychology is a science, and teaching is an art; and sciences never generate arts directly out of themselves. An intermediary inventive mind must make the application, by using its originality.

The science of logic never made a man reason rightly, and the science of ethics (if there be such a thing) never made a man behave rightly. The most such sciences can do is to help us to catch ourselves up and check ourselves, if we start to reason or to behave wrongly; and to criticise ourselves more articulately after we have made mistakes. A science only lays down lines within which the rules of the art must fall, laws which the follower of the art must not transgress; but what particular things he shall positively do within those lines is left exclusively to his own genius. One genius will do his work well and succeed in one way, while another succeeds as well quite differently; yet neither will transgress the lines.

The art of teaching grew up in the schoolroom, out of inventiveness and sympathetic concrete observation. Even where (as in the case of Herbart) the advancer of the art was also a psychologist, the pedagogics and the psychology ran side by side, and the former was not derived in any sense from the latter. The two were congruent, but neither was subordinate. And so everywhere the teaching must *agree* with the psychology, but need not necessarily be the only kind of teaching that would so agree; for many diverse methods of teaching may equally well agree with psychological laws.

To know psychology, therefore, is absolutely no guarantee that we shall be good teachers. To advance to that result, we must have an additional endowment altogether, a happy tact and ingenuity to tell us what definite things to say and do when the pupil is before us. That ingenuity in meeting and pursuing the pupil, that tact for the concrete situation, though they are the alpha and omega of the teacher's art, are things to which psychology cannot help us in the least.

The science of psychology, and whatever science of general pedagogics may be based on it, are in fact much like the science of war. Nothing is simpler or more definite than the principles of either. In war, all you have to do is to work your enemy into a position from which the natural obstacles prevent him from escaping if he tries to; then to fall on him in numbers superior to his own, at a moment when you have led him to think you far away; and so, with a minimum of exposure of your own troops, to hack his force to pieces, and take the remainder prisoners. Just so, in teaching, you must simply work your pupil into such a state of interest in what you are going to teach him that every other object of attention is banished from his mind; then reveal it to him so impressively that he will remember the occasion to his dying day; and finally fill him with devouring curiosity to know what the next steps in connection with the subject are. The principles being so plain, there would be nothing but victories for the masters of the science, either on the battlefield or in the schoolroom, if they did not both have to make their application to an incalculable quantity in the shape of the mind of their opponent. The mind of your own enemy, the pupil, is working away from you as keenly and eagerly as is the mind of the commander on the other side from the scientific general. Just what the respective enemies want and think, and what they know and do not know, are as hard things for the teacher as for the general to find out. Divination and perception, not psychological pedagogics or theoretic strategy, are the only helpers here.

But, if the use of psychological principles thus be negative rather than positive, it does not follow that it may not be a great use, all the same. It certainly narrows the path for experiments and trials. We know in advance, if we are psychologists, that certain methods will be wrong, so our psychology saves us from mistakes. It makes us, moreover, more clear as to what we are about. We gain confidence in respect to any method which we are using as soon as we believe that it has theory as well as practice at its back. Most of all, it fructifies our independence, and it reanimates our interest, to see our subject at two different angles—to get a stereoscopic view, so to speak, of the youthful organism who is our enemy, and, while handling him with all our concrete tact and divination, to be able, at the same time, to represent to ourselves the curious inner elements of his mental machine. Such a complete knowledge as this of the pupil, at once intuitive and analytic, is surely the knowledge at which every teacher ought to aim.

Fortunately for you teachers, the elements of the mental machine can be clearly apprehended, and their workings easily grasped. And, as the most general elements and workings are just those parts of psychology which the teacher finds most directly useful, it follows that the amount of this science which is necessary to all teachers need not be very great. Those who find themselves loving the subject may go as far as they please, and become possibly none the worse teachers for the fact, even though in some of them one might apprehend a little loss of balance from the tendency observable in all of us to overemphasize certain special parts of a subject when we are studying it intensely and abstractly. But for the great majority of you a general view is enough, provided it be a true one; and such a general view, one may say, might almost be written on the palm of one's hand.

Least of all need you, merely *as teachers,* deem it part of your duty to become contributors to psychological science or to make psychological observations in a methodical or responsible manner. I fear that some of the enthusiasts for child-study have thrown a certain burden on you in this way. By all means let child-study go on—it is refreshing all our sense of the child's life. There are teachers who take a spontaneous delight in filling syllabuses, inscribing observations, compiling statistics, and computing the per cent. Child-study will certainly enrich their lives. And, if its results, as treated statistically, would seem on the whole to have but trifling value, yet the anecdotes and observations of which it in part consists do certainly acquaint us more intimately with our pupils. Our eyes and ears grow quickened to discern in the child before us processes similar to those we have read of as noted in the children—processes of which we might otherwise have remained inobservant. But, for Heaven's sake, let the rank and file of teachers be passive readers if they so prefer, and feel free not to contribute to the accumulation. Let not the prosecution of it be preached as an imperative duty or imposed by regulation on those to whom it proves an exterminating bore, or who in any way whatever miss in themselves the appropriate vocation for it. I cannot too strongly agree with my colleague, Professor Munsterberg, when he says that the teacher's attitude toward the child, being concrete and ethical, is positively opposed to the psychological observer's, which is abstract and analytic. Although some of us may conjoin the attitudes successfully, in most of us they must conflict.

The worst thing that can happen to a good teacher is to get a bad conscience about her profession because she feels herself hopeless as a psychologist. Our teachers are overworked already. Everyone who adds a jot or tittle of unnecessary weight to their burden is a foe of education. A bad conscience increases the weight of every other burden; yet I know that child-study, and other pieces of psychology as well, have been productive of bad conscience in many a really innocent pedagogic breast. I should indeed be glad if this passing word from me might tend to dispel such a

The Vocation of Teaching

bad conscience, if any of you have it; for it is certainly one of those fruits of more or less systematic mystification of which I have already complained. The best teacher may be the poorest contributor of child-study material, and the best contributor may be the poorest teacher. No fact is more palpable than this.

So much for what seems the most reasonable general attitude of the teacher toward the subject which is to occupy our attention.

MINIMUM REQUIREMENTS FOR LOWEST REGULAR TEACHING CERTIFICATES *

	Elementary School			High School		
State	Degree or Number of Semester Hours Required	Professional Education Required, Semester Hours (Total)	Directed Teaching Required, Semester Hours (Included In Column 3)	Degree or Number of Semester Hours Required	Professional Education Required, Semester Hours (Total)	Directed Teaching Required, Semester Hours (Included In Column 6)
1	2	3	4	5	6	7
Alabama	B	30	3	B	24	3
Alaska	90	16	4	B	16	4
Arizona	B	18	6	5	18	6
Arkansas	60	12	3	60	12	3
California	B	24	8	5	22	6
Colorado	60 [1]	20	4	B	20	4
Connecticut	B	30	6	B	18	6
Delaware	B	30	6	B	18	6
District	B	40	6	5	24	6
Florida	B	20	6	B	20	6
Georgia	B	18	6	B	18	6
Hawaii	B	18	AC	B	18	AC
Idaho	B	20	6	B	20	5 [2]
Illinois	B	16	5	B	16	5
Indiana	B	35	6	B	18	5
Iowa	60	20	5	B	20	5
Kansas	60	6	0	B	18	3
Kentucky	B [3]	28	8	B	18	8
Louisiana	B	24	4	B	18	4
Maine	96	AC	AC	B	12	0
Maryland	B	32 [4]	6 [5]	B	16 [6]	3 [5]
Massachusetts	B [7]	18	2	B	12	2
Michigan	B [8]	20	5	B	20	5
Minnesota	B [9]	30	6	B	18	4
Mississippi	B	24	6	B	18	6
Missouri	64	5	0	B	18	5
Montana	64 [10]	30	10	B	16	3
Nebraska	12 [11]	6	0	B	18	3
Nevada	B [12]	18	4	B	18	4
New Hampshire	B	AC	6	B	21	6
New Jersey	B	30	6	B	18	6
New Mexico	B	24	6	B	24	6
New York	B	36	12	5 [13]	18	2
North Carolina	B	18	3	B	18	3
North Dakota	32 [14]	16	3	B	16	3
Ohio	B	28	6	B	17	6
Oklahoma	B [15]	12	0	B	12	0
Oregon	B	20	4	B [16]	24	6
Pennsylvania	B	30	6	B	12	6
Puerto Rico	67	30	6	B	21	5

* W. Earl Armstrong and T. M. Stinnett, *A Manual on Certification Requirements for School Personnel in the United States* (Washington, D. C., National Educational Association, 1957), pp. 19, 20.

His Education and Certification

| | Elementary School ||| High School |||
State	Degree or Number of Semester Hours Required	Professional Education Required, Semester Hours (Total)	Directed Teaching Required, Semester Hours (Included In Column 3)	Degree or Number of Semester Hours Required	Professional Education Required, Semester Hours (Total)	Directed Teaching Required, Semester Hours (Included In Column 6)
1	2	3	4	5	6	7
Rhode Island	B	30	6	B	24	6
South Carolina	B	21	6	B	18	6
South Dakota	30 [17]	5	2	B	20	5
Tennessee	B	24	4	B	24	4
Texas	B	24	6	B	24	6
Utah	B	30	8	B	22	8
Vermont	B	18	6	B	18	6
Virginia	B	24	100 CH	B	18	100 CH
Washington	B [18]	27	10	B [18]	27	10
West Virginia	64	11	3	B	20	5
Wisconsin	64	26	8	B	18	5
Wyoming	60	NS	NS	B	20	C

Legend: B means bachelor's degree of specified preparation; 5 means bachelor's degree plus a fifth year of appropriate preparation, not necessarily completion of master's degree; AC means approved curriculum; C means a course; NS means not specified; CH means clock hours.

[1] Colorado. Minimum requirement for out-of-state applicants is 90 semester hours.
[2] Idaho. Will increase to 6 semester hours September 1, 1958.
[3] Kentucky. Kentucky was reported in the 1953 and 1955 editions of the Manual as enforcing the degree requirement, effective September 1, 1953. When this date was reached, it was decided to continue issuing the temporary elementary certificate (based upon 64 semester hours) until 1956; and in 1956, the date for dropping this certificate was postponed to 1958. Thus, technically Kentucky is still at the 60-hour level and will be until September 1, 1958. The master's degree is required for the standard certificate. Beginning in 1953, the degree required for professional certificate; 64 semester hours for temporary elementary certificate.
[4] Maryland. Reduction to 26 semester hours under consideration.
[5] Maryland. Change to 8 semester hours under consideration.
[6] Maryland. Increase to 18 semester hours under consideration.
[7] Massachusetts. Completion of bachelor's degree or graduation from an approved four-year normal school.
[8] Michigan. Will continue until June 30, 1960, to certificate graduates of 12 county normals (one college year) for teaching in primary school districts not employing more than two teachers. These certificates are valid only in county of issuance for a term of one year. About 150 certificates are issued annually.
Michigan will continue until June 30, 1960, to issue the State Limited Certificate (based upon 60 semester hours), valid only for teaching at the elementary level in non-high school districts for a term of one year. About 500 of these certificates are issued annually.
Both of the certificates mentioned above are considered as sub-standard.
[9] Minnesota. Minnesota has three high school normal training departments which offer a one-year course, following high school graduation, qualifying students to teach in ungraded elementary schools. Also a provisional elementary certificate is issued on 90 semester hours; both are considered as temporary, substandard certificates.
[10] Montana. Graduation from an approved two-year program. Bill is in Legislature to make a degree basis for certification.
[11] Nebraska. Teachers for elementary grades in rural schools are required to be graduates of normal training high school courses and to complete 12 semester hours of college credit; or if non-normal training graduates 30 semester hours including 8 in education, of which 2 are in directed teaching, and recommendation of teacher training institution. For town schools minimum of 60 semester hours, 15 in education, 3 in directed teaching, and recommendation of teacher training institution.
[12] Nevada. Bachelor's degree requirement will become effective September 1, 1957.
[13] New York. Effective September 1, 1958, a provisional high school certificate will be issued for the academic fields, based upon completion of the bachelor's degree, with 18 semester hours in education, including student teaching; valid for five years; non-renewable; holder must complete requirements for permanent certificate. Effective same date, permanent certificate will require 24 semester hours in education, including 6 in student teaching.
[14] North Dakota. Requirement for teaching in rural schools; for teaching in graded schools, 64 semester hours is minimum requirement.
[15] Oklahoma. Minimum requirement, fixed by law, was 124 semester hours; but degree is now required.
[16] Oregon. Provisional certificate only; five years required for standard certification. Fifth year must be completed within five years after provisional certificate is issued.
[17] South Dakota. Requirement for teaching in rural schools. For town schools, minimum requirement is 60 semester hours.
[18] Washington. Provisional certificate only; five years required for standard certification. Fifth year must be completed within five years after provisional certificate is issued.

Part 2

▼

Schooling for All

Contents of Part 2

Schooling for All

BEGINNINGS IN THE EAST

BEGINNINGS IN THE SOUTH

AMERICAN STATESMEN ON EDUCATION

EARLY LEGISLATION AFTER THE UNION

THE DEBATE ON PUBLIC EDUCATION

THE EDUCATION OF NEGROES IN BOSTON BEFORE THE CIVIL WAR

TOWARD UNIVERSAL SCHOOLING

Schooling for All

The United States has pioneered in the development of free, universal compulsory schooling, but the ideal of universal education is by no means local to the United States. On the contrary, it has come to be a world-wide aspiration, officially recognized by the United Nations' *Declaration of Human Rights,* by the establishment of UNESCO, and by UNESCO activities. The democracies of the world and the totalitarian states of the world are as eager in their rivalry to have educated populations as in their rivalry for armaments.

Compulsory education in modern times did not begin in the United States. It began in Prussia. The United States has no unchallenged claim to the most effective system of universal education. There are countries (the Scandinavian countries) in which there are fewer illiterates (smaller percentages of illiterates) than in the United States. If this is a measure, it might mean that Scandinavian schooling is either more universal or more effective or both. Nevertheless, nowhere in the world in any time or place has there been such a sustained effort as in the United States to make so much schooling available to so many people. The people of this country, through the governments they have controlled (local, state, and national governments) and through the charities to which they have contributed, have from the beginning of our history recognized an obligation to provide education for their children, and the obligation has been given high priority. They have achieved a system of public and private schools that has become for all its faults a model for the world.

It is no great distortion of the facts, then, to speak of universal free education in the United States. The American school system has come so close to achieving this goal that it is taken for granted. A newer aspiration is to provide more years of appropriate schooling for all people. It is well to remember, however, that universal education is not a fact the world over. There are probably more people in the world who have never been to school than people who have, and there are still societies in which there are no schools at all. It is well to remember also that even in the United States there are exceptions to the rule of universal education. In the United States, 11 per cent of the adult population over twenty-five are classified as "functionally illiterate" because they have completed less than five years of school. There are still so many functionally illiterate young men that during World War II the armed forces of the United States found it advisable to establish special classes for men whose reading skills were below the fourth grade level, which is the minimum requirement for military service in a print-and-paper culture. Thousands of young men learned to read in order to exercise the citizen's privilege and obligation of serving in the army. This is the adult population and represents lack of school opportunities in the recent past, but there are still so many exceptions to the rule of universal education that Herold Hunt, in an essay included in this volume, could ask in 1956 whether we mean it when we speak of "education for all."

On the whole, the people of the United States do mean it, as their action in building our system of public and private schools clearly shows. In this country, the question "Who should go to school?" has been answered by the emphatic affirmation that everyone should go to school; and almost everyone does. There is more general agreement on this question than on most important matters of public policy, but there are related questions on which educational policy remains to be defined or redefined.

THE DEVELOPMENT OF FREE PUBLIC SCHOOLS

The public and private schools of the United States reflect the aspirations of the American people toward religious faith and moral virtue, toward an able and responsible citizenry, toward equality of opportunity, toward national solidarity and economic security.

> After God had carried us safe to New England, and we had built our houses, provided necessaries for our livelihood, reared convenient places for God's worship, and settled the civil government, one of the next things we longed for and looked after was to advance learning and perpetuate it to posterity, dreading to leave an illiterate ministry to the churches when our present ministers shall lie in the dust.

So begins the account of the founding of Harvard College in the famous *First Fruits of New England,* written in 1642. The religious motive was very strong in the beginnings of education in the American colonies, not only in the founding of the colleges. The first education law of Massachusetts, also in 1642, directs that children be taught "especially to read and understand the principles of religion and the capital laws of this country."

This introduces the second motive, citizenship and informed political leadership, which grew in importance with growing democracy and which looms very large indeed in Jefferson's plan for education in Virginia almost a century and a half later. The third motive, the desire for economic competence, was also very important in this first law, which required that children be taught "employments profitable to the Commonwealth"; but training for jobs was undertaken by means of apprenticeship or in the home-shop or farm. The law gave selectmen power, with approval of a magistrate, to take away and apprentice children whose parents were not "able and fit to employ them and bring them up." Public education, when it came into being in New England, continued to have as its goals the inculcation of religion, morality, and good citizenship and gave some attention to ability to earn a living. Schools in other colonies, founded by the several churches or by private charity, or conducted by schoolmasters and dames as private businesses, shared these aspirations.

There have been other motives as well. The American commitment to equality of opportunity for all and humanitarian concern for the welfare of children have been important. So has American nationalism, for the schools have had the task of helping to assimilate into American society the children of each of the immigrant waves that have built America.

Time and a changing world have shifted emphases, but these aspirations remain. American schools still seek to foster religious and moral values, good citizenship in the local community, the nation, and the family of nations, and to develop economic competence. And they are outstanding instruments of equality.

Although the people of the United States and their colonial forebears have placed a high priority on education in most times and places and have regarded schools as an important means of pursuing these aspirations, public schools have not always been taken for granted and they did not come into being without opposition. The decision that everyone should go to school and the assignment of responsibility for schools to the government were not immediate. On the contrary, the system of public education which seems commonplace today came into being through a series of revolutionary proposals and warm political debates. The use of public funds for elementary education had its opponents; use of public funds for high schools was fought up to the Supreme Court of the State of Michigan in the famous "Kalamazoo Case" as late as 1874. Proposals for compulsory schooling and related child labor legislation were opposed, successfully, well into the twentieth century. The existence of enormous school systems sponsored by several religious groups and the willingness of millions of people taxed for public schools to pay also for schools operated by their churches are evidence enough that not everyone regards the public schools as a final and satisfactory solution of educational problems. Public schools may seem commonplace, but there is nothing commonplace about the American aspiration to provide appropriate schooling for every child nor about the system of public schools by which the American people seek to satisfy this aspiration.

The first education law on this continent, the Massachusetts Bay Law of 1642, formulated the aspirations, but it did not provide for schools. It directed parents and masters of apprentices to see to it that the children for whom they were responsible were taught certain things, and it authorized fines for parents and masters who neglected the education of their children. But it assumed education to be a parental responsibility, not a function of government. Five years later, to be sure, a second Massachusetts law directed each township with more than a specified number of families to designate a teacher and at a larger population level to establish a grammar school that would prepare youths for college. Alternatively, the town could contribute to the support of the nearest grammar school in a neighboring town, but it was left to decide for itself whether school bills should be paid from public funds or by charges to parents whose children attended school. There was no requirement that parents send children to school.

When the theocracy of New England established government schools, it did not deny church responsibility for schools. In effect, the government was controlled by the church. In other colonies, where church and state were not so closely related, churches and private charities rather than the government established schools. The "Society for the establishment of a Free School in the City of New York," founded in 1805, illustrates the assumption that schooling was primarily a church function. Its purpose was to make schooling available to poor children "who do not belong to or are not provided for by any religious society."

It also illustrates the persistence of the assumption that free schools are for the poor, and church and charitable schools characteristically carried on the identification of free schools with the English tradition of pauper schools. When schooling at public expense came into being, it too was likely to be free only to the poor. In 1790 the Constitution of Pennsylvania provided that "the legislature shall, as soon as conveniently may be, provide by law for the establishment of schools throughout the state in such manner that the poor may be taught gratis." The enabling legislation, more than a score of years later, provided only that private school tuition fees might be paid from public funds for children whose parents declared themselves paupers.

Schooling for All

The "common school," the public elementary school, was widespread in America long before there was compulsory education. A period of rapid growth came during the first half of the nineteenth century. But the common schools, although publicly supported and publicly controlled, did not provide free education for a long time. There were many devices for financing them besides state and local taxes. Following precedents from colonial New England, some schools were supported in part from earmarked license fees—marriage licenses and liquor licenses, for example—and by lotteries and land grants. Beginning in 1802, National Land Grants provided funds for public education throughout the new states but did not apply to the sixteen states which constituted the Union at that time. But funds raised by means of land grants, lotteries, and license fees were not always used at once. People were reluctant to make indefinite commitments for annual taxes, assessments, or contributions and hoped to build endowments that would establish and support schools without continuous taxation. In some communities, private rather than public agencies undertook the task. The public schools of today's New York City stem from the activities of the "Society for establishing a Free School in the City of New York," which received public support soon after its organization in 1805.

Charges prorated among parents whose children attended the school were a very common means of school support. These "rate-bills," often the chief source of school income, charged parents specified sums for each day of attendance by each child. No attendance, no charge. A Livingston County, New York, rate-bill of 1825, for example, charges Amos Avery ten cents for fifteen days of school attendance for his child, and Job Holbrook 56 cents for 83 days of school attendance by his children. The total school cost billed to all parents was $11.81, from which the collector's fee of 56 cents was deducted. The resulting $11.25 was supplemented by $4.75 of "public money" to make up the teacher's wage of $16.00.[1] Some rate-bills itemized accounts and charged parents for "Amount of School Bill," "Assessor's fees thereon," and "Amount for Fuel." Parents who delivered wood for the school stove were exempted from the fuel bill. Usually, teachers took part of their pay in "board," and "boarded around" with the parents of their pupils.

School rates were collected as taxes, but they were not a tax on property or occupation or income; they were a tax on children. They did not constitute a general tax on children, however. The childless did not pay them, of course, but neither did parents who sent their children to private schools or who engaged private tutors or governesses for them. And the poor could avoid the tax by not sending their children to school at all. As long as part

---

[1] Ellwood P. Cubberley, *Readings in Public Education in the United States* (Boston, Houghton Mifflin, 1934), p. 185.

of the cost of schools was paid by rate-bills, schooling was not entirely a charge on the public purse. In New York State generally, rate-bills produced about half the sum paid to teachers, and rate-bills were not discontinued in New York until 1867. Other states using them discontinued them at different dates between 1834 and 1871. With their disappearance, schools became cost-free to those who were within reach of them and chose to send their children, and over the years since 1871 new schools and rapidly spreading compulsory education laws have put schools within the reach of most children.

That the development took so long is evidence that it was not unopposed. The cost of education was a large stumbling block, of course, but there were other arguments against free public schools. Echoes of some of them are still heard. It was argued that education would make the poor discontented with their lot—as if they ought not be—and might endanger the stability of society. The world must have "hewers of wood and drawers of water," and education, or "too much education," makes people restive in lowly occupations and inferior status. Southern laws making it illegal to teach slaves to read and write constituted a special instance of this view, of course, but it was widely held in the North as well. It is still used as an argument against providing higher education for "too many people." College graduates, it is assumed, will go into the professions or into "professional level" jobs in business and industry. From this it is argued that the number who go to college should reflect the number of appropriate jobs that will be available. If there are too many graduates, some will be discontented with their lot and will be a source of social unrest.

Cost-free schools were described as offensively paternalistic. Establishment of them, some said, would constitute an invasion of the right of the parent to determine the upbringing of his own children. Schooling at public expense was said to be a form of agrarianism or socialism, amounting to confiscation of property.

> It would be [said a newspaper editorial of 1830] a compulsory application of the means of the richer, for the direct use of the poorer classes; and so far an arbitrary division of property among them.

Other people urged that many are not capable of education, that the attempt to give it to them is futile and wasteful and deprives the more gifted of the quality of education that they ought to have. Leveling is always down, they said, never up.

Some objected on religious grounds: to require members of religious bodies that have their own schools to support through taxes other schools in which their consciences would not let them enter their children was a violation of conscience on the one hand and a form of double taxation on the other. Some objected that public schools are necessarily "godless" schools. This was a great debate, in which Horace Mann took a leading part as champion of the common school. The separation of church and state which characterizes our government makes it illegal for public schools to teach any particular religion. To leave religion out of education, Mann's opponents said, to teach important subjects—moral values, for example —without relating them to religious truths is to inculcate irreligion.

Perhaps as great an obstacle to the growth of free public schools as these arguments against them was the identification of free schools with "pauper schools." Charity schools, pauper schools, schools for the poor, whether privately or publicly supported, and provisions for children of paupers to attend private schools at public expense were steps on the way to a system of free public schools for all children. They were also obstacles to the development of such a system, for attendance at them was invidious and humiliating.

Something of the tradition remains. Although attendance at public schools and colleges is no longer a sign of poverty, attendance at some private schools and colleges is regarded as a sign of wealth and social status. Educational values are supplemented by the values that Thorstein Veblen called "conspicuous consumption." Because in our society poverty has sometimes been viewed as a form of unworthiness and wealth as a form of merit, attendance at free schools seemed a degradation, and the acceptance of free schooling was impeded as long as eligibility for free schooling depended on poverty.

Despite the opposition, the progress toward universal free schooling was steady throughout the nineteenth century. The forces that fostered it are summarized as follows by Quillen:

> The founding of tax-supported elementary schools was furthered in the early and mid-nineteenth century by such forces as nationalism, democracy, industrialism, and the humanitarian movement. Nationalism, which increased in intensity during and after the War of 1812, brought a demand for education to further national loyalty and patriotism. The spread of democracy brought the need for education for voters and office-holders. Industrialism both increased the need for more highly educated workers and the financial resources to support education. The humanitarian movement sought a general amelioration of life. It was an attempt to extend the rights and improve the living conditions of various groups. As the humanitarian movement developed, more and more emphasis was given to education, universal education, as a panacea for social ills. In fact, the potentialities of the school were perhaps exag-

gerated; and since that time the American people may have generally expected too much from schools.[2]

By the Civil War, the advocates of the common school had won their fight in principle, and public elementary schools had spread throughout many parts of the country.

After the Civil War, the humanitarian movement continued, and our industrial development also took on great impetus. Higher standards of living freed more and more children from the necessity to labor, and the demand for more schooling for more and more children continued. Massachusetts had passed a compulsory attendance law in 1852. After the Civil War, other states followed rapidly. All states had compulsory education laws by 1918. During the twentieth century, continuing humanitarian interest and continuing industrial development resulted in child labor laws as well.

After the Civil War, especially after the Kalamazoo decision affirmed that local school districts could legally spend public funds for secondary education, high schools began to multiply, as extensions of the common school.

The first secondary schools in colonial New England had been "Grammar Schools"—Latin grammar schools, designed to prepare boys for Harvard, where entrance requirements were "perfect" knowledge of the paradigms of Greek nouns and verbs and ability "to understand Tully, or such like classical Latin author *extempore,* and make and speak true Latin in verse and prose." Although in New England these schools were required by law in the towns of larger population, they were schools for a select few, for the most part those destined for the professions. But they were commonly extensions of schools in which younger children were taught by the same master to read and write English. Latin schools with no Latin students in them were not unknown. Edwards and Richey point out that the law requiring large towns to maintain Latin schools in effect required them to have college graduates as schoolmasters, there and ready to teach Latin if anyone came for it, but available to teach the reading and writing of English to the children who did come.[3]

The Latin schools were the first public secondary schools, but the "Academy" was perhaps a more direct ancestor of the modern American high school. It was a later development, for which Benjamin Franklin is given credit, although the school he founded in 1750 with privately contributed funds merely extended and gave firmer establishment to what had

---

[2] James Quillen, "The Evolving Objectives of Education in American Life," *The Educational Record,* July 1958, pp. 224-5.

[3] Newton Edwards and Herman G. Richey, *The School in the American Social Order* (Boston, Houghton Mifflin, 1947), p. 64.

Schooling for All

previously been done by private schoolmasters in such urban communities as Boston, New York, and Philadelphia.

The academy was a practical school, designed to give terminal, vocational education. It taught Latin and Greek, of course, but it undertook to teach modern languages as well: English, French, and German. To languages it added, according to its first advertisement,

> History, Geography, Chronology, Logic, and Rhetoric; also Writing, Arithmetic, Merchants Accounts, Geometry, Algebra, Surveying, Gauging, Navigation, Astronomy, Drawing in Perspective, and other mathematical Sciences; with natural and mechanical Philosophy, &c. agreeable to the Constitutions heretofore published, at the rate of Four Pounds per annum, and Twenty Shillings entrance.

Early in the nineteenth century, the academy had become the dominant secondary school in America, existing sometimes as a private school, sometimes as an endowed school with tax exemptions, sometimes also with public support.

It is not hard to see the high school in this ancestor, but the high school is the descendant of the Grammar School as well. It prepares some youths for college and offers practical, terminal education for others. Nevertheless, like the Latin Grammar School, the high school remained primarily a college-preparatory school for a long time. In 1900 only 11 per cent of the youth of high school age were in school and only a little more than half of them graduated. But the high school had both functions, and because it had both it was a departure from the "two-track" educational system characteristic of European education and reflected in grammar schools that prepared for college and academies that prepared for work. Today, 89 per cent of the high school age-group are in school. Half of them graduate, and about one-third go to college. For the rest, high school is the terminal school.

Thus the American high school has come close to providing universal secondary education. The elementary school is even closer to universality. Insofar as they are co-ordinated parts of a single-track educational program, they reflect and enhance the American tradition of equality of opportunity.

SCHOOLS AND EQUALITY

When free public schools had been established as precedents and the principle of public secular education had been accepted with reservations and limitations and regional lags, universal schooling remained to be achieved. Schools did not build themselves and there were too few of them for a long time. Schools that existed were not equally good nor equally appropriate for the children who went to them. For many children in a sparsely populated country, schools were not and hardly could be available before the days of good roads and school buses. Where there were schools, many parents did not recognize the importance of schooling, others could not afford to clothe their children for school, or could not dispense with the earnings of their children. Until school attendance was compulsory and until compulsory school laws were enforced, because the people believed in them, education was far from universal. Passing a law does not necessarily solve a problem, although the law itself may help to change an attitude.

Nor did the first compulsory school laws require very much in comparison with current requirements. Massachusetts had the first modern American compulsory school law in 1852. In 1866, in support of this law, a factory in Framingham refused to employ children under fifteen if they did not have certificates to the effect that they had been satisfactorily in attendance at school for eleven weeks during the year. Typical later nineteenth-century laws required children from eight to fourteen years old to attend school from twelve to sixteen weeks each year. A child might satisfy requirements, therefore, by attending school for the equivalent of less than six semesters as we think of them. And not infrequently, communities ran out of money and were unable to keep schools open the required time. As late as 1900 only 49.6 per cent of the children between five and seventeen attended school and only for an average of seventy-two days a year. The schools themselves were open for an average of 144 days. Half the children, then, were in school. This half attended on the average for about the equivalent of fourteen weeks during the year, but by no means necessarily for consecutive weeks or for consecutive days in a given week. Moreover, an average implies many who attended fewer than seventy-two days just as it implies many who attended more than that. The late-nineteenth-century teacher, the teacher in 1900, could only guess which half of his mixed bag of pupils of different ages and competencies would appear for a given day's teaching. By way of contrast, in 1940, 74 per cent of youth aged five to seventeen went to school for an average of 129 days in schools open on the average for 175 days.[4] Attendance has continued to grow. In 1957, 93 per cent in this age group were in school.

The growth of school attendance during the nineteenth and twentieth centuries reflects the growing belief in education among the people of the United States, growing insistence on equality of opportunity for all children, a growing humanitarianism, and a growing economy, which all together resulted in the spread of compulsory school laws and in child labor legislation in the several states. The laws came late, however. Between 1870 and 1881 nineteen states and territories passed compulsory school laws. By 1898, twelve more. In 1918, but not until 1918, all states and ter-

[4] Newton Edwards and Herman G. Richey, op. cit. pp. 121-3.

ritories had compulsory school laws. Many college students reading this volume may reflect that no law compelled their grandparents to attend school. Where laws did exist, they did not require much, provided for numerous exemptions, and were often unenforced.

There are many illustrations of unenforced laws. The law of 1642 requiring parents and masters of apprentices to teach the children in their care what are now called "school subjects" might be disobeyed. The second Massachusetts law implies that the first was not enforceable, and later New England laws refer again and again to "shameful neglect" of earlier ones. Towns required by the General Court to employ schoolmasters did not always do it. In 1713 the town of Andover, indicted for failure to provide a schoolmaster, in effect pleaded not guilty by reason of the teacher shortage. A schoolmaster had been appointed but he left for a better job. The town was unable to replace him, "perhaps by reason we do lie so exposed to our Indian enemies." [5]

Literal obedience to the law may not achieve the intention of the law. In colonial New England the law was satisfied if there were a schoolmaster in a New England town. But the aspirations of children or of their parents for them need not have been. Towns in colonial New England covered large areas—twenty to forty square miles—and were sparsely populated. The single schoolmaster serving an entire town could not be within reach of all children. One common practice was for the schoolmaster to move around the township—a few months in this settlement, where there were twenty families, a few months in that settlement, where there were fifteen families. Any house could do for a school, and the law required the town to hire a schoolmaster, not to build a school. In the town of Harwich in 1725 the several moves of the schoolmaster were fully planned. After stated intervals he was to move from one to another of six neighborhoods, and the length of time he remained in the different neighborhoods varied. A child attended school—or rather, attended the schoolmaster—for four months, six months, or eight months, while the master resided in his neighborhood. Then he waited from thirty-two to thirty-six months for another opportunity to go to school. If all the children had lived in the same settlement and had attended the single schoolmaster at the same time, or if there had been roads and school buses, he would have had an ungraded class of 254 children.[6]

A law of 1898 requiring parents to send their children to school might also be disobeyed. Or the law might be obeyed without satisfying its intention. Even in the twentieth century, superintendents of schools have sometimes been authorized to exempt children because of poverty, because of

[5] Ibid. p. 105.
[6] Ibid. pp. 111-12.

lack of access to a school, or for other reasons. Of course it is cheaper to exempt children than to build and staff a school within walking distance of every home, and school budgets are always too small to do everything. Quite obviously the existence of public schools does not guarantee an educated people. There must be enough schools, children must be free to go to them, and people must value and be able to afford the opportunity for their children.

The American school system has not yet gone all the way. Ginzberg and Bray estimate that "each year 125,000 illiterate children are moving past the compulsory attendance ages" and attribute part of the failure to inadequate elementary schools and lax enforcement of compulsory attendance laws.[7]

When there are enough schools and when children are free to go to them, schools may indeed be, as the White House Conference Committee said American schools are, "a major tool for creating a Nation without rigid class barriers." No one will deny that the American school has been a "great equalizer of the conditions of men." But it is not essential to the nature of schools that they result in a mobile or relatively classless society. Whether they do or not depends on what kind of schools they are, how they are conducted, for whom they are conducted, for what purposes, and by whom they are controlled. The Supreme Court decision on segregated schools affirms that segregated schools violate a first principle of democracy—the principle of equal rights—when it affirms that "separate educational facilities are inherently unequal" and bases this conclusion on the effect of segregation on "the hearts and minds of children." Different kinds of schools, pay or free, private or public, white or Negro, classical or vocational, may themselves be marks of caste, high or low.

A seventeenth-century English proposal illustrates the fact that schools may be instruments of inequality in a class-conscious society as easily as they may be instruments of equality in an egalitarian society. The great English philosopher John Locke was frequently asked by his friends for advice about bringing up their children. The result is his little book *Some Thoughts Concerning Education*. In it he describes the education appropriate for a young gentleman, a member of the ruling class in the class-conscious society of seventeenth-century England. For the young gentleman, Locke recommends a carefully selected private tutor, not a school.

Later in his life, as a government official, Locke turned his attention to the education of the poor and prepared a plan for bringing up the children of paupers. This time he did not propose private tutors: he proposed a vocational school. "The children of labouring people," he begins, "are

[7] Eli Ginzberg and Douglas W. Bray, *The Uneducated* (New York, Columbia University Press), 1953, p. 234.

an ordinary burthen to the parish, and are usually maintained in idleness, so that their labour also is generally lost to the public till they are twelve or fourteen years old."

"The most effectual remedy" that Locke can propose (not for their ignorance but for their lack of productivity) is to establish in each parish a "working school" to which unemployed children of indigent parents will be required to come and where they will be given work which will make them self-sustaining. (At age three, Locke thinks, they may not be able to earn their whole keep; but they can soon after that and in the long pull they will cost the parish nothing.) It will not cost much to feed them: "for a baker may be agreed with to furnish and bring into the school-house every day the allowance of bread necessary for all the scholars that are there. And to this may be also added, without any trouble, in cold weather, if it be thought needful, a little warm water-gruel; for the same fire that warms the room may be made use of to boil a pot of it." [8]

This was the advanced and liberal proposal of a humane and thoughtful man. If it had been acted upon, if it had not been in advance of its age, many unhappy children might have benefited. But it is no part of the concept of this working school that it be a "tool for creating a Nation without rigid class barriers." In Locke's plan, the young gentleman does not go to school; he is educated at home by a tutor, preferably but not usually his father. Freedom from school is a privilege of his wealth and rank. For the children of paupers, however, school is a place of productive employment, a place of custody until they reach the age for apprenticeship, and almost incidentally a place where children will learn spinning, knitting, weaving, and habits of industry and piety that will be valuable to society and to the individual children. Vocational schools in our own system need not necessarily be viewed as agencies of a mobile society either. The boy of fourteen who chooses a Mechanical Trades High School or whose parents choose it for him makes himself ineligible for college four years later and thus cuts himself off from the easiest and most direct road to white-collar or professional employment. The kind of school may be a mark of caste.

Locke's plan may be reversed completely, of course, and more often has been. In England and in New England a hundred years ago prosperous children went to school. Poor children went to work if there was work for them. Those in modest circumstances were likely to be apprenticed.

Clearly the school is an instrument of equality only in a society that values equality. In general, it is in America. Although it is part of the Jacksonian tradition that an unschooled man may become president of

[8] John Locke, *Report of the Board of Trade to the Lord Justices, in the year 1697, Respecting the Relief and Employment of the Poor,* no publisher, no date.

anything, including the country, schools have been very important instruments of "upward mobility" and of equality. The self-made man sends his son to school. Many self-made men have also made their own way through school. Some of them have endowed schools. If one generation has raised its economic level, schools help the next generation to raise its cultural level.

The school has also been an instrument of "Americanization," a means by which the foreign-born and the children of the foreign-born are helped to make their way in a new society and to win social equality in it. It has been a means of spreading a common culture. Denis Brogan, a British observer of America, comments on this:

> Of those millions [of high school students] a large section will be children of immigrants to whom English is still largely a foreign tongue. Of these millions, a very large portion will be the children of migrants from different parts of the United States. Others will be the children of rural-bred parents, forced to adjust themselves to the new urban world. They have to learn a common language, common habits, common tolerance, a common political and national faith. And they do.[9]

The particular conspicuous social or political contribution of the American school, then, is its lessening of inequalities of opportunity, whatever their origin, whatever their kind. Of course there are failures and partial successes. Some schools are better than others. The schools of some neighborhoods and some whole regions are better than those of others by every common test of schools. Some teachers are superior to others in character and competence. The child who finds himself in an inferior school or in the classroom of an incompetent or indifferent teacher does not have an opportunity for education equal to that of a child in the classroom of a competent and sympathetic teacher in a well-planned, well-equipped, and well-conducted school.

Some schools, then, inferior in one way or another, do not contribute what they should to equality of opportunity. Segregated schools extend and perpetuate existing inequalities. The public schools of fashionable suburbs and of urban slums extend and perpetuate other inequalities of opportunity. Perhaps different kinds of school programs sometimes do the same thing. In the main, however, the schools in the United States have been equalizers of the conditions of men. They could not have been and could not continue to be, however, if the people of the United States had not answered the question "Who should go to school?" by saying that everyone should go to school and by seeing to it that almost everyone

[9] Denis W. Brogan, *The American Character* (New York, Alfred A. Knopf, 1944), p. 135.

does. If the schools have not yet devised an educational program that is appropriate for everyone or different programs appropriate for all kinds of students, this is a problem that has grown with the schools and the schools have not ignored it.

Different Schools for Different Children

This problem of providing different educational programs appropriate for different kinds of students exists throughout the school system, but it is focused most sharply in the high school.

Early high schools were preparatory schools for college. For those who did not plan to go to college but who chose to go to high school anyway, the schools provided the same kind of education as for the potential college student. The student who from lack of ability or lack of interest did not do well in the academic program did not remain in school. He withdrew on his own initiative or on the school's initiative. He fit himself to the school or his schooling ended.

With the coming of compulsory school laws requiring attendance to age fourteen, sixteen (and now in some states eighteen), high schools became terminal schools for the overwhelming majority of their students, in theory as in fact. Moreover, they were required to retain the kinds of students who did not continue in high school before compulsory education was extended into the teens and for whom the academic program as it existed was unsuitable. Schools perforce began to plan and to conduct educational programs for different kinds of students instead of requiring all students to fit themselves to a single program.

The new school programs developed during the present century include training for a great variety of vocations. Writing in 1905, the famous Juvenile Court judge, Ben R. Lindsey, observed that only in reform schools could a boy learn a trade. "I ask you," he said,

> is it fair, just or decent that in most of the cities of this country an American boy has no opportunity to learn a trade, to capacitate himself for joyous, useful work with his hands, unless he commits a crime?

Ten years later, in 1915, John and Evelyn Dewey observed that school education "until recently" had met the needs

> of only one class of people, those who are interested in knowledge for its own sake, teachers, scholars, and research workers. The idea that training is necessary for the man who works with his hands is still so new that the schools are only just beginning to admit that control of the material things of life is knowledge at all. Until very recently schools have neglected the class of people who are numerically the largest and upon whom the whole world depends for its supply of necessities. . . .

The Deweys were arguing not merely in terms of the economic value of vocational training, however. They were urging

> a reorganization of the ordinary school work to meet the needs of this class of pupils, so that they will wish to stay in school for the value of what they are learning. . . .

They were proposing vocational or "non-academic" schooling in terms of the different clientele coming into the schools, a clientele for whom they questioned the value of traditional academic study.

Half a century later there are innumerable vocational high schools, and most comprehensive high schools have vocational programs. For most occupations, school rather than apprenticeship provides the first job training, and for many occupations the high school has seemed to be the appropriate school.

The introduction of a variety of vocational programs is not the only way in which school programs have multiplied. They have multiplied also because universal compulsory education assumes that everyone is educable and requires the school to provide for everyone.

At first there were many exceptions. Women needed little education and were likely to become "unwomanly" if they had too much. And by many they were thought to be incapable of "real" education. In the South in the days of slavery the law sometimes forbade teaching slaves to read because it was dangerous and unsuitable, but there was also a widely held view that Negroes are inferior and incapable of learning. In the North, men of property sometimes argued against the education of "the laboring classes" because it was dangerous and unsuitable, but again there was a frequent assumption of differences by social classes. Poverty was thought to be a result of incapacity and a sign of incapacity rather than, frequently, a cause of it. Besides, the necessity to labor made education impracticable, for education depends on leisure. "The 'peasant' must labor," says an editorial of 1830. "The mechanic cannot abandon the operations of his trade, for general studies." The victory of women in the war of the sexes, the emancipation and enfranchisement of slaves, and the growth of an economy that lets parents dispense with the miserable earnings of miserable children, and child labor laws that require them to do it, have shown these to be myths.

The handicapped were thought to be ineducable—the blind and the deaf because they were cut off from the means of communication used in education, the lame because they could not get to school. A school for the deaf was founded in Connecticut in 1816 and a school for the blind in Massachusetts in 1829, both taking form and inspiration from earlier schools in Paris. Special residential schools for the blind and the deaf were

Schooling for All

established in one state after another throughout the nineteenth century, and special schools for children with other physical handicaps were also established, but not until 1900 were there non-residential public school classes for handicapped children.

It was not necessary to change the definition of educability implicit in early schools because of physical differences among children. The educable were those who could learn what was taught in the schools. The tall and the short, the thin and the fat, the dark and the light, the lame, even the blind and the deaf (when techniques of teaching them had been developed) could learn to spell, to read, and to cipher.

Differences in interest and intelligence were another matter, for children of different mental capacities cannot learn the same things or cannot learn them at the same rate or do not learn them in the same way. As schooling becomes more nearly universal, the school population is no longer predominated by "interested, highly verbal, academic-minded, upper-class children" destined for intellectual occupations. It also includes those who are destined to work with their hands. And it includes the apathetic, the unwilling, the verbally inept, the physically handicapped, the mentally handicapped, and the morally delinquent. When the school includes nearly the whole child population, the educable are no longer only those who can learn what the school has traditionally taught. When the parent cannot withdraw the child nor the school expel him, the school must undertake the education of all kinds of children, of children representing almost the whole range of interest and ability. If the child cannot learn what the school teaches in the way it is taught, the school must find new ways of teaching that will enable him to learn or must find out what he can learn and teach him that.

The great variety of school programs that constitutes the American school system today reflects growing recognition of individual differences and growing insistence upon their importance in education. Special schools have been established for some groups, special programs for others. Vocational programs have multiplied in separate schools and in comprehensive high schools and in junior colleges, technical institutes, and colleges. "Opportunity rooms" are planned to help the mentally retarded, "advanced standing programs" and "enrichment programs" are planned for the intellectually gifted. Other special provisions are made for the delinquent and recalcitrant. For the problem of more schooling for all is a problem of providing meaningful and valuable education for different students—students with different interests, different aspirations, different abilities, different gifts, different handicaps, and different social advantages and disadvantages. Equality of opportunity for education is not interpreted to mean that everyone must have the same education. It means that everyone should have a chance at the education most appropriate for him.

How Much School?

Neither does equality of educational opportunity mean that everyone should have the same amount of schooling. In general, higher school ability is thought to justify more years of school as well as the more traditional kinds of schooling.

Every state in the Union now requires all children to go to school until they reach a specified age, most states until they are sixteen and some until they are eighteen, with specified exceptions. Currently, exceptions to the general requirement are urged occasionally, and the question whether a school system should have the right to expel unruly students who are still of compulsory school age is an issue in the news. In large cities, special schools for such students are a more likely development, and such schools have recently been established in New York City.

But American communities are not alike in the amount of free schooling that they provide for their residents. In most communities, free schooling (voluntary after the minimum age for leaving school is reached) is available only through high school. In other places, public junior colleges, community colleges, and technical institutes give youth an opportunity for two years of public schooling beyond the high school, and community colleges and technical institutes are multiplying and growing rapidly. Some cities (New York City, for example, through its four great city colleges) provide free public education through the bachelor's degree, for qualified students. Many states provide free or low-cost higher education for their residents through state universities and colleges. Even private colleges and universities, for the most part, however high their tuition charges may seem, give qualified students higher education, including professional and graduate education, at much less than cost. Scholarship and fellowship programs, privately or publicly supported, give substantial assistance to many students through the highest levels of education. In general, however, education is publicly supported and cost-free only through high school. Beyond high school, even though it may be free or partially subsidized, schooling is available not to everyone but only to students selected or retained on the basis of achievement and ability.

And only to those who can afford it. The existence of free or low-cost schooling does not mean that relative poverty and relative wealth have nothing to do with who goes to school. Organized labor in general has been a staunch advocate of free education, but when the Free Academy which became the College of the City of New York was first proposed in 1847, it was opposed by a labor journalist named Mike Walsh on the ground that it was another instance of privilege for those in "comfortable circumstances"—those who could afford to live without the earnings of their children.[10] There are still many families in the United States too poor to live without the earnings of their children or to support them to the age of twenty or twenty-one. There are many young people who are good students who do not finish high school because they do not want to or because they feel compelled to become self-supporting in spite of the willingness of their parents to see them through. There are many more who do not go to college because they do not want to; but there are others who do not because they cannot afford to.

A report of the Educational Policies Commission, *Higher Education in a Decade of Decision,* published in 1957, points out that

> While most college students today are of upper-level ability, not all upper-ability college-age persons are enrolled. There are barriers to college attendance for many students who are well able to profit by even the most rigorous advanced training. The most important problem is not that of preventing individuals who lack the requisite ability or preparation from going to college, but is that of attracting the many able students who do not now receive education beyond the high school.[11]

First among the barriers discussed by the Commission are "financial obstacles." Others include distance from college and lack of interest or motivation (called "the most pervasive barrier"). Nothing is said in the report about the difficulties of members of certain minority groups in different parts of the country, but we may add this barrier to the list for ourselves.

If the American people have decided that everyone should go to high school, the question who should go to college is one of the current educational controversies. Some think more and more colleges should be built for more and more students, others that too many people are in college already. Meanwhile, during recent years, in spite of the barriers noted by the Educational Policies Commission, larger and larger percentages of high school graduates have gone on to college. Going to college in many communities has become as commonplace for the present school generation as going to high school was for their parents. In 1930 there were fifty young people in high school for every hundred in the age group fourteen through seventeen. In 1957 there were eighty-nine for each hundred in the age group. In 1930 there were twelve young people in colleges and universities for every hundred in the age group eighteen through twenty-one; in 1955 there were thirty-two for each hundred in the age group. The

---

[10] Mario E. Cozenza, *The Establishment of the College of the City of New York* (Published by the Associate Alumni of CCNY, New York, 1925), pp. 139-40.

[11] Educational Policies Commission, *Higher Education in a Decade of Decision* (Washington, D. C., National Education Association, 1957), pp. 25-6.

numbers in these age groups are increasing rapidly and the percentages of those who complete high school and of those who enter college are also increasing.

During the past few years, as the population in elementary school age groups has increased, there has been an enormous expansion of school facilities, but building has not kept up with the flood of pupils. Teachers' salaries have risen sharply and there have been vigorous attempts to recruit more and more teachers, but there have not been enough teachers. More recently the "population bulge" has reached the high schools and brought to them the same problems of building and recruiting and comparable shortages of facilities and staff. Elementary schools and high schools are inadequately housed and inadequately staffed and are staffed in part by undereducated teachers. Now that the "bulge" has reached the colleges, higher education faces the same problems.

Year by year the age at which people leave school rises. More people finish high school and more go to college and stay in college longer. Robert Ulich points out, however, that "Prolongation of the school age is in itself not a blessing but may even be a curse to a civilization unless there goes together with the prolongation a revolutionary rethinking of the total educational system from the secondary schools upward. . . ." [12]

With reference to higher education there is a real issue and a lively controversy. Since colleges expect to have no trouble filling their dormitories and classrooms during the foreseeable future, there is widespread advocacy of "raising standards," of separating out from the mass of men for higher education the intellectual elite. Douglas Bush, like Robert Ulich a professor at Harvard University, argues in an article called "Education for All Is Education for None" that education of high quality is possible only with carefully selected especially able students.[13] Dr. James R. Killian, former president of the Massachusetts Institute of Technology, has affirmed again and again that our schools can win our scientific and technological competition with the Russians only if they stress the quality, not the quantity, of scientific education. Dr. James B. Conant, former president of Harvard, proposes the multiplication of terminal junior colleges for the many who will insist on education beyond the high school, so that the universities may concern themselves only with the selected few who may go into the professions or into other occupations and positions of "leadership." [14]

There are other views, of course. In 1945 the President's Commission

[12] Robert Ulich, *Crisis and Hope in American Education* (Boston, Beacon Press, 1951), p. 28.
[13] *The New York Times Magazine,* January 9, 1955.
[14] James B. Conant, *Education and Liberty* (Cambridge, Harvard University Press, 1953), pp. 57-8.

on Higher Education concluded that 49 per cent of all youth of college age have academic ability for two years of college and that 32 per cent could undertake more advanced college and professional programs. The United States Office of Education proposes research programs in the problems of "educating the gifted," but it does not assume that only the gifted should be educated nor that the gifted should necessarily be given more years of education than the less gifted. Almost the entire issue of the *Journal of Higher Education* for April 1956 was devoted to the question of "elitism vs. education for all," and other journals, popular and professional, have included repeated discussions of the question. An unpublished memorandum prepared for the Commission on Trends in Education of the Modern Language Association reports that

> . . . one leafs through the file of these discussions with the impression that those who write from the point of view of the public schools assume that all the educable must be educated, but that the college and university professors who are aware of the "rising tide of numbers" look forward to the day when they need admit to college only those elite students who insist on learning in spite of anything the faculty may do.

In effect, the debate is between those who think the important thing is to prevent unqualified students from entering college—because they interfere with the education of the qualified and because facilities are limited—and those who agree with the Educational Policies Commission report that the important problem is to attract the qualified student. There are also different views about what constitutes qualification for college. Not everyone accepts the estimate of the President's Commission that 49 per cent of the college-age population can benefit from college, and others think they can only if the colleges discard some of their inherited preconceptions of students and of what constitutes "college level education." The several views may be summarized as follows: that quality education is impossible if everyone is to be educated, and quality is more important than quantity; that some quality must be sacrificed because there is a commitment and an obligation to provide education for all who seek it; that mass education may be quality education and that the problem is to learn how to make it quality education; that mass education should be provided for "the masses" and quality education for the elite. It is worth noting, however, that those who advocate higher education "for all" are really advocating higher education for 49 per cent of the population. No one proposes four years of college for everybody.

Every state in the Union has decided, then, that everyone should have an opportunity for a high school education. Who should continue schooling beyond high school remains an open question. In both high school and college, what should be taught is another issue, also in terms of different kinds of students. In some ways, the question at issue is the point at which general education should end and specialized education begin—or rather, the point at which emphasis should shift from general to specialized education. The question "How much schooling?" is thus as closely related to the purposes of education as the question "Who should go to school?"

Judge Lindsey, in the context of schooling that ended at fourteen, asked for "an opportunity between the sixth and eighth grades . . . for children of the toiling masses to learn some kind of useful trade. . . ." He was looking forward to the time when a boy of fourteen could be "a valuable help to the plumber, the carpenter, or the printer at a decent wage, instead of going to the messenger service or the street." In short, he was thinking of terminal schooling at an earlier age than that specified by the several states today and he was mindful that most people in this country go to work when they finish school. The vocational training he recommended was to be the last stage of schooling.

The Deweys were also thinking of terminal schooling in terms of the new school population. They proposed vocational programs so that students would wish to stay in school longer, to learn useful trades.

At whatever level, the normal pattern of education in America puts specialized, vocational education last, whether in high school, in the undergraduate college, or in the graduate school of medicine or law. The longer people go to school, the later their vocational education is likely to begin.

At present, depending largely on how much schooling the student expects to complete, specialized education begins at very different points for different students, depending on how long they intend to continue in school. It begins at about fourteen for boys and girls who attend vocational high schools. It begins at about eighteen for those who graduate from general or college-preparatory high school programs and pursue their further education in technical institutes or in the commercial programs of business colleges or community colleges, who enter such undergraduate professional schools as those in engineering or pharmacy, or who go from high school into on-the-job training programs conducted by their employers. It begins at approximately the sophomore year in college for the pre-medical student, at graduation from college for many who go from college into on-the-job training or who enter graduate or professional schools.

At each point, the student's decision is more or less irrevocable except at considerable cost in time and money. In many urban universities there are more adult students enrolled in evening classes than there are college-age students enrolled in undergraduate day classes. Many of them are rectifying earlier compulsions to quit school or earlier choices of the "wrong" schooling. The point is worth repeating that the student who enters a vocational high school or program at fourteen has at that imprudent age made the decision not to go to college.

The diversity of our school programs, we may conclude, reflects in part the diversity of the school population under a system of universal education. When school is compulsory or when other pressures than the law impel a large proportion of the total population to continue in school beyond the compulsory school age, the school population will be diverse and there will be diverse school programs. Students (or someone for them) must choose among the different kinds of education available.

There are different opinions about how significant a diverse population is to education, about the extent to which a diverse population requires different educational goals, and about the validity of student interest as a guide in determining school programs. But everyone agrees that educational programs should not be identical for all students, even though some believe that the ultimate aims of education are the same for all. Everyone agrees that each student must be guided (some say *forced*) into the right direction for him. More and better testing and counseling, so that students will not make premature and unwise decisions, is perhaps the most frequent proposal. Since qualified school counselors are even less plentiful than qualified teachers, however, and since even the best counseling is not infallible, this proposal introduces a new set of problems to be pondered. They are problems inherent in the public decision that everyone should go to high school and in the private decision to go to college that more and more young people are making each year.

WHAT DOES THE READER DO?

To understand the past out of which the present and the future grow requires an active imagination. From hints here and there the student of the past builds an image, checking it against his other knowledge, rechecking it as he gathers more knowledge, and exercising special care not to build the past in the image of the present that he knows so much more directly.

A description of an early American school may help to remind the reader that schools to which children have been privileged or required to go at different times and places in the past have differed from one another and from modern schools in what was taught, in the qualifications of the teacher, in the materials of instruction, in methods of instruction, and in almost anything else he can think of. He must remember not to picture early schools of which he reads in the image of schools he has attended himself.

In 1816, William A. Alcott, aged eighteen, became the schoolmaster of the New England district in which he lived. He has left a detailed account of ten years of "school-keeping." [15]

Alcott was prepared for his profession of teaching by attendance at the district school of his neighborhood for a period of three to four months each winter from the age of four to the age of thirteen and for a few months each summer from age four to eight. Between thirteen and seventeen he attended "a kind of high school" conducted each winter by the parish minister—"in all about six months." He had a good reputation for learning. In the district school he had "usually succeeded in attaining and keeping at the head of the class," because rank in class was based on the spelling lesson and he was a good speller. His reputation was so good that the school committee sought him out for the district school.

The first school which Alcott "kept" had "thirty-five or forty pupils," ranging in age from barely four to his own age of eighteen. The school term was determined by the stipend of the teacher—school kept for four months if the teacher could be secured for eight dollars a month, for three months if he cost ten dollars. Since Alcott was expected to board himself, instead of "boarding around" at the homes of his pupils, his wage was ten dollars and the school term was set at three months.

Among the pupils, three were abecedarians, i.e. beginners who had been sent to learn the alphabet, their ABC's. Others were spellers, readers, and writers. The abecedarians (four- and five-year-olds, presumably)

> during the first hour of the day, were destitute of any employment. All they were permitted to do, was to "sit still," "fold up their arms," "avoid playing and whispering," and "hear the rest." . . . How much they were edified by hearing the exercises of the older pupils, I will not now undertake to determine.

What they "sat still" on was a plank bench. It was not until his sixth year of teaching that Alcott, assisted by the mothers of some of his pupils, introduced into another school the innovation of backs on school benches, out of concern for "fifteen abecedarians, most of whom were scarcely four."

When the older members of the school had recited for an hour and a half, Alcott could turn to the four-year-olds.

> One at a time they were summoned to appear before me. "What's that?" said I, pointing to A. . . . This the pupil usually happened to know something of; so after casting a side glance on the school, in order to discover how many eyes were upon him, he ventured, in a trembling voice, to falter its name. Pointing to B, I proceeded—"What's that?" C, "What's that?"

[15] *Confessions of a Schoolmaster* (Andover, Newman and Saxon, 1839).

When the child reached the end of his knowledge in the alphabet of capital letters, the teacher pronounced the letter's name for him. "Most of my abecedarians 'learned their letters,' " Alcott says, "in the course of three months; but I hardly know how." After two years (six to eight months of school) they had progressed to reading words of one syllable.

Spelling was the first business of older pupils and remained as it had in Alcott's school days the basis for rank in class. The best speller remained at the head of the class until some other pupil spelled a word he could not spell.

> My lessons in spelling were usually long, and I pronounced words very rapidly, and required each pupil to spell without much hesitation and with the utmost rapidity . . . How often I have boasted that we spelled *more,* in *our* school, than in any other school in the town!

After spelling, reading was the important exercise. There were three texts: the *New Testament,* the *American Preceptor,* and the reading lessons in *Webster's Spelling Book.*

> . . . in reading the New Testament, it was customary for each pupil to read, at once two verses. The exercise was usually begun by myself. I named the chapter, and after ascertaining that every pupil had his place, read two verses; then the scholar at the head read two, then the next; and so on. I was to make the corrections—if anything was wrong —unless occupied in writing copies, or in some other way, in which case the head pupil supplied my place. . . .
>
> Thus we went on, till one hour was passed, when another class took their reading books, and the same scene, in substance, was acted over again.

The occupation of "writing copies" which interrupted the teacher's work with the readers was for the sake of the "writers." Each child in the first and second (highest) classes had a writing book. But writing did not mean composition; it meant copying for the sake of penmanship. It was the teacher's task to prepare a model for each pupil to copy, to make quill pens for each pupil and repair them at need.

So much for the curriculum. Three months soon passed. In three months the school had read through the *Testament,* the *American Preceptor,* and the reading lessons of *Webster's Spelling Book.* Spellers had spelled all the columns in the spelling book. Older pupils had memorized the abbreviations, the rules for "pauses," and the Introduction to the *Spelling Book.* "Writers" had copied a given number of sheets in "coarse hand" and "fine hand."

And that was it. Alcott's school committee was a conservative one whose members wanted no curricular frills and fads. "Arithmetic, grammar, and geography were not permitted in the school," although Alcott, a progressive teacher, thought they ought to be and in later years gave instruction in them in evening classes for eager pupils willing to return after official school hours.

Discipline was a constant problem. Alcott prided himself on sparing use of corporal punishment and for a year prided himself on not using the rod at all. This, however, he felt to be a mistake. The alternative punishments of boxing ears, hitting a pupil on the head with a book, striking him with a ferule, and on one occasion hanging a small boy up by his heels, seemed to him, after he had tried them, worse than the standard punishment of switching. A humane man, he was careful that his rods were not too big; a rod, not a club, he thought the proper instrument and much safer than the alternatives common among parents and teachers of the day. He prided himself on a school well-disciplined with minimum use of corporal punishment, and he prided himself on the respect and affection of the children in his school.

Alcott's school will serve, even in this brief description, to remind the reader that early schools were not like those of today. The reader must use the same kind of historical imagination in reading other educational news of the past. A law directing a "town" to employ a "schoolmaster" requires the reader to remember that a colonial New England town was not a modern city but an expanse of sparsely populated, partly cultivated land, perhaps "exposed to Indian enemies." He must realize that a schoolmaster does not necessarily imply that all children went to school nor that those who did had continuous schooling.

When the student reads later in American history of provisions for "gratis" schooling for the poor, he must realize that these provisions restricted free schooling to the poor and must imagine the emotional responses of both the poor and the prosperous. When he reads proposals or arguments for school programs, he must not confuse proposals with actions. When he reads old laws (or new ones) he must remember that they point to abuses or needs that they are designed to remedy more surely than they guarantee immediate correction of abuses. There would have been no Prohibition Amendment if there had been no abuses of alcohol. There would have been no need for compulsory school laws if all children had been in school and no need for child labor legislation if no children had been laboring beyond their capacity and health. But neither should the reader assume immediate and perfect enforcement of laws. A Prohibition Amendment does not end abuses of alcohol. Passage of child labor legislation does not immediately guarantee that no under-age children will be illegally employed. Compulsory school laws do not guarantee that all children will be in school nor that they will learn much when they are there.

Schooling for All

"Everything that can be said about American schools is true somewhere," says a publication of the American Association of School Administrators, and present American schools are as diverse as that statement implies. Generalizations about the schools of the past are equally suspect: any generalization is likely to be true somewhere sometime but not to be universally true. Alcott's school reminds the student that early American schools were different from the schools of 1960, but it is not a model of all early schools. Schools, schooling, and the general attitude toward schooling differed in Connecticut and Virginia, in Texas and Michigan, in Pennsylvania and Georgia. They may have differed almost equally in adjacent townships or in the same township as schoolmasters changed. No single illustration of past attitudes or practices is a safe basis for unqualified generalization.

The reader of history must guard also against merging all of the past into a single uniform period uniformly different from the present. An illustration drawn from colonial times may help to explain a situation in the 1890's, another in 1925, and still another in 1960. But 1740 and 1925 are not to be thought of, as if they were alike, simply as "olden days." The past tends to collapse like a squeezed accordion. The student of the past must extend it to its full length if he is to be aware of all its folds.

The documents that follow this introduction are historical documents for the most part, illustrative of several stages in the development of the American system of free universal education. They do not tell the story and from them alone the story cannot be reconstructed in full. But they must be read with historical imagination. Old schools were not merely quaint oddities; they were the schools to which very real children were sent to learn. These children were the ancestors of many of us, and what they learned had some part in shaping us, a great part in shaping the nation. The better we understand the schools and the children, the better we will understand today's schools and ourselves.

Beginnings in the East

A MASSACHUSETTS BAY LAW OF 1642 *

. . . This Court, taking into consideration the great neglect of many parents and masters in training up their children in learning and labor and other employments which may be profitable to the commonwealth, do hereupon order and decree that in every town the chosen men appointed for managing the prudential affairs of the same shall henceforth stand charged with the care of the redress of this evil, so as they shall be sufficiently punished by fines for the neglect thereof, upon presentment of the grand jury, or other information or complaint in any Court within this jurisdiction; and for this end they, or the greater number of them, shall have power to take account from time to time of all parents and masters, and of their children, concerning their calling and employment of their children, especially of their ability to read and understand the principles of religion and the capital laws of this country, and to impose fines upon such as shall refuse to render such accounts to them when they shall be required; and they shall have power, with consent of any Court or the magistrate, to put forth apprentices the children of such as they shall (find) not to be able and fit to employ and bring them up. . . . They are also to provide that a sufficient quantity of materials, as hemp, flax, etc., may be raised in their several towns, and tools and implements provided for working out the same; and for their assistance in this so needful and beneficial employment, if they meet with any difficulty or opposition which they cannot well master by their own power, they may have recourse to some of the magistrates,

* Massachusetts (Colony), *Records of the Governor and Company of the Massachusetts Bay in New England* (Boston, William White, 1853), II, pp. 6-7. (Spelling is modernized)

who shall take such course for their help and encouragement as the occasion shall require according to justice; and the said townsmen, at the next Court in these limits, after the end of their year, shall give a brief account in writing of their proceedings herein. . . .

A GRANT OF LAND FOR SCHOOLS, DEDHAM, MASSACHUSETTS, 1643 *

January 2, 1643. . . . Also it was with an unanimous consent concluded that some portion of land in this intended division should be set apart for public use; viz. for the Town, the Church, and a free School; viz.: 40 acres at the least or 60 acres at the most.

January 1, 1645. . . . The said inhabitants taking into consideration the great necessity of providing some means for the education of the youth in our said town did with an unanimous consent declare by vote their willingness to promote that work promising to put to their hands to provide maintenance for a free school in our said town.

And farther did resolve and consent testifying it by vote to raise the sum of twenty pounds per annum towards the maintaining of a school master to keep a free school in our said town.

And also did resolve and consent to betrust the said twenty pounds per annum and certain lands in our town formerly set apart for public use: into the hand of trustees to be presently chosen by themselves to employ the said twenty pounds and the land aforesaid to be improved for the use of the said school: that as the profits shall arise from the said land every man may be proportionately abated of his sum of said twenty pounds aforesaid. . . .

THE OLD DELUDER, SATAN— A MASSACHUSETTS BAY LAW OF 1647 **

. . . It being one chief project of the old deluder, Satan, to keep men from the knowledge of the Scriptures, as in former times by keeping them

---

* Dedham, Massachusetts, *Early Records of the Town of Dedham, Massachusetts. 1636-1659. A Complete transcript of Book One of the General Records of the town, together with the selectmen's day book, covering a portion of the same period, being Volume Three of the printed records of the town* . . . (Dedham, Massachusetts, Printed at the Office of the Dedham Transcript, 1892) pp. 92, 105. (Modernized)

** Massachusetts (Colony), *Records of the Governor and Company of the Massachusetts Bay in New England* (Boston, William White, 1853), II, p. 203. (Spelling is modernized) in an unknown tongue, so in these latter times by persuading from the use of tongues, that so at least the true sense and meaning of the original might be clouded by false glosses of saint seeming deceivers, that learning may not be buried in the grave of our fathers in the church and commonwealth, the Lord assisting our endeavors,—

It is therefore ordered that every township in this jurisdiction, after the Lord hath increased them to the number of fifty householders, shall then forthwith appoint one within their town to teach all such children as shall resort to him to write and read, whose wages shall be paid either by the parents or masters of such children, or by the inhabitants in general, by way of supply, as the major part of those that order the prudentials of the town shall appoint; provided, those that send their children be not oppressed by paying much more than they can have them taught for in other towns; and it is further ordered, that where any town shall increase to the number of one hundred families or householders, they shall set up a grammar school, the master thereof being able to instruct youth so far as they shall be fitted for the university, provided, that if any town neglect the performance hereof above one year, that every such town shall pay 5 £ to the next school till they shall perform this order. . . .

Beginnings in the South

THE WILL OF BENJAMIN SYMS, 1634 *

In the name of God Amen this Twelfth day of Febry Anno Domini one thousand Six hundred and thirty four I Benjamin Syms being of perfect health, & memory praised be God make & ordain this my last Will and testament, in manner & forme following Viz

    I commend my soul into the hands of God my Creator and Redeemer and my body to the Earth from whence it came to have Christian burial whereas there is due to me two hundred acres of land lying in the old Poquoson River and Eight Milch cows—I bequeath it as followth Viz The use of the said land with the milk and Increase Male of the said cattle to be for the mantayance of an honest & learned man to keep upon the said Ground a free School to Educate & teach the Children of the adjoining Parishes of Elizb City & Poquoton from Mary's Mount downwards to the Poquoson River.

Item My Will and desire is that the Worshipful the Commander and ye rest of the Commissioners of this liberty with the ministers and Church Wardens of the said Parish where the said School is founded to see it from time to time justly & truly performed.

Item My Will and Desire is that when it please God there is sufficient Increase of the said cattle yt some part of them be saved for the erecting a very sufficient School house and the Rest of the Increase that are left to be disposed of before nominated and in Repairing the said School.

* Edgar W. Knight, *A Documentary History of Education in the South before 1860* (Chapel Hill, The University of North Carolina Press, 1949), pp. 203-5.

Item My Will is that the Increase of the said Cattle after the said School Master is sufficiently stocked for his maintaynance shall be spent according to the directions of the said Commander & Commitions with the rest of them to manteyne poor children, or decayed or maimed persons of the said parish

In witness whereof I have hereunto set my hand and seal the day and year first above written . . .

his mark
Benjamin Syms

THE LEGISLATURE CONFIRMS THE WILL, 1642 *

Be it also enacted and confirmed upon consideration had of the godly disposition and good intent of Benjamin Symms, dec. in founding by his last will and testament a freeschool in Elizabeth county, for the incouragement of all others in the like pious performances, that the said will and testament with all donations therein contained concerning the freeschool and the scituation thereof in the said county and the land appurteining to the same, shall be confirmed according to the true meaning and godly intent of the said testator without any alienation or conversion thereof to any place or county.

—March, 1642-3: 18th Charles 1st Hening, *Statutes at Large,* I, 252.

PROPAGATING THE XTIAN KNOWLEDGE **

. . . I shou'd say something of Propagating the Xtian Knowledge: We want a Schoolmaster in parish for our White peoples Children but as for the Negroes or Indians with all submission I wou'd desire that such a thing shou'd be taken into Consideration as the importance of the matter and the Consequences wch may follow do deserve. The best Scholar of all the Negroes in my Parish and a very sober and honest Liver, thro' his Learning was like to Create some Confusion among all the Negroes in this Country; he had a Book wherein he read some description of the several judgmts. that Chastise Men because of their Sins in these latter days, that description made an Impression upon his Spirit, and he told his Master

* Edgar W. Knight, *A Documentary History of Education in the South Before 1860* (Chapel Hill, The University of North Carolina Press, 1949), p. 205.
** Francis Le Jau. *The Carolina Chronicle of Dr. Francis Le Jau, 1706-1717* (Berkeley and Los Angeles, California, University of California Press, 1956), pp. 69-70.

abruptly there wou'd be a dismal time and the Moon wou'd be turned into Blood, and there wou'd be dearth of darkness and went away: When I heard of that I sent for the Negroe who ingeniously told me he had read so in a Book; I advised him and Charged him not to speak so, which he promised to me but yet wou'd never shew me the Book; but when he spoke those few Words to his Master, some Negroe overheard a part, and it was publickly blazed abroad that an Angel came and spake to the man, he had seen a hand that gave him a Book, he had heard Voices, seen fires &c. As I had opportunities I took care to undeceive those who asked me about it; now it is over. I fear that these Men have not judgment enough to make a good use of their Learning; and I have thought most convenient not to urge too far that Indians and Negroes shou'd be indifferently admitted to learn to read, but I leave it to the discretion of their Masters whom I exhort to examine well their Inclinations. I have often observed and lately hear that it had been better if persons of a Melancholy Constitution or those that run into the Search after Curious matter had never seen a Book . . .

PROHIBITION AGAINST TEACHING SLAVES IN SOUTH CAROLINA TO WRITE, 1740 *

XLIV. And whereas, the having of slaves taught to write, or suffering them to be employed in writing, may be attended with great inconveniences; *Be it enacted by etc.* that all and every person and persons whatsoever, who shall hereafter teach, or cause any slave or slaves to be taught to write, or shall use or employ any slave as a scribe in any matter of writing whatsoever, hereafter taught to write; every such person and persons, shall, for every such offence, forfeit the sum of £100 current money.

* *An Act for the Better Ordering and Governing Negroes and Other Slaves in this Province,* in South Carolina, Statutes, *The Public Laws of the State of South Carolina from its Establishment as a British Province down to the Year 1790, inclusive* (Philadelphia, R. Aitkin & Son, 1790), p. 174.

American Statesmen on Education

TO DIFFUSE KNOWLEDGE MORE GENERALLY *

Another object of the revisal is, to diffuse knowledge more generally through the mass of the people. This bill proposes to lay off every county into small districts of five or six miles square, called hundreds and in each of them to establish a school for teaching, reading, writing, and arithmetic. The tutor to be supported by the hundred, and every person in it entitled to send their children three years gratis, and as much longer as they please, paying for it. These schools to be under a visitor who is annually to chuse the boy of best genius in the school, of those whose parents are too poor to give them further education, and to send him forward to one of the grammar schools, of which twenty are proposed to be erected in different parts of the country, for teaching Greek, Latin, geography, and the higher branches of numerical arithmetic. Of the boys thus sent in any one year, trial is to be made at the grammar schools one or two years, and the best genius of the whole selected, and continued six years, and the residue dismissed. By this means twenty of the best geniuses will be raked from the rubbish annually, and be instructed, at the public expense, so far as the grammar schools go. At the end of six years instruction, one half are to be discontinued (from among whom the grammar schools will probably be supplied with future masters); and the other half, who are to be chosen for the superiority of their parts and disposition, are to be sent and continued three years in the study of such sciences as they shall chuse, at William and

* Thomas Jefferson, Notes on Virginia (1782), in *The Works of Thomas Jefferson, Collected and Edited by Paul Leicester Ford, Volume IV* (New York and London, G. P. Putnam, 1904), pp. 60-65.

Mary college, the plan of which is proposed to be enlarged, as will be hereafter explained, and extended to all the useful sciences. The ultimate result of the whole scheme of education would be the teaching all the children of the State reading, writing, and common arithmetic; turning out ten annually, of superior genius, well taught in Greek, Latin, geography, and the higher branches of arithmetic; turning out ten others annually, of genius, who, to those branches of learning, shall have added such of the sciences as their genius shall have led them to; the furnishing to the wealthier part of the people convenient schools at which their children may be educated at their own expence.—The general objects of this law are to provide an education adapted to the years, to the capacity, and the condition of every one, and directed to their freedom and happiness. Specific details were not proper for the law. These must be the business of the visitors entrusted with its execution. The first stage of this education being the schools of the hundreds, wherein the great mass of people will receive instruction, the principal foundations of future order will be laid here. Instead, therefore, of putting the Bible and Testament into the hands of the children at an age when their judgments are not sufficiently matured for religious inquiries, their memories may here be stored with the most useful facts from Grecian, Roman, European, and American history. The first elements of morality too may be instilled into their minds; such as, when further developed as their judgments advance in strength, may teach them how to work out their own greatest happiness, by shewing them that it does not depend on the condition of life in which chance has placed them, but is always the result of a good conscience, good health, occupation, and freedom in all just pursuits.—

Those whom either the wealth of their parents or the adoption of the state shall destine to higher degrees of learning, will go on to the grammar schools, which constitute the next stage, there to be instructed in the languages. The learning Greek and Latin, I am told, is going into disuse in Europe. I know not what their manners and occupations may call for: but it would be very ill-judged in us to follow their example in this instance. There is a certain period of life, say from eight to fifteen or sixteen years of age, when the mind like the body is not yet firm enough for laborious and close operations. If applied to such, it falls an early victim of premature exertion; exhibiting, indeed, at first, in these young and tender subjects, the flattering appearance of their being men while they are yet children, but ending in reducing them to be children when they should be men. The memory is then most susceptible and tenacious of impressions; and the learning of languages being chiefly a work of memory, it seems precisely fitted to the powers of this period, which is long enough too for acquiring the most useful languages, ancient and modern. I do not pretend that language is science. It is only an instrument for the attainment of science. But that time is not lost which is employed in providing tools for future operations; more especially as in this case the books put into the hands of youth for this purpose may be such as will at the same time impress their minds with useful facts and good principles. If this period be suffered to pass in idleness, the mind becomes lethargic and impotent, as would the body it inhabits if unexercised during the same time. The sympathy between body and mind during their rise, progress and decline, is too strict and obvious to endanger our being misled while we reason from the one to the other.—As soon as they are of sufficient age, it is supposed they will be sent on from the grammar schools to the university, which constitutes our third and last stage, there to study those sciences which may be adapted to their views.—By that part of our plan which prescribes the selection of the youths of genius from among the classes of the poor, we hope to avail the state of those talents which nature has sown as liberally among the poor as the rich, but which perish without use, if not sought for and cultivated.— But of all the views of this law none is more important, none more legitimate, than that of rendering the people the safe, as they are the ultimate guardians of their own liberty. For this purpose the reading in the first stage, where *they* will receive their whole education, is proposed, as has been said, to be chiefly historical. History, by apprising them of the past, will enable them to judge of the future; it will avail them of the experience of other times and other nations; it will enable them to know ambition under every disguise it may assume; and knowing it, to defeat its views. In every government on earth is some trace of human weakness, some germ of corruption and degeneracy, which cunning will discover, and wickedness insensibly open, cultivate, and improve. Every government degenerates when trusted to the rulers of the people alone. The people themselves therefore are its only safe depositories. And to render even them safe, their minds must be improved to a certain degree. This indeed is not all that is necessary, though it be essentially necessary. An amendment of our constitution must here come in aid of the public education. The influence over government must be shared among all the people. If every individual which composes their mass participates of the ultimate authority, the government will be safe; because the corrupting of the whole mass will exceed any private resources of wealth and public ones cannot be provided but by levies on the people. In this case every man would have to pay his own price. The government of Great Britain has been corrupted, because but one man in ten has a right to vote for members of parliament. The sellers of the government, therefore, get nine-tenths of their price clear. It has been thought that corruption is restrained by confining the right of suffrage to a few of the wealthier of the people; but it would be more effectually restrained by an extension of that right to such numbers as would bid defiance to the means of corruption. . . .

TO QUALIFY THOSE RESTORED TO FREEDOM *

An Address to the Public; from the Pennsylvania Society for Promoting the Abolition of Slavery and the Relief of Free Negroes Unlawfully Held in Bondage. (1789) Plan for Improving the Condition of the Free Blacks.

. . . Slavery is such an atrocious debasement of human nature that its very extirpation, if not performed with solicitous care, may sometimes open a source of serious evils.

The unhappy man, who has long been treated as a brute animal, too frequently sinks beneath the common standards of the human species. The galling chains that bind his body do also fetter his intellectual faculties and impair the social affections of his heart. . . .

Under such circumstances, freedom may often prove a misfortune to himself and prejudicial to society.

Attention to emancipated black people, it is therefore to be hoped, will become a branch of our national policy; but as far as we contribute to promote this emancipation, so far that attention is evidently a serious duty incumbent on us, and which we mean to discharge to the best of our judgment and abilities.

To instruct, to advise, to qualify those who have been restored to freedom for the exercise and enjoyment of civil liberty, to promote in them habits of industry, to furnish them with employments suited to their age, sex, talents, and other circumstances, and to procure their children an education calculated for their future situation in life; these are the great outlines of the annexed plan, which we have adopted and which we conceive will essentially promote the public good and the happiness of these our hitherto too much neglected fellow-creatures . . .

PLAN FOR IMPROVING THE CONDITION OF THE FREE BLACKS

The business relative to free blacks shall be transacted by a committee of twenty-four persons, annually elected by ballot, at the meeting of the Society in the month called April; and, in order to perform the different services with expedition, regularity, and energy, this committee shall resolve itself into the following subcommittees, viz.

I. A Committee of Inspection, who shall superintend the morals, gen-

---

* Benjamin Franklin in *The Works of Benjamin Franklin* ed. by Jared Sparks (Boston, Whittemore, Niles and Hall, 1856), II, pp. 515-16, 513-14.

eral conduct, and ordinary situation of the free negroes and afford them advice and instruction, protection from wrongs, and other friendly offices.

II. A Committee of Guardians, who shall place out children and young people with suitable persons that they may (during a moderate time of apprenticeship or servitude) learn some trade or other business of subsistence. The committee may effect this partly by persuasive influence on parents and the persons concerned, and partly by cooperating with the laws which are or may be enacted for this and similar purposes. In forming contracts on these occasions, the committee shall secure to the Society, as far as may be practicable, the right of guardianship over the persons so bound.

III. A Committee of Education, who shall superintend the school instruction of the children and youth of the free blacks. They may either influence them to attend regularly the schools already established in this city, or form others with this view; they shall, in either case, provide that the pupils may receive such learning as is necessary for their future situation in life, and especially a deep impression of the most important and generally acknowledged moral and religious principles. They shall also procure and preserve a regular record of the marriages, births, and manumissions of all free blacks.

IV. A Committee of Employ, who shall endeavor to procure constant employment for those free negroes who are able to work, as the want of this would occasion poverty, idleness, and many vicious habits. This committee will, by sedulous inquiry, be enabled to find common labor for a great number; they will also provide that such as indicate proper talents may learn various trades, which may be done by prevailing upon them to bind themselves for such a term of years as shall compensate their masters for the expense and trouble of instruction and maintenance. The committee may attempt the institution of some useful and simple manufactures which require but little skill and also may assist in commencing business such as appear to be qualified for it. . . .

A PETITION OF THE LEFT HAND *

To those who have the superintendency of education

I address myself to all the friends of youth, and conjure them to direct their compassionate regards to my unhappy fate, in order to remove the prejudices of which I am the victim. There are twin sisters of us; and the

* Benjamin Franklin in *The Works of Benjamin Franklin* ed. by Jared Sparks (Boston, Whittemore, Niles and Hall, 1856), II, pp. 183-4.

two eyes of man do not more resemble, nor are capable of being upon better terms with each other, than my sister and myself, were it not for the partiality of our parents, who make the most injurious distinctions between us. From my infancy, I have been led to consider my sister as a being of more elevated rank. I was suffered to grow up without the least instruction, while nothing was spared in her education. She had masters to teach her writing, drawing, music, and other accomplishments; but if by chance I touched a pencil, a pen, or a needle, I was bitterly rebuked; and more than once I have been beaten for being awkward, and wanting a graceful manner. It is true, my sister associated me with her upon some occasions; but she always made a point of taking the lead, calling upon me only from necessity, or to figure by her side.

But conceive not, Sirs, that my complaints are instigated merely by vanity. No; my uneasiness is occasioned by an object much more serious. It is the practice in our family, that the whole business of providing for its subsistence falls upon my sister and myself. If any disposition should attack my sister,—and I mention it in confidence upon this occasion, that she is subject to the gout, the rheumatism, and cramp, without making mention of other accidents,—what would be the fate of our poor family? Must not the regret of our parents be excessive, at having placed so great a difference between sisters who are so perfectly equal? Alas! we must perish from distress; for it would not be in my power even to scrawl a suppliant petition for relief, having been obliged to employ the hand of another in transcribing the request which I have now the honor to prefer to you.

Condescend, Sirs, to make my parents sensible of the injustice of an exclusive tenderness, and of the necessity of distributing their care and affection among all their children equally. I am, with a profound respect, Sirs, your obedient servant,

The Left Hand.

THE TIME IS COME *

It is with indescribable regret, that I have seen the youth of the United States migrating to foreign countries, in order to acquire the higher branches of erudition, and to obtain a knowledge of the Sciences. Altho' it would be injustice to many to pronounce the certainty of their imbibing maxims, not congenial with republicanism; it must nevertheless be admitted, that a seri-

---

* George Washington, 1795, in Edgar W. Knight and Clifton L. Hall, *Readings in American Educational History* (New York, Appleton-Century-Crofts, 1951), p. 97.

ous danger is encountered, by sending abroad among other political systems those, who have not well learned the value of their own.

The time is therefore come, when a plan of Universal education ought to be adopted in the United States. . . .

NO PRIVILEGED ORDERS *

An Address by De Witt Clinton of the Public School Society, December 11, 1809

On an occasion so interesting to this institution, when it is about to assume a more reputable shape, and to acquire a spacious and permanent habitation, it is no more than a becoming mark of attention to its patrons, benefactors, and friends, assembled for the first time in this place, to delineate its origin, its progress, and its present situation. . . .

In casting a view over the civilized world, we find an universal accordance in opinion on the benefits of education but the practical exposition of this opinion exhibits a deplorable contrast. While magnificent colleges and universities are erected and endowed and dedicated to literature, we behold few liberal appropriations for diffusing the blessings of knowledge among all descriptions of people. The fundamental error of Europe has been, to confine the light of knowledge to the wealthy and the great, while the humble and the depressed have been as sedulously excluded from its participation, as the wretched criminal, immured in a dungeon, is from the light of heaven. This cardinal mistake is not only to be found in the institutions of the Old World, and in the condition of its inhabitants, but it is to be seen in most of the books which have been written on the subject of education. The celebrated Locke, whose treatises on government and the human understanding have crowned him with immortal glory, devoted the powers of his mighty intellect to the elucidation of education; but in the very threshold of his book we discover this radical error: his treatise is professedly intended for the children of gentlemen. "If those of that rank (says he) are, by their education, once set right, they will quickly bring all the rest in order;" and he appears to consider the education of other children as of little importance. The consequence of this monstrous heresy has been, that ignorance, the prolific parent of every crime and vice, has predominated over the great body of the people, and a correspondent moral debasement has prevailed. "Man differs more from man than man from beast," says a writer (Montaigne's Essays), once celebrated. This remark,

* William Oland Bourne, *History of the Public School Society of New York* (New York, William Wood and Company, 1870), pp. 14-24.

however generally false, will certainly apply with great force to a man in a state of high mental cultivation, and man in a state of extreme ignorance.

This view of human nature is indeed calculated to excite the most painful feelings, and it entirely originates from a consideration of the predominating error which I have expressed. To this source must the crimes and the calamities of the Old World be principally imputed. Ignorance is the cause as well as the effect of bad governments, and without the cultivation of our rational powers, we can entertain no just ideas of the obligations of morality or the excellences of religion. Although England is justly renowned for its cultivation of the arts and sciences, and although the poor-rates of that country exceed five millions sterling per annum, yet (I adopt the words of an eminent British writer) "there is no Protestant country where the education of the poor has been so grossly and infamously neglected as in England." (Edinburgh Review) If one tenth part of that sum had been applied to the education of the poor, the blessings of order, knowledge, and innocence would have been diffused among them, the evil would have been attacked at the fountain-head, and a total revolution would have taken place in the habits and lives of the people, favorable to the cause of industry, good morals, good order, and rational religion.

More just and rational views have been entertained on this subject in the United States. Here, no privileged orders, no factitious distinctions in society, no hereditary nobility, no established religion, no royal prerogatives, exist to interpose barriers between the people, and to create distinct classifications in society. All men being considered as enjoying an equality of rights, the propriety and necessity of dispensing, without distinction, the blessings of education, followed of course. In New England, the greatest attention has been invariably given to this important object. In Connecticut, particularly, the schools are supported, at least three fourths of the year, by the interest of a very large fund created for that purpose, and a small tax on the people; the whole amounting to seventy-eight thousand dollars per annum. The result of this beneficial arrangement is obvious and striking. Our Eastern brethren are a well-informed and moral people. In those States it is as uncommon to find a poor man who cannot read and write, as it is rare to see one in Europe who can.

Pennsylvania has followed the noble example of New England. On the 4th of April last, a law was passed in that State, entitled "An Act to provide for the education of the poor, gratis." The expense of educating them is made a county charge, and the county commissioners are directed to carry the law into execution.

New York has proceeded in the same course, but on a different, and, perhaps, more eligible plan. For a few years back a fund has been accumulating with great celerity, solemnly appropriated to the support of Common

Schools. . . . It is highly probable that the whole fund will, in a few years, amount to twelve hundred and fifty thousand dollars, yielding a yearly income of seventy-five thousand dollars. If population is taken as the ratio of distribution, the quota of this city will amount to seven thousand five hundred dollars—a sum amply sufficient on the plan of our establishment, if judiciously applied, to accommodate all our poor with a gratuitous education.

On a comparison of the plan of this State with that of Pennsylvania, it will probably be found that we are entitled to the palm of superior excellence. Our capital is already created, and nothing more is requisite than a judicious distribution; whereas the expense of school establishments in that State is to be satisfied by annual burdens. The people of Pennsylvania are therefore interested against a faithful execution of the plan, because the less that is applied to education, the less they will have to pay in taxation. Abuses and perversions will of course arise and multiply in the administration of the public bounty. And the laws of that State being liable to alteration or repeal, her system has not that permanency and stability to which ours can lay claim. It is true that our Legislature may divert this fund; but it would justly be considered a violation of public faith, and a measure of a very violent character. As long as the public sentiment is correct in this respect, we have no reason to apprehend that any Legislature will be hardy enough to encounter the odium of their constituents and the indignation of posterity. . . .

A number of benevolent persons had seen, with concern, the increasing vices of the city, arising, in a great degree, from the neglected education of the poor. Great cities are, at all times, the nurseries and hot-beds of crimes. Bad men from all quarters repair to them, in order to obtain the benefit of concealment, and to enjoy in a superior degree the advantages of rapine and fraud. And the dreadful examples of vice which are presented to youth, and the alluring forms in which it is arrayed, connected with a spirit of extravagance and luxury, the never-failing attendant of great wealth and extensive business, cannot fail of augmenting the mass of moral depravity. . . . There can be no doubt that hundreds are in . . . this city, prowling about our streets for prey, the victims of intemperance, the slaves of idleness, and ready to fall into any vice, rather than to cultivate industry and good order. How can it be expected that persons so careless of themselves, will pay any attention to their children? The mendicant parent bequeaths his squalid poverty to his offspring, and the hardened thief transmits a legacy of infamy to his unfortunate and depraved descendants. Instances have occurred of little children, arraigned at the bar of our criminal courts, who have been derelict and abandoned, without a hand to protect, or a voice to guide them, through life. When interrogated as to their connections, they have replied that they were without home and without friends. . . .

True it is that charity schools, entitled to eminent praise, were established in this city; but they were attached to particular sects, and did not embrace children of different persuasions. Add to this that some denominations were not provided with these establishments, and that children the most in want of instruction were necessarily excluded, by the irreligion of their parents, from the benefit of education.

After a full view of the case, those persons of whom I have spoken agreed that the evil must be corrected at its source, and that education was the sovereign prescription. Under this impression they petitioned the Legislature, who, agreeably to their application, passed a law, on the 9th of April, 1805, entitled "An Act to incorporate the Society instituted in the city of New York, for the establishment of a free school for the education of poor children who do not belong to, or are not provided for by, any religious society." Thirteen trustees were elected under this act, on the first Monday of the ensuing May, with power to manage the affairs of the corporation. On convening together, they found that they had undertaken a great task and encountered an important responsibility; without funds, without teachers, without a house in which to instruct, and without a system of instruction; and that their only reliance must be on their own industry, on the liberality of the public, on the bounty of the constituted authorities, and the smiles of the Almighty Dispenser of all good.

In the year 1798, an obscure man of the name of Joseph Lancaster, possessed of an original genius and a most sagacious mind, and animated by a sublime benevolence, devoted himself to the education of the poor of Great Britain. Wherever he turned his eyes he saw the deplorable state to which they were reduced by the prevalence of ignorance and vice. He first planted his standard of charity in the city of London, where it was calculated that forty thousand children were left as destitute of instruction as the savages of the desert. And he proceeded, by degrees, to form and perfect a system which is, in education, what the neat finished machines for abridging labor and expense are in the mechanic arts.

It comprehends reading, writing, arithmetic, and the knowledge of the Holy Scriptures. It arrives at its object with the least possible trouble and at the least possible expense. Its distinguishing characters are economy, facility, and expedition, and its peculiar improvements are cheapness, activity, order, and emulation. It is impossible on this occasion to give a detailed view of the system. For this I refer you to a publication entitled "Improvements in Education, &c., by Joseph Lancaster"; and for its practical exposition I beg you to look at the operations of this seminary. Reading, in all its processes, from the alphabet upwards, is taught at the same time with writing, commencing with sand, proceeding to the slate, and from thence to the copy-book. And, to borrow a most just and striking remark, "the beauty of the system is, that nothing is trusted to the boy himself; he does not only *repeat* the lesson before a superior, but he *learns* before a superior." (Edinburgh Review) Solitary study does not exist in the establishment. The children are taught in companies. Constant habits of attention and vigilance are formed, and an ardent spirit of emulation kept continually alive. Instruction is performed through the instrumentality of the scholars. The school is divided into classes of ten, and a chief, denominated a monitor, is appointed over each class, who exercises a didactic and supervisional authority. The discipline of the school is enforced by shame, rather than by the infliction of pain. The punishments are varied with circumstances; and a judicious distribution of rewards, calculated to engage the infant mind in the discharge of its duty, forms the keystone—which binds together the whole edifice. . . .

When I perceive that many boys in our school have been taught to read and write in two months, who did not before know the alphabet, and that even one has accomplished it in three weeks—when I view all the bearings and tendencies of this system—when I contemplate the habits of order which it forms, the spirit of emulation which it excites, the rapid improvement which it produces, the purity of morals which it inculcates—when I behold the extraordinary union of celerity in instruction and economy of expense—and when I perceive one great assembly of a thousand children, under the eye of a single teacher, marching, with unexampled rapidity and with perfect discipline, to the goal of knowledge, I confess that I recognize in Lancaster the benefactor of the human race. I consider his system as creating a new era in education, as a blessing sent down from heaven to redeem the poor and distressed of this world from the power and dominion of ignorance.

Although the merits of this apostle of benevolence have been generally acknowledged in his own country, and he has received the countenance and protection of the first men of Great Britain, yet calumny has lifted up her voice against him, and attempts have been made to rob him of his laurels. Danger to the Established Church and to Government has been apprehended from his endeavors to pour light upon mankind. This insinuation has been abundantly repelled by the tenor of his life—his carefully steering clear, in his instructions, of any peculiar creed, and his confining himself to the general truths of Christianity. "I have," says Lancaster, "been eight years engaged in the benevolent work of superintending the education of the poor. I have had three thousand children, who owe their education to me, some of whom have left school, are apprenticed or in place, and are going on well. I have had great influence with both parents and children, among whom there is, nevertheless, no one instance of a convert to my religious profession." That knowledge is the parent of sedition and insurrection and that, in proportion as the public mind is illuminated, the principles of anarchy are disseminated, is a proposition that can never admit of debate, at least in this country. . . .

The trustees of this institution, after due deliberation, did not hesitate to adopt the system of Lancaster; and, in carrying it into effect, they derived essential aid from one of their body who had seen it practised in England, and who had had personal communication with its author. A teacher was also selected who has fully answered every reasonable expectation. He has generally followed the prescribed plan. Wherever he has deviated, he has improved. A more numerous, a better governed school, affording equal facilities to improvement, is not to be found in the United States.

Provided thus with an excellent system and an able teacher, the school was opened on the 6th of May, 1806, in a small apartment in Bancker street. This was the first scion of the Lancaster stock in the United States; and, from this humble beginning, in the course of little more than three years, you all observe the rapidity with which we have ascended.

One great desideratum still remained to be supplied. Without sufficient funds, nothing could be efficiently done. Animated appeals were made to the bounty of our citizens, and five thousand six hundred and forty-eight dollars were collected by subscription. Application was also made to the Legislature of this State for assistance, and on the 27th of February, 1807, a law was passed appropriating four thousand dollars, "for the purpose of erecting a suitable building, or buildings, for the instruction of poor children; and every year thereafter, the sum of one thousand dollars, for the purpose of promoting the benevolent objects of the Society." The preamble of this liberal act contains a legislative declaration of the excellence of the Lancaster system, in the following words: *"Whereas,* the Trustees of the Society for establishing a Free School in the City of New York for the education of such poor children as do not belong to, or are not provided for by, any religious society, have, by their memorial, solicited the aid of the Legislature; and whereas their plan of extending the benefits of education to poor children, and the excellent mode of instruction adopted by them, are highly deserving of the encouragement of Government."

Application was also made to the Corporation of the city for assistance; and the tenement in Bancker street being in all respects inadequate to the accommodation of the increasing establishment, that body appropriated a building adjacent to the Almshouse, for the temporary accommodation of the school, and the sum of five hundred dollars towards putting it in repair; the Society agreeing to receive and educate fifty children from the Almshouse. To this place the school was removed on the 1st of May, 1807, where it has continued until today.

The Corporation also presented the ground of this edifice, on which was an arsenal, to the Society, on condition of their educating the children of the Almshouse gratuitously; and also the sum of fifteen hundred dollars to aid in the completion of this building. . . . This room will contain nearly six hundred scholars, and below there are apartments for the family of the teacher, for the meeting of the trustees, and for a female school, which may contain one hundred scholars, and may be considered as an useful adjunct to this institution. This seminary was established about twelve years ago by a number of young women belonging to, or professing with, the Society of Friends, who have, with meritorious zeal and exemplary industry, devoted much of their personal attention, and all their influence, to the education of poor girls in the elementary parts of education and needle-work. The signal success which attended this Free School animated the trustees with a desire to extend its usefulness, and to render it coextensive with the wants of the community and commensurate with the objects of public bounty. A statute was accordingly passed, on their application, on the 1st of April, 1808, altering the style of this corporation, denominating it "The Free-School Society of New York," and extending its powers to all children who are the objects of a gratuitous education. . . .

An economical school, whose principal object is the instruction of the children of the refugees from the West Indies, was opened some time since in this city, where, in addition to the elementary parts of education, grammar, history, geography, and the French language are taught. It is conducted on the plan of Lancaster, with modifications and extensions, and is patronized and cherished by French and American gentlemen of great worth and respectability, who are entitled to every praise for their benevolence. Children of either sex are admitted, without distinction of nation, religion, or fortune. This seminary is in a flourishing condition, and contains two hundred scholars. There are two masters in this seminary, and two women who teach needle-work; and there is a printing-press, where such as have any talents in that way are taught that important art.

We have also the satisfaction of seeing the benefits of this system extended, either in whole or in part, to the charity schools of the Dutch, Episcopal, and Methodist Churches, and of the Presbyterian Church in Rutgers street; and also to the school founded by the Manumission Society, for the education of the people of color, which has, in consequence of this amelioration, been augmented from seventy to one hundred and thirty children. . . .

After our youth are instructed in the elements of useful knowledge, it is indispensable to their future usefulness that some calling should be marked out for them. As most of them will undoubtedly be brought up in useful trades, pecuniary means to facilitate their progress to this object would, if properly applied, greatly redound to the benefit of the individual, as well as to the poor of the community.

In such an extensive and comprehensive establishment we are to expect, according to the course of human events, that children of extraordinary genius and merit will rise up, entitled to extraordinary patronage. To select such from the common mass—to watch over their future destiny—to advance them through all the stages of education and through all the grades of knowledge, and to settle them in useful and honorable professions, are duties of primary importance, and indispensable obligations. This, however, will require considerable funds; but of what estimation are pecuniary sacrifices, when put in the scale against the important benefits that may result? And if we could draw aside the veil of futurity, perhaps we might see in the offspring of this establishment, so patronized and so encouraged, characters that will do honor to human nature—that will have it in their power

> The applause of listening senates to command,
> The threats of pain and ruin to despise;
> To scatter plenty o'er a smiling land,
> And read their history in a nation's eyes. . . .

Early Legislation After the Union

EARLY CONSTITUTIONAL PROVISIONS *

Pennsylvania, 1776
> Sec. 44. A school or schools shall be established in every county by the legislature, for the convenient instruction of youth, with such salaries to the masters, paid by the public, as may enable them to instruct youth at low prices; and all useful learning shall be duly encouraged and promoted in one or more universities.

North Carolina, 1776
> 41. That a school or schools shall be established by the legislature, for the convenient instruction of youth, with such salaries to the masters, paid by the public, as may enable them to instruct at low prices; and all useful learning shall be duly encouraged, and promoted, in one or more universities.

Northwest Ordinance, 1787
> Article III. Religion, morality and knowledge being necessary to good government and the happiness of mankind, schools and the means of education shall forever be encouraged.

* B. F. Poore, *The Federal and State Constitutions, Colonial Charters, and Other Organic Laws of the United States* (Washington, D. C., Government Printing Office, 1877).

GEORGIA MAKES ALIENS OF THOSE WHO STUDY ABROAD, 1785 *

And be it enacted, by the authority aforesaid that if any Person or persons under the age of sixteen years shall after the passing of this Act be sent abroad without the limits of the United States and reside there three years for the purpose of receiving an education under a foreign power. Such person or persons after their return to this State shall for three Years be considered and treated as aliens in so far as not to be eligible to a Seat in the Legislature or Executive authority or to hold any office civil or military in the State for that term and so in proportion for any greater number of years as he or they shall be absent as aforesaid, but shall not be injured or disqualified in any other respect.

FIRST CONSTITUTION OF INDIANA, 1816 **

ARTICLE IX

Sec. 1. Knowledge and learning, generally diffused through a community, being essential to the preservation of a free government, and spreading the opportunities and advantages of education through the various parts of the country being highly conducive to this end, it shall be the duty of the general assembly, to provide by law for the improvement of such lands as are, or hereafter may be, granted by the United States to this State for the use of schools, and to apply any funds which may be raised from such lands, or from any other quarter, to the accomplishment of the grand object for which they are or may be intended. . . . The general assembly shall, from time to time, pass such laws as shall be calculated to encourage intellectual, scientific, and agricultural improvements by allowing rewards and immunities for the promotion and improvement of arts, sciences, commerce, manufactures, and natural history; and to countenance and encourage the principles of humanity, industry, and morality.

Sec. 2. It shall be the duty of the general assembly, as soon as circumstances will permit, to provide, by law, for a general system of education,

---

* Allen D. Candler (comp.), *The Colonial Records of the State of Georgia*, XIX, Part II, p. 378.

** *The Constitution of the State of Indiana; adopted in convention at Corydon, on the Twenty-ninth Day of June, in the year of our Lord Eighteen Hundred and Sixteen and of the United States, the Fortieth* (Louisville, Butler and Wood, 1816), pp. 18-19.

ascending in a regular gradation from township schools to a state university, wherein tuition shall be gratis, and equally open to all.

Sec. 3. And for the promotion of such salutary end, the money which shall be paid as an equivalent by persons exempt from military duty, except in times of war, shall be exclusively, and in equal proportions, applied to the support of county seminaries; also, all fines assessed for any breach of the penal laws shall be applied to said seminaries, in the counties wherein they shall be assessed. . . .

The Debate on Public Education in the 1830's

PUBLIC EDUCATION AND PAUPERISM *

With the exception of this city and county, the city and incorporated borough of Lancaster, and the city of Pittsburgh, erected into "school districts" since 1818, it appears that the entire state is destitute of any provisions for public instruction, except those furnished by the enactment of 1809. This law requires the assessors of the several counties to ascertain and return the number of children whose parents are unable, through poverty, to educate them; and such children are permitted to be instructed at the most convenient schools at the expense of their respective counties.

The provisions of this act, however, are incomplete and frequently inoperative. . . .

The elementary schools throughout the state are irresponsible institutions, established by individuals, from mere motives of private speculation or gain, who are sometimes destitute of character, and frequently, of the requisite attainments and abilities. From the circumstance of the schools being the absolute property of individuals, no supervision or effectual control can be exercised over them; hence, ignorance, inattention, and even immorality, prevail to a lamentable extent among their teachers.

In some districts, no schools whatever exist! . . .

* Report of the Joint Committees of the City and County of Philadelphia, appointed September 1829, to ascertain the state of public instruction in Pennsylvania and to digest and propose such improvements in education as may be deemed essential to the intellectual and moral prosperity of the people, *The New York Sentinel and the Working Man's Advocate*, Vol. I, No. 19 (March 6, 1830), p. 1, col. 3-5.

But the principles on which these "school districts" are founded, are yet, in the opinion of the committees, extremely defective and inefficient. Their leading feature is pauperism! They are confined exclusively to the children of *the poor,* while there are, perhaps, thousands of children whose parents are unable to afford for them, a good private education, yet whose standing, professions or connexions in society effectually exclude them from taking the benefit of a *poor law.* There are great numbers, even of the poorest parents, who hold a dependence on the public bounty to be incompatible with the rights and liberties of an American citizen, and whose deep and cherished consciousness of *independence* determines them rather to starve the intellect of their offspring, than submit to become the objects of public charity.

There are, also, many poor families, who are totally unable to maintain and clothe their children, while at the schools; and who are compelled to place them, *at a very early age,* at some kind of labor that may assist in supporting them, or to bind them out as apprentices to relieve themselves entirely of the burthen of their maintenance and education, while the practice formerly universal, of schooling apprentices, has, of late years, greatly diminished and is still diminishing.

Another radical and glaring defect in the existing public school system is the very limited amount of instruction it affords, even to the comparatively small number of youth, who enjoy its benefits. It extends, in no case, further than a tolerable proficiency in reading, writing, and arithmetic, and sometimes to a slight acquaintance with geography. Besides these, the girls are taught a few simple branches of industry. A great proportion of scholars, however, from the causes already enumerated, acquire but a very slight and partial knowledge of these branches.

The present public school system . . . makes no provision for the care and instruction of children under five years old. This class of children is numerous, especially among the poor, and it frequently happens that the parents, or *parent,* (perhaps a widow) whose only resource for a livelihood is her needle or wash tub, is compelled to keep her elder children from the school to take charge of the younger ones, while her own hands are industriously employed in procuring a subsistence for them. Such instances are far from being rare, and form a very prominent and lamentable drawback on the utility of the schools in these districts. The care thus bestowed on infants, is insufficient and very partial. They are frequently exposed to the most pernicious influences and impressions. The seeds of vice, thus early scattered over the infant soil, are too often permitted to ripen, as life advances, till they fill society with violence and outrage, and yield an abundant harvest for magdalens and penitentiaries.

An opinion is entertained by many good and wise persons, and supported to a considerable extent, by actual experiment, that proper schools for supplying a judicious infant training, would effectually prevent much of that vicious depravity of character which penal codes and punishments are vainly intended to counteract. Such schools would, at least, relieve, in a great measure, many indigent parents, from the care of children, which in many cases occupies as much of their time as would be necessary to earn the children a subsistence. They would also afford many youth an opportunity of participating in the benefits of the public schools, who otherwise must, of necessity, be detained from them. . . .

In a republic, the people constitute the government, and by wielding its powers in accordance with the dictates, either of their intelligence or their ignorance; of their judgment or their caprices, are the makers and the rulers of their own good or evil destiny. They frame the laws and create the institutions, that promote their happiness or produce their destruction. If they be wise and intelligent, no laws but what are just and equal will receive their approbation, or be sustained by their suffrages. If they be ignorant and capricious, they will be deceived by mistaken or designing rulers, into the support of laws that are unequal or unjust.

It appears, therefore, to the committees that there can be no real liberty without a wide diffusion of real intelligence; that the members of a republic, should all be alike instructed in the nature and character of their equal rights and duties, as human beings, and as citizens; and that education, instead of being limited as in our public poor schools, to a simple acquaintance with words and cyphers, should tend, as far as possible, to the production of a just disposition, virtuous habits, and a rational self governing character.

When the committees contemplate their own condition, and that of the great mass of their fellow laborers; when they look around on the glaring inequality of society, they are constrained to believe, that until the means of equal instruction shall be equally secured to all, liberty is but an unmeaning word, and equality an empty shadow, whose substance to be realized must first be planted by an equal education and proper training in the minds, in the habits, in the manners, and in the feelings of the community.

EQUALITY ONLY IN CUSTODY?*

From the Minority Report

... The principle that your Committee would repeat, is, that Public Education ought to be *equal, republican, open to all, and the best that can be devised.*

If State Schools are to be, as now in New England, common day-schools only, we do not perceive how either of these requisitions are to be fulfilled. In republican schools, there must be no temptation to aristocratical prejudices. The pupils must learn to consider themselves as fellow-citizens, as equals. ... Yet if the children from these State Schools are to go every evening, the one to his wealthy parents' soft carpeted drawing-room, and the other to his poor father's, or widowed mother's comfortless cabin, will they return next day as friends and equals? He knows little of human nature who thinks they will. ...

But again: is that education the best, which teaches children the common branches of education during six or seven hours each day, and then leaves them to all the bad habits, which children suffered to run will acquire? Here in the city, for instance; is that education *the best,* by which children spend five or six hours out of the twenty-four in the streets, learning rudeness, impertinent language, vulgar manners, and vicious habits? Will any advantages in school compensate for the disadvantages out of it? ...

For our own parts, we understand education to mean, every thing which influences directly or indirectly the child's character. To see his companions smoke segars is a part of his education; to hear oaths is a part of his education; to see and laugh at drunken men in the street is part of his education; to witness vulgar merriment or coarse brawls is a part of his education. And if any one thinks that an education like this (which is daily obtained in the streets of our city) will be counteracted and neutralized by half a dozen hours of daily schooling, we are not of his opinion. We had almost as soon see a child of ours brought up among the Indians, as have him frequent a common day school one half the day, and wander about the streets the other half.

But even if none of these reasons existed, how is the poor laborer or the poorer widow, to keep her children at a day school, until they have received an education equal to that of their richer neighbors? Can the laborer

* Reports on Education, New York Working Men's Party (Extracts), Minority Report: June 19, 1830; Full Committee Report: May 29, 1830. Published in *The New York Sentinel and Working Man's Advocate,* Vol. 1, No. 36 (June 19, 1830); Vol. 1, No. 31 (May 29, 1830).

or the widow afford to support their children until they are twelve, fourteen, or sixteen years old, while they peruse the page of science, and obtain the acquirements and accomplishments which form the enlightened, well educated man? Even if no children's tax be levied on them, can they furnish food and decent clothing for their children during the necessary term? And if they cannot clothe their children as well as their neighbors clothe theirs, will they send them to school to be looked down upon or laughed at? If day schools alone are provided, therefore, *would not those very children who most require instruction be virtually excluded?* . . .

We conceive, then, that State Schools, to be republican, efficient and acceptable to all, must receive the children, not for six hours a day, but altogether; must feed them, clothe them, lodge them, must direct not their studies only, but their occupations and amusements; must care for them until their education is completed, and then only abandon them to the world, as useful, intelligent, virtuous citizens. . . .

Your Committee propose therefore, a System of Public Education, which shall provide for all children, at all times, receiving them at the earliest age their parents choose to entrust them to the national care; feeding, clothing, and educating them to the age of maturity.

Your Committee propose . . . that nothing savoring of inequality, nothing reminding them of the pride of riches, or the contempt of poverty, should be suffered to enter these republican safeguards of a young nation of equals. We propose that the destitute widow's child or the orphan boy should share the public care equally with the heir to a princely estate; so that all may become, not in word, but in deed and in feeling, free and equal. . . .

From the Report of the Full Committee

Resolved, that the report on the subject of education, submitted to your committee by a minority, embracing a system of guardianship and support, is unwise in its details, impolitic in its operations, at variance with the best feelings of our nature, and based upon the doctrines of infidelity.

Resolved, that the report be rejected.

Resolved, that we utterly disapprove of those journals which have endeavored to palm upon the public *this system* as one that is approved by the great body of the working men.

Resolved, that this report and these resolutions be signed by the Chairman and Secretary, and published.[1]

H. G. Guyon, Chairman.   A. L. Balch, Secretary.

[1] *The New York Sentinel and Working Man's Advocate* of June 19, 1830, notes that the report of the minority sub-committee was "rejected and denounced by the twenty-five members of the committee without having been read before them and (that this minority report) embraces all the principles upon which the charge of 'Infidelity' and 'Agrarianism' are founded against us and all others who have advocated such a system." (Editor's note)

THE MECHANIC MUST LABOR *

We remark the following toast in one of the lists which nearly fill the papers at this season.

"*Education and general information*—these must *indeed* constitute our only true *National Bulwark*. May the day soon come when in point of literary acquirements the poorest peasant shall stand on a level with his more wealthy neighbours."

It is our strong inclination and our obvious interest that literary acquirements should be *universal;* but we should be guilty of imposture, if we professed to believe in the possibility of that consummation. Literature cannot be acquired without leisure, and wealth gives leisure. Universal opulence, or even competency, is a chimera, as man and society are constituted. There will ever be distinctions of condition, of capacity, of knowledge and ignorance, in spite of all the fond conceits that may be indulged, or the wild projects which may be tried, to the contrary. The "peasant" must labor during those hours of the day, which his wealthy neighbor can give to the abstract culture of his mind; otherwise, the earth would not yield enough for the subsistence of all: the mechanic cannot abandon the operations of his trade, for general studies; if he should, most of the conveniences of life and objects of existence would be wanting; languor, decay, poverty, discontent would soon be visible among all classes. No government, no statesman, no philanthropist, can furnish what is incompatible with the very organization and being of civil society. Education, the most comprehensive, should be, and is, open to the whole community; but it must cost to every one, *time and money;* and those are means which every one cannot possess simultaneously. Doubtless, more of education and of information is attainable for all in this republic, than can be had any where else by the poor or the operatives, so called.

WHY SHOULD THE PROPERTIED CLASSES PAY? **

We can readily pardon the editor of the United States Gazette for not perceiving that the scheme of Universal Equal Education at the expense of the State, is virtually "Agrarianism." It would be a compulsory application of the means of the richer, for the direct use of the poorer classes; and

---

* *The National Gazette and Literary Register,* Editorial, Vol. X, No. 2931 (July 10, 1830).
** *National Gazette (Philadelphia National Gazette,* daily edition), Editorial, August 19, 1830, p. 2, cols. 1, 2.

so far *an arbitrary division of property among them.* The declared object is, to procure the opportunity of instruction for the child or children of every citizen; to elevate the standard of the education of the working classes, *or equalize the standard for all classes;* which would, doubtless, be to lower or narrow that which the rich may now compass. But the most sensible and reflecting possessors of property sufficient to enable them to educate their children in the most liberal and efficacious way, and upon the broadest scale, would prefer to share their means for any other purpose, or in any other mode, than such as would injuriously affect or circumscribe the proficiency of their offspring. A public meeting of "the Mechanics and other Working Men of the City and County of New York," was held in the city, on the 17th inst., and among the principles for which they have "resolved" to contend, we find the following:

"*In Education*—The adoption of a general system of instruction, at the expense of the State, which shall afford to children, however rich or poor, equal means to obtain useful learning. To effect this, it is believed that a system of direct taxation will not be necessary, as the surplus revenue of the State and United States Governments will, in a very few years, afford ample means—but even if it were necessary to resort to direct taxation to accomplish this all-important object, and the amount paid by the wealthy should be far greater than that paid by our less eligibly situated fellow-citizens, an equivalent to them would be found in the increased ability and usefulness of the educated citizen to serve and to promote the best interests of the State; in the increased permanency of our institutions—and in the superior protection of liberty, person, and property."

Thus, a direct tax for "the equal means of obtaining useful learning" is not deemed improbable, and it is admitted that the amount which would be paid by the wealthy would be "far greater" than that paid by their "less eligibly situated fellow citizens." Here, we contend, would be the action, if not the name, of the Agrarian system. Authority—that is, the State—is to force the more eligibly situated citizens to contribute a part (which might be very considerable) of their means, for the accommodation of the rest; and this is equivalent to the idea of an actual, compulsory partition of their substance. The more thriving members of the "mechanical and other working classes" would themselves feel the evil of the direct taxation; they would find that they had toiled for the benefit of other families than their own. One of the chief excitements to industry, among those classes, is the hope of earning the means of educating their children respectably or liberally: that incentive would be removed, and the scheme of State and equal education be thus a premium for comparative idleness, to be taken out of the pockets of the laborious. . . .

We have no confidence in any compulsory equalizations; it has been well observed that they pull down what is above, but never much raise what is below, and often "depress high and low together beneath the level of what was originally lowest." By no possibility could a perfect equality be procured. . . .

GROSS INJUSTICE IN SOME OF OUR MANUFACTORIES EXPOSED *

. . . It is a well known fact, that the principal part of the helps in cotton factories consist of boys and girls, we may safely say from six to seventeen years of age, and are confined to steady employment during the longest days of the year, from daylight until dark, allowing, at the outside, one hour and a half per day. In consequence of this close confinement, it renders it entirely impossible for the parents of such children to obtain for them any education or knowledge, save that of working that machine, which they are compelled to work, and that too with a small sum, that is hardly sufficient to support nature, while they on the other hand are rolling in wealth, of the vitals of these poor children every day. . . . We have known many instances where parents who are capable of giving their children a trifling education one at a time, deprived of that opportunity by their employer's threats, that if they did take one child from their employ, (a short time for school) such family must leave the employment—and we have even known these threats put in execution. Now . . . we may establish schools and academies, and devise every means for the instruction of youth in vain, unless we also give time for application; we have heard it remarked to some employers, that it would be commendable to congress to shorten the hours of labour in factories; the reply was: it would be an infringement on the rights of the people. We know the average number of hands employed by one manufacturer to be, at the lowest estimate, fifty men, women and children. Now the query is: whether this individual, or this number employed by him, is the people? . . .

[signed] Many Operatives.

* *Mechanic's Free Press* (*Philadelphia Times*), August 21, 1830, p. 2, cols. 3, 4.

The Education of Negroes in Boston Before the Civil War

RESOLUTION OF BOSTON NEGROES AGAINST SEGREGATED SCHOOLS *

Resolved, That, impelled by a deep sense of gratitude, we tender to Dr. H. Storer our unfeigned thanks for his successful efforts in instituting the late investigation of affairs connected with the Smith School, and for his unremitting attention to the same from the commencement to the close.

Resolved, That we present our most grateful acknowledgments to the Hon. John C. Park, for the late voluntary and disinterested devotion of his time and eminent talents in the cause of the wronged and neglected colored children of this city.

Whereas, we, the colored citizens of the city of Boston have recently sent a petition to the School Committee, respectfully praying for the abolition of the separate schools for colored children, and asking for the rights and privileges extended to other citizens in respect to the common school system—viz. the right to send our children to the schools established in the respective districts in which we reside; and

Whereas, the School Committee, at their last meeting, passed a vote stating, in substance, that the prayer of our petition would not be granted, and that the separate schools for colored children would be continued; and

Whereas, we believe, and have the opinion of eminent counsel, that the institution and support of separate schools at the public charge, for any

* *The Liberator,* Vol. XIV, No. 26 (June 28, 1844), p. 103.

one class of the inhabitants in exclusion of any other class, is contrary to the laws of this Commonwealth; therefore,

Resolved, That we consider the late action of the School Committee, in regard to our petition asking for the entire abolition of separate schools for colored children, as erroneous and unsatisfactory.

Resolved, That while we would not turn aside from our main object, the abolition of the separate colored schools, we cannot allow this occasion to pass without an expression of our surprise and regret at the recent acquittal by the School Committee of Abner Forbes, Principal of the Smith School, and of our deep conviction that he is totally unworthy of his present responsible station; and that the colored parents of this city are recommended to withdraw their children from the exclusive school established in contravention of that equality of privileges which is the vital principle of the school system of Massachusetts.

Resolved, That a copy of the above preamble and resolutions be sent to the Chairman of the School Committee, with a request that the petition heretofore presented may be reconsidered, and that we be allowed a hearing on said petition before them.

Resolved, That the heartfelt thanks of the colored citizens of Boston are due to Messrs. George S. Hillard and John T. Sargent for the humane and independent stand recently taken by them in the School Committee, in behalf of the rights and welfare of the colored children.

Resolved, That the expression of the sense of this meeting be transmitted to the several gentlemen named in the foregoing resolutions, and be also published in the city papers.

John T. Hilton, President

REPORT ON THE SMITH SCHOOL [*]

In regard to the Smith school, we have come to the conclusion that it is not only in an unsatisfactory, but in a deplorable condition. The attainments of the scholars are of the lowest grade; a few can read aloud from the first class reader, but cannot understand any other than the simplest passages. Their chattering about grammar shows only the power of their memories to retain the names of things which they do not understand; and their knowledge of geography is nothing but the faculty of repeating imper-

[*] Report of the Subcommittee Appointed for the Purpose of Making Annual Examinations in the Grammar Department of All the Schools (May 6, 1845), City of Boston. From Otis W. Caldwell and Stuart A. Courtis, *Then and Now in Education, 1845-1923* (Yonkers-on-Hudson, New York, World Book Company, 1925), Appendix I, pp. 185-6.

fectly names of states, towns, rivers, etc. There are certain parts of physical and political geography which we supposed might be made most interesting to colored children, those relating to the West India Islands, the condition of the colored race in Cuba, Jamaica, Hayti, etc.; the colonies in Africa, the condition of the natives, etc.; but the scholars of the Smith school seemed to know nothing about them. They supposed Cuba to be smaller than Massachusetts, knew little or nothing of the other islands, and though one or two had heard of the emancipation act, the class knew nothing about it. They had only the most crude and vague notions of history; and, as for mathematical geography, astronomy, or natural philosophy, the master declined any examination.

But the intellectual deficiency which prevails in this school is not its worst feature; there is a want of discipline; an indifference to verbal requests for order, which indicates the frequency of appeal to more stirring motives; a want of respectful attention, and many indefinable but clear indications of a low moral tone.

Your Committee are aware, that there are many circumstances to be considered before blame should be laid on any individual, for the present low state of the school; they are aware of the difficulties in obtaining a good average attendance, and they will not say that another individual could at once inspire the colored population with more interest in the school, could secure a more punctual attendance, or could awaken the faculties and interest the attention of the scholars. But they do believe that there is good sense enough among the parents, and intellect enough among the children, if fairly enlisted in the subject, and directed by a zealous and discreet friend, to create a school which shall reach at least to the rank now attained by one half of the city schools.

It is to be regretted that the present incumbent has not more faith in the desire of the colored population for the education of their children, and in the capacities of the children themselves; for we fear that, without much faith, and even some enthusiasm, no great harvest can follow the teacher's labors. We think this school calls loudly for improvement.

Toward Universal Schooling

FIRST MORRILL (LAND-GRANT) ACT *

Chap. CXXX.—An Act Donating Public Lands to the several States and Territories which may provide Colleges for the benefit of Agriculture and the Mechanic Arts.

Be it enacted by the Senate and House of Representatives of the United States of America, in Congress assembled, that there be granted to the several States, for the purposes hereinafter mentioned, an amount of public land, to be apportioned to each State a quantity equal to thirty thousand acres for each senator and representative in Congress to which the States are respectively entitled by the apportionment under the census of eighteen hundred and sixty: *Provided,* that no mineral lands shall be selected or purchased under the provisions of this act. . . .

Section 4. *And be it further enacted,* That all moneys derived from the sale of the lands aforesaid by the States . . . shall be invested in stocks of the United States or of the States, or some other safe stocks, yielding not less than five per centum upon the par value of said stocks; and that the moneys so invested shall constitute a perpetual fund, the capital of which shall remain forever undiminished (except so far as may be provided in section fifth of this act), and the interest of which shall be inviolably appropriated, by each State which may take and claim the benefit of this act, to the endowment, support, and maintenance of at least one college where the leading object shall be, without excluding other scientific

* United States Congress, *Statutes at Large,* Chapter 130 (1862) (Boston, Little, Brown, 1863), XII, pp. 503-4.

and classical studies, and including military tactics, to teach such branches of learning as are related to agriculture and the mechanic arts, in such manner as the legislatures of the States may respectively prescribe, in order to promote the liberal and practical education of the industrial classes in the several pursuits and professions in life. . . .

Approved July 2, 1862.

SCHOOL COMMITTEE REPORT FOR THE CITY OF FRAMINGHAM, MASSACHUSETTS *

The law in regard to the employment of children in manufacturing establishments has been faithfully carried out in districts 9 and 10. The Saxonville mills, in this respect, furnish a model worthy of imitation by all similar establishments. All applicants for employment, under fifteen years of age, are required to bring written certificates from their teachers or the school committee, stating the time they have attended school during the year. It is not enough to be connected with the school for eleven weeks. The rule adopted requires a certificate from the register of actual attendance the full time specified in the statute. The parents least interested in schools appreciate some of the evils of irregular attendance on finding, to their surprise, that their children, by reason of absence, have not been at school the required time.

Punctuality is also promoted by the ringing of the "factory bell" fifteen minutes before the daily sessions. For the purpose of promoting good order in school, the rule has been enforced for many years, "that no person who is disorderly in school shall be employed by the company." This regulation has effectually secured the co-operation of those parents who were proposing to get work for the children in the mills. Though this rule has been strictly carried out, but four applicants for employment during the last ten years have been rejected on the ground of their misconduct at school. One Irish boy last summer, expelled from school for misconduct, found his name at once on the "black-list" in the counting-room. But the next morning, melted by the tears of his mother, and thoroughly subdued by the sterner treatment of his father, he begged for re-admission to school, made an humble apology to the teacher before the school and the committee, and became one of the most obedient boys in the school. It hardly need be added, his name was erased from the black-list.

The schools falling short in time during the current year, by reason of advanced expenses and wages of teachers, were continued four weeks by

* Twenty-ninth Annual Report of the Board of Education, Commonwealth of Massachusetts, pp. 84-5. (1866)

the generosity of the leading owner of these mills. It was a pleasant scene to witness the interest with which all, even the poorest children in these schools, sought to express their appreciation of this benefaction, by their little contributions, and the evident pride and pleasure with which they presented an elegant copy of the new Webster's Dictionary, bearing in gilt letters the fitting inscription,

M. H. Simpson, Esq.,
A THANK OFFERING
From the Children in the Schools of Saxonville.

COMPULSORY EDUCATION *

As a means to attain the most perfect results, and make the public school system practically efficient, compulsory attendance at school during a portion of every year, up to a certain age, is suggested. This suggestion is about to be put upon probation in several of the states. . . .

The object sought in this paper is a resume of opinions obtained from the different sources used. . . .

REPORT OF SUPERINTENDENT RANDALL, NEW YORK CITY

Superintendent Randall, of the city of New York, says in his report, 1864, "Making the most liberal estimate of the number under instruction, we cannot escape the conviction that not far from 100,000 children in the city either attend no school, or attend a very brief period." Of 204,000 reported enrolled, 40,000, being 20 per cent, attended less than two months. Yet, startling as the figures are, Mr. Randall was not prepared, in 1868, to recommend a compulsory system, which he thinks would not agree with the genius of our free institutions.

ABSENTEEISM IN CONNECTICUT

Under the head of *absenteeism* in the Connecticut report of 1868, the secretary says, "less than one-half the children of this State are on an average found in our public schools." The school visitors in their reports, 1869, tell the same story and suggest the enforcement of truant laws to remedy the evil and bring into the schools "children who are wandering about the streets without parental control or useful employment."

* L. Van Bokkelen, *Compulsory Education* (A Circular of Information of the U.S. Bureau of Education), Dec. 1871 (Washington, D. C., U.S. Government Printing Office, 1872), pp. 5, 9-17.

Compulsory Enactments in Maryland

The school system for Maryland as reported by the superintendent of public instruction . . . , in 1865, contained compulsory enactments, of which he says, "The design is to compel parents to send their children to school, and to prevent manufacturers from employing children who cannot read and write, unless they provide facilities for such moderate degree of instruction. It is only simple justice to those who are taxed to build school-houses and pay teachers that the benefit designed to be secured should reach its object. The child must be sent to school. This is the duty of parents and guardians, but if they fail, it becomes the duty of the State. The law intimates no interference with parental rights. It guards the rights of the child when the parent neglects them."

Compulsory Measures in Several States

Several states have already adopted such measures. The State of Massachusetts embodies two modes of partial compulsion in its school system, the *truant* law and the law requiring annually three months' attendance at school as a condition of employment in mills and factories. The nature of the truant law and its results are well known to all interested in popular education. It is fully discussed in reports of the superintendent of public schools in Boston, Hon. J. D. Philbrick, 1861. . . .

Truancy in Boston

The Boston School committee in their report, 1863, say "No one who passes through our streets, in school hours, but must be painfully impressed with the conviction that we are very far from having yet successfully grappled with this momentous evil." The same doubt is expressed in the report of 1867, and the further confession made that though the truant laws are enforced in a spirit of wise moderation, yet the discipline of truants "is not an agreeable feature in our system of public instruction." The law evidently is not entirely acceptable, and they who administer it are apprehensive lest it may interfere with individual liberty of action and punish as a crime the vagrancy or truancy which is a misfortune. It also involves the broad question of the comparative right of the State and of parents over children during school-hours, and as commitment to a reformatory for one or more years is one of the penalties of truancy, the question has already been brought into the courts on the plea that such commitment is unconstitutional, it being imprisonment without due process of law, and a violation of the bill of rights, which declares all men to have certain inherent rights, among which is liberty.

ADVERSE DECISION OF THE SUPREME COURT OF ILLINOIS

On these grounds the supreme court of Illinois has discharged from custody a boy who had been committed to the reform school of Chicago, on the plea that the good of society required he should be sent to said school for instruction, employment, and reformation. The opinion of the court is followed by annotations. . . .

We make the following extracts from these annotations: "The principle of the absorption of the child in and its complete subjection to the despotism of the State is wholly inadmissible in the civilized world."

"The education of children is a branch of parental duty, and the municipal law should not disturb this relation except for the strongest reasons."

"The absorption of this relation" by the State "would not only tend to wither motives to action, but necessarily in time alienate the father's natural affections."

"If a father imprisoned his child for one year, the majesty of the law would frown upon the unnatural act. Can the State exceed the power of the parent, except in punishing crime?"

"If, without crime, without the conviction of any offense, the children of the State are to be confined for the good of society, then society had better be reduced to its original elements, and free government acknowledged a failure. . . ."

Although it is very evident that this Illinois case does not touch what is technically understood by compulsory education—a law obliging parents to provide a reasonable amount of instruction for children, either in schools of their own selection or in the public schools—yet it suffices to show that neither society nor the courts are unanimous upon the main question, and hence whatever laws are enacted should be the result of wisdom tempered by prudence, protecting society against the dangers of ignorance, the child against cruel exactions of avaricious parents, tax-payers against the squandering of their money, and also taking care lest parents or children suffer by summary proceedings or harsh judgments. The law ought to bear upon parents to compel them to place their children at school, and should not visit upon the children the sin of the parents, which generally is the cause of truancy. . . .

AMERICAN COMPULSORY LAWS

Compulsory laws and truant-laws to prevent the increasing evils of absenteeism have in modified forms been enacted in several States, the results of which will be as a lamp of experience to guide other States in their school legislation. We give below the text of the laws lately enacted . . .

Legislation in Texas

An Act to organize and maintain a system of public free schools.
Approved April 24, 1871.

Sec. 6. The board of school directors shall require the attendance in the public schools of their respective districts of all the scholastic population thereof, for a term of at least four months of each and every year; and should any of said scholastic population neglect or refuse to attend said schools, each and every parent or guardian of such child or ward neglecting or refusing to attend shall be deemed guilty of a misdemeanor, and upon trial and conviction thereof before any court of competent jurisdiction shall be fined in a sum not to exceed twenty-five dollars for each and every such offense, and shall pay the costs of the prosecution; and all moneys collected for fines, under the provision of this section, shall be paid into and become a part of the public school fund of the district where the penalty was incurred: *Provided,* that when any child or ward of scholastic age may be shown to have received regular instruction from any private teacher having a proper certificate of competency, or when it may be shown that said child or ward was prevented by ill health from attending school, or that there was no public school within three miles of the residence of said child or ward, or that said absence was caused by reason of danger from hostile Indians, this shall exempt from the operation of the penalty contemplated by this section: *And provided further,* that nothing in this act shall be so construed as to compel the attendance of a child under ten years of age in the public free schools when there is no school established within one mile of the residence of said child or ward.

Legislation in Michigan

(*Enacted and amended by the legislature at its session in 1871.*)
An Act to compel children to attend school.

Section 1. *The People of the State of Michigan enact,* That every parent, guardian, or other person in the State of Michigan having control and charge of a child or children between the ages of eight and fourteen years, shall be required to send any such child or children to a public school for a period of at least twelve weeks in each school year, commencing on the first Monday of September, in the year of our Lord eighteen hundred and seventy-one, at least six weeks of which shall be consecutive, unless such child or children are excused from such attendance by the board of the school district in which such parents or guardians reside, upon its being shown to their satisfaction that his bodily or mental condition has been such as to prevent his attendance at school or application to study for the period required, or that such child or children are taught in a private school, or at home, in such branches as are usually taught in the public school: *Provided,* In case a public school shall not be taught for three months during the year, within two miles by the nearest traveled road, of the residence of any person within the school district, he shall not be liable to the provisions of this act. . . .

LEGISLATION IN NEW HAMPSHIRE

An Act to compel children to attend school.
Approved July 14, 1871.

Section 1. *Be it enacted by the senate and house of representatives, in general court convened:* That every parent, guardian, master, or other person having the custody, control, or charge, of any child between the age of eight and fourteen years, residing in any school district in which a public school is annually taught for the period of twelve weeks or more, within two miles by the nearest traveled road from his residence, shall cause such child to attend such public school for twelve weeks at least in every year, from and after the 1st day of September next, six weeks at least of which attendance shall be consecutive, unless such child shall be excused from such attendance by the school committee of the town, or the board of education, or the superintending school committee of such district, upon its being shown to their satisfaction that the physical or mental condition of such child was such as to prevent his attendance at school for the period required, or that such child was instructed in a private school, or at home, for at least twelve weeks during such year, in the branches of education required to be taught in the public schools, or, having acquired those branches, in other more advanced studies. . . .

HISTORICAL SKETCH OF COMPULSORY EDUCATION

For a clearer understanding of this subject it is well to inquire what nations have adopted the compulsory system, and how has that system been enforced. It is not a novel expedient, nor the decree of despotic governments. It dates from the era of Solon, and is incorporated in the legislation of the most enlightened European nations. . . . The laws of Solon prescribed "that every man should have his son instructed in music and gymnastics."

In Sparta, according to the laws of Lycurgus, the State took the education of children, from their seventh year, entirely into its own hands.

Charlemagne founded primary schools and compelled the children of all his courtiers to attend them.

Martin Luther said, "It is my opinion that the government ought to *compel* parents to send their children to school." It is a characteristic of the reformers that they considered the school an essential instrument in the service of God. Attendance upon catechism was compulsory, and for every child found in the street, during the hour of religious instruction, the parents had to pay a fine, which went into the poor-box.

In 1649, the synod of Würtemberg made attendance at school compulsory under penalty of a fine. In 1787 this attendance was required from the sixth to the fourteenth year.

In Saxony the law of 1773 made attendance at school compulsory from the fifth to the fourteenth year, and provided that children who went to service before their fourteenth year should attend school two hours daily at the expense of their masters. The law of 1804 was more stringent, and imposed a heavy fine upon delinquents. A similar law was enacted in Bavaria in 1802.

In France, says M. Durny, "Compulsory education is ancient and of noble origin." In 1795 it was ordered that all children throughout the republic should be compelled to attend school; but this regulation, like many others during that sad period, remained a dead letter, nor was it revived by the admirable law of 1833, nor the more recent law of 1850. The attendance at school is consequently very irregular, nor was the late Emperor able to prevent it. The consequence of this has been signally exemplified by late events.

In Prussia compulsory education has been most efficiently enforced, and its practical results can be easily computed. The first attempt at more regular attendance at school was in 1658. This was repeated in 1716. By a regulation of August 12, 1763, it was ordered that all children be sent to school from the fifth to the fourteenth year. This order was revived in 1794, and in 1819 severe penalties were imposed. The result is that in 1864, out of three million children of school-age, only 130,000 did not attend school, and an officer at Potsdam, having in charge the examination of recruits for the army, received in the space of twelve years only three soldiers who could neither read nor write. In country districts where children live farther than two miles from the school, they are not obliged to attend before the completion of the sixth year; when the distance is greater, not before the seventh year. Similar laws prevail in all the German States.

In Sweden, Norway, and Denmark, parents who do not send their children to school are subject to a fine, and, either from this cause or the conviction of the value of education, out of 385,000 Swedish children in 1862, only 9,131 were uninstructed.

In all Switzerland, except four cantons, education is obligatory. In Zurich the school-age extends from five to sixteen, inclusive. Not only parents and guardians, but also masters of trades are required to have children attend school. In the canton of Berne, young soldiers must read, write, and solve ordinary examples in arithmetic, or attend school in the barracks. Ordinarily not more than three or five in a hundred are of this class. M. Baudouin, the French school commissioner to Switzerland in 1865, says: "When one travels in this country, not to admire the beauty of the landscapes, but to examine the institutions, and to seek counsel in results, he has no need to look at territorial limits to know that he is passing from a canton in which education has been neglected, into another in which it has been carefully cultivated."

In view of the amount of gross ignorance that has so far prevailed in England, the two extremes of the most stolid ignorance and the highest culture existing in close contact, many influential Englishmen have publicly declared that the remedy is to be found in compulsory education.

THE KALAMAZOO DECISION *

(Mr. Justice Cooley delivered the opinion of the Court.)

The bill in this case is filed to restrain the collection of such portion of the school taxes assessed against complainants for the year 1872, as have been voted for the support of the high school in that village, and for the payment of the salary of the superintendent. While, nominally, this is the end sought to be attained by the bill, the real purpose of the suit is wider and vastly more comprehensive than this brief statement would indicate, inasmuch as it seeks a judicial determination of the right of school authorities, in what are called union school districts of the state, to levy taxes upon the general public for the support of what in this state are known as high schools, and to make free by such taxation the instruction of children in other languages than the English.

The more general question which the record presents we shall endeavor to state in our own language, but so as to make it stand out distinctly as a naked question of law, disconnected from all considerations of policy or expediency; in which light alone are we at liberty to consider it. It is, as we understand it, that there is no authority in this state to make the high schools free by taxation levied on the people at large. The argument is that while there may be no constitutional provision expressly prohibiting such taxation, the general course of legislation in the state and the general understanding of the people have been such as to require us to regard the instruction in the classics and in living modern languages in these schools as in the nature not of practical and therefore necessary instruction for the benefit of the people at large, but rather as accomplishments for the

* *Stuart v. School District No. 1 of Kalamazoo,* 30 Mich. 69 (1874).

Toward Universal Schooling

few, to be sought after in the main by those best able to pay for them, and to be paid for by those who seek them, and not by general tax. And not only has this been the general state policy, but this higher learning of itself, when supplied by the state, is so far a matter of private concern to those who receive it that the courts ought to declare it incompetent to supply it wholly at the public expense. This is in substance, as we understand it, the position of the complainants in this suit.

When this doctrine was broached to us, we must confess to no little surprise that the legislation and policy of our state were appealed to against the right of the state to furnish a liberal education to the youth of the state in schools brought within the reach of all classes. We supposed it had always been understood in this state that education, not merely in the rudiments, but in an enlarged sense, was regarded as an important practical advantage to be supplied at their option to rich and poor alike, and not as something pertaining merely to culture and accomplishment to be brought as such within the reach of those whose accumulated wealth enabled them to pay for it. As this, however, is now so seriously disputed, it may be necessary, perhaps, to take a brief survey of the legislation and general course, not only of the state, but of the antecedent territory, on the subject.

In 1827 the educational system was supplemented by "an act for the establishment of common schools," which is also worthy of special attention and reflection, as indicating what was understood at that day by the common schools which were proposed to be established.

The first section of that act provided "that every township within this territory, containing fifty families or householders, shall be provided with a good schoolmaster or schoolmasters, of good morals, to teach children to read and write, and to instruct them in the English or French language, as well as in arithmetic, orthography, and decent behavior, for such term of time as shall be equivalent to six months for one school in each year. And every township containing one hundred families or householders, shall be provided with such schoolmaster or teacher for such term of time as shall be equivalent to twelve months for one school in each year. And every township containing one hundred and fifty families or householders shall be provided with such schoolmaster or teacher for such term of time as shall be equivalent to six months in each year, and shall, in addition thereto, be provided with a schoolmaster or teacher, as above described, to instruct children in the English language for such term of time as shall be equivalent to twelve months for one school in each year. And every township containing two hundred families or householders shall be provided with a grammar schoolmaster, of good morals, *well instructed in the Latin, French and English languages,* and shall, in addition thereto, be provided with a schoolmaster or teacher, as above described, to instruct children in the English language, for such term of time as shall be equivalent to twelve months for each of said schools in each year." And the townships respectively were required under a heavy penalty, to be levied in case of default on the inhabitants generally, to keep and maintain the schools so provided for.—*Code of 1827, p. 448; Territorial Laws, Vol. 2, p. 472.*

Here, then, was a general law, which, under the name of common schools, required not only schools for elementary instruction, but also grammar schools to be maintained. The qualifications required in teachers of grammar schools were such as to leave it open to no doubt that grammar schools in the sense understood in England and the Eastern states were intended, in which instruction in the classics should be given, as well as in such higher branches of learning as would not usually be taught in the schools of lowest grade. How is it possible, then, to say, as the exigencies of complainants' case require them to do, that the term common or primary schools, as made use of in our legislation, has a known and definite meaning which limits it to the ordinary district schools, and that consequently the legislative authority to levy taxes for the primary schools cannot be held to embrace taxation for the schools supported by village and city districts in which a higher grade of learning is imparted.

It is probable that this act, like that of 1817, was found in advance of the demands of the people of the territory, or of their ability to support high schools, and it was repealed in 1833, and another passed which did not expressly require the establishment or support of schools of secondary grade, but which provided only for school directors, who must maintain a district school at least three months in each year.—*Code of 1833, p. 129.* The act contains no express limitations upon their powers, but it is not important now to consider whether or not they extended to the establishment of grammar schools as district schools, where, in their judgment, they might be required. Such schools would certainly not be out of harmony with any territorial policy that as yet had been developed or indicated.

Thus stood the law when the constitution of 1835 was adopted. The article on education in that instrument contained the following provisions:

"2. The legislature shall encourage by all suitable means the promotion of intellectual, scientific and agricultural improvement. The proceeds of all lands that have been, or hereafter may be, granted by the United States to this state for the support of schools, which shall hereafter be sold or disposed of, shall be and remain a perpetual fund, the interest of which, together with the rents of all such unsold lands, shall be inviolably appropriated to the support of schools throughout the state.

"3. The legislature shall provide for a system of common schools, by which a school shall be kept up and supported in each school district at

Toward Universal Schooling 199

least three months in every year; and any school district neglecting to keep up and support such a school may be deprived of its equal proportion of the interest of the public fund."

The fifth section provided for the support of the university, "with such branches as the public convenience may hereafter demand for the promotion of literature, the arts and sciences," etc. Two things are specially noticeable in these provisions: *first,* that they contemplated provision by the state for a complete system of instruction, beginning with that of the primary school and ending with that of the university; *second,* that while the legislature was required to make provision for district schools for at least three months in each year, no restriction was imposed upon its power to establish schools intermediate the common district school and the university, and we find nothing to indicate an intent to limit their discretion as to the class or grade of schools to which the proceeds of school lands might be devoted, or as to the range of studies or grade of instruction which might be provided for in the district schools.

In the very first executive message after the constitution went into effect, the governor, in view of the fact that "our institutions have leveled the artificial distinctions existing in the societies of other countries, and have left open to every one the avenues to distinction and honor," admonished the legislature that it was their "imperious duty to secure to the state a general diffusion of knowledge," and that "this can in no wise be so certainly effected as by the perfect organization of a uniform and liberal system of common schools." Their "attention was therefore called to the effectuation of a perfect school system, open to all classes, as the surest basis of public happiness and prosperity." In his second message he repeated his admonitions, advising that provision be made for ample compensation to teachers, that those of the highest character, both moral and intellectual, might be secured, and urging that the "youth be taught the first principles in morals, in science, and in government, commencing their studies in the primary schools, elevating its grades as you approach the district seminary, and continue its progress till you arrive at the university." This message indicated no plan, but referred the legislature to the report of the superintendent, who would recommend a general system.

The system reported by superintendent Pierce contemplated a university, with branches in different parts of the state as preparatory schools, and district schools. This is the parent of our present system, and though its author did not find the legislature prepared to accept all his views, the result has demonstrated that he was only a few years in advance of his generation, and that the changes in our school system which have since been adopted have been in the direction of the views which he then held and urged upon the public. And an examination of his official report for

1837 will show that the free schools he then favored were schools which taught something more than the rudiments of a common education; which were to give to the poor the advantages of the rich, and enable both alike to obtain within the state an education broad and liberal, as well as practical.

It would be instructive to make liberal extracts from this report did time and space permit. The superintendent would have teachers thoroughly trained, and he would have the great object of common schools "to furnish good instruction in all the elementary and common branches of knowledge, for all classes of community, *as good, indeed, for the poorest boy of the state as the rich man can furnish for his children with all his wealth.*" The context shows that he had the systems of Prussia and of New England in view, and that he proposed by a free school system to fit the children of the poor as well as of the rich for the highest spheres of activity and influence.

It might also be useful in this connection to show that the Prussian system and that "of the Puritans," of which he speaks in such terms of praise, resemble in their main features, so far as bringing within the reach of all a regular gradation of schools is concerned, the system of public instruction as it prevails in this state to-day. But it is not necessary for the purposes of the present case to enter upon this subject. It must suffice to say that the law of 1827, which provided for grammar schools as a grade of common schools, was adopted from laws which from a very early period had been in existence in Massachusetts, and which in like manner, under heavy penalties, compelled the support of these grammar schools in every considerable town.—See *Mass. Laws, 1789, p. 39;* compare *General Stat., 1860, p. 215,* § 2.

It now becomes important to see whether the constitutional convention and the people, in 1850, did any thing to undo what previously had been accomplished towards furnishing high schools as a part of the primary school system. The convention certainly did nothing to that end. On the contrary, they demonstrated in the most unmistakable manner that they cherished no such desire or purpose. The article on education as originally reported, while providing for free schools to be kept in each district at least three months in every year, added that "the English language and no other shall be taught in such schools." Attention was called to this provision, and it was amended so as to read that instruction should be "conducted in the English language." The reason for the change was fully given, that as it was reported it might be understood to prohibit the teaching of other languages than the English in the primary schools; a result that was not desired. Judge Whipple stated in the convention that, in the section from which he came, French and German were taught, and "it is a most valuable improvement of the common school system." The late superintendent Pierce said that in some schools Latin was taught, and that he himself had taught Latin in a common school. He would not adopt any provision by which any knowledge would be excluded. "All that we ought to do is this: we should say the legislature shall establish primary schools." This, in his opinion, would give full power, and the details could be left to legislation.—See *Debates of the Convention, 269, 549.*

The instrument submitted by the convention to the people and adopted by them provided for the establishment of free schools in every school district for at least three months in each year, and for the university. By the aid of these we have every reason to believe the people expected a complete collegiate education might be obtained. The branches of the university had ceased to exist; the university had no preparatory department, and it must either have been understood that young men were to be prepared for the university in the common schools, or else that they should go abroad for the purpose, or be prepared in private schools. Private schools adapted to the purpose were almost unknown in the state, and comparatively a very few persons were at that time of sufficient pecuniary ability to educate their children abroad. The inference seems irresistible that the people expected the tendency towards the establishment of high schools in the primary school districts would continue until every locality capable of supporting one was supplied. And this inference is strengthened by the fact that a considerable number of our union schools date their establishment from the year 1850 and the two or three years following.

If these facts do not demonstrate clearly and conclusively a general state policy, beginning in 1817 and continuing until after the adoption of the present constitution, in the direction of free schools in which education, and at their option the elements of classical education, might be brought within the reach of all the children of the state, then, as it seems to us, nothing can demonstrate it.

We might follow the subject further, and show that the subsequent legislation has all concurred with this policy, but it would be a waste of time and labor. We content ourselves with the statement that neither in our state policy, in our constitution, or in our laws, do we find the primary school districts restricted in the branches of knowledge which their officers may cause to be taught, or the grade of instruction that may be given, if their voters consent in regular form to bear the expense and raise the taxes for the purpose.

It follows that the decree dismissing the bill was right, and should be affirmed.

The other Justices concurred.

EFFECTS OF THE COMPULSORY EDUCATION ACT IN NEW YORK CITY [*]

During the year the Board of Education added to the number of "attendance officers" employed for the enforcement of the Compulsory Education Act, and, also, it took measures looking to the providing and equipping of a "truant school."

Much of the time of the attendance officers was employed in work connected with the "biennial school census," which was taken for the first time in 1895, yet they found time to make 62,485 visits to homes, schools, stores, factories, etc.

As a result of their labors, 16,603 cases were investigated and closed. They returned to school 3,655 truants and placed in school 1,728 non-attendants. Nine truants and non-attendants were committed to reformatory institutions by parents through attendance officers. . . .

The following Table, [adapted] *obtained from the Records of the Police Department, shows the number of children between eight and fourteen years of age arrested for five years preceding the enactment of the* [compulsory education] *law, and for the last five years, together with the cause of arrest:*

CAUSE OF ARREST	1870-1874	1891-1895
Truancy	493	140
Vagrancy	999	254
Disorderly conduct	1,067	503
Violating city ordinance	114	83
Assault and battery	92	45
Malicious mischief	40	36
Intoxication	103	19
Felonious assault	14	28
Petty larceny	1,195	344
Larceny from the person	80	6
Grand larceny	132	56
Burglary	107	134
Robbery	21	2
Suspicious persons	109	128
Held for further examination	1,424	754
All other causes	114	14
TOTAL	6,105	2,546

[*] Fifty-fourth Annual Report of the Board of Education, New York City, for the year 1895, pp. 152-3.

CHILD REFORM THROUGH EDUCATION FOR A TRADE *

. . . my experience is that most boys will work if given any kind of an encouraging opportunity. The lack of a chance is often responsible for idleness. Ninety-six per cent of our boys and girls are forced out of the grammar school to fight the battles of life. They must have a chance to earn a living under such reasonably favorable conditions as not to destroy all chance of happiness or else they must become idlers and loafers. My own experience is that our common school education too often fails to equip them for earning more than the most scanty wages. An opportunity between the sixth and eighth grades in our city schools for children of the toiling masses to learn some kind of useful trade or valuable work with the hands —to learn to do what their fathers do—is a reform in our educational system which the champions of child labor must, in my opinion, espouse if they would round out a systematic and consistent plan of battle in this fight for the salvation of the children. I want to see the time come in this country when a boy of fourteen years of age up may be a valuable help to the plumber, the carpenter or the printer at a decent wage, instead of going to the messenger service and the street. I do not believe that juvenile labor should trespass upon the legitimate occupations of men and women, but we must equip these children for some kind of industrial efficiency and usefulness, or enlarge our reformatories and prisons for their care and maintenance. One of the saddest things in my experience as judge of the juvenile court has been the little fellows who have requested me to send them to the reform school in order that they might learn a trade. The principal of a school once said to me: "Judge, why don't you send that boy to the reform school so that he can learn a trade?" On behalf of the boy, I replied: "In God's name, why don't you people on the Board of Education give him an opportunity to learn a trade at home?" I ask you, is it fair, just or decent that in most of the cities of this country an American boy has no opportunity to learn a trade, to capacitate himself for joyous, useful work with his hands, unless he commits a crime? And yet, I am compelled to say to you, that such is the condition in this country.

* Ben R. Lindsey, "Child Labor Legislation in the Western States," in *The Addresses at the Annual Meeting of the National Child Labor Committee, The Annals of the American Academy of Political and Social Science,* Vol. 25, May 1905, p. xxx.

THE OREGON DECISION *

(Mr. Justice McReynolds delivered the opinion of the Court.)

These appeals are from decrees, based upon undenied allegations, which granted preliminary orders restraining appellants from threatening or attempting to enforce the Compulsory Education Act adopted November 7, 1922, under the initiative provision of her Constitution by the voters of Oregon. Jud. Code, § 266. They present the same points of law; there are no controverted questions of fact. Rights said to be guaranteed by the federal Constitution were specially set up, and appropriate prayers asked for their protection.

The challenged Act, effective September 1, 1926, requires every parent, guardian or other person having control or charge or custody of a child between eight and sixteen years to send him "to a public school for the period of time a public school shall be held during the current year" in the district where the child resides; and failure so to do is declared a misdemeanor. There are exemptions—not specially important here—for children who are not normal, or who have completed the eighth grade, or who reside at considerable distances from any public school, or whose parents or guardians hold special permits from the County Superintendent. The manifest purpose is to compel general attendance at public schools by normal children, between eight and sixteen, who have not completed the eighth grade. And without doubt enforcement of the statute would seriously impair, perhaps destroy, the profitable features of appellees' business and greatly diminish the value of their property.

Appellee, the Society of Sisters, is an Oregon corporation, organized in 1880, with power to care for orphans, educate and instruct the youth, establish and maintain academies or schools, and acquire necessary real and personal property. It has long devoted its property and effort to the secular and religious education and care of children, and has acquired the valuable good will of many parents and guardians. It conducts interdependent primary and high schools and junior colleges, and maintains orphanages for the custody and control of children between eight and sixteen. In its primary schools many children between those ages are taught the subjects usually pursued in Oregon public schools during the first eight years. Systematic religious instruction and moral training according to the tenets of the Roman Catholic Church are also regularly provided. All courses of study, both temporal and religious, contemplate continuity of training under appellee's charge; the primary schools are essential to

---

* *Pierce v. Society of Sisters,* 268 U.S. 510 (1925).

the system and the most profitable. It owns valuable buildings, especially constructed and equipped for school purposes. The business is remunerative—the annual income from primary schools exceeds thirty thousand dollars—and the successful conduct of this requires long time contracts with teachers and parents. The Compulsory Education Act of 1922 has already caused the withdrawal from its schools of children who would otherwise continue, and their income has steadily declined. The appellants, public officers, have proclaimed their purpose strictly to enforce the statute.

After setting out the above facts the Society's bill alleges that the enactment conflicts with the right of parents to choose schools where their children will receive appropriate mental and religious training, the right of the child to influence the parents' choice of a school, the right of schools and teachers therein to engage in a useful business or profession, and is accordingly repugnant to the Constitution and void. And, further, that unless enforcement of the measure is enjoined the corporation's business and property will suffer irreparable injury.

Appellee, Hill Military Academy, is a private corporation organized in 1908 under the laws of Oregon, engaged in owning, operating and conducting for profit an elementary, college preparatory and military training school for boys between the ages of five and twenty-one years. The average attendance is one hundred, and the annual fees received for each student amount to some eight hundred dollars. The elementary department is divided into eight grades, as in the public schools; the college preparatory department has four grades, similar to those of the public high schools; the courses of study conform to the requirements of the State Board of Education. Military instruction and training are also given, under the supervision of an Army officer. It owns considerable real and personal property, some useful only for school purposes. The business and incident good will are very valuable. In order to conduct its affairs long time contracts must be made for supplies, equipment, teachers and pupils. Appellants, law officers of the State and County, have publicly announced that the Act of November 7, 1922, is valid and have declared their intention to enforce it. By reason of the statute and threat of enforcement appellee's business is being destroyed and its property depreciated; parents and guardians are refusing to make contracts for the future instruction of their sons, and some are being withdrawn.

The Academy's bill states the foregoing facts and then alleges that the challenged Act contravenes the corporation's rights guaranteed by the Fourteenth Amendment and that unless appellants are restrained from proclaiming its validity and threatening to enforce it irreparable injury will result. The prayer is for an appropriate injunction.

No answer was interposed in either cause, and after proper notices they were heard by three judges (Jud. Code § 266) on motions for preliminary injunctions upon the specifically alleged facts. The court ruled that the Fourteenth Amendment guaranteed appellees against the deprivation of their property without due process of law consequent upon the unlawful interference by appellants with the free choice of patrons, present and prospective. It declared the right to conduct schools was property and that parents and guardians, as a part of their liberty, might direct the education of children by selecting reputable teachers and places. Also, that these schools were not unfit or harmful to the public, and that enforcement of the challenged statute would unlawfully deprive them of patronage and thereby destroy their owners' business and property. Finally, that the threats to enforce the Act would continue to cause irreparable injury; and the suits were not premature.

No question is raised concerning the power of the State reasonably to regulate all schools, to inspect, supervise and examine them, their teachers and pupils; to require that all children of proper age attend some school, that teachers shall be of good moral character and patriotic disposition, that certain studies plainly essential to good citizenship must be taught, and that nothing be taught which is manifestly inimical to the public welfare.

The inevitable practical result of enforcing the Act under consideration would be destruction of appellees' primary schools, and perhaps all other private primary schools for normal children within the State of Oregon. These parties are engaged in a kind of undertaking not inherently harmful, but long regarded as useful and meritorious. Certainly there is nothing in the present records to indicate that they have failed to discharge their obligations to patrons, students or the State. And there are no peculiar circumstances or present emergencies which demand extraordinary measures relative to primary education.

Under the doctrine of *Meyer* v. *Nebraska,* 262 U.S. 390, we think it entirely plain that the Act of 1922 unreasonably interferes with the liberty of parents and guardians to direct the upbringing and education of children under their control. As often heretofore pointed out, rights guaranteed by the Constitution may not be abridged by legislation which has no reasonable relation to some purpose within the competency of the State. The fundamental theory of liberty upon which all governments in this Union repose excludes any general power of the State to standardize its children by forcing them to accept instruction from public teachers only. The child is not the mere creature of the State; those who nurture him and direct his destiny have the right, coupled with the high duty, to recognize and prepare him for additional obligations. . . .

Generally it is entirely true, as urged by counsel, that no person in any business has such an interest in possible customers as to enable him to restrain exercise of proper power of the State upon the ground that he will be deprived of patronage. But the injunctions here sought are not against the exercise of any *proper* power. Plaintiffs asked protection against arbitrary, unreasonable and unlawful interference with their patrons and the consequent destruction of their business and property. Their interest is clear and immediate, within the rule approved in *Truax* v. *Raich, Truax* v. *Corrigan* and *Terrace* v. *Thompson, supra,* and many other cases where injunctions have issued to protect business enterprises against interference with the freedom of patrons or customers. *Hitchman Coal & Coke Co.* v. *Mitchell,* 245 U.S. 229; *Duplex Printing Press Co.* v. *Deering,* 254 U.S. 443; *American Steel Foundries* v. *Tri-City Central Trades Council,* 257 U.S. 184; *Nebraska District* v. *McKelvie,* 262 U.S. 404; *Truax* v. *Corrigan, supra,* and cases there cited.

The suits were not premature. The injury to appellees was present and very real, not a mere possibility in the remote future. If no relief had been possible prior to the effective date of the Act, the injury would have become irreparable. Prevention of impending injury by unlawful action is a well recognized function of courts of equity.

The decrees below are

Affirmed.

THE SORTING MACHINE *

The educational system may be thought of as an enormous complicated machine for sorting and ticketing and routing children through life. Young children are fed in at one end to a moving belt which conveys them past all sorts of inspecting stations. One large group is almost immediately brushed off into a bin labeled "nonreaders," "first-grade repeaters," or "opportunity class" where they stay for eight or ten years and are then released through a chute to the outside world to become "hewers of wood and drawers of water." The great body of children move ahead on the main belt, losing a few here and there who are "kept back" for repeated inspection.

At a station labeled "high school" there are several types of inspection and the main belt divides into smaller belts which diverge slightly from each other. From some of the belts the children, now become youths, are unceremoniously dumped down chutes into the outside world, while the other belts, labeled "college preparatory," "commercial," "vocational" roll

* W. Lloyd Warner et al., *Who Shall Be Educated?* (New York, Harper, 1944), pp. 49-54.

steadily on. The young people are inspected not only for brains and learning ability, but also for skin color, pronunciation, cut of clothes, table manners, parental bank account. Strangely enough they are not inspected for moral integrity, honesty, or other qualities which go under the name of "character."

At the end of the high-school division several of the belts project their human freight into the outside labor market, and the sorting machine is now much smaller, housing a few narrow conveyors labeled "college," "professional school," and "trade school." The inspectors quickly shunt aside the majority of this small band of young men and women into the labor market, leaving a few indeed who reach the next station, labeled "bachelor's degree," which is the end of the machine really, though there is a small extension called "graduate school."

Whatever figure of speech we use, the school system appears to be a sorting device with various selective principles operating. In addition to the principle of intellectual ability, there are such principles of selection as economic status, social class, and social personality. There is little or no selection for moral character.

The Hometown school has already sorted out Tom Brown from Bob Jones. Tom will be promoted regularly and readied for college. Bob will be dropped as soon as possible. It is not yet clear what will happen to Joe Sienkowitz, but it appears that he will finish high school and because of his talent his teachers may help him to get a scholarship for study of music. There are probably two or three other boys in Tom Brown's class, fully as able as Tom, but without any special artistic talent, who will have to stop their education at the end of high school because their way into college is blocked by lack of money.

We can see how much selection takes place by looking at the figures for the numbers of young people who reach various levels of the educational ladder. Table I gives the number of youth out of a thousand who were reaching certain rungs of the ladder on two dates a generation apart, 1938 and 1910. The high school is much less selective at present than it was a generation ago. The college has also lost some of its selective quality though it remains a highly selective institution.

Through its function as a sorting agency the educational system is supposed to sift out the people with best brains and ability and to help them rise to the top. Thus the school is not only a system of education, it is also a system of elections. In America this system of elections is not 100 per cent efficient. That is, it does not succeed in selecting all the people with the best brains and ability and helping them to rise in the status system.

TABLE I

THE SCHOOL AS A SELECTING AGENCY *

Number of People out of Every Thousand Who Reach a Given Educational Level

Level	1938	1910
First year high school (age 14)	850	310
Third year high school (age 16)	580	140
Graduation from high school (age 18)	450	93
Entrance to college or a similar educational institution	150	67
Graduation from college (Bachelor's degree)	70	23
Master's degree	9	1.5
Doctor of Philosophy	1.3	

* These figures are based on enrollment figures for school and college appearing in the Biennial Surveys of the United States Office of Education.

EDUCATIONAL OPPORTUNITY IS NOT EQUALLY AVAILABLE TO ALL

There are two senses in which we might say that educational opportunity is equally available to all children. We could speak of equal educational opportunity if all children and young people went to schools of their own choosing as long as they or their parents pleased. In that sense we fall far short of providing equal educational opportunity and we shall probably never attain such a goal.

In a more limited sense we might speak of equality of educational opportunity if all children and young people exceeding a given level of intellectual ability were enabled to attend schools and colleges up to some specified level. This is the only practicable kind of equality of educational opportunity. For example, if all boys and girls with I.Q.'s over 100 were able to attend high school up to the age of eighteen, and if all young people with I.Q.'s over 110 were able to attend college for four years, we could say that equality of educational opportunity existed to a considerable degree.

It is possible to investigate the availability of educational opportunity in this sense in various parts of the country. For example, a study of youth in Pennsylvania was conducted about a decade ago by the State Department of Public Instruction and the American Youth Commission.[1] The socio-

[1] Harlan Updegraff, *Inventory of Youth in Pennsylvania* (Washington, D. C., American Youth Commission, American Council on Education, 1936. Mimeographed). Data used here are taken from Tables 3, 4, 5, 6, and 14 of the Appendix. Names of pupils were obtained from the sixth-grade rolls of 1926 in school districts distributed so as to be proportional to the number of public-school pupils enrolled

economic status [2] and educational history were ascertained for a group of 910 pupils with intelligence quotients of 110 or above. It is generally assumed that pupils with intelligence quotients above 110 are good college material. This group of superior pupils was divided into two subgroups on the basis of socio-economic status. Of the upper socio-economic group, 93 per cent graduated from high school and 57 per cent attended college. Of the lower socio-economic group, 72 per cent graduated from high school and 13 per cent attended college. Further study of the data in Table II will show even more clearly that the group with below-average socio-economic status had relatively less educational opportunity than the group with above-average socio-economic status, although both groups were about equal in intellectual ability.

A similar conclusion must be drawn from a study made by Helen B. Goetsch [3] on 1,023 able students who graduated from Milwaukee high schools in 1937 and 1938. These students all had I.Q.'s of 117 or above. The income of their parents is directly related to college attendance, as is

in each of the various types of districts and communities in the state. Data concerning 3,022 of these pupils were available in 1934-35, giving their intelligence quotients, scores on the Chapman-Sims socio-economic scale, and educational history. There were 910 of these pupils with intelligence quotients of 110 or more. The mean score on the Chapman-Sims scale was 5.0 for the group of 3,022 pupils. Accordingly we shall divide the group of superior intelligence into a subgroup with above-average socio-economic status, as indicated by a Chapman-Sims score of 5 or by a Chapman-Sims score of less than 5. The data are presented in Table II. From this table the disadvantage of the group with below-average socio-economic status is at once evident.

[2] Socio-economic status is not the same as social class, although in many ways they are the same. Those who study the first emphasize economic criteria such as occupation and income; those who study social class emphasize participation in such social institutions as the family, cliques, associations, and churches within a community and the evaluation and ranking of this behavior by members of the same community. The Chapman-Sims scale takes into account the size of one's library, possession of automobile, telephone, etc. If people were ranked on the basis of socio-economic status, the great majority of them, probably more than four-fifths, would have the same position relative to others that their social class position gives them. Since there have been no studies of education in relation to social class position aside from the few that are reported in this book, we must rely upon the studies of education in relation to socio-economic status for information that certainly is relevant to our interests in this book.

[3] Helen B. Goetsch, *Parental Income and College Opportunities* (Teachers College Contributions to Education, No. 795, New York, Teachers College, Columbia University, 1940). This group fell within percentiles 86-100 on a state-wide scholastic aptitude test given to high-school seniors. Their I.Q.'s ranged from 117 to 146. In April, 1938, 34.5 per cent were in college full-time. The distribution of parental income for this group was not much different from the income distribution for a cross section of Milwaukee families. The relation of full-time college attendance (as of April 1938) and parental income is shown in Table III. The median parental income for those who were in college full- or part-time was $1,721, while the median parental income for those not in college was $1,285.

Table II

RELATION OF INTELLIGENCE TO EDUCATIONAL OPPORTUNITY

(Record of Students with Intelligence Quotients of 110 or Above)

Educational Advance	Socio-economic Status Above Average No.	Per Cent	Socio-economic Status Below Average No.	Per Cent	Total Group No.	Per Cent
Dropped school at eighth grade or below	4	0.7	27	7.9	31	3.4
Completed ninth, tenth, or eleventh grade but did not graduate from high school	36	6.2	69	20.2	105	11.6
Graduated from high school but did not attend college	206	36.3	202	59.0	408	44.8
Attended college	322	56.8	44	12.9	366	40.2
Total	568	100.0	342	100.0	910	100.0

Table III

RELATION OF PARENTAL INCOME TO FULL-TIME COLLEGE ATTENDANCE OF SUPERIOR MILWAUKEE HIGH SCHOOL GRADUATES

Parental Income	Per Cent in College Full-time
$8,000+	100.0
5,000-7,999	92.0
3,000-4,999	72.9
2,000-2,999	44.4
1,500-1,999	28.9
1,000-1,499	25.5
500-999	26.8
Under 500	20.4

shown in Table III. The higher the parents' income, the greater is the proportion who went to college.

The same general result is found in the data of the National Health Survey, which was conducted in eighty-three cities in eighteen states during the winter of 1935-36. When boys and girls of ages sixteen to twenty-four are classified by family income, school attendance increases markedly with increase in family income.[4]

It might be argued, in the face of these facts, that children of families in the lower socio-economic levels do not desire as much education as those from the middle and upper levels. Thus, if public grants were available to pay the living expenses of all high-school pupils who wished to go to school and needed financial help, we might still find that more children of the upper economic levels were attending school. But there are three lines of evidence which indicate that children at the lower economic levels do not have all the educational opportunity they or their parents desire. One is the frequency with which "lack of money" is given as a reason for quitting school.[5] Another is the sharp increase in college and high-school enrollment that came with the establishing of the National Youth Administration student-aid program in 1935. A third is the fact that there is a substantial out-of-pocket cost attached to attendance at a "free" high school. Hand has summarized a number of studies on the cash cost of going to a public high school. He finds this to average $125 a year in several cities.[6] Students can go to school and spend little or no money. But they are then barred from many of the school activities, they cannot even take regular laboratory courses, and they must go around in what is to high-school youngsters the supremely embarrassing condition of having no change to rattle in their pockets, no money to contribute to a party, no possibility of being independent in their dealings with their friends.

[4] Bernard D. Karpinos, "School Attendance as Affected by Prevailing Socio-Economic Factors," *School Review,* 51:39-49 (January 1943).

[5] Howard M. Bell, *Youth Tell Their Story* (American Council on Education, Washington, D. C., 1938), pp. 64ff.

[6] Harold C. Hand, in *General Education in the American High School* (pp. 17-20), by a Committee of the North Central Association of Colleges and Secondary Schools (Chicago: Scott, Foresman and Company, 1942). This money goes for class dues, club dues, fee for laboratory science, mechanical drawing, woodworking, etc., courses; charges for towels, lockers, and gym clothing; band and orchestra instruments and uniforms; textbooks, workbooks, pencils, ink, paper, etc.; subscriptions to school yearbooks, newspapers, magazines, etc.; photos for school yearbooks, excursion costs; graduation announcements, photographs, diploma fees, cap and gown rental; and so on.

THE DESEGREGATION DECISION *

(Mr. Chief Justice Warren delivered the opinion of the Court.)

These cases come to us from the States of Kansas, South Carolina, Virginia, and Delaware. They are premised on different facts and different local conditions, but a common legal question justifies their consideration together in this consolidated opinion.

In each of the cases, minors of the Negro race, through their legal representatives, seek the aid of the courts in obtaining admission to the public schools of their community on a nonsegregated basis. In each instance, they had been denied admission to schools attended by white children under laws requiring or permitting segregation according to race. This segregation was alleged to deprive the plaintiffs of the equal protection of the laws under the Fourteenth Amendment. In each of the cases other than the Delaware case, a three-judge federal district court denied relief to the plaintiffs on the so-called "separate but equal" doctrine announced by this Court in Plessy v. Ferguson, 163 US 537, 41 L ed 256, 16 S Ct 1138. Under that doctrine, equality of treatment is accorded when the races are provided substantially equal facilities, even though these facilities be separate. In the Delaware case, the Supreme Court of Delaware adhered to that doctrine, but ordered that the plaintiffs be admitted to the white schools because of their superiority to the Negro schools.

The plaintiffs contend that segregated public schools are not "equal" and cannot be made "equal," and that hence they are deprived of the equal protection of the laws. Because of the obvious importance of the question presented, the Court took jurisdiction. Argument was heard in the 1952 Term, and reargument was heard this Term on certain questions propounded by the Court.

Reargument was largely devoted to the circumstances surrounding the adoption of the Fourteenth Amendment in 1868. It covered exhaustively consideration of the Amendment in Congress, ratification by the states, then existing practices in racial segregation, and the views of proponents and opponents of the Amendment. This discussion and our own investigation convince us that, although these sources cast some light, it is not enough to resolve the problem with which we are faced. At best, they are inconclusive. The most avid proponents of the post-War Amendments undoubtedly intended them to remove all legal distinctions among "all persons born or naturalized in the United States." Their opponents, just as certainly, were antagonistic to both the letter and the spirit of the

* *Brown v. Board of Education* 347 US 483 (1954) (Notes abridged).

214   *Schooling for All*

Amendments and wished them to have the most limited effect. What others in Congress and the state legislatures had in mind cannot be determined with any degree of certainty.

An additional reason for the inconclusive nature of the Amendment's history, with respect to segregated schools, is the status of public education at that time.[1] In the South, the movement toward free common schools, supported by general taxation, had not yet taken hold. Education of white children was largely in the hands of private groups. Education of Negroes was almost nonexistent, and practically all of the race were illiterate. In fact, any education of Negroes was forbidden by law in some states. Today, in contrast, many Negroes have achieved outstanding success in the arts and sciences as well as in the business and professional world. It is true that public school education at the time of the Amendment had advanced further in the North, but the effect of the Amendment on Northern States was generally ignored in the congressional debates. Even in the North, the conditions of public education did not approximate those existing today. The curriculum was usually rudimentary; ungraded schools were common in rural areas; the school term was but three months a year in many states; and compulsory school attendance was virtually unknown. As a consequence, it is not surprising that there should be so little in the history of the Fourteenth Amendment relating to its intended effect on public education.

In the first cases in this Court construing the Fourteenth Amendment, decided shortly after its adoption, the Court interpreted it as proscribing all state-imposed discriminations against the Negro race.[2] The doctrine

---

[1] For a general study of the development of public education prior to the Amendment, see Butts and Cremin, A History of Education in American Culture (1953), Pts. I, II; Cubberley, Public Education in the United States (1934 ed), chs II-XII. School practices current at the time of the adoption of the Fourteenth Amendment are described in Butts and Cremin, supra, at 269-275; Cubberley, supra, at 288-339, 408-431; Knight, Public Education in the South (1922), chs VIII, IX. See also H Ex Doc No. 315, 41st Cong, 2d Sess (1871). Although the demand for free public schools followed substantially the same pattern in both the North and the South, the development in the South did not begin to gain momentum until about 1850, some twenty years after that in the North. The reasons for the somewhat slower development in the South (e. g., the rural character of the South and the different regional attitudes toward state assistance) are well explained in Cubberley, supra, at 408-423. In the country as a whole, but particularly in the South, the War virtually stopped all progress in public education. Id., at 427-428. The low status of Negro education in all sections of the country, both before and immediately after the War, is described in Beale, A History of Freedom of Teaching in American Schools (1941), 112-132, 175-195. Compulsory school attendance laws were not generally adopted until after the ratification of the Fourteenth Amendment, and it was not until 1918 that such laws were in force in all the states. Cubberley, supra, at 563-565.

[2] Slaughter-House Cases (US) 16 Wall 36, 67-72, 21 L ed 394, 405-407 (1873); Strauder v. West Virginia, 100 US 303, 307, 308, 25 L ed 664-666 (1880):

"It ordains that no State shall deprive any person of life, liberty, or property,

of "separate but equal" did not make its appearance in this Court until 1896 in the case of Plessy v. Ferguson (US) supra, involving not education but transportation.[3] American courts have since labored with the doctrine for over half a century. In this Court, there have been six cases involving the "separate but equal" doctrine in the field of public education. In Cumming v. County Board of Education, 175 US 528, 44 L ed 262, 20 S Ct 197, and Gong Lum v. Rice, 275 US 78, 72 L ed 172, 48 S Ct 91, the validity of the doctrine itself was not challenged.[4] In more recent cases, all on the graduate school level, inequality was found in that specific benefits enjoyed by white students were denied to Negro students of the same educational qualifications. Missouri ex rel. Gaines v. Canada, 305 US 337, 83 L ed 208, 59 S Ct 232; Sipuel v. University of Oklahoma, 332 US 631, 92 L ed 247, 68 S Ct 299; Sweatt v. Painter, 339 US 629, 94 L ed 1114, 70 S Ct 848; McLaurin v. Oklahoma State Regents, 339 US 637, 94 L ed 1149, 70 S Ct 851. In none of these cases was it necessary to reexamine the doctrine to grant relief to the Negro plaintiff. And in Sweatt v. Painter (US) supra, the Court expressly reserved decision on the question whether Plessy v. Ferguson should be held inapplicable to public education.

In the instant cases, that question is directly presented. Here, unlike Sweatt v. Painter, there are findings below that the Negro and white schools involved have been equalized, or are being equalized, with respect to

---

without due process of law, or deny to any person within its jurisdiction the equal protection of the laws. What is this but declaring that the law in the States shall be the same for the black as for the white; that all persons, whether colored or white, shall stand equal before the laws of the States, and, in regard to the colored race, for whose protection the amendment was primarily designed, that no discrimination shall be made against them by law because of their color? The words of the amendment, it is true, are prohibitory, but they contain a necessary implication of a positive immunity, or right, most valuable to the colored race,—the right to exemption from unfriendly legislation against them distinctively as colored,—exemption from legal discriminations, implying inferiority in civil society, lessening the security of their enjoyment of the rights which others enjoy, and discriminations which are steps towards reducing them to the condition of a subject race."

[3] The doctrine apparently originated in Roberts v. Boston, 5 Cush 198, 206 (1850, Mass), upholding school segregation against attack as being violative of a state constitutional guarantee of equality. Segregation in Boston public schools was eliminated in 1855. Mass Acts 1855, ch 256. But elsewhere in the North segregation in public education has persisted in some communities until recent years. It is apparent that such segregation has long been a nationwide problem, not merely one of sectional concern.

[4] In the Cumming Case, Negro taxpayers sought an injunction requiring the defendent school board to discontinue the operation of a high school for white children until the board resumed operation of a high school for Negro children. Similarly, in the Gong Lum Case, the plaintiff, a child of Chinese descent, contended only that state authorities had misapplied the doctrine by classifying him with Negro children and requiring him to attend a Negro school.

buildings, curricula, qualifications and salaries of teachers, and other "tangible" factors. Our decision, therefore, cannot turn on merely a comparison of these tangible factors in the Negro and white schools involved in each of the cases. We must look instead to the effect of segregation itself on public education.

In approaching this problem, we cannot turn the clock back to 1868 when the Amendment was adopted, or even to 1896 when Plessy v. Ferguson was written. We must consider public education in the light of its full development and its present place in American life throughout the Nation. Only in this way can it be determined if segregation in public schools deprives these plaintiffs of the equal protection of the laws.

Today, education is perhaps the most important function of state and local governments. Compulsory school attendance laws and the great expenditures for education both demonstrate our recognition of the importance of education to our democratic society. It is required in the performance of our most basic public responsibilities, even service in the armed forces. It is the very foundation of good citizenship. Today it is a principal instrument in awakening the child to cultural values, in preparing him for later professional training, and in helping him to adjust normally to his environment. In these days, it is doubtful that any child may reasonably be expected to succeed in life if he is denied the opportunity of an education. Such an opportunity, where the state has undertaken to provide it, is a right which must be made available to all on equal terms.

We come then to the question presented: Does segregation of children in public schools solely on the basis of race, even though the physical facilities and other "tangible" factors may be equal, deprive the children of the minority group of equal educational opportunities? We believe that it does.

In Sweatt v. Painter (US) supra, in finding that a segregated law school for Negroes could not provide them equal educational opportunities, this Court relied in large part on "those qualities which are incapable of objective measurement but which make for greatness in a law school." In McLaurin v. Oklahoma State Regents, 339 US 637, 94 L ed 1149, 70 S Ct 851, supra, the Court, in requiring that a Negro admitted to a white graduate school be treated like all other students, again resorted to intangible considerations: ". . . his ability to study, to engage in discussions and exchange views with other students, and, in general, to learn his profession." Such considerations apply with added force to children in grade and high schools. To separate them from others of similar age and qualifications solely because of their race generates a feeling of inferiority as to their status in the community that may affect their hearts and minds in a way unlikely ever to be undone. The effect of this separation on their educational opportunities was well stated by a finding in the Kansas case by a court which nevertheless felt compelled to rule against the Negro plaintiffs:

"Segregation of white and colored children in public schools has a detrimental effect upon the colored children. The impact is greater when it has the sanction of the law; for the policy of separating the races is usually interpreted as denoting the inferiority of the Negro group. A sense of inferiority affects the motivation of a child to learn. Segregation with the sanction of law, therefore, has a tendency to [retard] the educational and mental development of Negro children and to deprive them of some of the benefits they would receive in a racial[ly] integrated school system."

Whatever may have been the extent of psychological knowledge at the time of Plessy v. Ferguson, this finding is amply supported by modern authority.[5] Any language in Plessy v. Ferguson contrary to this finding is rejected.

We conclude that in the field of public education the doctrine of "separate but equal" has no place. Separate educational facilities are inherently unequal. Therefore, we hold that the plaintiffs and others similarly situated for whom the actions have been brought are, by reason of the segregation complained of, deprived of the equal protection of the laws guaranteed by the Fourteenth Amendment. This disposition makes unnecessary any discussion whether such segregation also violates the Due Process Clause of the Fourteenth Amendment.

Because these are class actions, because of the wide applicability of this decision, and because of the great variety of local conditions, the formulation of decrees in these cases presents problems of considerable complexity. On reargument, the consideration of appropriate relief was necessarily subordinated to the primary question—the constitutionality of segregation in public education. We have now announced that such segregation is a denial of the equal protection of the laws. In order that we may have the full assistance of the parties in formulating decrees, the cases will be restored to the docket, and the parties are requested to present further argument on Questions 4 and 5 previously propounded by the Court for

[5] K. B. Clark, Effect of Prejudice and Discrimination on Personality Development (Midcentury White House Conference on Children and Youth, 1950); Witmer and Kotinsky, Personality in the Making (1952), ch VI; Deutscher and Chein, The Psychological Effects of Enforced Segregation: A Survey of Social Science Opinion, 26 J Psychol 259 (1948); Chein, What are the Psychological Effects of Segregation Under Conditions of Equal Facilities?, 3 Int J Opinion and Attitude Res 229 (1949); Brameld, Educational Costs, in Discrimination and National Welfare (MacIver, ed, 1949), 44-48; Frazier, The Negro in the United States (1949), 674-681. And see generally Myrdal, An American Dilemma (1944).

the reargument this Term.[6] The Attorney General of the United States is again invited to participate. The Attorneys General of the states requiring or permitting segregation in public education will also be permitted to appear as amici curiae upon request to do so by September 15, 1954, and submission of briefs by October 1, 1954.

It is so ordered.

EDUCATION FOR ALL, DO WE MEAN IT? [*]

We Americans believe in education for all. We believe that every child in our land has the right—and it is a sacred right—to develop his talents to the fullest, to participate actively in our society.

The founding fathers took no more significant action than the rejection of the European idea of education by selection—the idea that education was so precious that it should be reserved for those born to an elevated station in life. Every page in American history has been influenced by this great decision. Our states provide free public education for all children and require by law that they attend school up to a certain age.

In the early days, free education was provided only through the elementary grades, then later through the high school. Year after year, decade after decade citizens and educators, working together, have made steady progress. Through their efforts the knowledge of the ages is being brought to more and more children, preparing them for earning a living and participating in our democratic life.

[6] "4. Assuming it is decided that segregation in public schools violates the Fourteenth Amendment

"(a) would a decree necessarily follow providing that, within the limits set by normal geographic school districting, Negro children should forthwith be admitted to schools of their choice, or

"(b) may this Court, in the exercise of its equity powers, permit an effective gradual adjustment to be brought about from existing segregated systems to a system not based on color distinctions?

"5. On the assumption on which questions 4 (a) and (b) are based, and assuming further that this Court will exercise its equity powers to the end described in question 4 (b),

"(a) should this Court formulate detailed decrees in these cases;

"(b) if so, what specific issues should the decrees reach;

"(c) should this Court appoint a special master to hear evidence with a view to recommending specific terms for such decrees;

"(d) should this Court remand to the courts of first instance with directions to frame decrees in these cases, and if so what general directions should the decrees of this Court include and what procedures should the courts of first instance follow in arriving at the specific terms of more detailed decrees?"

[*] Herold C. Hunt, "Education for All, Do We Mean It?," *National Parent-Teacher, The P.T.A. Magazine*, April 1956, pp. 16-18.

The school record of two succeeding generations indicates the striding pace at which we are moving. According to the 1950 census, 28 per cent of those between the ages of forty-five and fifty-four had completed high school. But look at the record of the next generation—those between the ages of twenty-five and twenty-nine. Fifty-two per cent of them are high school graduates! This record of improvement should stimulate our efforts to press on toward our cherished aim of education for all.

But what level of education do we set as our goal? The recent White House Conference on Education reported that "each state has the responsibility to provide for all its children an opportunity for a minimum of twelve years of public school education."

This is not to imply that every child has the capacity to achieve the educational level generally represented by graduation from high school. Nor does it suggest that scholarship requirements be lowered so that every child may receive a high school diploma. Rather it recognizes a concept universally accepted—that the years of youth are years of preparation, when every young person should be busy acquiring the skills and the knowledge that will mold him into a contributing, responsible member of society.

Unfortunately, however, there are millions of school-age children who are not in school. These boys and girls make up the large segment—48 per cent—of all those who do not graduate from high school.

Who are these boys and girls? The physically and mentally handicapped, the children in isolated rural areas, the children of migrant workers, and the children who for some reason or other leave their classes after seven, eight, or more years of schooling.

The Handicapped and the Isolated. More than three and a half million exceptional children, it is estimated, need special help from the schools. In these boys and girls we have a large reservoir of potentially useful citizens—*if* they get adequate care and a suitable education during childhood. To fail them is to add to human misery and place a continuing economic burden on their families and society.

More than half of these three and a half million youngsters are handicapped physically. They are hampered by poor eyesight, hearing loss, speech defects, or other impairments. The rest of the group is made up of children who are handicapped mentally, seriously disturbed emotionally, or socially maladjusted. All of them need special educational services, which cost from two to five times what it costs to educate a normal child. For some handicaps—speech impediments, for example—the cost may be less; for severe handicaps, it may be more. Even so, the cost of educating these exceptional children is in the long run still far below that of supporting a noncontributing member of society.

Thousands of our handicapped boys and girls are not enrolled in school. Some are in hospitals where no education programs are provided; others, confined to their own homes, never see a visiting teacher; and some of the mentally retarded live in counties that do not have programs for them.

Increasingly, however, our schools are providing opportunities for exceptional children. Increasingly, also, citizens are accepting their obligation for aiding these children. Yet even with the recent rapid development of special programs, much remains to be done. Not more than one fourth of the nation's handicapped are receiving the help they need. In most cases the lack of qualified teaching personnel and the high cost of special programs are the basic reasons for this unfortunate situation.

Although the youth of rural America are getting more and better education than did their fathers, there are still certain sections of the country where an alarming number of children under seventeen do not attend any school. Recently the Department of Agriculture made a survey of the enrollments of farm children from seven to seventeen years of age and found that far too many rural children in twelve southern states are not enrolled in school. In one of these states, for example, 13.8 per cent of the children between seven and thirteen were not enrolled. The figures were poorer still for the older children; 22 per cent for the fourteen- and fifteen-year-olds; 50 per cent for the sixteen- and seventeen-year-olds.

To help explain this record, we need to know that the breadwinners of almost four million families in the twelve states work in agriculture, forestry, or fishing. About a million of these families have a cash income of less than a thousand dollars a year. Such meager incomes contribute to low enrollments. Because of economic hardship children past fourteen years of age are inclined to leave school to work on the family farm or to hire out to other farmers.

What of the parents? Don't they encourage attendance at school? Having little formal education themselves—and here may lie the reason for their low income—the parents do not always appreciate the benefits that adequate schooling can bring. As a result, some of their children may never be exposed to the inspiration for fuller living that our schools impart to millions of other young people. And so the low-income, little-schooling, low-income cycle continues from one generation to the next.

Children Who Follow the Crops. Every spring in Florida and Georgia trucks loaded with men, women, and children of all ages pull onto the main highways and head for fields in the north. The migrant workers are off to harvest fruits and vegetables for our tables. Trucks stream out, too, on highways in the Midwest and in California, Oregon, and Washington— a transient labor force that is essential to farmers in many states. While we do not know exactly how many school-age children accompany their parents as they move from field to field, from job to job, the number may be close to half a million.

These boys and girls face almost insurmountable obstacles to school attendance. Their families leave home in the spring before school is out. They return in the fall after school has started. And during the months in between, many of the youngsters never see the inside of a classroom.

Why not? For one thing, the children themselves may be working. Sometimes parents (and employers) urge the youngsters to help with the harvest, though it is illegal for boys and girls of school age to work during school hours. Sometimes parents are not interested in having their children attend school. Sometimes local communities, already burdened by teacher shortages and crowded classrooms, make no effort to get the children into school. And all too frequently nearly everybody concerned shrugs off the issue with the excuse that the children will be moving along in a few days anyway.

There are other reasons why some of these boys and girls seldom answer the summoning school bell. They haven't food for lunch. They haven't clothing for the classroom. And somebody has to stay home to look after the younger children while mothers and fathers work in the fields.

In recent years migrant children have been spending more days at school, especially while they are in their "home" state. This is encouraging. Even so, those who do attend are usually two to five years behind their fellow students in school achievement.

What does this picture from our fields and orchards suggest? That in our own migrant children here in the United States we have one of our largest single groups of potential illiterates.

Children Who Drop Out. We have still another group of children who do not complete high school—the largest one of all. They are not the physically or mentally handicapped. They are not the children in isolated rural areas, and their parents are not migrant workers. They are the boys and girls who do get to school, attend for several years, and then for a variety of reasons drop out before graduation.

The United States Office of Education estimates that of every thousand students who entered high school in 1951, only 675, or 67.5 per cent, graduated in 1955. Why did these students drop out? Lack of money, ill-health, dissatisfaction with some part of school life, and unsatisfactory progress are the reasons most often given.

Can the high schools do anything to increase their holding power? Schoolmen can give the problem special attention. They can provide more health services, hire more visiting teachers, offer improved student guidance and a more flexible curriculum.

When it comes to winning a diploma, though, one other factor may be decisive: the willingness of both parents and children to accept sacrifices. There are thousands of students who, despite handicaps, doggedly persist in their studies—and eventually graduate. These are usually the boys and girls who come from homes that appreciate the lifetime benefits of school, homes where both parents and students have a "will to win" that carries them over the rough spots both at home and at school. In these families nothing is permitted to become an obstacle in the pursuit of learning. Students manage to take things in stride—from run-ins with teachers and impatience with required courses to an undernourished family purse. Perhaps renewed emphasis on "sticking-to-it-no-matter-what" could pay rich dividends.

Working Out Ways. To a nation that has displayed a genius for the large task, the obstacles to our goal of education for all are not insurmountable. We can point to some encouraging signs. The U.S. Office of Education is planning to sponsor research on teaching the mentally retarded and on expanding the specialized training required of teachers. President Eisenhower's Committee on Migratory Labor has placed emphasis on the "need for providing opportunities for the education of migrant children." Many states and local communities have active projects under way to encourage the school attendance of migrant children and to make their experiences worthwhile.

Schools and the communities they serve can, by renewed efforts, help many more boys and girls to complete their schooling. The holding power of the schools can be enhanced by modern buildings, adequate equipment, understanding and carefully prepared teachers, interesting and varied curriculums, health services, vocational guidance, and special provisions for teaching the mentally retarded and slow learners. Surely dropouts for financial reasons can be curtailed if students from low-income families are not confronted with fees for textbooks, laboratory equipment, athletic equipment, school papers, tickets to sports events, and graduation expenses. Some communities have been eminently successful in providing such help without embarrassment to the students.

Education for all? We can have it. Parents and teachers, mustering their resources and those of their communities, can speed us along toward that goal.

EXCELLENCE IN A DEMOCRACY *

It is now widely recognized that our society has given too little attention to the individual of unusual talent or potentialities. To make such an assertion is not to deplore the unprecedented time and money we have devoted to raising the general level of achievement. It would serve no purpose to replace our neglect of the gifted by neglect of everyone else. We are all too prone to such wild swings of the pendulum in our national life. We must learn to view these matters in a perspective which will permit us to repair one omission without creating others.

It has not always been easy for Americans to think clearly about excellence. At the heart of the matter is a seeming paradox in democracy as we know it. On the one hand, ours is the form of society which says most convincingly, "Let the best man win," and rewards winners regardless of origin. On the other, it is the form of society which gives those who do not come out on top the widest latitude in rewriting the rules of the contest. It is crucial to understand this tug of war between equality and excellence in a democracy. When the rewriting of the rules is prompted by the standards of fair play, by elementary considerations of justice, by basic value judgments as to what sort of a "best man" the society wants, democracy can have no quarrel with it. Indeed, it is the core process of a democracy. But when the rewriting of the rules is designed to banish excellence, to rule out distinguished attainment, to inhibit spirited individuals, then all who have a stake in the continued vitality of democracy must protest.

Every democracy *must* encourage high individual performance. If it does not, it closes itself off from the main springs of its dynamism and talent and imagination, and the traditional democratic invitation to the individual to realize his full potentialities becomes meaningless. More, perhaps, than any other form of government, a democracy must maintain what Ralph Barton Perry has called "an express insistence upon quality and distinction."

The eighteenth-century philosophers who made equality a central term in our political vocabulary never meant to imply that men are equal in all respects. Nor do Americans today take such a view. It is possible to state in fairly simple terms the views concerning equality which would

---

* *The Pursuit of Excellence; Education and The Future of America.* Special Studies Project Report V, Rockefeller Brothers Fund (New York, Doubleday & Company, Inc., 1958), pp. 15-17. © 1958 by Rockefeller Brothers Fund, Inc. Reprinted by permission of Doubleday & Co., Inc.

receive most widespread endorsement in our country today. The fundamental view is that in the final matters of human existence all men are equally worthy of our care and concern. Further, we believe that men should be equal in enjoyment of certain familiar legal, civil and political rights. They should, as the phrase goes, be equal before the law.

But men are unequal in their native capacities and their motivations, and therefore in their attainments. In elaborating our national views of equality, the most widely accepted means of dealing with this problem has been to emphasize *equality of opportunity*. The great advantage of the conception of equality of opportunity is that it candidly recognizes differences in endowment and motivation and accepts the certainty of differences in achievement. By allowing free play to these differences, it preserves the freedom to excel which counts for so much in terms of individual aspirations, and has produced so much of mankind's greatness.

Having committed ourselves to equality of opportunity, we must strive incessantly to make it a reality in our society. This is a task which will concern us at many points in the present report.

With respect to the pursuit of excellence there are several considerations that we must keep firmly in mind.

First, we must not make the mistake of adopting a narrow or constricting view of excellence. *Our conception of excellence must embrace many kinds of achievement at many levels.* There is no single scale or simple set of categories in terms of which to measure excellence. There is excellence in abstract intellectual activity, in art, in music, in managerial activities, in craftsmanship, in human relations, in technical work.

Second, we must not assume that native capacity is the sole ingredient in superior performance. Excellence, as we shall later have occasion to note, is a product of ability and motivation and character. And the more one observes high performance in the dust and heat of daily life, the more one is likely to be impressed with the contribution made by the latter two ingredients.

Finally, we must recognize that judgments of differences in talent are not judgments of differences in human worth.

To sum up, it is possible for us to cultivate the ideal of excellence while retaining the moral values of equality. Whether we shall succeed in doing so is perhaps the fundamental issue in the development of our human resources. A challenge must be recognized before it can be met. Our society will have passed an important milestone of maturity when those who are the most enthusiastic proponents of a democratic way of life are also the most vigorous proponents of excellence.

Part 3

▼

The Purposes of Education

Contents of Part 3

The Purposes of Education

FORMULATIONS AND DISCUSSIONS

ILLUSTRATIONS

The Language Arts
The Social Studies
Mathematics and Science
Education for Life Adjustment
Education in Moral and Spiritual Values
Student Evaluation

The Purposes of Education

Who Formulates Aims?

Aims of education have been formulated by philosophers and theologians, by statesmen and educators, by legislatures and courts, by councils and committees of citizens. In this volume there are statements by Aristotle and Spencer, Luther and Pius XI, Plutarch and Jefferson, Comenius and Horace Mann, the Massachusetts Bay Company and the Supreme Court of the United States, the Mid-Century Committee on Outcomes of Education and the White House Conference on Education. Today in America formulation of aims for schools is everybody's business.

Especially it is part of the teacher's business. When he prepares a lesson plan, he begins with a statement of objectives for the lesson. When he prepares a larger unit, he begins by asking himself what he hopes his students will accomplish. Even when he decides that children should have a part in formulating goals for a unit or course, he does so in terms of his conception of the purposes of education. When he finds himself on a committee with other teachers and administrators to formulate a statement of his school's "philosophy," the committee begins with a statement of aims. Accrediting commissions ask for such statements. If he meets with committees of laymen, again they begin with aims. If he confers with parents, individually or at PTA meetings, he is sure to be asked "Why?" Why is my son required to take mathematics? Or why isn't he? Why does the school give money and energy to driver education? Or why doesn't it? Why do you teach social studies instead of history? What good is General Language? Why not teach French instead? As he tries to answer these questions, he must do so in terms of the purposes of education.

228 The Purposes of Education

They are legitimate questions because the formulation of aims for American education is everybody's business. It has not always been so. In general, the formulation of school aims by groups of laymen (through committees, through such local, regional, and national organizations and activities as parents' associations, taxpayers' associations, the National Congress of Parents and Teachers, and the White House Conference on Education) is a recent development. No doubt there are precedents—in the Town Meetings of New England, for example—but they are modern precedents. For this development is a phenomenon of modern democracy and of the universal franchise. It has its beginnings in the Reformation and the rise of parliamentary government, especially during and since the seventeenth century.

In America, in early colonial days, the influence of the Reformation is clear in the first school law of New England, "the old Deluder, Satan" law. And the political reference is clear in Jefferson's *Notes on Virginia,* a century later. A key purpose of his proposed school system is "that of rendering the people safe, as they are the ultimate guardians of their own liberty."

When the individual has been made responsible for his own reading and interpretation of Scripture and for the formulation of his own religious views and when he is expected to exercise his voice in government, it is not a long step for him to demand a voice in determining the education of his children, especially when education is affirmed to be the responsibility of the government in which he has a voice. They are his children, it is his government, they are his schools, and he pays taxes to support them.

As individuals and in committee, then, for thousands of years—literally for thousands of years—men have sought definitions of the purpose or purposes for which they have established educational institutions and educational routines. They have sought satisfactory formulations of the aims of education. Now every citizen, every taxpayer, certainly every parent, inescapably every teacher has an interest in and may if he wishes have a voice in the formulation of the "ends of education," for the centuries have not settled the questions; they are still open questions.

IDEAS MAKE A DIFFERENCE

There are those who think there can be no final answers to these questions and that it is futile to seek them, because the aims of education change with changes in the social environment or in our knowledge of men and of society, and because fixed aims stop educational progress. This is implied in Harold Benjamin's *Saber-Tooth Curriculum,* for example. "Clubbing little wooly horses" is a legitimate school subject, and teaching children to club them a legitimate school aim, when people have to club horses in order to eat. When the horses disappear, it becomes pointless. New aims must be established for the schools in a new economy.

Others think the ends of education do not change. Only the means change, if we get the ends right. Robert M. Hutchins describes the one view and advocates the other:

> Our erroneous notion of progress has . . . made education the servant of any contemporary movements in society, no matter how superficial. . . . We have felt that it was our duty to educate the young so that they would be prepared for further political, social, and economic changes. Some of us have thought we should try to figure out what the impending changes would be and frame a curriculum that embodied them. Others have even thought that we should decide what changes are desirable and then educate our students not merely to anticipate them, but also to bring them about.
>
> One purpose of education is to draw out the elements of our common human nature. These elements are the same in any time or place. The notion of educating a man to live in any particular time or place, to adjust him to any particular environment, is therefore foreign to a true conception of education. . . . I suggest that the heart of any course of study designed for the whole people will be, if education is rightly understood, the same in any time, in any place, under any political, social, or economic conditions.[1]

Mr. Hutchins would not agree that clubbing little wooly horses ever was an appropriate school subject.

Those who think, as Harold Benjamin does, that aims of education must change with different times and circumstances do not always agree about what the times require. A Sputnik may be taken as an urgent call for school emphasis on the training of applied scientists, or for new emphasis on global education, or for both. A depression may call for intensification of job-training or may be used to illustrate the futility of training for particular jobs. Men in different societies will interpret quite differently the charge to educate for the sake of the social order. Thomas Jefferson for the young republic wished to make every man in some measure a statesman and the guardian of his own liberties, an independent thinker about politics. A Soviet text in pedagogy describes the "basic traits of discipline required of the Soviet pupil." One stated quality of discipline is that it requires "unquestioned obedience and submission to the leader, the teacher, or the organizer. Without this there is no discipline; submission to the will of the leader is a necessary and essential mark of discipline."

There is also disagreement among those who think the aims of educa-

[1] Robert M. Hutchins, *The Higher Learning in America* (New Haven, Yale University Press, 1936), pp. 65-6.

tion remain constant. There have been many different formulations of "the" end of education or of "the primary end." Perfection or cultivation of the intellect, salvation, social-self-realization, ability to make rational decisions—these are only a few of many succinct statements of "the end" of education.

These differences reflect different views of the nature of man, the nature of society, the nature of the good life. Mr. Hutchins, for example, and Mortimer J. Adler in the essay included in these readings, begin with an ideal of human nature that stresses intellect, from which it follows that the good life is the contemplative life. Man is a rational animal. From the point of view of the school, the significant thing is his rationality. The first object of education is to help him become more rational. "One purpose of education is to draw out the elements of our common nature." The intellect is the element of our common nature that is the first and chief concern of the schools.

For other writers, differences in aims established for schools have reflected changing perceptions of man's nature and of his place in the universe. With the rise of modern science, there came a new source of authority for knowledge of human nature and the relationships of men to one another in society. Science began to vie with revelation and with philosophy as a source of knowledge, and the findings of science have changed the schools. Two great intellectual revolutions may be cited as cases in point. After Copernicus, man and the planet he inhabits were no longer the center of the universe. It was not so self-evident any more that Creation was for man and that man existed solely for God's glory. In 1611, John Donne wrote as follows of the new science:

> And new Philosophy calls all in doubt,
> The Element of fire is quite put out;
> The Sun is lost, and th'earth, and no mans wit
> Can well direct him where to look for it.
> . . .
> 'Tis all in peeces, all cohaerence gone;
> All just supply, and all Relation.

After Lyell and Darwin in the nineteenth century, there came another new view of men, one in which man seemed as closely related to the apes as to the angels. Before Darwin, Herbert Spencer would not have defined as most important among human activities, and therefore for education, those which "directly minister to self-preservation." Nor would he have ranked after them in order of importance those that minister indirectly to self-preservation, those that assure continuance of the human race, those that preserve human society, and finally the occupations of leisure. "As

The Purposes of Education

they occupy the leisure part of life, so should they occupy the leisure part of education."

Spencer's analysis provides a rationale for much that has happened in the schools during the twentieth century. It provides a rationale for safety education and health education, the simple, common, frequently heard defense of which might come straight from his argument: you can teach a child nothing if he does not get to school alive. It provides a rationale for vocational education: in order to live in our society one must have means of earning a living; learning a trade contributes indirectly to self-preservation. It provides a rationale for parent and family-life education, which are conducive to the preservation of the race and of society. It may seem a long way from the voyage of the *Beagle* and the publication of *The Origin of Species* to the establishment of vocational high schools and the initiation of marriage courses, but the steps are direct.

It is not merely the language that is different, then. The concept of man and of the good life are different, and different educational programs follow. Again we may contrast Adler and Spencer, beginning with Adler's statement that "all the quarrels that exist in educational philosophy exist because men have different conceptions of what the good life is, of what is good for man, of the conditions under which man is improved or bettered." For Adler the good life is the contemplative life, not the active life, and it is for this that education should prepare the pupil. He distinguishes between learning for the sake of learning and for the sake of earning. "School is a place of learning for the sake of learning. . . . No one should have to take vocational training without compensation because it is not self-rewarding. To include vocational training in school *without compensation* is to suppose that it is education, which it is not at all."

This is in direct contradiction of Spencer, Dewey, and Benjamin. For Spencer, the first step in determining the ends of education and establishing priorities among them is "to clarify, in the order of their importance, the leading kinds of activity which constitute human life." John and Evelyn Dewey, in *Schools of Tomorrow,* affirm the obligation of schools to give the future worker in industry an education that will make him economically independent. And New-Fist-Hammer-Maker in Harold Benjamin's fable seems to have read Spencer, for he begins his curriculum planning by asking the question, "What things must we know how to do, in order to live with full bellies, warm backs, and minds free from fear?" In each case the stress is on what men do, on the active life, not the contemplative life. Where Adler would educate for leisure, Spencer and Benjamin put leisure last and educate for survival and for work.

The difference is one of priorities. Spencer would also educate for leisure, in the leisure part of education, when more fundamental needs are cared for. Adler does not suggest that vocational training can be dispensed with. He thinks it should be given on the job, that the learner should be paid, and that the school should devote itself to the more important task of educating for leisure. "The good life *depends on labor,* but it consists of leisure." The end is more important than the means.

Paul Woodring in his recent book, *A Fourth of a Nation,* describes the major controversy in contemporary education as between a "classic thesis" and a "pragmatic antithesis." The classic position is represented by such writers as Hutchins, Adler, and Bestor; the pragmatic antithesis by such writers as Dewey and Benjamin.

The classic view seeks the development of the individual in terms of an ideal of human nature. "The objective of living and learning," H. H. Horne said, "is to develop the natural man into the ideal man."

The classic tradition sees man as having a dual nature, spiritual and physical. It asserts that intellect is part of the spiritual nature, that it can be cultivated or developed toward perfection, and that this is the chief concern of education. As Cardinal Newman described it, the university exists for the perfection of the intellect as the hospital and gymnasium exist for the perfection of the body and the Church for the perfection of the moral nature, and he deplored the absence of an English word to describe the perfection of the intellect as *health* describes the perfection of the body and *virtue* the perfection of the moral nature. The analogy with health and virtue describes the concept. The classic position holds that essential human nature is always the same, that truth exists to be discovered and does not change, that values are permanent, and consequently that the best education for one age or place will be best for all. The problem is to discover what is best.

Inasmuch as the classic point of view begins with an ideal of human nature which stresses intellect, it is not surprising that its representatives plan educational programs in which the lower schools emphasize verbal and mathematical skills and are regarded as preparation for higher education. The program of higher education in turn emphasizes the great intellectual achievements of the past equally with those of the present—the great issues, the great books, the great ideas. Because the position asserts absolute values as well as absolute truth, it places great stress on the inculcation of values. As Plato put it, the aim is to teach children to love what they ought to love and hate what they ought to hate. And because values are the concern of the humanities, not of the sciences, the humanities have the dominant position in the curriculum. Because man is thought not to change in his essential nature and because the nature of man is the source of ends for education, new social situations and new knowledge of psychology, sociology, and other young sciences do not change the purpose of education. They only give better means by which to pursue old ends. And finally, because the educational purpose is to approximate an ideal of human nature, it is the same for all men; individual differences only call for different educational methods and result in different degrees of success. As the name Woodring gives it implies, the classic position represents an old tradition, but it is very much alive.

The "pragmatic antithesis" is younger and also very much alive. It denies each point of the classic position: "It denies that man is dual in his nature, that mind can be sharply distinguished from behavior. It denies that final truth or positive knowledge is available to man or, indeed, that such truth or knowledge exists. It denies all dogmas, absolutes, and the permanence and universality of values. . . ." [2] Instead of seeking the development of the individual in terms of an ideal of human nature, the pragmatic view seeks development of his ability to do what he must do in the world of today or tomorrow.

Because this view insists on the unity of man's nature, it denies that education can properly be limited to the cultivation of the intellect. The whole behavior of the child—the whole child, to use the popular phrase—is the concern of the school. Accordingly, the school built on this view of human nature will have a much broader curriculum and will not make sharp distinctions between curricular and extra-curricular activities. Because this view denies the existence of final "external" ends, it does not seek to approximate an ideal of human nature common to all men; its program is described and designed only to promote growth: "Since growth is the characteristic of life, education is all one with growing; it has no end beyond itself." [3] Because truth is relative and recognizable only in terms of its application, in its value as a predictor, in its use, the stress in education is on activity. Truth is what works when it is tried, in scientific experiment or in establishing social relations. If the world changes or if our knowledge changes, truths may change. Because the eternality of values is also denied, because values are also asserted to be relative to time, place, and situation, the aim is not as Plato put it to teach children to love what they ought to love; it is rather to enable them to build their own value systems.

Finally this view puts much greater stress on individual differences. Educational programs must be planned not in terms of some non-existent ideal of human nature, but in terms of the very different natures of different men. The classic position does not deny individual differences; it

[2] Paul Woodring, *A Fourth of a Nation* (New York, McGraw-Hill Book Company, 1957), p. 54.
[3] John Dewey, *Democracy and Education* (New York, The Macmillan Company, 1917), p. 62.

denies that they are the proper basis for an educational program. The pragmatic position denies that any ideal of human nature is best for every time, place, or society and insists that the ends of education as well as the means must be adapted to the capacities and interests of the individual.

The school based on this position will be very different from that based on the classic position. If it were possible, there would be a different program for each child, since each child has unique capacities and interests. Failing this, the curriculum must in any event be much broader and more varied in order to meet different needs of different pupils. It will change from time to time as the world changes, it will be different in different communities and for different groups of children. Standards of achievement will not be established in terms of knowledge to be mastered but in terms of the potentialities of each pupil. Because "education is all one with growing," each school activity must be assessed in terms of its present relevance to the interests and needs of the pupil as well as in terms of its potential future usefulness. Because the whole child, not his intellect alone, is the concern of the school, school activities will be less exclusively verbal and bookish. There will be more use of visual aids, more manual activities, more observation and experiment, more doing. Because men in modern society work, and because education prepares for the world we live in, vocational education is welcomed into the program rather than resisted. Indeed, the distinction between vocational and liberal pursuits that is so important in the classic position hardly exists at all.

Of course this discussion is an over-simplification, and it states extreme views. It would be hard to find a school to illustrate either extreme position in detail, although there are classrooms that do because there are teachers who hold these positions. Ideas do indeed make a difference. Because they do, one thing a teacher cannot do is have no opinions at all. The sensitive question of the social or political aims of education will serve to illustrate. The schools are regarded by some as an important means of preserving the *status quo.* The Constitution, the Bill of Rights, our system of free enterprise, capitalism, representative government are so important to the "American Way" that some think the main purpose of American schools is to preserve them. On the other hand, poverty, disease, inequality of opportunity, race bias, special privilege, and special handicaps are realities in American life and constitute limitations on our social democracy. There are those who think it the main function of schools to criticize our society and to take the lead in reforming it. John Dewey, in his most influential book, says that a curriculum "must select with the intention of improving the life we live in common so that the future shall be better than the past," and some of his followers have argued that it is the function of the school "to teach what the next society should be." And finally there are those who think schools (and teachers) should take no stand at all on social or political questions. Still others point out that this means that the school can deal adequately and honestly with nothing important, and every teacher knows how difficult it is to discuss with a heterogeneous class those topics which seem really important to young people and toward which different groups in the community take widely different views, e.g. religion, sex, politics, economics.

The question of the social function of the school and the social role of the teacher becomes more difficult as different groups of people enter the schools in large numbers and as different groups become more articulate in the community. When schooling was not regarded as necessary for the "laboring classes"—or when special schools isolate different economic groups—a dominant view of economics could be presented. When the schools include children of parents with widely different economic creeds, the social studies teacher and the curriculum committee have a different problem. The difference between "races" and the rationale of Southern society are not likely to be discussed in the same way in segregated and in integrated schools, or in Northern schools and Southern schools. Yet surely the educational aims of the school and the social science teacher may require him to discuss with his classes the key social problems of the day.

One thing is sure. The teacher must have goals—educational goals—for his pupils. He must understand the goals of his school and be willing to work toward them; it is his task to implement them. The school serves multiple publics and is sensitive to their demands. When those demands are contradictory, the school and the teacher come to the point at which they cannot depend uncritically on the expressed desires of members of the community.

THE MULTIPLICITY OF AIMS

"Education as such has no aims," said John Dewey, and he was careful to call his chapter "Aims *in* Education." "Only persons, parents, and teachers, etc., have aims, not an abstract idea like education."

Whether or not there are aims inherent in the idea of education, certainly people have aims for education; and they differ. Nor are they often defined in terms of a carefully thought out philosophy. People simply tell the schools more or less impulsively what they think the schools should do, and the schools are pressed to establish a great variety of different programs to serve the ends of different individuals and groups. For the school like any other social agency (educational or not) serves the public, and the public communicates what it asks of the school in a variety of ways. But in a complex and diverse society, there are many publics. There are school children and older students. There are their parents. There are employers, labor unions, church groups, government agencies, professional organizations, civic organizations. There are as many employer groups as there are industries or types of business, as many citizens' groups as there are economic or social classes in our society, as many professional organizations as there are professions—each with its special demands upon the school.

The same person may belong to several articulate publics. Associations of parents want the school systems among other things to produce more and better teachers. A father who urges this through the Parent-Teacher Association, as a member of the Chamber of Commerce urges the same schools to stress education that will produce more competent business executives, on the one hand, and employees devoted to private enterprise on the other. Through his industrial association he asks for more electrical engineers. As a good church member, he deplores the lack of promising young men among the clergy, and as a board member of the city hospital he knows of the acute shortages of competent, trained personnel in the health sciences and applied social sciences. He urges the school system to attack this problem, too. If the school system is an agency which screens, recruits, and educates people for a variety of specialized occupations, these diverse demands are seen not to be contradictory—except in so far as all these and many more occupations are competing for the same people and asking the schools to do their screening and recruiting for them.

In the pressures brought on schools, there is competition not only for the same people as potential practitioners of different vocations but also for the limited time of the same pupil, because special interests of different groups also lead them to call upon the schools to teach many things to all pupils. The school in the United States is asked to teach reading, music and cabinet-making, geography and automobile driving, English composition and the principles and practice of democracy, independence of thought and committee procedures, religious and moral values and the will to win, biology and finger painting, geology and thrift, astronomy, sex hygiene, and typing, cooking and the appreciation of poetry, respect for elders and self-reliance, farm practices and the multiplication table, clothing design and the origins of the Bill of Rights.

There is no dearth of special spokesmen to urge duties on the school. An automobile insurance company states the aims of education by giving lower rates to families whose younger members have had high school driver education. A hunting and fishing magazine proposes high school "fire arms education" as prerequisite to a first hunting license. Savings banks and the United States Treasury Department foster school "Thrift Days." Labor unions, consumer co-operatives, and manufacturers' associations urge realistic "economic education" (not always meaning the same thing). A bar association provides funds for a study of "Constitutional Education" in its community. Patriotic organizations urge special "citizenship education" defined in their own terms, sometimes with only rhetorical references to the Constitution. Different church groups argue differently about the public school's responsibility for religious education. Parents and police chiefs want the schools to "do something" about juvenile delinquency.

Special interests not only tell the schools about their duties, they also provide materials for school use. School supply manufacturers provide consultants to help teachers teach more effectively by means of their supplies. The oil industry provides free educational materials for use in classes studying petroleum and its place in our economy. Insurance companies provide free materials for health education. Dictionary makers provide word study guides as teacher aids. The Chamber of Commerce provides free materials for economic education. The National Congress of Parents and Teachers has published a "Teachers Guide to the PTA" for use in colleges for teacher education. Automobile dealers provide driver-training aids, fishing tackle manufacturers provide equipment for fishing classes, the Modern Language Association develops materials for teaching foreign languages in the third grade, and a manufacturer of hair oil provides a comic book to be used as a high school text in good grooming, with suggestions for classroom use. Each of these (and the list might be expanded indefinitely) implies another objective for the schools, an expression by a "public" of what the school is expected to teach; and each of them is evidence that some schools have undertaken to do it.

This is a departure from history. It is the modern school, the modern American school in particular, that is asked to assume the obligation, and sometimes seems to have accepted it, to teach almost everything that anyone needs to know. It is also asked to accept other responsibilities besides teaching. It is made responsible for the health of children and for their recreation. It provides safe custody for them until they are old enough to go to work. It is an employment agency serving its graduates and its local industry and it is a resource for national manpower. It teaches parents as well as children and it sometimes serves as a community social center.

There is a current controversy about the scope of school responsibility, closely related to the controversy between the "classic" and the "pragmatic" views of education. S. T. Torsten Lund and others, for example, urge "school-centered communities," in which the school would be a central agency for practically all worthy community activities and would coincide in breadth with the community and in duration with the lives of its residents. Robert M. Hutchins, on the contrary, observes that a need of our time is for "unspecialized men and specialized institutions."

The issue is a fairly clear one: What is the limit of the educational responsibility of an educational agency? Should the school try to teach everyone everything he needs to know? The White House Conference Committee says, "Yes," and observes that ". . . Although it is new, this ideal of schools which do everything possible for all children is a natural development in the United States. . . ."

Arthur Bestor, however, thinks this development fatal to the success of our schools if it is not reversed:

> The idea that the school must undertake to meet every need that some other agency is failing to meet, regardless of the suitability of the schoolroom to the task, is a preposterous delusion that in the end can wreck the educational system without in any way contributing to the salvation of society.

This is another open question, which is dealt with further in Part 4 of this volume.

There are many different purposes, then, for which the schools are expected to establish special programs or activities. There is another way in which schools have diverse aims, however; for the same educational activity may have different purposes for different people and more than one purpose for the same person. Both government and industry these days need large numbers of highly trained scientists and technicians—physicists, for example—and anticipate need for more and more of them over the years to come. As potential employers, spokesmen for government and for industry urge the high schools and colleges to persuade more and more young men and women to study sciences, physics in particular. Both government and industry help to pay the bill. From the point of view of government, the distant goal may be national security; a more immediate goal is to fill vacant or anticipated jobs. From the point of view of the manufacturer of electronic equipment, the distant goals may be new products, higher production, successful competition with other manufacturers (sustained profits, in short). A more immediate goal may be a supply of young physicists to fill vacant or anticipated jobs. For both government and industry there are very particular things to be done by the physicists they seek, and these also are aims of education as viewed by spokesmen for government and industry.

The young man studying physics in college is interested in his country's security and in increased industrial power and production. But his primary aim in studying physics, if he can identify one, is not likely to be preparation for a particular job with a particular employer, as it is the aim of government or industry to fill particular jobs. He is fortunate that he is becoming a physicist when he will have a choice of jobs and is sure of good employment. If there were a surplus of physicists, he might choose another specialty. But this is not the same as having a particular job in mind. The statement of his primary aim is likely to be very simple: he is studying physics because he wants to be a physicist. His educational aim is learning to be one: he is interested in physics and wants to know about it.

Then there is the professor. Among his general aims may be the advancement of the science to which he is devoted, an aim which he hopes to achieve by training young physicists as well as by his own study. He gets his greatest satisfaction from students who come to surpass his own knowledge.

There is the parent, too; for most students of physics, as of other specialties, are in school partly at the expense of their parents, and their parents have an interest in their schooling. The parent's aim in sending his son or daughter to college may be very different from the student's aim. He need not share his son's interest in physics at all nor be very much concerned that his son make a direct contribution either to national security or to industrial power. In the most general terms, he wants "what is best" for his child. What is best in his view may be a white-collar job, a comfortable income, doing what he wants to do, personal satisfaction and security, social status, achievement of the parent's unrealized aspirations, or a great many other things. Whatever the parent's aspiration for his son, he regards going to college as a means by which his son may more nearly achieve it. He leaves more particular choices of specialization and professional aspiration to his offspring.

Or he may not, of course. Matthew Arnold tells us of "Mrs. Gooch's Golden Rule, or the Divine Injunction 'Be ye Perfect' done into British,— the sentence Sir Daniel Gooch's mother repeated to him every morning when he was a boy going to work: *'Ever remember, my dear Dan, that you should look forward to being some day manager of that concern!'* " Like Sir Daniel, many sons and daughters are expected to achieve their parents' aspirations for them. Some in these circumstances have the same aspirations as their parents; some do not.

Any individual, of course, has many aims—sometimes many aims that may be served by the same means. The professor of physics or the manufacturer may also be parent; both are citizens and may be government officials. In their different roles they may have different interests that are served simultaneously by the physics course. Diversity of aims, whether they are the diverse aims of the same person or of different people, may or may not mean conflict of aims. The aim of the student and the aims of government and industry as we have described them in this example are not contradictory. When industry and government attract science teachers away from the schools into more remunerative jobs, however, the future supply of physicists may be jeopardized. Near and distant goals of government and industry may thus be contradictory.

A single physics course, then, although itself only a small part of an educational program, from different points of view may serve many ends: national security, increased industrial production, preparation for a profession, assurance of white-collar status and a comfortable income for a son or daughter, or the advancement of science. A formulation of its aims might list all of these and many more. When at the semester's end the professor wishes to appraise his success and the student's, however, he does it not in these terms but in terms of objectives stated so precisely and so particularly that he can frame questions that will test the student's knowledge. He has the general and distant aim of advancing science, but he has the more particular and more immediate aim of encouraging his student to master very specific skills and knowledge. This he seeks not merely because such achievement is easier to measure but also because it is a step on the way to making a physicist, and this in turn is a step on the way to all the more general and more remote objectives of education in physics.

Near and Distant Goals

Ends, in education as in other activities, may be near or remote, and they may be desired for themselves or for the sake of something else—"learning for the sake of learning," Adler says, "or learning for the sake of earning."

Ends may be near or remote. A distinguished journalist recently described his daughter as "fourteen going on eighteen." The phrase wraps up many of the hopes and sorrows of adolescence. To be eighteen! Eighteen is a golden age from the point of view of fourteen—as from the point of view of forty. Young, but mature; independent, but carefree; the peak of life. But to be eighteen one must become fourteen and a half, fifteen, sixteen, seventeen, and then survive twelve endless months before he can be eighteen, with a driver's license, permission to use the car, a later curfew, a larger allowance or a self-supporting job, self-chosen clothes, and all the other symbols of maturity.

But to be eighteen, much as it may be desired, is not an aim, because there is nothing one can do to become eighteen except wait. Aims govern our actions. They are goals toward which we can strive but which we cannot achieve by mere waiting. "The aim of a foreseen end," says Dewey in the essay included in these readings, "gives direction to the activity; it is not an idle view of a mere spectator." To become a teacher, for example, one must have a certificate. It is a means to being a teacher, but to get it is an aim. To get a certificate, one must have certain knowledge and skills attested either by examination or by completing specified college courses.

The Purposes of Education

This also is an aim, less remote. To enter college, one must complete high school. The members of "Future Teachers of America" now in high school have before them the distant aim of becoming teachers and the intermediate aims of graduation from college, certification, mastery of relevant knowledge and skills, and employment by a school. Again Dewey: "Every means is a temporary end until we have attained it. Every end becomes a means of carrying activity further as soon as it is achieved."

John Dewey does not regard "ultimate ends," ends which lead to no further activity if achieved, as meaningful. Another view distinguishes between intermediate ends and ultimate ends and places greatest importance upon the ultimate. Intermediate ends are things desired for the sake of more distant goals; ultimate ends are desired for themselves. Being ultimate, they have the characteristic that we can never cease striving for them—they cannot be achieved or cannot be retained without continuing effort. Aristotle gives us a working definition of this kind of finality in the *Nichomachean Ethics* and also identifies happiness as the end, the good to which in his judgment we subordinate all other things and for the sake of which we desire all other things:

> If . . . there is some end of the things we do, which we desire for its own sake (everything else being desired for the sake of this) and if we do not choose everything for the sake of something else (for at that rate the process would go on to infinity so that our desire would be empty and vain,) clearly this must be the good and the chief good. Will not knowledge of it, then, have a great influence on life? Shall we not, like archers who have a mark to aim at, be more likely to hit upon what is right? . . .
>
> Let us again return to the good we are seeking, and ask what it can be. It seems different in different actions and arts; it is different in medicine, in strategy, and in the other arts likewise. What then is the good of each? Surely that for whose sake everything else is done. In medicine this is health, in strategy victory, in architecture a house, and in any other sphere something else, and in every action and pursuit the end; for it is for the sake of this that all men do whatever else they do. Therefore if there is an end for all that we do, this will be the good achievable by action. . . . We call final without qualification that which is always desirable in itself and never for the sake of something else.
>
> Now such a thing happiness, above all else, is held to be; for this we always choose for itself and never for the sake of something else, but honour, pleasure, reason, and every virtue we choose indeed for themselves (for if nothing resulted from them we should still choose each of them,) but we choose them also for the sake of happiness, judging that by means of them we shall be happy. Happiness, on the other hand, no

one chooses for the sake of these, nor, in general, for anything other than itself.[4]

Other philosophers have identified other things than happiness as the final good or have defined happiness differently from Aristotle, who devotes many pages to its definition. Some deny that there is any single final good to which all others are subordinate.

Things that are desired for their own sakes, even though they may also be desired for the sake of something else, we may regard as ultimate ends, if not the chief end. Whether or not wisdom, for example, is desired for the sake of happiness, it is desirable for itself. In this sense, different human activities may have different final goals. If wisdom, for example, is the final goal of education, then everything that we do in education is for the sake of wisdom. Lesser goods to be achieved are steps on the way.

Almost any college catalogue will illustrate the point. That of Mount Holyoke College, for example, does affirm wisdom to be the end of "liberal education." Then it amplifies:

> Without offering vocational training, Mount Holyoke awakens the life in which the good vocations are found; without imposing philosophies, it shows what a sound philosophy is; without professing final answers, it finds what questions need answers. In itself, it cannot save the individual, or democracy, or the world; but to every student willing to learn, it shows both what is there to be saved and what they must know who will save it.

Typical course descriptions in the same catalogue, however, are in these terms:

> QUANTITATIVE ANALYSIS. A study of chemical equilibrium and other chemical principles with applications to analytical separations. Semi-micro methods of analysis are used in the laboratory.
> HISTORY OF THE IBERIAN PENINSULA SINCE 711 A.D. Aspects of medieval and early modern Spain and Portugal, with emphasis on the period of Spanish ascendance in Europe and the Western Hemisphere.

Two important current statements of the purposes of schools in the United States today also illustrate the difference between intermediate ends and ultimate ends. The White House Conference on Education affirms that

> We believe education is necessary for the fullest development and enrichment of the individual,

and that

[4] *Ethica Nichomachea,* tr. by W. D. Ross, in *The Basic Works of Aristotle,* ed. by Richard McKeon (New York: Random House, 1941), pp. 935, 941-2.

The Purposes of Education 243

The continued success of our democratic way of life requires that every individual be afforded that education necessary to enable him to make an intelligent choice and to effect necessary compromises on questions of public policy.

"Full development and enrichment of the individual," and "the democratic way of life" are infinitely pursuable ends and are the stated general aims of education agreed upon by the White House Conference. They are followed by fourteen less general statements of less remote aims: e.g. "It is the consensus of these groups that the schools should continue to develop" such things as "physical and mental health," "wise use of time," and "ability to think and evaluate constructively and creatively."

Mental health, wisdom of any kind, and ability to think creatively and constructively are still very general aims, however. The Mid-Century Committee on Outcomes in Elementary Education formulates "outcomes" with much more particularity than the White House Conference. It makes its statement in terms of intermediate ends, telling us that at age nine a child (if education has been successful to that point) "skips to music in unison with others," "eats wholesome food, chews it well," can "recognize the most obvious jokes," "is beginning to understand the purpose of the school" [sic!], knows how "to assume group leadership," should "be able to read a map of his own city or town," "should be able to operate a radio and television set," "can use clay in simple pottery forms," "in third grade material, he reads with a comprehension score of 80 per cent," "reads poetry and stories for personal pleasure," "can count by 2's, 3's, 4's, 5's, and 10's up to 50 or 100," and "is able to handle his own financial transactions." None of these accomplishments, perhaps, is indispensable to wisdom. Taken together they are still a long way from wisdom. Yet each may be a step on the way.

Just as the program of a school is planned in terms of near and distant goals, so is each class. A distant objective of any reading instruction may be assumed to be to develop life-long habits of reading for power and for pleasure, the capacity and the desire to use the printed page as a source of knowledge and a source of wisdom and joy. But the teacher in the early grades does not seek to interest his children in Shakespeare's plays or Winston Churchill's *History of the English Speaking Peoples*. He is content if his pupils learn to read what they can understand, read it with pleasure, and learn to use print as a source of the kind of knowledge that is meaningful to them. Before they reach that goal, there are many nearer intermediate aims to be achieved. Similarly in any other subject: the objective of a geography unit in the fifth grade social science classes of one city school system is affirmed to be understanding the way of life of other people in the world. Subsidiary objectives include understanding the globe as a symbol of the earth. This is an intermediate end on the way to the remoter end, itself an intermediate end on the way to better citizenship in a spherical world. Throughout the whole school system, teachers and pupils establish one goal after another on the endless road of education, at each stage seeking the means that will advance them most rapidly.

MEANS AND ENDS

Because the readings that follow deal with the end or ends of education, they deal also at least by implication with the means. If the object is to teach children to spell, the teacher may follow the old practice of requiring them to memorize long lists of words classified by the number of syllables. A young schoolmaster in the early part of the nineteenth century boasted that he could "not only spell all the common words of the spelling book, but also recollect them if they were separated from their companions." If the object is not to teach spelling for its own sake but rather to teach children to communicate on paper, the teacher may only insist that they learn to spell words of which they know the meaning and that they learn to use the dictionary. Extracts from textbooks, sample tests, and lesson plans included in the readings that follow illustrate the relationship between means and end.

An end is that which is desired or sought whether for itself or for the sake of something else. A means is that through which or with the aid of which an end is approached or achieved. An end—happiness, for example —may be desired only for its own sake. It is good but not good *for* anything. An end may also be desired both for its own sake and for the sake of something else, as knowledge is. That is, we may desire knowledge whether we have a specific use for it or not; we can also use it. Some things are desirable only for what we can do with them. Money, for example, is essentially a means. It is desirable because we can do things with it: we can exchange it for goods and services. If men regard it as an end, love it, and desire it for itself, we attribute avarice to them and call them misers. When Robinson Crusoe finds money in the ship he is stripping of things that will be useful on his island, he is too thoroughly European to leave it behind, but he exclaims upon its uselessness:

> "What art thou good for? . . . one of those knives is worth this heap. I have no manner of use for thee." However, [he adds] on second thoughts, I took it away.

Like money, tools of various kinds are essentially means, not ends. A hammer is desirable because it can be used to drive nails, a screwdriver because it can be used to drive screws, a slide-projector because it can cast pictures on a screen. None of these has value unless there are nails or screws to be driven or pictures to be projected. Spelling is a valuable accomplishment only if there are words to be spelled and an occasion to spell them.

Means and ends are inseparably related. Robinson Crusoe could not continue his journal because he ran out of ink and could invent no satisfactory substitute. He lost one load of goods from the ship because his raft—his means of transportation—was inadequate for the load he put on it. He could not launch his first canoe because he built it too far from the sea and had no adequate means to move it. The fences he built were even better than he planned because the green stakes cut from his tropical trees sprouted and grew luxuriantly.

Crusoe's account of his conquest of the tropic island is almost a treatise on the adjustment of means and ends to one another. When Crusoe could not devise sufficient means to achieve his purposes, he changed his goals. It is after building his first canoe that he comments on "the folly of beginning a work before we count the cost, and before we judge rightly of our own strength to go through with it." When the smaller canoe is finished, he has given up hope of a vessel large enough to enable him to seek the mainland. "The smallness of my boat assisted to put an end to that design and now I thought no more of it." On the other hand, when Crusoe discovered that his fence-posts grew, he trained them for shade and planted more for additional protection and shade.

Like Robinson Crusoe, the teacher is wiser in action if he remembers that means must be commensurate with ends. Like Crusoe, when means are inadequate to ends, the teacher must seek other means or change his ends, or both.

> The aim as it first emerges [says John Dewey] is a mere tentative sketch. If it suffices to direct activity successfully, nothing more is required, since its whole function is to set a mark in advance. . . . But usually . . . acting upon it brings to light conditions which had been overlooked. This calls for revision of the original aim; it has to be added to and subtracted from.

Alfred North Whitehead states a different view:

> In the schools of antiquity, philosophers aspired to impart wisdom, in modern colleges our humbler aim is to teach subjects. . . . At the dawn of our European civilization, men started with the full ideals which should inspire education, and . . . gradually our ideals have sunk to square with our practice.[5]

[5] Alfred North Whitehead, *The Aims of Education* (New York, The Macmillan Company), 1929, p. 45.

Whitehead does not argue, of course, that the ancients succeeded in imparting wisdom, and he does imply that we achieve at least partial success in "teaching subjects." He recommends, by implication, that modern education return to the old aspiration, not in the hope that it can be achieved but in order to keep schools alert for means that may enable them to approach it more nearly. "When ideals have sunk to the level of practice," he says, "the result is stagnation." Rabbi Ben Ezra in Browning's poem also testifies to the value of unachieved aspirations:

> What I aspired to be,
> And was not, comforts me.

At Mount Holyoke, as our quotation from the catalogue indicates, there is an aspiration to wisdom. There is also the aim of teaching subjects, with the presumption that study of chemistry, classics, history, and the other subjects that make up a college curriculum is the means through which later "ripeness of thought and wisdom of action" are achieved. A key question for any agency of education lies in this presumption, the question whether the means available are adequate to the end in view.

In his *Notes on Virginia,* Thomas Jefferson proposed a system of schools and schooling designed in effect to make every man a statesman. Jefferson proposed for this purpose three years of elementary schooling open to all, during which the reading was to be "chiefly historical" because the goal was effective citizenship.

There are and have been good and effective citizens who have never been to school, and there are educated rascals—some of them very effective bad citizens. Nevertheless, our schools have retained Jefferson's goal and his faith that schooling can help make every man a good citizen, in some measure a statesman. But now eight, twelve, or fourteen years of schooling are required "to make a citizen." The three short years that Jefferson proposed have been found inadequate, perhaps partly because the concept of citizenship has been broadened, partly because the duties of citizenship seem more difficult to perform in the twentieth century, but also because the twentieth century knows more about children and their learning. Psychologists and educators today make a different appraisal of how much children can learn in three years, how much they retain and apply when they reach maturity. They make a different appraisal of how meaningful "historical reading" done and finished in the third grade will be when the third-grader has grown up. On many grounds the twentieth century has made the judgment that the means proposed by Jefferson are disproportionate to the end, inadequate to achieve it.

There have been other changes in the concept of appropriate means than length of time. Accordingly, twentieth-century schools have devised

The Purposes of Education

other aids to school learning than books and other school activities than reading and recitation. "Historical reading" remains an important component in education for citizenship, but the curriculum now includes other social studies, too. Moreover, the climate and organization of the schools have changed, so that children not only read about citizenship and government but practice citizenship and observe governments. There are student organizations and school elections. There are school community chests and school service clubs and school neighborhood-improvement programs. Units of study in many classes are planned by committees of students, and class projects in many other classes are undertaken by committees. Children have a voice in determining school activities and are expected to learn how to work with others by democratic procedures. Some report cards report on "citizenship" as well as upon achievement in listed school subjects. Field trips to government agencies and installations, visits to city, county, state, and federal government agencies are commonplace. The policeman, the fireman, the postman, or the elected official may explain his duties to a class, and children in any grade are likely to be engaged in field studies of their neighborhoods.

And still, even from our highest schools, enough indifferent citizens and enough educated rascals graduate to show that the means devised for citizenship education (more broadly, for moral education) are inadequate for complete and universal achievement of the exalted goal. Every man is not a statesman. The objective has not been abandoned. It has been redefined and the means by which it is sought have been changed and no doubt will be changed again and again as long as the goal is retained but imperfectly achieved.

Like other distant goals, it is sought in stages, more or less clearly defined—by way of intermediate ends which are established in terms of the means available. It is always easier to aim at the nearer goal, which may itself be a means toward the more distant goal. Local, regional, state, and national meetings of the White House Conference on Education, for example, began with the question of ends or aims. "What should our schools accomplish?" was the conference formulation of the question, and this question was given priority over other questions because (so the sponsors of the conference affirmed) the means cannot be determined until the ends are established. The questions of means that were then raised were as follows: How can we organize our school systems more efficiently and economically? What are our school building needs? How can we get enough good teachers and keep them? How can we finance our schools—build and operate them? How can we obtain a continuing public interest in education? These are intermediate ends as well as means. Just as we must manufacture tools before we can manufacture automobiles, so we must build schools before we can educate children in them.

Some participants in the conference objected, however, to the consideration of ends separately from the means available. "It would seem," says a minority report in one state,

> that all the broad and general objectives and recommendations of the Report cannot come within the finances reasonably to be expected in the near future. Therefore a selective priority—either absolute or partial—between the various objectives and recommendations is necessary.

This is to say that ends cannot be finally determined until the means are known, or that it is unwise to formulate ends without an appraisal of the means available to achieve them. Like Robinson Crusoe, the writers of the minority report are commenting on "the folly of beginning a work . . . before we judge rightly of our own strength to go through with it." In their view, appraisal of the means available is part of the process of establishing goals.

The warning sign in an office-building elevator, "Unsafe for more than 20 persons or 3,000 pounds" is an appraisal of the adequacy of means to ends, and it is foolhardy to ignore it. Similarly, airlines do not schedule flights beyond the gasoline capacity of their planes, and it is a first principle of military strategy not to attempt more than can be accomplished with the forces available. But designers are constantly seeking to increase the load capacity and flying range of airplanes, and military commanders seek to build their strength until it is adequate for the preconceived objective.

Schools operate this way, too. A school without a library and a librarian may try very hard to inculcate the library habit in its pupils. Teachers lend their own books, establish cordial relations with public libraries, and do what they can without a library. Meanwhile, school budget authorities seek funds to establish a library so that teachers can do their job better.

In the schoolroom, too, the teacher strives constantly to find means that will enable his students to achieve more and more while he does the best he can with the means at his disposal. Every time he chooses a new text, every new exercise he devises, every new task he sets, every sketch he draws on the blackboard, every activity he suggests to a child, every clipping added to the classroom bulletin board, every object brought for observation, every new story told, every game played is an attempt by the teacher to find better means to achieve immediate and distant goals.

WHAT DOES THE READER DO?

Faced with different views of man and different views of education, faced even with different meanings for the same word as he finds it used by different writers, what does the reader do?

The Purposes of Education

As he reads, he should be aware that different formulations of the purposes of education may reflect quite different views of the nature of man, the good life, and society. He should ask himself what presuppositions underlie each formulation of the aims of education.

The reader should remember that the aims of education may be viewed from the point of view of an individual or individuals with personal and possibly unique aims or aspirations and capacities. (It is an illuminating exercise for a college student to write what he thinks the aims of education should be from the point of view of a college and then to write a statement of why he is in college. The two statements do not always look alike. It is illuminating for a teacher to state his objectives for a class, then for one member of it, and then to compare his statements with one prepared by the student.)

Education may be viewed, the reader should remember, from the point of view of the common interest of some special group: workers, consumers, employers; neighbors, a community, or a nation; parents or teachers. When a boy is urged to study the physical sciences because we may be on the verge of atomic war, is it for the good of the nation or the good of the boy or both? When a junior college in a center of the chemical industry is urged to establish training programs for chemical technicians, is it for the good of the boy or the good of the industry?

Finally, education may be viewed as reflecting an ideal of human nature relevant to all men. Thus the betterment of mankind, Mortimer Adler says, may be viewed "with respect to their differences" or "with respect to the *similarities* that all men have." Programs of vocational education which prepare students for a wide variety of different occupations are based on one view, Adler says. Programs of "common learnings" in which all children are taught the same skills—such skills as reading and arithmetic, presumably—represent the other view.

There are other distinctions which should be kept in mind. Some things —some qualities, habits of mind, states of being, some kinds of knowledge, some activities—like life itself or like health or happiness may be desirable for their own sakes. Other things are desirable only because they lead to something else. Still others may be desirable both for their own sakes and for the sake of something else, as Aristotle says, we value honor and pleasure for their own sakes but also for the sake of happiness. Money, on the other hand, is valuable only for the sake of other things. Accordingly, the aims of education may be formulated in terms of ultimate ends—things desirable for their own sakes—or in terms of intermediate ends—things desirable for the sake of something else to which they are the means. Thus Pius XI states the ultimate end of education as follows:

> . . . since education consists essentially in preparing man for what he must be and for what he must do here below, in order to attain the sublime end for which he was created, it is clear that there can be no true education which is not wholly directed to man's last end. . . .

But there are intermediate ends as well, which as they are achieved become means to the ultimate end. Pope Pius quotes Tertullian to show that neither Christianity nor Christian education implies withdrawal from the world:

> . . . we do not shun your forums, your markets, your baths, your shops, your factories, your stables, your places of business and traffic. We take ship with you and serve in your armies, we are farmers and merchants with you. . . .

"The true Christian," Pope Pius adds, "does not renounce the activities of this life, he does not stunt his natural faculties; but he develops and perfects them with the supernatural."

Here is a clear distinction between ultimate and intermediate ends. Men learn what they must do here below as a means to the ultimate end of salvation.

Some ends are remote, sometimes so remote that although they may be approached more and more nearly, they are not to be achieved fully in this life. Democracy, wisdom, security, virtue, perfection, culture may be such ends. Other goals are so near that they can be achieved in school in a single lesson and retained for life: a child can learn a few new words, a principle of perspective—what we see from above should be drawn rising —another portion of the "times table," a fact of history, or to tip his hat to a lady; and we can measure his achievement. Perhaps achievement of any of these goals is a step on the way to wisdom, culture, security, socialization, democracy, virtue, self-realization, or happiness—or toward all of them. They are also steps on the way to nearer goals. New words mean better communication, reading and writing, listening and speaking. A new insight into perspective means better drawing, sharper observation, keener enjoyment, and so on. All of them mean increased capacity to learn.

It is well for the reader to remember that distant goals may determine the nearer goals to be achieved on the way. In planning an automobile trip from Chicago to New York, the driver may set as the first day's objective a motel near Pittsburgh. In seeking to develop good citizenship, the teacher may set as the objective of a unit "understanding of the globe as a symbol of the earth."

The reader's object in reading about the aims of education (the aim of this particular educational exercise) is to clarify his own thinking about them. His first task, as a means to that end, is to understand what the writer he reads intends to say. Acceptance, rejection, or modification of the views of an author—or indifference to them—should follow understanding. If any of these attitudes comes first, understanding is not so likely to follow.

To understand one author may help to understand another. To compare the views of different writers may help to understand all of them. The critical reader will keep in mind the questions that have been raised here and will ask other questions of his own. If the authors he reads are not in agreement, are they writing about the same thing or about different things? Is one writer concerned with immediate goals, for example, and another with remote or ultimate goals? Is one writing from the point of view of the student, another from the point of view of society? The Mid-Century Committee states the objectives of education in the specific terms that have been quoted (a child of nine can "count by 2's, 3's, 4's, 5's, and 10's up to 50 or 100"). Does this contradict Horace Mann's more general assertion that an end of education is "to counterwork the tendency to the domination of capital and the servility of labor"? Does it supplement Mann's statement? Or are the two statements not meaningfully related because they are about different things? Do the different formulations reflect the different times at which they were written? If so, are earlier statements rendered invalid, or do they become both clearer and more relevant if we view them in historical perspective? "What we see from above should be drawn rising" is perhaps a historical principle as well as a principle of pictorial art.

Not all of these questions can be answered about all the readings presented here, for most of the readings are extracts from longer discussions and all of them are but part of the whole thought of their authors; and what one thinks about education, one's philosophy of education, is part of a larger philosophy. Each statement of an educational aim is partial if it is divorced from its context. To understand fully the brief statement from Aristotle's *Politics,* for example, to know all of the assumptions and all of the arguments that underlie Aristotle's conclusions about education, we ought to read the rest of the book and his works on ethics and on other subjects as well. And perhaps to understand those works more fully, we need to know Plato, who taught Aristotle, and a good deal about Greek society. The chapter from John Dewey's *Democracy and Education* is clarified, too, if we read the rest of the volume and other works by Dewey. No doubt it would be further clarified if we could know in detail Dewey's work with the laboratory school he headed as a young man at the University of Chicago.

Few of us can undertake the work that this kind of mastery suggests, and complete mastery of educational philosophy is one of those unachievable goals to which some men devote their whole lives. We do the best we can with the time and the books and the experience available, suiting the means to the end and defining the end in terms of the means available.

But acquaintance with the thought of a variety of writers on education is not the end. Having understood what others think, having examined the views of men who have thought much on the subject, the student has a basis on which to build his own thought, to examine and to clarify it. Indeed, he formulates, examines, and reformulates his own views as he reads—and presumably for the rest of his life as he gathers experience and as he reads further.

The history of Western thought has been described as a great conversation, and this is an insightful description. But there are many conversations, not only one. The writer we read today may not be responding directly to the remarks of the writer we read yesterday. And even in the great conversation among great writers, as in lesser conversations among ourselves, the speakers sometimes use terms differently, sometimes shift the focus of discussion, sometimes change the subject, sometimes seek to win an argument rather than to explore an idea. The perceptive reader takes an active part in the conversation and has some of the functions of a discussion leader. He defines for himself the point at issue, he summarizes, he calls on different speakers for their special contributions to the discussion, and he brings the discussion back to the point at issue when it digresses. The task requires all the reader's alertness, but he learns much more than he will as a mere eavesdropper on the conversation.

Why should he bother? Simply because education is important and (since he is a student) important to him. A publication of the National Manpower Council, *A Policy for Skilled Manpower,* tells us that many of us have and use concepts of the aims proper to education, although we may not know it:

> What is the purpose of secondary education? An attempt to answer this question is implicit in every current dispute over our public educational system. This is true whether the speaker bewails the alleged inability of contemporary students to write, read, or mind their manners; whether he insists that more education for all is the surest way to cure the world's ills; whether he protests that too many people are getting too much education; or whether he calls for larger appropriations for school buildings and teachers' salaries. No matter what his point of view, he bases his arguments and his judgments on his concept—frequently unstated and unexamined—of what our educational system should accomplish.[6]

[6] National Manpower Council, *A Policy for Skilled Manpower* (New York, Columbia University Press, 1954), p. 136.

The Purposes of Education

In debate about schools, our words and our arguments are shaped by our concept of the purposes of education. Our concept shapes our actions, too. The present life of a student and the whole professional life of a teacher are shaped by views of the purposes of education, their own and others. Ignorance is always a handicap, in thought and in action; not to know what one thinks is one of the most incapacitating forms of ignorance. One of the aims of higher education, in the view of the editors of this volume, is to encourage students to think seriously about serious things.

Formulations and Discussions

SABER-TOOTH CURRICULUM *

The first great educational theorist and practitioner of whom my imagination has any record (began Dr. Peddiwell in his best professorial tone) was a man of Chellean times whose full name was *New-Fist-Hammer-Maker* but whom, for convenience, I shall hereafter call *New-Fist*.

New-Fist was a doer, in spite of the fact that there was little in his environment with which to do anything very complex. You have undoubtedly heard of the pear-shaped, chipped-stone tool which archeologists call the *coup-de-poing* or fist hammer. New-Fist gained his name and a considerable local prestige by producing one of these artifacts in a less rough and more useful form than any previously known to his tribe. His hunting clubs were generally superior weapons, moreover, and his fire-using techniques were patterns of simplicity and precision. He knew how to do things his community needed to have done, and he had the energy and will to go ahead and do them. By virtue of these characteristics he was an educated man.

New-Fist was also a thinker. Then, as now, there were few lengths to which men would not go to avoid the labor and pain of thought. More readily than his fellows, New-Fist pushed himself beyond those lengths to the point where cerebration was inevitable. The same quality of intelligence which led him into the socially approved activity of producing a superior artifact also led him to engage in the socially disapproved prac-

---

* Harold Benjamin, *Saber-Tooth Curriculum* (New York and London, McGraw-Hill, 1939), pp. 24-44. Copyright 1939 by McGraw-Hill Book Co., Inc.

tice of thinking. When other men gorged themselves on the proceeds of a successful hunt and vegetated in dull stupor for many hours thereafter, New-Fist ate a little less heartily, slept a little less stupidly, and arose a little earlier than his comrades to sit by the fire and think. He would stare moodily at the flickering flames and wonder about various parts of his environment until he finally got to the point where he became strongly dissatisfied with the accustomed ways of his tribe. He began to catch glimpses of ways in which life might be made better for himself, his family, and his group. By virtue of this development, he became a dangerous man.

This was the background that made this doer and thinker hit upon the concept of a conscious, systematic education. The immediate stimulus which put him directly into the practice of education came from watching his children at play. He saw these children at the cave entrance before the fire engaged in activity with bones and sticks and brightly colored pebbles. He noted that they seemed to have no purpose in their play beyond immediate pleasure in the activity itself. He compared their activity with that of the grown-up members of the tribe. The children played for fun; the adults worked for security and enrichment of their lives. The children dealt with bones, sticks, and pebbles; the adults dealt with food, shelter, and clothing. The children protected themselves from boredom; the adults protected themselves from danger.

"If I could only get these children to do the things that will give more and better food, shelter, clothing, and security," thought New-Fist, "I would be helping this tribe to have a better life. When the children became grown, they would have more meat to eat, more skins to keep them warm, better caves in which to sleep, and less danger from the striped death with the curving teeth that walks these trails by night."

Having set up an educational goal, New-Fist proceeded to construct a curriculum for reaching that goal. "What things must we tribesmen know how to do in order to live with full bellies, warm backs, and minds free from fear?" he asked himself.

To answer this question, he ran various activities over in his mind. "We have to catch fish with our bare hands in the pool far up the creek beyond that big bend," he said to himself. "We have to catch fish with our bare hands in the pool right at the bend. We have to catch them in the same way in the pool just this side of the bend. And so we catch them in the next pool and the next and the next. Always we catch them with our bare hands."

Thus New-Fist discovered the first subject of the first curriculum—fish-grabbing-with-the-bare-hands.

"Also we club the little woolly horses," he continued with his analysis.

"We club them along the bank of the creek where they come down to drink. We club them in the thickets where they lie down to sleep. We club them in the upland meadow where they graze. Wherever we find them we club them."

So woolly-horse-clubbing was seen to be the second main subject in the curriculum.

"And finally, we drive away the saber-tooth tigers with fire," New-Fist went on in his thinking. "We drive them from the mouth of our cave with fire. We drive them from our trail with burning branches. We wave firebrands to drive them from our drinking hole. Always we have to drive them away, and always we drive them with fire."

Thus was discovered the third subject—saber-tooth-tiger-scaring-with-fire.

Having developed a curriculum, New-Fist took his children with him as he went about his activities. He gave them an opportunity to practice these three subjects. The children liked to learn. It was more fun for them to engage in these purposeful activities than to play with colored stones just for the fun of it. They learned the new activities well, and so the educational system was a success.

As New-Fist's children grew older, it was plain to see that they had an advantage in good and safe living over other children who had never been educated systematically. Some of the more intelligent members of the tribe began to do as New-Fist had done, and the teaching of fish-grabbing, horse-clubbing, and tiger-scaring came more and more to be accepted as the heart of real education.

For a long time, however, there were certain more conservative members of the tribe who resisted the new, formal educational system on religious grounds. "The Great Mystery who speaks in thunder and moves in lightning," they announced impressively, "the Great Mystery who gives men life and takes it from them as he wills—if that Great Mystery had wanted children to practice fish-grabbing, horse-clubbing, and tiger-scaring before they were grown up, he would have taught them these activities himself by implanting in their natures instincts for fish-grabbing, horse-clubbing, and tiger-scaring. New-Fist is not only impious to attempt something the Great Mystery never intended to have done; he is also a damned fool for trying to change human nature."

Whereupon approximately half of these critics took up the solemn chant, "If you oppose the will of the Great Mystery, you must die," and the remainder sang derisively in unison, "You can't change human nature."

Being an educational statesman as well as an educational administrator and theorist, New-Fist replied politely to both arguments. To the more theologically minded, he said that, as a matter of fact, the Great Mystery had ordered this new work done, that he even did the work himself by causing children to want to learn, that children could not learn by themselves without divine aid, that they could not learn at all except through the power of the Great Mystery, and that nobody could really understand the will of the Great Mystery concerning fish, horses, and saber-tooth tigers unless he had been well grounded in the three fundamental subjects of the New-Fist school. To the human-nature-cannot-be-changed shouters, New-Fist pointed out the fact that paleolithic culture had attained its high level by changes in human nature and that it seemed almost unpatriotic to deny the very process which had made the community great.

"I know you, my fellow tribesmen," the pioneer educator ended his argument gravely, "I know you as humble and devoted servants of the Great Mystery. I know that you would not for one moment consciously oppose yourselves to his will. I know you as intelligent and loyal citizens of this great cave-realm, and I know that your pure and noble patriotism will not permit you to do anything which will block the development of that most cave-realmish of all our institutions—the paleolithic educational system. Now that you understand the true nature and purpose of this institution, I am serenely confident that there are no reasonable lengths to which you will not go in its defense and its support."

By this appeal the forces of conservatism were won over to the side of the new school, and in due time everybody who was anybody in the community knew that the heart of good education lay in the three subjects of fish-grabbing, horse-clubbing, and tiger-scaring. New-Fist and his contemporaries grew old and were gathered by the Great Mystery to the Land of the Sunset far down the creek. Other men followed their educational ways more and more, until at last all the children of the tribe were practiced systematically in the three fundamentals. Thus the tribe prospered and was happy in the possession of adequate meat, skins, and security.

It is to be supposed that all would have gone well forever with this good educational system if conditions of life in that community had remained forever the same. But conditions changed, and life which had once been so safe and happy in the cave-realm valley became insecure and disturbing.

A new ice age was approaching in that part of the world. A great glacier came down from the neighboring mountain range to the north. Year after year it crept closer and closer to the headwaters of the creek which ran through the tribe's valley, until at length it reached the stream and began to melt into the water. Dirt and gravel which the glacier had collected on its long journey were dropped into the creek. The water grew muddy. What had once been a crystal-clear stream in which one could see easily to the bottom was now a milky stream into which one could not see at all.

At once the life of the community was changed in one very important respect. It was no longer possible to catch fish with the bare hands. The fish could not be seen in the muddy water. For some years, moreover, the fish in this creek had been getting more timid, agile, and intelligent. The stupid, clumsy, brave fish, of which originally there had been a great many, had been caught with the bare hands for fish generation after fish generation, until only fish of superior intelligence and agility were left. These smart fish, hiding in the muddy water under the newly deposited glacial boulders, eluded the hands of the most expertly trained fish-grabbers. Those tribesmen who had studied advanced fish-grabbing in the secondary school could do no better than their less well-educated fellows who had taken only an elementary course in the subject, and even the university graduates with majors in ichthyology were baffled by the problem. No matter how good a man's fish-grabbing education had been, he could not grab fish when he could not find fish to grab.

The melting waters of the approaching ice sheet also made the country wetter. The ground became marshy far back from the banks of the creek. The stupid woolly horses, standing only five or six hands high and running on four-toed front feet and three-toed hind feet, although admirable objects for clubbing, had one dangerous characteristic. They were ambitious. They all wanted to learn to run on their middle toes. They all had visions of becoming powerful and aggressive animals instead of little and timid ones. They dreamed of a far-distant day when some of their descendants would be sixteen hands high, weigh more than half a ton, and be able to pitch their would-be riders into the dirt. They knew they could never attain these goals in a wet, marshy country, so they all went east to the dry, open plains, far from the paleolithic hunting grounds. Their places were taken by little antelopes who came down with the ice sheet and were so shy and speedy and had so keen a scent for danger that no one could approach them closely enough to club them.

The best trained horse-clubbers of the tribe went out day after day and employed the most efficient techniques taught in the schools, but day after day they returned empty-handed. A horse-clubbing education of the highest type could get no results when there were no horses to club.

Finally, to complete the disruption of paleolithic life and education, the new dampness in the air gave the saber-tooth tigers pneumonia, a disease to which these animals were peculiarly susceptible and to which most of them succumbed. A few moth-eaten specimens crept south to the desert, it is true, but they were pitifully few and weak representatives of a once numerous and powerful race.

So there were no more tigers to scare in the paleolithic community, and the best tiger-scaring techniques became only academic exercises, good in themselves, perhaps, but not necessary for tribal security. Yet this danger

Formulations and Discussions 259

to the people was lost only to be replaced by another and even greater danger, for with the advancing ice sheet came ferocious glacial bears which were not afraid of fire, which walked the trails by day as well as by night, and which could not be driven away by the most advanced methods developed in the tiger-scaring courses of the schools.

The community was now in a very difficult situation. There was no fish or meat for food, no hides for clothing, and no security from the hairy death that walked the trails day and night. Adjustment to this difficulty had to be made at once if the tribe was not to become extinct.

Fortunately, for the tribe, however, there were men in it of the old New-Fist breed, men who had the ability to do and the daring to think. One of them stood by the muddy stream, his stomach contracting with hunger pains, longing for some way to get a fish to eat. Again and again he had tried the old fish-grabbing technique that day, hoping desperately that at last it might work, but now in black despair he finally rejected all that he had learned in the schools and looked about him for some new way to get fish from that stream. There were stout but slender vines hanging from trees along the bank. He pulled them down and began to fasten them together more or less aimlessly. As he worked, the vision of what he might do to satisfy his hunger and that of his crying children back in the cave grew clearer. His black despair lightened a little. He worked more rapidly and intelligently. At last he had it—a net, a crude seine. He called a companion and explained the device. The two men took the net into the water, into pool after pool, and in one hour they caught more fish—intelligent fish in muddy water—than the whole tribe could have caught in a day under the best fish-grabbing conditions.

Another intelligent member of the tribe wandered hungrily through the woods where once the stupid little horses had abounded but where now only the elusive antelope could be seen. He had tried the horse-clubbing technique on the antelope until he was fully convinced of its futility. He knew that one would starve who relied on school learning to get him meat in those woods. Thus it was that he too, like the fish-net inventor, was finally impelled by hunger to new ways. He bent a strong, springy young tree over an antelope trail, hung a noosed vine therefrom, and fastened the whole device in so ingenious a fashion that the passing animal would release a trigger and be snared neatly when the tree jerked upright. By setting a line of these snares, he was able in one night to secure more meat and skins than a dozen horse-clubbers in the old days had secured in a week.

A third tribesman, determined to meet the problem of the ferocious bears, also forgot what he had been taught in school and began to think in direct and radical fashion. Finally, as a result of this thinking, he dug a deep pit in a bear trail, covered it with branches in such a way that a bear would walk out on it unsuspectingly, fall through to the bottom, and remain trapped until the tribesmen could come up and dispatch him with sticks and stones at their leisure. The inventor showed his friends how to dig and camouflage other pits until all the trails around the community were furnished with them. Thus the tribe had even more security than before and in addition had the great additional store of meat and skins which they secured from captured bears.

As the knowledge of these new inventions spread, all the members of the tribe were engaged in familiarizing themselves with the new ways of living. Men worked hard at making fish nets, setting antelope snares, and digging bear pits. The tribe was busy and prosperous.

There were a few thoughtful men who asked questions as they worked. Some of them even criticized the schools.

"These new activities of net-making and operating, snare-setting, and pit-digging are indispensable to modern existence," they said. "Why can't they be taught in school?"

The safe and sober majority had a quick reply to this naive question. "School!" they snorted derisively. "You aren't in school now. You are out here in the dirt working to preserve the life and happiness of the tribe. What have these practical activities got to do with schools? You're not saying lessons now. You'd better forget your lessons and your academic ideals of fish-grabbing, horse-clubbing, and tiger-scaring if you want to eat, keep warm, and have some measure of security from sudden death."

The radicals persisted a little in their questioning. "Fishnet-making and using, antelope-snare construction and operation, and bear-catching and killing," they pointed out, "require intelligence and skills—things we claim to develop in schools. They are also activities we need to know. Why can't the schools teach them?"

But most of the tribe, and particularly the wise old men who controlled the school, smiled indulgently at this suggestion. "That wouldn't be *education*," they said gently.

"But why wouldn't it be?" asked the radicals.

"Because it would be mere training," explained the old men patiently. "With all the intricate details of fish-grabbing, horse-clubbing, and tiger-scaring—the standard cultural subjects—the school curriculum is too crowded now. We can't add these fads and frills of net-making, antelope-snaring, and—of all things—bear-killing. Why, at the very thought, the body of the great New-Fist, founder of our paleolithic educational system, would turn over in its burial cairn. What we need to do is to give our young people a more thorough grounding in the fundamentals. Even the graduates of the secondary schools don't know the art of fish-grabbing in any complete sense nowadays, they swing their horse clubs awkwardly too, and as for the old science of tiger-scaring—well, even the teachers seem to lack the real flair for the subject which we oldsters got in our teens and never forgot."

"But, damn it," exploded one of the radicals, "how can any person with good sense be interested in such useless activities? What is the point of trying to catch fish with the bare hands when it just can't be done any more? How can a boy learn to club horses when there are no horses left to club? And why in hell should children try to scare tigers with fire when the tigers are dead and gone?"

"Don't be foolish," said the wise old men, smiling most kindly smiles. "We don't teach fish-grabbing to grab fish; we teach it to develop a generalized agility which can never be developed by mere training. We don't teach horse-clubbing to club horses; we teach it to develop a generalized strength in the learner which he can never get from so prosaic and specialized a thing as antelope-snare-setting. We don't teach tiger-scaring to scare tigers; we teach it for the purpose of giving that noble courage which carries over into all the affairs of life and which can never come from so base an activity as bear-killing."

All the radicals were silenced by this statement, all except the one who was most radical of all. He felt abashed, it is true, but he was so radical that he made one last protest.

"But—but anyway," he suggested, "you will have to admit that times have changed. Couldn't you please *try* these other more up-to-date activities? Maybe they have *some* educational value after all?"

Even the man's fellow radicals felt that this was going a little too far.

The wise old men were indignant. Their kindly smiles faded. "If you had any education yourself," they said severely, "you would know that the essence of true education is timelessness. It is something that endures through changing conditions like a solid rock standing squarely and firmly in the middle of a raging torrent. You must know that there are some eternal verities, and the saber-tooth curriculum is one of them!"

ARISTOTLE ON EDUCATION *

But of all the things which I have mentioned, that which most contributes to the permanence of constitutions is the adaptation of education to the form of government, and yet in our own day this principle is uni-

* *Aristoteles (in English), The Politics of Aristotle,* Translated into English with Introduction, Marginal Analysis, Essays, Notes and Indices by B. Jowett. Vol. 1 (Oxford, The Clarendon Press, 1885), pp. 168, 169, 231, 232, 233. 234, 244, 245, 256. (Fourth century B.C.)

versally neglected. The best laws, though sanctioned by every citizen of the state, will be of no avail unless the young are trained by habit and education in the spirit of the constitution, if the laws are democratical, democratically, or oligarchically if the laws are oligarchical. For there may be a want of self-discipline in states as well as in individuals. Now, to have been educated in the spirit of the constitution is not to perform the actions in which oligarchs or democrats delight, but those by which the existence of an oligarchy or of the democracy is made possible. Whereas among ourselves the sons of the ruling class in an oligarchy live in luxury, but the sons of the poor are hardened by exercise and toil, and hence they are both more inclined and better able to make a revolution. And in democracies of the more extreme type there has arisen a false idea of freedom which is contradictory to the true interests of the state. For two principles are characteristic of democracy, the government of the majority and freedom. Men think that what is just is equal; and that equality is the supremacy of the popular will; and that freedom and equality mean the doing what a man likes. In such democracies everyone lives as he pleases, or in the words of Euripides, "according to his fancy." But this is all wrong; men should not think it slavery to live according to the rule of the constitution; for it is their salvation.

. . . virtue and goodness in the state are not a matter of chance but the result of knowledge and purpose. A city can be virtuous only when the citizens who have a share in the government are virtuous, and in our state all the citizens share in the government; let us then inquire how a man becomes virtuous. For even if we could suppose all the citizens to be virtuous, and not each of them, yet the latter would be better, for in the virtue of each the virtue of all is involved.

There are three things which make men good and virtuous: these are nature, habit, reason. In the first place, everyone must be born a man and not some other animal; in the second place, he must have a certain character, both of body and soul. But some qualities there is no use in having at birth, for they are altered by habit, and there are some gifts which by nature are made to be turned by habit to good or bad. Most animals lead a life of nature, although in lesser particulars some are influenced by habit as well. Man has reason, in addition, and man only. Wherefore nature, habit, reason must be in harmony with one another; [for they do not always agree]; men do many things against habit and nature, if rational principle persuades them that they ought. We have already determined what natures are likely to be most easily moulded by the hands of the legislator. All else is the work of education; we learn some things by habit and some by instruction.

Formulations and Discussions

Since every political society is composed of rulers and subjects let us consider whether the relations of one to the other should interchange or be permanent. For the education of the citizens will necessarily vary with the answer given to this question. Now, if some men excelled others in the same degree in which gods and heroes are supposed to excel mankind in general, having in the first place a great advantage even in their bodies, and secondly in their minds, so that the superiority of the governors over their subjects was patent and undisputed, it would clearly be better that once for all the one class should rule and the others serve. But since this is unattainable, and kings have no marked superiority over their subjects, such as Scylax affirms to be found among the Indians, it is obviously necessary on many grounds that all the citizens alike should take their turn of governing and being governed. Equality consists in the same treatment of similar persons, and no government can stand which is not founded on justice. For [if the government be unjust] everyone in the country unites with the governed in the desire to have a revolution, and it is an impossibility that the members of the government can be so numerous as to be stronger than all their enemies put together. Yet that governors should excel their subjects is undeniable. How all this is to be effected, and in what way they will respectively share in the government, the legislature has to consider. The subject has been already mentioned. Nature herself has given the principle of choice when she made a difference between old and young (though they are really the same in kind), of whom she fitted the one to govern and the other to be governed. No one takes offence at being governed when he is young, nor does he think himself better than his governors, especially if he will enjoy the same privilege when he reaches the required age.

We conclude that from one point of view governors and governed are identical, and from another different. And therefore their education must be the same and also different. For he who would learn to command well must, as men say, first of all learn to obey. As I observed in the first part of this treatise, there is one rule which is for the sake of the rulers and another rule which is for the sake of the ruled; the former is a despotic, the latter a free government. Some commands differ not in the thing commanded, but in the intention with which they are imposed. Wherefore, many apparently menial offices are an honour to the free youth by whom they are performed; for actions do not differ as honourable or dishonourable in themselves so much as in the end and intention of them. But since we say that the virtue of the citizen and ruler is the same as that of a good man, and that the same person must first be a subject and then a ruler, the legislator has to see that they become good men, and by what means this may be accomplished, and what is the end of the perfect life.

Now the soul of man is divided into two parts, one of which has reason in itself, and the other, not having reason in itself, is able to obey reason. And we call a man good because he has the virtues of these two parts. In which of them the end is more likely to be found is no matter of doubt to those who adopt our division; for in the world both of nature and of art the inferior always exists for the sake of the better or superior, and the better or superior is that which has reason. The reason, too, in our ordinary way of speaking, is divided into two kinds, for there is a practical and a speculative reason. And there must be a corresponding division of actions; the actions of the naturally better part are to be preferred by those who have it in their power to attain to both or to all, for that is always to everyone that most eligible which is the highest attainable by him. The whole of life is further divided into two parts, business and leisure, war and peace, and all actions into those which are necessary and useful, and those which are honourable. And the preference given to one or the other class of actions must necessarily be like the preference given to one or other part of the soul and its actions over the other; there must be war for the sake of peace, business for the sake of leisure, things useful and necessary for the sake of things honourable. All these points the statesman should keep in view when he frames his laws; he should consider the parts of the soul and their functions, and above all the better and the end; he should also remember the diversities of human lives and actions. For men must be able to engage in business and go to war, but leisure and peace are better; they must do what is necessary and useful, but what is honourable is better. In such principles children and persons of every age which requires education should be trained. . . .

No one will doubt that the legislator should direct his attention above all to the education of youth, or that the neglect of education does harm to states. The citizen should be moulded to suit the form of government under which he lives. For each government has a peculiar character which originally formed and which continues to preserve it. The character of democracy creates democracy, and the character of oligarchy creates oligarchy; and always the better the character, the better the government.

Now, for the exercise of any faculty or art a previous training and habituation are required; clearly therefore for the practice of virtue. And since the whole city has one end, it is manifest that education should be one and the same for all, and that it should be public, and not private—not as at present, when every one looks after his own children separately, and gives them separate instruction of the sort which he thinks best; the training in things which are of common interest should be the same for all. Neither must we suppose that any one of the citizens belongs to himself, for they all belong to the state, and are each of them a part of the state,

Formulations and Discussions

and the care of each part is inseparable from the care of the whole. In this particular the Lacedaemonians are to be praised, for they take the greatest pains about their children, and make education the business of the state.

That education should be regulated by law and should be an affair of state is not to be denied, but what should be the character of this public education, and how young persons should be educated, are questions which remain to be considered. As things are, there is disagreement about the subjects. For mankind are by no means agreed about the things to be taught, whether we look to virtue or the best life. Neither is it clear, whether education is more concerned with intellectual or moral virtue. The existing practice is perplexing; no one knows on what principle we should proceed—should the useful in life, or should virtue, or should the higher knowledge, be the aim of our training; all three opinions have been entertained. Again about the means there is no agreement; for different persons, starting with different ideas about the nature of virtue, naturally disagree about the practice of it. There can be no doubt that children should be taught those useful things which are really necessary, but not all things; for occupations are divided into liberal and illiberal; and to young children should be imparted only such kinds of knowledge as will be useful to them without vulgarizing them. And any occupation, art, or science, which makes the body or soul or mind of the freeman less fit for the practice or exercise of virtue, is vulgar; wherefore we call those arts vulgar which tend to deform the body, and likewise all paid employments, for they absorb and degrade the mind. There are only some liberal arts quite proper for a freeman to acquire, but only in a certain degree, and if he attend to them too closely, in order to attain perfection in them, the same evil effects will follow. The object also which a man sets before him makes a great difference; if he does or learns anything for his own sake or for the sake of his friends, or with a view to excellence, the action will not appear illiberal; but if done for the sake of others, the very same action will be thought menial and servile. The received subjects of instruction, as I have already remarked, are partly of a liberal and partly of an illiberal character.

LYCURGUS OF SPARTA *

. . . Lycurgus would never reduce his laws into writing; nay, there is a Rhetra expressly to forbid it. For he thought that the most material points,

---

* Plutarch, *Plutarch's Lives, The Translation called Dryden's, Corrected from the Greek and Revised by A. H. Clough*, Vol. I (Boston, Little, Brown & Co., 1906), pp. 99, 101-2, 104-8, 115, 116, 125. (Second century A.D.)

and such as most directly tended to the public welfare, being imprinted on the hearts of their youth by a good discipline, would be sure to remain and would find a stronger security, than any compulsion would be, in the principles of action formed in them by their best lawgiver, education. . . . Every end and object of law and enactment it was his design education should effect. . . .

In order to the good education of their youth (which, as I said before, he thought the most important and noblest work of a lawgiver), he went so far back as to take into consideration their very conception and birth, by regulating their marriages. . . .

And indeed, Lycurgus was of a persuasion that children were not so much the property of their parents as of the whole commonwealth, and, therefore, would not have his citizens begot by the first comers, but by the best men that could be found. . . .

Nor was it in the power of the father to dispose of the child as he thought fit; he was obliged to carry it before certain triers at a place called Lesche; these were some of the elders of the tribe to which the child belonged; their business it was carefully to view the infant, and, if they found it stout and well made, they gave order for its rearing, and allotted to it one of the nine thousand shares of land above mentioned for its maintenance, but, if they found it puny and ill-shaped, ordered it to be taken to what was called the Apothetae, a sort of chasm under Taygetus; as thinking it neither for the good of the child itself, nor for the public interest, that it should be brought up, if it did not, from the very outset, appear made to be healthy and vigorous. . . .

Lycurgus . . . would not have masters bought out of the market for his young Spartans, no such as should sell their pains; nor was it lawful, indeed, for the father himself to breed up the children after his own fancy; but as soon as they were seven years old they were to be enrolled in certain companies and classes, where they all lived under the same order and discipline, doing their exercises and taking their play together. Of these, he who showed the most conduct and courage was made captain; they had their eyes always upon him, obeyed his orders, and underwent patiently whatsoever punishment he inflicted; so that the whole course of their education was one continued exercise of a ready and perfect obedience. The old men, too, were spectators of their performances, and often raised quarrels and disputes among them, to have a good opportunity of finding out their different characters, and of seeing which would be valiant, which a coward, when they should come to more dangerous encounters. Reading and writing they gave them, just enough to serve their turn; their chief care was to make them good subjects, and to teach them to endure pain and conquer in battle. To this end, as they grew in years, their discipline was proportionately increased; their heads were close clipped, they were accustomed to go barefoot, and for the most part to play naked.

After they are twelve years old, they were no longer allowed to wear any undergarments; they had one coat to serve them a year; their bodies were hard and dry, with but little acquaintance of baths and unguents; these human indulgences they were allowed only on some few particular days in the year. They lodged together in little bands upon beds made of the rushes which grew by the banks of the river Eurotas, which they were to break off with their hands without a knife; if it were winter, they mingled some thistle-down with their rushes, which it was thought had the property of giving warmth. By the time they were come to this age, there was not any of the more hopeful boys who had not a lover to bear him company. The old men, too, had an eye upon them, coming often to the grounds to hear and see them contend either in wit or strength with one another, and this as seriously and with as much concern as if they were their fathers, their tutors, or their magistrates; so that there scarcely was any time or place without some one present to put them in mind of their duty, and punish them if they neglected it.

Besides all this, there was always one of the best and honestest men in the city appointed to undertake the charge and governance of them; he again arranged them into their several bands, and set over each of them for their captain the most temperate and boldest of those they called Irens, who were usually twenty years old, two years out of the boys; and the oldest of the boys, again, were Mell-Irens, as much as to say, who would shortly be men. This young man, therefore, was their captain when they fought and their master at home, using them for the offices of his house; sending the oldest of them to fetch wood, and the weaker and less able, to gather salads and herbs, and these they must either go without or steal; which they did by creeping into the gardens, or conveying themselves cunningly and closely into the eating-houses; if they were taken in the fact, they were whipped without mercy, for thieving so ill and awkwardly. They stole, too, all other meat they could lay their hands on, looking out and watching all opportunities, when people were asleep or more careless than usual. If they were caught, they were not only punished with whipping, but hunger, too, being reduced to their ordinary allowance, which was but very slender, and so contrived on purpose, that they might set about to help themselves, and be forced to exercise their energy and address. This was the principal design of their hard fare; there was another not inconsiderable, that they might grow taller; for the vital spirits, not being overburdened and oppressed by too great a quantity of nourishment, which necessarily discharges itself into thickness and breadth, do, by their natural lightness, rise; and the body, giving and yielding because it is pliant, grows in height. . . .

To return from whence we have digressed. So seriously did the Lacedaemonian children go about their stealing, that a youth, having stolen a young fox and hid it under his coat, suffered it to tear out his very bowels with its teeth and claws, and died upon the place, rather than let it be seen. What is practised to this very day in Lacedaemon is enough to gain credit to this story, for I myself have seen several of the youths endure whipping to death at the foot of the altar of Diana surnamed Orthia. . . .

. . . Their discipline continued still after they were full grown men. No one was allowed to live after his own fancy; but the city was a sort of camp, in which every man had his share of provisions and business set out, and looked upon himself not so much born to serve his own ends as the interest of his country. Therefore if they were commanded nothing else, they went to see the boys perform their exercises, to teach them something useful or to learn it themselves of those who knew better. And indeed one of the greatest and highest blessings Lycurgus procured his people was the abundance of leisure which proceeded from his forbidding to them the exercise of any mean and mechanical trade. Of the money-making that depends on troublesome going about and seeing people and doing business, they had no need at all in a state where wealth obtained no honor or respect. The Helots tilled their ground for them, and paid them yearly in kind the appointed quantity, without any trouble of theirs. To this purpose there goes a story of a Lacedaemonian who, happening to be at Athens when the courts were sitting, was told of a citizen that had been fined for living an idle life, and was being escorted home in much distress of mind by his condoling friends; the Lacedaemonian was much surprised at it and desired his friend to show him the man who was condemned for living like a freeman. So much beneath them did they esteem the frivolous devotion of time and attention to the mechanical arts and to money-making. . . .

However, it was not the design of Lycurgus that his city should govern a great many others; he thought rather that the happiness of a state, as of a private man, consisted chiefly in the exercise of virtue, and in the concord of the inhabitants; his aim, therefore, in all his arrangements, was to make and keep them free-minded, self-dependent, and temperate. And therefore all those who have written well on politics, as Plato, Diogenes, and Zeno, have taken Lycurgus for their model, leaving behind them, however, mere projects and words; whereas Lycurgus was the author, not in writing but in reality, of a government which none else could so much as copy; and while men in general have treated the individual philosophic character as unattainable, he, by the example of a complete philosophic state, raised himself high above all other lawgivers of Greece. . . .

INSTRUCTION FOR THE PRESENT AND THE FUTURE LIFE *

THE GREAT DIDACTIC

Setting forth

The whole Art of Teaching
all Things to all Men

or

A certain Inducement to found such Schools in all
the Parishes, Towns, and Villages of every
Christian Kingdom, that the entire
Youth of both Sexes, none
being excepted, shall

QUICKLY, PLEASANTLY, & THOROUGHLY

Become learned in the Sciences, pure in Morals
trained to Piety, and in this manner
instructed in all things necessary
for the present and for
the future life,

in which, with respect to everything that is suggested,

Its Fundamental Principles are set forth from the essential nature of the matter,

Its Truth is proved by examples from the several mechanical arts,

Its Order is clearly set forth in years, months, days, and hours, and, finally,

An Easy and sure Method is shown, by which it can be pleasantly brought into existence.

Let the main object of this, our Didactic, be as follows: To seek and to find a method of instruction, by which teachers may teach less, but learners may learn more; by which schools may be the scene of less noise, aversion, and

* John Amos Comenius, *The Great Didactic,* The Great Didactic of John Amos Comenius now for the first time Englished, M. W. Keatinge, ed. and trans. (London, Adam and Charles Black, 1896), title page and verso, pp. 155, 156, 188-90, 204-8. (First published 1628-32.)

useless labour, but of more leisure, enjoyment, and solid progress; and through which the Christian community may have less darkness, perplexity, and dissension, but on the other hand more light, orderliness, peace, and rest.

God be merciful unto us and bless us, and cause his face to shine upon us: That thy way may be known upon earth, thy saving health among all nations.—Psalm lxvii. 1, 2.

From Chapter IV: There are three stages in the preparation for eternity: to know oneself (and with oneself all things); to rule oneself; and to direct oneself to God.

1. It is evident, then, that the ultimate end of man is eternal happiness with God. The subordinate ends, also, at which we aim in this transitory life, are evident from the words of the divine soliloquy which the Creator uttered when about to make man. "Let us make man," He said, "in our image, after our likeness; and let them have dominion over the fish of the sea, and over the fowl of the air, and over the cattle, and over all the earth, and over every creeping thing that creepeth upon the earth" (Gen. i. 26).

2. From which it is plain that man is situated among visible creatures so as to be

(i) A rational creature.
(ii) The Lord of all creatures.
(iii) A creature which is the image and joy of its Creator.

These three aspects are so joined together that they cannot be separated, for in them is laid the basis of the future and of the present life.

3. To be a rational creature is to name all things, and to speculate and reason about everything that the world contains, as we find it in Gen. ii, 19, or, in the words of Solomon (Wisdom vii. 17), to know how the world was made and the operation of the elements; the beginning, ending, and midst of the times; the alterations of the turning of the sun, and the change of seasons; the circuits of years and the positions of stars; the natures of living things and the furies of wild beasts; the violence of winds and the reasonings of men; the diversities of plants and the virtues of roots; in a word, everything that is secret and that is manifest. To man belong the knowledge of handicrafts and the art of speaking, lest (as says the son of Sirach) anything should remain unknown, be it small or great, in any department of knowledge (Eccles. v. 12). For thus, if he know the properties of all things, will he be able to justify his title of "rational being."

4. To be the lord of all creatures consists in subjecting everything to his own use by contriving that its legitimate end be suitably fulfilled; in

conducting himself royally, that is, gravely and righteously, among creatures (adoring only one above him, his Creator; recognising God's angels, man's fellow-servants, as his equals, and considering all other things as far beneath him). Thus will he preserve the dignity which has been granted to him. He should enslave himself to no creature, not even to his own flesh and blood; but should use all freely in his service, and not be ignorant where, when, how, and to what extent each may prudently be used, how far the body should be gratified, and how far our neighbour's interests should be consulted. In a word, he should be able to control with prudence his own movements and actions, external and internal, as well as those of others.

5. Finally, to be the image of God is to represent the perfection of his Archetype, who says Himself "Ye shall be holy, for I the Lord your God am holy" (Lev. xix. 2).

6. From this it follows that man is naturally required to be: (1) acquainted with all things; (2) endowed with power over all things and over himself; (3) to refer himself and all things to God, the source of all. Now, if we wish to express these three things by three well-known words, these will be:

(i) Erudition.
(ii) Virtue or seemly morals.
(iii) Religion or piety.

Under Erudition we comprehend the knowledge of all things, arts, and tongues; under Virtue, not only external decorum, but the whole disposition of our movements, internal and external; while by Religion we understand that inner veneration by which the mind of man attaches and binds itself to the supreme Godhead.

7. In these three things is situated the whole excellence of man, for they alone are the foundation of the present and of the future life. All other things (health, strength, beauty, riches, honour, friendship, good-fortune, long life) are as nothing. . . .

From Chapter VI: If a man is to be produced, it is necessary that he be formed by education.

1. The seeds of knowledge, of virtue, and of piety are, as we have seen, naturally implanted in us; but the actual knowledge, virtue, and piety are not so given. These must be acquired by prayer, by education, and by action. He gave no bad definition who said that man was a "teachable animal." And indeed it is only by a proper education that he can become a man.

2. For, if we consider knowledge, we see that it is the peculiar attribute

of God to know all things by a single and simple intuition without beginning, without progress, and without end. For man and for angels this is impossible, because they do not possess infinity and eternity, that is to say, divinity. It is enough for them to have received sufficient keenness of intellect to comprehend the works of God, and to gather a wealth of knowledge from them. As regards angels, it is certain that they also learn by perception (1 Peter i. 12; Ephes. iii. 10; 1 Kings xxii. 20; Job i. 6), and that their knowledge, like our own, is derived from experience.

3. Let none believe, therefore, that any can really be a man, unless he have learned to act like one, that is, have been trained in those elements which constitute a man. . . .

4. Man, as far as his body is concerned, is born to labour; and yet we see that nothing but the bare aptitude is born in him. He needs instruction before he can sit, stand, walk, or use his hands. Why, therefore, should it be claimed for our mind that, of itself, it can exist in its full development, and without any previous preparation; since it is the law of all things created that they take their origin from nothing and develope themselves gradually, in respect both of their material and of the process of development? For it is well known, and we showed in our last chapter, that the angels, whose perfection comes very near to that of the Almighty, are not omniscient, but make gradual advances in their knowledge of the marvellous wisdom of God.

5. It is evident, too, that even before the Fall, a school in which he might make gradual progress was opened for man in Paradise. For, although the first created, as soon as they came into being, lacked neither the power of walking erect, nor speech, nor reason, it is manifest, from the conversation of Eve with the serpent, that the knowledge of things which is derived from experience was entirely wanting. For Eve, had she had more experience, would have known that the serpent is unable to speak, and that there must therefore be some deceit.

Much more, therefore, in this state of corruption must it be necessary to learn by experience, since the understanding which we bring with us is an empty form, like a bare tablet, and since we are unskilled to do, speak, or know anything; for all these faculties do but exist potentially and need development. . . .

6. Examples show that those who in their infancy have been seized by wild animals, and have been brought up among them, have not risen above the level of brutes in intellect, and would not have been able to make more use of their tongues, their hands, and their feet than beasts can, had they not once more come into the society of men. . . .

7. Education is indeed necessary for all, and this is evident if we consider the different degrees of ability. No one doubts that those who are

stupid need instruction, that they may shake off their natural dullness. But in reality those who are clever need it far more, since an active mind, if not occupied with useful things, will busy itself with what is useless, curious, and pernicious; and, just as the more fertile a field is, the richer the crop of thorns and of thistles that it can produce, so an excellent intelligence becomes filled with fanciful notions, if it be not sown with the seeds of wisdom and of virtue. . . .

10. We see then that all who are born to man's estate have need of instruction, since it is necessary that, being men, they should not be wild beasts, savage brutes, or inert logs. It follows also that one man excels another in exact proportion as he has received more instruction. We may conclude this chapter with the words of the "Wise Man." "He who deems wisdom and discipline of no avail is wretched: his hopes (of attaining his desire) are vain, his labour is fruitless, and his work idle" (Wisdom iii. 11).

PROPOSALS RELATING TO THE EDUCATION OF YOUTH IN PENNSYLVANIA *

. . . As to their studies, it would be well if they could be taught everything that is useful and everything that is ornamental: but art is long, and their time is short. It is therefore proposed that they learn those things that are likely to be most useful and most ornamental. Regard being had to the several professions for which they are intended.

All should be taught to write a fair hand, and swift, as that is useful to all. And with it may be learnt something of drawing,[17] by imitation of prints, and some of the first principles of perspective. Arithmetic,[18] accounts, and some of the first principles of geometry and astronomy. The English language might be taught by grammar;[19] in which some of our best writers, as Tillotson, Addison, Pope, Algernon Sidney, Cato's *Letters*, etc. should be classics. The styles principally to be cultivated, being the clear and the concise. Reading should also be taught, and pronouncing, properly, distinctly, emphatically, not with an even tone, which under-does, nor a theatrical, which over-does nature.

To form their style they should be put on writing letters[20] to each other, making abstracts of what they read or writing the same things in their own words; telling or writing stories lately read, in their own expres-

* Benjamin Franklin, *Proposals Relating to the Education of Youth in Pennsylvania, 1749,* in *Educational Views of Benjamin Franklin,* edited by Thomas Woody (New York, McGraw-Hill, 1931), pp. 158-79. Modernized text. (Abridged footnotes by Franklin follow the text of the *Proposals.*)

sions. All to be revised and corrected by the tutor who should give his reasons, explain the force and import of words, etc.

To form their pronunciation,[21] they may be put on making declamations, repeating speeches, delivering orations, etc. The tutor assisting at the rehearsals, teaching, advising, correcting their accent, etc.

But if history [22] be made a constant part of their reading, such as the translations of the Greek and Roman historians and the modern histories of ancient Greece and Rome, etc., may not almost all kinds of useful knowledge be that way introduced to advantage, and with pleasure to the student? As

Geography, by reading with maps and being required to point out the places where the greatest actions were done, to give their old and new names, with the bounds, situation, extent of the countries concerned, etc.

Chronology, by the help of Helvicus or some other writer of the kind who will enable them to tell when those events happened, what princes were contemporaries, what states or famous men flourished about that time, etc. The several principal epochs to be first well fixed in their memories.

Ancient customs, religious and civil, being frequently mentioned in history, will give occasion for explaining them, in which the prints of medals,[23] basso-reliévos and ancient monuments will greatly assist.

Morality,[24] by descanting and making continual observations on the causes of the rise or fall of any man's character, fortune, power, etc., mentioned in history; the advantages of temperance, order, frugality, industry, perseverance, etc. etc.[25] Indeed the general natural tendency of reading good history must be to fix in the minds of youth deep impressions of the beauty and usefulness of virtue of all kinds, public spirit, fortitude, etc.

History will show the wonderful effects of oratory in governing, turning and leading great bodies of mankind, armies, cities, nations. When the minds of youth are struck with admiration at this,[26] then is the time to give them the principles of that art, which they will study with taste and application. Then they may be made acquainted with the best models among the ancients, their beauties being particularly pointed out to them. Modern political oratory being chiefly performed by the pen and press, its advantages over the ancient in some respects are to be shown, as that its effects are more extensive, more lasting, etc.

History will also afford frequent opportunities of showing the necessity of a public religion, from its usefulness to the public; the advantage of a religious character among private persons; the mischiefs of superstition, etc. and the excellency of the Christian religion above all others ancient or modern.[27]

History will also give occasion to expatiate on the advantage of civil orders and constitutions, how men and their properties are protected by joining in societies and establishing government, their industry encouraged and rewarded, arts invented, and life made more comfortable: the advantages of liberty, mischiefs of licentiousness, benefits arising from good laws and a due execution of justice, etc. Thus may the first principles of sound politics [28] be fixed in the minds of youth.

On historical occasions questions of right and wrong, justice and injustice, will naturally arise, and may be put to youth, which they may debate in conversation and in writing.[29] When they ardently desire victory for the sake of the praise attending it they will begin to feel the want and be sensible of the use of logic, or the art of reasoning to discover truth, and of arguing to defend it, and convince adversaries. This would be the time to acquaint them with the principles of that art. Grotius, Puffendorff, and some other writers of the same kind, may be used on these occasions to decide their disputes. Public disputes [30] warm the imagination, whet the industry, and strengthen the natural abilities.

When youth are told that the great men whose lives and actions they read in history spoke two of the best languages that ever were, the most expressive, copious, beautiful; and that the finest writings, the most correct compositions, the most perfect productions of human wit and wisdom, are in those languages, which have endured ages and will endure while there are men; that no translation can do them justice or give the pleasure found in reading the originals; that those languages contain all science; that one of them is become almost universal, being the language of learned men in all countries; that to understand them is a distinguishing ornament, etc. they may be thereby made desirous of learning those languages, and their industry sharpened in the acquisition of them. All intended for divinity should be taught the Latin and Greek; for physic, the Latin, Greek, and French; for law, the Latin and French; merchants, the French, German, and Spanish; and though all should not be compelled to learn Latin, Greek, or the modern foreign languages, yet none that have an ardent desire to learn them should be refused; their English, arithmetic, and other studies absolutely necessary being at the same time not neglected.

If the new *Universal History* were also read it would give a connected idea of human affairs, so far as it goes, which should be followed by the best modern histories, particularly of our mother country; then of these colonies; which should be accompanied with observations on their rise, increase, use to Great Britain, encouragements, discouragements, etc. the means to make them flourish, secure their liberties, etc.

With the history of men, times, and nations, should be read, at proper hours or days, some of the best histories of nature,[31] which would not only be delightful to youth and furnish them with matter for their letters, etc. as well as other history, but afterwards of great use to them, whether they are merchants, handicrafts, or divines, enabling the first the better to understand many commodities, drugs, etc. the second to improve his trade or handicraft by new mixtures, materials, etc. and the last to adorn his discourses by beautiful comparisons and strengthen them by new proofs of Divine Providence. The conversation of all will be improved by it, as occasions frequently occur of making natural observations, which are instructive, agreeable, and entertaining in almost all companies. Natural history will also afford opportunities of introducing many observations relating to the preservation of health, which may be afterwards of great use. Arbuthnot on air and aliment, Sanctorius on perspiration, Lemery on foods and some others, may now be read, and a very little explanation will make them sufficiently intelligible to youth.

While they are reading natural history might not a little gardening, planting, grafting, inoculating, etc. be taught and practised and now and then excursions made to the neighboring plantations of the best farmers, their methods observed and reasoned upon for the information of youth. The improvement of agriculture being useful to all,[32] and skill in it no disparagement to any.

The history of commerce, of the invention of arts, rise of manufactures, progress of trade, change of its seats, with the reasons, causes, etc. may also be made entertaining to youth, and will be useful to all. And this, with the accounts in other history of the prodigious force and effect of engines and machines used in war, will naturally introduce a desire to be instructed in mechanics,[33] and to be informed of the principles of that art by which weak men perform such wonders, labor is saved, manufactures expedited, etc. etc. This will be the time to show them prints of ancient and modern machines, to explain them, to let them be copied,[34] and to give lectures in mechanical philosophy.

With the whole should be constantly inculcated and cultivated that benignity of mind,[35] which shows itself in searching for and seizing every opportunity to serve and to oblige; and is the foundation of what is called good breeding; highly useful to the possessor, and most agreeable to all.[36]

The idea of what is true merit should also be often presented to youth, explained and impressed on their minds, as consisting in an inclination joined with an ability to serve mankind, one's country, friends and family; which ability is (with the blessing of God) to be acquired or greatly increased by true learning; and should indeed be the great aim and end [37] of all learning.

Franklin's Footnotes to the Foregoing "Proposals Relating to the Education of Youth in Pennsylvania."

17. Drawing is a kind of universal language, understood by all nations. A man may often express his ideas, even to his own countrymen, more clearly with a lead pencil, or a bit of chalk, than with his tongue. And many can understand a figure, that do not comprehend a description in words, though ever so properly chosen. All boys have an early inclination to this improvement, and begin to make figures of animals, ships, machines, etc. as soon as they can use a pen, but for want of a little instruction at that time generally are discouraged, and quit the pursuit.

Mr. Locke says, p. 234: "When your son can write well and quick, I think it may be convenient not only to continue the exercise of his hand in writing, but also to improve the use of it further in drawing; a thing very useful to a gentleman on several occasions; . . ."

Drawing is no less useful to a mechanic than to a gentleman. Several handicrafts seem to require it; as the carpenter's, shipwright's, engraver's, painter's, carver's, cabinet-maker's, gardener's, and other businesses. By a little skill of this kind, the workman may perfect his own idea of the thing to be done, before he begins to work; and show a draft for the encouragement and satisfaction of his employer.

18. Mr. Locke is of opinion, p. 269, that a child should be early entered in arithmetic, geography, chronology, history and geometry. . . .

Not only the skill, but the habit of keeping accounts, should be acquired by all, as being necessary to all.

19. Mr. Locke, speaking of grammar, p. 252, says, "That to those the greatest part of whose business in this world is to be done with their tongues, and with their pens, it is convenient, if not necessary, that they should speak properly and correctly, whereby they may let their thoughts into other men's minds the more easily, and with the greater impression. Upon this account it is that any sort of speaking so as will make him be understood is not thought enough for a gentleman. He ought to study grammar, among the other helps of speaking well, but it must be the grammar of his own tongue, of the language he uses, that he may understand his own country speech nicely, and speak it properly, without shocking the ears of those it is addressed to with solecisms and offensive irregularities. And to this purpose grammar is necessary; but it is the grammar only of their own proper tongues. . . . If this be so (as I suppose it is) it will be matter of wonder, why young gentlemen are forced to learn the grammars of foreign and dead languages, and are never once told of the grammar of their own tongues. They do not so much as know there is any such thing, much less is it made their business to be instructed in it. . . . Page 255,

the same author adds, that "if grammar ought to be taught at any time, it must be to one who can speak the language already; how else can he be taught the grammar of it? . . ."

20. This Mr. Locke recommends, *Education,* p. 284, and says, "The writing of letters has so much to do in all the occurrences of human life that no gentleman can avoid showing himself in this kind of writing. . . . Had the methods of education been directed to their right end, one would have thought this so necessary a part could not have been neglected, whilst themes and verses in Latin, of no use at all, were so constantly everywhere pressed, to the racking of children's inventions beyond their strength and hindering their cheerful progress by unnatural difficulties . . . since 'tis English that an Englishman will have constant use of, that is the language he should chiefly cultivate and wherein most care should be taken to polish and correct his style. . . . This I find universally neglected. . . .

21. By pronunciation is here meant the proper modulation of the voice to suit the subject with due emphasis, action, etc. In delivering a discourse in public, designed to persuade, the manner, perhaps, contributes more to success than either the matter or method. Yet the two latter seem to engross the attention of most preachers and other public speakers, and the former to be almost totally neglected.

22. As nothing teaches (saith Mr. Locke) so nothing delights more than history. The first of these recommends it to the study of grown men, the latter makes me think it the fittest for a young lad who as soon as he is instructed in chronology and acquainted with the several epochs in use in this part of the world, and can reduce them to the Julian period, should then have some history put into his hand. *Education,* p. 276.

Mons. Rollin . . . lays down the following rules for studying history, viz. 1. To reduce the study to order and method. 2. To observe what relates to usages and customs. 3. To enquire particularly, and above all things, after the truth. 4. To endeavor to find out the causes of the rise and fall of states, of the gaining or losing of battles, and other events of importance. 5. To study the character of the nations and great men mentioned in history. 6. To be attentive to such instructions as concern moral excellency and the conduct of life. 7. Carefully to note everything that relates to religion. (*Belles Lettres*) Vol. 3, p. 146.

23. Plenty of these are to be met with in Montfaucon, and other books of antiquities.

24. For the importance and necessity of moral instructions to youth see the latter notes.

25. Dr. Turnbull, *Liberal Education,* p. 371, says, "That the useful lessons which ought to be inculcated upon youth are much better taught and enforced from characters, actions and events, developing the inward

springs of human conduct and the different consequences of actions, whether with respect to private or public good, than by abstract philosophical lectures. . . ."

26. "Rules are best understood when examples that confirm them and point out their fitness or necessity naturally lead one, as it were by the hand, to take notice of them. One who is persuaded and moved by a speech, and heartily admires its force and beauty, will with pleasure enter into a critical examination of its excellencies and willingly lay up in his mind the rules of rhetoric such an example of eloquence plainly suggests. . . ." Turnbull, p. 410.

27. See Turnbull on this head, from p. 386 to 390, very much to the purpose but too long to be transcribed here.

28. Thus, as Milton says, *Education,* p. 381, should they be instructed in the beginning, end and reasons of political societies; that they may not, in a dangerous fit of the commonwealth, be such poor, shaken, uncertain reeds, of such a tottering conscience as many of our great counsellors have lately shown themselves, but steadfast pillars of the state.

29. . . . "When he has pretty well digested Tully's *Offices,*" says Mr. Locke, p. 277, "and added to it Puffendorff *de Officio Hominis & Civis,* it may be reasonable to set him upon Grotius, *de Jure Belli & Pacis,* or which is perhaps the better of the two, Puffendorff *de Jure Naturali & Gentium;* wherein he will be instructed in the natural rights of men, and the original and foundations of society and the duties resulting from thence. . . . A virtuous and well-behaved young man that is well versed in the general part of the civil law (which concerns not the chicane of private cases but the affairs and intercourse of civilized nations in general, grounded upon principles of reason) understands Latin well, and can write a good hand, one may turn loose into the world with great assurance that he will find employment and esteem everywhere."

30. Mr. Walker, in his excellent *Treatise of the Education of Young Gentlemen,* speaking of public and open argumentation pro and con, says, p. 124: ". . . This warms and activates the spirit in the search of truth, excites notions, . . . puts them upon a continual stretch of their wits to defend their cause. . . ."

31. Rollin, Vol. 4, p. 211, speaking of natural philosophy, says, . . . "I say that even children are capable of studying nature, for they have eyes and don't want curiosity; they ask questions and love to be informed; and here we need only awaken and keep up in them the desire of learning and knowing, which is natural to all mankind. . . . It is inconceivable how many things children are capable of if all the opportunities of instructing them were laid hold of, with which they themselves supply us.

"A garden, a country, a plantation are all so many books which lie open to them; but they must have been taught and accustomed to read in them. Nothing is more common amongst us than the use of bread and linen. How seldom do children know how either of them are prepared, through how many operations and hands the corn and flax must pass, before they are turned into bread and linen . . . why should not children be instructed in these wonderful works of nature and art which they every day make use of without reflecting upon them?"

He adds, that a careful master may in this way enrich the mind of his disciple with a great number of useful and agreeable ideas, and by a proper mixture of short reflections will at the same time take care to form his heart and lead him by nature to religion. . . .

32. Milton would have the Latin authors on agriculture taught at school . . . "here will be an occasion of inciting and enabling them hereafter to improve the tillage of their country, to recover the bad soil and to remedy the waste that is made of good; for this was one of Hercules' praises." *Education,* p. 379. . . .

33. How many mills are built and machines constructed, at great and fruitless expense, which a little knowledge in the principles of mechanics would have prevented?

34. We are often told in the journals of travellers that such and such things are done in foreign countries, by which labor is saved and manufactures expedited, etc., but their description of the machines or instruments used are quite unintelligible for want of good drafts. . . .

35. "Upon this excellent disposition (says Turnbull, p. 326) it will be easy to build that amiable quality commonly called good breeding, and upon no other foundation can it be raised. For whence else can it spring but from a general good-will and regard for all people, deeply rooted in the heart, which makes any one that has it careful not to show in his carriage, any contempt, disrespect, or neglect of them, but to express a value and respect for them according to their rank and condition, suitable to the fashion and way of their country? . . ."

36. "It is this lovely quality which gives true beauty to all other accomplishments or renders them useful to their possessor, in procuring him the esteem and goodwill of all that he comes near. Without it, his other qualities, however good in themselves, make him but pass for proud, conceited, vain or foolish. Courage, says an excellent writer, in an ill-bred man has the air and escapes not the opinion of brutality; learning becomes pedantry; wit, buffoonery; plainness, rusticity; and there cannot be a good quality in him which ill-breeding will not warp and disfigure to his disadvantage." Turnbull, p. 327.

37. To have in view the glory and service of God, as some express themselves, is only the same thing in other words. For doing good to men is

the only service of God in our power; and to imitate His beneficence is to glorify Him. Hence Milton says, "The end of learning is to repair the ruins of our first parents, by regaining to know God aright, and out of that knowledge to love him, to imitate him, to be like him, as we may the nearest by possessing our souls of true virtue." *Education*, p. 373.

EDUCATION FOR THE DIFFERENT CLASSES *

The idea of elementary training, in the theoretical and practical exposition of which I have spent the greater part of my later years, is nothing else than the idea of conformity to nature in the unfolding and development of the capacities and powers of the human race. . . .

Just as this lofty idea of Elementary Method requires careful attention to the psychological foundation of the sequence of the means of education and harmony among these, it demands also that these should be in harmony with conditions and circumstances peculiar to the different social ranks, respectively. Attention to this ensures that the child in all social ranks, learns to love what is worthy of love in his peculiar station, to think about that in his surroundings which appeals to thought and that he learns from the cradle up, to act, wish, hope and strive for that which, in his condition in life, seems desirable, necessary, and useful. . . . If it is the child of a peasant the Elementary Methods of training will make of him, neither as regards his feelings, his intellect nor his practical skill, a dreamy impractical creature, an outcast from the peasant class, incapable of rightly estimating the worth of his class or of contributing to its improvement. . . .

The rehabilitation of the different classes requires different measures. The urban classes do not need a more thorough general training than the peasant but they need a notably different kind of training. If the adequately trained peasant must be trained so that he will not have to call in the cabinet-maker whenever a board has to be planed, nor the blacksmith and locksmith whenever a nail is to be driven into the wall, so the city artisan must be trained to appreciate the different objects of art needed in the different vocations with mathematical accuracy and esthetic taste, to solve number problems algebraically and to handle problems of form with trained inventiveness and mathematical correctness.

The welfare of the urban middle class depends upon the extent to which they as a class are trained to participate personally in the various trades and occupations. . . .

* Johann Pestalozzi, "The Swan Song" (first published in 1826) in Lewis Flint Anderson, *Pestalozzi* (New York and London, McGraw-Hill Book Company, Inc., 1931), pp. 218-19, 276-8.

282 The Purposes of Education

This is not the case with the aristocracy. They neither can nor should be led through manual to intellectual activity nor through these to the elevation of their emotional nature. . . .

The prosperity of the productive classes, urban as well as rural, depends upon the cultivation of their ability to do. The extension of knowledge contributes very little. The upper classes, on the other hand, need as a distinguishing characteristic of their system of education, a considerable extension of knowledge, but of knowledge based upon personal observation. . . . Those who are to be trained for the learned class should have an education distinguished by a more thoroughly intellectual and investigative enquiry into the real inner nature of the objects, the scientific investigation and intellectual treatment of which, is their vocation.

The question arises, "What does Nature contribute toward the attainment of the educational ends peculiar to the different social classes, respectively?"

The reply is that the best means of training are to be found in the immediate environment of the individuals of these different classes, respectively, and especially in those objects which normally occasion activity. . . .

The consequences of this are of the highest importance. Certainly the unrest of our time and all its bloody and windy phenomena have their origin in the ever-growing weakness of our individual powers for self-help which is every day intensified by the artificial tendencies of the present.

THE EDUCATION OF MAN *

I. GROUNDWORK OF THE WHOLE

1. In all things there lives and reigns an eternal law. . . . This all-controlling law is necessarily based on an all-pervading, energetic, living, self-conscious, and hence eternal Unity. . . . This Unity is God. All things have come from the Divine Unity, from God, and have their origin in the Divine Unity, in God alone. God is the sole source of all things. In all things there lives and reigns the Divine Unity, God. All things live and have their being in and through the Divine Unity, in and through God. All things are only through the divine effluence that lives in them. The divine effluence that lives in each thing is the essence of each thing.

2. It is the destiny and life-work of all things to unfold their essence, hence their divine being, and, therefore, the Divine Unity itself—to reveal

* Friedrich Froebel, *The Education of Man,* International Education Series, Vol. V (New York, D. Appleton, 1896), pp. 1-5. (First published in 1826.)

Formulations and Discussions

God in their external and transient being. It is the special destiny and life-work of man, as an intelligent and rational being, to become fully, vividly, and clearly conscious of his essence, of the divine effluence in him, and, therefore, of God; to become fully, vividly, and clearly conscious of his destiny and life-work; and to accomplish this, to render it (his essence) active, to reveal it in his own life with self-determination and freedom.

Education consists in leading man, as a thinking, intelligent being, growing into self-consciousness, to a pure and unsullied, conscious and free representation of the inner law of Divine Unity, and in teaching him ways and means thereto.

3. The knowledge of that eternal law, the insight into its origin, into its essence, into the totality, the connection, and intensity of its effects, the knowledge of life in its totality, constitute *science, the science of life;* and, referred by the self-conscious, thinking, intelligent being to representation and practice through and in himself, this becomes *the science of education.*

The system of directions, derived from the knowledge and study of that law, to guide thinking, intelligent beings in the apprehension of their life-work and in the accomplishment of their destiny, is *the theory of education.*

The self-active application of this knowledge in the direct development and cultivation of rational beings toward the attainment of their destiny, is *the practice of education.*

The object of education is the realization of a faithful, pure, inviolate, and hence holy life.

Knowledge and application, consciousness and realization in life, united in the service of a faithful, pure, and holy life, constitute the *wisdom of life,* pure wisdom. . . .

4. *To be wise is the highest aim of man,* is the most exalted achievement of human self-determination.

To educate one's self and others, with consciousness, freedom, and self-determination, is a two-fold achievement of wisdom . . . it *begins now* to proclaim itself as a necessary, universal requirement of humanity, and to be heard and heeded as such . . .

5. By education, then the divine essence of man should be unfolded, brought out, lifted into consciousness, and man himself raised into free, conscious obedience to the divine principle that lives in him, and to a free representation of this principle in his life. . . .

Education as a whole, by means of instruction and training, should bring to man's consciousness, and render efficient in his life, the fact that man and nature proceed from God and are conditioned by him—that both have their being in God.

Education should lead and guide man to clearness concerning himself and in himself, to peace with nature, and to unity with God; hence it should lift him to a knowledge of himself and of mankind, to a knowledge of God and of nature, and to the pure and holy life to which such knowledge leads.

THE BUSINESS OF THE SCHOOLROOM IS THE INTERESTS OF SOCIETY *

I proceed, then, in endeavoring to show how the true business of the schoolroom connects itself, and becomes identical, with the great interests of society. The former is the infant, immature state of those interests; the latter their developed, adult state. As "the child is father to the man," so may the training of the schoolroom expand into the institutions and fortunes of the State.

PHYSICAL EDUCATION

In the worldly prosperity of mankind, health and strength are indispensable ingredients. . . .

Now, modern science has made nothing more certain than that both good and ill health are the direct result of causes mainly within our own control. In other words, the health of the race is dependent upon the conduct of the race. . . .

My general conclusion, then, under this head, is, that it is the duty of all the governing minds in society—whether in office or out of it—to diffuse a knowledge of these beautiful and beneficent laws of health and life throughout the length and breadth of the State; to popularize them; to make them, in the first place, the common acquisition of all, and, through education and custom, the common inheritance of all, so that the healthful habits naturally growing out of their observance shall be inbred in the people, exemplified in the personal regimen of each individual, incorporated into the economy of every household, observable in all private dwellings, and in all public edifices, especially in those buildings which are erected by capitalists for the residence of their work-people, or for renting to the poorer classes; obeyed, by supplying cities with pure water; by providing public baths, public walks, and public squares; by rural cemeteries; the drainage and sewerage of populous towns, and by whatever else may promote the general salubrity of the atmosphere; in fine, by a religious observance of all those sanitary regulations with which modern science has blessed the world.

* Horace Mann, *Life and Works of Horace Mann, Vol. IV; Annual Reports of the Secretary of the Board of Education of Massachusetts for the years 1845-1848. Report for 1848* (Boston, Lee and Shepard, 1891), pp. 233, 235, 243-52, 259-60, 268, 269, 277-80, 282, 283, 286-8, 291, 292, 298, 311, 312, 317-19, 335-8.

For this thorough diffusion of sanitary intelligence, the common school is the only agency. It is, however, an adequate agency. Let human physiology be introduced as an indispensable branch of study into our public schools; let no teacher be approved who is not master of its leading principles, and of their applications to the varying circumstances of life; let all the older classes in the schools be regularly and rigidly examined upon this study by the school-committees,—and a speedy change would come over our personal habits, over our domestic usages, and over the public arrangements of society. Temperance and moderation would not be such strangers at the table. Fashion, like European sovereigns, if not compelled to abdicate and fly, would be forced to compromise for the continued possession of her throne by the surrender of her subjects of many of their natural rights. A sixth order of architecture would be invented,—the hygienic,—which, without subtracting at all from the beauty of any other order, would add a new element of utility to them all. The "health-regulations" of cities would be issued in a revised code,—a code that would bear the scrutiny of science. And, as the result and reward of all, a race of men and women, loftier in stature, firmer in structure, fairer in form, and better able to perform the duties and bear the burdens of life, would revisit the earth. The minikin specimens of the race, who now go on dwindling and tapering from parent to child, would re-ascend to manhood and womanhood. Just in proportion as the laws of health and life were discovered and obeyed would pain, disease, insanity, and untimely death, cease from among men. Consumption would remain; but it would be consumption in the active sense.

INTELLECTUAL EDUCATION AS A MEANS OF REMOVING POVERTY, AND SECURING ABUNDANCE

Another cardinal object which the government of Massachusetts, and all influential men in the State, should propose to themselves is, the physical well-being of all the people,—the sufficiency, comfort, competence, of every individual in regard to food, raiment, and shelter. And these necessaries and conveniences of life should be obtained by each individual for himself, or by each family for themselves, rather than accepted from the hand of charity or extorted by poor-laws. It is not averred that this most desirable result can, in all instances, be obtained; but it is, nevertheless, the end to be aimed at. True statesmanship and true political economy, not less than true philanthropy, present this perfect theory as the goal, to be more and more closely approximated by our imperfect practice. The desire to achieve such a result cannot be regarded as an unreasonable ambition; for, though all mankind were well fed, well clothed, and well housed, they might still be but half civilized. . . .

According to the European theory, men are divided into classes,—some to toil and earn, others to seize and enjoy. . . .

Our ambition as a State should trace itself to a different origin, and propose to itself a different object. Its flame should be lighted at the skies. Its radiance and its warmth should reach the darkest and coldest abodes of men. It should seek the solution of such problems as these: To what extent can competence displace pauperism? How nearly can we free ourselves from the low-minded and the vicious, not by their expatriation, but by their elevation? To what extent can the resources and powers of Nature be converted into human welfare, the peaceful arts of life be advanced, and the vast treasures of human talent and genius be developed? How much of suffering, in all its forms, can be relieved? or, what is better than relief, how much can be prevented? Cannot the classes of crimes be lessened, and the number of criminals in each class be diminished? Our exemplars, both for public and for private imitation, should be the parables of the lost sheep and of the lost piece of silver. When we have spread competence through all the abodes of poverty, when we have substituted knowledge for ignorance in the minds of the whole people, when we have reformed the vicious and reclaimed the criminal, then may we invite all neighboring nations to behold the spectacle, and say to them, in the conscious elation of virtue, "Rejoice with me," for I have found that which was lost. Until that day shall arrive, our duties will not be wholly fulfilled, and our ambition will have new honors to win. . . .

I suppose it to be the universal sentiment of all those who mingle any ingredient of benevolence with their notions on political economy, that vast and overshadowing private fortunes are among the greatest dangers to which the happiness of the people in a republic can be subjected. Such fortunes would create a feudalism of a new kind, but one more oppressive and unrelenting than that of the middle ages. . . . Are we not in danger of naturalizing and domesticating among ourselves those hideous evils which are always engendered between capital and labor, when all the capital is in the hands of one class, and all the labor is thrown upon another?

Now, surely nothing but universal education can counterwork this tendency to the domination of capital and the servility of labor. If one class possesses all the wealth and the education, while the residue of society is ignorant and poor, it matters not by what name the relation between them may be called: the latter, in fact and in truth, will be the servile dependents, and subjects of the former. But, if education be equally diffused, it will draw property after it by the strongest of all attractions; for such a thing never did happen, and never can happen, as that an intelligent and practical body of men should be permanently poor. . . .

Education, then, beyond all other devices of human origin, is the great equalizer of the conditions of men,—the balance-wheel of the social machinery. I do not here mean that it so elevates the moral nature as to make men disdain and abhor the oppression of their fellow-men. This idea pertains to another of its attributes. But I mean that it gives each man the independence and the means by which he can resist the selfishness of other men. It does better than to disarm the poor of their hostility towards the rich: it prevents being poor. . . . The spread of education, by enlarging the cultivated class or caste, will open a wider area over which the social feelings will expand; and, if this education should be universal and complete, it would do more than all things else to obliterate factitious distinctions in society. . . .

For the creation of wealth, then,—for the existence of a wealthy people and a wealthy nation,—intelligence is the grand condition. The number of improvers will increase as the intellectual constituency, if I may so call it, increases. In former times, and in most parts of the world even at the present day, not one man in a million has ever had such a development of mind as made it possible for him to become a contributor to art or science. Let this development precede, and contributions, numberless, and of inestimable value, will be sure to follow. That political economy, therefore, which busies itself about capital and labor, supply and demand, interest and rents, favorable and unfavorable balances of trade, but leaves out of account the element of a widespread mental development, is nought but stupendous folly. The greatest of all arts in political economy is to change a consumer into a producer; and the next greatest is to increase the producer's producing power,—an end to be directly attained by increasing his intelligence. For mere delving, an ignorant man is but little better than a swine, whom he so much resembles in his appetites and surpasses in his powers of mischief. . . .

POLITICAL EDUCATION

The necessity of general intelligence,—that is, of education (for I use the terms as substantially synonymous, because general intelligence can never exist without general education, and general education will be sure to produce general intelligence),—the necessity of general intelligence under a republican form of government, like most other very important truths, has become a very trite one. It is so trite, indeed, as to have lost much of its force by its familiarity. Almost all the champions of education seize on this argument first of all, because it is so simple as to be understood by the ignorant, and so strong as to convince the skeptical. Nothing would be easier than to follow in the train of so many writers, and to demonstrate by logic, by history, and by the nature of the case, that a republican form of government, without intelligence in the people, must be, on a vast scale, what a mad-house, without superintendent or keepers, would be on a small one,—the despotism of a few succeeded by universal anarchy, and anarchy by despotism, with no change but from bad to worse. . . .

However elevated the moral character of a constituency may be, however well informed in matters of general science or history, yet they must, if citizens of a republic, understand something of the true nature and functions of the government under which they live. That any one, who is to participate in the government of a country when he becomes a man, should receive no instruction respecting the nature and functions of the government he is afterwards to administer, is a political solecism. In all nations, hardly excepting the most rude and barbarous, the future sovereign receives some training which is supposed to fit him for the exercise of the powers and duties of his anticipated station. Where, by force of law, the government devolves upon the heir while yet in a state of legal infancy, some regency, or other substitute is appointed to act in his stead until his arrival at mature age; and, in the mean time, he is subjected to such a course of study and discipline as will tend to prepare him, according to the political theory of the time and place, to assume the reins of authority at the appointed age. If in England, or in the most enlightened European monarchies, it would be a proof of restored barbarism to permit the future sovereign to grow up without any knowledge of his duties,—and who can doubt that it would be such a proof?—then, surely, it would be not less a proof of restored or of never-removed barbarism amongst us to empower any individual to use the elective franchise without preparing him for so momentous a trust. Hence the Constitution of the United States, and of our own State, should be made a study in our public schools. . . .

But perhaps it will be objected, that the Constitution is subject to different readings, or that the policy of different administrations has become the subject of party strife; and, therefore, if any thing of constitutional or political law is introduced into our schools, there is danger that teachers will be chosen on account of their affinities to this or that political party, or that teachers will feign affinities which they do not feel in order that they may be chosen; and so each school-room will at length become a miniature political club-room, exploding with political resolves, or flaming out with political addresses, prepared by beardless boys in scarcely legible hand-writing and worse grammar.

With the most limited exercise of discretion, all apprehensions of this kind are wholly groundless. There are different readings of the Constitution, it is true; and there are partisan topics which agitate the country from side to side: but the controverted points, compared with those about which there is no dispute, do not bear the proportion of one to a hundred. And, what is more, no man is qualified, or can be qualified, to discuss the disputable questions, unless previously and thoroughly versed in those questions about which there is no dispute. In the terms and principles common to all, and recognized by all, is to be found the only common medium of language and of idea by which the parties can become intelligible to each other; and there, too, is the only common ground whence the arguments of the disputants can be drawn.

It is obvious, on the other hand, that, if the tempest of political strife were to be let loose upon our common schools, they would be overwhelmed with sudden ruin. . . .

But to avoid such a catastrophe, shall all teaching relative to the nature of our government be banished from our schools? and shall our children be permitted to grow up in entire ignorance of the political history of their country? In the schools of a republic, shall the children be left without any distinct knowledge of the nature of a republican government, or only with such knowledge as they may pick up from angry political discussions, or from party newspapers, from caucus speeches, or Fourth-of-July orations, —the Apocrypha of Apocrypha?

Surely, between these extremes, there must be a medium not difficult to be found. And is not this middle course, which all sensible and judicious men, all patriots, and all genuine republicans, must approve?—namely, that those articles in the creed of republicanism which are accepted by all, believed in by all, and which form the common basis of our political faith, shall be taught to all. But when the teacher, in the course of his lessons or lectures on the fundamental law, arrives at a controverted text, he is either to read it without comment or remark; or, at most, he is only to say that the passage is the subject of disputation, and that the schoolroom is neither the tribunal to adjudicate, nor the forum to discuss it.

Such being the rule established by common consent, and such the practice observed with fidelity under it, it will come to be universally understood that political proselytism is no function of the school, but that indoctrination into matters of controversy between hostile political parties is to be elsewhere sought for, and elsewhere imparted. Thus may all the children of the Commonwealth receive instruction in all the great essentials of political knowledge,—in those elementary ideas without which they will never be able to investigate more recondite and debatable questions; thus will the only practicable method be adopted for discovering new truths, and for discarding, instead of perpetuating, old errors; and thus, too, will the pernicious race of intolerant zealots, whose whole faith may be summed up in two articles—that they themselves are always infallibly right, and that all dissenters are certainly wrong,—be extinguished,—extinguished, not by violence, nor by proscription, but by the more copious inflowing of the light of truth.

MORAL EDUCATION

Moral education is a primal necessity of social existence. The unrestrained passions of men are not only homicidal, but suicidal; and a community without a conscience would soon extinguish itself. . . .

The race has existed long enough to try many experiments for the solution of this greatest problem ever submitted to its hands; and the race has experimented, without stint of time or circumscription of space to mar or modify legitimate results. Mankind have tried despotisms, monarchies, and republican forms of government. They have tried the extremes of anarchy and of autocracy. They have tried Draconian codes of law; and, for the lightest offences, have extinguished the life of the offender. They have established theological standards, claiming for them the sanction of divine authority, and the attributes of a perfect and infallible law; and then they have imprisoned, burnt, massacred, not individuals only, but whole communities at a time, for not bowing down to idols which ecclesiastical authority had set up. These and other great systems of measures have been adopted as barriers against error and guilt: they have been extended over empires, prolonged through centuries, and administered with terrible energy; and yet the great ocean of vice and crime overleaps every embankment, pours down upon our heads, saps the foundations under our feet, and sweeps away the securities of social order, of property, liberty, and life.

At length, these experiments have been so numerous, and all of them have terminated so disastrously, that a body of men has risen up in later times, powerful in influence, and not inconsiderable in numbers, who, if I may use a mercantile phrase, would abandon the world as a total loss; who mock at the idea of its having a benevolent or even an intelligent Author or Governor; and who, therefore, would give over the race to the dominion of chance, or to that of their own licentious passions, whose rule would be more fatal than chance.

But to all doubters, disbelievers, or despairers in human progress, it may still be said, there is one experiment which has never yet been tried. It is an experiment, which, even before its inception, offers the highest authority for its ultimate success. Its formula is intelligible to all; and it is as legible as though written in starry letters on an azure sky. It is expressed in these few and simple words: "Train up a child in the way he should go; and, when he is old, he will not depart from it." This declaration is positive. If the conditions are complied with, it makes no provision for failure. Though pertaining to morals, yet, if the terms of the direction are observed, there is no more reason to doubt the result than there would be in an optical or a chemical experiment.

But this experiment has never yet been tried. Education has never been brought to bear with one-hundredth part of its potential force upon the natures of children, and, through them, upon the character of men and of the race. In all the attempts to reform mankind which have hitherto been made, whether by changing the frame of government, by aggravating or softening the severity of the penal code, or by substituting a government-created for a God-created religion—in all these attempts, the infantile and youthful mind, its amenability to influences, and the enduring and self-operating character of the influences it receives, have been almost wholly unrecognized. Here, then, is a new agency, whose powers are but just beginning to be understood, and whose mighty energies hitherto have been but feebly invoked; and yet, from our experience, limited and imperfect as it is, we do know, that, far beyond any other earthly instrumentality, it is comprehensive and decisive. . . .

So far as human instrumentalities are concerned, we have abundant means for surrounding every child in the State with preservative and moral influences as extensive and as efficient as those under which the present industrious, worthy, and virtuous members of the community were reared. And as to all those things in regard to which we are directly dependent upon the divine favor, have we not the promise, explicit and unconditional, that the men SHALL NOT depart from the way in which they should go, if the children are trained up in it? It has been overlooked that this promise is not restricted to parents, but seems to be addressed indiscriminately to all, whether parents, communities, states, or mankind.

RELIGIOUS EDUCATION

But it will be said that this grand result in practical morals is a consummation of blessedness that can never be attained without religion, and that no community will ever be religious without religious education. Both these propositions I regard as eternal and immutable truths. . . .

. . . our noble system of free schools for the whole people is strenuously opposed by a few persons in our own State, and by no inconsiderable numbers in some of the other states in this Union; and . . . a rival system of "parochial" or "sectarian schools" is now urged upon the public by a numerous, a powerful, and a well-organized body of men. It has pleased the advocates of this rival system, in various public addresses, in reports, and through periodicals devoted to their cause, to denounce our system as irreligious and anti-Christian. They do not trouble themselves to describe what our system is, but adopt a more summary way to forestall public opinion against it by using general epithets of reproach, and signals of alarm. . . .

That our public schools are not theological seminaries, is admitted. That they are debarred by law from inculcating the peculiar and distinctive doctrines of any one religious denomination amongst us, is claimed; and they are also prohibited from ever teaching that what they do teach is the whole of religion, or all that is essential to religion or to salvation, is equally certain. But our system earnestly inculcates all Christian morals; it founds its morals on the basis of religion; it welcomes the religion of the Bible; and, in receiving the Bible, it allows it to do what it is allowed to do in no other system,—*to speak for itself*. But here it stops, not because it claims to have compassed all truth, but because it disclaims to act as an umpire between hostile religions. . . .

If the Bible, then, is the exponent of Christianity; if the Bible contains the communications, precepts, and doctrines which make up the religious system called and known as Christianity; if the Bible makes known those truths, which, according to the faith of Christians, are able to make men wise unto salvation; and if this Bible is in the schools,—how can it be said that Christianity is excluded from the schools? or how can it be said that the school-system which adopts and uses the Bible is an anti-Christian or an un-Christian system? If that which is the acknowledged exponent and basis of Christianity is in the schools, by what tergiversation in language, or paralogism in logic, can Christianity be said to be shut out from the schools? . . .

Is it not, indeed, too plain to require the formality of a syllogism, that if any man's creed is to be found in the Bible, and the Bible is in the schools, then that man's creed is in the schools? . . .

And further: our law explicitly and solemnly enjoins it upon all teachers without any exception, "to exert their best endeavors to impress on the minds of children and youth committed to their care and instruction the principles of piety, justice, and a sacred regard to truth, love to their country, humanity, and universal benevolence, sobriety, industry, and frugality, chastity, moderation, and temperance, and those other virtues which are the ornament of human society, and the basis upon which a republican constitution is founded." Are not these virtues and graces part and parcel of Christianity? In other words, can there be Christianity without them? While these virtues and these duties towards God and man are inculcated in our schools, any one who says that the schools are anti-Christian or un-Christian expressly affirms that his own system of Christianity does not embrace any one of this radiant catalogue; that it rejects them all; that it embraces their opposites. . . .

In justice to my own name and memory; in justice to the Board of which

I was originally a member, and from which I have always sought counsel and guidance; and in justice to thousands of the most wise, upright, and religious-minded men in Massachusetts, who have been my fellow-laborers in advancing the great cause of popular education, under the auspices of this system,—I have felt bound to vindicate it from the aspersions cast upon it, and to show its consonance with the eternal principles of equity and justice. I have felt bound to show, that so far from its being an irreligious, an anti-Christian, or an un-Christian system, it is a system which recognizes religious obligations in their fullest extent; that it is a system which invokes a religious spirit, and can never be fitly administered without such a spirit; that it inculcates the great commands upon which hang all the law and the prophets; that it welcomes the Bible, and therefore welcomes all the doctrines which the Bible really contains; and that it listens to these doctrines so reverently, that, for the time being, it will not suffer any rash mortal to thrust in his interpolations of their meaning, or overlay the text with any of the "many inventions" which the heart of man has sought out. It is a system, however, which leaves open all other means of instruction—the pulpits, the Sunday schools, the Bible classes, the catechisms, of all denominations,—to be employed according to the preferences of individual parents. It is a system which restrains itself from teaching that what it does teach is all that needs to be taught, or that should be taught; but leaves this to be decided by each man for himself, according to the light of his reason and conscience, and on his responsibility to that Great Being, who, in holding him to account for the things done in the body, will hold him to the strictest account for the manner in which he has "trained up" his children. . . .

How divinely wise were our Pilgrim Fathers when they foresaw, that, if they could give knowledge and virtue to their children, they gave them all things. . . . *We have our futurity as they had theirs,*—a futurity rapidly hastening upon us,—a futurity now fluid,—ready, as clay in the hands of the potter, to be moulded into every form of beauty and excellence; but so soon as it reaches our hands, so soon as it receives the impress of our plastic touch, whether this touch be for good or for evil, it is to be struck into the adamant of the unchanging and unchangeable past. Into whose form and likeness shall we fashion this flowing futurity,—of Mammon, of Moloch, or of Jesus? Clear, and more clear, out of the dimness of coming time, emerge to the vision of faith the myriad hosts of the generations that shall succeed us. Those generations are to stand in our places, to be called by our names, and to accept the heritage of joy or of woe which we shall bequeath them. Shall they look back upon us with veneration for our wisdom and beneficent forecast, or with shame at our selfishness and degeneracy? Our ancestors were noble examples to us; shall we be ignoble examples to our posterity? They gave from their penury, and shall we withhold from our abundance? Let us not dishonor our lineage. Let us remember that generosity is not to be measured by the largeness of the sum which a man may give, but by the smallness of the sum which remains after his gift. Let us remember that the fortunes of our children, and of their descendants, hang upon our fidelity, just as our fortunes were suspended upon the fidelity of our fathers. Deeds survive the doers. In the highest and most philosophic sense, the asserted brevity of human life is a fiction. The act remains, though the hand that wrought it may have perished. And when our spirits shall have gone to their account, and the dust of our bodies shall be blown about by the winds, or mingled with the waves, the force which our life shall have impressed upon the machinery of things, will continue its momentum, and work out its destiny upon the character and happiness of our descendants.

WHAT KNOWLEDGE IS MOST WORTH? *

. . . How to live?—that is the essential question for us. Not how to live in the mere material sense only, but in the widest sense. The general problem which comprehends every special problem is—the right ruling of conduct in all directions under all circumstances. In what way to treat the body; in what way to treat the mind; in what way to manage our affairs; in what way to bring up a family; in what way to behave as a citizen; in what way to utilize all those resources of happiness which nature supplies —how to use all our faculties to the greatest advantage of ourselves and others—how to live completely? And this being the great thing needful for us to learn, is, by consequence, the great thing which education has to teach. To prepare us for complete living is the function which education has to discharge; and the only rational mode of judging of any educational course is, to judge in what degree it discharges such function. . . .

Our first step must obviously be to classify, in the order of their importance, the leading kinds of activity which constitute human life. They may be naturally arranged into:—1. Those activities which directly minister to self-preservation; 2. Those activities which, by securing the necessaries of life, indirectly minister to self-preservation; 3. Those activities which have for their end the rearing and discipline of offspring; 4. Those activities which are involved in the maintenance of proper social and political rela-

* Herbert Spencer, *Education: Intellectual, Moral and Physical* (New York, D. Appleton, 1897), pp. 30-32, 37-49, 51, 52, 54-60, 62, 64, 65, 67-75. (First published in 1861.)

Formulations and Discussions

tions; 5. Those miscellaneous activities which make up the leisure part of life, devoted to the gratification of the tastes and feelings.

That these stand in something like their true order of subordination, it needs no long consideration to show. . . .

Happily, that all-important part of education which goes to secure direct self-preservation, is in great part already provided for. Too momentous to be left to our blundering, Nature takes it into her own hands. While yet in its nurse's arms, the infant, by hiding its face and crying at the sight of a stranger, shows the dawning instinct to attain safety by flying from that which is unknown and may be dangerous; and when it can walk, the terror it manifests if an unfamiliar dog comes near, or the screams with which it runs to its mother after any startling sight or sound, shows this instinct further developed. Moreover, knowledge subserving direct self-preservation is that which it is chiefly busied in acquiring from hour to hour. How to balance its body; how to control its movements so as to avoid collisions; what objects are hard, and will hurt if struck; what objects are heavy, and injure if they fall on the limbs; which things will bear the weight of the body, and which not; the pains inflicted by fire, by missiles, by sharp instruments—these, and various other pieces of information needful for the avoidance of death or accident, it is ever learning. . . . Being thus, as we say, so well cared for by Nature, this fundamental education needs comparatively little care from us. What we are chiefly called upon to see, is, that there shall be free scope for gaining this experience, and receiving this discipline. . . .

This, however, is by no means all that is comprehended in the education that prepares for direct self-preservation. Besides guarding the body against mechanical damage or destruction, it has to be guarded against injury from other causes—against disease and death that follow breaches of physiologic law. For complete living it is necessary, not only that sudden annihilations of life shall be warded off; but also that there shall be escaped the incapacities and the slow annihilation which unwise habits entail. . . .

If any one doubts the importance of an acquaintance with the fundamental principles of physiology as a means to complete living, let him look around and see how many men and women he can find in middle or later life who are thoroughly well. Occasionally only do we meet with an example of vigorous health continued to old age; hourly do we meet with examples of acute disorder, chronic ailment, general debility, premature decrepitude. Scarcely is there one to whom you put the question, who has not, in the course of his life, brought upon himself illnesses which a little knowledge would have saved him from. Here is a case of heart disease consequent on a rheumatic fever that followed reckless exposure. There is a case of eyes spoiled for life by overstudy. . . . Now we hear of an irremediable injury that followed some silly feat of strength; and, again, of a constitution that has never recovered from the effects of excessive work needlessly undertaken. While on all sides we see the perpetual minor ailments which accompany feebleness. Not to dwell on the natural pain, the weariness, the gloom, the waste of time and money thus entailed, only consider how greatly ill-health hinders the discharge of all duties—makes business often impossible, and always more difficult; produces an irritability fatal to the right management of children; puts the functions of citizenship out of the question; and makes amusement a bore. Is it not clear that the physical sins—partly our forefathers' and partly our own—which produce this ill-health, deduct more from complete living than anything else? and to a great extent make life a failure and a burden instead of a benefaction and a pleasure?

To all which add the fact, that life, besides being thus immensely deteriorated, is also cut short. It is not true, as we commonly suppose, that a disorder or disease from which we have recovered leaves us as before. . . . Through the accumulation of small injuries it is that constitutions are commonly undermined, and break down, long before their time. And if we call to mind how far the average duration of life falls below the possible duration, we see how immense is the loss. When, to the numerous partial deductions which bad health entails, we add this great final deduction, it results that ordinarily more than one-half of life is thrown away.

Hence, knowledge which subserves direct self-preservation by preventing this loss of health, is of primary importance. . . . We infer that as vigorous health and its accompanying high spirits are larger elements of happiness than any other things whatever, the teaching how to maintain them is a teaching that yields in moment to no other whatever. And therefore we assert that such a course of physiology as is needful for the comprehension of its general truths, and their bearings on daily conduct, is an all-essential part of a rational education.

Strange that the assertion should need making! Stranger still that it should need defending! Yet are there not a few by whom such a proposition will be received with something approaching to derision. Men who would blush if caught saying Iphige′nia instead of Iphigeni′a, or would resent as an insult any imputation of ignorance respecting the fabled labours of a fabled demi-god, show not the slightest shame in confessing that they do not know where the Eustachian tubes are, what are the actions of the spinal cord, what is the normal rate of pulsation, or how the lungs are inflated. While anxious that their sons should be well up in the superstitions of two thousand years ago, they care not that they should be taught anything about the structure and functions of their own bodies—nay, would even disapprove such instruction. So overwhelming is the influence of established routine! So terribly in our education does the ornamental override the useful!

We need not insist on the value of that knowledge which aids indirect self-preservation by facilitating the gaining of a livelihood. This is admitted by all; and, indeed, by the mass is perhaps too exclusively regarded as the end of education. But while every one is ready to endorse the abstract proposition that instruction fitting youths for the business of life is of high importance, or even to consider it of supreme importance; yet scarcely any inquire what instruction will so fit them. It is true that reading, writing, and arithmetic are taught with an intelligent appreciation of their uses; but when we have said this we have said nearly all. While the great bulk of what else is acquired has no bearing on the industrial activities, an immensity of information that has a direct bearing on the industrial activities is entirely passed over.

For, leaving out only some very small classes, what are all men employed in? They are employed in the production, preparation, and distribution of commodities. And on what does efficiency in the production, preparation, and distribution of commodities depend? It depends on the use of methods fitted to the respective natures of these commodities; it depends on an adequate knowledge of their physical, chemical, or vital properties, as the case may be; that is, it depends on Science. . . .

For all the higher arts of construction, some acquaintance with Mathematics is indispensable. The village carpenter, who, lacking rational instruction, lays out his work by empirical rules learnt in his apprenticeship, equally with the builder of a Britannia Bridge, makes hourly reference to the laws of quantitative relations. The surveyor on whose survey the land is purchased; the architect in designing a mansion to be built on it; the builder in preparing his estimates; his foreman in laying out the foundations; the masons in cutting the stones; and the various artisans who put up the fittings; all are guided by geometrical truths. Railway-making is regulated from beginning to end by mathematics: alike in the preparation of plans and sections; in staking out the line; in the mensuration of cuttings and embankments; in the designing, estimating, and building of bridges, culverts, viaducts, tunnels, stations. And similarly with the harbours, docks, piers, and various engineering and architectural works that fringe the coasts and overspread the face of the country; as well as the mines that run underneath it. Out of geometry, too, as applied to astronomy, the art of navigation has grown; and so, by this science, has been made possible that enormous foreign commerce which supports a large part of our population, and supplies us with many necessaries and most of our luxuries. . . . And then let it be remembered that according as the principles of mechanics are well or ill used to these ends, comes success or failure—individual and national. The engineer who misapplies his formulae for the strength of materials, builds a bridge that breaks down. The manufacturer whose apparatus is badly devised, cannot compete with another whose apparatus wastes less in friction and inertia. The ship-builder adhering to the old model, is outsailed by one who builds on the mechanically-justified wave-line principle. And as the ability of a nation to hold its own against other nations depends on the skilled activity of its units, we see that on such knowledge may turn the national fate. Judge then the worth of mathematics.

Pass next to Physics. Joined with mathematics, it has given us the steam-engine, which does the work of millions of labourers. That section of physics which deals with the laws of heat, has taught us how to economise fuel in our various industries; how to increase the produce of our smelting furnaces by substituting the hot for the cold blast; how to ventilate our mines; how to prevent explosions by using the safety-lamp, and, through the thermometer, how to regulate innumerable processes. That division which has the phenomena of light for its subject, gives eyes to the old and the myopic; aids through the microscope in detecting diseases and adulterations; and by improved lighthouses prevents shipwrecks. Researches in electricity and magnetism have saved incalculable life and property by the compass; have subserved sundry arts by the electrotype; and now, in the telegraph, have supplied us with the agency by which for the future all mercantile transactions will be regulated, political intercourse carried on, and perhaps national quarrels often avoided. While in the details of indoor life, from the improved kitchen-range up to the stereoscope on the drawing-room table, the applications of advanced physics underlie our comforts and gratifications.

Still more numerous are the bearings of Chemistry on those activities by which men obtain the means of living. The bleacher, the dyer, the calico-printer, are severally occupied in processes that are well or ill done according as they do or do not conform to chemical laws. The economical reduction from their ores of copper, tin, zinc, lead, silver, iron, are in a great measure questions of chemistry. Sugar-refining, gas-making, soap-boiling, gun-powder manufacture, are operations all partly chemical; as are also those by which are produced glass and porcelain. Whether the distiller's wort stops at the alcoholic fermentation or passes into the acetous, is a chemical question on which hangs his profit or loss; and the brewer, if his business is sufficiently large, finds it pays to keep a chemist on his premises. . . .

And then the science of life—Biology: does not this, too, bear fundamentally upon these processes of indirect self-preservation? With what we ordinarily call manufactures, it has, indeed, little connection; but with the all-essential manufacture—that of food—it is inseparably connected. As agriculture must conform its methods to the phenomena of vegetable and animal life, it follows necessarily that the science of these phenomena is the rational basis of agriculture. . . .

Yet one more science have we to note as bearing directly on industrial success—the Science of Society. Without knowing it, men who daily look at the state of the money-market, glance over prices current, discuss the probable crops of corn, cotton, sugar, wool, silk, weigh the chances of war, and from all those data decide on their mercantile operations, are students of social science: empirical and blundering students it may be; but still, students who gain the prizes or are plucked of their profits, according as they do or do not reach the right conclusion. Not only the manufacturer and the merchant must guide their transactions by calculations of supply and demand, based on numerous facts; but even the retailer must do the like: his prosperity very greatly depending upon the correctness of his judgments respecting the future wholesale prices and the future rates of consumption. Manifestly, all who take part in the entangled commercial activities of a community, are vitally interested in understanding the laws according to which those activities vary.

Thus, to all such as are occupied in the production, exchange, or distribution of commodities, acquaintance with science in some of its departments, is of fundamental importance. Whoever is immediately or remotely implicated in any form of industry (and few are not) has a direct interest in understanding something of the mathematical, physical, and chemical properties of things; perhaps, also, has a direct interest in biology; and certainly has in sociology. Whether he does or does not succeed well in that indirect self-preservation which we call getting a good livelihood, depends in a great degree on his knowledge of one or more of these sciences: not, it may be, a rational knowledge; but still a knowledge, though empirical. For what we call learning a business, really implies learning the science involved in it; though not perhaps under the name of science. And hence a grounding in science is of great importance, both because it prepares for all this, and because rational knowledge has an immense superiority over empirical knowledge. . . .

That which our school courses leave almost entirely out, we thus find to be that which most nearly concerns the business of life. All our industries would cease, were it not for that information which men begin to acquire as they best may after their education is said to be finished. And were it not for this information, that has been from age to age accumulated and spread by unofficial means, these industries would never have existed. Had there been no teaching but such as is given in our public schools, England would now be what it was in feudal times. That increasing acquaintance with the laws of phenomena which has through successive ages enabled us to subjugate Nature to our needs, and in these days gives the common labourer comforts which a few centuries ago kings could not purchase, is scarcely in any degree owed to the appointed means of instructing our youth. The vital knowledge—that by which we have grown as a nation to what we are, and which now underlies our whole existence, is a knowledge that has got itself taught in nooks and corners; while the ordained agencies for teaching have been mumbling little else but dead formulas.

We come now to the third great division of human activities—a division for which no preparation whatever is made. If by some strange chance not a vestige of us descended to the remote future save a pile of our schoolbooks or some college examination papers, we may imagine how puzzled an antiquary of the period would be on finding in them no indication that the learners were ever likely to be parents. "This must have been the *curriculum* for their celibates," we may fancy him concluding. "I perceive here an elaborate preparation for many things: especially for reading the books cf extinct nations and of co-existing nations (from which indeed it seems clear that these people had very little worth reading in their own tongue); but I find no reference whatever to the bringing up of children. They could not have been so absurd as to omit all training for this gravest of responsibilities. Evidently then, this was the school course of one of their monastic orders."

Seriously, is it not an astonishing fact, that though on the treatment of offspring depend their lives or deaths, and their moral welfare or ruin; yet not one word of instruction on the treatment of offspring is ever given to those who will hereafter be parents? Is it not monstrous that the fate of a new generation should be left to the chances of unreasoning custom, impulse, fancy—joined with the suggestions of ignorant nurses and the prejudiced counsel of grandmothers? If a merchant commenced business without any knowledge of arithmetic and book-keeping, we should exclaim at his folly, and look for disastrous consequences. Or if, before studying anatomy, a man set up as a surgical operator, we should wonder at his audacity and pity his patients. But that parents should begin the difficult task of rearing children without ever having given a thought to the principles—physical, moral, or intellectual—which ought to guide them, excites neither surprise at the actors nor pity for their victims.

To tens of thousands that are killed, add hundreds of thousands that survive with feeble constitutions, and millions that grow up with constitutions not so strong as they should be; and you will have some idea of the curse inflicted on their offspring by parents ignorant of the laws of life. . . . When sons and daughters grow up sickly and feeble, parents commonly regard the event as a misfortune—as a visitation of Providence. Thinking after the prevalent chaotic fashion, they assume that these evils come without causes; or that the causes are supernatural. Nothing of the kind. In some cases the causes are doubtless inherited; but in most cases foolish regulations are the causes. Very generally parents themselves are responsible for all this pain, this debility, this depression, this misery. They have undertaken to control the lives of their offspring from hour to hour; with cruel carelessness they have neglected to learn anything about these vital processes which they are unceasingly affecting by their commands and prohibitions; in utter ignorance of the simplest physiologic laws, they have been year by year undermining the constitutions of their children; and have so inflicted disease and premature death, not only on them but on their descendants.

Equally great are the ignorance and consequent injury, when we turn from physical training to moral training. Consider the young mother and her nursery legislation. But a few years ago she was at school, where her memory was crammed with words, and names, and dates, and her reflective faculties scarcely in the slightest degree exercised—where not one idea was given her respecting the methods of dealing with the opening mind of childhood; and where her discipline did not in the least fit her for thinking out methods of her own. The intervening years have been passed in practising music, in fancy-work, in novel-reading, and in party-going: no thought having yet been given to the grave responsibilities of maternity; and scarcely any of that solid intellectual culture obtained which would be some preparation for such responsibilities. And now see her with an unfolding human character committed to her charge—see her profoundly ignorant of the phenomena with which she has to deal, undertaking to do that which can be done but imperfectly even with the aid of the profoundest knowledge. She knows nothing about the nature of the emotions, their order of evolution, their functions, or where use ends and abuse begins. She is under the impression that some of the feelings are wholly bad, which is not true of any one of them; and that others are good, however far they may be carried, which is also not true of any one of them. And then, ignorant as she is of that with which she has to deal, she is equally ignorant of the effects that will be produced on it by this or that treatment. What can be more inevitable than the disastrous results we see hourly arising? Lacking knowledge of mental phenomena, with their causes and consequences, her interference is frequently more mischievous than absolute passivity would have been. This and that kind of action, which are quite normal and beneficial, she perpetually thwarts; and so diminishes the child's happiness and profit, injures its temper and her own, and produces estrangement. Deeds which she thinks it desirable to encourage, she gets performed by threats and bribes, or by exciting a desire for applause: considering little what the inward motive may be, so long as the outward conduct conforms; and thus cultivating hypocrisy, and fear, and selfishness, in place of good feeling. While insisting on truthfulness, she constantly sets an example of untruth, by threatening penalties which she does not inflict. While inculcating self-control, she hourly visits on her little ones angry scoldings for acts that do not call for them. She has not the remotest idea that in the nursery, as in the world, that alone is the truly salutary discipline which visits on all conduct, good and bad, the natural consequences—the consequences, pleasurable or painful, which in the nature of things such conduct tends to bring. Being thus without theoretic guidance, and quite incapable of guiding herself by tracing the mental processes going on in her children, her rule is impulsive, inconsistent, mischievous, often, in the highest degree; and would indeed be generally ruinous, were it not that the overwhelming tendency of the growing mind to assume the moral type of the race, usually subordinates all minor influences.

And then the culture of the intellect—is not this, too, mismanaged in a similar manner? Grant that the phenomena of intelligence conform to laws; grant that the evolution of intelligence in a child also conforms to laws; and it follows inevitably that education can be rightly guided only by a knowledge of these laws. To suppose that you can properly regulate this process of forming and accumulating ideas, without understanding the nature of the process, is absurd. How widely, then, must teaching as it is, differ from teaching as it should be; when hardly any parents, and but few teachers, know anything about psychology. . . . See the results. What with perceptions unnaturally dulled by early thwarting, and a coerced attention to books—what with the mental confusion produced by teaching subjects before they can be understood, and in each of them giving generalizations before the facts of which these are the generalizations—what with making the pupil a mere passive recipient of others' ideas, and not in the least leading him to be an active inquirer or self-instructor—and what with taxing the faculties to excess; there are very few minds that become as efficient as they might be. Examinations being once passed, books are laid aside; the greater part of what has been acquired, being unorganized, soon drops out of recollection; what remains is mostly inert—the art of applying knowledge not having been cultivated; and there is but little power either of accurate observation or independent thinking. To all which add, that while much of the information gained is of relatively small value, an immense mass of information of transcendent value is entirely passed over.

Thus we find the facts to be such as might have been inferred *a priori*. The training of children—physical, moral, and intellectual—is dreadfully defective. And in great measure it is so, because parents are devoid of that knowledge by which this training can alone be rightly guided. . . .

From the parental functions let us pass now to the functions of the citizen. We have here to inquire what knowledge best fits a man for the discharge of these functions. It cannot be alleged, as in the last case, that the need for knowledge fitting him for these functions is wholly overlooked; for our school courses contain certain studies which, nominally at least, bear upon political and social duties. Of these the only one that occupies a prominent place is History.

But, as already more than once hinted, the historic information commonly given is almost valueless for purposes of guidance. Scarcely any of the facts set down in our school-histories, and very few even of those contained in the more elaborate works written for adults, give any clue to the right principles of political action. The biographies of monarchs (and our children commonly learn little else) throw scarcely any light upon the science of society. . . .

. . . That which it really concerns us to know, is the natural history of society. We want all facts which help us to understand how a nation has grown and organized itself. Among these, let us of course have an account of its government; with as little as may be of gossip about the men who officered it, and as much as possible about the structure, principles, methods, prejudices, corruptions, &c., which it exhibited: and let this account not only include the nature and actions of the central government, but also those of local governments, down to their minutest ramifications. Let us of course also have a parallel description of the ecclesiastical government—its organization, its conduct, its power, its relations to the State: and accompanying this, the ceremonial, the creed, and religious ideas—not only those nominally believed, but those really believed and acted upon. Let us at the same time be informed of the control exercised by class over class, as displayed in all social observances—in titles, salutations, and forms of address. Let us know, too, what were all the other customs which regulated the popular life out of doors and in-doors: including those which concern the relations of the sexes, and the relations of parents to children. The superstitions, also, from the more important myths down to the charms in common use, should be indicated. Next should come a delineation of the industrial system: showing to what extent the division of labour was carried; how trades were regulated, whether by caste, guilds, or otherwise; what was the connection between employers and employed; what were the agencies for distributing commodities; what were the means of communication; what was the circulating medium. Accompanying all which should be given an account of the industrial arts technically considered: stating the processes in use, the quality of the products. Further, the intellectual condition of the nation in its various grades should be depicted: not only with respect to the kind and amount of education, but with respect to the progress made in science, and the prevailing manner of thinking. The degree of aesthetic culture, as displayed in architecture, sculpture, painting, dress, music, poetry, and fiction, should be described. Nor should there be omitted a sketch of the daily lives of the people—their food, their homes, and their amusements. And lastly, to connect the whole, should be exhibited the morals, theoretical and practical, of all classes: as indicated in their laws, habits, proverbs, deeds . . . Such alone is the kind of information respecting past times, which can be of service to the citizen for the regulation of his conduct. The only history that is of practical value is what may be called Descriptive Sociology. And the highest office which the historian can discharge, is that of so narrating the lives of nations, as to furnish materials for a Comparative Sociology; and for the subsequent determination of the ultimate laws to which social phenomena conform. . . .

And now we come to that remaining division of human life which includes the relaxations, pleasures, and amusements filling leisure hours. After considering what training best fits for self-preservation, for the obtainment of sustenance, for the discharge of parental duties, and for the regulation of social and political conduct; we have now to consider what training best fits for the miscellaneous ends not included in these—for the enjoyments of Nature, of Literature, and of the Fine Arts, in all their forms. Postponing them as we do to things that bear more vitally upon human welfare; and bringing everything, as we have, to the test of actual value; it will perhaps be inferred that we are inclined to slight these less essential things. No greater mistake could be made, however. We yield to none in the value we attach to aesthetic culture and its pleasures. Without painting, sculpture, music, poetry, and the emotions produced by natural beauty of every kind, life would lose half its charm. So far from thinking that the training and gratification of the tastes are unimportant, we believe the time will come when they will occupy a much larger share of human life than now. When the forces of Nature have been fully conquered to man's use—when the means of production have been brought to perfection—when labour has been economized to the highest degree—when education has been so systematized that a preparation for the more essential activities may be made with comparative rapidity—and when, consequently, there is a great increase of spare time; then will the poetry, both of Art and Nature, rightly fill a large space in the minds of all.

But it is one thing to admit that aesthetic culture is in a high degree conducive to human happiness; and another thing to admit that it is a fundamental requisite to human happiness. However important it may be, it must yield precedence to those kinds of culture which bear more directly upon the duties of life. . . .

And here we see most distinctly the vice of our educational system. It neglects the plant for the sake of the flower. In anxiety for elegance, it forgets substance. While it gives no knowledge conducive to self-preservation—while of knowledge that facilitates gaining a livelihood it gives but the rudiments, and leaves the greater part to be picked up any how in after life—while for the discharge of parental functions it makes not the slightest provision—and while for the duties of citizenship it prepares by imparting a mass of facts, most of which are irrelevant, and the rest without key; it is diligent in teaching every thing that adds to refinement, polish, éclat. However fully we may admit that extensive acquaintance with modern languages is a valuable accomplishment, which, through reading, conversation, and travel, aids in giving a certain finish; it by no means follows that this result is rightly purchased at the cost of that vitally important knowledge sacrificed to it. Supposing it true that classical education conduces to elegance and correctness of style; it cannot be said that elegance and correctness of style are comparable in importance to a familiarity with the principles that should guide the rearing of children. Grant that the taste may be greatly improved by reading all the poetry written in extinct languages; yet it is not to be inferred that such improvement of taste is equivalent in value to an acquaintance with the laws of health. Accomplishments, the fine arts, *belles-lettres,* and all those things which, as we say, constitute the efflorescence of civilization, should be wholly subordinate to that knowledge and discipline in which civilization rests. *As they occupy the leisure part of life, so should they occupy the leisure part of education.* . . .

CAST DOWN YOUR BUCKET WHERE YOU ARE! *

. . . Ignorant and inexperienced, it is not strange that in the first years of our new life we began at the top instead of at the bottom; that a seat in Congress or the State Legislature was more sought than real estate or industrial skill; that the political convention or stump-speaking had more attraction than starting a dairy farm or truck garden.

A ship lost at sea for many days suddenly sighted a friendly vessel. From the mast of the unfortunate vessel was seen a signal: "Water, water; we die of thirst!" The answer from the friendly vessel at once came back: "Cast down your bucket where you are." A second time the signal, "Water,

---

* Booker T. Washington, *Atlanta Exposition Address,* delivered at the opening of the Cotton States' Exposition, Atlanta, Georgia, September 1895; in *Selected Speeches of Booker T. Washington* (New York, Doubleday, Doran & Co., Inc., 1932), pp. 31-4, 35, 36. Copyright 1932 by Doubleday and Co., Inc. Reprinted by permission of the publishers.

water; send us water!" ran up from the distressed vessel, and was answered: "Cast down your bucket where you are." And a third and fourth signal for water was answered, "Cast down your bucket where you are." The captain of the distressed vessel, at last heeding the injunction, cast down his bucket, and it came up full of fresh, sparkling water from the mouth of the Amazon River. To those of my race who depend upon bettering their condition in a foreign land, or who underestimate the importance of cultivating friendly relations with the Southern white man who is their next-door neighbor, I would say: "Cast down your bucket where you are" —cast it down in making friends, in every manly way, of the people of all races by whom we are surrounded.

Cast it down in agriculture, mechanics, in commerce, in domestic service, and in the professions. And in this connection it is well to bear in mind that whatever other sins the South may be called to bear, when it comes to business, pure and simple, it is in the South that the Negro is given a man's chance in the commercial world, and in nothing is this Exposition more eloquent than in emphasizing this chance. Our greatest danger is that in the great leap from slavery to freedom we may overlook the fact that the masses of us are to live by the productions of our hands, and fail to keep in mind that we shall prosper in proportion as we learn to dignify and glorify common labor, and put brains and skill into the common occupations of life; shall prosper in proportion as we learn to draw the line between the superficial and the substantial, the ornamental gewgaws of life and the useful. No race can prosper till it learns that there is as much dignity in tilling a field as in writing a poem. It is at the bottom of life we must begin, and not at the top. Nor should we permit our grievances to overshadow our opportunities. As we have proved our loyalty to you in the past, in nursing your children, watching by the sick bed of your mothers and fathers, and often following them with tear-dimmed eyes to their graves, so in the future, in our humble way, we shall stand by you with a devotion that no foreigner can approach, ready to lay down our lives, if need be, in defense of yours, interlacing our industrial, commercial, civil, and religious life with yours in a way that shall make the interests of both races one. In all things that are purely social we can be as separate as the fingers, yet one as the hand in all things essential to mutual progress. . . .

Gentlemen of the Exposition, as we present to you our humble effort at an exhibition of our progress, you must not expect over-much. Starting thirty years ago with ownership here and there in a few quilts and pumpkins and chickens (gathered from miscellaneous sources), remember the path that has led from these to the inventions and production of agricultural implements, buggies, steam-engines, newspapers, books, statuary, carving, paintings, the management of drugstores and banks, has not been trodden without contact with thorns and thistles. While we take pride in what we exhibit as a result of our independent efforts, we do not for a moment forget that our part in this exhibition would fall far short of your expectations but for the constant help that has come to our educational life, not only from the Southern states, but especially from Northern philanthropists, who have made their gifts a constant stream of blessing and encouragement. The wisest among my race understand that the agitation of questions of social equality is the extremest folly, and that progress in the enjoyment of all the privileges that will come to us must be the results of severe and constant struggle rather than of artificial forcing. No race that has anything to contribute to the markets of the world is long, in any degree, ostracized. It is important and right that all privileges of the law be ours, but it is vastly more important that we be prepared for the exercise of those privileges. The opportunity to earn a dollar in a factory just now is worth infinitely more than the opportunity to spend a dollar in an opera house. . . .

CARDINAL PRINCIPLES OF SECONDARY EDUCATION *

The Need for Reorganization

Secondary education should be determined by the needs of the society to be served, the character of the individuals to be educated, and the knowledge of educational theory and practice available. These factors are by no means static. Society is always in process of development; the character of the secondary-school population undergoes modification; and the sciences on which educational theory and practice depend constantly furnish new information. Secondary education, however, like any other established agency of society, is conservative and tends to resist modification. Failure to make adjustments when the need arises leads to the necessity for extensive reorganization at irregular intervals. The evidence is strong that such a comprehensive reorganization of secondary education is imperative at the present time. . . .

The Goal of Education in a Democracy

Education in the United States should be guided by a clear conception of the meaning of democracy. It is the ideal of democracy that the individual and society may find fulfillment each in the other. Democracy

---

* Commission on the Reorganization of Secondary Education, National Education Association, *Cardinal Principles of Secondary Education* (Washington, D. C., United States Government Printing Office, Bulletin, No. 35, 1918), pp. 7-16.

sanctions neither the exploitation of the individual by society, nor the disregard of the interests of society by the individual. More explicitly—

The purpose of democracy is so to organize society that each member may develop his personality primarily through activities designed for the well-being of his fellow members and of society as a whole.

This ideal demands that human activities be placed upon a high level of efficiency; that to this efficiency be added an appreciation of the significance of these activities and loyalty to the best ideals involved; and that the individual choose that vocation and those forms of social service in which his personality may develop and become most effective. For the achievement of these ends democracy must place chief reliance upon education.

Consequently, education in a democracy, both within and without the school, should develop in each individual the knowledge, interests, ideals, habits, and powers whereby he will find his place and use that place to shape both himself and society toward ever nobler ends. . . .

THE ROLE OF SECONDARY EDUCATION IN ACHIEVING THESE OBJECTIVES

The objectives outlined above apply to education as a whole—elementary, secondary, and higher. It is the purpose of this section to consider specifically the role of secondary education in achieving each of these objectives.

For reasons stated in section X, this commission favors such reorganization that secondary education may be defined as applying to all pupils of approximately 12 to 18 years of age.

1. *Health.*—Health needs can not be neglected during the period of secondary education without serious danger to the individual and the race. The secondary school should therefore provide health instruction, inculcate health habits, organize an effective program of physical activities, regard health needs in planning work and play, and cooperate with home and community in safe-guarding and promoting health interests.

To carry out such a program it is necessary to arouse the public to recognize that the health needs of young people are of vital importance to society, to secure teachers competent to ascertain and meet the needs of individual pupils and able to inculcate in the entire student body a love for clean sport, to furnish adequate equipment for physical activities, and to make the school building, its rooms and surroundings, conform to the best standards of hygiene and sanitation.

2. *Command of fundamental processes.*—Much of the energy of the elementary school is properly devoted to teaching certain fundamental processes, such as reading, writing, arithmetical computations, and the

elements of oral and written expression. The facility that a child of 12 or 14 may acquire in the use of these tools is not sufficient for the needs of modern life. This is particularly true of the mother tongue. Proficiency in many of these processes may be increased more effectively by their application to new material than by the formal reviews commonly employed in grades seven and eight. Throughout the secondary school, instruction and practice must go hand in hand, but as indicated in the report of the committee on English, only so much theory should be taught at any one time as will show results in practice.

3. *Worthy home-membership.*—Worthy home-membership as an objective calls for the development of those qualities that make the individual a worthy member of a family, both contributing to and deriving benefit from that membership.

This objective applies to both boys and girls. The social studies should deal with the home as a fundamental social institution and clarify its relation to the wider interests outside. Literature should interpret and idealize the human elements that go to make the home. Music and art should result in more beautiful homes and in greater joy therein. The coeducational school with a faculty of men and women should, in its organization and its activities, exemplify wholesome relations between boys and girls and men and women.

Home membership as an objective should not be thought of solely with reference to future duties. These are the better guaranteed if the school helps the pupils to take the right attitude toward present home responsibilities and interprets to them the contribution of the home to their development.

In the education of every high-school girl, the household arts should have a prominent place because of their importance to the girl herself and to others whose welfare will be directly in her keeping. The attention now devoted to this phase of education is inadequate, and especially so for girls preparing for occupations not related to the household arts and for girls planning for higher institutions. The majority of girls who enter wage-earning occupations directly from the high school remain in them for only a few years, after which home making becomes their lifelong occupation. For them the high-school period offers the only assured opportunity to prepare for that lifelong occupation, and it is during this period that they are most likely to form their ideals of life's duties and responsibilities. For girls planning to enter higher institutions—

> our traditional ideals of preparation for higher institutions are particularly incongruous with the actual needs and future responsibilities of girls. It would seem that such high-school work as is carefully designed to develop capacity for, and interest in, the proper management and con-

duct of a home should be regarded as of importance at least equal to that of any other work. We do not understand how society can properly continue to sanction for girls high-school curriculums that disregard this fundamental need, even though such curriculums are planned in response to the demands made by some of the colleges for women.[1]

In the education of boys, some opportunity should be found to give them a basis for the intelligent appreciation of the value of the well-appointed home and of the labor and skill required to maintain such a home, to the end that they may cooperate more effectively. For instance, they should understand the essentials of food values, of sanitation, and of household budgets.

4. *Vocation.*—Vocational education should equip the individual to secure a livelihood for himself and those dependent on him, to serve society well through his vocation, to maintain the right relationships toward his fellow workers and society, and, as far as possible, to find in that vocation his own best development.

This ideal demands that the pupil explore his own capacities and aptitudes, and make a survey of the world's work, to the end that he may select his vocation wisely. Hence, an effective program of vocational guidance in the secondary school is essential.

Vocational education should aim to develop an appreciation of the significance of the vocation to the community, and a clear conception of right relations between the members of the chosen vocation, between different vocational groups, between employer and employee, and between producer and consumer. These aspects of vocational education, heretofore neglected, demand emphatic attention.

The extent to which the secondary school should offer training for a specific vocation depends upon the vocation, the facilities that the school can acquire, and the opportunity that the pupil may have to obtain such training later. To obtain satisfactory results those proficient in that vocation should be employed as instructors and the actual conditions of the vocation should be utilized either within the high school or in cooperation with the home, farm, shop, or office. Much of the pupil's time will be required to produce such efficiency.

5. *Civic education* should develop in the individual those qualities whereby he will act well his part as a member of neighborhood, town or city, State, and Nation, and give him a basis for understanding international problems.

For such citizenship the following are essential: A many-sided interest in the welfare of the communities to which one belongs; loyalty to ideals of civic righteousness, practical knowledge of social agencies and institu-

[1] Report of the Committee on the Articulation of High School and College, 1911.

Formulations and Discussions

tions; good judgment as to means and methods that will promote one social end without defeating others; and as putting all these into effect, habits of cordial cooperation in social undertakings.

The school should develop the concept that the civic duties of men and women, while in part identical, are also in part supplementary. Differentiation in civic activities is to be encouraged, but not to the extent of loss of interest in the common problems with which all should cope.

Among the means for developing attitudes and habits important in a democracy are the assignment of projects and problems to groups of pupils for cooperative solution and the socialized recitation whereby the class as a whole develops a sense of collective responsibility. Both of these devices give training in collective thinking. Moreover, the democratic organization and administration of the school itself, as well as the cooperative relations of pupils and teacher, pupil and pupil, and teacher and teacher, are indispensable.

While all subjects should contribute to good citizenship, the social studies —geography, history, civics, and economics—should have this as their dominant aim. Too frequently, however, does mere information, conventional in value and remote in its bearing, make up the content of the social studies. History should so treat the growth of institutions that their present value may be appreciated. Geography should show the interdependence of men while it shows their common dependence on nature. Civics should concern itself less with constitutional questions and remote governmental functions, and should direct attention to social agencies close at hand and to the informal activities of daily life that regard and seek the common good. Such agencies as child-welfare organizations and consumers' leagues afford specific opportunities for the expression of civic qualities by the older pupils.

The work in English should kindle social ideals and give insight into social conditions and into personal character as related to these conditions. Hence the emphasis by the committee on English on the importance of a knowledge of social activities, social movements, and social needs on the part of the teacher of English.

The comprehension of the ideals of American democracy and loyalty to them should be a prominent aim of civic education. The pupil should feel that he will be responsible, in cooperation with others, for keeping the Nation true to the best inherited conceptions of democracy, and he should also realize that democracy itself is an ideal to be wrought out by his own and succeeding generations.

Civic education should consider other nations also. As a people we should try to understand their aspirations and ideals that we may deal more sympathetically and intelligently with the immigrant coming to our shores, and have a basis for a wiser and more sympathetic approach to international problems. Our pupils should learn that each nation, at least potentially, has something of worth to contribute to civilization and that humanity would be incomplete without that contribution. This means a study of specific nations, their achievements and possibilities, not ignoring their limitations. Such a study of dissimilar contributions in the light of the ideal of human brotherhood should help to establish a genuine internationalism, free from sentimentality, founded on fact, and actually operative in the affairs of nations.

6. *Worthy use of leisure.*—Education should equip the individual to secure from his leisure the re-creation of body, mind, and spirit, and the enrichment and enlargement of his personality.

This objective calls for the ability to utilize the common means of enjoyment, such as music, art, literature, drama, and social intercourse, together with the fostering in each individual of one or more special avocational interests.

Heretofore the high school has given little conscious attention to this objective. It has so exclusively sought intellectual discipline that it has seldom treated literature, art, and music so as to evoke right emotional response and produce positive enjoyment. Its presentation of science should aim, in part, to arouse a genuine appreciation of nature.

The school has failed also to organize and direct the social activities of young people as it should. One of the surest ways in which to prepare pupils worthily to utilize leisure in adult life is by guiding and directing their use of leisure in youth. The school should, therefore, see that adequate recreation is provided both within the school and by other proper agencies in the community. The school, however, has a unique opportunity in this field because it includes in its membership representatives from all classes of society and consequently is able through social relationships to establish bonds of friendship and common understanding that can not be furnished by other agencies. Moreover, the school can so organize recreational activities that they will contribute simultaneously to other ends of education, as in the case of the school pageant or festival.

7. *Ethical character.*—In a democratic society ethical character becomes paramount among the objectives of the secondary school. Among the means for developing ethical character may be mentioned the wise selection of content and methods of instruction in all subjects of study, the social contacts of pupils with one another and with their teachers, the opportunities afforded by the organization and administration of the school for the development on the part of pupils of the sense of personal responsibility and initiative, and, above all, the spirit of service and the principles

of true democracy which should permeate the entire school—principal, teachers, and pupils.

Specific consideration is given to the moral values to be obtained from the organization of the school and the subjects of study in the report of this commission entitled "Moral Values in Secondary Education." That report considers also the conditions under which it may be advisable to supplement the other activities of the school by offering a distinct course in moral instruction.

THE NEBRASKA DECISION *

(Mr. Justice McReynolds delivered the opinion of the Court.)

Plaintiff in error was tried and convicted in the District Court for Hamilton County, Nebraska, under an information which charged that on May 25, 1920, while an instructor in Zion Parochial School, he unlawfully taught the subject of reading in the German language to Raymond Parpart, a child of ten years, who had not attained and successfully passed the eighth grade. The information is based upon "An act relating to the teaching of foreign languages in the State of Nebraska," approved April 9, 1919, which follows [Laws 1919, c. 249.]:

"Section 1. No person, individually or as a teacher, shall, in any private, denominational, parochial or public school, teach any subject to any person in any language other than the English language.

"Sec. 2. Languages, other than the English language, may be taught as languages only after a pupil shall have attained and successfully passed the eighth grade as evidenced by a certificate of graduation issued by the county superintendent of the county in which the child resides.

"Sec. 3. Any person who violates any of the provisions of this act shall be deemed guilty of a misdemeanor and upon conviction, shall be subject to a fine of not less than twenty-five dollars ($25), nor more than one hundred dollars ($100) or be confined in the county jail for any period not exceeding thirty days for each offense.

"Sec. 4. Whereas, an emergency exists, this act shall be in force from and after its passage and approval."

The Supreme Court of the State affirmed the judgment of conviction. 107 Neb. 657. It declared the offense charged and established was "the direct and intentional teaching of the German language as a distinct subject to a child who had not passed the eighth grade," in the parochial school maintained by Zion Evangelical Lutheran Congregation, a collec-

* *Meyer v. Nebraska*, 262 U.S. 390 (1923).

tion of Biblical stories being used therefor. And it held that the statute forbidding this did not conflict with the Fourteenth Amendment, but was a valid exercise of the police power. . . .

The American people have always regarded education and acquisition of knowledge as matters of supreme importance which should be diligently promoted. The Ordinance of 1787 declares, "Religion, morality, and knowledge being necessary to good government and the happiness of mankind, schools and the means of education shall forever be encouraged." Corresponding to the right of control, it is the natural duty of the parent to give his children education suitable to their station in life; and nearly all the States, including Nebraska, enforce this obligation by compulsory laws.

Practically, education of the young is only possible in schools conducted by especially qualified persons who devote themselves thereto. The calling always has been regarded as useful and honorable, essential, indeed, to the public welfare. Mere knowledge of the German language cannot reasonably be regarded as harmful. Heretofore it has been commonly looked upon as helpful and desirable. Plaintiff in error taught this language in school as part of his occupation. His right thus to teach and the right of parents to engage him so to instruct their children, we think, are within the liberty of the Amendment.

The challenged statute forbids the teaching in school of any subject except in English; also the teaching of any other language until the pupil has attained and successfully passed the eighth grade, which is not usually accomplished before the age of twelve. The Supreme Court of the State has held that "the so-called ancient or dead languages" are not "within the spirit or the purpose of the act." *Nebraska District of Evangelical Lutheran Synod* v. *McKelvie,* 187 N. W. 927. Latin, Greek, Hebrew are not proscribed; but German, French, Spanish, Italian and every other alien speech are within the ban. Evidently the legislature has attempted materially to interfere with the calling of modern language teachers, with the opportunities of pupils to acquire knowledge, and with the power of parents to control the education of their own.

It is said the purpose of the legislation was to promote civic development by inhibiting training and education of the immature in foreign tongues and ideals before they could learn English and acquire American ideals; and "that the English language should be and become the mother tongue of all children reared in this State." It is also affirmed that the foreign born population is very large, that certain communities commonly use foreign words, follow foreign leaders, move in a foreign atmosphere, and that the children are thereby hindered from becoming citizens of the most useful type and the public safety is imperiled.

That the State may do much, go very far, indeed, in order to improve the quality of its citizens, physically, mentally and morally, is clear; but the individual has certain fundamental rights which must be respected. The protection of the Constitution extends to all, to those who speak other languages as well as to those born with English on the tongue. Perhaps it would be highly advantageous if all had ready understanding of our ordinary speech, but this cannot be coerced by methods which conflict with the Constitution—a desirable end cannot be promoted by prohibited means.

For the welfare of his Ideal Commonwealth, Plato suggested a law which should provide: "That the wives of our guardians are to be common, and their children are to be common, and no parent is to know his own child, nor any child his parent. . . . The proper officers will take the offspring of the good parents to the pen or fold, and there they will deposit them with certain nurses who dwell in a separate quarter; but the offspring of the inferior, or of the better when they chance to be deformed, will be put away in some mysterious, unknown place, as they should be." In order to submerge the individual and develop ideal citizens, Sparta assembled the males at seven into barracks and intrusted their subsequent education and training to official guardians. Although such measures have been deliberately approved by men of great genius, their ideas touching the relation between individual and State were wholly different from those upon which our institutions rest; and it hardly will be affirmed that any legislature could impose such restrictions upon the people of a State without doing violence to both letter and spirit of the Constitution.

The desire of the legislature to foster a homogeneous people with American ideals prepared readily to understand current discussions of civic matters is easy to appreciate. Unfortunate experiences during the late war and aversion toward every characteristic of truculent adversaries were certainly enough to quicken that aspiration. But the means adopted, we think, exceed the limitations upon the power of the State and conflict with rights assured to plaintiff in error. The interference is plain enough and no adequate reason therefor in time of peace and domestic tranquility has been shown.

The power of the State to compel attendance at some school and to make reasonable regulations for all schools, including a requirement that they shall give instructions in English, is not questioned. Nor has challenge been made of the State's power to prescribe a curriculum for institutions which it supports. Those matters are not within the present controversy. Our concern is with the prohibition approved by the Supreme Court. *Adams* v. *Tanner, supra,* p. 594, pointed out that mere abuse incident to an occupation ordinarily useful is not enough to justify its abolition, although regulation may be entirely proper. No emergency has arisen which renders knowledge by a child of some language other than English so clearly harmful as to justify its inhibition with the consequent infringement of rights long freely enjoyed. We are constrained to conclude that the statute as applied is arbitrary and without reasonable relation to any end within the competency of the State.

The judgment of the court below must be reversed and the cause remanded for further proceedings not inconsistent with this opinion.

Reversed.

ENCYCLICAL LETTER ON CHRISTIAN EDUCATION OF YOUTH *

REASONS FOR TREATING OF CHRISTIAN EDUCATION

. . . Never has there been so much discussion about education as nowadays; never have exponents of new pedagogical theories been so numerous, or so many methods and means devised, proposed and debated, not merely to facilitate education, but to create a new system infallibly efficacious, and capable of preparing the present generations for that earthly happiness which they so ardently desire.

The reason is that men, created by God, to His image and likeness and destined for Him Who is infinite perfection, realize today more than ever amid the most exuberant material progress, the insufficiency of earthly goods to produce true happiness either for the individual or for the nations. And hence they feel more keenly in themselves the impulse towards a perfection that is higher, which impulse is implanted in their rational nature by the Creator Himself. This perfection they seek to acquire by means of education. But many of them with, it would seem, too great insistence on the etymological meaning of the word, pretend to draw education out of human nature itself and evolve it by its own unaided powers. Such easily fall into error, because, instead of fixing their gaze on God, first principle and last end of the whole universe, they fall back upon themselves, becoming attached exclusively to passing things of earth; and thus their restlessness will never cease till they direct their attention and their efforts to God, the goal of all perfection, according to the profound saying of St. Augustine: "Thou didst create us, O Lord, for Thyself, and our heart is restless till it rest in Thee."

* Pius XI, "Full Text of Pope's Encyclical" (*Christian Education of Youth,* January 11, 1930), *Current History,* XXXI (March 1930), pp. 1091, 1092, 1098, 1099, 1103, 1104.

Nature, Importance and Excellence of Christian Education

It is therefore as important to make no mistake in education, as it is to make no mistake in the pursuit of the last end, with which the whole work of education is intimately and necessarily connected. In fact, since education consists essentially in preparing man for what he must be and for what he must do here below, in order to attain the sublime end for which he was created, it is clear that there can be no true education which is not wholly directed to man's last end, and that in the present order of Providence, since God has revealed Himself to us in the Person of His Only Begotten Son, Who alone is "the way, the truth and the life," there can be no ideally perfect education which is not Christian education.

From this we see the supreme importance of Christian education, not merely for each individual, but for families and for the whole of human society, whose perfection comes from the perfection of the elements that compose it. From these same principles, the excellence, we may well call it the unsurpassed excellence, of the work of Christian education becomes manifest and clear; for after all it aims at securing the Supreme Good, that is, God, for the souls of those who are being educated, and the maximum of well-being possible here below for human society. And this it does as efficaciously as man is capable of doing it, namely by cooperating with God in the perfecting of individuals and of society, in as much as education makes upon the soul the first, the most powerful and lasting impression for life, according to the well-known saying of the Wise Man, "A young man according to his way, even when he is old, he will not depart from it." With good reason therefore did St. John Chrysostom say, "What greater work is there than training the mind and forming the habits of the young?"

But nothing discloses to us the supernatural beauty and excellence of the work of Christian education better than the sublime expression of love of Our Blessed Lord, identifying Himself with children, "Whosoever shall receive one such child as this in My name, receiveth Me."

Now in order that no mistake be made in this work of utmost importance, and in order to conduct it in the best manner possible with the help of God's grace, it is necessary to have a clear and definite idea of Christian education in its essential aspects, viz., who has the mission to educate, who are the subjects to be educated, what are the necessary accompanying circumstances, what is the end and object proper to Christian education according to God's established order in the economy of His Divine Providence. . . .

Subject of Education

In fact it must never be forgotten that the subject of Christian education is man whole and entire, soul united to body in unity of nature, with all his faculties natural and supernatural, such as right reason and revelation show him to be; man, therefore, fallen from his original estate, but redeemed by Christ and restored to the supernatural condition of adopted son of God, though without the preternatural privileges of bodily immortality or perfect control of appetite. There remain therefore, in human nature the effects of original sin, the chief of which are weakness of will and disorderly inclinations.

"Folly is bound up in the heart of a child and the rod of correction shall drive it away." Disorderly inclinations then must be corrected, good tendencies encouraged and regulated from tender childhood, and above all the mind must be enlightened and the will strengthened by supernatural truth and by the means of grace, without which it is impossible to control evil impulses, impossible to attain to the full and complete perfection of education intended by the Church, which Christ has endowed so richly with divine doctrine and with the Sacraments, the efficacious means of grace.

Naturalism in Education, False and Damaging

Hence every form of pedagogic naturalism which in any way excludes or weakens supernatural Christian formation in the teaching of youth, is false. Every method of education founded, wholly or in part, on the denial or forgetfulness of original sin and of grace, and relying on the sole powers of human nature, is unsound. Such, generally speaking, are those modern systems bearing various names which appeal to a pretended self-government and unrestrained freedom on the part of the child, and which diminish or even suppress the teacher's authority and action, attributing to the child an exclusive primacy of initiative, and an activity independent of any higher law, natural or divine, in the work of his education.

If any of these terms are used, less properly to denote the necessity of a gradually more active cooperation on the part of the pupil in his own education, if the intention is to banish from education despotism and violence, which, by the way, just punishment is not, this would be correct, but in no way new. It would mean only what has been taught and reduced to practise by the Church in traditional Christian education, in imitation of the method employed by God Himself towards His creatures, of whom He demands active cooperation according to the nature of each; for His Wisdom "reacheth from end to end mightily and ordereth all things sweetly."

But alas! It is clear from the obvious meaning of the words and from experience, that what is intended by not a few, is the withdrawal of education from every sort of dependence on the divine law. So today we see, strange sight indeed, educators and philosophers who spend their lives in searching for a universal moral code of education, as if there existed no decalogue, no gospel law, no law even of nature stamped by God on the heart of man, promulgated by right reason, and codified in positive revelation by God Himself in the ten commandments. These innovators are wont to refer contemptuously to Christian education as "heteronomous," "passive," "obsolete," because founded upon the authority of God and His holy law.

Such men are miserably deluded in their claim to emancipate, as they say, the child, while in reality they are making him the slave of his own blind pride and of his disorderly affections, which, as a logical consequence of this false system, come to be justified as legitimate demands of a so-called autonomous nature.

But what is worse is the claim, not only vain but false, irreverent and dangerous, to submit to research, experiment and conclusions of a purely natural and profane order, those matters of education which belong to the supernatural order; as for example questions of priestly or religious vocation, and in general the secret workings of grace which indeed elevate the natural powers, but are infinitely superior to them, and may nowise be subjected to physical laws, for "the Spirit breatheth where He will." . . .

To Form the True Christian

Hence the true Christian, product of Christian education, is the supernatural man who thinks, judges and acts constantly and consistently in accordance with right reason illumined by the supernatural light of the example and teaching of Christ; in other words, to use the current term, the true and finished man of character. For, it is not every kind of consistency and firmness of conduct based on subjective principles that makes true character, but only constancy in following the eternal principles of justice, as is admitted even by the pagan poet when he praises as one and the same "the man who is just and firm of purpose." And on the other hand, there cannot be full justice except in giving to God what is due to God, as the true Christian does.

The scope and aim of Christian education as here described, appears to the worldly as an abstraction, or rather as something that cannot be attained without the suppression or dwarfing of the natural faculties, and without a renunciation of the activities of the present life, and hence inimical to social life and temporal prosperity, and contrary to all progress in letters, arts and sciences, and all the other elements of civilization. To a like objection raised by the ignorance and the prejudice of even cultured pagans of a former day, and repeated with greater frequency and insistence in modern times, Tertullian has replied as follows: "We are not strangers to life. We are fully aware of the gratitude we owe to God, Our Lord and Creator. We reject none of the fruits of His handiwork; we only abstain from their immoderate or unlawful use. We are living in the world with you; we do not shun your forum, your markets, your baths, your shops, your factories, your stables, your places of business and traffic. We take ship with you and we serve in your armies, we are farmers and merchants with you; we interchange skilled labor and display our works in public for your service. How we can seem unprofitable to you with whom we live and of whom we are, I know not."

The true Christian does not renounce the activities of this life, he does not stunt his natural faculties; but he develops and perfects them, by coordinating them with the supernatural. He thus ennobles what is merely natural in life and secures for it new strength in the material and temporal order, no less than in the spiritual and eternal. . . .

AIMS IN EDUCATION *

Our first question is to define the nature of an aim so far as it falls within an activity, instead of being furnished from without. We approach the definition by a contrast of mere *results* with *ends*. Any exhibition of energy has results. The wind blows about the sands of the desert; the position of the grains is changed. Here is a result, an effect, but not an *end*. For there is nothing in the outcome which completes or fulfills what went before it. There is mere spatial redistribution. One state of affairs is just as good as any other. Consequently there is no basis upon which to select an earlier state of affairs as a beginning, a later as an end, and to consider what intervenes as a process of transformation and realization.

Consider for example the activities of bees in contrast with the changes in the sands when the wind blows them about. The results of the bees' actions may be called ends not because they are designed or consciously intended, but because they are true terminations or completions of what has preceded. When the bees gather pollen and make wax and build cells, each step prepares the way for the next. When cells are built, the queen lays eggs in them; when eggs are laid, they are sealed and bees brood them and keep them at a temperature required to hatch them. When they are

---

* John Dewey, *Democracy and Education* (New York, The Macmillan Company, 1935), pp. 117-29. Copyright 1935 by The Macmillan Company. (First published in 1916.)

Formulations and Discussions

hatched, bees feed the young till they can take care of themselves. Now we are so familiar with such facts, that we are apt to dismiss them on the ground that life and instinct are a kind of miraculous thing anyway. Thus we fail to note what the essential characteristic of the event is; namely, the significance of the temporal place and order of each element; the way each prior event leads into its successor while the successor takes up what is furnished and utilizes it for some other stage, until we arrive at the end, which, as it were, summarizes and finishes off the process.

Since aims relate always to results, the first thing to look to when it is a question of aims, is whether the work assigned possesses intrinsic continuity. Or is it a mere serial aggregate of acts, first doing one thing and then another? To talk about an educational aim when approximately each act of a pupil is dictated by the teacher, when the only order in the sequence of his acts is that which comes from the assignment of lessons and the giving of directions by another, is to talk nonsense. It is equally fatal to an aim to permit capricious or discontinuous action in the name of spontaneous self-expression. An aim implies an orderly and ordered activity, one in which the order consists in the progressive completing of a process. Given an activity having a time span and cumulative growth within the time succession, an aim means foresight in advance of the end or possible termination. If bees anticipated the consequences of their activity, if they perceived their end in imaginative foresight, they would have the primary element in an aim. Hence it is nonsense to talk about the aim of education —or any other undertaking—where conditions do not permit of foresight of results, and do not stimulate a person to look ahead to see what the outcome of a given activity is to be.

In the next place the aim as a foreseen end gives direction to the activity; it is not an idle view of a mere spectator, but influences the steps taken to reach the end. The foresight functions in three ways. In the first place, it involves careful observation of the given conditions to see what are the means available for reaching the end, and to discover the hindrances in the way. In the second place, it suggests the proper order or sequence in the use of means. It facilitates an economical selection and arrangement. In the third place, it makes choice of alternatives possible. If we can predict the outcome of acting this way or that, we can then compare the value of the two courses of action; we can pass judgment upon their relative desirability. If we know that stagnant water breeds mosquitoes and that they are likely to carry disease, we can, disliking that anticipated result, take steps to avert it. Since we do not anticipate results as mere intellectual onlookers, but as persons concerned in the outcome, we are partakers in the process which produces the result. We intervene to bring about this result or that.

Of course these three points are closely connected with one another.

We can definitely foresee results only as we make careful scrutiny of present conditions, and the importance of the outcome supplies the motive for observations. The more adequate our observations, the more varied is the scene of conditions and obstructions that presents itself, and the more numerous are the alternatives between which choice may be made. In turn, the more numerous the recognized possibilities of the situation, or alternatives of action, the more meaning does the chosen activity possess, and the more flexibly controllable is it. Where only a single outcome has been thought of, the mind has nothing else to think of; the meaning attaching to the act is limited. One only steams ahead toward the mark. Sometimes such a narrow course may be effective. But if unexpected difficulties offer themselves, one has not as many resources at command as if he had chosen the same line of action after a broader survey of the possibilities of the field. He cannot make needed readjustments readily.

The net conclusion is that acting with an aim is all one with acting intelligently. To foresee a terminus of an act is to have a basis upon which to observe, to select, and to order objects and our own capacities. To do these things means to have a mind—for mind is precisely intentional purposeful activity controlled by perception of facts and their relationships to one another. To have a mind to do a thing is to foresee a future possibility; it is to have a plan for its accomplishment; it is to note the means which make the plan capable of execution and the obstructions in the way,—or, if it is really a *mind* to do the thing and not a vague aspiration—it is to have a plan which takes account of resources and difficulties. Mind is capacity to refer present conditions to future results, and future consequences to present conditions. And these traits are just what is meant by having an aim or a purpose. A man is stupid or blind or unintelligent—lacking in mind—just in the degree in which in any activity he does not know what he is about, namely, the probable consequences of his acts. A man is imperfectly intelligent when he contents himself with looser guesses about the outcome than is needful, just taking a chance with his luck, or when he forms plans apart from study of the actual conditions, including his own capacities. Such relative absence of mind means to make our feelings the measure of what is to happen. To be intelligent we must "stop, look, listen" in making the plan of an activity.

To identify acting with an aim and intelligent activity is enough to show its value—its function in experience. We are only too given to making an entity out of the abstract noun "consciousness." We forget that it comes from the adjective "conscious." To be conscious is to be aware of what we are about; conscious signifies the deliberate, observant, planning traits of activity. Consciousness is nothing which we have which gazes idly on the scene around one or which has impressions made upon it by physical things; it is a name for the purposeful quality of an activity, for the fact that it is directed by an aim. Put the other way about, to have an aim is to act with meaning, not like an automatic machine; it is to *mean* to do something and to perceive the meaning of things in the light of that intent.

The Criteria of Good Aims.—We may apply the results of our discussion to a consideration of the criteria involved in a correct establishing of aims. (1) The aim set up must be an outgrowth of existing conditions. It must be based upon a consideration of what is already going on; upon the resources and difficulties of the situation. Theories about the proper end of our activities—educational and moral theories—often violate this principle. They assume ends lying *outside* our activities; ends foreign to the concrete makeup of the situation; ends which issue from some outside source. Then the problem is to bring our activities to bear upon the realization of these externally supplied ends. They are something for which we *ought* to act. In any case such "aims" limit intelligence; they are not the expression of mind in foresight, observation, and choice of the better among alternative possibilities. They limit intelligence because, given ready-made, they must be imposed by some authority external to intelligence, leaving to the latter nothing but a mechanical choice of means.

(2) We have spoken as if aims could be completely formed prior to the attempt to realize them. This impression must now be qualified. The aim as it first emerges is a mere tentative sketch. The act of striving to realize it tests its worth. If it suffices to direct activity successfully, nothing more is required, since its whole function is to set a mark in advance; and at times a mere hint may suffice. But usually—at least in complicated situations—acting upon it brings to light conditions which had been overlooked. This calls for revision of the original aim; it has to be added to and subtracted from. An aim must, then, be *flexible;* it must be capable of alteration to meet circumstances. An end established externally to the process of action is always rigid. Being inserted or imposed from without, it is not supposed to have a working relationship to the concrete conditions of the situation. What happens in the course of action neither confirms, refutes, nor alters it. Such an end can only be insisted upon. The failure that results from its lack of adaptation is attributed simply to the perverseness of conditions, not to the fact that the end is not reasonable under the circumstances. The value of a legitimate aim, on the contrary, lies in the fact that we can use it to change conditions. It is a method for dealing with conditions so as to effect desirable alterations in them. A farmer who should passively accept things just as he finds them would make as great a mistake as he who framed his plans in complete disregard of what soil, climate, etc., permit. One of the evils of an abstract or remote external aim in education is that its very inapplicability in practice is likely to react

into a haphazard snatching at immediate conditions. A good aim surveys the present state of experience of pupils, and forming a tentative plan of treatment, keeps the plan constantly in view and yet modifies it as conditions develop. The aim, in short, is experimental, and hence constantly growing as it is tested in action.

(3) The aim must always represent a freeing of activities. The term *end in view* is suggestive, for it puts before the mind the termination or conclusion of some process. The only way in which we can define an activity is by putting before ourselves the objects in which it terminates—as one's aim in shooting is the target. But we must remember that the *object* is only a mark or sign by which the mind specifies the *activity* one desires to carry out. Strictly speaking, not the target but *hitting* the target is the end in view; one *takes* aim by means of the target, but also by the sight on the gun. The different objects which are thought of are means of *directing* the activity. Thus one aims at, say, a rabbit; what he wants is to shoot straight: a certain kind of activity. Or, if it is the rabbit he wants, it is not rabbit apart from his activity, but as a factor in activity; he wants to eat the rabbit, or to show it as evidence of his marksmanship—he wants to do something with it. The doing with the thing, not the thing in isolation, is his end. The object is but a phase of the active end,—continuing the activity successfully. This is what is meant by the phrase, used above, "freeing activity."

In contrast with fulfilling some process in order that activity may go on, stands the static character of an end which is imposed from without the activity. It is always conceived of as fixed; it is *something* to be attained and possessed. When one has such a notion, activity is a mere unavoidable means to something else; it is not significant or important on its own account. As compared with the end it is but a necessary evil; something which must be gone through before one can reach the object which is alone worth while. In other words, the external idea of the aim leads to a separation of means from end, while an end which grows up within an activity as plan for its direction is always both ends and means, the distinction being only one of convenience. Every means is a temporary end until we have attained it. Every end becomes a means of carrying activity further as soon as it is achieved. We call it end when it marks off the future direction of the activity in which we are engaged; means when it marks off the present direction. Every divorce of end from means diminishes by that much the significance of the activity and tends to reduce it to a drudgery from which one would escape if he could. A farmer has to use plants and animals to carry on his farming activities. It certainly makes a great difference to his life whether he is fond of them, or whether he regards them merely as means which he has to employ to get something else in which alone he is interested. In the former case, his entire course of activity is significant; each phase of it has its own value. He has the experience of realizing his end at every stage; the postponed aim, or end in view, being merely a sight ahead by which to keep his activity going fully and freely. For if he does not look ahead, he is more likely to find himself blocked. The aim is as definitely a *means* of action as is any other portion of an activity.

Applications in Education.—There is nothing peculiar about educational aims. They are just like aims in any directed occupation. The educator, like the farmer, has certain things to do, certain resources with which to do, and certain obstacles with which to contend. The conditions with which the farmer deals, whether as obstacles or resources, have their own structure and operation independently of any purpose of his. Seeds sprout, rain falls, the sun shines, insects devour, blight comes, the seasons change. His aim is simply to utilize these various conditions; to make his activities and their energies work together, instead of against one another. It would be absurd if the farmer set up a purpose of farming, without any reference to these conditions of soil, climate, characteristic of plant growth, etc. His purpose is simply a foresight of the consequences of his energies connected with those of the things about him, a foresight used to direct his movements from day to day. Foresight of possible consequences leads to more careful and extensive observation of the nature and performances of the things he had to do with, and to laying out a plan—that is, of a certain order in the acts to be performed.

It is the same with the educator, whether parent or teacher. It is as absurd for the latter to set up their "own" aims as the proper objects of the growth of the children as it would be for the farmer to set up an ideal of farming irrespective of conditions. Aims mean acceptance of responsibility for the observations, anticipations, and arrangements required in carrying on a function—whether farming or educating. Any aim is of value so far as it assists observation, choice, and planning in carrying on activity from moment to moment and hour to hour; if it gets in the way of the individual's own common sense (as it will surely do if imposed from without or accepted on authority) it does harm.

And it is well to remind ourselves that education as such has no aims. Only persons, parents, and teachers, etc., have aims, not an abstract idea like education. And consequently their purposes are indefinitely varied, differing with different children, changing as children grow and with the growth of experience on the part of the one who teaches. Even the most valid aims which can be put in words will, as words, do more harm than good unless one recognizes that they are not aims, but rather suggestions to educators as to how to observe, how to look ahead, and how to choose in liberating and directing the energies of the concrete situations in which they find themselves. As a recent writer has said: "To lead this boy to read Scott's novels instead of old Sleuth's stories; to teach this girl to sew; to root out the habit of bullying from John's make up; to prepare this class to study medicine,—these are samples of the millions of aims we have actually before us in the concrete work of education."

Bearing these qualifications in mind, we shall proceed to state some of the characteristics found in all good educational aims. (1) An educational aim must be founded upon the intrinsic activities and needs (including original instincts and acquired habits) of the given individual to be educated. The tendency of such an aim as preparation is, as we have seen, to omit existing powers, and find the aim in some remote accomplishment or responsibility. In general, there is a disposition to take considerations which are dear to the hearts of adults and set them up as ends irrespective of the capacities of those educated. There is also an inclination to propound aims which are so uniform as to neglect the specific powers and requirements of an individual, forgetting that all learning is something which happens to an individual at a given time and place. The larger range of perception of the adult is of great value in observing the abilities and weaknesses of the young, in deciding what they may amount to. Thus the artistic capacities of the adult exhibit what certain tendencies of the child are capable of; if we did not have the adult achievements we should be without assurance as to the significance of the drawing, reproducing, modeling, coloring activities of childhood. So if it were not for adult language, we should not be able to see the import of the babbling impulses of infancy. But it is one thing to use adult accomplishments as a context in which to place and survey the doings of childhood and youth; it is quite another to set them up as a fixed aim without regard to the concrete activities of those educated.

(2) An aim must be capable of translation into a method of cooperating with the activities of those undergoing instruction. It must suggest the kind of environment needed to liberate and to organize *their* capacities. Unless it lends itself to the construction of specific procedures, and unless these procedures test, correct, and amplify the aims, the latter is worthless. Instead of helping the specific task of teaching, it prevents the use of ordinary judgment in observing and sizing up the situation. It operates to exclude recognition of everything except what squares up with the fixed end in view. Every rigid aim just because it is rigidly given seems to render it unnecessary to give careful attention to concrete conditions. Since it *must* apply anyhow, what is the use of noting details which do not count?

The vice of externally imposed ends has deep roots. Teachers receive them from superior authorities; these authorities accept them from what is current in the community. The teachers impose them upon children. As a

Formulations and Discussions

first consequence, the intelligence of the teacher is not free; it is confined to receiving the aims laid down from above. Too rarely is the individual teacher so free from the dictation of authoritative supervisor, textbook on methods, prescribed course of study, etc., that he can let his mind come to close quarters with the pupil's mind and the subject matter. This distrust of the teacher's experience is then reflected in lack of confidence in the responses of pupils. The latter receive their aims through a double or treble external imposition, and are constantly confused by the conflict between the aims which are natural to their own experience at the time and those in which they are taught to acquiesce. Until the democratic criterion of the intrinsic significance of every growing experience is recognized, we shall be intellectually confused by the demand for adaptation to external aims.

(3) Educators have to be on their guard against ends that are alleged to be general and ultimate. Every activity, however specific, is, of course, general in its ramified connections, for it leads out indefinitely into other things. So far as a general idea makes us more alive to these connections, it cannot be too general. But "general" also means "abstract," or detached from all specific context. And such abstractness means remoteness, and throws us back, once more, upon teaching and learning as mere means of getting ready for an end disconnected from the means. That education is literally and all the time its own reward means that no alleged study or discipline is educative unless it is worth while in its own immediate having. A truly general aim broadens the outlook; it stimulates one to take more consequences (connections) into account. This means a wider and more flexible observation of means. The more interacting forces, for example, the farmer takes into account, the more varied will be his immediate resources. He will see a greater number of possible starting places, and a greater number of ways of getting at what he wants to do. The fuller one's conception of possible future achievements, the less his present activity is tied down to a small number of alternatives. If one knew enough, one could start almost anywhere and sustain his activities continuously and fruitfully.

Understanding then the term general or comprehensive aim simply in the sense of a broad survey of the field of present activities, we shall take up some of the larger ends which have currency in the educational theories of the day, and consider what light they throw upon the immediate concrete and diversified aims which are always the educator's real concern. We premise (as indeed immediately follows from what has been said) that there is no need of making a choice among them or regarding them as competitors. When we come to act in a tangible way we have to select or choose a particular act at a particular time, but any number of comprehensive ends may exist without competition, since they mean simply different ways of looking at the same scene. One cannot climb a number of different mountains simultaneously, but the views had when different mountains are ascended supplement one another: they do not set up incompatible, competing worlds. Or, putting the matter in a slightly different way, one statement of an end may suggest certain questions and observations, and another statement another set of questions, calling for other observations. Then the more general ends we have, the better. One statement will emphasize what another slurs over. What a plurality of hypotheses does for the scientific investigator, a plurality of stated aims may do for the instructor.

THE CONCEPT OF NEEDS IN EDUCATION *

Any discussion among "progressive" educators is likely to bring in an early reference to the "needs" of pupils. In former years the phrase "felt needs" had considerable currency. The qualifying adjective had the great merit of providing an indication of what was meant by needs. A felt need was identical with desire; it was generated by the nature of the pupil and it pointed to an appropriate course of action. Consequently, an inquiry into needs was supposed to have a quality of objectivity comparable to that of studies dealing with the stratification of rocks or with spots on the sun. A felt need was a desire; although there seems to have been some hesitation about classifying all desires as needs. The hankering of an old soak for another drink, for example, or the yearning of a small boy to punch his playmate's nose, might not qualify as a real need in the mind of a pious educator. Labelling a desire as a need gives it a preferred status; the implication of the term "need" is that we are dealing with a legitimate claim and that something should be done about it.

If, then, we take the concept of felt needs as our point of departure, we at once encounter a problem. How are we to distinguish between desires which are to be recognized as "needs" and those which are not? Even if the desires which we encounter are innocent in themselves, their number and variety are such that we cannot give recognition to all of them. There are no discoverable limits to human desires. As William James says, "Not that I would not, if I could, be both handsome and fat and well dressed, and a great athlete, and make a million a year, be a wit, a *bon-vivant,* and a lady-killer, as well as a philosopher; philanthropist, statesman, warrior, and African explorer, as well as a 'tone-poet' and saint. But the thing is

* Boyd H. Bode, "The Concept of Needs in Education," *Progressive Education,* XV, January 1938, pp. 7-9.

Formulations and Discussions

simply impossible. The millionaire's work would run counter to the saint's; the *bon-vivant* and the philanthropist would trip each other up; the philosopher and the lady-killer could not well keep house in the same tenement of clay." [1]

In principle there is no difference in this respect between adults and younger people. When desires conflict, as they constantly do, a decision, to be intelligent, must be based, not on the quality or urgency of the desires, but on a long-range program. It is the program, the more remote aim or purpose, that decides which desires are relevant and which are interlopers. Even so elementary a craving as hunger, for example, must be dealt with in this way. Perhaps the person concerned has what he considers to be an unesthetic tendency towards overweight; perhaps he deems it his duty to tighten his belt and help conserve the national food supply; perhaps he believes that eternal salvation can be won only through complete subjugation of the body; or again he may have a primitive conviction that the world owes him a living and act accordingly. It all depends. The fact that he is hungry does not in itself give a clue to his needs. The need is determined in each case by the end to be achieved, by the underlying philosophy. It is related that a man once said to the celebrated Dr. Samuel Johnson: "But doctor, a man has to live!" To which the crusty old doctor replied: "Sir, I do not see the necessity."

We may assume then that some kind of guidance and selection is indispensable. It is different, of course, if we start with Rousseau's assumption that the patterns for development are inherent in our nature because man is created in the image of God. In that case it is reasonable to suppose that desires are the expression of this inherent pattern or divine image and therefore not subject to regulation of any kind. We can understand, too, how a believer in the instinct theory might reach such a conclusion, since the instinct theory merely changes Rousseau's terminology without changing anything else. In either case we have the idea of an inherent pattern from which education is to take its clues. We can then base education on the nurture of "needs" or desires as they happen to arise, with the comforting assurance that such procedure has the endorsement both of the Almighty and of science. This is logical, even if it does not make sense.

We usually assume that these older views have long since been abandoned. But perhaps this assumption is not wholly warranted. It is true that we place more emphasis on guidance and that we are less inclined than formerly to take the "feltness" of a desire as evidence of a need. A need, it seems, may be a real need, even if it is not recognized as such by the person concerned. Thus a man may be deemed to be greatly in need of a

---

[1] James, W. *Psychology,* Vol. I, p. 311.

noble woman who loves him and has faith in him, even though the man himself be wholly unable to diagnose his case in any such fashion. In other words, we grant that needs are not the result of purely inner determination, but we seem to persist in the belief that we can ascertain, in an objective way, what the nature of the individual calls for, if we interpret this nature in the light of surrounding circumstances. This is not a surrender of the old point of view, but a refinement of it.

Antecedently the presumption is all against the notion that adolescent needs, for example, can be ascertained by a detailed study of the individual in relation to his social environment. If there is no fixed pattern either in the individual or in the social environment, it is altogether unlikely that such a pattern will be found if we take the two together. Yet, as was said before, the only way to discover a need is in terms of a "pattern" or scheme of values. Let us suppose, for illustration, that a youngster is found to be maladjusted with respect to parental relationships. What light does this shed on his "needs"? This depends altogether on our theory of what these relationships ought to be. According to one view, he may be sadly lacking in the virtue of obedience to parental authority. According to another view, he may be in urgent need of a clearer insight into the limitations of this authority, so that he may persist in his course without being oppressed by a sense of guilt. Either of these views will provide a basis for the determination of needs, but neither one can be regarded as inherent in the nature of the individual or in the cosmic structure of things. Studies of adolescence may be immensely valuable as portrayals of the difficulties that beset modern youth. But it is misleading to call them studies of needs, because the needs still remain to be determined after the investigation is completed. The claim that needs are discoverable in this way would have to be rated, not as a scientific truth but as academic bootlegging. To expect "needs" to emerge from such studies is like expecting an architectural design to result from a study of the structural materials that are to be used for a building.

All this is but a roundabout way of saying that needs refer to ends or aims. In specific situations where the end in view may be taken for granted, it is entirely appropriate to speak of needs, since the end or purpose furnishes a point of reference for judging the needs. But to undertake to build an educational program by starting with needs is quite another matter. Unless we assume that there is a predestined end for human living and that we are in on the know as to what this end is, there is no justification whatsoever for talking so blithely about needs. An authoritarian scheme of education could make excellent use of a doctrine of needs, for it would be in a position to know at every point what it was talking about. In a democratic system of education the center of the plot must always be the continuous rebuilding of the scheme of values, the underlying philosophy or social outlook, by the pupil, as a basis for determining his needs. At most the social and material environment can only furnish an opportunity to choose between alternative conceptions of needs—and even this opportunity is largely dependent on co-operation by the school in supplying the conditions for making an intelligent choice.

The point at issue is far more than the verbal question of how the term "need" is to be employed. It concerns the question of what education should be primarily concerned to achieve. The failure to emancipate ourselves completely from Rousseauism and the instinct psychology is responsible for most, if not all, the weaknesses of the progressive movement in education. The attitude of superstitious reverence for childhood is still with us. The insistence that we must stick like a leech at all times to the "needs" of childhood has bred a spirit of anti-intellectualism, which is reflected in the reliance on improvising instead of long-range organization, in the overemphasis of the here and now, in the indiscriminate tirades against "subjects," in the absurdities of pupil planning, and in the lack of continuity in the educational program. It has frequently resulted in an unhealthy attitude towards children, an attitude which suggests that there is no such thing as a normal child, and that we must be everlastingly exploring his insides, like a Calvinist taking himself apart day after day to discover evidences of sin.

It is a commonplace that the infant's only chance to grow into a human being is through social relationships. This is only another way of saying that growth is not directed from within but by the "patterns" embodied in the social order. If we believe in progress, in a democratic sense, we must believe that these patterns require continuous revision. As they actually exist in our complex modern world, they not only present conflicting types, but the basic patterns are severally incoherent and internally contradictory. In business, for example, we accept both the profit motive and the ideal of social service; in government we hold to both rugged individualism and the ideal of social security; in the field of esthetics we find that standards are both absolute and relative. Yet these are the patterns which must serve as instrumentalities for "growth." In a properly organized educational system this confusion in our cultural heritage will be the constant point of reference, instead of being merely appended, like the tail to the kite, as an additional item after we have set up the program in terms of "needs," the concept of needs thus making a red herring drawn across the trail. What we need is a moratorium on needs, so that we can get down to serious business and bring to fruition the splendid promise that is contained in the philosophy of progressive education.

THE PURPOSES OF EDUCATION IN AMERICAN DEMOCRACY*

... Four aspects of educational purpose have been identified. These aspects center around the person himself, his relationships to others in home and community, the creation and use of material wealth, and sociocivic activities. ... The four great groups of objectives thus defined are:

1. The Objectives of Self-Realization
2. The Objectives of Human Relationship
3. The Objectives of Economic Efficiency
4. The Objectives of Civic Responsibility ...

THE OBJECTIVES OF SELF-REALIZATION

The Inquiring Mind. The educated person has an appetite for learning.
Speech. The educated person can speak the mother tongue clearly.
Reading. The educated person reads the mother tongue efficiently.
Writing. The educated person writes the mother tongue effectively.
Number. The educated person solves his problems of counting and calculating.
Sight and Hearing. The educated person is skilled in listening and observing.
Health Knowledge. The educated person understands the basic facts concerning health and disease.
Health Habits. The educated person protects his own health and that of his dependents.
Public Health. The educated person works to improve the health of the community.
Recreation. The educated person is a participant and spectator in many sports and other pastimes.
Intellectual Interests. The educated person has mental resources for the use of leisure.
Esthetic Interests. The educated person appreciates beauty.
Character. The educated person gives responsible direction to his own life.

THE OBJECTIVES OF HUMAN RELATIONSHIP

Respect for Humanity. The educated person puts human relationships first.
Friendships. The educated person enjoys a rich, sincere, and varied social life.

* National Education Association, Educational Policies Commission, *The Purposes of Education in American Democracy* (Washington, D. C., National Education Association of the United States, 1938), pp. 47, 50, 72, 90, 108.

Formulations and Discussions

Cooperation. The educated person can work and play with others.
Courtesy. The educated person observes the amenities of social behavior.
Appreciation of the Home. The educated person appreciates the family as a social institution.
Conservation of the Home. The educated person conserves ideals.
Homemaking. The educated person is skilled in homemaking.
Democracy in the Home. The educated person maintains democratic family relationships.

THE OBJECTIVES OF ECONOMIC EFFICIENCY

Work. The educated producer knows the satisfaction of good workmanship.
Occupational Information. The educated producer understands the requirements and opportunities for various jobs.
Occupational Choice. The educated producer has *selected* his occupation.
Occupational Efficiency. The educated producer succeeds in his chosen vocation.
Occupational Adjustment. The educated producer maintains and improves his efficiency.
Occupational Appreciation. The educated producer appreciates the social value of his work.
Personal Economics. The educated consumer plans the economics of his own life.
Consumer Judgment. The educated consumer develops standards for guiding his expenditures.
Efficiency in Buying. The educated consumer is an informed and skillful buyer.
Consumer Protection. The educated consumer takes appropriate measures to safeguard his interests.

THE OBJECTIVES OF CIVIC RESPONSIBILITY

Social Justice. The educated citizen is sensitive to the disparities of human circumstance.
Social Activity. The educated citizen acts to correct unsatisfactory conditions.
Social Understanding. The educated citizen seeks to understand social structures and social processes.
Critical Judgment. The educated citizen has defenses against propaganda.
Tolerance. The educated citizen respects honest differences of opinion.
Conservation. The educated citizen has a regard for the nation's resources.
Social Applications of Science. The educated citizen measures scientific advance by its contribution to the general welfare.

World Citizenship. The educated citizen is a cooperating member of the world community.
Law Observance. The educated citizen respects the law.
Economic Literacy. The educated citizen is economically literate.
Political Citizenship. The educated citizen accepts his civic duties.
Devotion to Democracy. The educated citizen acts upon an unswerving loyalty to democratic ideals.

CHARACTER EDUCATION *

1. *Essential elements of education in communist morality.* Communist morality serves our general purposes and is wholly linked with the building of a new communist society.

The Stalin Constitution declares the defense of the fatherland to be the duty of every Soviet citizen. It speaks of the obligation to guard public property, and of the obligation to observe the rules of socialist life.

A morally educated individual, according to our understanding, is one who in his conduct subordinates his own interests to the service of his Motherland and his people. Such service presupposes wrath and hatred toward the enemies of the Motherland who imperil the battle-won rights of the people and all that has been created in the realm of material and cultural life by both the older and the younger generation. Communist morality presupposes action and makes struggle obligatory. . . .

The entire work of the school must be directed toward the education of children in communist morality. In giving knowledge to pupils and in formulating their world outlook, the school must cultivate in them the habits of communist conduct. . . .

3. *Consciousness of the learner.* Moral conduct does not have great value if the individual complies with regulations merely because "he is told" or because he is threatened with some unpleasant consequences in the event of their violation . . . it is important that we behave in accordance with the canons of communist morality because of inner *conviction*. . . .

While giving foremost place to methods of persuasion, Soviet pedagogy does not repudiate methods of coercion. In our socialist society there are no requirements governing the conduct of adults and children which would do injury to the dignity and the rights of personality. The young are not

* B. P. Yesipov and N. K. Goncharov, *I Want To Be Like Stalin,* translated by George S. Counts and Nucia P. Lodge (New York, The John Day Company, 1947), pp. 42, 43, 45, 95, 141-2.

Formulations and Discussions

confronted with rules which are unreasonable. If the learner grasps the essence of a given rule, he will understand why it should be obeyed; but if he still fails to conform and violates the established procedures, he must be forced to observe them. Indulgence of and indifference to violations of moral requirements will bring harm to society and to the learner himself. If the teacher overlooks such violations, the child will permit himself to disregard moral rules and standards in the future. . . .

Chapter VI: FOR ORDER AND DISCIPLINE

1. *Basic traits of discipline required of the Soviet pupil.* The discipline which we cultivate in our children under socialist conditions is characterized by the following qualities: In the first place it is *conscious,* that is, it is founded on an inner conviction of the necessity of following definite rules and regulations in conduct which in turn are based on an understanding of their meaning and significance. In the second place, discipline is *self-initiated,* that is, it is not a discipline of simple obedience but rather a discipline which is linked with the desire to fulfill in the best possible manner a given assignment, order, or commission. More than this, it is linked with a readiness always to do one's duty, not waiting for an order or a reminder, but displaying initiative. In the third place, discipline is *firm,* that is, it is unquestioned obedience and submission to the leader, the teacher, or the organizer. Without this there is no discipline; submission to the will of the leader is a necessary and essential mark of discipline. In the fourth place, discipline is *organizational,* that is, it is a discipline which prompts and habituates the pupil to the precise organization of individual and collective work, to organization in games and life. In the fifth place, discipline is *comradely,* that is, it is founded on mutual respect of the members of the collective. In the sixth place, discipline is *resolute,* that is, it surmounts difficulties, prompts the completion of every task, subjects conduct to high purposes, and conquers motives of low degree.

Chapter VIII: FOR ALL MANKIND

The overruling purpose of the school, according to Lenin, must be the cultivation of communist morality in the pupils. The entire business of the education of contemporary youth must be the development in them of communist morality.

Lenin showed that eternal and unchanging ethical standards do not exist. Ethical standards are determined by the development of society and by social relations. Also for every concrete social form there are corresponding ethical standards. The conduct of the individual is determined by social relations and by social position. The ruling ethics in society is the ethics of the ruling class. Wealthy classes, as Lenin says, regard their morality as the morality of all mankind and founded on "the commandments of god." "We reject any such morality which is derived from extra-human or extra-class conceptions. We say that it is a fraud, that it is a deception designed to dull the minds of workers and peasants in the interests of landlords and capitalists."

In place of such ethics, created in the interests of exploiters, the working class creates a new ethics, which develops out of the interests of the struggle for a new society in which there will be no exploitation of man by man. The new ethics, the ethics of the forward-looking class, serves the cause of the reconstruction of society. Communist ethics unites the workers for the struggle for the welfare of all mankind, for deliverance from oppression and violence. Communist ethics therefore is the most advanced, the most human, and the most noble; and it is devoted to the purpose of creating a communist society. "To this end," says Lenin, "we need a generation of youth transformed into responsible people by the conditions attending a disciplined and desperate struggle with the bourgeoisie. In this struggle genuine communists will be developed; to this struggle must be subjected and with this struggle must be linked every step in the education of youth."

LABOR, LEISURE, AND LIBERAL EDUCATION [*]

Although the title of this paper is "Labor, Leisure, and Liberal Education" and although it begins and ends with a consideration of liberal education, its main concern is with the distinction between labor and leisure. This is so because I have found it almost impossible, in my own thinking about the subject, to understand liberal education except in terms of what its *end* is. And the end of liberal education, it seems to me, lies in the use we make of our leisure, in the activities with which occupy our leisure time.

In support of this thesis, that liberal education is to be understood in terms of leisure, I should like to proceed in the following order: first, to make some approximations to a definition of liberal education in terms of leisure; second, to try to reach—and this is the main part of the article—a deeper understanding of the significance of this definition by examining more closely the distinctions between work or labor, on the one hand (I shall use the words "work" and "labor" interchangeably), and leisure, on the other; and, third, to draw from this analysis, some implications or con-

[*] Mortimer J. Adler, "Labor, Leisure and Liberal Education," *Journal of General Education*, VI, October 1951, pp. 33-7, 43-5. Reprinted by permission of the University of Chicago Press.

sequences for the place of liberal education in an industrial democracy like ours.

Let me begin where anyone has to begin—with a tentative definition of education. Education is a practical activity. It is concerned with means to be employed or devised for the achievement of an end. The broadest definition with which no one, I think, can disagree is that education is a process which aims at the improvement or betterment of men, in themselves and in relation to society. Few will quarrel with this definition because most people are willing to say that education is good; and its being good requires it to do something that is good for men. The definition says precisely this: that education improves men or makes them better.

All the quarrels that exist in educational philosophy exist because men have different conceptions of what the good life is, of what is good for man, of the conditions under which man is improved or bettered. Within that large area of controversy about education, there is one fundamental distinction that I should like to call to your attention.

There seem to be two ways in which men can be bettered or improved: first, with respect to special functions or talents and, second, with respect to the capacities and functions which are common to all men. Let me explain. In civilized societies, and even in primitive societies, there is always a rudimentary, and often a very complex, division of labor. Society exists through a diversity of occupations, through different groups of men performing different functions. In addition to the division of labor and the consequent diversity of functions, there is the simple natural fact of individual differences. So one view of education is that which takes these individual and functional *differences* into consideration and says that men are made better by adjusting them to their occupations, by making them better carpenters or better dentists or better bricklayers, by improving them, in other words, in the direction of their own special talents.

The other view differs from this, in that it makes the primary aim of education the betterment of men not with respect to their differences but with respect to the *similarities* which all men have. According to this theory, if there are certain things that all men *can* do, or certain things that all men *must* do, it is with these that education is chiefly concerned.

This simple distinction leads us to differentiate between specialized education and general education. There is some ground for identifying specialized education with vocational education, largely because specialization has some reference to the division of labor and the diversity of occupations, and for identifying general education with liberal education because the efforts of general education are directed toward the liberal training of man *as man*.

There is still another way of differentiating education in terms of its ends. Aristotle often talks about the difference between the useful and the honorable. What he means by the "useful" and the "honorable" can sometimes be translated into extrinsic and intrinsic ends. An educational process has an *intrinsic* end if its result lies entirely within the *person* being educated, an excellence or perfection of his person, an improvement built right into his nature as a good habit is part of the nature of the person in whom a power is habituated. An *extrinsic* end of education, on the other hand, lies in the goodness of an *operation,* not as reflecting the goodness of the operator but rather the perfection of something else as a result of the operation being performed well.

Thus, for example, there can be two reasons for learning carpentry. One might wish to learn carpentry simply to acquire the skill or art of using tools to fabricate things out of wood, an art or skill that anyone is better for having. Or one might wish to learn carpentry in order to make good tables and chairs, not as works of art which reflect the excellence of the artist, but as commodities to sell. This distinction between the two reasons for learning carpentry is connected in my mind with the difference or distinction between liberal and vocational education. This carpentry is the same in both cases, but the first reason for learning carpentry is liberal, the second vocational.

All of this, I think, leads directly to the heart of the matter: that vocational training is training for work or labor; it is specialized rather than general; it is for an extrinsic end; and ultimately it is the education of slaves or workers. And from my point of view it makes no difference whether you say slaves or workers, for you mean that the worker is a man who does nothing but work—a state of affairs which has obtained, by the way, during the whole industrial period, from its beginning *almost* to our day. . . .

I would like, however, to add one basic qualification at this point. According to this definition or conception of liberal education, it is not restricted in any way to training in the liberal arts. We often too narrowly identify liberal education with those arts which are genuinely the liberal arts—grammar, rhetoric, and logic and the mathematical disciplines—because that is one of the traditional meanings of liberal education. But, as I am using the term "liberal" here, in contradistinction to "vocational," I am not confining liberal education to intellectual education or to the cultivation of the mind. On the contrary, as I am using the phrase, liberal education has three large departments, according to the division of human excellences or modes of perfection. Physical training, or gymnastics in the Platonic sense, if its aim is to produce a good co-ordination of the body, is liberal education. So also is moral training, if its aim is to produce moral perfections, good moral habits or virtues; and so also is intellectual training, if its aim is the production of good intellectual habits or virtues. All three are liberal as distinguished from vocational. This is not, in a sense, a deviation from the conception of liberal education as being concerned only with the mind, for in all three of these the mind plays a role. All bodily skills are arts; all moral habits involve prudence; so the mind is not left out of the picture even when one is talking about moral and physical training. . . .

Vocational training is learning for the sake of earning. I hope I step on nobody's toes too hard when I say, as I must say, that therefore it is an absolute misuse of school to include any vocational training at all. School is a place of learning for the sake of learning, not for the sake of earning. It is as simple as that. Please understand that I do not mean vocational training can be totally dispensed with; I mean only that it should be done on the job. It should be done as preparatory to work; and as preparatory to work, it should be compensated. No one should have to take vocational training without compensation, because it is not self-rewarding. To include vocational training in school *without compensation* is to suppose that it is education, which it is not at all. In contrast to vocational training, liberal education is learning for its own sake or for the sake of further education. It is learning for the sake of all those self-rewarding activities which include the political, aesthetic, and speculative.

There are three further comments I should like to make on this distinction. First, professional education can be both vocational and liberal, because the kind of work for which it is the preliminary training is essentially liberal work. The work of a lawyer is liberal, not servile, work. In Greece freemen who were citizens were all lawyers; there education for legal practice was liberal education. Professional education is vocational only in so far as this kind of leisure activity happens to be a way that some men, in our division of labor, earn their compensation.

Second, liberal education can involve work simply because we find it necessary to compel children to begin, and for some years to continue, their educations. Whenever you find an adult, a chronological adult, who thinks that learning or study is work, let me say that you have met a child. One sign that you are grown up, that you are no longer a child, is that you never regard any part of study or learning as work. As long as learning or study has anything compulsory about it, you are still in the condition of childhood. The mark of truly adult learning is that it is done with no thought of labor or work at all, with no sense of the compulsory. It is entirely voluntary. Liberal education at the adult level can, therefore, be superior to liberal education in school, where learning is identified with work.

Third, if schooling is equivalent to the proper use of leisure time in youth, then the proper use of leisure time in adult life should obviously include the continuation of schooling—without teachers, without compulsion, without assignments—the kind of learning that adults do outside school, the kind they do in conversations and discussions, in reading and study.

Finally, we may ask the place of liberal education in an industrial democracy. We can do this quickly by considering two basic errors or fallacies peculiar to our society: the first I would call the aristocratic error; the second, the industrial fallacy.

The aristocratic error is simply the error of dividing men into free men and slaves or workers, into a leisure class and a working class, instead of dividing the time of each human life into working time and leisure time. In the last few weeks I have been reading Karl Marx's *Capital* and, quite apart from the theory of surplus value—Marx's special notion of capitalist production—the book, as you know, is filled with the horrible facts about the life of the laboring classes until almost our own day. We must face the fact that, until very recently, the working classes did nothing but *sleep and work*. When we realize that children started to work at the age of seven; that whole families worked—men, women, and children; that the hours of working time were often twelve and fourteen hours a day, sometimes seven days a week, then we realize that the distinction between the leisure class and the working class is something you and I no longer can appreciate because it has disappeared from our society. It does not exist in the world today, at least not in the United States. But, if we consider the past, in which workers were like slaves, the aristocratic error consisted in the division of mankind into two classes, a leisure class and a working class.

To correct this error, we must say not only that all men are free but also that all men must work for their subsistence (which is nothing but a democratic or socialist variant on the biblical admonition that man must eat by the sweat of his brow). You will see the educational consequences of this fallacy when you stop to think how little point there would have been in talking about liberal education for all men in the eighteenth and nineteenth centuries, when much more than half the population had no time for education. It would have been just as meaningless for them to have been given a liberal education, doomed as they were to lead lives of work and sleep.

The second fallacy arises from the fact that industrial production has created an abundance of leisure time for all. I do not mean that the working classes today have as much leisure time as the leisure classes of other centuries. I mean simply that more leisure exists today, *per capita,* than ever existed before. Though industrial production has produced this abundance of leisure, industrialism as such has made all men servants of productivity; and, when productivity itself is regarded as the highest good, leisure is debased to the level of play or idleness, which can be justified only as recreation. The man of leisure is regarded by industrialists, interested solely in productivity, as either a playboy or a dilettante. Leisure loses its meaning when industrial society reduces it to an incidental by-product of productivity.

If these two fallacies are corrected, we reach, I think, the obvious conclusion that in a rightly conceived industrial democracy, liberal education *should be* and *can be* for all men. It should be because they are all equal as persons, as citizens, from a democratic point of view. It can be because industrialism can emancipate all men from slavery and because workers in our day need not spend their entire lives earning their livings. Liberal education in the future of democracy should be and should do for all men what it once was and did for the few in the aristocracies of the past. It should be part of the lives of all men.

But I may be asked whether I have forgotten about individual differences. Even if all men are citizens, even if they are emancipated from the complete drudgery of labor, it still is not true that all men are equally endowed with talent or have an equal capacity to lead the good life. Let me give you an un-Aristotelian answer to this objection, because I cannot help feeling that Aristotle's opinions on such matters were affected, to some extent at least, by the fact that he lived in a slave society.

The good or happy life is a life lived in the cultivation of virtue. Another way of saying this is that the good life or the happy life is concerned with leisure. The good life *depends on labor,* but it *consists of leisure.* Labor and all conditions that go with labor are the antecedent means of happiness. They are external goods, that is, *wealth.* Leisure activities are the ends for which wealth is the means. Leisure activities are the constituents of happiness. Leisure activities constitute not mere living but living well. They are what Aristotle calls "virtuous activities" or the "good of the soul."

Happiness so conceived is open to all men, *when all men are both workers and free men.* As regards both work and leisure, each man should do the best work and participate in the best sort of leisure activities of which he is capable, the highest for which his talents equip him. So conceived, happiness is the same for all men, though it differs in actual content, in degree of intensity, according to the individual differences of men.

It is clear, I think, that liberal education is absolutely necessary for human happiness, for living a good human life. The most prevalent of all human ills are these two: a man's discontent with the work he does and the necessity of having to kill time. Both these ills can be, in part, cured by liberal education. Liberal schooling prepares for a life of learning and for the leisure activities of a whole lifetime. Adult liberal education is an indispensable part of the life of leisure, which is a life of learning.

ELEMENTARY SCHOOL OBJECTIVES—
"PRIMARY PERIOD" *

[Kearney and his associates formulate objectives for the "primary period" —ending with the third grade, age about nine—under nine headings: (1) Physical Development, Health and Body Care; (2) Individual Social and Emotional Development; (3) Ethical Behavior, Standards, Values; (4) Social Relations; (5) The Social World; (6) The Physical World (The Natural Environment); (7) Esthetic Development; (8) Communication; (9) Quantitative Relationships. What is presented here is the statement of objectives to be achieved at the end of the third grade under the headings "Physical Development, Health and Body Care" and "Communication."]

1. PHYSICAL DEVELOPMENT, HEALTH AND BODY CARE

A. Knowledge and Understanding. The child knows that there is value in pure air, good food, proper exercise, clean hands, good health habits, adequate sleep, simple preventive medication. He knows how and when to brush his teeth and has some knowledge of how infections are spread. He practices safe behavior in crossing streets, and in using fire, knives, machinery. He knows that animals and plants provide foods for man. He is aware of the dangers of strange dogs, animals in the zoo, unknown vegetables and berries. He knows that medicines, the unknown contents of bottles, or things that look edible may be poisonous. He knows the meaning of the skull and crossbones on bottles and boxes.

B. Skill and Competence. In his play the child can skip, hop on one foot, climb, descend, jump, jump rope, suspend from bar, run with ease, and perform stunts appropriate for his age and grade. He identifies and can perform various steps in folk dances, imitative plays, circle games, and other group games. He skips to music in unison with others. He tries to use hands skillfully and to develop eye-hand coordination. He can throw and catch a large softball; build boats and houses of blocks; handle pencils and paint brushes; use hammer, saw, screw driver, broom, mop, dust brush, dust cloth. When climbing, he hangs on "tight." He cares for his own person: hair, teeth, nails, and skin. He dresses himself, managing

* Nolan C. Kearney, *Elementary School Objectives* (New York, Russell Sage Foundation, 1953), pp. 52, 54, 55, 56-7, 102, 104-6, 110, 111.

shoelaces, buttons, zippers, and fasteners. He eats without undue spilling of food.

C. Attitude and Interest. The child shows interest in his own growth and development; begins to accept his own physical and intellectual limitations, including handicaps that cannot be corrected. He is eager to learn new games and try them out, and plays games without fear. He has a broad and generalized eagerness to learn about the many interesting and stimulating things that concern his adjustment to life around him.

D. Action Pattern. The child is becoming used to washing his hands before eating and after going to the toilet. He is growing in habitual attention to personal cleanliness; covers nose and mouth with handkerchief when sneezing or coughing, keeps hands and objects out of mouth, uses only his own towels, toothbrush, and other personal articles. He eats wholesome food, chews it well, and accepts it in some variety. Although he ordinarily does not require a nap during the day, he rests when tired, engages in quiet activities right after eating, and gets adequate sleep according to his needs. He habitually engages in active play. He stays away from other people when he or they have communicable diseases, and has no undue fear of a doctor, dentist, or nurse. He shows some concern for proper room temperature, good light for reading, and safety conditions when playing and working. He practices safe behavior with fire, with tools, with sharp objects, with matches, and with traffic, traffic signals, traffic regulations, bicycles, and public vehicles.

8. COMMUNICATION

A. Knowledge and Understanding. The child should be able to recognize at once the words that are part of his basic reading sight-vocabulary, and to define many common words that he uses orally, including common abstract terms. He knows how to read the period at the end of sentences (and some children will read quotation marks around direct quotations, question marks, and exclamation marks). He should be building a proper acquaintance with children's literature. He should understand that many words "pair off" as opposites. He should be able to distinguish between the names of persons and things and the action words. Basic to his understanding of communication is his growing recognition that words and sentences are useful only as they have meaning for him.

He should be able to name and recognize all the letters of the alphabet in random order and to repeat the alphabet. He should be able to spell from dictation 7 out of 10 unfamiliar one-syllable words if they are completely phonetic. He should be able to spell 500 to 700 of the most commonly used words. Children should know the common sounds (in words) that go with the letters that represent them. They should recognize simple phonetic clues in spelling and use simple word-analysis techniques as an aid in spelling. They should know the standards for letter formation, spacing and alignment, in manuscript or cursive form.

B. Skill and Competence. (*Reading*) The child does assigned reading by himself. He reads, first, to get the whole story, anticipates the story from its title, picks out the chief sentences, and is able to tell what each says. He reads to find answers—what, where, when, why. He can recall the sequence of a story or the facts read in a story. He can read a simple narrative of ten pages with comprehension and pleasure, if there are but few unfamiliar words. He can indicate the interesting features of a book by describing or dramatizing them. He can distinguish the chief elements of a story and repeat them. He can repeat the narrative of a story for children in the language of the author. He reads simple informational material with comprehension. He handles second-grade material in silent or oral reading easily, reading or pronouncing most of the words accurately. In third-grade material, he reads with a comprehension score of 80 per cent. He can read 7 out of 10 paragraphs of third-grade material and recognize many of the main ideas. Silent-reading rate should be between 95 and 120 words a minute; not over 140 fixations per 100 words of easy reading material. He makes but few reversals on letter forms, as "b" for "d," and rarely does he reverse letter sequence, writing "not" for "ton." He has a recognition span of at least four-letter words, such as "come" or "hand." He reads with rhythmic eye movement and without lip movements or whispering.

(*Word Study*) He recognizes and produces the individual letter signs for the common blends. He can fuse two- or three-letter sounds into a single word and can recognize letters by their sound. He can recite the alphabet. He can sound out 6 out of 10 completely phonetic unfamiliar words. He grows in skill in attacking unfamiliar words: picks out new words in a story, notes how they differ from similar words, and notes context in an effort to find meanings.

(*Book and Library Skills*) He handles books properly, begins to use the index and table of contents in his search for information, and uses a children's dictionary or a picture dictionary to locate words or to find their spelling and meaning.

(*Speaking*) He converses easily, fearlessly, confidently, and fluently with children and with adults. He gives simple oral directions clearly, makes telephone calls efficiently and courteously, gives interesting reports on personal and group experiences, choosing interesting incidents to relate.

He contributes to group sessions and enterprises by sharing his experiences, giving directions to others, suggesting activities, and arranging classroom furniture for effective work and communication. He suggests reasonable solutions to immediate problems of group behavior.

He can plan a short talk, can make oral announcements, give clear directions, describe and discuss ideas obtained from reading, motion pictures, and the like. He can present short reports on trips, interviews, books. He can dramatize stories, impersonate characters, develop dialogue, and pronounce correctly the words he uses. He speaks with sufficient volume and clarity and does not use baby-talk or show evidence of avoidable speech defects. In speaking, he avoids errors that are not common in his home or community.

(*Spelling*) He can spell 400 common one- or two-syllable words. He uses simple generalizations and some knowledge of phonetics, consonants, and vowel sounds as aids in spelling. He knows how to use an apostrophe in a few simple words such as "don't." He is able to form simple plurals.

(*Handwriting*) He can write legibly with a pencil and perhaps with a ball-point or fountain pen (either manuscript or cursive writing). He keeps a reasonably even margin, and is able to form most capital and small letters correctly if given time. He writes his own name well, maintains good posture in writing, and can write legibly 40 letters a minute or 60 letters a minute if the material is repetitive (quality of 50 on Ayres scale is sometimes recommended). Not more than 3 out of 25 of his written words should require study before they can be read. He should be able to form the letters of the alphabet in their correct proportions, and to space properly above and below the base line.

(*Composition*) He is acquiring a "sentence sense." He uses capitals to begin sentences and for proper names, uses a period at the end of sentences, and groups together two or more sentences that follow each other easily.

He is able to compose and write simple letters independently with at least a realization that there should be a heading, salutation, message, complimentary close, and signature. He should be able to copy forms for writing friendly notes, letters of thanks, letters of request, and letters of invitation. He should be able to write notes to parents about school events.

He should be able to write a one-paragraph story, using some descriptive words about people. He should be able to write his street address (city, state, and country) and the date.

(*Listening*) He listens carefully in order to comprehend simple statements in direct conversation or in audiences, and puts in writing ideas that concern him. He is able to remember a series of three or more steps when listening to directions, and can write a short sentence from dictation.

C. Attitude and Interest. The child likes to write short friendly notes, to read for recreation or information, to talk and listen to others respectfully and thoughtfully, to recite poems, and to retell favorite stories. He is interested in the sounds of words in word-families, in rhymes, in secret languages and codes. He characterizes his efforts in absolute terms of good and bad. He begins to develop attitudes toward radio and television programs.

D. Action Pattern. The child habitually listens to others while they talk or give reports and he waits until they have finished or for an appropriate opportunity to speak. He finds good reading materials and shares them with others, both through reading aloud and through recommending poems, stories, plays, and news items. He habitually reads to others to inform, to help solve a group problem, and to entertain. He reads more rapidly silently than orally. He looks for information in books and reads for meaning. He voluntarily reads magazines and newspapers and books designed for children, and reads poetry and stories for personal pleasure.

He uses the picture dictionary in the library, and habitually studies new words and words he is uncertain about spelling. He writes occasional brief stories for fun. He contributes to class discussions at least briefly each day, and asks questions about topics that interest him. He tries to establish habits of correct usage in oral communication.

THE SCHOOL AND THE PRACTICAL NEEDS OF YOUTH [*]

. . . As a matter of fact, to define the school as an agency of intellectual training does not preclude the carrying out by the school of many ancillary tasks, important to the child and to society. The school does bring together almost all the children of the community. Consequently many health and welfare services can reach children and their families most conveniently through the school. Instructions concerning health and safety precautions, including emergency and civil defense arrangements, can be disseminated most efficiently through the school. The school ordinarily conducts a program of social activities, and some of the niceties of social intercourse can receive unobtrusive attention in connection therewith. A pupil is better known to his teachers than to anyone else save his parents, hence the school can engage in certain kinds of counselling and can refer problems to agencies that might otherwise never learn of them.

So far as the school is able to do so without interfering with its essential programs of study, it should make its facilities available for these services. The list I have just given, however, indicates the variety of demands that can be made upon its time. It is all too easy for a school administrator to give in to the pressures that are brought upon him by well-meaning groups of various kinds, and to allow the school's own program to be engulfed by

[*] Arthur Eugene Bestor, *Educational Wastelands: The Retreat from Learning in Our Public Schools* (Urbana, Illinois, University of Illinois Press, 1953), pp. 73-7.

activities only distantly related to its central purpose. This has actually happened to an almost unbelievable extent in many American public schools. Only a firm conviction of the importance of fundamental intellectual training, and a stern insistence upon subordinating all other activities to this one, can enable teachers and administrators to preserve the educational system from utter chaos.

It is this fact which renders so objectionable the effort of many modern educationists to redefine the purposes of the school explicitly in terms of the needs of youth. Let me quote one of the most influential statements of this point of view:

> Youth have specific needs they recognize; society makes certain requirements of all youth; together these form a pattern of common educational needs, which may be expressed as follows:
>
> 1. All youth need to develop salable skills.
> 2. All youth need to develop and maintain good health and physical fitness.
> 3. All youth need to understand the rights and duties of the citizen of a democratic society.
> 4. All youth need to understand the significance of the family for the individual and society.
> 5. All youth need to know how to purchase and use goods and services intelligently.
> 6. All youth need to understand the influence of science on human life.
> 7. All youth need an appreciation of literature, art, music, and nature.
> 8. All youth need to be able to use their leisure time well and to budget it wisely.
> 9. All youth need to develop respect for other persons.
> 10. All youth need to grow in their ability to think rationally.
>
> *It Is the Job of the School to Meet the Common and the Specific Individual Needs of Youth.*[1]

No one can take serious exception to these ten items in themselves. Young men and women do have these needs. One must, however, point out that the needs of the nation, not the needs of young people alone, are at stake. The pupils in a schoolroom are children, of course, and the school must make its first appeal to the interests which they have as children. The purpose of the school, however, is not primarily to teach children to

[1] National Association of Secondary-School Principals, *Planning for American Youth: An Educational Program for Youth of Secondary School Age* (Washington, D. C., 1944).

solve children's problems, but to prepare them to solve the problems of the men and women which they are to become.

This is a fundamental defect of the statement, but there are many shortcomings of a more specific sort. Why should not students understand science itself, rather than merely "the influence of science on human life"? What exactly is meant by the "appreciation" of nature? Why is nothing said about understanding the past in order to grasp the problems of the present? Why is it not considered important for young men and women to be able to express themselves clearly and accurately in their mother tongue? Why is there not even an indirect reference to arithmetic or to the more advanced forms of quantitative thinking? Is provincialism so desirable that students have no need to understand the world outside the boundaries of their own country and time by studying geography, or comparative government, or foreign languages, to say nothing of history?

Weaknesses of logic are also apparent in the statement, or rather in the philosophy behind it. A fundamental ambiguity of thought is concealed within its vague inclusiveness. An attempt is being made to define education exclusively in terms of the needs of youth, without reference to the capabilities of the school. The attempt ends in a *reductio ad absurdum,* embodied in the last sentence, a sentence that is fantastically untrue. It is *not* the job—it cannot possibly be the job—of the school to meet the common and the specific individual needs of youth. If it were, then the school should undertake to meet needs even more basic than any mentioned in the list: All youth need food, clothing, and shelter.

The idea that the school must undertake to meet every need that some other agency is failing to meet, regardless of the suitability of the schoolroom to the task, is a preposterous delusion that in the end can wreck the educational system without in any way contributing to the salvation of society. Much of the cant about education for "home and family living" is a disguised way of saying that the school must take the responsibility for things that the family today is supposedly failing to do. If family life is in a parlous state, that is a national calamity. But it does not mean that we can or should reproduce its intimacies in the schoolroom. Even if it were true, for example, that parents are not giving adequate sex instruction to their children (and I suspect that they are giving it more fully and explicitly than in any earlier period) does anyone seriously expect an embarrassed school teacher to explain the physiology of human reproduction to boys and girls in public, and to use franker and more explicit terms than their parents are willing to employ in private?

The school promises too much on the one hand, and too little on the other, when it begins to think so loosely about its functions. In order to reason logically about education we require two premises: one concerning the needs of youth, the other concerning the nature and capabilities of the school. The two matters are not identical, and neither can be deduced from the other. The nature of the school—what it is designed to do, and what it is able to do—is a fundamental consideration. The school is a particular kind of institution, and, like every institution, it has a definite field of competence and definite limitations. We must know what these are before we can determine *which* needs of youth the school is in a position to satisfy. And only by considering this question can we decide which responsibilities of the school are primary and inescapable, and which are secondary and optional.

A failure to distinguish between men's needs in general and their specifically educational needs is one basic cause of the anti-intellectualism so rampant in the American public schools. Regressive education is a monstrosity in the literal sense of that word. It consists in the abnormal overdevelopment of certain features of the school program and the withering away of other and more important features. It is a vicious educational program, not because the elements in it are bad, but because they are completely out of balance. A well-intentioned but incidental concern with the personal problems of adolescents has grown so excessive as to push into the background what should be the school's central concern, the intellectual development of its students. To such an extreme have many educationists gone that they seem anxious for the school to satisfy all imaginable needs except those of the mind.

Genuine liberal education is not a course in first aid. It is a serious effort to train men to recognize symptoms, to trace them to fundamental causes, and to deal intelligently with the latter. When education becomes completely enmeshed in the petty, surface details of a student's everyday life, it loses the opportunity of equipping him with the intellectual powers that he will need to solve the deeper problems that lie beneath the surface. By frittering time away upon the "felt needs" of adolescents, the school runs the risk of leaving its students helpless in the presence of the real "real-life" needs that will come later and that will put to the test all the resources of a mature and disciplined intelligence.

In a vast number of American schools, the greatest of all the contributions which the school can make to society—the production of well-informed and intelligent citizens—is being sacrificed in favor of a multitude of minor social services which, even in the aggregate, are of far less ultimate consequence than the things that are being irretrievably lost. . . .

REPORT OF THE COMMITTEE FOR THE WHITE HOUSE CONFERENCE ON EDUCATION *

From the work of the Committee for the White House Conference on Education, one fundamental fact emerges: schools now affect the welfare of the United States more than ever before in history, and this new importance of education has been dangerously underestimated for a long time.

Some of the reasons for the rapidly increasing importance of the schools have been often noted. Ignorance is a far greater handicap to an individual than it was a generation ago, and an uneducated populace is a greater handicap to a nation. This trend is obviously going to continue and quicken.

An equally important and less frequently mentioned reason for the growing importance of education is the plain fact that the schools have become the chief instrument for keeping this Nation the fabled land of opportunity it started out to be. In other decades, the opportunities of America lay primarily in escape from the rigid class barriers of Europe, the availability of free land at the frontier, and the excitement of a violently growing nation, where farms often became villages and villages became cities within the span of one human life. When the frontier was closed, it would have been easy for opportunities to dry up in this Nation, and for rigid class barriers to develop. It has been primarily the schools which have prevented this from happening. As long as good schools are available, a man is not frozen at any level of our economy, nor is his son. Schools free men to rise to the level of their natural abilities. Hope for personal advancement and the advancement of one's children is, of course, one of the great wellsprings of human energy. The schools, more than any other agency, supply this hope in America today. By providing a channel for ambition, they have taken the place of the frontier, and in a highly technical era, have preserved the independent spirit of a pioneer nation. The schools stand as the chief expression of the American tradition of fair play for everyone, and a fresh start for each generation.

It is this fundamental conception of schools designed to give a fresh start to each generation that has broadened the ideals of education in America so much in the past 25 years. It is no longer thought proper to restrict educational programs to the skills of the mind, even though those skills remain of fundamental importance. Schools also attempt to improve

* *A Report to the President, the Committee for the White House Conference on Education, Full Report, April 1956* (Washington, D. C., United States Government Printing Office, 1956), pp. 4-5, 8-13.

children's health, to provide vocational training, and to do anything else which will help bring a child up to the starting line of adult life as even with his contemporaries as native differences in ability permit.

The most practical aspect of this new concept of education is that it calls for the most careful mining and refining of all human talents in the land—it is in itself a kind of law against waste. This new educational ideal represents the fullest flowering of the long western tradition of emphasizing the dignity of the individual. Many difficulties, of course, attend its development, but the members of this Committee believe that in essence it is noble and right, and that in the long run it will prove to be one of the great strengths of America.

It is, of course, obvious that much progress has been made toward realizing this new educational ideal in the United States during the recent past. It is the belief of this Committee, however, that improvement has been nowhere near fast enough. The onrush of science has outstripped the schools. What is even more important, ideals of human conduct have in some areas advanced as rapidly as technology. Many a school which seemed good enough a generation ago now seems a disgrace to the community where it stands.

The schools have fallen far behind both the aspirations of the American people and their capabilities. In the opinion of this Committee, there is growing resolve throughout the Nation to close the gap between educational ideals and educational realities. . . .

WHAT SHOULD OUR SCHOOLS ACCOMPLISH?

What should our schools accomplish? No attempt has been made to answer from the point of view of ultimate philosophical objectives which could be read into the question. The Committee has deliberately limited its considerations to the responsibilities of elementary and secondary schools in the contemporary American scene. As a lay group, the Committee has felt it inappropriate to undertake a discussion of curriculum content in specific detail. It has sought instead to reaffirm those current objectives of our schools that it believes to be desirable and to suggest those new emphases which will enable our schools to adjust to the changing needs of our society.

It is relatively easy to observe what the schools *try* to accomplish. The list is startling to anyone who remembers schools a generation back, even more startling to historians who recall the original task assigned to schools: the teaching of reading and ciphering. What schools try to do varies widely. People in suburbs demand different services from those expected by residents in rural areas. In spite of this, it is not difficult to draw up a list of purposes shared by most schools, however widely the technique for fulfilling them may vary. For good or ill, most modern school systems are normally asked to provide something like the following:

1. A general education as good as or better than that offered in the past, with increased emphasis on the physical and social sciences.
2. Programs designed to develop patriotism and good citizenship.
3. Programs designed to foster moral, ethical, and spiritual values.
4. Vocational education tailored to the abilities of each pupil and to the needs of community and Nation.
5. Courses designed to teach domestic skills.
6. Training in leisure-time activities such as music, dancing, avocational reading, and hobbies.
7. A variety of health services for all children, including both physical and dental inspections, and instruction aimed at bettering health knowledge and habits.
8. Special treatment for children with speech or reading difficulties and other handicaps.
9. Physical education, ranging from systematic exercises, physical therapy, and intramural sports, to interscholastic athletic competition.
10. Instruction to meet the needs of the abler students.
11. Programs designed to acquaint students with countries other than their own in an effort to help them understand the problems America faces in international relations.
12. Programs designed to foster mental health.
13. Programs designed to foster wholesome family life.
14. Organized recreational and social activities.
15. Courses designed to promote safety. These include instruction in driving automobiles, swimming, civil defense, etc.

THE GROWTH OF SCHOOL GOALS

During the past two generations, this list of school goals has grown with increased speed. This is a phenomenon which has excited both admiration and dismay. After several decades of experimentation, should this broadening of the goals be recognized as legitimate?

This Committee answers *Yes*. Nothing was more evident at the White House Conference on Education than the fact that these goals, representing as they do an enormously wide range of purposes, are the answer to a genuine public demand. These goals have, after all, been hammered out at countless school board meetings during the past quarter-century throughout the land. The basic responsibility of the schools is the development of the skills of the mind, but the overall mission has been enlarged. Schools are now asked to help children to acquire any skill or characteristic which a majority of the community deems worthwhile. The order given by the American people to the schools is grand in its simplicity: in addition to intellectual achievement, foster morality, happiness, and any useful ability. The talent of each child is to be sought out and developed to the fullest. Each weakness is to be studied and, so far as possible, corrected. This is truly a majestic ideal, and an astonishingly new one. Schools of that kind have never been provided for more than a small fraction of mankind.

Although it is new, this ideal of schools which do everything possible for all children is a natural development in the United States. The moving spirit of this Nation has been from the beginning a sense of fairness. Nowadays equality of opportunity for adults means little without equality of educational opportunity for children. Ignorance is a greater obstacle than ever to success of most kinds. The schools have become a major tool for creating a Nation without rigid class barriers. *It is primarily the schools which allow no man's failure to prevent the success of his son.*

In still another way, this new ideal for the schools is a natural development of this country: it recognizes the paramount importance of the individual in a free society. Our schools are asked to teach skills currently needed by the Nation, but never at the expense of the individual. This policy of encouraging each child to develop his individual talents will be of the greatest use to the Nation, for in the long run, if no talent is wasted in our land, no skill will be lacking. . . .

RECOMMENDATIONS

1. As the duties of the schools expand, the establishment of priorities in education should be studied by every board of education. This Committee believes that the development of the intellectual powers of young people, each to the limit of his capacity, is the first responsibility of schools. Beyond this basic task, all kinds of instruction are not equally important for all children, and their importance varies from community to community. This Committee also recognizes the need to invoke priorities in extracurricular activities. Athletics must be controlled, for instance, so that they serve young people rather than use them to enhance the competitive standing of a school or community. A primary responsibility of any local school authority is to establish priorities of significance among basic general education, specialized education of all kinds, and extracurricular activities.

In this era of international stress, the United States has unusual demands for good scientists and engineers, in addition to other specialists. There is a necessity for broad understanding of the meaning of citizenship in the United States. America must have citizens who know something of other nations and are equipped to understand their own Nation's role in international affairs. These special needs can be assigned a high priority by schools which are pursuing the broad list of objectives currently demanded by the people. In adding new, worthwhile activities to the curriculum, nothing of value has to be subtracted if a proper sense of proportion is maintained and enough resources are provided.

2. Overspecialization of vocational education should be avoided. There are almost 50,000 trades in this country, and specialized instruction for all of them cannot be provided. Broadly conceived programs of vocational education must be maintained which are not likely to be outmoded rapidly by technological change and which offer basic instruction that can be useful in many jobs.

3. Just as good schools permit flexibility in this whole Nation by allowing individuals to achieve the level of accomplishment their abilities deserve, the school system must be flexible within itself. Pupils should be able to shift from one program to another as they grow and change in interests and abilities. This Committee thinks that for every child to have, throughout his school career, the chance to change to the kind of education found best for him is more important than the time saved by choosing a few pupils early in their lives for accelerated, specialized programs, as is often done in Europe. The American people have time as well as the physical resources to allow this kind of flexibility.

4. Educational programs which fully exercise and develop the abilities of especially brilliant students must be maintained. A system which wastes the talents of those who have the most to offer has no part in the new American ideal for the schools. Social equality can be maintained by the schools without hampering the intellectual progress of the unusually able. Increased stress must be placed on meeting the challenge of those students who have the capacity for the greatest intellectual growth. Improved provision for these talented young people should be the next great advance in our public school system. This Committee believes it possible to achieve this goal and still handle the tidal wave of new students which is expected. The real and fundamental manpower scarcity at the present time is a scarcity of quality and not of numbers. Consequently, the identification and careful handling of talented youth are urgent and commanding requirements.

5. School leaders should *help* foster all desirable characteristics in children, but they should not be tempted to consider themselves the only agency in the field. The major influence upon children is their home and the whole community in which they are raised. It is right for people to expect the schools to help forward all worthy causes, but entirely wrong to abnegate responsibility in hope that the schools will take up the slack.

Formulations and Discussions

Schools can never take the place of a warm family life, a vigorous church, and a wholesome community, although they must be strong allies. Where other good influences are lacking, schools should and do try to repair the damage, but they cannot do the job alone.

In conclusion, this Committee believes that the new goals for the schools demanded by the American people reflect a determination to leave nothing that can be done for each generation of children undone. Far from seeking the abandonment of the ideals of the past, the people have called for a quickened pursuit of those ideals. At the same time, they have decided to use the schools in a variety of new ways, sometimes as an ally of other agencies, sometimes as a replacement for other agencies which have failed. Controversy has often surrounded questions of procedure and relative importance, but the nobility of intent implicit in this new concept is beyond doubt. There is far more to be proud of in today's schools than there is to criticize. Their weaknesses usually stem from a lack of means, rather than any defect in their goal. Efforts to work out ways in which school, family, church, and many other agencies can best work together for the fullest development of every child must be a continuous process in every community. To avoid a general dilution of education, the multiplication of school duties must be accompanied by a proportionate increase of school resources. We must never lose sight of the insistent need to increase the excellence of our schools while increasing their scope; the two goals are not incompatible except under conditions of bad management or inadequate resources. The problems of the schools are great, but they never should be allowed to obscure the worthiness of their goals. In the judgment of this Committee, the people will probably continue to insist that all needs of all children be met, one way or another. The attempt to provide schools capable of playing their full part in making that ideal a reality may well prove to be one of the wisest decisions ever made by the American people.

Illustrations

The selections and illustrations that follow show how educational purposes are revealed in teaching materials. Sometimes, as in Lindlay Murray's "Address to Young Students," the author makes his purpose quite explicit; sometimes, as in "The Term Begins," the authors' aims—in this instance to develop social as well as language skills—are implicit in the activities suggested. Typically, textbook writers, like teachers generally, have more than a single aim in mind. The authors of the *New England Primer* were clearly as concerned that children learn piety as that they learn their alphabet: indeed, the latter was justified as a means to the former. The excerpts from early and current histories and geographies demonstrate efforts to inculcate attitudes toward the child's own and other nations and political systems as well as to teach specific dates, names, and places.

Since educational purposes are themselves based on more or less conscious ideas about human nature and learning, it is not surprising to find that textbooks and the methods of teaching and grading children exemplify these different ideas. The selections from Rousseau and from J. E. Worcester, for example, stem from quite different theories about child development and learning. Memorization and deductive thinking characterize some texts; problem solving is emphasized in others. The accounts by Horne and by Rugg of Asiatic immigration differ not only in the authors' attitudes toward this social phenomenon but also in their approach to learning.

School regulations and report cards, like textbooks, exemplify different educational purposes. The U.S.S.R. "Rules for School Children" and "The American Pupils' Creed" written by seventh graders in a Maryland school both illustrate the school's interest in teaching children respect for school and teachers, but the emphasis in each reflects aims peculiar to each society.

As the reader studies each of these selections and examines other early and contemporary texts and instructional materials he should look for concomitant as well as subject-centered aims, for reflections of the values of particular periods and societies, and for basic assumptions about human nature, the nature of knowledge, and the processes of learning.

THE CURRICULUM *

Among the investigations in psychology which have had a tremendous influence upon educational theory and practice, must be included the studies of the problem of formal discipline, made by Thorndike and Woodworth in 1902. At that time, educational theory and practice were largely founded on the idea that the mind consisted of a number of powers or faculties which it was the main task of education to improve. The school should devote itself to developing memory, imagination, will, reasoning, and other powers. It was assumed that these faculties had an organic basis which might be compared to a muscle and that systematic and rigid training would develop the power as a whole, as the muscle is developed by any one of many sorts of formal and exacting exercises. This general theory led to the development of the curriculum which included a large number of problems introduced not because of their direct utility or even their reality, but because of the mental exercise which they provided. In many cases it was assumed that the more formal and difficult and exacting the mental work, the more beneficial the results. Guided by such a theory, the curriculum was narrow and formal in character and contained a large number of such problems as the following, which I am taking, with certain modifications, from E. L. Thorndike's "Psychology of Arithmetic." First are certain problems, which to quote Thorndike, "would occur in real life only in an insane asylum."

Alice has $3/8$ of a dollar, Bertha $11/16$, Mary $3/25$ and Nan $3/4$. How much have they together?

Consider the following ingenious method of finding how many pints there are in a large pile of nuts. The problem is as follows:

There are 9 nuts in a pint. How many pints in a pile of 6,789,582 nuts?

By implication, the child is advised first to count the nuts in the pile and then the number in the pint, and divide the former by the latter.

* Arthur I. Gates, "Psychology and Education," in Paul S. Achilles, editor, *Psychology at Work* (New York, Whittlesey House, 1932), pp. 60-63.

Consider the following clever way suggested to the child as a means of finding the thickness of a board:

> A nail 5 inches long is driven through a board so that it projects 2.419 inches on one side and 1.706 on the other. How thick is the board?

Offer the following problem to any sensible farmer and ask him how often he has been required to figure it out:

> Just after a ton of hay was weighed in market a horse ate 1 pound of it. What was the ratio of what he ate to what was left?

Consider also the thoughtfulness of this horse in eating exactly 16 ounces of hay.

The studies published by Thorndike and Woodworth in 1903 resulted in a complete overthrow of the older educational theory of formal discipline. In place of this doctrine was offered the theory of transfer of training, which, in brief, states that improvement in thinking, reasoning, neatness, honesty, and the like is to be found in the development of innumerable particular habits, and that these habits are likely to remain imbedded in the situation in which they are developed. A corollary to the theory is that such habits transfer from a situation in which they were developed to other situations roughly in proportion to the degree to which the two settings have elements in common. This doctrine at once led to the educational theory that the school should attempt to teach primarily those facts and skills, attitudes and habits which are required in the affairs of everyday life.

The impetus given by this revolutionary doctrine led rapidly to a host of studies designed to determine the frequency and importance of operations in arithmetic, facts and principles in history and science, and information and skills required in other subjects, in the lives of children and adults as they are today, or, as they are likely to be presently. In one such study made by a student of Professor Thorndike, Dr. G. M. Wilson, a survey of the actual arithmetical operations used by representative adults in all walks of life and in all the activities of life was made. This investigation showed not only that the arithmetics included an enormous amount of fantastic and misleading problems, like those cited before, but a large number of operations, which, though of value to certain specialists, are rarely if ever used by a typical child or adult. The following are examples: The greatest common divisor and the least common multiple, long and complex problems in compound fractions, reductions to denominate numbers, apothecary weight, computation of the square and cube root, problems in proportion, problems in ratio beyond limits set by fractions, problems in mensuration, such as those concerning the trapezium, polygons, spheres, problems in discounts except as they are concerned with United

States money, partial payments, compound interest, and many others.

Similar investigations have been made in other fields. For example, spelling books in common use fifteen years ago often included as many as 7,500 words, a considerable proportion of which were such demons as the following: *marasmus, hychopathy, varioloid, quassia, valerian, badinage, chirography,* and several more difficult ones that many people today would hesitate even to pronounce in public.

What to teach in spelling has since been determined by counts of millions of words found in the written composition of children of all ages, and of adults. As a result of extensive investigations of these types, it has been found that approximately four thousand words comprise about 98 per cent of those used in the written composition of both children and adults. Such words as the demons listed above are not written once a year by more than perhaps one person in a million. It is, of course, a sheer waste of time to teach all of the children to spell all these words, which they will never use and probably never understand. It is furthermore true that study of such words is a less effective means of developing spelling ability than study of the words that one will actually use in writing.

All along the line the misleading formal and futile materials have been eliminated from the curriculum, with the result that there has been an enormous reduction in the needless difficulties in the elementary school. On the other hand, the curriculum has been tremendously broadened. Instead of struggling despairingly with problems and exercises introduced merely because they were difficult and therefore presumably designed to improve the mind, the children are now engaged in learning facts about food and clothing, hygiene and health, the nature of the physical world immediately about them, how to get along with each other, the significant facts of social, political, and economic institutions, and other things that will be of vital importance in their everyday life.

The Language Arts

ENGLISH: THE LEADING LANGUAGE *

1. Language, or the expression of ideas by words, is peculiar to man alone of all created beings.

2. In the early ages of the world, as we learn from the Bible, the whole earth was of one language and of one speech, and so continued until the building of the Tower of Babel, when the Creator, doubtless for wise pur-

* S. A. Mitchell, *Mitchell's Intermediate or Secondary Geography,* Phila., 1868, p. 11.

poses, confounded the language of men, so that they could no longer understand one another.

3. There are now, it is estimated, 80 distinct languages spoken in the world; and 3664 dialects have sprung from them, of which 1624 are American.

4. The languages of civilized nations are both written and spoken, but those of savages and barbarians are merely verbal. The latter have, therefore, no learning and no books.

5. The English language is the most widely spread; it is spoken wherever Americans or Britons are settled. There are more books and newspapers printed in it than in any other, whence information is spread amongst all classes, and the Americans and English are in consequence the most intelligent people in the world.

6. The German, French, Spanish, and Italian, are, next to the English, the most extensively spoken of the European tongues; the books printed in them, especially in the first two named, are numerous, and embrace works on every subject.

7. The Persians, Turks, Arabians, Moors, and some other nations, are acquainted with letters, but are ignorant of printing; their books are therefore limited in number, and exist only in manuscript: the mass of the people are consequently very ignorant, few except the priests being able to read and write.

Questions—1. What is language? 2. What do we learn from the Bible? When did men cease to speak one language? What then occurred? 3. How many languages and dialects are now spoken? 4. What is said of the languages of civilized nations? Of savages and barbarians? 5. What is said of the English tongue? Of the books and newspapers printed in it? Of the Americans and English? 6. What is said of the German, French, Spanish and Italian languages? 7. Of the Persians, Turks, Arabians, Moors, &c.? What is said of their books? The mass of the people?

LANGUAGES OF THE WORLD *

LANGUAGES AND THE MAP

For a few minutes think about the people living on the various continents and islands of the world and about the languages they speak. Write a list

* Lou LaBrant et al., *Your Language, Book 3* (New York, McGraw-Hill Book Company, Inc., 1956), pp. 138, 139, 141, 142.

of the names of fifteen countries, and beside each name, write the name of the language (or languages) spoken in that country. When you have finished your list, look at it to see whether you have listed any of the same languages for more than one country. If you have covered a large part of the world in your list, you will probably find certain languages repeated. Among languages used by the greatest number of people are English, French, Chinese, Spanish, and the languages of India. Many of these languages of the world are related to each other, through the way words are put together into sentences, or through the words they have in common.

The name of a country does not always tell you what language its people speak. In India more than 170 languages are spoken. The people of North China have a spoken language different from that used in South China. In South America, the native language in most countries is Spanish, but in the great country of Brazil, the native language is Portuguese. In the United States, some groups use other languages than English. Spanish, French, and the American Indian languages, for example, are used by groups of people in different parts of our country.

LANGUAGES AROUND YOU

Begin today your study of the languages of the world by investigating the languages that members of your own class know about.

Your great-grandparents probably thought a trip to another continent was a great event, but today there is scarcely a town in the United States without some citizens who have been to Africa, Asia, South America, Europe, or Australia. Do you know of people in your community who have visited these parts of the world? Find out, if you do not know. Now work out answers to the following questions about your own class. Find out how much your class knows, as a group, about languages.

1. How many in the class can speak a foreign language well enough to carry on a simple conversation?
2. How many others are beginning to study some foreign language?
3. What languages, in addition to English, are spoken or understood by members of your class?
4. How many members of your class, although they cannot really speak in another language, know a few words from a foreign language (*adios,* for *good-by,* for example)? What are these languages that members of your class have sampled?
5. How many students have at least one parent who speaks or reads a foreign language? Which parent? What other relatives (include living uncles, aunts, cousins, and grandparents)? What are the languages?
6. What languages have you heard spoken by persons you have seen? On the radio or television? In foreign movies?

English Among World Languages [1]

In the world there are today more than two billion people. About one-fourth of a billion (250 million) speak English. That is, for every person born into an English speaking family, there are eight or ten born into families speaking other tongues. At the United Nations you will find five official languages—French, English, Spanish, Russian, and Chinese—and two called "working languages"—English and French.

Every treaty or document filed with the United Nations must appear in the two working languages, and translations of speeches are made in all five. Indeed, every nation that is a member of the United Nations has its official interpreters and translators, and they are constantly at work putting speeches and reports into the languages of their own countries. This work involves telephone wires, offices for cabling, mimeographers, and a great number of people busily using machines and papers, to get what is said in one language into the ears of people who speak various languages of the world.

If you visit the sessions of the United Nations, you will find at your seat a headpiece, which you may wear. It is connected with the translation bureau. By turning a little dial, you will be connected with a translator of the language you prefer. In front of you, speaking to other members of the conference, may be a man using Spanish, Turkish, or Chinese. He usually speaks slowly; as he pauses, the translator quickly puts the words into his own language. You, with your headpiece, hear a low voice saying into your ears, in English or French or whatever you have chosen (of the official languages), the speech the man in front of you is giving in his own tongue.

What part is English playing? English is one of the official languages of the United Nations, and it is also one of the working languages. The doors in the United Nations buildings are marked with English and French. All official documents are originally issued in these languages. Why is this so?

The reason lies in many situations. For a long time French was the official language of all European and American treaties. (At a time before that, Latin was called the universal language.) Gradually the English-speaking nations scattered around the globe, and English also grew in international importance. Now English is one of the languages taught in many countries as a foreign language, just as German, French, Spanish, or Latin is taught in most of our high schools. For these and many political and economic reasons, our language has become influential in many parts of the world.

[1] It is possible that your English teacher will want to work with your social studies teacher in developing a joint unit on this work.

We must not think, however, that English is the property only of North Americans or of the people of the United States. It belongs to all the people who have learned to speak it. We must also remember that it was spoken in England before America was discovered and that the English carried their language not only to America but to Australia, to parts of Asia, and to large areas in South Africa.

ADDRESS TO YOUNG STUDENTS *

The Compiler of these elements of the English language, hopes it will not be deemed inconsistent with the nature and design of his work, to make a short address to the young persons engaged in the study of it, respecting their future walks in the paths of literature, and the chief purpose to which they should apply their acquisitions.

In forming this grammar, and the volume of Illustrations connected with it, the author was influenced by a desire to facilitate your progress in learning, and, at the same time, to impress on your minds principles of piety and virtue. He wished also to assist, in some degree, the labours of those who are cultivating your understandings, and providing for you a fund of rational and useful employment; an employment calculated to exclude those frivolous pursuits, and that love of ease and sensual pleasure, which enfeeble and corrupt the minds of many inconsiderate youth, and render them useless to society.

Without your own best exertions, the concern of others for your welfare, will be of little avail: with them, you may fairly promise yourself success. The writer of this address, therefore, recommends to you, an earnest co-operation with the endeavours of your friends to promote your improvement and happiness. This co-operation, whilst it secures your own progress, will afford you the heart-felt satisfaction, of knowing that you are cherishing the hopes, and augmenting the pleasures, of those with whom you are connected by the most endearing ties. He recommends to you also, serious and elevated views of the studies in which you may be engaged. Whatever may be your attainments, never allow yourselves to rest satisfied with mere literary acquisitions, nor with a selfish or contracted application of them. . . . The great business of this life is to prepare, and qualify us, for the enjoyment of a better, by cultivating a pure and humble state of mind, and cherishing habits of piety towards God, and benevolence to men. . . .

* Lindley Murray, *English Grammar, Adapted to the Different Classes of Learners; with an Appendix containing Rules and Observations for assisting the more advanced students to write with perspicuity and accuracy* (Boston, T. Bedlington, 1825), pp. 335-7.

But if you counteract the hopes of your friends, and the tendency of these attainments; if you grow vain of your real or imaginary distinctions, and regard with contempt, the virtuous, untutored mind; if you suffer yourselves, to be absorbed in over-curious or trifling speculations; if your heart and principles be debased and poisoned, by the influence of corrupting and pernicious books, for which no elegance of composition can make amends; if you spend so much of your time in literary engagements, as to make them interfere with higher occupations, and lead you to forget, that pious and benevolent action is the great end of your being; if such be the unhappy mis-application of your acquisitions and advantages,—instead of becoming a blessing to you, they will prove the occasion of greater condemnation; and, in the hour of serious thought, they may excite the painful reflections,—that it would have been better for you, to have remained illiterate and unaspiring; to have been confined to the humblest walks of life; and to have been even hewers of wood and drawers of water all your days.

THE TERM BEGINS *

You are beginning a new term. For some months, you will be part of the group that makes up your English class. Probably this group is different from any group that has worked together before.

You must know by this time that the people with whom you work have a great deal to do with your own particular accomplishment, and that you have an effect on theirs. During the coming months it will be important for members of this class to work together, listening to each other and talking over questions and ideas.

Before you begin to share this experience, you and your classmates will need to become acquainted. During this first hour of the English class, learn the names of the other members of the class if you do not already know them.

A name is not, of course, the most important part of a person, and you will want to learn more about your classmates than just their names. You will find that every member of your class knows some things that the others do not know, that they do not all like and dislike the same things, and that some have had unusual experiences.

One good way for classmates to get acquainted is for each to tell what he does best and what he has found interesting during the last six months. Sometimes a student will believe that he does not have anything to tell

* Lou LaBrant et al., *Your Language, Book 3* (New York, McGraw-Hill Book Co., Inc., 1956), pp. 1-3.

about, but everyone is a specialist in something. Some members of the class may be specialists in the subject of baseball; some may work with amateur radio sets; some may be good cooks; others may be athletes, enjoying tennis, swimming, hiking, or football. One girl might know the history of several old buildings in her neighborhood. Another student might be able to name the birds in your part of the country. Almost everyone belongs to a club, a Sunday school class, or a team. Perhaps there are Boy Scouts in the class. Others may have gone camping or boating. Several members of your class may have read some interesting books or magazines.

In many classes there are students who have already begun to earn money. They may explain to the others how they do so. You may also want to know who can paint, draw, take care of plants and animals, sew, or do shopwork. Such skills may be necessary in carrying on studies or in producing plays. In one class, two boys knew a great deal about map making. They drew a large map on which the class marked spots of interest for study.

A quick method of becoming acquainted with at least one member of your class is to talk with a neighbor for a few minutes. If several students already know their neighbors, your class may want to have each person write his name on a paper, so that the slips may be drawn by lot and partners chosen. Then each couple may talk quietly together. Inquire where your partner has lived and where he has gone to school. Find out whether he has decided what he wants to do after he finishes school, or ask about his favorite movies and radio or television programs.

After these informal conversations, the students seated in one row or at one table, or six or eight seated alphabetically, may hold a conference to compare notes on each other's experience and knowledge. Then one or two in each group may tell the class what they have learned about their classmates. Perhaps the teacher will join one group; certainly he has had interesting experiences. Those who volunteer to report to the class may say something like this:

> In our group we learned that we have a new student who once lived in Japan. When Tom's father was in the Army, his family lived near Tokyo for two years. We asked Tom many questions about Japanese people, and I know all of us will want him to tell us someday about his life over there and the customs he noticed in Japan.

THE FIRST PICTURED ALPHABET FOR CHILDREN *

	Cornix cornicatur,	*á á*	A a
	The Crow crieth.		
	Agnus balat.	*b é é é*	B b
	The Lamb blaiteth.		
	Cicáda ſtridet.	*ci ci*	C c
	The Graſhopper chirpeth.		
	Upupa dicit.	*du du*	D d
	The Whooppoo faith.		
	Infans ejulat.	*é é é*	E e
	The Infant cryeth.		
	Ventus flat.	*fi fi*	F f
	The Wind bloweth.		
	Anſur gingrit.	*ga ga*	G g
	The Gooſe gagleth.		
	Os halat.	*háh háh*	H h
	The mouth breatheth out.		
	Mus mintrit.	*í í í*	I i
	The Mouſe chirpeth.		
	Anas tetrinnit.	*kha kha*	K k
	The Duck quaketh.		
	Lupus ululat.	*lu ulu*	L l
	The Wolf howleth.		
	Urſus murmurat.	*mum mum*	M m
	The Bear grumbleth.		

B 2

* Johann Amos Comenius, *Orbis Sensualium Pictus* (first published 1658). Translated by Charles Hoole, M.A. (London: John Sprint, 1700), p. 3.

366

A PRIMER FOR PIETY *

Words of four Syllables.
Ac-com-pa-ny	Accompany
Be-ne-vo-lence	Benevolence
Ce-re-mo-ny	Ceremony
Dif-con-tent-ed	Difcontented
E-ver-laft-ing	Everlafting
Fi-de-li-ty	Fidelity
Glo-ri-fy-ing	Glorifying
Hu-mi-li-ty	Humility
In-fir-mi-ty	Infirmity.

Words of five Syllables.
Ad-mi-ra-ti-on	Admiration
Be-ne-fi-ci-al	Beneficial
Con-fo-la-ti-on	Confolation
De-cla-ra-ti-on	Declaration
Ex-hor-ta-ti-on	Exhortation
For-ni-ca-ti-on	Fornication
Ge-ne-ra-ti-on	Generation
Ha-bi-ta-ti-on	Habitation
In-vi-ta-ti-on	Invitation

A — In *Adam's* Fall / We Sinned all.

B — Thy Life to Mend / This *Book* Attend.

C — The *Cat* doth play / And after flay.

D — A *Dog* will bite / A Thief at night.

E — An *Eagles* flight / Is out of fight.

F — The Idle *Fool* / Is whipt at School.

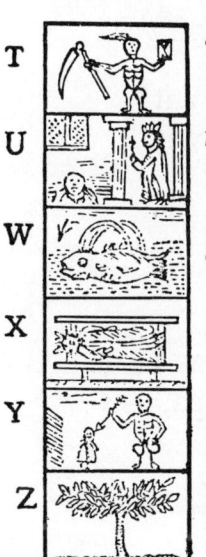

T — *Time* cuts down all / Both great and fmall.

U — *Uriah's* beauteous Wife / Made *David* feek his Life.

W — *Whales* in the Sea / God's Voice obey.

X — *Xerxes* the great did die, / And fo muft you & I.

Y — *Youth* forward flips / Death fooneft nips.

Z — *Zacheus* he / Did climb the Tree / His Lord to fee.

Now the *Child* being entred in his *Letters* and *Spelling,* let him learn thefe and fuch like Sentences by *Heart*, whereby he will be both *inftructed* in his *Duty*, and encouraged in his *Learning*.

The Dutiful Child's Promifes,

I Will fear GOD, and honour the KING.
I will honour my Father & Mother.
I will Obey my Superiours.
I will Submit to my Elders.
I will Love my Friends.
I will hate no Man.
I will forgive my Enemies, and pray to God for them.
I will as much as in me lies keep all God's Holy Commandments.

* *The New England Primer* (Boston: E. Draper, 1727), unpaged. (First published before 1690.)

A LOGICAL BEGINNING *
READING IN TWO LETTERS.

I am in.   He is in.
We go in.   Do go in.

He is by me.   Am I by it?
No, I am on it.   He is by it.

Go in if I go.   He is in, as I am.
My ma is in.   So is my pa.
If he is in, so am I.

* Campbell and Dunn, *The Child's First Book* (Richmond: Ayres and Wade, 1864), p. 12.

BEGINNING WITH THE CHILD'S EXPERIENCE *

THE LITTLE WORD I

Look at the little word I in this story. Do you see that it is a capital letter?

Billy and I have a red wagon. I wanted Happy to pull us. Billy and I were the ones who did the pulling.

The word I is a capital letter.

Can you copy these sentences?

1. I could not get Happy to pull us.
2. Billy and I talked to him.
3. Then he and I gave up.
4. Billy and I pulled Happy down the street.
5. I think Happy had a good time.

Write one sentence telling about something you like to do.

* Matilda Bailey and Edna M. Horrocks, *Our English Language* (New York: American Book Company, 1956), p. 17.

The Social Studies

HOW EMILE LEARNS GEOGRAPHY *

. . . Let the senses be the only guide for the first workings of reason. No book but the world, no teaching but that of fact. The child who reads ceases to think, he only reads. He is acquiring words not knowledge.

Teach your scholar to observe the phenomena of nature; you will soon rouse his curiosity, but if you would have it grow, do not be in too great a hurry to satisfy this curiosity. Put the problems before him and let him solve them himself. Let him know nothing because you have told him, but because he has learnt it for himself. Let him not be taught science, let him discover it. If ever you substitute authority for reason he will cease to reason; he will be a mere plaything of other people's thoughts.

You wish to teach this child geography and you provide him with globes, sphere, and maps. What elaborate preparations! What is the use of all these symbols; why not begin by showing him the real thing so that he may at least know what you are talking about?

One fine evening we are walking in a suitable place where the wide horizon gives us a full view of the setting sun and we note the objects which mark the place where it sets. Next morning we return to the same place for a breath of fresh air before sun-rise. We see the rays of light which announce the sun's approach; the glow increases, the east seems afire, and long before the sun appears the light leads us to expect its return. Every moment you expect to see it. There it is at last! A shining point appears like a flash of lightning and soon fills the whole space; the veil of darkness rolls away, man perceives his dwelling place in fresh beauty. . . .

Fired with this enthusiasm, the master wishes to impart it to the child. He expects to rouse his emotion by drawing attention to his own. Mere folly! The splendour of nature lives in man's heart; to be seen, it must be felt. The child sees the objects themselves, but does not perceive their relations, and cannot hear their harmony. It needs knowledge he has not yet acquired, feelings he has not yet experienced, to receive the complex impression which results from all these separate sensations. . . .

Never tell the child what he cannot understand: no descriptions, no eloquence, no figures of speech, no poetry. The time has not come for feeling or taste. Continue to be clear and cold; the time will come only too soon when you must adopt another tone.

* Jean Jacques Rousseau, *Emile, or Education,* translated by Barbara Foxley. Everyman's Library. Reprinted by permission of E. P. Dutton & Co., Inc., pp. 131-4. (First published in 1762.)

Brought up in the spirit of our maxims, accustomed to make his own tools and not to appeal to others until he has tried and failed, he will examine everything he sees carefully and in silence. He thinks rather than questions. Be content, therefore, to show him things at a fit season; then, when you see that his curiosity is thoroughly aroused, put some brief question which will set him trying to discover the answer.

On the present occasion when you and he have carefully observed the rising sun, when you have called his attention to the mountains and other objects visible from the same spot, after he has chattered freely about them, keep quiet for a few minutes as if lost in thought and then say, "I think the sun set over there last night; it rose here this morning. How can that be?" Say no more; if he asks questions, do not answer them; talk of something else. Let him alone, and be sure he will think about it.

To train a child to be really attentive so that he may be really impressed by any truth of experience, he must spend anxious days before he discovers that truth. If he does not learn enough in this way, there is another way of drawing his attention to the matter. Turn the question about. If he does not know how the sun gets from the place where it sets to where it rises, he knows at least how it travels from sunrise to sunset, his eyes teach him that. Use the second question to throw light on the first; either your pupil is a regular dunce or the analogy is too clear to be missed. This is his first lesson in cosmography.

As we always advance slowly from one sensible idea to another, and as we give time enough to each for him to become really familiar with it before we go on to another, and lastly as we never force our scholar's attention, we are still a long way from a knowledge of the course of the sun or the shape of the earth; but as all the apparent movements of the celestial bodies depend on the same principle, and the first observation leads on to all the rest, less effort is needed, though more time, to proceed from the diurnal revolution to the calculation of eclipses, than to get a thorough understanding of day and night.

Since the sun revolves round the earth it describes a circle, and every circle must have a centre; that we know already. This centre is invisible, it is in the middle of the earth, but we can mark out two opposite points on the earth's surface which correspond to it. A skewer passed through the three points and prolonged to the sky at either end would represent the earth's axis and the sun's daily course. A round teetotum revolving on its point represents the sky turning on its axis, the two points of the teetotum are the two poles; the child will be delighted to find one of them, and I show him the tail of the Little Bear. Here is another game for the dark. Little by little we get to know the stars, and from this comes a wish to know the planets and observe the constellations.

We saw the sun rise at midsummer, we shall see it rise at Christmas or some other fine winter's day; for you know we are no lie-a-beds and we enjoy the cold. I take care to make this second observation in the same place as the first, and if skilfully led up to, one or other will certainly exclaim, "What a funny thing! The sun is not rising in the same place; here are our landmarks, but it is rising over there. So there is the summer east and the winter east, etc." Young teacher, you are on the right track. These examples should show you how to teach the sphere without any difficulty, taking the earth for the earth and the sun for the sun.

As a general rule—never substitute the symbol for the thing signified, unless it is impossible to show the thing itself; for the child's attention is so taken up with the symbol that he will forget what it signifies.

I consider the armillary sphere a clumsy disproportioned bit of apparatus. The confused circles and the strange figures described on it suggest witchcraft and frighten the child. The earth is too small, the circles too large and too numerous, some of them, the colures, for instance, are quite useless, and the thickness of the pasteboard gives them an appearance of solidity so that they are taken for circular masses having a real existence, and when you tell the child that these are imaginary circles, he does not know what he is looking at and is none the wiser.

We are unable to put ourselves in the child's place, we fail to enter into his thoughts, we invest him with our own ideas, and while we are following our own chain of reasoning, we merely fill his head with errors and absurdities. . . .

His geography will begin with the town he lives in and his father's country house, then the places between them, the rivers near them and then the sun's aspect and how to find one's way by its aid. This is the meeting place. Let him make his own map, a very simple map, at first containing only two places; others may be added from time to time, as he is able to estimate their distance and position. You see at once what a good start we have given him by making his eye his compass.

No doubt he will require some guidance in spite of this, but very little, and that little without his knowing it. If he goes wrong let him alone, do not correct his mistakes; hold your tongue till he finds them out for himself and corrects them, or at most arrange something, as opportunity offers, which may show him his mistakes. If he never makes mistakes he will never learn anything thoroughly. Moreover, what he needs is not an exact knowledge of local topography, but how to find out for himself. No matter whether he carries maps in his head provided he understands what they mean, and has a clear idea of the art of making them. See what a difference there is already between the knowledge of your scholars and the ignorance of mine. They learn maps, he makes them. . . .

GEOGRAPHY OF THE WORLD *

ENGLAND

Q. Are there any curiosities in England?

A. There are many both natural and artificial. The artificial are either British, Norman, Saxon or Danish and Anglo-Normanic. The Stonehenge, in Wiltshire, a religious and Druidical structure, is the most remarkable of any of the British antiquities. It is a monument composed of stones, raised within the compass of a ditch, consisting of two circles and two ovals. The upright stones are three feet and a half asunder, and their tops are connected by overthwart stone, fitted with tenons and mortices. Some of these stones are of great size, viz six feet broad, three in thickness, and twenty-one feet in height. The outer circle is one hundred and eighty feet in diameter, the space between which and the next circle form a walk of three hundred feet in circumference, whose appearance is awfully sublime. Similar monuments are found in various parts of the kingdom.

Q. What are the Roman antiquities?

A. They are principally the remains of their camps and military ways; and of the walls built by Agricola and Severus, in the north of England.

Q. What are the Saxon antiquities?

A. They consist principally of religious edifices and places of strength.

Q. What are the natural curiosities of England?

A. Medicinal springs of various kinds: The Mother Tower in Derbyshire, which is constantly mouldering away, but never diminishes; Elden-Hole which has not been fathomed; Poole's-Hole, and several other remarkable caverns.

Q. What other artificial curiosities are there?

A. Many works of architecture, both ancient and modern. The church of St. Paul's in London, which was begun and finished by Sir Christopher Wren in twenty-seven years, is the greatest work ever accomplished by one man: It is built of stone in the form of a cross, and is the largest Protestant church in the world, being five hundred feet long, and three hundred and forty high. It occupies six acres of ground. Other respectable edifices are London, Westminster, and Blackfriar's Bridges; Westminster Abbey, the church of St. Stephens, Walbrook, Westminster Hall, and the monument built in commemoration of the fire which happened in 1666, with many others.

* Nathaniel Dwight, *A Short but Comprehensive System of the Geography of the World: by way of questions and answers, principally designed for Children and Common Schools* (Northampton, Mass., 1807), pp. 32-3, 42-3. (First published in 1795.)

Q. What is the capital city of England?

A. London, standing on both sides of the river Thames, about sixty miles from the sea shore, towards the south part of the island. It is in 51 degrees and 31 minutes of north latitude, and on the first meridian, as the English geographers reckon longitude.

Q. Give a concise description of London.

A. London is regularly built, contains about one million of inhabitants, and including Westminster and Southwark, is about eighteen miles in circumference. There are three hundred and five places devoted to religious worship in London, besides methodists' tabernacles, and exclusive of twenty-one out-parishes. There are also one hundred alms-houses, twenty hospitals and infirmaries, three colleges, ten public prisons, fifteen flesh markets, one for live cattle, two for herbs, and twenty-three others for corn, coal, hay, &c., fifteen inns of court, twenty-seven public squares, three bridges, forty-nine halls, eight public schools, one hundred and thirty-one charity schools, two hundred and seven inns, four hundred and forty-seven taverns, five hundred and fifty-one coffee-houses, five thousand and seventy-five ale-houses, one thousand hackney coaches, four hundred chairs, seven thousand streets, and one hundred and fifty thousand dwelling houses. There are no elegant royal palaces in London. Windsor Castle is the best.

Q. What other cities of importance are there in England?

A. There are many; particularly Bristol, in the southwest part of the kingdom, containing fifteen thousand houses, and ninety-five thousand inhabitants; York, Exeter, Gloucester, Litchfield, Chester, Warwick, Coventry, Salisbury, Bath, and many others. Many of these cities are diminishing, whilst London is increasing.

Q. What is the present state of the English commerce and manufacture?

A. They have a very extensive commerce, and have excelled in almost all kinds of manufactures.

FRANCE

Q. What number of inhabitants are there in France?

A. It is said to contain about 28,000,000.

Q. What are the characteristics of the French?

A. They are generally inferior to the English in stature, complexion and beauty; their disposition is gay and lively, and distinguished by quickness and violence of passion. They are very fond of dress and gallantry, and are inferior to no nation in courage or activity: are polite and complaisant to strangers. Their ladies, sensible and handsome, are singularly easy in their behaviour, and distinguished by wit and sprightliness.

Q. What are the diversions of the French?

A. They consist of dancing, hunting, fencing and riding, in which they excel all their neighbors in skill and gracefulness.

Q. What is the dress of the French?

A. It was formerly very various, changing almost as often as the moon No object more wholly engrossed the thoughts of the French than fashions and ceremony. But since the revolution, they are as remarkable for plainness as before for tinsel.

Q. What is the established religion of France?

A. The Roman Catholic religion was for a long time the established religion in that kingdom, and the French Kings were so constant in it that the pope conferred on them the title of "Most Christian," and styled the reigning monarch the "Eldest Son of the Church." Since the revolution all denominations are, in a sense, tolerated. They profess to worship God under the title of the Supreme Being, and pay a kind of public homage to certain virtues, public opinion, liberty, equality, &c.

Q. What is the language of France?

A. It is radically Latin, and mixed with many German words. It is one of the most universal of the living languages, and is calculated rather to express familiar sentiments than sublime ones.

THAT USEFUL SCIENCE, GEOGRAPHY *

Elements of Geography.

CONTAINING

A CONCISE AND COMPREHENSIVE VIEW

OF THAT

Useful Science,

AS DIVIDED INTO

1. ASTRONOMICAL---2. PHYSICAL, OR NATURAL---3. POLITICAL GEOGRAPHY.

ON A NEW PLAN...ADAPTED TO THE CAPACITIES OF CHILDREN AND YOUTH:

DESIGNED FOR

A READING AND CLASSICAL BOOK IN COMMON SCHOOLS, AND AS A USEFUL WINTER EVENINGS ENTERTAINMENT FOR YOUNG PEOPLE IN PRIVATE FAMILIES.

Illuftrated with a neat Map of the United States, and a beautiful Chart of the whole World.

BY JEDIDIAH MORSE, D. D.

Minifter of the Congregation in Charleftown, Maff.—Author of the American Univerfal Geography, American Gazetteer, &c.

" Thofe branches of Science which lead the mind to attend to the appearances of nature, are fuited to raife excited thoughts of the Great CREATOR."——*Backus.*

Fifth Edition===Improved.

PUBLISHED ACCORDING TO ACT OF CONGRESS.

---

* Jedidiah Morse, *Elements of Geography* (Boston: Thomas and Andrews, 1804), title page, preface, p. 62.

Preface

On the early and proper education of children depends in a great measure, their own happiness, that of their parents, their country, and posterity. The continuance and security of true Religion, and of civil Liberty, among any people, must result from their being enlightened by true and useful knowledge. The foundation of this knowledge is laid in Schools and Families, where its rudiments are, or should be taught. It is of the first importance, therefore, that *school books* should be accurately composed, and printed on a good type and paper, and be in all respects adapted, as to their subjects and manner of execution, to the capacities of youth, and to gratify and improve their minds.

Too little regard has hitherto been paid to these things in this country. The *cheapest* books, however incorrectly composed, and badly printed, and however illy adapted, as to the subjects, for the improvement of the youthful understanding, have too commonly been considered by parents as the *best*. Hence children have often spent years at school with little apparent advantage, and have sometimes been taught error instead of truth. I am happy to have it in my power to add, that great improvements, in these respects, have been made within a few years past.

Curiosity is the most prominent feature in the youthful mind, and it is the business of parents and instructors to guide and to gratify it; and by skilful management, it may be made to subserve the most useful purposes. No science is *better* adapted to gratify the *rational* curiosity of youth than GEOGRAPHY. Mr. Locke was of the opinion, that *"youth* ought to begin with this Science as an introduction to their future studies." . . .

The Author has endeavoured, in this little volume, to blend *entertainment* with *improvement;* and to comprise in it as much information as was consistent with perspicuity to the minds of children, with a view particularly to render the book cheap, and thereby to diffuse useful knowledge extensively among all classes of people, the poor as well as the rich.

He has aimed to adapt it to the use of common schools in the capital and country towns, to be read, and if thought proper, studied and recited by the scholars in classes: in this way they will be pleased and entertained, and their curiosity gratified, at the same time that they are making progress in the art of reading, and in the science of Geography.

· · ·

Of Deists

All such as assert the sufficiency, universality, and absolute perfection of *natural religion,* with a view to discredit and discard all extraordinary *revelation,* as useless and needless, are called *Deists.*

Deists are no where to be found, but in Christian countries; the reason probably is, that without the light of revelation, which gives consistency and beauty to *natural religion,* its sufficiency and absolute perfection has never yet been admitted by sensible men in any age. Deists have been compared to the *wiseacre,* who thought the sun useless, because he shined only when we had *the light of the day.*

Lord Herbert in the 17th century, was the first who reduced *Deism* to a system. Deists are not agreed among themselves. Some acknowledge a future state; others deny it. Others again, which perhaps form the most numerous class, think it a very doubtful question, Whether the soul exists after death?

In France, Deists are very numerous; and in England, and other European countries; and in the United States, their number is not inconsiderable, and is probably increasing.

THE SCIENCE OF HISTORY *

Discovery and Settlement of America

It was the practice of Europeans to take possession of the parts of America which they visited, by the pretended right of discovery. The original inhabitants were treated as if they had no rights, and were no more owners of the soil than the beasts of the forest. This example was set by *Columbus* himself. He landed upon St. Salvador, the first island discovered, in a gorgeous dress, with a drawn sword in his hand, and the royal standard displayed, and took possession of the island for the crown of Castile and Leon; and in conformity to this practice, it was inscribed on his tomb, that to this crown he "had given a new world."

The pope, in accordance with principles that were acted upon in an age of ignorance and superstition, granted to the sovereigns of Spain the countries discovered by their subjects in the new world. The propagation of Christianity was held out as the chief reason for taking possession of America; and the promotion of a religion which breathes "peace on earth and good will towards men," was made the pretext for every species of injustice, cruelty, bloodshed, and slavery, which the defenceless inhabitants of America were destined to experience from Cortez, Pizarro, and other unprincipled invaders.

The Spaniards who first came to America, were stimulated by the desire and expectation of finding the precious metals, gold and silver. So powerful was this passion for gold, that the first adventurers encountered every possible hardship and danger in search of it, and sacrificed millions of the

* J. E. Worcester, A.A.S., S.H.S., *Elements of History, Ancient and Modern: with Historical Charts* (Boston, 1834), pp. 240, 241-2, 311-12.

wretched natives, whom they compelled to work in the mines. The unfortunate Indians were subjected to the *meta,* a kind of annual conscription, by which they were forced to perform, in the mines, for their avaricious task-masters, a service so hard and unhealthy, that it proved fatal to as many as about one third of every conscription.

The discovery and settlement of America also gave rise to that foul stigma on Christendom, *the African slave-trade,* which was commenced soon after the first colony was established, and has been continued to the present time. By this infamous traffic, millions of the unhappy Africans have been torn from their native country, and doomed to a miserable servitude.

• • •

SETTLEMENT AND EARLY HISTORY OF THE COLONIES

The vanity of nations, like that of families, inclines them to lay claim to a high antiquity; and the obscurity in which their early history is, in most instances, involved, affords them an opportunity to indulge this propensity. But with regard to the United States, circumstances are different. The vanity of the people of this country inclines them to dwell upon their recent origin, and their rapid growth; and the promise which these afford of future greatness. Of all independent nations of any importance, now existing, this has had the most recent origin, and its early history is the best known: nor do the annals of the world afford another instance of a nation rising, in so short a space of time from its first settlement, to an equal degree of power and freedom.

Various circumstances have concurred to promote the rapid increase in population and wealth, and the progress of society, which have been witnessed in this country. The first settlers were emigrants from countries advanced in civilization, and they brought with them the arts of civilized life. A great portion of them were men distinguished for intelligence and enterprise, and were strenuous advocates for civil and religious liberty; and at the first foundation of their settlements, they paid particular attention to the promotion of education. A vast field of enterprise has been constantly presented before them, with ample rewards to industry. The means of subsistence have been abundant and easily obtained; and extensive tracts of fertile and unoccupied lands, suitable for new settlements, have always been procurable on moderate terms. The political and commercial relations of the inhabitants have connected them with the most enlightened nations in the world; and have afforded them the means of being acquainted with the progress of literature and science, and with the various improvements in the arts of civilized life.

• • •

380 The Purposes of Education

CHRONOLOGICAL TABLE

In the following table the most important epochs are given, together with a system of *Artificial Memory,* to facilitate the recollecting of dates. This system is derived chiefly from Dr. Grey's *Memoria Technica.*

In order to facilitate remembering dates, a word is formed of the *name* recorded, or of the first syllables of it, together with one or more syllables added to it, and made up of *numeral letters.* For this purpose, a vowel and a consonant are assigned to each digit, and *a* or *b* denote 1; *e* or *d* 2; *i* or *t* 3; *o* or *f* 4; and so on, in the following series:

a	e	i	o	u	au	oi	oo	ou	ai
1	2	3	4	5	6	7	8	9	0
b	d	t	f	v	s		p	k	n z

These letters may easily be remembered by considering that the first five vowels represent 1, 2, 3, 4, 5; that the diphthong *au,* which is composed of *a* 1 and *u* 5, denotes 6; that *oi,* for the same reason, denotes 7, *oo* 8, and *ou,* 9. The diphthong *ai* is put for the cipher 0, but without any similar reason.

The *first* consonant, *b,* denotes 1; *d,* the first letter of *duo,* the Latin for *two,* denotes 2; *t,* the initial of the word *three,* is put for 3; *f,* for the same reason, for 4; *v* (V being the Roman numeral for *five*) denotes 5; *s,* the initial of *six,* is put for 6; *p,* from se*p*tem, the Latin for *seven,* denotes 7; *k,* from the Greek o*k*to, *eight,* is put for 8; *n,* the initial of the word *nine,* denotes 9; and *z,* the final letter, is put for 0.

Having perfectly learned the foregoing series, the student may proceed to exercise himself in the formation and resolution of dates, in the following manner:

10   189   342   390   659   1492   1776   1830

az   boon   tod   tonz   sun   afne   apois   booiz

The system may be extended at pleasure; and by the formation of words in the manner described, it will be easy to fix in the mind the time of the death of illustrious men, the commencement of the reigns of kings, and other events, of which it is desirable to remember the date. It will be easy to remember whether the event took place *before* or *after* Christ.—Besides the series of letters already explained, *g* may denote a hundred, and *th* a thousand.

TABLE

4004	Creation of the world	Cre-*faizo*
2348	Deluge	Del-*etok*
2247	Babel built; mankind dispersed	Bab-*edop*
2188	The kingdom of Egypt commences	Egypt-*ebook*
1921	Calling of Abraham	Abrah-*aneb*
1556	Athens founded by Cecrops	Ath-*avus*
1493	Cadmus brings letters into Greece and builds Thebes	Cadmus-*hont*
1491	Israelites brought out of Egypt by Moses	Israel-*bona*
1263	Argonautic expedition	Argonaut-*best*
1184	Troy taken and burnt by the Greeks	Troy-*bako*
1075	Saul King of Israel	Saul-*azpu*
1012	The Temple of Solomon founded	Templ-*azad*
884	Lycurgus reforms the laws of Lacedaemon	Lycurg-*ooko*
776	The first Olympiad begins	Olym-*pois*
753	Rome founded by Romulus	Rom-*put*
536	Cyrus founds the Persian empire	Cyru-*vis*
509	Tarquin expelled from Rome	Tarquin-*vain*
490	Battle of Marathon	Marath-*onz*
400	Socrates put to death	Socrat-*ozai*
324	Alexander the Great dies at Babylon	Alexand-*ido*
312	The era of the Seleucidae	Seleucid-*ibe*
146	Greece reduced to a Roman province	Greece-*bos*
31	Battle of Actium; end of Roman Commonwealth	Actium-*ta*

Birth of Christ; 4 years before the vulgar era.

CAUSES OF THE REVOLUTIONARY WAR [*]

1. We come now to trace the causes by which England lost her colonies, and America gained her independence. We should always remember that there is a GREAT FIRST CAUSE,—even God our Creator and Ruler. We should observe with thankfulness, by what steps, He led our forefathers, and how He made them a way across the deep, and gave them a place, wherein to plant a great nation. In His providence, the time was approaching, when the bonds were to be severed, which bound this country to the parent land.

2. But the First Cause, uses, as His agents, the opinions and wills of men, which guide their conduct. The men in Great Britain, who took at this time, the lead in the government, had haughty and wrong notions, of the power, which England had a right to exercise over her distant colonies. They forgot, that the American people were children of the same forefathers with themselves, and heirs of the same political rights. They held the Americans in comparative contempt, as those whose labors and money, must, if *they* demanded, be given to them; without, or against their owner's consent.

[*] Emma Willard, *Abridged History of the United States; or Republic of America* (New York, A. S. Barnes & Co., 1851), pp. 175-9.

3. Had the rulers in England, undertaken to oppress the people there in the same manner, *they* would have rebelled; much more the Americans. They, as we have seen, had grown up in their new countries, with a deep sense of the rights of the people. Toil and danger had made them strong and brave. When they saw that the rulers in Great Britain, had determined on making them submit to their unrighteous will, they became alarmed. They resolved, that they would first endeavor, by petitions, to bring them to a better mind. If after that, they persisted in their oppressions, they would refuse to submit; and if force was employed against them, repel it by force; trusting, that a righteous God, would aid their cause.

4. During the French war, the English wanted the services of the Americans; and, besides, those were in power, who opposed the high government party. But the war was no sooner at an end, than this party took the lead, with Lord Grenville at its head.

5. In 1764, Lord Grenville gave notice to the American agents in London, that it was his intention to draw a revenue from the colonies, and that he should, in the ensuing session of parliament, propose a duty on stamps.

6. The colonial agents in London informed their respective colonies of the intended system of taxation. Massachusetts instructed her agents, to deny the right of parliament to impose taxes upon those, who were not represented in the house of commons. The house of burgesses of Virginia appointed a committee to prepare an address to the king and parliament. The assembly of New York also sent petitions, which, in a spirit more bold and decided, than those from any other colony, asserted their own rights, and the limitations of British power.

7. Associations were formed in all the colonies to encourage home manufactures, and prohibit, as much as possible, the use of British goods. The tendency of this judicious measure, was to make the colonists less dependent, and, by operating injuriously on the British merchants, to make them a party against the ministry.

8. Notwithstanding the opposition, which, in truth, was not unexpected, Lord Grenville, introduced into the British parliament, his plan for taxing America, to commence with duties on stamps. In the house of commons, the project, though ably supported, met with ardent and animated opposition.

9. "Children planted by your care!" exclaimed Colonel Barre, in answer to one who spoke against the Americans. "No! Your oppressions planted them in America! They fled from your tyranny to an uncultivated land, where they were exposed to all the hardships to which human nature is liable.

10. "They nourished by your indulgence! No! They grew by your neglect! When you began to care about them, that care was exercised in send-

ing persons to rule over them, whose character and conduct has caused the blood of these sons of liberty to recoil within them. They protected by your arms! They have nobly taken up arms in your defense! The people of America are loyal, but a people jealous of their liberties, and they will vindicate them."

11. Neither the eloquence of Colonel Barre and others, nor the remonstrances of the colonists, could prevent the passage of the stamp act. Of three hundred, who voted in the house of commons, only fifty were against it; in the house of lords there was not a single dissenting voice; and the royal assent was readily obtained.

12. By this act, no written instrument could be legal, unless the paper was stamped on which it was drawn; and this stamped paper was to be purchased, at an exorbitant price, of the agents of the British government.

13. Provision was made for the recovery of penalties for the breach of this act, as of all others relating to trade and revenue, in any admiralty, or king's marine court, throughout the colonies. These courts proceeded in trials, without the intervention of a jury. This act, suspending trial by jury, and making the colonists liable to be called to trial, for real or supposed offences, to distant provinces, was highly displeasing to the Americans.

14. Anticipating opposition to these measures, parliament passed laws for sending troops to America, and obliging the inhabitants of those colonies to which they should be sent, to furnish them with quarters, and all necessary supplies.

15. Great was the grief and indignation caused in America by the news of the stamp act. The Virginia legislature, called the house of burgesses, was in session. The eloquent PATRICK HENRY introduced the five celebrated resolutions, which constituted the first public opposition to the odious act. The last of these declared in express terms that they were not bound to obey any law imposing taxes, unless made by their representatives.

THE STAMP TAX *

In 1765 Parliament decided that the colonists should pay a stamp tax. This meant that they were to buy stamps and place them on important papers and on some of the things they bought and sold. This was not an unusual kind of tax. There was a stamp tax in England. Even now stamp taxes are collected. You may have seen the small stamp on a package of cigarettes.

Sometimes people could not get the stamps easily when they needed

* R. W. Cordier and E. B. Robert, *History of Young America* (Chicago, Rand McNally & Company), 1954, pp. 117-19.

them. It was not really the inconvenience they minded, however. It was not even the amount of the tax. The colonists objected to being taxed at all by the English Parliament.

A young man in the Virginia Assembly became famous because of his opposition to the Stamp Act. His name was Patrick Henry. He made a speech in which he said that Englishmen carried their rights with them wherever they went. One of their rights was not to be taxed except by their own representatives. In England the members of Parliament were elected by the English people. They represented the people, and they decided what taxes the English people should pay. The colonists did not elect members of Parliament. They had representatives only in their own assemblies. Only their own assemblies, therefore, should tax them.

So the colonists asked to have the Stamp Act *repealed*. Lawmakers who can make a law can also repeal it. When a law has been repealed, that law no longer exists. Many people in England thought the colonists were right. No one wanted to make the colonists angry. Parliament repealed the Stamp Act in 1766.

In 1767 a new tax law was passed by Parliament. This law placed customs duties on imported paper, paint, and tea. All tea and most paper and paint were imported. The taxes were not at all high, but the colonists still objected to being taxed by Parliament.

The colonists opposed the new taxes just as they had opposed the stamp tax. They would not buy the taxed goods and quarreled with government officials over the taxes. Parliament had made another mistake. All the new tax laws were repealed, except for a very small duty on tea—less than the people in England had to pay. Members of Parliament thought the colonists would not object to this small tax.

The colonists believed that if they paid even a small tax they would be admitting that Parliament had a right to tax them. When tea came to America, colonial merchants would not buy it. At several ports it was placed in warehouses and left there. In some places it was destroyed. In Boston a whole shipload of tea was thrown into the harbor. This action became famous as the Boston Tea Party.

The colonists did not agree among themselves about opposing these new laws. Many of them thought the laws should be obeyed. Members of Parliament and English officers did not agree, either. Many thought the English government had no right to tax the colonists. New ideas were appearing in the world, as new ideas had appeared many times before.

New ideas nearly always come into the world very much in this way. Some people accept them at once and others do not. After a time the people who accept the new ideas and those who do not will probably quarrel. If the new ideas are good, more and more people accept them as time passes. If they are not good, they will usually be forgotten after a while.

THIS SAD WAR *

```
 1   2    3     4      5    1    2    3    1    2    3         1
note, not, move, dove, book—tube, tub,full— type,hymn myrrh— dew
```

TEMPERANCE BADGE:
No. 22.—XXII.

This sad war is a bad thing.

My pa-pa went, and died in the army.

My big broth-er went too, and got shot. A bomb shell took off his head.

My aunt had three sons, and all have died in the army. Now she and the girls have to work for bread.

I will work for my ma and sis-ters.

I hope we will have peace by the time am old enough to go to war.

If I were a man, and had to make laws, I would not have any war, if I could help it.

If little boys fight, old folks whip them for it; but when men fight, they say "how brave!"

I do not know how this is, but I think there is a better way, if folks could find it.

But if I were a man, and the laws said I must go to war, I would not run away-like some do.

We must obey the laws of the land; and if they are not good laws, those who made them are to blame.

I saw a poor man who had run away from the army, and he must have felt badly, for he was in a sad plight.

I would soon-er die at my post than de-sert.

And O if my pa-pa had run a-way, and been shot for it, how sad I must have felt all my life!

This is a sad world at best. But if we pray to God to help us, and try to do the best we can, it is not *so* bad at last.

I will pray God to help me to do well, that I may grow up to be a good and a wise man.

---

* Mrs. M. B. Moore, *The Dixie Speller* (Raleigh: Branson and Farrar, 1864), p. 23.

OLD AUNT ANN *

1. Here comes old Aunt Ann. She is quite old. See how she leans on her stick.
2. When she was young she did good work, but now she can not work much. But she is not like a poor white woman.
3. Aunt Ann knows that her young Miss, as she calls her, will take care of her as long as she lives.
4. Many poor white folks would be glad to live in her house, and eat what Miss Kate sends out for dinner.

STORY OF THE TREATMENT OF AFRICAN SLAVES †

STORY OF THE TREATMENT OF AFRICAN SLAVES.

WHEN a ſhip arrives in Africa for ſlaves, the tribes go to war with their nabors, and take as many priſoners as poſſible. Theſe priſoners are ſold to the white people, or bartered for iron, rum and trinkets. Sometimes a ſtout negro is ſold for a piſtol.

When the ſlaves come into the hands of their new maſters, they are marked, either by a hot iron or a

---

* Mrs. M. B. Moore, *The First Dixie Reader* (Raleigh, Branson, Farrar, and Co., 1864), p. 22.

† Noah Webster, *The Little Reader's Assistant* (Hartford: Elisha Babcock, 1790), p. 40f.

gafh in the cheek. They are then chained together, or tied with lethern thongs and driven to the veſſels by the laſh of the whip. Many of them are loaded with elephants teeth, and as they often come thro large barren defarts, they are forced to carry all their water and proviſion on their ſhoulders.

When they arrive at the ſhip, they are often crouded together in the hold in ſuch numbers, as to breed a peſtilential air, which cauſes ſickneſs, and multitudes die on the paſſage. When the voyage is long and proviſion fails, hundreds of them are ſometimes thrown into the ſea. Sometimes when they are brot upon deck for the benefit of freſh air, the poor wretches, refenting their ſlavery, and reſolved to be free, plunge into the ocean, and thus happily eſcape a life

ASIATIC IMMIGRATION FIRST BROUGHT A NEW PROBLEM *

By the twentieth century the conditions surrounding immigration had widely changed from those of earlier generations. We had to face new facts. The change first became noticeable on our Pacific coast; there the Chinese and after a while the Japanese began an extensive immigration into our land.

At first we welcomed them. The Japanese were mostly scholars, who came here to learn our civilization; and we felt a special pride in aiding Japan, as the protegé brought to us by Commodore Perry. But as the number of immigrants of the yellow races increased, and as the later comers proved to be almost wholly of the poorest or "coolie" class, our viewpoint changed. We had been able to absorb vast numbers of Europeans, because their ancestry was the same as ours. We could scarcely hope to turn these oriental peoples into "Americans." They were too wholly different in race.

This was the beginning of our "Asiatic problem." Many of our leaders still wanted to welcome all comers as of old. Others argued that the yellow races would always remain aliens among us, "undigested," an obstacle to our government and to our social organization. The "African problem" of the negro was ours; it had come down to us through history, and we could not evade it. But it would be folly for us to take up deliberately a "Chinese problem" of equal difficulty.

WE NEEDED PROTECTION FROM EASTERN LIVING STANDARDS

There was also another danger in Asiatic immigration, one that organized labor was quick to see. The orientals were accustomed to far lower standards of living than we. They expected to toil long hours for small returns; and they lived on such cheap foods that they could afford to work for prices at which Americans would starve. A vast Chinese immigration, if our own labor had to compete with it, would drag us all down to the oriental level of living.

From 1875 onward our Pacific States began a vigorous resistance to either Chinese or Japanese immigration. They fought it in every possible way, and gradually brought the rest of the nation to see the necessity of supporting them.

* Charles F. Horne, *The Story of Our American People* (New York, United States History Publishing Company, 1925).

AMERICAN EDUCATION COMES TO JAPAN *

McGUFFEY'S

NEW

ECLECTIC PRIMER.

英 蒙 學 米
卷 之 壹

* Title page of McGuffey's *New Eclectic Primer* (1871).

WHY DO OUR LAWS FORBID THE IMMIGRATION OF LABORERS FROM CHINA AND JAPAN BUT ALLOW THE IMMIGRATION OF CHINESE AND JAPANESE BUSINESS MEN AND SCHOLARS? *

There are several answers to the question of why Chinese and Japanese laborers no longer enter the United States. . . .

In the graph [omitted] you will notice that before 1853 there was practically no Chinese immigration to this country, and then in a very short time more than thirteen thousand Chinese came across the Pacific. How do you account for this? Who, do you suppose, furnished the money for their transportation all the way from China? In 1849 the gold-rush started in California. Four years later (1853) thousands of fortune seekers had crossed the continent, mining companies were being formed, roads had to be made, there was a great demand for cheap labor. But it was almost impossible to get cheap labor from the East. The journey across the continent was long, expensive, and dangerous. What was more natural than that the development companies in California should turn to China for help. The coolies (Chinese laborers) were glad to come; transportation was cheaper from China than from New York; and the Chinese laborer was willing to work for lower wages than the "white" laborer.

Look at the graph again: what do you think caused the great increase in Chinese immigration between 1860 and 1870? Can you recall when the first trans-continental railroad was built? Had this any bearing on Chinese immigration? Look in *Mechanical Conquest of America,* pp. 199-203. . . .

The Exclusion Act, you will notice, came years after railroads had joined the East and the West. There was no longer the same necessity for importing labor from the Orient. The coolies were wanted chiefly because they demanded less money than the American workers. . . . What effect do you think this had upon the American and European workers in California? What effect do you think the arrival of thousands of new immigrants from China had upon the Chinese workers who had been in America for ten or fifteen years, and had grown accustomed to American conditions?

The feeling of American laborers toward the Chinese was very bitter during the 1870's. The following statement by Frank M. Pixley, editor of the *Argonaut,* shows you how prejudiced many people were in those days:

* Harold Rugg, *America and Her Immigrants.* The Social Science Pamphlets. (The Lincoln School, New York, 1926), pp. 192-4. Copyright 1926 by Harold Rugg.

Illustrations 391

"The Chinese are inferior to any race God ever made . . . their people have got the perfection of crimes of 4,000 years. . . . I believe that the Chinese have no souls to save, and if they have they are not worth the saving." [1]

On the other hand, an official report of the same date on Chinese immigration says:

"As a body in this country . . . they (Chinese) are a quiet, inoffensive, docile people. There are none among them like the hoodlum elements among our lawless boys and girls. . . ." [2]

In 1877 there were some very bad race riots in California, hundreds of Chinese laborers were driven out of the towns into the country and into the mountains; many were beaten and stoned; some were shot; and some even were burned.

. . . as soon as immigration was cut off the Chinese began to raise their standard of living toward that of the western working man. . . . But now let us see what the people who wanted cheap labor did to get around the Exclusion Law. Look at the graph and you can see quickly enough what they did. They sent to Japan.

Of course the story was repeated. Only the characters in the story were different. The same classes and communities who had hated the Chinese began to hate the Japanese and praise the Chinese.

STUDENTS DISCUSS THE CONSTITUTIONAL RIGHTS OF THOSE WHO OPPOSE DEMOCRACY *

A social studies class in the John W. Weeks Junior High School, Newton, Massachusetts, was observed while talking about the constitutional rights of American citizens who are members of organizations advocating radical changes in government. This class was visited in October 1939.

Throughout the discussion, the teacher was concerned that students should be able to support their statements with evidence, and that this evidence should be reliable.

The class session opened with a "current events" report by a student panel. Included in this student report was a statement relating to the al-

[1] K. K. Kawakami, *The Real Japanese Question* (New York, Macmillan, 1921), p. 129.
[2] J. S. Tow, *The Real Chinese in America* (New York, The Academy Press, 1923), p. 66.
* National Education Association, Educational Policies Commission, *Learning the Ways of Democracy* (Washington, D. C., National Education Association, 1940), pp. 174-6.

leged communist domination of the American League for Peace and Democracy, as reported in the press. Following the report, the class turned to discussion:

Boy 1: I think the statement that the people on the mailing lists of the American League for Peace and Democracy are communists, is just propaganda.

Teacher: We certainly have to have something more than these press reports to justify us in believing that statement, especially when we see the list of the names of people involved, and their replies to the charges.

Boy 2: What can they do about it even if they find these organizations are giving out literature? Don't we have freedom of speech and freedom of the press under the Constitution?

Boy 3: The Dies Committee can prosecute them if they violate the laws.

Teacher: (correcting the student's statement) A committee of Congress can summon witnesses and can punish them if they do not appear, or punish them if they tell untruths, but it can not prosecute them for the violation of laws.

Boy 4: What good does the Dies Committee do, if it can't punish people for violating laws?

Boy 5: The "Bund" may not go as far as it would otherwise, because the Dies Committee is acting.

Boy 6: I think the "Bund" influences weak Americans.

Girl 1: What do you mean by "weak" Americans?

Boy 6: Oh, I don't know, the feeble-minded, I suppose.

Boy 1: I suppose they influence illiterates.

Girl 1: Well, organizations like that and the communists' organizations may influence poor people who live in slums, but they don't have much effect on the rest of us.

Teacher: Should the Nazis and Communists in this country have the right of free speech?

Girl 2: Yes.

Girl 3: Most of them are American citizens the same as everyone else, but there ought to be a law that if they are going to do anything to harm our government they can be stopped.

Boy 6: I don't see why they are American citizens and then plot against the United States.

Teacher: How do you know that they are plotting against the United States? What evidence do we have on that point?

Boy 6: Well, they do something at these meetings. They are probably doing that.

Girl 4: Can't people be punished for un-American acts?

Teacher: It can be done, but the government hesitates to do it. In our history we have several times had "field days" of persecuting people who didn't agree with us. Should they have freedom of speech, even if they are advocating something which we believe is wrong? If your answer is "yes," where will you draw the line for subversive activities? If your answer is "no," are you denying these people rights guaranteed by the Constitution?

TO THE TEACHERS OF MODERN HISTORY IN THE USSR *

The course in Modern History acquaints the pupils with the history of capitalism in other countries, from the English bourgeois revolution of the mid-seventeenth century up to the Great October Socialist Revolution and the end of the First World War.

In studying the course pupils should acquire a knowledge of the main events and facts in chronological order, and should learn to understand concepts such as "the proletariat," "the bourgeoisie," "capitalism," "bourgeois revolution," "proletariat revolution," "dictatorship of the proletariat," "socialism" and "communism" correctly, from the concrete historical material.

The teacher should explain that the first period of modern history starts with the English bourgeois revolution in the seventeenth century, as a result of which the feudal order was destroyed in England and a capitalist order established, which was progressive for that time.

A most important event during the first period of modern history is the formation of the proletariat, the growth of the labour movement and the rise of scientific communism. The same period sees the plundering of the feudal countries of the East by the capitalist states of the West. The invasion of the countries of the East by the capitalist states led to the strengthening in the former countries of popular movements: the Boxer rising in China and the national (sepoy) rising in India (known in Britain as the Indian Mutiny).

The second period of modern history, taken in Class 9, starts with the Franco-Prussian War of 1870-71 and the Paris Commune, and ends with the Great October Socialist Revolution in Russia and the end of the First World War. "This is the period of the decline of capitalism already begun, of the first blow to capitalism, struck by the Paris Commune, of the transition of the old 'free' capitalism into imperialism and of the overthrow

* Translated from "Programmy Srednei Shkoly na 1956-57 uchebuy god. Istoriya SSSR, Novaya Istoriya," in *SCR Soviet Education Bulletin*, Vol. 5, No. 1, May 1958, pp. 1-7.

of capitalism in the USSR by the forces of the October Revolution, marking the beginning of a new era in the history of mankind." [1]

The Great October Socialist Revolution was a break-through on the front of imperialism. Russia through revolution fell out of the war and was lost to the capitalist system. Capitalism ceased to be the basic system in the world's economy, and the world was split into two social systems, the capitalist and the socialist.

The Modern History course is of great importance in forming the communist world outlook of the pupils. This course provides a characterisation, through concrete historical material, of capitalism at different stages of its development, reveals the irreconcilable contradictions of capitalism, shows how the class struggle in capitalist society leads, under definite actual historical conditions, to proletarian revolution and the dictatorship of the proletariat. Here the teacher should explain that at the present time, owing to far-reaching historical changes in the international scene, to the advantage of socialism, new prospects are now open for the transition of countries from capitalism to socialism, and that different forms of this transition are possible. . . .

The increasing attacks of the capitalists on the working class, reductions in wages, mass unemployment, the plundering of the colonies, all these facts and phenomena are characteristic of the true nature of bourgeois democracy. Demonstration of the wretched situation of the workers and peasants in the capitalist and colonial countries should occupy a considerable place in the teaching of modern history. . . .

The pupils must grasp the lesson of the ever-increasing part played by the masses of the people during the age of capitalism, and of the decisive part assigned to the working class, as the only class consistently revolutionary. . . .

Outstanding personalities play an important part in history only to the extent to which they correctly express the interests and needs of the progressive classes. History is not made by heroes, but moved forward by the people, which also creates heroes. This important thesis of Marxist historical theory must be properly grasped by the pupils. . . .

One of the most important themes in this section of the course is the American Civil War of 1861-65. In the course of the fight to put down the revolt of the slave-owning planters, negro slavery was abolished and a bourgeois-democratic agrarian reform carried through. In dealing with this theme the part played by the masses of the people in the civil war must be made clear. At the same time the teacher must stress that although negro slavery was then formally abolished in the USA, in fact the negroes

[1] J. Stalin, S. Kirov, A. Zhdanov, *Notes on Outline of Textbook of Modern History*. Pub. in essays *On the Study of History*, 1937. Partizdat of C.C. of CPSU (b), p. 26.

remain to this day the most oppressed section of the US population, deprived of rights. . . .

It must be explained to the pupils that in history there are two kinds of wars: just wars of liberation; and unjust aggressive wars. The American people's war of independence against English colonial oppression in 1775-82, for example, was a just war . . . the war fought by the Hungarian people in 1848-49 against the oppression of the Austrian monarchy and the intervention of Tsarist Russia was a just war.

Examples of unjust wars are the wars of the USA against the peoples of Mexico, the Philippines and Cuba.

The 1914-18 World War was an imperialist war, unjust on both sides. . . .

Further, it must be explained that a policy of aggression is inherent in all capitalist states.

As long as capitalism exists in the world, reactionary forces representing the interests of capitalistic monopolies will continue to attempt aggression and will try to unleash war. But there is today no inexorable inevitability about war, since there are now in existence mighty social and political forces having at their disposal real means of preventing the imperialists from unleashing war.

Here it should be stressed that from the very beginning of its existence the Soviet Union has consistently pursued a peace-loving foreign policy, a policy of preserving peace throughout the world, which is in the most vital interests of the peoples of all countries.

Mathematics and Science

SOCRATES ELICITS A GEOMETRIC THEOREM FROM A SLAVE BOY *

Socrates. . . . The soul, then, as being immortal, and having been born again many times, and having seen all things that exist, whether in this world or the world below, has knowledge of them all; and it is no wonder that she should be able to call to remembrance all that she ever knew about virtue, and about everything; for as all nature is akin, and the soul has learned all things, there is no difficulty in her eliciting or as men say learning, out of a single recollection all the rest, if a man is strenuous

---

* *The Dialogues of Plato,* trans. into English by B. Jowett, M. A. (New York: Random House, 1937), *Meno,* pp. 360-65. (Fourth century B.C.)

and does not faint; for all enquiry and all learning is but recollection. . . .

Meno. Yes, Socrates; but what do you mean by saying that we do not learn, and that what we call learning is only a process of recollection? Can you teach me how this is?

Soc. I told you, Meno, just now that you were a rogue, and now you ask whether I can teach you, when I am saying that there is no teaching, but only recollection; and thus you imagine that you will involve me in a contradiction.

Men. Indeed, Socrates, I protest that I had no such intention. I only asked the question from habit; but if you can prove to me that what you say is true, I wish that you would.

Soc. It will be no easy matter, but I will try to please you to the utmost of my power. Suppose that you call one of your numerous attendants, that I may demonstrate on him.

Men. Certainly. Come hither, boy.

Soc. He is Greek, and speaks Greek, does he not?

Men. Yes, indeed; he was born in the house.

Soc. Attend now to the questions which I ask him, and observe.

Soc. Tell me, boy, do you know that a square figure is like this? (Socrates draws in the sand)

Boy. I do.

Soc. Now, a square figure has these lines, four in number, all equal?

Boy. Certainly.

Soc. And these, drawn through the middle are equal too, are they not?

Boy. Yes.

Soc. And a figure of this sort may be larger or smaller?

Boy. To be sure.

Soc. Now if this side were two feet and that also two, how many feet would the whole be? Or let me put it thus: if one way it were two feet, and only one foot the other, of course the space would be two feet taken once?

Boy. Yes.

Soc. But as it is two feet also on that side, it must be twice two feet?

Boy. It is.

Soc. Then the space is twice two feet?

Boy. Yes.

Soc. Well, how many are twice two feet? Count and tell me.

Boy. Four, Socrates.

Soc. And might there not be another figure twice the size of this, but of the same sort, with all its sides equal like this one?

Boy. Yes.

Soc. Then how many feet will it be?

Boy. Eight.

Soc. Come now, try and tell me how long will each side of that figure be. This one is two feet long: what will be the side of the other, which is double in size?

Boy. Clearly, Socrates, double.

Soc. Tell me, boy, do you say we get the double space from the double line? The space I speak of is not long one way and short the other, but must be equal each way like this one, while being double its size—eight square feet. Now see if you still think we get this from a double length of line.

Boy. I do.

Soc. Well, this line is doubled, if we add here another of the same length?

Boy. Certainly.

Soc. And you say we shall get our eight-foot space from four lines of this length?

Boy. Yes.

Soc. Then let us describe the square, drawing four equal lines of that length. This will be what you say is the eight-foot figure, will it not?

Boy. Certainly.

Soc. And here, contained in it, have we not four squares, each of which is equal to this space of four feet?

Boy. Yes.

Soc. Then how large is the whole? Four times that space, is it not?

Boy. It must be.

Soc. And is four times equal to double?

Boy. No, to be sure.

Soc. But how much is it?

Boy. Fourfold.

Soc. Thus, from the double-sized line, boy, we get a space, not of double, but of fourfold size.

Boy. That is true.

Soc. And if it is four times four it is sixteen, is it not?

Boy. Yes.

Soc. What line will give us a space of eight feet? This one gives us a fourfold space, does it not?

Boy. It does.

Soc. And a space of four feet is made from this line of half the length?

Boy. Yes.

Soc. Very well; and is not a space of eight feet double the size of this one, and half the size of this other?

Boy. Yes.

Soc. Will it not be made from a line longer than the one of these, and shorter than the other?

Boy. I think so.

Soc. . . . Now tell me, did we not draw this line two feet, and that four?

Boy. Yes.

Soc. Then the line on the side of the eight-foot figure should be more than this of two feet, and less than the other of four?

Boy. It should.

Soc. Try and tell me how much you would say it is.

Boy. Three feet.

Soc. Then if it is to be three feet, we shall add a half to this one, and so make it three feet? For here we have two, and here one more, and so again on that side there are two, and another one; and that makes the figure of which you speak. Now if it be three this way and three that way, the whole space will be thrice three feet, will it not?

Boy. So it seems.

Soc. And thrice three feet are how many?

Boy. Nine.

Soc. And how many feet was that double one to be?

Boy. Eight.

Soc. So we fail to get our eight-foot figure from this three-foot line.

Boy. Yes, indeed.

Soc. But from what line shall we get it? Try and tell us exactly; and if you would rather not reckon it out, just show what line it is.

Boy. Well, on my word. Socrates, I for one do not know.

Soc. Tell me, boy: here we have a square of four feet, have we not?

Boy. Yes.

Soc. And here we add another square equal to it?

Boy. Yes.

Soc. And here a third, equal to either of them?

Boy. Yes.

Soc. Now shall we fill up this vacant space in the corner, so that we shall have four equal spaces?

Boy. Yes.

Soc. Well now, how many times larger is this whole space than the original one we started with?

Boy. Four times.

Soc. But it was to have been only twice, you remember?

Boy. To be sure.

Soc. And does this line (BD), drawn from corner to corner, cut in two each of these spaces?

Boy. Yes.

Soc. And have we here four equal lines (BD, DF, FH, HB) contained in this space?

Boy. We have.
Soc. Now consider how large this space is (BDFH).
Boy. I do not understand.
Soc. Has not each of the inside lines cut off half of each of these four spaces?
Boy. Yes.
Soc. And how many spaces of that size are there in this part?
Boy. Four.
Soc. And how many in this (ABCD)?
Boy. Two.
Soc. And four is how many times two?
Boy. Twice.
Soc. And how many feet is this space (BDFH)?
Boy. Eight feet.
Soc. From what line do we get this figure?
Boy. From this.
Soc. From the line drawn corner-wise across the four foot figure?
Boy. Yes.
Soc. The professors call it the diagonal: so if the diagonal is its name, then according to you, Meno's boy, the double space is the square of the diagonal.
Boy. Yes, certainly it is, Socrates.

THE NUMBER THREE *

NUMBER LESSON FOR THE FIRST GRADE

(This lesson is taken from Rein's "Das Erste Schuljahr," and is an example of a highly elaborated method. The children have learned a story, in the language-work, about a poor little girl whose father and mother had died; and the number of persons represented forms the starting-point of the new lesson.)

Aim.—We will find out how many persons there were in the house of the little Star Dollar Girl while her father and mother were still alive.

Part I.—ADDITION AND SUBTRACTION

(A.)

(1) Preparation.—We have counted many things. How many walls has the schoolroom? How many windows? How many panes has the lower sash? The upper? Both? How many maps hang on the wall?

* Charles DeGarmo, *The Essentials of Method* (Boston, D. C. Heath and Company, 1892), pp. 100-101.

(2) Presentation.—(1) The three persons.

(a) There was first the father (1), then the mother (1 + 1 = 2), then their little girl (2 + 1 = 3). How many people were there? Three. Who were they? Father, mother, and child. How many are father and mother together? Two. How many are father, mother, and child? Three. Count them. Father, 1; mother, 2; child, 3; 1, 2, 3.

(b) But the three did not remain together. The father died and was buried. How many were left in the house? Now the mother died. How many were left? Finally the little girl went away; then there was no one left in the house. One away from 3 leaves 2, 1 from 2 leaves 1, 1 from 1 leaves nothing (zero); 3, 2, 1.

(3) Transition from persons to balls upon the Abacus, three balls being set off upon a horizontal wire, the following being said: That is the father, that is the mother, that is the child.

(a) Repetition of the foregoing exercise in connection with the balls:— The father = 1 person; father and mother = 2 persons; father and mother and child = 3 persons.

Three persons − 1 person = 2 persons; two persons − 1 person = 1 person; one person − 1 person = 0 persons.

ARITHMETICAL LANGUAGE *

1. **Arithmetic** is the science of numbers and the art of computing with them.

2. A **Unit** is a single thing or *one*. A thing is a *concrete unit;* one is an *abstract unit*.

3. A **Number** is a unit or a collection of units. Numbers are *concrete* and *abstract*.

4. A **Concrete Number** is one in which the kind of unit is named; as, two *yards,* five *books*.

5. An **Abstract Number** is one in which the kind of unit is not named; as, *two, four,* etc.

* * *

14. **Arithmetical Language** is of two kinds, *Oral* and *Written*. The former is called *Numeration* and the latter is called *Notation*.

---
* Edward Brooks, *The Normal Union Arithmetic, Graded Course*. Part II. (Philadelphia, Christopher Sower Co., 1877), p. 9f.

SEEING AND COUNTING *

Fun with Boats

1. How many boats do you see?
   7 boats and 1 boat are 8 boats.
   1 boat and 7 boats are 8 boats.

   7 and 1 are ...
   1 and 7 are ...

   $\frac{7}{1}$ $\frac{1}{7}$
   $\frac{1}{8}$ $\frac{7}{8}$

2. How many children do you see? How many are boys? How many are girls?
   5 boys and 2 girls are 7 children.

   2 and 5 are ...
   5 and 2 are ...

   $\frac{5}{2}$ $\frac{2}{5}$
   $\frac{2}{7}$ $\frac{5}{7}$

* Clifford B. Upton, *First Days with Numbers* (New York: American Book Company, 1958), p. 33.

STUDYING SCIENCE IN FIFTH GRADE *

"In studying science you must plan to do three things. You must observe the world around you. You must read and study to find what the things you observe really are, and what they mean. Then you must ask questions and experiment to find the answers."

THINGS TO REMEMBER

We learn by observation when we look at, handle, or use something.
We do an experiment to find the answer to a question.
In doing an experiment we usually compare one thing with another.
What we learn in science is true because it was first learned by observation and experiment.

THINGS TO THINK ABOUT

In how many ways is a science lesson different from a fairy story?
Why does this book not have pictures of animals acting like people?
How does science differ from history?
What is the difference between playing with science equipment and experimenting with it?
When you read everything to do in an experiment from a book, are you really experimenting or making an observation?

EXPERIMENTS TO DO

Obtain an alcohol lamp and a kerosene lamp or lantern and do the experiment described.
Learn by experiments the best way to heat water in your classroom.
Find by doing experiments with lamps, chimneys, and bottles what is gained by using chimneys on lamps and stoves.

EARLY MAN †

The earth is more than two billion years old. It is so old that we can hardly imagine how many years it has existed. Scientists can tell the age of the earth by studying the changes which have taken place in the layers of rock and sand and soil that are near the earth's surface.

---

* Victor C. Smith and Barbara Henderson, *Science Through the Seasons* (Chicago, J. B. Lippincott Company, 1956), pp. 18-19.
† Howard E. Wilson et al., *Out of the Past* (New York, American Book Company, 1954), pp. 3, 4, 11-14.

A half a billion years ago plants, animals, fish, and reptiles were living on the earth. About 200,000,000 years ago was the "age of dinosaurs" (dī′nō·sôr). Those heavy, stupid animals roamed the earth for many centuries. Skeletons of some of the dinosaurs have been found, and we know a great deal about how these heavy beasts lived. But the dinosaurs finally died out. Like many other early animals and plants, they have become extinct.

THE EARLIEST PEOPLE

About a million years ago, the first people lived on the earth. A million years is such a long period of time that it is difficult to imagine how far those years stretch into the past. If we think of one million years as sixty minutes on a giant time clock, a minute is 16,000 years long. People have been civilized for less than half a minute on this giant clock. . . .

We do not know much about the earliest people who lived on the earth. Only small pieces of their skeletons have been found. In 1891 a Dutch scholar named Eugene Dubois (dü·bwä′) found a part of a skull and some teeth in Java. He found them deep in a layer of soil that had been on the surface of the earth a million years ago. Dubois could tell from the skull and teeth about how their owner looked. This ancient ancestor of ours was called Java Man by the scholars. He was perhaps the earliest man of whom we have any record. . . .

THINGS TO DO

I. Questions and Answers. After studying carefully this chapter, "Early Man," answer these questions and others your teacher may ask.

1. How old do we think the earth is? When were the dinosaurs living on the earth?
2. How long do some scientists think that people have lived on the earth?
3. Who was Java Man? Pekin Man? . . .

II. History Definitions and New Words. You will understand better the history you study if you make sure that you know the meaning of certain important words and phrases that explain the story of the past. Copy neatly in your notebook the words that are given below. After each word or group of words write a short definition that explains it. Put a copy of the best definitions in your Class Book, too.

| *history* | *prehistoric times* | *dinosaur* | *Old Stone Age* |
| *historic times* | *scientist* | *extinct* | *New Stone Age* |

III. The Main Ideas. In each chapter that you study there will be some very important ideas that you should remember. The headings in black capital letters on the pages will help you to find those important ideas. On a sheet of paper, copy the black heading in this chapter on Early Man. Under this heading write a few sentences in your own words that tell the main ideas of the chapter. Your teacher will help you to do this as a class exercise before you do it alone. Put your completed work in your notebook.

IV. A Chart of Early Man. Divide a sheet of paper into three columns so that it looks like this.

Prehistoric People   When They Lived   Where They Lived

In the first column list the names of prehistoric people who have been studied by scientists. Start your list in the first column with the name of the earliest people discovered so far, and keep the other names in order, according to the time that scientists think they lived. In the second column put the dates when they lived. In the third column put the names of the places on the earth where their remains were discovered.

V. The Map Tells a Story. Appoint a class committee to make a large map of the world. On the map draw pictures of early people. Show where their remains have been discovered. Label the pictures with the names of the people, the places their remains were found, and the approximate dates when they lived.

VI. The Clock Game. Appoint a committee to make a giant time piece for your classroom like the one on page 4. You can play a game with the clock by having one of your classmates place the hand at a certain date while someone names the prehistoric people who lived at that time. Another way to play the clock game is to have someone name a group of prehistoric people while a classmate places the hand at the date. . . .

VIII. Eugene Dubois Writes a Letter. Imagine that you are Eugene Dubois and that you are in Java. Write a letter to a friend in Europe telling what you are doing in Java and why you are there. Look for information in library books and in encyclopedias. . . .

X. A Radio Broadcast. A group may pretend that they are scientific detectives giving a radio broadcast to an audience that does not understand how scientists have unlocked the secrets of the past. Explain to the audience how scientists have solved the mysteries of prehistoric man. The following are some suggested topics for the broadcasters:

1. Relics of the Past, or Pieces of the Puzzle
2. The Crust of the Earth Holds Evidence
3. The Glaciers Tell a Story
4. Scientists Are Detectives
5. Eugene Dubois, the Bone Hunter
6. Putting the Puzzle Together

COMPARISON OF SCIENCE TOPICS IN SCHOOLS IN FLORIDA AND THE SOVIET UNION *

Florida	Soviet		
	Natural	Chemistry	Physics
Grades 1-3 (age 5 yrs. and 9 mo.-9). Study sky, land, air, plant and animal life, light, earth, seasons, water and its forms, food, reproduction of animals and plants, magnets, motion of earth, sources of food and heat, and soil.	Grades 1-3 (age 7-10). Study of seasons of year, trees, regions of USSR, animals, birds, forest, gardening, vegetables, grain, fruit trees, hygiene.	No Course	No Course
Grades 4-6 (age 10-12). Study solar system, plants and animals, electricity, light, adaptation, survival, seasons, air, conservation, weather, climate, sound, energy, care of body.	Grades 4-6 (age 11-13). Study air, water, mineral resources, soil, practical work, excursions, vegetables, basis for classifying plants.	No Course	Grade 6. Pupils study rudiments of mechanics and motors. Have classes 2 hours each week and is presented in simple and descriptive form.
Grade 7 (age 13). Program centered around understanding environment. Pupils study nature, air, heat, soil, weather, constellations.	Grade 7 (age 14). Pupils study the anatomy and physiology of man, hygiene and sex instruction.	Grade 7. Pupils study air, water, hydrogen, short outline of main chemical concepts, substances, elements, atomic molecular structure, oxides, salts, laws of weight.	Grade 7. Pupils study heat, light, and electricity. Have classes 3 hours each week and material presented in simple and descriptive form.
Grade 8 (age 14). Pupils study use of power, the weather, energy, water, reproduction, planets, earth's surface.	Grade 8 (age 15). No Course	Grade 8. Study inorganic chemistry.	Grade 8. Systematic study of mechanics, heat, light, electricity. Material covered in grade 7 repeated in a more extensive and detailed manner.

* Fred Turner and Sara de Keni, *Schools in Florida and in the U.S.S.R.* (Tallahassee, The Florida School Bulletin, State Department of Education, March 1958), pp. 14-16.

| | Soviet | | |
Florida	Natural	Chemistry	Physics
Grade 9 (age 15). Study solar system, formation of earth, plants, animals, conservation, light, lenses, color, sound, communications, motors.	Grade 9 (age 16). Study the principles of Darwin.	Grade 9. Study inorganic chemistry.	Grade 9. Study of molecular physics and heat. Materials in grade 8 repeated in a more extensive and detailed form.
Grade 10 (age 16). Systematic study of biology. It includes classification of plants and animals; structure of plants; conservation; structure of body; effects of alcohol, tobacco and narcotics on the body; diseases and their cure; genetics; reproduction; mental health. Laboratory experiences are given, when possible.	Grade 10 (age 17). Study general psychology, including the main concepts of logic.	Grade 10. An introduction to organic chemistry.	Grade 10. Pupils study electricity, optics, and sound. Repeat subject matter previously covered.
Grade 11 (age 17). A systematic course in chemistry is taught. Laboratory experiences and demonstrations are given when possible. The study includes the preparation, properties, and use of elements and compounds; equations; problems in relative weights, relative valence and percentage composition; common light and heavy metals; introduction to nuclear fission.	No Grade	No Grade	No Grade
Grade 12 (age 18). A systematic course in physics is taught. Laboratory experiences and demonstrations are given when possible. Included in the study are the laws of the mechanics of solids, liquids, and gases; method of heat transfer; use of simple machines; heat engines; pressure indicators; laws of magnetism, electrostatics, electrical currents, sound, light, and nuclear physics.	No Grade	No Grade	No Grade

Education for Life Adjustment

ADJUSTMENT TO AN AGRICULTURAL ECONOMY *

THE

Farmer's Catechizm ;

CONTAINING

Plain rules of Hufbandry—And calculated for the ufe of Schools.

Q. WHAT is the beft bufinefs a man can do?
A. Tilling the ground, or farming.
Q. Why is farming the *beft* bufinefs?
A. Becaufe it is the moft neceffary, the moft helthy, the moft innocent, and moft agreeable employment of men.
Q. Why is farming (or agriculture) the moft *neceffary* employment?
A. Becaufe by tilling the ground, we obtain food, without which, we could not live much better than the brutes.
Q. Why is farming the moft *helthy* bufinefs?
A. Becaufe labor and exercize are neceffary to ftrengthen the body, to make it digeft food, keep the blood in due circulation, and throw off any offending matter that might bring on difeafes. Befides, men who cultivate the earth liv in the open country, and breethe a pure air.
Q. Why is farming the moft *innocent* employment?

* Noah Webster, *The Little Reader's Assistant* (Hartford: Elisha Babcock, 1790), first page following p. 8d.

EXERCISES SUBSERVIENT TO FUTURE EMPLOYMENTS *

... I would propose that the amusements of our youth, at school, should consist of such exercises as will be most subservient to their future employments in life. These are: 1. agriculture; 2. mechanical occupations; and 3. the business of the learned professions.

I. There is a variety in the employments of agriculture which may readily be suited to the genius, taste, and strength of young people. An experiment has been made of the efficacy of these employments, as amusements, in the Methodist College of Abington, in Maryland; and, I have been informed, with the happiest effects. A large lot is divided between the scholars, and premiums are adjudged to those of them who produce the most vegetables from their grounds, or who keep them in the best order.

II. As the employments of agriculture cannot afford amusement at all seasons of the year, or in cities I would propose, that children should be allured to seek amusements in such of the mechanical arts as are suited to their strength and capacities. Where is the boy who does not delight in the use of a hammer—a chisel—or a saw? and who has not enjoyed a high degree of pleasure in his youth, in constructing a miniature house?

III. To train the youth who are intended for the learned professions or for merchandize, to the duties of their future employments, by means of useful amusements, which are *related* to those employments, will be impracticable; but their amusements may be derived from cultivating a spot of ground; for where is the lawyer, the physician, the divine, or the merchant, who has not indulged or felt a passion, in some part of his life, for rural improvements?—Indeed I conceive the seeds of knowledge in agriculture will be most productive, when they are planted in the minds of this class of scholars.

I have only to add under this head, that the common amusements of children have no connection with their future occupations. Many of them injure their clothes, some of them waste their strength, and impair their health, and all of them prove more or less, the means of producing noise, or of exciting angry passions, both of which are calculated to beget vulgar manners. The Methodists have wisely banished every species of play from their college. Even the healthy and pleasurable exercise of swimming, is not permitted to their scholars, except in the presence of one of their masters.

* Benjamin Rush, *The Selected Writings of Benjamin Rush*, D. D. Runes, ed. (New York, Philosophical Library, Inc., 1947), p. 106f. (Originally published 1790.)

THIRD GRADE CLOTHING PROJECTS FOR PUBLIC AND PAROCHIAL SCHOOL CHILDREN *

THE TOGGERY SHOP [From the public school edition.]

"I keep outgrowing my clothes," said Dick. "When I can't get into them any longer, my parents have to buy new ones."

"We might work out some way to sell or exchange things we have outgrown," said Miss Reed.

The children liked the idea. They were eager to do something about it. They decided to set up a Toggery Shop. The principal said they could have a small storeroom for their shop.

The boys and girls brought all sorts of outgrown or old clothes. These were to be sold or traded. Each piece had to be clean before it could be brought to the shop. Some had to be mended or repaired.

The children made labels for each piece of clothing. These told the price, size, kind of material, and owner's name. They labeled the clothes for sale or trade. They brought shoes, rubbers, suits, coats, dresses, and gloves.

The children chose Paul to be the first manager of the shop. He had many assistants and sales people. All the children took turns at the different jobs.

Paul traded the overshoes he had outgrown for a good pair of leather gloves. Jane sold a pair of shoes.

Other children traded many kinds of clothes. They bought and sold some, too.

OTHER THINGS TO DO

1. The children talked to people at a laundry and at a dry-cleaning place to find out how they wash and clean clothes.
2. The children brought clothes to school to mend. They learned how to sew on buttons, hooks and eyes, and snaps. They also learned how to darn socks.
3. Some boys and girls made a Clothes Care Center in a corner of their room. There they brushed their clothes, shined their shoes, or mended their clothes.

* Alta McIntire, Wilhelmina Hill, and William P. Finley, *Working Together* (Chicago, Follett Publishing Company, 1957). Parallel pages (p. 120f.) from the regular and Catholic editions of the Follett New Unified Social Studies Series.

A Clothing Drive [From the Catholic school edition.]

"Who can remember what Father Dunn's sermon was about last Sunday?" asked Sister one day.

"It was about poor people in other countries," said Nancy. "Some people are too poor to buy the clothes they need. And he asked us to help them."

"That's right," said Sister. "He talked about a clothing drive for the Catholic Relief Services. Would you like to take part in this clothing drive?"

"Yes," said Dick. "I have shoes at home that are small for me."

"And I have a heavy jacket that I can't wear any more," said Billy. "Can we fix the zipper on it?"

"Of course," said Sister Ann. "We can fix rips and tears and sew on missing buttons."

The boys and girls brought all sorts of outgrown or old clothing. Each piece had to be clean before it could be brought from home. At school they sorted the clothes. They put all the shoes together. They put sweaters in another pile.

"I like doing this," said Nancy one day. "It makes me feel good to know that some other little girl will be able to wear my blue sweater."

The children invited Father Dunn to come to class one afternoon.

"What a wonderful surprise," said Father. He looked all around at the piles of clothes. He smiled. "God will bless you for your good work! And many poor people in far-off lands will be praying for you. Thank you, my children."

The children were happy when men from the parish came to pick up the clothes. They decided to take good care of their clothes so that they could have another clothing drive next year.

Other Things to Do

1. The children talked to people at a laundry and at a dry-cleaning place to learn about their work.
2. Some boys and girls made a Clothes Care Center in a corner of their room. There they brushed their clothes, shined their shoes, or mended their clothes.

ADJUSTING TO A NEW CULTURE *

NUTRITION—A BALANCED DIET

Wheel of Health

Be healthy.
Eat *wisely*.
Spend money *carefully*.
Think before buying.
A few cents will buy good foods, but we must learn how.
Remember to drink milk and eat eggs, meat, fruit, and vegetables every day.

Vocabulary

be healthy: consérvate saludable

eat wisely: come inteligentemente

* "A Doorway to Science," Related Curriculum Materials Series, *The Puerto Rican Study* (New York City: Board of Education, 1958), p. 35.

TOPICS FOR RURAL ELEMENTARY GRADES, USSR *

First and Second Grades
First steps at school
Autumn work in the family
Health
Preparation for the winter, types of winter work
Life and work in winter
The approach of spring and preparation for spring work
Spring work and the participation of children in it
Organization of celebrations . . . October Revolution, Lenin's Day . . .

Children were made to understand that work is the basis of human life, that collective work alone is progressive and productive, that nature is no object for passive contemplation but a source of natural forces to be put to use for the benefit of man. They learnt, too, that in capitalist countries the toilers are deprived of the fruits of their labour by the exploiting classes, while in the Land of Socialism peasant and worker toil for the common good.

ADOLESCENTS STUDY THEMSELVES †

OUR GROUP GOALS FOR THE YEAR—We need and want to learn more about:
1. Ourselves as adolescents
2. Our American history
3. American democracy
4. Our world and its problems
5. Communicating effectively
6. Controlling our emotions
7. Sports as spectator—participant
8. Independent study skills

COMMITTEES (Ourselves as adolescents)
1. What is "teen-age" behavior? What are some causes?
    (Bob, Katherine, Leslie, Joe)
2. What changes do we make from childhood to adolescence?
    (Neil, Bill, Lenny, Iris, Bonnie, Kathy)
3. What do we need to know to get along with the opposite sex?
    (Stephen, Phil, Randy, Janet, Ann, Kathy, Jo)
4. How can we develop personal health, attractiveness, mental skills?
    (Linda, David, Hugh, Stan, Kippy)
5. What about "juvenile delinquency"?
    (Pat, Carol, Van, Charles, Wayne, Lynn)

* E. Kontaissoff, "Soviet Education and the New Man," *Soviet Studies*, Vol. V, No. 2, October 1953, p. 108.
† Wm. M. Stewart School, University of Utah, Fall 1958. Student statements of study goals and committee study questions.

Education in Moral and Spiritual Values

"TO BEGET A LOVE OF ORDER AND PROPRIETY" *

The pupil should stand erect,—his heels near together,—toes turned out,—and his eyes directed to the face of the person speaking to him.

Fig. 1. Represents the Book-Monitor with a pile of books across his left arm, with the backs from him, and with the top of the page to the right hand.

Fig. 2. The Book-Monitor, with the right hand, hands the book to the pupil; who receives it in his right hand with the back of the book to the left; and then passes it into the left hand, where it is held with the back upwards, and with the thumb extended at an angle of forty-five degrees with the edge of the book, (as in fig. 2), until a further order is given.

Fig. 3. When the page is given out, the book is turned by the thumb on the side; and, while held with both hands, is turned with the back downwards, with the thumbs meeting across the leaves, at a point judged to be nearest the place to be found. On opening the book, the left hand slides down to the bottom, and thence to the middle, where the thumb and little finger are made to press on the two opposite pages. If the pupils should have thus lit upon the page sought for, he lets fall the right hand by the side, and his position is that of fig. 3.

Fig. 4. But, if he has opened short of the page required, the thumb of the right hand is to be placed near the upper corner of the page, as seen in fig. 4; while the forefinger lifts the leaves to bring into view the number of the page. If he finds he has not raised enough, the forefinger and thumb hold those already raised while the second finger lifts the leaves, and brings

---

* "Looking Backward One Hundred Years," *Annual Report of the Superintendent of Schools, City of New York*, 1953-54, Part IV, p. 22.

Illustrations

them within the grasp of the thumb and finger. When the page required is found, all the fingers are to be passed under the leaves, and the whole turned at once. Should the Pupil, on the contrary, have opened too far, and be obliged to turn back he places the right thumb, in like manner, on the left hand page, and the leaves are lifted as before described.

Fig. 5. Should the book be old, or so large as to [be] wearisome to hold, the right hand may sustain the left, as seen in fig. 5.

Fig. 6, 7. While reading, as the eye rises to the top of the right hand page, the right hand is brought to the position seen in fig. 4; and, with the forefinger under the leaf, the hand is slid down to the lower corner, and retained there during the reading of this page, as seen in fig. 6. This also is the position in which the book is to be held when about to be closed; in doing which, the left hand, being carried up to the side, supports the book firmly and unmoved, while the right hand turns the part it supports over on the left thumb, as seen in fig. 7. The thumb will then be drawn out from between the leaves, and placed on the cover; when the right hand will fall by the side, as seen in fig. 2.

Fig. 8. But if the reading has ended, the right hand retains the book, and the left hand falls by the side, as seen in fig. 8. The book will now be in a position to be handed to the Book-Monitor, who receives it in his right hand, and places it on his left arm, with the back towards the body; the books are now in the most suitable situation for being passed to the shelves or drawers, where, without being crowded, they should be placed with uniformity and care.

In conclusion, it may be proper to remark, that however trivial these minute directions may appear to some minds, it will be found on experience, that books thus treated, may be made to last double the time that they will do, under the usual management in schools. Nor is this attainment of a correct and graceful mode of handling a book the only benefit received by the pupil. The use of this manual is calculated to beget a love of *order* and *propriety;* and disposes him more readily to adopt the habit generally, of doing things in a methodical and systematical manner.

From Report of City Superintendent, 1855

THE FACE *

1. The face is the index to the heart of man. As you look on the face of a clock, and tell the time of day; so you may look on the human face and read the heart.

* Mrs. M. B. Moore, *The First Dixie Reader* (Raleigh, Branson, Farrar, and Co., 1864) p. 47f.

2. If you notice the faces of small babies they look nearly alike. Some eyes are black, some blue, and some hazel; while the noses of some are larger than others.
3. But when children begin to grow, and some to have bad tempers, you perceive a great difference.
4. The child who has a bad temper, and cries, and pouts, and quarrels, is almost sure to have red eyes, thick ugly lips and often a red nose.
5. Other children are too proud to cry, and sulk; but they smile a bitter smile, and utter a few biting words; while their eyes look like those of an angry snake.
6. These tempers, too, tell upon the face. The lips will fit tight together, while you can almost see the sparks of malice dart from under the eyelids. Such faces are not called handsome—people fear them.
7. So you see the way to have a pretty face, is to feel pretty, and always try to do right. An honest face is the prettiest face yet. All can have this.

THE HONEST INDIAN *

An Indian once met one of his white friends, who lived in a village not far from the Indian's wigwam, and asked him for a little tobacco to smoke his pipe. The white man took a handful of loose tobacco out of his pocket, and gave it to him.

The next day the Indian came to the village and enquired for the gentleman who had given him the tobacco. He said he had found a piece of money in the tobacco, and he wished to restore it to the owner.

The person to whom he addressed himself, told him the money was his, for it had been given to him; and that he ought to keep it, and not say anything about it. But this advice did not please the honest Indian.

He pointed to his breast and said: "I got a good man, and a bad man in here. The good man say, 'This money is not yours; you must return it to the owner.' The bad man say, 'It *is* yours; for he gave it to you.' The good man say, 'That is not right; he gave you the tobacco, but not the money.' The bad man say, 'Never mind, you got it; go buy some dram.' The good man say, 'No, no, you must not do so.' "

"So I don't know what to do, and I try to go to sleep; but the good man and the bad man kept talking all night, and trouble me; and now I bring the money back I feel good."

* Richard M. Smith, *The Confederate First Reader* (Richmond, Va., G. L. Bidgood, 121 Main Street, 1864), p. 11.

SANCTIONS *

... If certain values are accepted as guides to conduct, and if there is general agreement as to the kind of conduct desired, does it make any practical difference *why* the values are approved? Does it really matter that different people have different explanations and that many people have no explanation at all? ...

Whether or not sanctions, as such, are important is a theoretical question which we need not discuss here. It is clear, however, that *from the point of view of educational policy and program,* sanctions are of primary importance.

Children and young people typically, and sometimes annoyingly, want to know *why*. They do not readily believe, or trust, or act upon, the instruction of those who tell them there is no reason at all for preferring one kind of conduct over another, or that any reason at all will do equally well. Nor, even if it were pedagogically effective, could the doctrine of "never-mind-why" be acceptable to any but an authoritarian state or a dictatorial school system. On neither pedagogical nor on ideological grounds can the schools ignore the problem of sanctions.

... Let us survey some of the many possibilities in terms of a situation which is imaginary in its detail but typical of the decisions that teachers and children make many times a day in their life together in the school.

> Johnny dug from his pocket a shiny new dime, his weekly allowance. ... He indicated his purchase to the clerk and laid his dime on the counter. The clerk picked it up ... and placed four coins in change on the counter. Johnny scooped up coins and candy together and ran on to school.
>
> As he hung up his jacket, he removed his precious change and counted it—one penny, two pennies, three pennies, four—no, that's not a penny! That's a dime. ... Overjoyed, he ran to his teacher. ... "Look," he cried, "the man at the store gave me a dime instead of a penny, and now I can have two more candy bars and one peppermint stick this week. ..."
>
> Miss Williams put her pencil down on the desk. "Johnny," she said, "your arithmetic is just right! But don't you think you should return the dime and ask the clerk to give you a penny instead?"
>
> The light vanished from Johnny's face and he looked suddenly stricken. "But why, Miss Williams? He gave it to me. Why can't I keep it? Why?"

* Educational Policies Commission, *Moral and Spiritual Values in the Public Schools* (Washington, D. C., National Education Association, 1951), pp. 37-45.

Sanction No. 1   Justice

Miss Williams: Because the dime doesn't belong to you. You did not earn it and your father didn't give it to you.

Johnny: No, but the man at the candy store did.

Miss Williams: He thought it was a penny.

Johnny: But what difference does it make?

Miss Williams: When he counts the day's receipts, he will be short nine cents. The owner of the store will make the clerk pay it. Perhaps the clerk has a little boy. Would you want that other boy to go without his candy?

Johnny: His father should be more careful.

Miss Williams: Perhaps. Nevertheless, if all business were run on the basis of keep-what-you-get, whether it is fair or not, our whole country would be in serious trouble.

Johnny: But what difference would two candy bars make to the whole country?

Miss Williams: It isn't just the two candy bars. It isn't fair for you to profit by the clerk's error. The principle of fair play is important to all of us.

Sanction No. 2   The Law
(Another teacher, Miss Brown, handles the situation)

Miss Brown: Because if you kept the dime, it would be the same as if you had stolen it, and the law punishes people who steal.

Johnny: But how can the clerk know who has this dime?

Miss Brown: The clerk may not know, but I know. You told me.

Johnny: Are you going to tell a policeman?

Miss Brown: No, I am not. Instead I am going to ask you to return the dime. You wouldn't be put in jail for keeping the dime, because you are so young and it is a small sum. But if you were older, and the sum were larger, you might be. . . . We have laws against stealing. If we don't respect our laws, society will punish us. . . .

Sanction No. 3   Property Rights
(Another teacher, Mrs. Smith, handles the situation)

Mrs. Smith: Do you want to keep property that doesn't belong to you?

Johnny: But it does belong to me. The man gave it to me. . . .

Mrs. Smith: . . . Suppose you had given someone a dime by mistake. Wouldn't you expect him to return it?

Johnny: Maybe. Yes, I probably would. But the clerk at the store must have more money than I do. He won't need this change very much. . . .

Mrs. Smith: You see, you admit that it would be wrong to keep a larger sum. But it isn't the amount that matters. It's the principle that counts.

It isn't right to take another person's property. Just remember that, and you will get along fine.

Sanction No. 4 — Integrity
(Another teacher, Miss Johnson, handles the situation)

Johnny: But why should I care if no one knew about it?
Miss Johnson: Oh, but *you* would know about it. How could you respect yourself if you had done something you knew was wrong? If you knew someone else had done such a thing, would you respect him? . . .
Johnny: I don't suppose so—no, I wouldn't. Not if it was my dime.
Miss Johnson: Yet you would probably be reminded of that clerk's wrongdoing only when you saw him. On the other hand, you cannot get away from yourself, and you would be reminded of your own wrongdoing all the time. Are two candy bars worth a guilty feeling?

Sanction No. 5 — Group Approval
(Another teacher, Mrs. Miller, handles the situation)

Mrs. Miller: If you don't return the dime, what will people think? Do you want your friends to know that you would steal? . . .

Sanction No. 6 — Authority
(Another teacher, Miss Jones, handles the situation)

Miss Jones: Because it's wrong to keep the dime.
Johnny: But the man gave it to me.
Miss Jones: By mistake. He didn't mean to give you a dime. We have to live by rules. I tell you that it is wrong for you to keep the dime.
Johnny: I still don't see *why* it should be wrong.
Miss Jones: People give many reasons why it is wrong but nobody disputes the fact that it is wrong. You must learn what is wrong and right. One reason I am here as your teacher is to teach you these duties.
Johnny: I never had three candy bars in one week before. I don't see why I can't have them just this once.
Miss Jones: Johnny, unless you take that dime straight back I shall keep you after school. Is that clear, young man? That's why you must return the dime, without any more argument.

Sanction No. 7 — Guidance
(Another teacher, Miss Wright, handles the situation)

Miss Wright: Had you thought about the clerk?
Johnny: He's dumb, not to be able to tell a dime from a penny.
Miss Wright: Did you know you had a dime when you picked it up?
Johnny: No, I thought I had four cents until I got upstairs.
Miss Wright: Then, at first glance, you couldn't tell the difference?
Johnny: Well, if I'd looked closely, I could.

Miss Wright: Did the clerk look closely?
Johnny: Well, I guess we can all make mistakes.
Miss Wright: If you had made the mistake, how would you feel about it?
Johnny: I suppose I'd be sorry. . . .
Miss Wright: If the clerk had given you a ten-dollar bill instead of a one, what would you have done?
Johnny: Oh, I'd take it right back. I wouldn't want him to lose nine dollars.
Miss Wright: But it's all right for him to lose nine cents?
Johnny: That's not much money.
Miss Wright: How much money would it have to be before you thought you ought to take it back?
Johnny: I don't know. I hadn't thought about it that way. Do you think I ought to take back the dime?
Miss Wright: What do *you* think, Johnny?

RULES FOR SCHOOL CHILDREN *

It is the duty of every school child:
1. To strive with tenacity and perseverance to master knowledge, in order to become an educated and cultured citizen *and* to serve most fully the Soviet Motherland.
2. To be diligent in study and punctual in attendance, never being late to classes.
3. To obey without question the orders of school director and teachers.
4. To bring to school all necessary books and writing materials, to have everything ready before the arrival of the teacher.
5. To appear at school washed, combed, and neatly dressed.
6. To keep his desk in the classroom clean and orderly.
7. To enter the classroom and take his seat immediately after the ringing of the bell, to enter or leave the classroom during the lesson period only with the permission of the teacher.
8. To sit erect during the lesson period, not leaning on the elbows or slouching in the seat; to attend closely to the explanations of the teacher and the responses of the pupils, not talking or engaging in mischief.
9. To rise as the teacher or the director enters or leaves the classroom.

* Adopted by the Soviet of People's Commissars of the RSFSR, August 2, 1943. Quoted in *I Want To Be Like Stalin,* by George S. Counts and Nucia P. Lodge (New York, The John Day Company, 1947), pp. 149f.

10. To rise and stand erect while reciting; to sit down only on permission of the teacher; to raise the hand when desiring to answer or ask a question.
11. To make accurate notes of the teacher's assignment for the next lesson, to show these notes to the parents, and to do all homework without assistance.
12. To be respectful to the school director and the teachers, to greet them on the street with a polite bow, boys removing their hats.
13. To be polite to his elders, to conduct himself modestly and properly in school, on the street, and in public places.
14. To abstain from using bad language, from smoking and gambling.
15. To take good care of school property, to guard well his own possessions and those of his comrades.
16. To be courteous and considerate toward little children, toward the aged, the weak, and the sick, to give them the seat on the trolley or the right of way on the street, to help them in every way.
17. To obey his parents and assist in the care of little brothers and sisters.
18. To maintain cleanliness in the home by keeping his own clothes, shoes, and bed in order.
19. To carry always his pupil's card, guarding it carefully, not passing it to other children, but presenting it on request of the director or the teacher of the school.
20. To prize the honor of his school and his class as his very own. For violation of these rules the pupil is subject to punishment, even to expulsion from school.

THE AMERICAN PUPIL'S CREED [*]

I believe in the schools of the United States of America and in the democratic principles for which they stand; schools which our forefathers devoted their lives to establish so that education might be free for every boy and girl in our land; schools in which, under the guidance of a counselor trained to advise wisely, each pupil may choose his course of study and prepare for a vocation of his preference; schools which have grown and must continue to grow through the years to meet the needs of an ever-changing civilization.

[*] "For Florida's Children—Florida Education or Soviet Training?" in The Florida School Bulletin, State Department of Education, March 1958.

I, therefore, believe it is my duty as an American student to attend school regularly unless I am ill; to cooperate with my teachers and fellow students; to use my time and energy wisely; to participate in democratic discussions; to obey and help to enforce the rules and regulations of my school; to develop my interests, ideals, habits, skills, and powers in the right way so that I may become a worthy member of the United States of America, which offers me, as part of my American heritage, a better chance for an education than any other country in the world.

7A Social Studies Class
Hereford High School
Baltimore County, Maryland

Student Evaluation

AN EIGHTH GRADER WRITES A LETTER OF SELF-EVALUATION

Wm. M. Stewart School
University of Utah
Salt Lake City, 12, Utah
December 1, 1958

Dear Mom and Dad,

We are asked to write a self evaluation letter each year and this is it. I'll start with Friends;

I think I have a lot of friends and I guess I could have a few more. One reason is that I don't talk enough but I am trying to get over it.

My personality is pretty good although sometimes I am mad and gripey but not too often.

My physical well being is pretty good. I am not usually too tired and I feel good most of the time but sometimes I could get to bed earlier.

When I am with the people I go around with I will bring up something I could do better. I think if I did try to talk more in class and when around the other places, it would help.

I do not participate too much so if I try and make myself do it a few times it will come easier.

Reporting; I have given one report so far and I think I could have done better but if I keep doing it it would be easier for me.

Love,
M_____

REPORTING PUPIL DILIGENCE AT HOME AND AT SCHOOL *

DILIGENCE CARD

Name of Child.................... School................ Month.......... Grade............19....

Totals, I.... II.... III....
Promoted................

	Teacher	Parent
1. Class Work		
2. Examination		

Columns (read vertically):
Cleanliness
Deportment
Effort
Proficiency
Times Absent
Reading
Writing
Spelling
English
Arithmetic
Drawing
Physiology
Geography
U. S. History
Nature Study
Music
Algebra
Spelling Contest
Physical Training

HOME (FOR PARENTS) **REPORT** (OPTIONAL)

I. For Credit on Exam. in Arith., Eng., Geog., Hist., Alg., Draw., 10%

1. HOME STUDY, 4%..................minutes daily
2. LIBRARY READING, 3%...............minutes daily
3. HELPING PARENTS, 3%...............minutes daily

Does child overstudy?..................

II. For Credit on Physiology Ex. only, 10%
(Write "Yes")

1. Hair Combed daily, 2%..........
2. Hands and Nails cleaned daily, 2%..........
3. Brushing Teeth daily, 2%..........
4. Sleeping with open window, 2%..........
5. Bathing weekly at least, 2%..........

III. For Credit on Nature Study Ex. only, 10%
(Write "Yes" and answer any two—5% each)

1. Caring for Fowls..........
2. Caring for Stock..........
3. Caring For Birds..........
4. Caring for Garden..........
5. Caring for Flower Beds..........
6. Caring for Lawn..........
7. Destroying Weeds..........
8. Destroying Bad Insects..........
9. Experiments..........

.... Parent

The other side of the card contains the pupil's report.

PUPIL'S REPORT
(Pupil may fill in if credit on Home Report is expected.)

1. Lessons studied at home....................................
2. Books read at home (give author also)....................
   ....
3. Chores done for Parents....................................

.... Student.

* Part of the "Diligence Card" in use in Wantagh School, Wantagh, Long Island, in 1918, reprinted from Ruth Strang, *How to Report Pupil Progress* (Chicago: Science Research Associates, Inc., 1955), p. 36.

423

EVALUATING PUPIL GROWTH *

	OBSERVATIONS OF TEACHERS								
GOALS TOWARD WHICH WE ARE WORKING	Soc. Studies–English	Mathematics	Science	Art	Home Economics	Industrial Arts	Music	Physical Education	

I. CITIZENSHIP — INDIVIDUAL RESPONSIBILITY:

a. Accepts personal responsibility for his own actions in halls, rooms, playgrounds, going to and from school, etc.
b. Shows evidence of willingness to serve the entire group in school projects and activities.
c. Demonstrates respect and care in the use of public property and consideration for his personal property and that of his classmates.
d. Demonstrates a growing ability and insight in analyzing situations and problems which he faces and in reacting appropriately to them.
e. Shows ability to relate himself to his classmates in a variety of ways — personal friends, participation in games, committee membership.
f. Demonstrates ability to accept differences among his classmates and others with whom he comes in contact.
g. Shows courtesy, consideration, and a willingness to accept and act on suggestions from classmates and teachers.
h. Shows insight into personal hygiene as evidenced by good grooming, appropriate dress and cleanliness.
i. Shows growth in health knowledge and practices as evidenced by physical condition and control.
j. Reports to all classes promptly or presents legitimate excuse for absence or tardiness.

HOMEROOM TEACHER COMMENTS:

II. LEARNING AND STUDY SKILLS:

a. Uses a variety of resources such as people, books, magazines, pamphlets, pictures, etc., for needed information. Organizes this information wisely for specific use.
b. Participates constructively in classroom discussions and other school activities.
c. Accepts responsibility for assignments and completes them promptly.
d. Shows a willingness to work beyond minimum requirements.
e. Complies with legitimate requests willingly and promptly and does not alibi.
f. Places proper emphasis on accomplishment and is not overly concerned about immediate rewards.
g. Initiates new activities, presents additional ideas.
h. Budgets time in respect to a given need or program of activities.
i. Willingly spends extra time to complete work.
j. Provides the necessary materials with which to do the work at hand.
k. Shows willingness to work experimentally.
l. Applies previously acquired knowledge and experience to new situations.
m. Shows increasing ability to work alone or with the group according to need.
n. Exercises independence in seeking extra aid when need is indicated.

* Part of the "Report to Parents" form from the William M. Stewart School, University of Utah, Salt Lake City, 1958.

HOMEROOM TEACHER COMMENTS:

III. COMMUNICATIVE SKILLS:
   a. Shows growth in ability to communicate informally with classmates, teachers, and other adults.
   b. Shows growth and ability to phrase a request, to organize ideas, to present a point of view, to relate an experience.
   c. Shows growth in ability and willingness to present ideas in writing.
   d. Keeps records useful for himself and/or for the group.
   e. Shows growth in the mechanical aspects of writing:
      sentence structure
      spelling
      punctuation and capitalization
      penmanship
   f. Uses graphic material, statistical tables, charts, maps, etc.
   g. Chooses to read in free time; reads a variety of material, much of which he locates independently.
   h. Shows growth in ability to adjust rate of reading to purpose.
   i. Shows growth in effective comprehension of reading.
   j. Shows evidence of understanding and relating sound mathematical and science concepts to everyday living.
   k. Demonstrates ability to recognize the elements of a problem and to use the scientific method in its solution.

HOMEROOM TEACHER COMMENTS:

IV. CREATIVE ASPECTS OF LIVING:
   a. Shows a growing awareness of, and an appreciation for, the creative arts such as literature, music, art, design, crafts, homemaking, etc.
   b. Recognizes his own creative abilities, accepts his personal limitations, and consciously develops the capabilities which he does possess.
   c. Seeks to discover new ways of expressing himself creatively.
   d. Shows recognition and acceptance of the talent and special ability of others.
   e. Recognizes that freedom and a permissive atmosphere are necessary for effective exploration and creativity.

HOMEROOM TEACHER COMMENTS:

Part 4

▼

The School in Context

Contents of Part 4

The School in Context

GROWING UP IN TWO CULTURES

EDUCATION AND THE FAMILY

RELIGION AND EDUCATION

COMMUNICATIONS AND EDUCATION

EDUCATION AND THE SOCIAL ORDER

The School in Context

"The little Manus becomes the big Manus, the little Indian, the big Indian." So Margaret Mead summarizes the complex process of growing up. And, she points out, the cardinal fact in the American child's life is that whatever else befalls him, he will grow up to be a big American.

For little Americans school is now a compulsory experience on their way to becoming big Americans. But it was not always so. Most of the men and women who founded and developed the United States had little if any schooling; many of the readers of this book have grandparents who were good men and women, effective in their work, and loyal and law-abiding citizens, though unschooled or almost so. The prospective teacher understandably views the school as central, even as indispensable. In this he shares a belief widespread among Americans. Indeed, it has often been said that belief in the importance of education is peculiarly American. C. H. Dobinson, comparing English and Russian education in one of the readings in this section, comments on national differences in what is expected of education. "Certainly the Russians, like the Americans," he writes, "have demonstrated that education, even if it can not do everything, can do a great deal more to a nation than Englishmen, even today, believe." Another Englishman, Denis Brogan, is similarly struck by the extent to which Americans have looked to the school to carry almost the entire responsibility for the education of the young. He sees the American school "undertaking to do more than it can (which is very American) and doing much more than it seems to do (which is also very American)."

There remain the Manus, the Arapesh, the Balinese, the Trobriand Islanders in the Pacific, most of the populations of most of the countries and territories of Africa and Asia, in fact, at least half of the world who grow to adulthood unschooled. These peoples live lives very different from those of the peoples in more highly civilized areas, but though they are not schooled, they are not uncultured. Through anthropologists' accounts of the life histories and the complex societies of many of these non-literate and non-mechanized groups, our notions of the educational process have been broadened and deepened. Education through the anthropologist's eyes is the sum of all of the experiences by which the infant becomes a member of a particular society. The methods by which the individual is "educated," or, in the anthropologist's terms, socialized, are as various as the cultures within which the process takes place. The agents that accomplish the process are various, too: the family, the individual's age and sex mates, religious leaders and groups, occupational groups, even the geographic and climatic character of the physical environment to which a group must accommodate itself. In some cultures, notably those which have previously developed complex technologies and a written language, there is another agent, the school.

Once the social invention, the school, has been created, does it necessarily become the chief agent for the education of the young? In all modern societies the school is the chief agent through which children and adolescents learn the fundamental intellectual skills, and are made acquainted with the historical, literary, and scientific heritage of their culture. Whether the school *should* do more is, as the readings and discussion in Part 3 on "The Purposes of Education" show, a matter of debate. It is a matter of debate, too, whether the school, which is only one of many educative agencies in society, *can* do all that some spokesmen would have it do. The development of a system of formal schooling does not mean that families, churches, playmates, wars, depressions, and laws cease to educate. Indeed, the development of new agencies and forces—the school, TV, unions, or "The Organization"—further complicates the problems of jurisdiction among them all. Some of the most critical issues in education, then, are best approached by looking away from the school and focusing instead on education as a pervasive cultural process and on the relationship of the school to some of the other institutions which help to make big Americans out of little Americans.

NATURE AND NURTURE

Long before the development of sociology, social psychology, and cultural anthropology as discrete disciplines, men had pondered the relative importance of inheritance and environment in shaping the character of individual men and groups of men. Though Plato's *Republic* was predicated on the existence of categories of men significantly different in native qualities and capacities, he repeatedly acknowledges the influence of en-

The School in Context

vironment on character. Whether he uses the metaphor of the wool dyers, who knew that only certain fleece would take the true sea-purple, or that of the seed and its nurturing soil, Plato reminds us that what men are depends at least in part on what they have experienced. The relationship of nature and nurture is as clearly suggested in Socrates' words to Adeimantus as in modern psychological formulations.

> Why, I said, we know that all germs or seeds, whether vegetable or animal, when they fail to meet with proper nutriment or climate or soil, in proportion to their vigour, are all the more sensitive to the want of a suitable environment. . . .

The idea of the relationship between man's nature and the nurture he receives is an old and persistent one. What has changed in different periods and in the theories of different men is, first, the weight given to one or the other of the two components in the relationship, and, second, the definition of the two components themselves. To the question, What in man is inherited? there have been various answers: his physical characteristics primarily; his character; his intelligence; all of these. Philosophers and scientists have varied, too, in their views of the mutability of man's inherited characteristics. Frequently, especially in earlier ages, they have been thought to be fully present at birth, in the sense that the butterfly is present in the chrysalis, as "the folded leaf is wooed from out the bud." According to this view the environment may stunt or foster or destroy, but its effects are strictly limited; the end result is predetermined by the qualities of the encapsulated organism. Only the emperor cocoon will yield the emperor moth, the maple bud the maple leaf. Colloquially we hear, "You can't make a silk purse out of a sow's ear."

At the other pole are beliefs that stress the power of environment to determine what a man becomes. Understandably, many educators have leaned toward this view. To the extent that man is conceived as a plastic, mutable being shaped by social institutions and experience the importance of education is heightened. If, as Helvetius thought, the qualities of men are not differentiated at birth but are the same in all men, then education might accomplish almost anything. Rousseau, his contemporary, was equally impressed with the power of society, though his concern was rather to protect the child from what he considered its distorting effects than to construct social institutions that would mold him into an ideal man. A tendency to weigh heavily the effects of environment has been generally characteristic of Utopian theorists and their projects. In Robert Owen's dream, ideal villages were to cultivate ideal men, and schools were an integral and essential means. The founders of new political systems—in Italy, Germany, and Russia as well as in the United States—are almost of necessity committed to belief in the ability of a controlled environment to shape new kinds of men.

Each of these positions is current still. "The stuff out of which an individual is made can be and is molded by the social environment into one shape or another," declares Abraham Myerson, a physician whose physiological approach to human nature was modified by subsequent psychoanalytical studies. On the other hand, Wayne Dennis observes that the adaptability of human nature to social patterns is circumscribed by tendencies within the individual toward patterns of its own. While anthropologists like Margaret Mead remind us that even the temperamental characteristics associated with masculinity and femininity are culturally determined, the physiological psychologists like Sanford find that characteristics such as self-sufficiency and social responsiveness correlate with physical properties such as body build.

Today most widely accepted theories of the relationship of nature and nurture, inheritance and environment, emphasize the interaction of these components. Gardner Murphy describes the relationship as bio-social. Man, he declares, is more accurately viewed as a creature enmeshed in his physical and social environments—neither dominated by them or independent of them. Because of his nature he must eat and he must love. But the rhythm of his hunger and what he finds appetizing or revolting to his taste depend upon his constitutional needs, the physical resources of his geographical location, and the patterns of nursing, food preparation, and eating to which he is exposed.

Though the controversy over the relative importance of nature and nurture is a long-standing one, efforts to test opposing hypotheses experimentally are relatively recent. Experimental studies dealing with this issue are for the most part a twentieth-century development. These studies have been of two types: (1) those in which the subjects have had identical or very similar heredity—as in the case of identical twins or siblings reared in different environments; and (2) those in which subjects of different inheritance have been reared in similar environments—in the same socio-economic class or ethnic culture, for example. Teachers need to learn about this evidence systematically in their studies of human growth and development. Here it is sufficient to cite two generalizations that are supported by many studies dealing with this issue. Clearly environment, and particularly the social environment, contributes in different degrees to different aspects of the whole person. It is safe to generalize as follows: that nurture makes relatively little difference in physical characteristics, more in intellectual capacities as they are measured by intelligence tests, still more in motivation and achievement in education, most in attitudes and personality. That is to say, children of equivalent native capacities will be somewhat more robust and vigorous if they are reared under optimum physical conditions. Identical twins or infants with identical scores on intelligence tests in the first months of life will show gains or losses in intelligence scores depending on whether they are reared in environments that foster or inhibit intellectual interests and growth. They will take on the attitudes of the people around them. Their personality structure will be shaped by their interactions with the individuals closest and most important to them.

Studies of the second type indicate that people of widely different endowments share many qualities in common with other members of their group. The results of research by cultural anthropologists, sociologists, and social psychologists have clarified long-standing generalizations about national character. National types, contrary to de Gobineau, Houston Stewart Chamberlin, and other nineteenth-century racist theorists, are now recognized as the product of nurture rather than nature, as culturally determined rather than innate.

Germans, according to popular opinion, are given to unquestioning obedience to authority. They are thought to be disinclined to assume individual initiative or responsibility. The tragic experiences of thousands of anti-Nazis during the Hitler regime serve as indisputable evidence that exceptions to such generalizations exist and may be assumed to exist within any groups. Indeed, it is important to preface any consideration of national character or, to use Kardiner's term, basic personality, with the observation that in any culture there will be wide variations among individuals. Nevertheless, interviews, questionnaires, and systematic case studies conducted in Germany tend to confirm the idea of widespread common personality traits, attitudes, and beliefs that differentiate Germans from other national groups. A comparison of German and American adolescents by means of a questionnaire administered in 1945 illustrates this difference.[1] The questions called for judgments on such situations as these: is a soldier in wartime justified in refusing to obey an order to shoot innocent prisoners; should those who unjustly criticize government be jailed; is the son of a cruel father justified in running away? On these questions, which raised problems of conflict with authority, German youth favored obedience much more often than did the Americans, though there were in each instance some Americans whose answers were typically "Fascist" and some German youth, especially anti-Nazis, whose responses were "democratic." In both national groups girls tended to respond in typical national patterns more consistently than boys.

Children of foreign-born parents bring into American classrooms their parents' attitudes toward authority generally, toward the roles of men and

[1] Donald V. McGranahan and M. Janowitz, "Studies of German Youth," *Journal of Abnormal and Social Psychology* 41:3-14, January 1946.

women, toward property, even toward time. Western man, especially the American, is time conscious to a degree quite foreign, as Northrup observes, to Mexicans and, presumably, many Latin Americans. Our concern with being "on time," our adjurations not to "waste" time but to "make it count" may serve the purposes we intend with children and adults conditioned in our own or comparable cultures, and fail to move those not so oriented. Because Anglo-American educators have had little understanding of the radical differences in value orientations of Spanish-Americans, efforts to teach them, Florence R. Kluckhohn declares, have had little success.[2] In schools in which independence, self-determinism, future-mindedness, and doing are the ideals rewarded, children whose cultural heritage stresses dependent behavior, fatalism, concern with the present, and being are confused and frustrated. There are few things more important to the teacher than to develop a quick and genuine sensitivity to the distinctive values of the various ethnic groups he will encounter. The process of learning the ways of a new culture, of becoming acculturated, is always unsettling; it can be a traumatic experience.[3] Separate accounts of the Hopi Indians of northern Arizona testify to the painful disruption in cultural mores and values caused by the advent of the white man's laws and the white man's schools. Though middle-aged, the Hopi who were the informants in Eggan's study still recalled their fright when they were forcibly taken as children to the white man's school. They learned then that their parents were powerless to "save" them from being sent away for unwelcome schooling. Their hair was cut without their permission, washed, sometimes their clothes were burned; and they were given "American" names. Apparently all their parents had taught them was wrong. They felt bombarded with new ideas, manners, food, and prohibitions. They learned little that was useful to them when they returned to the Hopi village; often they learned only a dissatisfaction with it. For the Hopi boy schooling came just at the time when tribal custom had brought him out of the baby world of the women and home and into the freer world of men. Expecting to accompany the men to the fields and range more freely with them, he was deposited unceremoniously in the confines of a classroom under the domination of a woman. The reservation schools were not exceptionally rigid; on the whole they seem to have been what we would have considered progressive; the teachers were probably dedicated people. But still it was a strange and frightening world. Few readers of this book are likely to teach

[2] Florence R. Kluckhohn, "Dominant and Variant Value Orientations," in Clyde Kluckhohn, H. A. Murray, and D. M. Schneider (eds.), *Personality in Nature, Society and Culture* (New York, Knopf, 1953), p. 354.
[3] Dorothy Eggan, "The General Problem of Hopi Adjustment," *American Anthropologist* 45:357-73, July-September 1943; Laura Thompson and Alice Joseph, *The Hopi Way* (Chicago, University of Chicago Press, 1944).

in reservation schools, but many will have in their classrooms children who for one reason or another enter a strange culture when they enter the classroom door.

Cultural differences and discontinuities are not only national in their origins. Because the great influx of immigrants to the United States occurred between 1848 and 1915, American teachers today are less likely to find as many children of foreign-born parents in their classes as did their colleagues a generation ago. But cultural differences are still an important factor in the teacher's experience. Today's teacher, however, is more likely to be working with children whose differences are regional or socio-economic rather than national in their origins. Today, as a result of labor migrations, California teachers will have Deep South Negro children in their classes; Detroit teachers will find bewildered "poor white" children from the Kentucky mountains in theirs; uprooted Puerto Rican children face New York City teachers wonderingly. As the compulsory school leaving age has been raised, most high school classes include many adolescents "from across the tracks" who would have been at work or on the streets a generation ago.

Studies comparable to those that documented the concept of national character show that there are attitudes and ways of behaving that distinguish regional groups and socio-economic classes. Crèvecoeur described the distinguishing effects of regions on the "new race" of Americans one hundred and seventy-five years ago.

> Exclusive of those general characteristics, each province has its own, founded on the government, climate, mode of husbandry, customs, and peculiarity of circumstances. Europeans submit insensibly to these great powers, and become in the course of a few generations, not only Americans in general, but either Pennsylvanians, Virginians, or provincials under some other name.

Though the homogenizing effect of mass media has counteracted Crèvecoeur's anticipated sharpening of regional differences, they still exist. Observers of American life have persistently commented on the Boston state of mind, the frontier spirit—which Turner thought had its effect on the whole temper of American life—small town and big city cultures. "Mind takes form in the city; and in turn, urban forms condition mind," Mumford says. And, the sociologist would say, it takes particular forms in particular cities, at particular times. Dominant values in Middletown differ from those in Yankee City; but the Lynds found notable changes—as well as persistent patterns—within Middletown itself when they re-examined it only a decade after their first study. During this period, that of the depression, the old two-class system in Middletown was replaced by a three-class system. It is through the presence in their classes of children from different socio-economic groups that most teachers become acquainted with the effects of social environment.

During the past three decades sociologists and social psychologists have been particularly interested in class and caste as subcultures having important effects on personality, attitudes—including those toward school—and achievement. The Character Education Inquiry under Hartshorne and May in the mid-twenties showed a significant relationship between honesty and moral knowledge and the socio-economic background of the children studied. Children from middle-class homes that rewarded the same attitudes and values that were taught by the school were more likely to learn honesty and probity than children from homes where these values were disregarded. Re-evaluations of results of studies indicating that intelligence norms were lower for children from low income families than for those from upper income families called attention to the fact that not income alone but the total environment of these groups differed in ways that favored or handicapped children's achievement on intelligence tests. A series of studies sponsored by the American Council on Education in the 1940's delineated the effects of caste systems in shaping moral personalities of Northern and Southern, urban and rural Negro youth. Allison Davis, in particular, has written extensively on the effects of class and caste on Negro and white children. In general these studies show that children of either race reared in middle-class environments are much more likely to respond to challenges presented by school and society by striving to achieve than are children of lower socio-economic status. Children nurtured in different socio-economic environments will tend to differ with respect to what they consider acceptable aggressive behavior, age and sex roles, and authority. Their expectations and satisfactions differ also. Middle-class children have learned before they enter school and continue to be taught that physical aggression will be punished, that aggressive behavior in the form of initiative, ambition, or conventionally valued skills will be rewarded. Lower-class children, on the other hand, are unlikely to be punished and may be rewarded for physical aggressiveness. Davis says of these two groups, "What they fear, what they abhor, what they desire, what they crave, what they will work for, or fight for, what they consider valuable or sacred differ in almost every basic area of human relationships." In a comic vein Russell Lynes has popularized the distinctive tastes in clothing, food, furniture, and leisure activities of the different classes. In his way Lynes, like the social scientists, calls attention to the wide range of tastes, traits, and behavior that are acquired by members of various subcultures in a society.

Certain cautions must be continuously kept in mind if these generalizations from the social sciences are not to result in stereotyped thinking about

The School in Context

people. First, the concepts discussed—national character, socio-economic class—are abstractions constructed for their usefulness in certain kinds of discussion. They may serve to alert the teacher to the fact that when some children fight repeatedly with other children, are destructive of school property, and shrug off appeals to study harder, they may be behaving in ways that are customary and acceptable among the adults and children in their family and community. Beyond this the teacher must look, as few of these studies even attempt to do, at the whole child. The boy in the second seat, third row, is not a member of three separate subcultures: lower-class, Puerto Rican, and urban. He is a New York—middle-class—Puerto Rican —only child—of a devout Catholic widowed working mother. He is more. He is himself; he has experiences, qualities, capacities, that are unique, that may be affected by but are not identical with or limited to the statistical norms and classifications that identify his sociological groups.

Among the readings in this section two describe generalized personality types, the Manus and the American, which the authors present as typical in these societies. But every life history departs in some degree from the model type. *The Education of Henry Adams* reveals a Bostonian, a child of the seventeenth and eighteenth centuries living in the nineteenth and twentieth, born in the shadow of the Boston State House but losing his heart to and forming his habits in the fields around his grandfather's house in Quincy. Adams held a childhood illness accountable for stimulating in him the New England qualities to an extreme. His brothers, he thought, were the type; he was the variation. Doubtless each of the brothers thought himself a variation, and was. In Lillian Smith's *Killers of the Dream* we are shown white middle- and upper-class Southern children growing up in a culture that exerted constant and seemingly inescapable pressures on them to learn the lessons of race and the customs of segregation. But Lillian Smith herself, learning these lessons, squeezed into the cultural mold, broke through it to develop attitudes and opinions of her own. Reared in a tradition of white superiority and racial taboos, she became a proponent of racial equality. And, she reminds us, there are individuals and families throughout the South who do not accept the dominant tradition. Nor is it only the extraordinary and rare individual who departs from the norms of his community. Even though, as Reisman and Whyte insist, modern society puts a high premium on conforming to the ways of one's peers, to the expectations of "The Organization," protest and non-conformity are also to be found in all phases of our intellectual and institutional life. The lesson of the force of culture is incompletely learned unless we learn also that cultures are pluralistic, inter-penetrating, and only partially responsible for determining what a man becomes.

The Agents of Education

Evidence of the effects of nurture on man are merely preliminary to the question, "What is the part of the school in this process?" Educational entries in *Who's Who* might well list a man's place in his family constellation, his family's status index, his ethnic origins, the size and character of the community he grew up in. But in fact they list his public or private secondary school and his college or university if he has attended one. When parents discuss educational plans for their children, they talk about schools, perhaps about curricula in terms of prestige. Early recognition of the range of influences affecting the individual, even explicit definitions of education as more than schooling, have had relatively slight impact on educational practices. When the British Elementary Education Act was passed in 1870, it assumed that attendance at school constituted "education." Only three years before this date John Stuart Mill, in his inaugural address at St. Andrews, had formulated a far more comprehensive definition of education.

> Not only does education include whatever we do for ourselves and whatever is done for us by others for the express purpose of bringing us nearer to the perfection of our nature; it does more: in its largest acceptation it comprehends even the indirect effects produced on character, and on the human faculties, by things of which the direct purposes are quite different; by laws, by forms of government, by the industrial arts, by modes of social life, nay, even by physical facts not dependent on human will; by climate, soil, and local position.

It is, of course, hardly reasonable to expect educational legislation to legislate "things of which the direct purposes are quite different." On the other hand, is it reasonable to expect schooling, even universal, compulsory, ten-year schooling, to accomplish all that is implied in education so broadly conceived? If everything educates, does it follow that the school should educate in everything?

The preceding section of this discussion described some of the effects of the social environment on individuals and groups. It gave little attention to the agents through which these influences are channeled. Attitudes are not assimilated from an encompassing "social climate," though this is one way of describing a complex, still imperfectly understood process. It is probably more accurate, though still not fully descriptive of such phenomena, to say that attitudes, beliefs, and habits are taught by social institutions. In all societies the education of the young is a primary responsibility of the family; it is shared usually by children's age and sex mates and by some type of religious institution. In Western society the institution of the school has had increasing responsibility for the education of the young.

Very recently communications on a mass scale have come to play a significant part in the education of children. One of the major issues in contemporary American education is that of the jurisdiction of each of these agents in the total education of the child. For a variety of reasons, notably the need to find an agent of acculturation for hundreds of thousands of children with a foreign language and heritage, American schools now undertake to teach much that was formerly taught in the home, by other children, and by employers. Whether this extension of the function of the school has been delegated to it by parents, employers, the electorate, or whether "educationists" have usurped these responsibilities and prerogatives from an unwilling or unwitting public is debatable.

Legislation appropriating public funds for vocational education in agriculture, the mechanic arts, and home economics attests to popular support for delegating to the schools phases of education previously considered the responsibility of other agencies. Since most decisions about curriculum are approved or disapproved by locally elected boards of education, it might be assumed that the inclusion of courses in home and family life and driver education, to select two controversial additions to the conventional curriculum, have public support. Numerous state and national polls of public opinion on what the schools should teach conducted in the past decade show substantial support for the school's undertaking to teach vocational skills, build character, polish personality, and so on. The 1950 Roper survey of public opinion on education concludes:

> . . . Today's parent is inclined to feel that the school, good or bad, is just as responsible as he for most of the upbringing of his child. In the old days it was felt that the school's job was to teach reading, writing, arithmetic and little else. But now, the survey shows, some 90% of the general public feel that it is also the school's business to train the whole child—even to the extent of teaching him honesty, fair play, consideration of others and a sense of right and wrong.

The extensive surveys of opinion in the state of Illinois and surveys in Detroit and Michigan give much the same picture. American parents and taxpayers—to say nothing of students and teachers—look to the school as the agency chiefly responsible for the total education of the young. Even in the midst of widespread attacks on the school's failure to fulfill its narrowly conceived intellectual function, public opinion still seems to expect the school to undertake aspects of education formerly considered the prerogative and obligation of the family. David Reisman quotes a mother who is asked:

> Q. Do you think the teachers should punish the children for using make-up?

A. Yes, I think they should punish them, but understand, I'm a modern mother and while I'm strict with my daughters, I am still modern. You know you can't punish your children too much or they begin to think you are mean and other children will tell them you are mean.

Her response is consonant with the views reported in public opinion surveys. It is a long way from the time when "a licking at school meant a licking at home."

Arthur Bestor, one of the severest critics of modern education, attacks the findings of public opinion polls showing support of these expanded functions. The Illinois surveys in particular, Bestor considers, failed to present the public with adequate alternatives to education for personality development, marriage, management of personal finances, and the like. Though he does not present evidence to support his view, he remains convinced that parents must really agree with him that schools should concentrate their efforts on the three R's. The use of opinion polls, no matter who designs and sponsors them and whatever their outcome, raises a more fundamental question: Should decisions about the social function of the school be made on this basis?

Bestor's argument, however, does not rest primarily on the purported bias of specific opinion polls. Much more fundamental is his attack on the assumption that the school should undertake responsibility for things that other agencies fail to do. It is widely acknowledged that many children fail to secure adequate education about matters of health or morals from their parents. Indeed, parental neglect was advanced as a justification for compulsory schooling from the time of the earliest agitation for it. But though children need education for family life, it does not necessarily follow that the school is the proper agency to provide this education even if the family defaults. Bestor is willing to grant that the school, as the only institution reaching all of the children, is a strategic center for dispensing ancillary welfare and educational services—provided the responsibility for these resides with other agencies. The trend toward assigning to the school educational obligations formerly assumed by other agencies he terms "regressive."

In a changing society changes in educational needs and educative agencies are to be expected. Because the school once served solely as the agency for transmitting intellectual skills is not a good reason for restricting it permanently to this function any more than the failure of the family to fulfill its former function is a good reason for the school to expand its sphere. In a society on wheels, like that of the United States, few would dispute the desirability of driver education for most if not for all youth. But driver education may be conducted by the police, as in Montreal, by automobile companies, by voluntary citizens' organizations like the Auto

Clubs of some communities, as well as by the school. The existence of an educational need does not dictate the agency best suited to meet it.

Those who would have the school serve as the principal educative agency for youth do not rest their argument on the default of other agencies. They raise the following points in support of their position. First, the school is the only agency in our society that reaches all the children. Children, they point out, are in school more hours per day, more days in the year, and more of their growing years than in any other public agency common to all. The school, furthermore, is the only agency, aside from individual families, whose whole concern is the child and his growth and development. Finally, since the whole child, not merely his mind, comes to school, the school is inescapably involved in his whole education. In effect, those who would utilize the school as the major agency for child socialization hold that the school cannot teach arithmetic or spelling without teaching a whole complex of social attitudes and values concurrently. At first glance this generalization seems axiomatic. But observation of practices in other cultures demonstrates important differences in the number of things intentionally taught in connection with teaching basic intellectual skills.

Jules Henry, in a paper presented at a conference on anthropology and education in 1954, compares reports of teaching situations in China and in the United States to illustrate cultural differences in the number of things taught children simultaneously with lessons in their letters. The first is a description of how Chinese boys before the turn of the century were taught the characters of the language, which Henry quotes from the account of a British observer of nineteenth-century Chinese culture.

> If the boys are beginners, they are brought up in a line before the desk, holding san-tsz' King, or "Trimetrical Classic," in their hands, and taught to read off the first lines after the teacher until they can repeat them without help. He calls off the first four lines as follows:
>
> > Jin chi tsu, sing pun shen;
> > Sing siang kin, sih siang yuen;
>
> when his pupils simultaneously cry out:
>
> > Jin chi tsu, sing pun shen;
> > Sing siang kin, sih siang yuen.
>
> The tedium of memorizing these unmeaning sounds is relieved by writing the characters on thin paper placed over copy slips. The writing and reading lessons are the same, and both are continued for a year or two until the forms and sounds of a few thousand characters are made familiar, but no particular effort is made to teach their meanings. . . . No effort is made to facilitate the acquisition of the characters by the boys by arranging them according to their component parts; they are learned

one by one, as boys are taught the names and appearance of minerals in a cabinet.[4]

The second is a description of a spelling lesson in a fourth-grade class in the United States:

> Children form a line along the back of the room. There is to be "spelling baseball," and they have lined up to be chosen. There is much noise, but teacher quiets them. Teacher has selected one boy and one girl and sent them to front of room to choose their sides. As the boy and girl pick children to form their teams, each child chosen takes a seat in orderly succession around the room. Apparently they know the game well. . . . Now Tom, who has not yet been chosen, tries to call attention to himself, in order to be chosen. Dick shifts his position more in direct line of vision of the choosers so that he may be chosen. Jane, Tom and Dick, and one girl whose name Observer does not know, are the last to be chosen. . . . Teacher now has to remind choosers that Dick and Jane have not been chosen. . . . Teacher gives out words for children to spell, and they write them on the board. (Each word is a "pitched ball," and each correctly spelled word is a "base hit." The children move from "base to base" as their teammates spell the words correctly.) With some of the words the teacher gives a little phrase: "Tongue—watch your tongue; don't let it say things that aren't kind; butcher—the butcher is a good friend to have; dozen—12 of many things—knee—get down on your knee; pocket—keep your hands out of your pocket, and anybody else's. No talking!" Teacher says, "Three outs," and children say, "Oh, oh!" . . . "Outs" seem to increase in frequency as each side gets near the children chosen last. . . . Children have great difficulty spelling August. As children make mistakes those in seats say, "No." Teacher says, "Man on third." As child at board stops and thinks, teacher says, "There's a time limit; you can't take too long, honey." At last, after many children fail on August, a child gets it right, and returns grinning with pleasure to her seat. . . . (Observer notes: Motivational level in this game seems terrific. They all seem to watch the board, know what's right or wrong, and seem quite keyed up. No lagging in moving from base to base.) . . . Child who is now writing Thursday stops to think after first letter, and children snicker. Stops after another letter. More snickers. Gets word wrong. . . . (Frequent signs of joy from the children when their side is right.) [5]

In each instance the school is functioning as the agency for transmitting specific intellectual skills to children. In each instance, also, the children are learning other elements of their culture. But it is also evident that in

---

[4] Jules Henry, "Culture, Education, and Communications Theory," in G. D. Spindler (ed.), *Education and Anthropology* (Palo Alto, Stanford University Press, 1955), p. 193f.

[5] Ibid. pp. 203-4.

the United States example there is a more or less conscious effort to use the classroom situation to teach more elements of the culture than in the traditional Chinese instance. Lest the utilization of a play setting lead the reader to identify the second example with modern innovations, it is well to recall that efforts to combine the teaching of intellectual skills like reading with the indoctrination of cultural values date back to the *New England Primer*. Then too the American school taught more than the alphabet when it taught children their letters. Then, as throughout the American experience, the school was a consciously employed channel for teaching the ethical values of the culture. In Colonial America children learned that "A" stood for Adam—"in whose fall we sinned all." More than two hundred years later children in the New York City Schools were being taught their spelling in this fashion:

> H-a-y—hay; grass cut down and dried. What is hay? The Bible says, "Man comes up as a flower and is cut down—" A baby is like a bud—a child like an opening blossom—a young person like a full blown flower. Then comes the season of fruit—"good trees bear good fruit"—goodness is like fruit—how pleasant! Be a good child, and bear good fruit.[6]

One cannot help wondering how well the spelling was remembered.

If anything, the American habit of utilizing the schools as an agency for transmitting a relatively large segment of the culture to the young seems today to be more firmly entrenched than ever.

A final example may serve to highlight the problem of institutional responsibility for the education of youth. Probably no problem relating to youth has roused more private despair and more public concern than that of juvenile delinquency. Speeches and sermons are delivered on the subject. Novels and films—from *Oliver Twist* to *The Blackboard Jungle*—dramatize its details. Psychologists and sociologists study its origins and advise on its prevention and cure. Hours of testimony reported in thousands of pages, in the published *Hearings before the Subcommittee to Investigate Juvenile Delinquency* of the United States Senate Committee on the Judiciary, demonstrate official national attention to this problem. These hearings present the opinions and research findings of public officials and social scientists on the institutions and forces responsible for it. Juvenile delinquency, students of the problem declare, is a product of impoverished neighborhoods where children live in overcrowded, dilapidated housing and have inadequate recreational facilities; it is a consequence of disorganized, destructive family life; it is stimulated by comic books, radio, movies, and TV programs that glamorize crime; it is reinforced by gang activities

[6] "Looking Backward One Hundred Years," *Annual Report of the Superintendent of Schools, City of New York, 1953-54*, Part V.

and by the example of adult crime. The school, too, may contribute to the development of the juvenile delinquent by failing to meet children's needs and by making school for some children a daily experience of failure and frustration. All experts agree that delinquency is learned.

That the school may contribute to delinquency is a relatively new idea. On the contrary, belief in the efficacy of schooling to prevent delinquency was a major factor in the establishment of free compulsory education. DeWitt Clinton saw in the provision of free schooling for the children of the poor their salvation from a life of crime in the city streets. In Massachusetts in the following generation, Horace Mann saw the school and the teacher as the institution and the agent to bring children lost in despair, poverty, and vice into the sun of responsible citizenship. The report of the New York City Board of Education two years after the inauguration of the Compulsory Education Act of 1875 includes a table of comparative juvenile misdemeanor and crime rates before and after the Act. An increase in schooling is credited with a decrease in delinquency.

As time went on, the hope that universal schooling alone would prevent or correct juvenile delinquency faded. It became apparent to more and more people that as the origins of children's maladjustment to society were various and complex in their interrelationships, prevention and correction would also have to be many sided. Toward the end of the nineteenth century and throughout the twentieth, philanthropic efforts and public legislation and practice set up or strengthened other social institutions believed capable of preventing and correcting juvenile delinquency. Or, to describe these efforts in terms of the total education or socialization of the child, they established institutions that would prevent children from learning antisocial attitudes and behavior, teach them constructive social values and action, and assist them in un-learning delinquent habits. Slum clearance projects and housing that provide play space and play equipment; settlement houses that offer opportunities for constructive associations with other children; church sponsored activities that help children learn how to relate ethical values to social behavior—each of these developments may be considered educative or re-educative attacks on juvenile delinquency. Law enforcement agencies—courts and prisons—have assumed educative functions with respect to this problem. The police, we have discovered, can collaborate with other agencies in providing positive social education for children. Local, state, and federal funds have been employed to provide day-care centers for children of working mothers, child welfare services for troubled families and their children, nurtural foster home care for children without families or whose families are unable properly to care for them.

Where schools have effected major changes in the attitudes and behavior of socially maladjusted or delinquent children, they have taken on qualities of some of the other institutions through which children learn. This was true of Pestalozzi's school at Stanz for orphaned children. Here, as his letters report, the school was a home as well as a school, he was parent as well as teacher. It was true also of Makarenko's amazingly effective school described in his book, *The Road to Life,* and represented in the film of that name. In his school he reclaimed the "wild boys" displaced from their homes and communities by the cataclysm of the Russian Revolution. "I realized," Makarenko wrote, "there are no delinquents but rather people who have fallen upon hardship. . . . Any normal child in the streets, lacking any help, outside society, outside a community, without friends or experience, without hope, with frayed nerves, any normal child in such conditions would become delinquent. . . ." Makarenko provided more than a school for these boys; he made for them a work experience, a community, a home.

Does this mean that the school, as school, has nothing to do with delinquency? Increasing knowledge about the origins and dynamics of delinquency indicates that although schooling may not be the panacea it was once thought to be, it does, like all of the institutions with which children come in contact, have an educative or mis-educative effect on them. A judge of the Domestic Relations and Juvenile Court of Toledo, Ohio, who has first-hand knowledge of many troubled, wayward children, reminds us of the mis-educative effects of bad schools and bad teaching. He lists the following techniques for teaching delinquency:

. . . ridiculing the child; embarrassing him; comparing him unfavorably with another; shaming him publicly; unduly mistrusting him; allowing the other children to make fun of or take advantage of him; repeatedly imposing tasks too difficult for him or unsuited to his capacities; otherwise injuring his dignity; failing to provide at least an occasional opportunity for him to achieve, create, and, if possible, excel; providing inadequate opportunities for friendship, self-expression, recreation, adventure; impairing his sense of security, of "belonging;" laxity or inconsistency in maintaining discipline; regarding the maintenance of discipline as . . . "Teacher vs. Pupil," instead of a joint enterprise; and especially failing to recognize and report behavior problems in their incipient stage and follow up to see that they receive proper treatment.[7]

Most contemporary students of the problem, like Tappan and Kvaraceus, believe that the school's contribution can be a constructive one but that the school need not attempt to make a direct approach to the prevention and correction of juvenile delinquency. The school that is doing its best

[7] Paul W. Alexander, "Some Tested Techniques in Teaching Delinquency," *Educational Forum* 8:17-21, November 1943.

to fulfill the role peculiar to it, is at the same time making a contribution to the control of juvenile delinquency. By providing intellectual challenges appropriate to each child's interests and abilities, by recognizing and rewarding his intellectual growth, by helping him to develop the intellectual concepts and master the intellectual skills that will make it possible to find himself in his world, by establishing a social and emotional climate conducive to intellectual inquiry and progress the school makes its unique contribution. Beyond this, the school can assist those other institutions and agencies through which children learn behavior that is ethically defensible and socially acceptable. The school can watch for symptoms of pre-delinquent behavior; it can refer parents and children to welfare and recreational services in the community.

The Gluecks, perhaps the most highly regarded authorities on juvenile delinquency, view the task of educating youth for constructive participation in society as one in which many agencies have responsibilities. "This educational training," they declare, "must begin in the family group, continue in the school, be extended to the church and other social organizations of the community."

The family, church, the school, and other social organizations are inescapably involved in the total education of the child. Divided or at odds, they reduce the child himself to a battleground. Like the school they are interested parties; with the school they can form a partnership in which each will mutually reinforce the others' effectiveness in teaching children their cultural heritage.

THE HIGH WALL

The majority opinion of the United States Supreme Court on *Everson vs. the New Jersey Board of Education* (1947) concluded with this statement:

> The First Amendment has erected a wall between church and state. That wall must be kept high and impregnable. We could not approve the slightest breach.

With these words the Court announced a split decision favoring, five to four, the use of public funds to transport children to parochial schools in New Jersey. The dissenting Justices used the same reason for disapproving of the contested action. Such contradictory interpretations of the constitutional principle of the separation of church and state are characteristic of judicial opinions on this subject. They reflect a persistent and deep-seated dilemma in the American heritage.

The founders of the nation were, as a group, God-fearing men. Religious zeal was a primary motive for their undertaking the arduous and uncertain journey to an unknown territory. In New England the government was a

The School in Context

dissenting theocracy; in the South the Church of England was the official church. Yet the descendants of these colonists, also God-fearing men, erected a high wall between church and state. They agreed in their First Amendment to the new Constitution that "Congress shall make no law respecting the establishment of religion, or prohibiting the free exercise thereof. . . ." A system of public schools established originally for religious ends and under religious auspices has evolved into a school system secular in aims and control. Again and again the schools have been faced with questions that reveal the dilemma posed by the conflicting beliefs: that education was a moral enterprise and that men's religious beliefs should not be legislated. "Can religion be taught without sectarianism?" "Can morality be taught without religion?" "Is rigorous intellectual inquiry compatible with religious faith?" These questions have been raised for more than two hundred years. They are still debated not only in professional journals but also in community newspapers and court litigation.

The first schools in America, like their European antecedents, were religious in intent and control. The early colonists, though protestants against established state religions, had no wish to secularize education. Their concern was rather to establish schools that would perpetuate their particular religious beliefs. Indeed, education was their first line of defense against the Old Deluder Satan. In many parts of the South the Anglican Church enjoyed the status of a state religion. Here, too, education was religious in character. Among the motives for the establishment of the colony of Virginia was that the settlers might "preach and baptize into the Christian Religion and by propagation of the Gospel, to recover out of the armes of the Divell, a number of poore and miserable soules, wrapt up unto death, in almost invincible ignorance." The Society for the Propagation of the Gospel was a principal agent in the establishment of the first free schools in the South. Teachers in colonial schools were examined on their religious beliefs; schooling throughout the colonies included religious instruction. Dissenters and followers of the Church of England alike believed in God, heaven and hell, the decalogue, the divine origin of The Bible, and the observance of the Sabbath. The charters and seals of schools and colleges founded during the early years of the nation testify to the general conception of education as a religious enterprise. The seal of Harvard until recently carried the motto *Christo et ecclesiae*. The open Bible is featured in many of the seals of the early colleges. The charter of the University of Pennsylvania declares its hope to assure the "well-being of a society, as well as, in a great measure, the eternal welfare of every individual, by impressing on their tender minds principles of morality and religion." The announcement of the opening of King's College, now Columbia University, specified the arts and sciences, practical and cultural, in which instruction was to be offered appropriate to the Age of Reason. But such learning, the announcement made clear, was to lead youth "from the study of nature, to the knowledge of themselves, and of the God of nature, and their duty to Him, themselves, and one another. . . ." The announcement of King's College, however, recognized a spirit of religious toleration that marked an important change from earlier sectarianism. By the middle of the eighteenth century the idea of liberty for contesting religions that was to result in the adoption of the First Amendment in its last quarter was already evident in the King's College announcement. "It is understood," the advertisement went on, "that as to religion there is no intention to impose on the scholars, the particular tenets of any particular sect of Christians, but to inculcate upon their tender minds, the great Principles of Christianity and Morality in which true Christians of each Denomination are generally agreed."

During the first half of the century following the Revolution the problem of sectarianism in education was not a public issue. Although the Ordinance of 1787 insured religious liberty to the settlers in the Northwest Territory, it declared also that "religion, morality, and knowledge, being necessary to good government and the happiness of mankind, schools and the means of education shall forever be encouraged." In fact many years were to pass before the states or local communities realized these good intentions by authorizing public funds for the support of schools. In the interim children whose families could afford it were tutored or sent to private schools mainly denominational in character. Children of the poor might in some communities attend charity schools supported by various denominations. During this period public money could be and was used to send poor children to such sectarian schools. Even public schools offered religious instruction presumably non-sectarian in character. But this apparent contradiction in principle and practice may be explained by the fact that at this time the population of the United States was almost exclusively Protestant. In 1790, when the first Roman Catholic bishop was installed in America, Catholics constituted less than 1 per cent of the population, Protestants 99 per cent; Jews were an even smaller group than Catholics. As long as the King James Bible was acceptable—as it was to the Protestant sects—it was possible to have a system of education that was Christian but not necessarily sectarian. In the first quarter of the nineteenth century, however, a large Irish Catholic immigration began and was followed after 1848 by a large wave of German Catholics. By the middle of the nineteenth century the Catholic population had risen to about 7 per cent and a system of Catholic schools was being developed. In 1840 the Provincial Council of Baltimore expressed its opposition to the use of non-Catholic versions of The Bible in public schools attended by Catholic

The School in Context

children, interpretations of Protestant teachers, and the Protestant assumption that the individual can interpret the Bible. It was during these years also that the public school system was being established, with a consequent withdrawal of funds from sectarian schools. The conditions for what was to become a major debate were set.

Typical of this debate was the exchange of letters and pamphlets between Horace Mann and the Reverend Mr. Smith in 1846. The Reverend Mr. Smith held the Massachusetts State Board of Education and its secretary, Mr. Mann, responsible for "Godless schools," and a consequent increase in crime and immorality. Mann's response to the attack supports the reading of The Bible in schools, but without comment. But he rejects entirely the proposals that local communities be allowed to determine which doctrine shall be taught in their schools or that schools open their doors to the teaching of conflicting creeds. If either of these alternatives were to prevail, Mann believed, the schools would be turned into sectarian battlegrounds and children would be so confused that they would be more likely to end as atheists than as good Christians. Since Massachusetts was one of the centers of the new Irish Catholic immigration, it is not surprising to find Mann including Catholics as well as Baptists, Congregationalists, and other Protestant sects he feared would strive to control the schools. Once a particular religion was entrenched in the educational system, Mann warned, religious freedom in the political field would be undermined.

The position defended by Mann describes present practices in most states to this day. Eleven states include prohibition of sectarian teaching in their constitutions; these and others have enacted subsequent legislation of this kind. But most states permit and some require reading from the Bible as part of school exercises, though it is not customary to require children to participate in these exercises if their parents object. (The Supreme Court has never ruled directly on the constitutionality of Bible reading in the schools.) Religious instruction, once an integral part of schooling even, to a degree, of public schooling, has been legally barred and practically eliminated. The 1942 White House Conference on Children in a Democracy stated that "the primary responsibility in the religious development of the child rests upon the parents in the family."

In recent years a number of communities have experimented with various plans for religious instruction of children after school hours or during school hours but not as a part of the regular public school program. Two of these, the Champaign, Illinois, plan and the New York City plan, were carried to the Supreme Court of the United States. The Champaign plan, in which schools set aside one period a week for voluntary instruction in the school building by religious teachers, was declared unconstitutional in an eight to one decision (1948). Four years later the New York City plan was held constitutional, though by a split decision. The New York City plan differed from the Champaign plan in that children were "released" from school for religious instruction which was given off the school premises at the expense of the religious groups participating.

The critical difference between the affirming and dissenting justices in this case touches upon an issue even more fundamental than that of sectarianism. Justice Douglas wrote, in the majority decision, "We are a religious people whose institutions presuppose a Supreme Being." On this assumption he concludes that the principle of separation of church and state should not be interpreted as sanctioning "callous indifference" or hostility to the efforts of religious groups to provide sectarian education for their children. Though the state may not support, it should not hinder and may facilitate private religious instruction. Justice Black, dissenting, challenges the conclusion drawn by Justice Douglas from the assumption that Americans are "a religious people." Though this be true, it makes it the more incumbent upon us, he holds, to preserve the minority rights of agnostics and atheists. The Bill of Rights, he believes, must be viewed as guaranteeing man's right to doubt and disbelieve as well as to believe as his conscience directs him. By allying the school with any plan for religious instruction, releasing some children, but constraining those whose parents do not wish them to receive religious instruction to remain at school, the government through the schools is showing partiality to believers. Justice Jackson, also dissenting, characterizes the released time plan as "governmental constraint in support of religion." "The day that this country ceases to be free for irreligion," he declares, "it will cease to be free for religion."

It is at this point that the most fundamental question with respect to the school's involvement in religious education arises. The selections from Pope Pius XI and from John Dewey in this section of the readings illustrate what would appear to be an irreconcilable difference. Here the issue is not one of sectarian versus non-sectarian influences but rather of religious versus explicitly secular education.

The Catholic position, as set forth in this Encyclical, is that all phases of the child's education must be in harmony and all must be infused with the truth as it is propounded by the Church. "And this must be so," the Encyclical continues, ". . . because every form of instruction, no less than every human action, has a necessary connection with man's last end. . . ." The child exposed to tutelage about natural and social phenomena divorced from instruction in their origin and control by a Supreme Being is in mortal danger.

Dewey, like Peirce, on the other hand, argues that education conducted

The School in Context 451

within the framework of an over-arching religious dogma forfeits its birthright, the pursuit of truth. Dewey's objection to efforts to relate and harmonize education is at base not political but philosophical. He sees the progress of knowledge as a history of the rejection of supernatural interpretations of reality. It is not merely the avoidance of sectarianism that should deter the schools from religious instruction, but the school's commitment to intellectual inquiry, which Dewey views as an essentially secular enterprise.

Pius XI denies that religious and secular approaches to knowledge are in conflict. He reports the Vatican Council's position as follows: "Not only is it impossible for faith and reason to be at variance with each other, they are on the contrary of mutual help. For while right reason establishes the foundations of faith, and, by the help of its light, develops a knowledge of the things of God, faith on the other hand frees and preserves reason from error. . . ." But Dewey prefers scientific demonstration to right reason and is unwilling to have inquiry "protected" from error. The Encyclical grants that the sciences may have methods of their own, but holds that the Church rightly "takes every precaution to prevent them from falling into error by opposition to divine doctrine, or from over-stepping their proper limits and thus invading and disturbing the domain of faith." For Dewey there must be no limits on inquiry; everything must be open to question.

> All proffered samples of learning must go to the same assay-room and be subjected to common tests. It is the essence of all dogmatic faiths to hold that any such "show down" is sacrilegious and perverse. The characteristic of religion, from their point of view, is that it is—intellectually—secret, not public; peculiarly revealed, not generally known; authoritatively declared, not communicated and tested in ordinary ways.

Dewey suggests that the domain of the school is inquiry, not the propagation of faith, though he sees a spiritual import in man's progressive exploration of the universe, man's own nature, and relations with other men.

In practice American schools have not, however, accepted so rigorous a separation of religion and scientific inquiry as Dewey proposed. The alternative of collaboration with the churches in fostering out-of-school religious instruction through "released time" programs has already been considered. But this practice fails to take account of the moral implications inherent in all education. As our scientific study of human nature has progressed it has become more, not less, apparent that interest in the "meaning" of life, in good and evil, are irrepressible consequences of the child's maturation. It has become evident, too, that every subject and all methods of teaching are value laden. The teacher may declare his purpose to be to teach mathematical processes only. But his examples, especially at elementary levels, will be impregnated with cultural details. The first American arithmetic text (1785) listed among the items to be studied: Table to find Easter from the year 1753 to 4199, Plain Oblique Angular Trigonometry, To Measure a Rhombus, To gauge a Wash Tub, The Proportions and Tonnage of Noah's Ark. A mid-nineteenth century text propounded this problem:

> There were 7 farmers, 3 of whom drank rum and whiskey, and became miserable; the rest drank water, and were healthy and happy. How many drank water?

Children in the U.S.S.R. are put to computing man hours required to harvest grain on a collective farm. Of course these cultural elements may be avoided, and children drilled on numerical processes in the abstract. Even so, they will learn in addition to the 4 times table, that it is permissible or shameful to fail, to be prompted by or to prompt another child, that mathematics is more or less important than skill in singing or pitching ball. The values of a culture cannot be eliminated from the classroom. The school may decline to teach religion; it cannot escape teaching ethics. The very fact that school is made compulsory, that literacy is prerequisite to franchise, teaches the child that knowledge is considered a key to man's control of his destiny. The school may teach authoritarian or democratic ethics; what it cannot be is morally neutral. As John L. Childs declares, "It is because some conception of what is humanly significant and desirable is implicit in all nurture of the young that we may say without exaggeration that each program of deliberate education is, by nature, a moral undertaking."

Acceptance of this view has led some educators to propose that the schools make their teaching of moral and spiritual values explicit. They see in such an undertaking a defensible alternative to religious instruction in the schools. The Educational Policies Commission defends and elaborates this alternative in their recent publication, *Moral and Spiritual Values in the Public Schools*. They propose that the school deliberately teach those values which they consider generally accepted by American society. They believe, moreover, that these values—among them respect for the human personality, devotion to truth, institutions as the servants of men, common consent, brotherhood—can be taught without reference to sectarian doctrines, even without religious sanctions. Agreement on what constitutes moral behavior, the Educational Policies Commission believes, is much more general than agreement on their religious source and justification. All denominations believe that the ultimate sanction for moral behavior is religious. Other Americans, Dewey, for example, seek sanction for moral behavior in knowledge of man's nature and in comparative studies of various social and political organizations. The anthropologist Ashley Montagu locates sanctions in the nature of the human organism: "The basic test of a value is the extent to which it contributes to the survival of the organism as a healthy and harmonically functioning interdependent whole." The Educational Policies Commission illustrates its proposal for teaching moral behavior without recourse to religious sanctions in the series of teacher-pupil interchanges on the subject of honesty which is included among the selections under "Illustrations" in this book. Seven different approaches to a child's wish to keep a dime given him by a clerk who gave him more change than he was entitled to are presented. The methods and arguments used by the seven hypothetical teachers differ, but in no case is a religious sanction employed. The child is told in effect, "You will not like yourself," "Your friends will not like you," "You may be arrested for stealing," "Other people may take your property," or only, "It's wrong." He is not told, as a Teachers' Manual for New York City schools in 1830 directed:

Teacher. God always sees you. (Slowly, and in a soft tone.)
Scholar. God always sees me.
T. God hears all you say.
S. God hears all I say.
T. God knows all you do.
S. God knows all I do.
T. You should fear to offend Him, for He is most Holy.
S. I should fear to offend Him, for He is most Holy.

The Educational Policies Commission declares that "the powerful sanctions of religious creeds and doctrines . . . may not be explicitly invoked in the public school classroom," though it recognizes that these sanctions may be used in moral instruction in the home and church. The publication does not discuss the consequences of possible conflict among sanctions employed by the school, the home, and the church. Certainly systematic avoidance of religious sanctions in schools makes the school an advocate of a secular view of life. It is on this ground that those who believe deeply in the importance of imbuing the total education of the child with religious qualities defend parochial schools.

The rights of parents of this persuasion were affirmed in the United States by the Supreme Court decision in the Oregon case. In this case an Oregon law compelling parents to send their children to public schools was declared unconstitutional. In some countries these rights are recognized by provision of public support for parochial as well as public schools. In Scotland, since 1918, Roman Catholic, Anglican, and other denominational schools have been a part of the system of public education. The

Netherlands, Scotland, Canada, and France are among the countries that have also supported some type of dual system of public and parochial schools. In America this practice is not constitutional. But even in America some compromises with the principle of no public funds for the support of churches or church schools have been made. Breaches in the high wall separating church and state, public and parochial education, have been made and have been affirmed by court decisions. Public funds in various localities have been authorized for textbooks and for transportation for children in parochial schools. Where the courts have upheld these practices, however, it has been on the grounds that the money was being expended not in behalf of the parochial school but for the benefit of the child.

Although the church and the school are generally considered major agents in the education of the young, their participation can hardly be described as a genuine partnership. In the eyes of some they are competing agents, a situation variously judged undesirable and remediable or proper and unavoidable.

COMMUNICATIONS AS EDUCATION

When Socrates discusses the education of the young, he includes among the unofficial "educators" not only the stories children hear but the public spectacles young men attend. Even the reactions of the audience, he recognized, add to or subtract from the effect of what is heard and seen.

> "Why, when," I said, "the multitude are seated together in assemblies or in court-rooms or theatres or camps or any other public gatherings of a crowd, and with loud uproar censure some of the things that are said and done and approve others, both in excess, with full-throated clamour and clapping of hands, and thereto the rocks and the region round about re-echoing redouble the din of the censure and the praise. In such case how do you think the young man's heart, as the saying is, is moved within him? What private teaching do you think will hold out and not be swept away by the torrent of censure and applause, and borne off on its current, so that he will affirm the same things that they do to be honorable and base, and will do as they do, and be even such as they?"

Even though athletic contests or theatrical presentations are designedly recreational, they are rarely merely that. The gladiatorial contest, the bullfight, the baseball game inculcate admiration of qualities valued in particular cultures. Frequently the dramatist intends to teach. Man's duties to God and to other men were purposely taught by the Greek tragedies, and by medieval mysteries and moralities; they are taught today by *The Cocktail Party* and *The Diary of Anne Frank*. Properly speaking, however, the modern parallels to the Greek tragedies and the medieval moralities as "collective representations" transmitting cultural values are Hollywood and TV productions that reach mass audiences.

The effects of these mass media are described as revolutionary. So, too, was the invention and exploitation of printing. But the effects of the twentieth-century revolution in communications may exceed that of book publishing, especially on children. Printing made possible more schooling. Films and television provide mass education outside the schoolhouse. Though many of the most influential books in history also had their initial and primary effect outside school or college walls, they had their effect only on the literate. *Pilgrim's Progress, Uncle Tom's Cabin, The Jungle* changed men's minds long before anyone thought of including them in courses in literature. The effect of the *Federalist Papers* and *Common Sense* on American political ideas, of *On the Origin of Species* on religious beliefs and social theory did not originate in schools. "For books . . . contain a potency of life in them. . . . They are as lively, and as vigorously productive, as those fabulous dragon's teeth; and being sown up and down, may chance to spring up armed men." But books require readers, some books demand skilled and highly schooled readers. The film and the TV are accessible to children and non-reading adults.

As Riesman points out in the selection in these readings, children's acquaintance with the myths and tales of their culture formerly came through oral presentations by adults. Folk tales were recounted, cautionary tales were read to children of other centuries. Today's children are exposed not only to programs planned for them but to a flood of programs intended for adult audiences. Neither they nor their parents need seek out and buy a particular story; in the case of television they need not even travel outside the home to see a particular story. Ninety-five per cent of American homes have radios, operated on an average of two hours a day; 80 per cent have television sets, operated on the average more than four hours a day. In some areas percentages run even higher.

> The things heard and watched and read influence the behavior of today's American from the time he rises until he goes to bed; they affect the way business is operated, courtship conducted, freedom defined, and public policy made. Mass communication has become almost as much a part of the environment of today's American as the air he breathes.[8]

The fact that children see TV programs at home, often with parents, gives what they see a kind of sanction that may reinforce their effect. Group viewing of films by adolescents also reinforces the effect of what is seen in a way unlikely to accompany solitary reading of books.

[8] Educational Policies Commission, *Mass Communication and Education* (Washington, D. C., National Education Association, 1958), p. 7.

Films and television not only expose children earlier and more constantly to adult stories, problems, and values, they present these materials in a far more realistic medium than that of the written word. The dragons and giants of fairy stories, even the bad men of penny-dreadfuls, did not spit the real fire of bombers or bleed in technicolor. The fairy tale princess and Little Dorrit might be imagined in each child's own image; modern-day children know that heroes and heroines must look like the current movie stars. The "pictures in our heads," as Walter Lippmann calls the culturally derived stereotypes that shape our perception of people and events, are the more sharply engraved when they are derived from the realistic presentations of movies and TV. The opinions of news commentators and panelists gain prestige through presentation on radio or TV. They tend to become far more powerful influence figures for adolescents than their teachers. Film and television thus provide an omnipresent, highly realistic, adult-oriented education for children before they enter school and throughout their school years. "It seems self-evident," one analyst of the film industry declares, "that Hollywood represents a challenge to the sovereignty of church, school, and family in the realm of values."

Critics of mass media often talk as though their effects were entirely undesirable. Recently films, TV, and comic books have been the subject of special Senate hearings to investigate juvenile delinquency. The numerous authorities on child psychology and psychiatry who testified at these hearings differ substantially in the degree of relationship they believe exists between juvenile delinquency and the presentation of crimes of violence in films and on TV. Most of these experts agree that the causes of children's behavior are complex, and that mass media cannot be held primarily responsible. They also agree, however, that much of what is presented through these communication channels may lead children to regard violence as permissible. For children who have other reasons for being emotionally disturbed, films and TV programs depicting violence may trigger latent aggressive behavior and teach specific anti-social behaviors and techniques.

But the publicity accorded discussions of the adverse effects of mass media should not obscure their very positive effects. Children learn acceptable ways of behaving as well as techniques of law-breaking; if war pictures show magnified scenes of violence, they may also show the futility of war. If the films, through pictures like *The Birth of a Nation* and hundreds of portrayals of Negroes as figures of ridicule, have taught children and adults to regard Negroes as less than human, they have also, especially in recent years, shown Negroes as people of dignity and achievement—as people rather than stereotypes. Beyond any such particular effects, however, the major revolution brought about by the new mass media is the creation of a new kind of student.

The children who come to school today are, of course, still children. They have many of the qualities that children had when they came to the one-room schoolhouses of a hundred years ago. But today's child is likely to be much more widely informed than his grandfather or father, and this largely as a result of his exposure to mass media. Unlike his grandparents, the average American child has seen and heard the President of the United States and representatives to the United Nations from Africa, Asia, and Europe. He has almost surely seen a major league baseball game; he may also have seen an opera, the take-off and landing of great planes, the firing of a space rocket, a documentary film of life under the ocean. The modern child's horizons, his fund of secondary experience, have been enormously expanded. In this respect he comes to school with live images of many things—from the look of a steel mill in operation to the look of Congress in session—that children of an earlier age learned in school as verbal abstractions. On the other hand, the modern child may have gained this wealth of secondary information at the expense of first-hand experience. He may have seen major league players but have played little baseball himself. He is, especially if he lives in a city, more likely to have watched hours of Lassie on TV than to have owned a dog, ridden a horse, caught a catfish. Moreover, exposure to programs of an expanded, often sensationalized adult world may leave the child too over-stimulated to respond to the relatively undramatic events of the classroom. Elizabeth Bowen's comment on the impact of a technological society is particularly applicable to the effects of mass media on the child. "Overhung, as we are," she writes, "by the nominal, concrete 'marvels' of our century—the triumphs of science, the masterworks of technology—we are creatures of numbed fancy and stunned senses." Finally, though mass media depict cultural virtues as well as vices, many educators consider that they tend to celebrate a less idealized picture of the American way of life than the school endeavors to promulgate.

How can the schools respond to the challenge of the mass media? Whatever else they may do, they can hardly ignore them. A society convinced of their educational import may endeavor to control them, especially to control the communication media to which children are exposed. Plato suggests such a course in his design for a model republic. The U.S.S.R. exercises such control. George S. Counts, who has observed and written about Soviet education for a generation believes that a major strength of Soviet education is that it is conceived in extremely broad terms.

> . . . it embraces the entire cultural apparatus, all of the agencies involved in the molding and the informing of the minds of both young and

old. It includes the school system from nursery school and kindergarten to university and scientific institute . . . it also includes for all practical purposes the press in its many forms and manifestations—the newspaper, the periodical, the book, the library, the bookstore, and even the lowly calendar. It includes the newer media of mass communications such as the radio and television. It includes all agencies and entertainment—the theatre, the moving picture, the circus, the playground, the club, the museum, and the public park. . . . It includes the political and cultural aspects of all organizations and particularly the organizations for children and youth.[9]

The Soviet view of the dimensions of education is a realistic one. But their centralized control of all of these agencies and organs is completely at variance with the democratic tradition. In America even those who believe there is a direct relationship between crime and motion pictures and comics, are disinclined to call for official censorship. At most they recommend self-censorship by film makers and publishers at the source and by parents at the consumer level.

Probably the most promising alternative for the schools is to find ways of exploiting the strengths of the mass media. Schools can—and increasingly do—tap these new avenues of information for students and build upon them. New courses of study in the social sciences and the language arts include units designed to teach children to select and appraise these media critically. In the past ten years the aims of teaching English have widened to include listening and viewing as well as reading, writing, and speaking. The coming decade will doubtless see major developments in the adaptation of television techniques to classroom teaching. Properly exploited mass media techniques can dramatize the teaching of science, languages, mathematics, and the social studies in a way previously undreamed of.

THE SCHOOL AND THE SOCIAL ORDER

A current slogan, intended to promote public interest in education, declares: "Better schools build better citizens; better citizens build a strong community." Plato, too, thought that if youth were well educated the welfare of the state would be assured. Jefferson was convinced that the preservation of the government and the principles for which it stood could only be secured by educating the citizenry. And men have looked to education not only to preserve national governments, but also, especially in modern times, to preserve international peace. H. G. Wells's observation, "Human history becomes more and more a race between education and catastrophe," is often quoted by those who believe that, if only it were possible to edu-

[9] George S. Counts, *The Challenge of Soviet Education* (New York, McGraw-Hill, 1957), p. 5.

cate enough of the world's population, war would become a thing of the past. Unfortunately, there seems to be little relation between education as such and the liberal society envisioned by eighteenth-century philosophers and statesmen or the dream of a parliament of peaceful nations. On the contrary, the major wars of the nineteenth and twentieth centuries have been waged by more and more highly educated nations. It would appear to be about as accurate to say that wars are made possible by education as that they are averted by it.

Those who see a uniformly positive relationship between education and social well-being assume that education is something good in and of itself. Usually these and similar pronouncements assume also that education is always everywhere the same, and that it must result in producing reasonable men—who will agree with other reasonable men, like the proponent. But practical men and politicians have long recognized that the relationship between education and the social order is more than a generalized relationship. They have realized, as Aristotle did, that the relationship was a particular one, that different forms of government required education adapted to their forms. "The best laws," he declared, "though sanctioned by every citizen of the state, will be of no avail unless the young are trained by habit and education in the spirit of the constitution, if the laws are democratical, democratically, or oligarchically if the laws are oligarchical." When Prussian education was reorganized following the defeat by Napoleon at Jena, von Humboldt warned: "What you would put into the state, you must first put into the schools." In recent years Nazi Germany and the U.S.S.R. have provided striking demonstrations of the effects of reorganizing the schools to initiate and maintain a particular social order. These effects, however, were achieved under totalitarian systems in which not the schools alone but the whole fabric of society—including the entire range of educative institutions—could be remodeled more or less simultaneously. These examples give a spurious impression of the power of the schools to effect social change. In less centralized political systems the school may have an effect on the social order, but since it is only one of many institutions that form public opinion and inculcate attitudes, its effect may be counteracted, even nullified, by these other forces.

To what degree is the school a creature of society, molded in its image, limited in its function to reinforcing the status quo? Is the school, especially the modern school, as Karl Mannheim describes it, "a replica, on a small scale, of the conflicting purposes and tendencies which rage in society at large"? And if it is, how can it change the larger image? Dewey, who saw the school as a potential force for social change, believed at the same time that the schools should be made more life-like. But the life within the school he would have to some degree ordered, controlled, idealized from the life of the market place. The "progressive" movement in education was centrally concerned with the relationship of school and society. But its interest was not in adjusting the learner to society as it existed but in preparing him to improve it. When Dewey unscrewed the chairs in the classroom, encouraged pupil activity, set time schedules by the character of the task, and replaced recitations by individual and group projects, it was to prepare children to play an active part in shaping their society. Progressive educators deplored the practices of conventional schools described by the Lynds:

> The school like the factory, is a thoroughly regimented world. Immovable seats in orderly rows fix the sphere of activity of each child. . . . Bells divide the day into periods. For the six-year-olds the periods are short (fifteen to twenty-five minutes) and varied; in some they leave their seats, play games, and act out make-believe stories, although in "recitation periods" all movement is prohibited. As they grow older, the taboo upon physical activity becomes stricter, until by the third or fourth year practically all movement is forbidden except the marching from one set of seats to another between periods, a brief interval of prescribed exercise daily, and periods of manual training or home economics once or twice a week. There are "study periods" in which children learn "lessons" from "textbooks" prescribed by the state and "recitation periods" in which they tell an adult and each other what the book has said. . . .[10]

Their objections stemmed in part from their belief that these practices were antagonistic to what had been learned about child nature and development. But they objected, also, though not always explicitly, to the assumptions about society and the individual's role in it that seemed to underly these practices. They rejected the idea of a society as rigid as was suggested in existing school practices; they believed that children educated to give textbook answers would be unprepared to deal creatively with the problems of a changing society.

Current critics of American society frequently attribute to progressive education many of the changes in society and social character they deplore. The "new" education is held responsible for conformity, irresponsibility, and "creeping socialism." A common rebuttal on the part of progressive educators to such attacks is that in fact a relatively small proportion of our schools ever fully adopted the principles of progressive education. But though this assertion is undoubtedly true, it does not account for the substantial changes in twentieth-century school practices. More important, it does not consider the likelihood that many of these changes might have occurred independently of John Dewey and the "progressive" movement.

[10] R. S. Lynd and H. M. Lynd, *Middletown* (New York, Harcourt, Brace, 1929), p. 188f.

The School in Context

Sociologists like Lynd, Whyte, and Riesman remind us that other social forces in America have exerted powerful pressures toward conformity and personal irresponsibility. They hold the trend toward big government, big business, and mass media accountable for the individual's sense of separation from decision making, his predilection for security, his taste for an increasingly homogenized culture. Riesman reminds us further that these characteristics of American society and American culture are not recent in origin, that John Stuart Mill and de Tocqueville described the tendency to conformity in America a century ago—before the common school was sufficiently common to have had any mass effects.

Whatever its effects, the school itself is affected by the society of which it is a part. Commager's discussion of the interrelationship between school and society, included among the readings in this section, develops the thesis that the school is at once a reflection of its society and an instrument for its improvement. The aims of the schools in a democracy, he contends, should be in harmony with fundamental democratic principles: the exaltation of reason, enterprise, discipline, imaginative boldness, tolerance, pluralism, freedom, and faith. But if the schools are to succeed in these aims, Commager insists, society must exemplify them also. In this he echoes the views of John Stuart Mill, who considered the nature of a government's educative effect a major criterion of its goodness. "The first question in respect to any political institution is, how far they tend to foster in the members of the community the various desirable qualities, moral and intellectual." When the scramble for easy money and political corruption are tolerated in business and government, the school will find it difficult to teach honesty and integrity. Try as it will to inculcate respect for intelligence and intellectual achievement within classroom walls, the public comparison of the salary scales of public entertainers and of the country's top scientists constitutes an impressive lesson to the contrary. The weight of public approval for cars and houses and ideas that conform to current fashion places an almost insurmountable burden on the school that tries to encourage originality. Almost, Commager believes, but not wholly insurmountable. The schools can and have, he thinks, served as the conscience of society, constantly striving to pass on the best in our culture and at least partially succeeding.

In fact, American schools have had a major part in transforming an aggregate of widely diversified ethnic and religious groups into an American people. When Denis Brogan looks, as an Englishman, at the American school he is impressed with its success in teaching these diverse millions "a common language, common habits, common tolerances, a common political and national faith." This is an accomplishment of major dimensions. Margaret Mead, in another of the readings in this section, doubts that the school can effect changes of this magnitude. Significant modifications of an existing cultural pattern, she implies, can only be made through economic and political measures which change adults. Only what has become internalized in adult beliefs and habits can be successfully transmitted to the young. In its essential features the die is cast before the child comes to school and such changes as the school begins are likely to be recast by the world the child encounters when he leaves the school.

At first glance these two views—that the school has made the America we know and that the school is powerless to reconstruct society and social behavior—seem irreconcilable. They are not so. And the reason they are not, at least as far as the American character and the American culture are concerned, is that the American school, as Brogan perceives, is a new kind of school. Unlike the conventional schools of Europe, which educate a part of the population to carry on a part of the culture, the American school undertook to educate all of the people in all of a culture. Where conventional schools set themselves the task of teaching intellectual skills, the American school has undertaken to teach social skills and behavior. And it has succeeded in large measure precisely because it has taken on many of the features of other social institutions. It has adapted to its purposes some of the characteristics of the family, it has utilized the educative force of the child's peer group, it has taken on the attributes of religious ritual. In the American school children discuss the problems of family life in a setting that emulates that of the intimate family setting. They learn practical politics by campaigning for class and school officers. They learn a hard-headed tolerance through playing on basketball and football teams whose roster includes names from all the nations of Europe. Their national loyalty is shaped not only in formal classes in American history but in daily exercises in which they pledge allegiance to the Stars and Stripes and sing "America" and "The Star Spangled Banner." The school that teaches these things may accomplish less in teaching foreign languages and advanced mathematics than schools that concentrate on these academic matters. Unlike the European schools, the American schools were presented with an unprecedented social task.

Even so, there are many who decry the school's acceptance of tasks they think more proper to the family, church, and other social institutions. Robert Maynard Hutchins is one of the spokesmen for this view. "Today as yesterday," he thinks, "we may leave experience to other institutions and influence and emphasize in education the contribution that it is supremely fitted to make, the intellectual training of the young." It seems unlikely, however, that the American school will, at least in the near future, revert to its earlier focus on formal instruction only. Even the critics of the school's expanded function tend to argue for a revision of priorities, a redistribution of emphasis, rather than for the elimination of these newer functions. Certainly the American public continues to show its approval, in opinion polls, and in such pronouncements as that of the White House Conference on Education, for the efforts of the schools to educate for citizenship, for family life, for democratic human relations as well as in the intellectual disciplines. As Americans become increasingly informed about the intellectual achievements of the schools in other countries, Russia especially, they may come to demand that American schools emulate these achievements. But they are likely to demand more mathematics, science, and foreign language in addition to rather than in place of courses in Home Economics, Problems of Democracy, and the extensive extra-curricular activities that have become traditional in American schools. Educational patterns are not, as James B. Conant observes, "an exportable commodity." The solutions to the problems of scope, emphasis, and social influence of American schools must be sought within the context of American society and social institutions.

WHAT SHOULD THE READER DO?

It is a commonplace to remark that different epochs have distinctive qualities. The names conferred upon them—The Periclean Age, The Renaissance, The Reformation, The Age of Reason, The Romantic Era, The Flowering of New England, The Mauve Decade, The Age of Anxiety, The Space Age—memorialize men's efforts to epitomize these qualities. Relatively early in their educational experience students are acquainted with evidences of the influence of the dominant character of an era upon its architecture, its art, literature, even its dress. Somewhat later the student may come to see that these cultural and temporal influences have not only shaped a style of expression but have also put their mark on fundamental beliefs and ways of thinking. Exceptional men, of course, have broken through the patterns of their times and have themselves helped set the mold for the intellectual preoccupations of succeeding generations. But all educated men can achieve the satisfaction of learning to recognize in their own thinking its correspondence to or deviations from the intellectual temper of their time and place. His understanding of his tendency to feel and think like a man of the eighteenth century helped Henry Adams to understand the twentieth century or at the least to understand why it always escaped him. "The boy looked out on the world with the instinct of resistance; for numberless generations his predecessors had viewed the world chiefly as a thing to be reformed, filled with evil forces to be abolished. . . ." To the end Henry Adams looked thus on the life of his own time; but he had the measure of his lens.

This book generally and this section particularly bear the hallmark of the twentieth century: interest in process and interrelationships. It has become almost second nature for modern man to ask of any event or situation: How did it come about? What is involved? The public press no longer confines itself to reporting; it seeks, sometimes on insufficient bases, to analyze. Case studies, which present not only a chronology of events but also the motives, involvement, and interaction of individuals and institutions, are now standard journalistic procedure for murders, international situations, strikes, and Supreme Court decisions. When a child in school fails to learn or continuously disrupts classroom routines, no one any longer believes that a single cause or a single cure can be found. Even those who question the propriety of placing the responsibility for dealing with these problems exclusively on the school, agree that problems develop and do not merely occur. They expect also to find that the causes are many and complex in their relationship.

This habit of mind is a result of the gradual assimilation of the explorations of scholars into the interrelationships and interactions of forces and institutions previously studied as discrete entities. A list of germinal books in the social sciences written in the past half-century would demonstrate a persistent effort to relate different kinds of phenomena to each other. Charles H. Cooley, *Human Nature and the Social Order;* Frederick Jackson Turner, *The Significance of the Frontier in American History;* Charles Beard, *An Economic Interpretation of the Constitution;* J. G. Frazer, *The Golden Bough*—in each of these, and in others of comparable influence, the effects of one class of events upon another were examined. Human biology we learned is biosocial; geography and economic conditions affect the course of history; economic interests infiltrate political theory; religious beliefs are culturally conditioned. It is not surprising, then, that the single most influential book in education in the modern period, John Dewey's *Democracy and Education,* examined education in its social setting.

The reader has already been asked to consider as he reads how the purposes of the schools are affected not only by ideas of man's nature and end but also by the consequences of practical decisions about who shall go to school for how long. The reader has also been reminded that changes in school purposes and population raise problems and initiate changes in teacher selection and education. In this section of the text and readings the reader is urged to look at the entire educational enterprise as one figure in the web of culture. The introductory text and the selections in this part of the book are centered upon the concept of culture, one of the key integrative concepts of this era. The reader, it is hoped, will begin to realize that proposals to "raise standards" in high school, to lengthen the school day, to provide special schools for delinquent children cannot be considered in isolation. By raising standards of academic achievement the school may simplify its task—if its task be only intellectual training. But if it is to teach

Americans of all kinds to live and work together how can it achieve this end if the less able are debarred from the school community? If fourteen-year-olds are discharged from schools, can the labor market absorb them? If it cannot, what other provisions can be made for this group—which our culture does not regard as adult? As a prospective teacher, the reader may see merit in a longer school day, even a longer school year; if he takes the position of prospective parent, he must ask whether further extension of the school's jurisdiction over the child's life will not further disrupt a fragile and tenuous family life. As he follows current educational issues, the reader, if he has begun to sense the complexity and far-reaching implications of each individual proposal, will ask, "In whose interest?" "At what cost?" "With what effect on other social institutions?" Most if not all of the reader's subsequent professional education will require him to concentrate his attention on the school and the children in it. At this point then, it is particularly important that he learn as much as possible through reading about and observing other social institutions that educate the child.

The selection by Dobinson should serve to remind the reader that he can learn much about education in his own culture by comparing it with that in other cultures. For the first time the educational system of another country has become a topic of general interest in America. There will undoubtedly be many opportunities in the years to come for the readers of this book to learn more about Russian education and about education in other countries than has been customary among American teachers heretofore. There is probably no better vantage point for a critical view of native institutions and practices than that provided by knowledge of a different social order. At the same time, realization of the organic relationship between an educational system and its cultural setting should deter the informed from assuming that one nation's schools can be successfully modelled on those of another.

If, like Henry Adams, the reader is willing to try to recapture his own experiences and to put them on paper, he may learn more than reading can tell him about how he came to be the person he now is. "I am a part of all that I have met," Tennyson wrote in recollection. How the reader first came to school, why he learned to like it, or what taught him to dislike it, what attitudes of others, what experiences of his own led him to think of teaching are worth recollecting. Though what he discovers in this way may not fully explain even himself to himself, it will almost certainly give him some sense of the complexity of the educational process. Such an exercise together with these and further readings should initiate a habit of looking at all experience—his own, and eventually his students'—as educative. He will find himself facing a question that will probably engage him throughout his teaching career: Of all the educative experiences that affect the growing child, which are peculiarly the domain of the school?

Growing Up in Two Cultures

GROWING UP IN NEW GUINEA *

EARLY EDUCATION

The Manus baby is accustomed to water from the first years of his life. Lying on the slatted floor he watches the sunlight gleam on the surface of the lagoon as the changing tide passes and repasses beneath the house. When he is nine or ten months old his mother or father will often sit in the cool of the evening on the little verandah, and his eyes grow used to the sight of the passing canoes and the village set in the sea. When he is about a year old, he has learned to grasp his mother firmly about the throat, so that he can ride in safety, poised on the back of her neck. She has carried him up and down the long house, dodged under low-hanging shelves, and climbed up and down the rickety ladders which lead from house floor down to the landing verandah. The decisive, angry gesture with which he was reseated on his mother's neck whenever his grip tended to slacken has taught him to be alert and sure-handed. At last it is safe for his mother to take him out in a canoe, to punt or paddle the canoe herself while the baby clings to her neck. If a sudden wind roughens the lagoon or her punt catches in a rock, the canoe may swerve and precipitate mother and baby into the sea. The water is cold and dark, acrid in taste and blindingly salt; the descent into its depths is sudden, but the training within the house holds good. The baby does not loosen his grip while his mother rights the canoe and climbs out of the water.

* Margaret Mead, *Growing Up in New Guinea; a Comparative Study of Primitive Education* (New York, William Morrow & Company, 1930), pp. 23-50, 259-77, abridged. Copyright 1930 by Margaret Mead.

Growing Up in Two Cultures 467

Occasionally the child's introduction to the water comes at an even earlier age. The house floor is made of sections of slats, put together after the fashion of Venetian blinds. These break and bend and slip out of place until great gaps sometimes appear. The unwary child of a shiftless father may crawl over one of these gaps and slip through into the cold, repellent water beneath. But the mother is never far away; her attention is never wholly diverted from the child. She is out of the door, down the ladder, and into the sea in a twinkling; the baby is gathered safely into her arms and warmed and reassured by the fire. Although children frequently slip through the floor, I heard of no cases of drowning and later familiarity with the water seems to obliterate all traces of the shock, for there are no water phobias in evidence. In spite of an early ducking, the sea beckons as insistently to a Manus child as green lawns beckon to our children, tempting them forth to exploration and discovery.

For the first few months after he has begun to accompany his mother about the village, the baby rides quietly on her neck or sits in the bow of the canoe while his mother punts in the stern some ten feet away. The child sits quietly, schooled by the hazards to which he has been earlier exposed. There are no straps, no baby harnesses to detain him in his place. At the same time, if he should tumble overboard, there would be no tragedy. The fall into the water is painless. The mother or father is there to pick him up. Babies under two and a half or three are never trusted with older children or even with young people. The parents demand a speedy physical adjustment from the child, but they expose him to no unnecessary risks. He is never allowed to stray beyond the limits of safety and watchful adult care.

So the child confronts duckings, falls, dousings of cold water, or entanglements in slimy seaweed, but he never meets with the type of accident which will make him distrust the fundamental safety of his world. Although he himself may not yet have mastered the physical technique necessary for perfect comfort in the water, his parents have. A lifetime of dwelling on the water has made them perfectly at home there. They are sure-footed, clear-eyed, quick-handed. A baby is never dropped; his mother never lets him slip from her arms or carelessly bumps his head against door post or shelf. All her life she has balanced upon the inch-wide edges of canoe gunwales, gauged accurately the distance between house posts where she must moor her canoe without ramming the outrigger, lifted huge fragile water pots from shifting canoe platforms up rickety ladders. In the physical care of the child she makes no clumsy blunders. Her every move is a reassurance to the child, counteracting any doubts which he may have accumulated in the course of his own less sure-footed progress. So thoroughly do Manus children trust their parents that a child will leap from any height into an adult's outstretched arms, leap blindly and with complete confidence of being safely caught.

Side by side with the parents' watchfulness and care goes the demand that the child himself should make as much effort, acquire as much physical dexterity as possible. Every gain a child makes is noted, and the child is inexorably held to his past record. There are no cases of children who toddle a few steps, fall, bruise their noses, and refuse to take another step for three months. The rigorous way of life demands that the children be self-sufficient as early as possible. Until a child has learned to handle his own body, he is not safe in the house, in a canoe, or on the small islands. His mother or aunt is a slave, unable to leave him for a minute, never free of watching his wandering steps. So every new proficiency is encouraged and insisted upon. Whole groups of busy men and women cluster about the baby's first step, but there is no such delightful audience to bemoan his first fall. He is set upon his feet gently but firmly and told to try again. The only way in which he can keep the interest of his admiring audience *is* to try again. So self-pity is stifled and another step is attempted.

As soon as the baby can toddle uncertainly, he is put down into the water at low tide when parts of the lagoon are high and others only a few inches under water. Here the baby sits and plays in the water or takes a few hesitating steps in the yielding spongy mud. The mother does not leave his side, nor does she leave him there long enough to weary him. As he grows older, he is allowed to wade about at low tide. His elders keep a sharp lookout that he does not stray into deep water until he is old enough to swim. But the supervision is unobtrusive. Mother is always there if the child gets into difficulties, but he is not nagged and plagued with continual "don'ts." His whole play world is so arranged that he is permitted to make small mistakes from which he may learn better judgment and greater circumspection, but he is never allowed to make mistakes which are serious enough to permanently frighten him or inhibit his activity. He is a tightrope walker, learning feats which we would count outrageously difficult for little children, but his tightrope is stretched above a net of expert parental solicitude. If we are horrified to see a baby sitting all alone in the end of a canoe with nothing to prevent his clambering overboard into the water, the Manus would be equally horrified at the American mother who has to warn a ten-year-old child to keep his fingers from under a rocking-chair, or not to lean out of the side of the car. Equally repellent to them would be our notion of getting children used to the water by giving them compulsory duckings. The picture of an adult voluntarily subjecting the child to a painful situation, using his superior strength to bully the child into accepting the water, would fill them with righteous indignation. Expecting children to swim at three, to climb about like young monkeys even before that age, may look to us like forcing them; really it is simply a quiet insistence upon their exerting every particle of energy and strength which they possess.

Swimming is not taught: the small waders imitate their slightly older brothers and sisters, and after floundering about in waist-deep water begin to strike out for themselves. Surefootedness on land and swimming come almost together, so that the charm which is recited over a newly delivered woman says, "May you not have another child until this one can walk and swim." As soon as the children can swim a little, in a rough and tumble overhand stroke which has no style but great speed, they are given small canoes of their own. These little canoes are five or six feet long, most of them without outriggers, mere hollow troughs, difficult to steer and easy to upset. In the company of children a year or so older, the young initiates play all day in shallow water, paddling, punting, racing, making tandems of their small craft, upsetting their canoes, bailing them out again, shrieking with delight and with high spirits. The hottest sun does not drive them indoors; the fiercest rain only changes the appearance of their playground into a new and strange delight. Over half their waking hours are spent in the water, joyously learning to be at home in their water world.

Now that they have learned to swim a little, they climb freely about the large canoes, diving off the bow, climbing in again at the stern, or clambering out over the outrigger to swim along with one hand on the flexible outrigger float. The parents are never in such a hurry that they have to forbid this useful play.

The next step in water proficiency is reached when the child begins to punt a large canoe. Early in the morning the village is alive with canoes in which the elders sit sedately on the center platforms while small children of three punt the canoes which are three or four times as long as the children are tall. At first glance this procession looks like either the crudest sort of display of adult prestige or a particularly conspicuous form of child labor. The father sits in casual state, a man of five feet nine or ten, weighing a hundred and fifty pounds. The canoe is long and heavy, dug out of solid log; the unwieldy outrigger makes it difficult to steer. At the end of the long craft, perched precariously on the thin gunwales, his tiny brown feet curved tensely to keep his hold, stands a small brown baby, manfully straining at the six foot punt in his hands. He is so small that he looks more like an unobtrusive stern ornament than like the pilot of the lumbering craft. Slowly, with a great display of energy but not too much actual progress, the canoe moves through the village, among other canoes similarly manned by the merest tots. But this is neither child labor nor idle prestige hunting on the part of the parents. It is part of the whole system by which a child is encouraged to do his physical best. The father is in a hurry. He has much work to do during the day. He may be setting off for overseas, or planning an important feast. The work of punting a canoe within the lagoon is second nature to him, easier than walking. But that his small child may feel important and adequate to deal with the exacting water life, the father retires to the central platform and the infant pilot mans the canoe. And here again, there are no harsh words when the child steers clumsily, only a complete lack of interest. But the first sure deft stroke which guides the canoe back to its course is greeted with approval.

The test of this kind of training is in the results. The Manus children are perfectly at home in the water. They neither fear it nor regard it as presenting special difficulties and dangers. The demands upon them have made them keen-eyed, quick-witted, and physically competent like their parents. There is not a child of five who can't swim well. A Manus child who couldn't swim would be as aberrant, as definitely subnormal as an American child of five who couldn't walk. Before I went to Manus I was puzzled by the problem of how I would be able to collect the little children in one spot. I had visions of a kind of collecting canoe which would go about every morning and gather them aboard. I need not have worried. A child was never at a loss to get from house to house, whether he went in a large canoe or a small one, or swam the distance with a knife in his teeth.

In other aspects of adapting the children to the external world the same technique is followed. Every gain, every ambitious attempt is applauded; too ambitious projects are gently pushed out of the picture; small errors are simply ignored but important ones are punished. So a child who, after having learned to walk, slips and bumps his head, is not gathered up in kind, compassionate arms while mother kisses his tears away, thus establishing a fatal connection between physical disaster and extra cuddling. Instead the little stumbler is berated for his clumsiness, and if he has been very stupid, slapped soundly into the bargain. Or if his misstep has occurred in a canoe or on the verandah, the exasperated and disgusted adult may simply dump him contemptuously into the water to meditate upon his ineptness. The next time the child slips, he will not glance anxiously for an audience for his agony, as so many of our children do; he will nervously hope that no one has noticed his *faux pas*. This attitude, severe and unsympathetic as it appears on the surface, makes children develop perfect motor co-ordination. The child with slighter original proficiency cannot be distinguished among the fourteen-year-olds except in special pursuits like spear throwing, where a few will excel in skill. But in the everyday activities of swimming, paddling, punting, climbing, there is a general high level of excellence. And clumsiness, physical uncertainty and lack of poise, is unknown among adults. The Manus are alive to individual differences in skill or knowledge and quick to brand the stupid, the slow learner, the man or woman with poor memory. But they have no word for clumsiness. The child's lesser proficiency is simply described as "not understanding *yet*." That he should not understand the art of handling his body, his canoes well, very presently, is unthinkable.

In many societies children's walking means more trouble for the adults. Once able to walk, the children are a constant menace to property, breaking dishes, spilling the soup, tearing books, tangling the thread. But in Manus where property is sacred and one wails for lost property as for the dead, respect for property is taught children from their earliest years. Before they can walk they are rebuked and chastised for touching anything which does not belong to them. It was sometimes very tiresome to listen to the monotonous reiteration of some mother to her baby as it toddled about among our new and strange possessions: "That isn't yours. Put it down. That belongs to Piyap. That belongs to Piyap. That belongs to Piyap. Put it down." But we reaped the reward of this endless vigilance: all our possessions, fascinating red and yellow cans of food, photographic material, books, were safe from the two- and three-year-olds who would have been untamed vandals in a forest of loot in most societies. As in the attitude towards physical prowess, there is no attempt to make it easy for the child, to demand less than the child is capable of giving. Nothing is put out of the child's reach. The mother spreads her tiny brightly colored beads out on a mat, or in a shallow bowl, right on the floor within the reach of the crawling baby and the baby is taught not to touch them. Where even the dogs are so well trained that fish can be laid on the floor and left there for an hour without danger there are no excuses made for the tiny human beings. A good baby is a baby who never touches anything; a good child is one who never touches anything and never asks for anything not its own. These are the only important items of ethical behavior demanded of children. And as their physical trustworthiness makes it safe to leave children alone, so their well-schooled attitudes towards property make it safe to leave a crowd of romping children in a houseful of property. No pots will be disturbed, no smoked fish purloined from the hanging shelves, no string of shell money severed in a tug of war and sent into the sea. The slightest breakage is punished without mercy. Once a canoe from another village anchored near one of the small islands. Three little eight-year-old girls climbed on the deserted canoe and knocked a pot into the sea, where it struck a stone and broke. All night the village rang with drum calls and angry speeches, accusing, deprecating, apologizing for the damage done and denouncing the careless children. The fathers made speeches of angry shame and described how roundly they had beaten the young criminals.

The children's companions, far from admiring a daring crime, drew away from them in haughty disapproval and mocked them in chorus.

Any breakage, any carelessness, is punished. The parents do not condone the broken pot which was already cracked and then wax suddenly furious when a good pot is broken, after the fashion of American parents who let the child tear the almanac and the telephone book and then wonder at its grieved astonishment when it is slapped for tearing up the family Bible. The tail of a fish, the extra bit of taro, the half rotten betel nut, cannot be appropriated with any more impunity than can the bowl of feast food. In checking thefts, the same inexorableness is found. There was one little girl of twelve named Mentun who was said to be a thief and sometimes taunted with the fact by other children. Why? Because she had been seen to pick up objects floating in the water, a bit of food, a floating banana, which obviously must have fallen out of one of the half a dozen houses near by. To appropriate such booty without first making a round of the possible owners, was to steal. And Mentun would have to exercise the greatest circumspection for months if she were not to be blamed for every disappearance of property in the years to come. I never ceased to wonder at the children who, after picking up pieces of coveted paper off the verandah or the islet near our house, always brought them to me with the question, "Piyap, is this good or bad?" before carrying away the crumpled scraps.

The departments of knowledge which small children are expected to master are spoken of as "understanding the house," "understanding the fire," "understanding the canoe," and "understanding the sea."

"Understanding the house" includes care in walking over the uncertain floors, the ability to climb up the ladder or notched post from the verandah to the house floor, remembering to remove a slat of the floor for spitting or urinating, or discarding rubbish into the sea, respecting any property lying on the floor, not climbing on shelves nor on parts of the house which would give beneath weight, not bringing mud and rubbish into the house.

The fire is kept in one or all of the four fireplaces ranged two along each side wall, towards the center of the house. The fireplace is made of a thick bed of fine wood ash on a base of heavy mats edged by stout logs of hard wood. It is about three feet square. In the center are three or four boulders which serve as supports for the cooking pots. Cooking is done with small wood, but the fire is kept up by heavier logs. Neat piles of firewood, suspended on low shelves, flank the fireplaces. Swung low over the fire are the smoking shelves where the fish are preserved. Understanding of the fire means an understanding that the fire will burn the skin, or thatch, or light wood, or straw; that a smoldering cinder will flare if blown upon, that such cinders, if removed from the fireplace, must be carried with the greatest care and without slipping or bringing them in contact with other objects; that water will quench fire. "Understanding the fire" does not include making fire with the fire plow, an art learned much later when boys are twelve or thirteen. (Fire is never made by women, although they may assist by sheltering the kindling dust between their hands.)

Understanding canoe and sea come just a little later than the understanding of house and fire, which form part of the child's environment from birth. A child's knowledge of canoe is considered adequate if he can balance himself, feet planted on the two narrow rims, and punt the canoe with accuracy, paddle well enough to steer through a mild gale, run the canoe accurately under a house without jamming the outrigger, extricate a canoe from a flotilla of canoes crowded closely about a house platform or the edge of an islet, and bail out a canoe by a deft backward and forward movement which dips the bow and stern alternately. It does not include any sailing knowledge. Understanding of the sea includes swimming, diving, swimming under water, and a knowledge of how to get water out of the nose and throat by leaning the head forward and striking the back of the neck. Children of between five and six have mastered these four necessary departments.

Children are taught to talk through the men's and older boys' love of playing with children. There is no belief that it is necessary to give a child formal teaching, rather chance adult play devices are enlisted. One of these is the delight in repetition.

This random affection for repetitiousness makes an excellent atmosphere in which the child acquires facility in speech. There is no adult boredom with the few faulty words of babyhood. Instead these very groping words form an excellent excuse for indulging their own passion for repetition. So the baby says "me," and the adult says "me." The baby says "me" and the adult says "me," on and on in the same tone of voice. I have counted sixty repetitions of the same monosyllabic word, either a true word or a nonsense syllable. And at the end of the sixtieth repetition, neither baby nor adult was bored.

Other activities learned through imitation are dancing and drumming. The small girls learn to dance by standing beside their mothers and sisters at the turtle dance given to shake the dust out of the house of mourning. Occasionally a child is incited to dance at home while the mother taps on the house floor.

Similarly the art of war is learned by playful imitation. The men use spears with bamboo shafts and cruel arrow-shaped heads of obsidian. The children make small wooden spears, about two and a half feet in length and fasten tips of pith on them. Then pairs of small boys will stand on the little islets, each with a handful of spears, and simultaneously hurl spears at each other. Dodging is as important a skill as throwing, for the Manus used no shields and the avalanche of enemy spears could only be dodged. This is an art which requires early training for proficiency, and boys of ten and twelve are already experts with their light weapons. The older men and boys, canoe building on the islet, or paddling by, stop to cheer a good throw. Here again, the children are encouraged, never ridiculed nor mocked.

Fishing methods are also learned early. Older men make the small boys bows and arrows and tiny, pronged fish-spears. With these the children wander in groups about the lagoon at low tide, skirting the small rocky islands, threading their way through the rank sea undergrowth, spearing small fish for the sport of it. Their catch, except when they net a school of minnows in their spiderweb nets, is not large enough to eat. This toying with fishing is pursued in a desultory fashion by children from the ages of three to fifteen. Then they will go on expeditions of their own and sometimes join the young men on excursions to the north coast after turtle, dugong, and kingfish.

Small children are also sometimes taken fishing by their fathers. Here as little more than babies they watch the procedures which they will not be asked to practice until they are grown. Sometimes in the dawn a child's wail of anger will ring through the village; he has awakened to find his father gone fishing without him. But this applies only to small boys under six or seven. Older boys prefer the society of other children and of grown youths, but shun the company of adults. Boys of fourteen and fifteen never accompany their parents about their ordinary tasks except when a boy has fallen out with his playmates. For the few days of strain which follow he will cling closely to his parents and be officiously helpful, only to desert them again as soon as friendly relations are re-established.

Little girls do very little fishing. As very tiny children they may be taken fishing by their fathers, but this is a type of fishing which they will never be required to do as grown women. Women's fishing consists of reef fishing, fishing with hand nets, with scoop baskets and with bell-shaped baskets with an opening at the top for the hand. Girls do not begin this type of fishing until near puberty.

Of the techniques of handwork small boys learn but little. They know how to whiten the sides of their canoes with seaweed juices; they know how to tie a rattan strip so that it will remain fast; they have a rudimentary knowledge of whittling, but none of carving. They can fasten on a simple outrigger float if it breaks off. They know how to scorch the sides of their canoes with torches of coconut palm leaves, and how to make rude bamboo torches for expeditions after dark. They know nothing about carpentry except what they remember from their early childhood association with their fathers.

But children have learned all the physical skill necessary as a basis for a satisfactory physical adjustment for life. They can judge distances, throw straight, catch what is thrown to them, estimate distances for jumping and diving, climb anything, balance themselves on the most narrow and precarious footholds, handle themselves with poise, skill, and serenity either on land or sea. Their bodies are trained to the adult dance steps, their eye and hand trained to shooting and spearing fish, their voices accustomed to the song rhythms, their wrists flexible for the great speed of the drum sticks, their hands trained to the paddle and the punt. By a system of training which is sure, unhesitant, unremitting in its insistence and vigilance, the baby is given the necessary physical base upon which he builds through years of imitation of older children and adults. The most onerous part of his physical education is over by the time he is three. For the rest it is play for which he is provided with every necessary equipment, a safe and pleasant playground, a jolly group of companions of all ages and both sexes. He grows up to be an adult wholly admirable from a physical standpoint, skilled, alert, fearless, resourceful in the face of emergency, reliable under strain.

But the Manus' conception of social discipline is as loose as their standards of physical training are rigid. They demand nothing beyond physical efficiency and respect for property except a proper observance of the canons of shame. Children must learn privacy in excretion almost by the time they can walk; must get by heart the conventional attitudes of shame and embarrassment. This is communicated to them not by sternness and occasional chastisement, but through the emotions of their parents. The parents' horror, physical shrinking, and repugnance is communicated to the careless child. This adult attitude is so strong that it is as easy to impregnate the child with it as it is to communicate panic. When it is realized that men are fastidious about uncovering in each other's presence and that a grown girl is taught that if she even takes off her grass skirt in the presence of another woman the spirits will punish her, some conception of the depth of this feeling can be obtained. Prudery is never sacrificed to convenience; on sea voyages many hours in duration, if the sexes are mixed the most rigid convention is observed.

Into this atmosphere of prudery and shame the children are early initiated. They are wrapped about with this hot prickling cloak until the adults feel safe from embarrassing betrayal. And here social discipline ceases. The children are taught neither obedience nor deference to their parents' wishes. A two-year-old child is permitted to flout its mother's humble request that it come home with her. At night the children are supposed to be at home at dark, but this does not mean that they go home when called. Unless hunger drives them there the parents have to go about collecting them, often by force. A prohibition against going to the other end of the village to play lasts just as long as the vigilance of the prohibitor, who has only to turn back for the child to be off, swimming under water out of reach.

Manus cooking is arduous and exacting. The sago is cooked dry in a shallow pot stirred over a fire. It requires continuous stirring and is only good for about twenty minutes after being cooked. Yet the children are not expected to come home at mealtime. They run away in the morning before breakfast and come back an hour or so after, clamoring for food. Ten-year-olds will stand in the middle of the house floor and shriek monotonously until someone stops work to cook for them. A woman who has gone to the house of a relative to help with some task or to lay plans for a feast will be assaulted by her six-year-old child who will scream, pull at her, claw at her arms, kick and scratch, until she goes home to feed him.

The parents who were so firm in teaching the children their first steps have become wax in the young rebels' hands when it comes to any matter of social discipline. They eat when they like, play when they like, sleep when they see fit. They use no respect language to their parents and indeed are allowed more license in the use of obscenity than are their elders. The veriest urchin can shout defiance and contempt at the oldest man in the village. Children are never required to give up anything to parents: the choicest morsels of food are theirs by divine right. They can rally the devoted adults by a cry, bend or twist their parents to their will. They do no work. Girls, after they are eleven or twelve, perform some household tasks, boys hardly any until they are married. The community demands nothing from them except respect for property and the avoidance due to shame.

Undoubtedly this tremendous social freedom reinforces their physical efficiency. On a basis of motor skill is laid a superstructure of complete self-confidence. The child in Manus is lord of the universe, undisciplined, unchecked by any reverence or respect for his elders, free except for the narrow thread of shame which runs through his daily life. No other habits of self-control or of self-sacrifice have been laid. It is the typical psychology of the spoiled child. Manus children demand, never give. The one little girl in the village who, because her father was blind, had loving service demanded of her was a gentle generous child.

But from the others nothing was asked and nothing was given.

The Child's Dependence upon Tradition

We have followed the Manus baby through its formative years to adulthood, seen its indifference towards adult life turn into attentive participation, its idle scoffing at the supernatural change into an anxious sounding of the wishes of the spirits, its easy-going generous communism turn into grasping individualistic acquisitiveness. The process of education is complete. The Manus baby, born into the world without motor habits, without speech, without any definite forms of behavior, with neither beliefs nor enthusiasms, has become the Manus adult in every particular. No cultural item has slipped out of the stream of tradition which the elders transmit in this irregular unorganized fashion to their children, transmit by a method which seems to us so haphazard, so unpremeditated, so often definitely hostile to its ultimate ends.

And what is true of Manus education in this respect, is true of education in any untouched, homogeneous society. Whatever the method adopted, whether the young are disciplined, lectured, consciously taught, permitted to run wild or ever antagonized by the adult world—the result is the same. The little Manus becomes the big Manus, the little Indian, the big Indian. When it is a question of passing on the sum total of a simple tradition, the only conclusion which it is possible to draw from the diverse primitive material is that any method will do. The forces of imitation are so much more potent than any adult technique for exploiting them; the child's receptivity to its surroundings is so much more important than any methods of stimulation, that as long as every adult with whom he comes in contact is saturated with the tradition, he cannot escape a similar saturation.

It must be clearly understood that when I speak of education I speak only of that process by which the growing individual is inducted into his cultural inheritance, not of those specific ways in which the complex techniques of modern life are imparted to children arranged in serried ranks within the schoolroom. As the schoolroom is one, and an important, general educational agency, it is involved in this discussion; as it teaches one method of penmanship in preference to a more fatiguing one, it is not. This strictly professionalized education is a modern development, the end result of the invention of writing and the division of labor, a problem in quantitative cultural transmission rather than of qualitative. The striking contrast between the small number of things which the primitive child must learn compared with the necessary educational attainments of the American child only serves, however, to point the moral that whereas there is such a great quantitative difference, the process is qualitatively very similar.

After all, the little American must learn to become the big American, just as the little Manus becomes the big Manus. The continuity of our cultural life depends upon the way in which children in any event receive the indelible imprint of their social tradition. Whether they are cuddled or beaten, bribed or wheedled into adult life—they have little choice except to become adults like their parents.

When we look about us among different civilizations and observe the vastly different styles of life to which the individual has been made to conform, to the development of which he has been made to contribute, we take new hope for humanity and its potentialities. But these potentialities are passive not active, helpless without a cultural milieu in which to grow. So Manus children are given opportunity to develop generous social feeling; they are given a chance to exercise it in their play world. But these generous communistic sentiments cannot maintain themselves in the adult world which sets the price of survival at an individualistic selfish acquisitiveness. Men who as boys shared their only cigarette and halved their only *laplap,* will dun each other for a pot or a string of dogs' teeth.

So those who think they can make our society less militantly acquisitive by bringing children up in a world of share and share alike, bargain without their hosts. They can create such a world among a few children who are absolutely under their control, but they will have built up an attitude which will find no institutionalized path for adult expression. The child so trained might become a morbid misfit or an iconoclast, but he cannot make terms with his society without relinquishing the childhood attitudes for which his society has no use.

The spectacular experiment in Russia had first to be stabilized among adults before it could be taught to children. No child is equipped to create the necessary bridge between a perfectly alien point of view, and his society. Such bridges can only be built slowly, patiently, by the exceptionally gifted. The cultivation in children of traits, attitudes, habits foreign to their cultures is not the way to make over the world. Every new religion, every new political doctrine, has had first to make its adult converts, to create a small nuclear culture within whose guiding walls its children will flourish. "Middletown" illustrates how art and literature and music, history and the classics are taught in the schools, but completely neglected in adult life by the male members of the community. They are undoubtedly taught by teachers sadly lacking in real knowledge or enthusiasm, but even given the best possible teachers, the results of the teaching would not be able to hold out against the contrasting pressure of "Middletown" life. The little groups of painters and writers who cluster forlornly together in out of the way spots in America or gather in the cafes in Paris are earnest of this. Exposure to the ideas of other cultures has given them an impetus towards the artist's life which they cannot live out within their communities. And although the production of gifted artists who must flee the tradition which has but half nourished them, is better than the production of no artists at all, it is but a sorry cultural result when compared with what can be accomplished within the walls of a rich and vital tradition.

So, although it is possible to induct a few children into a cultural tradition to which they are not the lineal heirs, this is not a process by which the children are educated above their cultural background in its widest sense. The tradition of Italian painting is exchanged for the tradition of commercial success in Des Moines, Iowa; the canons of German musical life substituted for the canons of jazz. But the children have not developed a new thing; they have taken that which some adult wished to give them out of his cultural richness. Only by the contributions of adults are real changes brought about; only then can the enlistment of the next generation have important effects.

In either case, those who wish to alter our traditions and cherish the Utopian but perhaps not impossible hope that they can consciously do so, must first muster a large enough body of adults who with them wish to make the slight rearrangements of our traditional attitudes which present themselves to our culturally saturated minds. This is equally true of those who wish to import part of the developed tradition of other societies. They must, that is, create a coherent adult culture in miniature before they can hope to bring up children in the new tradition—even if they expect them to be brought up by radio. Such changes in adult attitudes come slowly, are more dependent upon specially gifted or wise individuals than upon wholesale educational schemes.

Besides encouraging a most unfounded optimism, this over-valuation of the educational process and under-valuation of the iron strength of the cultural walls within which any individual can operate, produces one other unfortunate result. It dooms every child born into American culture to victimization by a hundred self-conscious evangelists who will not pause long enough to build a distinctive culture in which the growing child may develop coherently. One such group negates the efforts of another and the modern child is subjected to miseries which the Manus child never knows, reared as it is with unself-conscious finality into a Manus adult. Not until we realize that a poor culture will never become rich, though it be filtered through the expert methods of unnumbered pedagogues, and that a rich culture with no system of education at all will leave its children better off than a poor culture with the best system in the world, will we begin to solve our educational problems. Once we lose faith in the blanket formula of education, in the magic fashion in which education, using the passive capacities of children, is to create something out of nothing, we can turn our attention to the vital matter of developing individuals, who as adults, can gradually mold our old patterns into new and richer forms.[1]

THE ALL-AMERICAN CHILD [*]

. . . In American psychoanalytical thinking, the child is born faultless, a tabula rasa, and any defects which subsequently develop are the fault of uncontrollable circumstances, or of the ignorance or malice of its parents who mar what should otherwise be a perfect, or at least perfectly adjusted, human being.

This is an interesting example of the way in which even the most intractable material will be modified until it is congruent with the major psychological emphases of a society; no theory could gain widespread acceptance in America which did not concede that the child was the hope for the future, and that he could, given the proper start in life, go further and fare better than his parents. This belief is basic in America; it probably gained its original impetus in the crucial second generation, when the child was to become the complete American the parents could never be; and it has been maintained by the best-beloved American myths and exemplars —from log cabin to White House, from newsboy to millionaire, from the ghetto to the Supreme Court, from slave to institute head. It only needs the proper upbringing to develop these potentialities in every newborn child.

But what is the proper upbringing? Ah, there's the rub. In all societies except the United States, and, to a lesser degree, the countries facing her across the Atlantic, at all periods except during the last hundred years, the answer could be given without hesitation: the proper way to bring up children is the way we were brought up. Whether the child was weaned at three months or three years, whether it was tightly swaddled or allowed complete freedom, whether it should be trained to cleanliness at the earliest possible moment or left until it could walk and talk, whether it should be allowed to crawl or be prevented from crawling, whether it should be sung to and cuddled or kept firmly apart from any contact with other people and refused all show of affection—these alternatives were simply not envisaged. There was the correct way of rearing children, and that was the end of it. When a woman bore her first child, she had the

[1] After World War II Margaret Mead revisited Manus, where the people had transformed their culture to a twentieth-century model, and in *New Lives for Old*, she re-evaluates the possible contributions of early childhood education to the new order in Manus.

[*] Geoffrey Gorer, "The All-American Child," *The American People* (New York, W. W. Norton & Co., 1948), pp. 70-105. Copyright 1948 by Geoffrey Gorer. Reprinted by permission of the publishers.

accumulated wisdom of her whole society to help her; the grandmothers, the midwives, the neighbors all spoke with one voice; every baby she had seen since she could first notice anything was being brought up in the same way; her path was clear. Of course there were individual variations, mothers who spoiled their children more, or were more severe to them, than was called for; but they were relatively narrow variations from a common pattern; and the pattern itself was unquestioned.

In America the situation is very different. Here again the second generation was crucial; the girl's mother's advice was suspect, for was it not tainted with the backwardness and superstition and unsanitariness of the old world? And even if she were inclined to follow it, there would probably be endless clashes with her husband and his mother who may have followed quite a different set of rules from quite a different country in Europe. And so they sought the American way to turn the whimpering bundle of beet-red flesh into the future president of the United States, the future dean of a women's college; they consulted the expert.

In the best mercantile tradition the demand created the supply, and experts on child rearing appeared in enormous numbers and of every degree of qualification. There were the dieticians, who gave advice as to how to make the baby as big (husky) and healthy as possible, there were the psychologists who gave advice as to how to make the baby as happy as possible, there were the disciplinarians who gave advice as to how to train the baby as early as possible, there were the romantics who gave advice as to how to keep the baby as uninhibited as possible, there were the medical men and the medicine men, the good plain quacks and the good plain crooks. The government itself was not indifferent to the demand and, through the Children's Bureau of the Department of Labor, put out pamphlets distributed by the million to tell young mothers how to bring up their offspring. These pamphlets are completely revised every few years; a comparison of the different editions gives an interesting synopsis of the vagaries of the most accepted theories of child rearing. . . .

In societies where the raising of children is patterned and consistent, detailed scientific investigation has always shown a clear and significant correspondence between the vicissitudes undergone by the young child and the most striking shared aspects of the adult character and the form and emphasis of the main institutions. What becomes of this theory if it is only by chance that two Americans have been brought up in the same way?

Despite the very great difference in practice—the extent of the difference can hardly be exaggerated—there are important regularities in the upbringing of American children which are as determining in the formation of adult character as the patterned practices are in other societies. . . .

Because of the great hopes placed on the baby, and because of the necessarily experimental manner in which it is being raised, the mother is anxious, from the very first, to find out if her baby is developing as it should. She has only one guide: comparison with the neighbor's children of similar age and social position, being raised on the same, or parallel, principles. The "science" of pediatrics is changing so rapidly that older children are no guide; they were raised under the disadvantage of old-fashioned, unscientific methods, and what may have been a good enough performance ten years ago may be quite inadequate now. And so from birth (the "correct" weight for a newborn child changes constantly, but there always is a "correct" weight) the child is placed in a competitive position vis-à-vis its age mates. The mother's pride in her child and her self-esteem as a mother depend on her baby's not falling below the average for its group. Its weight, its growth, its acquisition of bodily skills, its time of teething, its time of talking, are all points on the scale by which the baby's success is weighed. As Margaret Mead has pointed out in detail, the mother's love is conditional on the child's success in this competition with its peers; only if it is successful can the mother give it her unconditional love, for it proves she has been a success in her role as mother, that she has done her duty by the hope of the future and can look the world in the face without shame. This does not, of course, mean that the failures in this primal competition are unloved or neglected; on the contrary, even more anxious attention may be paid to their getting the proper diet, to helping them to catch up; but the love for the failures is mixed with a sense of guilt; such children are a constant reproach to the inadequacy of the mother.

As soon as a child has acquired sufficient physical independence to be let out of doors alone—certainly by the age of three, and often earlier—it will leave its family and spend most of its time with its competitors and rivals in the immediate neighborhood. It will have known and played with these children (provided the parents have stayed in the same neighborhood all the time) from the time that it could be safely taken out of the baby carriage; but this earlier sociability has taken place under the watchful and anxious eyes of the mothers. By the time the child is three the mother is likely to be occupied with a younger brother or sister; and even if she were not, even if she had complete leisure, she should be ashamed of keeping a constant eye on the child, keeping it permanently tied to her apron strings. By so doing, she would risk committing the greatest crime that an American parent can commit: she would risk turning her child into a sissy.

This concept of being a sissy is a key concept for the understanding of American character; it has no exact parallel in any other society. It has nowadays become a term of opprobrium which can be applied to anyone, regardless of age or sex; although it is analogous to some English terms of opprobrium (e.g. milksop, cry-baby, nancy, mother's darling) it is more

Growing Up in Two Cultures

than any of them. Schematically, it means showing more dependence or fear or lack of initiative or passivity than is suitable for the occasion. It can be applied to a gambler hesitant about risking his money, to a mother overanxious about the pain her child may suffer at the hands of a surgeon, to a boy shy about asking a popular girl for a "date," to stage fright, to overt apprehension about a visit to the dentist, to a little girl crying because her doll is broken, just as well as to occasions which directly elicit courage or initiative or independence and which may be responded to more or less adequately. It is the overriding fear of all American parents that their child will turn into a sissy; it is the overriding fear of all Americans from the moment that they can understand language that they may be taken for a sissy; and a very great deal of American speech and activity, so often misinterpreted by non-Americans, is designed solely to avert this damning judgment. Particularly self-confident Americans may say "I guess I'm just a sissy. . . ." when they feel quite sure that they are not. When applied to adult males (but only in that case) the term also implies sexual passivity.

To prevent this dread development, the American child is constantly urged toward independence and activity and initiative, greatly praised for every real or reported manifestation of these qualities, reproved or punished for failure. And its independent activity in the neighborhood playground is a first and most important testing ground.

This early introduction into social life away from constant parental supervision (the younger groups will normally be watched by one or two of the mothers) has a number of important consequences. First of all it presents the child with another source of authority, which it can oppose to and play against the parents. Few parents can stand against the plea of "Gee, I don't see why I shouldn't; all the other kids are allowed to," or even "John's (Mary's) mother lets him (her) do it and he's three months younger than I am." If one protects one's child more than the neighbors do, if one demands greater compliance, if one is more fussy, more anxious, does not one risk turning one's child into a sissy, or, at the very least, risk that it may be so regarded, and so taunted, by these neighbors' children, its playmates? Consequently the pace is constantly set for greater freedom, greater permissiveness, greater independence for the children. There is no absolute standard; what children of a given age are allowed or encouraged to do depends on the period, the region, the locality, the social standing and income of the parents; but what is consistent is the tendency toward greater permissiveness, greater freedom; the fiats and prohibitions of the greater number of American parents are constantly being overruled by an appeal to the authority and example of the neighbors. In this way each generation of Americans acquires in early childhood attitudes which will subsequently reinforce the belief in divided authority, the system of checks and balances, and the supreme importance of the neighbors as guides and exemplars.

With rare exceptions (as when an older brother or sister brings its junior along) the children of a play group are very much of an age, with a span of at most eighteen months to two years between the oldest and the youngest. This group of near equals is in many ways the primary group for Americans all their lives; it is against these that they must measure and prove themselves.

Although the parents no longer participate directly in much of the child's social life, the child quickly finds out that they have the keenest interest and anxiety as to how it is acquitting itself. The same competition is now going on, the same proving whether the parents have produced and reared a child up to, above, or below the average; but instead of the tests being scales or charts it is now the account that the child gives of its activities abroad when it returns home. So, from a very early age, the child finds itself a speaker before an attentive and appreciative audience of adults,[1] and discovers that what it tells produces praise or blame, love or the withdrawal of love. Again, a function of the mouth—speech—becomes of the greatest psychological importance. When the child starts to tell of its exploits and triumphs it is very small and weak, and its parents are, by comparison, very big and strong. To hold their interest, to extort their admiration and approval, the child inevitably starts to speak overemphatically, to exaggerate, to boast. The parents are so used to this (they did it themselves) that they allow it to go unchecked, mentally making the calculations which will separate the kernel of true achievement from the husk of infantile self-glorification and self-dramatization. Although as they grow up the disparity between the size and power of the speaker and the audience disappears, Americans tend to continue to talk about themselves and their accomplishments in the same manner as they did as little children; American audiences interpret this with ease; but non-Americans generally fail to, and consider it as excessive boasting and self-glorification—which it would be if they, with their quite different upbringing, spoke about themselves in the same terms and tone of voice.

In the crucial second generation there was the further complication that, in the majority of cases, parents and children had only a very limited vocabulary in common. The child's vocabulary was naturally limited by its years, that of the parents by the usual inadequacy with which untrained adults use a foreign language they have acquired only in maturity. As a consequence, most of the subtleties of English syntax and vocabulary were

[1] See Gregory Bateson, "Morale and National Character" in *Civilian Morale*, edited by Goodwin Watson (Boston, Houghton Mifflin Co., 1942).

lost; the most extreme and violent words and phrases were used to cover all gradations of meaning.

This heightened, over-dramatized, over-emphatic method of speaking is contagious; the child only half believes its own boasts and stories, and consequently only half believes what its parents say. To make the proper effect on their child, American parents must exaggerate in their turn, double the force and content of their threats and promises; a child only expects a portion of the promises (and practically none of the threats) to be carried out; but it is deeply mortified and disappointed if such promises are not made; it would suspect that it is not loved, not worthy. . . .

But although words are so important, they are never taken quite at their face value; the child never fully believes its own stories, nor its parents' threats and promises. All statements are regarded with some skepticism; there is always some exaggeration, some hokum; spoken or written words are never thought to be the whole truth. . . .

So far, in discussing the upbringing of the American child, I have avoided sex pronouns and, somewhat awkwardly, used the word "it"; unfortunately English lacks a single word for he-or-she, and it would have been necessary to use the phrase all the time, for the treatment given small boys and girls differs only slightly in degree, not at all in kind. There is, however, an important difference in effect. As was pointed out in the previous chapter, all Americans acquire a predominantly feminine conscience; and this faces the little boy with a dilemma which his sister does not experience. Because of the encapsulated mother, the little boy has doubts about his masculinity, whereas the little girl is reaffirmed in her femininity. To prove to himself, and to the world, that he is a real "he-man" (the reduplication in the term is in itself suggestive) the little boy has to be more strident, shout and boast more, call more attention to himself than his sister need. American children of both sexes are brought up very similarly, by and large face the same dilemmas, and acquire the same type of character; but all the overcompensations for insecurity—a great deal is demanded of American children, up to the limit of their powers—are far more developed in the boy.

The ideal American family consists of two children, an elder daughter and a younger son, generally known as "Sis" and "Buddy" (or "Junior"). This does not mean that this size of family, or order of birth, is statistically more common in the United States than in other countries of similar urbanization; but this is the typical composition when the average American family is pictured in illustration or advertisement, and very often in popular fiction and films. In narratives a third child, a still younger brother, is often introduced for dramatic effect.

In all societies everywhere the birth of a younger baby involves the older child in considerable psychological turmoil, if for no other reason, because the new arrival inevitably displaces the older child from the center of family love and attention. Different societies interpret this situation in different ways. Margaret Mead has suggested that the typical American reaction of the child to the newborn baby is one of resentment, because the new arrival is permitted all the babyish ways which the older child has had to abandon in its forced progress—up to the limit of its strength— toward independence and adulthood. From this initial situation she derives "the bitterness toward all those who 'have it soft,' 'get by,' 'get away with murder,' a bitterness combined with envy."

With the exception of a single combination, the relationship between brothers and sisters is without deep intensity. They have no special obligations toward one another (except to "agree," not to squabble too much); outside the rural South, the brother is not expected to defend his sister's honor, nor is he responsible for her fortune, her marriage, or her children. In the vast majority of cases brothers and sisters scatter as soon as they leave home; typically they follow different pursuits, live in different localities, and, if they go to a university, go to different ones.

The one important exception occurs when two children of the same sex, particularly two boys, are born within a short interval of each other—at the most, two years. In this case the elder brother is likely to introduce the younger brother into his play group, and later his gang; and this has some regular and typical results. The younger brother is a member of a group in the majority older than he is, and with standards of daring and accomplishment beyond the level of his years. Fired by the standard he is set, the younger brother (the "kid brother") becomes extravagantly rash in his words and actions, confident that he will be saved from the dangerous results of his behavior by his older brother's protection, by his superior strength and wisdom. . . .

As the child grows in independence and skill, its father becomes somewhat more important, particularly as an authority which can be opposed to that of the mother. Most mothers conscientiously try to build for their husbands the position of authority in the family, and tell their children to ask his permission; but they often override his decisions, on the ground that he is too severe or too lenient, that he doesn't make allowance for children or that he is spoiling them. Most American parents dislike accepting the onus of restricting their children's pleasure and amusement; and there is a very general tendency for the parent first approached to put the burden of decision on the other. Most children learn this early, and become adept at playing one parent against the other. In those households where the father controls the children's pocket money, a refused application from the father will often be made good by the mother from her domestic budget. In many families it seems as though the parents were in covert competition for their children's love.

In the September adjoining its sixth birthday every American child will go to its neighborhood school, with the insignificant exception of the very rich. This may well be in a different town or district from that in which it was born, for conscientious American parents will often, within the limits of possibility open to them, move their home to that neighborhood whose school offers the best opportunities to their offspring. Schools are rarely judged by scholastic standards or opportunities, for, within a given region, the variation is slight. They are judged by their size, by the splendor and modernity of their buildings, by the number and condition of the accessory structures—workshops, indoor gymnasiums, and the like—and often by the absence of Negro children, or too many children of the alien and foreign born. The town in which an American spends the greater part of his schooldays is known as his "home town."

At school the competition for success, by which the child can earn its parents' love and approval and rate itself in the world, is again partly formalized. In American schoolrooms scholastic performance is classified on a five-point scale, usually from A to E, though marks are sometimes used, and these grades are inscribed on the report cards which the child must take home monthly. Since C is the average for the child's peers, parents can see immediately how their child rates in his year's crop of young Americans, whether he is a credit to them and himself, and therefore worthy of unqualified love, or whether they have failed in their most important function.

School athletics are less important for the rating of young children, and, in a way, never very important for the vast majority of American children. All American boys are expected to enjoy unformalized sports, typified by the baseball game on the empty lot; but to "go out for" a school sport means to accept a quasi-professional status, to acknowledge athletic abilities above the average. Athletes as a class are admired, envied, and privileged; they represent their school against its neighbors and rivals; and all boys, at any rate, are meant to follow the fortune of their teams with the greatest enthusiasm and emotional involvement. Among the athletes themselves the competition for success, symbolized by the Letter, is extremely keen. But it is a matter of individual choice whether the boy will himself enter in this competition; extra praise and regard are given to those who successfully do so; but blame is not given to those who do not.

In the event of an inadequately equipped athlete engaging in a competition beyond his powers, the attitude of the noncompetitors and of those he competes with are strongly contrasting. The people who are not involved in the competition are likely to identify with this valiant "underdog," to admire and praise his courage, and get great vicarious satisfaction from any success against the mighty that he may achieve. In contrast, the competitors have little respect for a person "going out of his class" and are justified in using all their strength and skill to eliminate him.

As was stated earlier, the children find in the schoolteacher an authority who can nearly always be successfully opposed to the parents. The parents keep this acknowledged rival and superior under the closest scrutiny, demanding in her private life standards of conduct and moral rectitude far higher than those they apply to themselves or their neighbors. This supervision is formalized in the parent-teacher associations (P.T.A.) in which the most civic-minded parents meet with the teachers at regular intervals to discuss the school and their children. Though often in fact aided by grants from the federal or state treasury, the school is regarded as created and paid for by the initiative and taxes of the local inhabitants; it is their creation, and it is their duty to see that it compares favorably with its rivals. The American public school is justifiably one of the chief sources of American civic pride.

The American school is, in the first instance, a social device, and an extremely successful one, for stamping the American character on children, whatever their background and origins may be; it is only secondarily an institution for implanting and transmitting knowledge. Scholastic achievement is one of the few spheres where American children are not pushed to the limit of their strength; compared with any country of Western Europe, the standard required at any given age is low. Most Americans attend school for more years than most Western Europeans, however. Classwork has a few distinctive features: training is given in public speaking by the use of recitations (spoken themes) as well as by essays; civics is an important subject, often made vivid by visits to neighboring factories, constructions, police courts, and the like; biology and science are taught early; study of the dead languages, if taught at all, normally only starts at high school (from the age of fourteen); European history is practically not taught at all; growing use is made of radio and films as adjuncts to teaching; vocational training starts early (again from high school) and is given in a great number of subjects, with very complete technical equipment in the bigger urban schools. Apart from this direct vocational training, American public-school education is less directed toward equipping the children for adult life (except for the development of Americanism) than toward making their childhood enjoyable and significant; under the influence of John Dewey, most American teachers believe that "children are people"; and much class time is given over to communal tasks and discussions with little direct relevance to later life.

The constant pushing toward independence, toward adulthood, is con-

Growing Up in Two Cultures

tinued. Except for a few children of the protected rich, American boys are urged to earn, or at least supplement, their pocket money (spending money) by working after school hours. There are a number of jobs which are generally regarded as the special domain of schoolboys (except in a few states which have stringent child-labor laws); newspaper delivery in the first instance, often the delivery of groceries, the soliciting of subscriptions for, and the delivery of, magazines, mowing lawns in summer and clearing snow away from paths in winter, caddying at golf clubs, and so on. From high school onward these may be supplemented by other jobs: serving behind the ice-cream counter at a drugstore, tending furnaces, washing cars, and the like. Far from being stigmatized, these early gainful activities are universally approved; they are signs, not of parental poverty or stinginess, but of the individual's independence and self-reliance. Girls do not normally start earning as early as boys; but from high school onward they have varied opportunities for employment; of these the most general in recent years is "sitting," looking after babies or young children while the parents are out; by this means the girls simultaneously earn money (the job is well paid), demonstrate their independence, and get quiet and time for their homework.

When school starts, the mixed neighborhood play group typically gives way to gangs entirely or predominantly of one sex; and these gangs continue up to, and in some cases through, adolescence. The gang may engage in almost any kind of activity compatible with the strength and interests of its members; but nearly all the boys' gangs have one feature in common: they engage in illegal or extralegal activities. Most of these activities are harmless: robbing orchards in the country, trespassing on empty buildings, trying to get into circuses or baseball parks without paying, smoking cigarettes made of corn silk, using dirty words and engaging in sexual experimentation, staying away from school and avoiding the truant officer (a municipal official whose job it is to see that children are at school when they should be, and who can have complaints made to the parents if they are not), cheeking policemen, and the like. What is important about these activities is that they are not only tolerated but expected and praised by the adults, especially the fathers; the successful flouting of authority is a sign of independence, of growing manliness; a boy who never attempted to do so would show grave signs of turning into a sissy. One more lesson is given in the proper attitude for an American to take toward authority and the law.

The line between tolerated, venial illegalities and those which should be regarded seriously is so finely drawn that it is understandable that many youngsters overstep the mark. If it is laudable to take apples off other people's trees, why not off other people's barrows? If it is manly to smoke cigarettes made of corn silk, why not ones made of marijuana? Most children, and most gangs, do learn without committing serious harm; but when children come from neighborhoods where the law is regarded overlightly, where the concentration of immigrants is high, from the slum borders where black and white and Asiatic mingle, where Jewish-gentile strife is severe among the adults, they can and do commit really serious crimes: desecrate churchyards and synagogues, commit grievous assaults and robberies, engage in a smaller way in the type of gang activities which has made the word notorious wherever American films or detective stories have an audience. It is not uncommon for white teachers in Negro schools to be attacked with knives; and cases have occurred of young boys shooting and killing their teachers.

Only a tiny minority of American children and youths engage in such criminal activity, but there is a fear, albeit almost unformulated, on the part of the adult community that the young will carry their defiance of authority too far, beyond the necessity of independent manliness. Serious community efforts are made to channel these energies and activities into such socially approved institutions as the Boy Scouts, Sea Scouts, and Camp Fire Girls; but though these have taken on typically American forms, with enormous emphasis on the competition for badges, they still smack too much of authority and regulation to be altogether congenial to most young Americans.

Society has, however, found a far more effective way for channeling youthful energy into socially acceptable channels, and one which is thoroughly congruent with the major emphases, with the constant pushing toward adulthood, and with the belief in the superior moral nature of womanhood. Any boy or girl who is not a roughneck (the term for those who carry their independence and uncouthness too far) or a sissy will try to be as attractive as possible to the opposite sex, will engage in the patterned precourtship, heterosexual behavior called "dating." The formal beginning of this type of behavior is quite often the commencement dance at the end of the sixth grade of school, that is to say in the child's twelfth summer. Some may start earlier, particularly in the South, and some later; but for the greater number this is the formal occasion for their entry into this pre-adult world. For this dance the children usually are given their first formal party clothes, for the girls long organdie dresses with short sleeves and full skirts, for the boys white trousers and double-breasted dark coats (the fashions may have already changed). Each boy must invite one of his feminine classmates to accompany him, and happy is the mother whose daughter receives many early invitations. This is the final stretch of the competition in which the parents have vicariously engaged since they compared the babies' weights in the hospital; if one's schoolgirl daughter is in constant demand, is popular, then she has been as well-equipped as is possible, one has been a success as a mother; if she spends too many nights of the week alone, or with another unfortunate girl, that child has been a failure, and one had perhaps better concentrate on her education, so that her brains may give her the chance that her beauty and personality have failed to provide.

The mother cannot participate so directly in her son's successes, and the father is often somewhat ambivalent, feeling himself pushed aside by the rising generation, grudging the constantly increasing demands for money which numerous dates necessitate, disputing who shall have the evening use of the family car ("Gee, a girl won't look at you if you haven't got a car"). But though he may not participate so directly in the social triumphs of his son as the mother does in those of her daughter, yet he would be even more mortified if his son spent most of his evenings at home, or with other boys similarly unenterprising; for this would be proof that he had been a complete failure as an American father: he would have produced a sissy.

Education and the Family

FROM THESE I LEARNED *

1. From my grandfather Verus (I learned) good morals and the government of my temper.
2. From the reputation and remembrance of my father modesty and manly character.
3. From my mother, piety and beneficence, and abstinence, not only from evil deeds, but even from evil thoughts; and further, simplicity in my way of living, far removed from the habits of the rich.
4. From my great-grandfather, not to have frequented public schools, and to have had good teachers at home, and to know that on such things a man should spend liberally.
5. From my governor, . . . I learned endurance of labour, and to want little, and to work with my own hands, and not to meddle with other people's affairs, and not to be ready to listen to slander.
6. From Diognetus (my tutor), not to busy myself about trifling things, and not to give credit to what was said by miracle-workers and jugglers about incantations and the driving away of daemons and such things; and not to breed quails (for fighting), nor to give myself up passionately to such things; and to endure freedom of speech; and to have become intimate with philosophy; and to have been a hearer, first of Bacchius, then of Tandasis and Marcianus; and to have written dialogues in my youth; and to have desired a plank bed and skin, and whatever else of the kind belongs to the Grecian discipline.

* *The Thoughts of the Emperor M. Aurelius Antoninus.* (Second century A.D.) Translated by George Long (London, George Bell and Sons, 1887), pp. 68-75.

Education and the Family

7. From Rusticus I received the impression that my character required improvement and discipline; and from him I learned not to be led astray to sophistic emulation, nor to writing on speculative matters, nor to delivering little hortatory orations, nor to showing myself off as a man who practices much discipline, or does benevolent acts in order to make a display; and to abstain from rhetoric, and poetry, and fine writing; and not to walk about in the house in my outdoor dress, nor to do other things of the kind. . . .

8. From Apollonius I learned freedom of will and undeviating steadiness of purpose; and to look to nothing else, not even for a moment, except to reason: . . .

9. From Sextus, a benevolent disposition, and the example of a family governed in a fatherly manner, and the idea of living conformably to nature: . . .

10. From Alexander the grammarian, to refrain from fault-finding, and not in a reproachful way to chide those who uttered any barbarous or solecistic or strange-sounding expression: . . .

14. From my brother Severus, to love my kin, and to love truth, and to love justice; . . .

16. In my father I observed mildness of temper, and unchangeable resolution in the things which he had determined to do after due deliberation; and no vainglory in those things which men call honours; and a love of labour and perseverance; and a readiness to listen to those who had anything to propose for the common weal; and undeviating firmness in giving to every man according to his deserts; and a knowledge derived from experience of the occasions for vigorous action and for remission. . . . I observed too his habit of careful inquiry in all matters of deliberation, and his persistency, and that he never stopped his investigation through being satisfied with appearances which first present themselves and that his disposition was to keep his friends, and not to be soon tired of them, nor yet to be extravagant in his affection; and to be satisfied on all occasions, and cheerful; and to foresee things a long way off, and to provide for the smallest without display; and to check immediately popular applause and all flattery; and to be ever watchful over the things which were necessary for the administration of the empire, and to be a good manager for the expenditure, and patiently to endure the blame which he got for such conduct; and he was neither superstitious with respect to the gods, nor did he court men by gifts or by trying to please them, or by flattering the populace; but he showed sobriety in all things and firmness, and never any mean thoughts or action, nor love of novelty. . . . There was in him nothing harsh, nor implacable, nor violent, nor, as one may say anything carried to the sweating point; but he examined all things severally, as if

he had abundance of time, and without confusion, in an orderly way vigorously and consistently. And that might be applied to him which is recorded of Socrates, that he was able both to abstain from and to enjoy, those things which many are too weak to abstain from, and cannot enjoy without excess. But to be strong enough both to bear the one and to be sober in the other is the mark of a man who has a perfect and invincible soul, such as he showed in the illness of Maximus.

17. To the gods I am indebted for having good grandfathers, good parents, a good sister, good teachers, good associates, good kinsmen and friends, nearly everything good. . . .

LETTER TO THE MAYORS AND ALDERMEN OF ALL THE CITIES OF GERMANY *

. . . And what would it avail if we possessed and performed all else, and became perfect saints, if we neglect that for which we chiefly live, namely, to care for the young? In my judgment there is no other outward offense that in the sight of God so heavily burdens the world, and deserves such heavy chastisement, as the neglect to educate children. . . .

But all that, you say, is addressed to parents; what does it concern the members of the council and the mayors? That is true; but how, if parents neglect it? Who shall attend to it then? Shall we therefore let it alone, and suffer the children to be neglected? How will the mayors and council excuse themselves, and prove that such a duty does not belong to them?

Parents neglect this duty from various causes.

In the first place, there are some who are so lacking in piety and uprightness that they would not do it if they could, but like the ostrich, harden themselves against their own offspring, and do nothing for them. Nevertheless these children must live among us and with us. How then can reason and, above all, Christian charity, suffer them to grow up ill-bred, and to infect other children, till at last the whole city be destroyed, like Sodom, Gomorrah, and some other cities?

In the second place, the great majority of parents are unqualified for it, and do not understand how children should be brought up and taught. For they have learned nothing but to provide for their bodily wants; and in order to teach and train children thoroughly, a separate class is needed.

In the third place, even if parents were qualified and willing to do it

* *Luther on Education Including a Historical Introduction and a Translation of the Reformer's Two Most Important Educational Treatises*, F. V. N. Painter, editor and translator. Second Ed. (Philadelphia, Lutheran Publication Society, 1889), pp. 178, 179, 180, 181, 182, 249, 269, 270.

themselves, yet on account of other employments and household duties they have no time for it, so that necessity requires us to have teachers for public schools, unless each parent employ a private instructor. But that would be too expensive for persons of ordinary means and many a bright boy, on account of poverty, would be neglected. Besides, many parents die and leave orphans; and how they are usually cared for by guardians, we might learn, even if observation were not enough, from the sixty-eighth Psalm, where God calls himself the "Father of the fatherless," as those who are neglected by all others. Also there are some who have no children, and therefore feel no interest in them.

Therefore it will be the duty of the mayors and council to exercise the greatest care over the young. For since the happiness, honor, and life of the city are committed to their hands, they would be held recreant before God and the world, if they did not, day and night, with all their power, seek its welfare and improvement. Now the welfare of a city does not consist alone in great treasures, firm walls, beautiful houses, and munitions of war; indeed, where all these are found, and reckless fools come into power, the city sustains the greater injury. But the highest welfare, safety, and power of a city consists in able, learned, wise, upright, cultivated citizens, who can secure, and utilize every treasure and advantage. . . .

Since, then, a city must have well-trained people, and since the greatest need, lack, and lament is that such are not to be found, we must not wait till they grow up of themselves; neither can they be hewed out of stones nor cut out of wood; nor will God work miracles, so long as men can attain their object through means within their reach. Therefore we must see to it, and spare no trouble or expense to educate and form them ourselves. For whose fault is it that in all the cities there are at present so few skillful people except the rulers, who have allowed the young to grow up like trees in the forest, and have not cared how they were reared and taught? The growth, consequently has been so irregular that the forest furnishes no timber for building purposes, but like a useless hedge, is good only for fuel. . . .

Wittenberg, 1524

LUTHER'S SERMON ON THE DUTY OF SENDING CHILDREN TO SCHOOL, 1530

. . . "If now you have a son capable of learning; if you can send him to school, but do not do it and go your way asking nothing about temporal government, law, peace, and so on; you are, to the extent of your ability, opposing civil authority like the Turk, yea, like the devil himself. For you withhold from the empire, principality, state, city, a saviour, comforter, corner-stone, helper; and so far as you are concerned, the emperor loses both his sword and crown, the state loses protection and peace, and it is through your fault (as much as lies in you) that no man can hold in security his body, wife, child, house, property. On the contrary, you freely offer them all upon a butcher's block, and give occasion for men to degenerate into brutes, and at last to devour one another. All this you certainly do, especially if you on purpose withdraw your child from such a salutary station out of regard for his physical wants. Are you not a pretty and useful man in society! You daily enjoy the benefits of the government, and then as a return rob it of your son, dedicating him to avarice, and thus strive with all your might not to maintain government, law, and peace, but to destroy social order, though you possess and hold your body, life, property, and honor, through secular authority . . .

But I maintain that the civil authorities are under obligation to compel the people to send their children to school, especially such as are promising, as has elsewhere been said. For our rulers are certainly bound to maintain the spiritual and secular offices and callings, so that there may always be preachers, jurists, pastors, scribes, physicians, school-masters, and the like; for these can not be dispensed with. If the government can compel such citizens as are fit for military service to bear spear and rifle, to mount ramparts, and perform other martial duties in time of war; how much more has it a right to compel the people to send their children to school, because in this case we are warring with the devil, whose object it is secretly to exhaust our cities and principalities of their strong men, to destroy the kernel and leave a shell of ignorant and helpless people, whom he can sport and juggle with at pleasure. That is starving out a city or country, destroying it without a struggle and without its knowledge. The Turk does differently, and takes every third child in his empire to educate for whatever he pleases. How much more should our rulers require children to be sent to school, who, however, are not taken from their parents, but are educated for their own and the general good, in an office where they have an adequate support.

Therefore, let him who can watch; and wherever the government sees a promising boy, let him be sent to school. . . .

HOME! THOU SCHOOL OF MORALS AND OF THE STATE! *

The power developed through interaction with the immediate environment is always the source of the wisdom and power of man in dealing with the more remote.

* Johann Heinrich Pestalozzi, *The Evening Hours of a Hermit,* translated by F. L. Anderson in *Pestalozzi* (New York and London: McGraw-Hill, 1931), p. 21. (First published 1790.)

A fatherly spirit fits one for the position of ruler, a brotherly spirit for that of the citizen; both give rise to system and order in the home and the state.

The domestic relationships of mankind are the earliest and the most excellent of the relationships of Nature.

Man labors at his vocation and bears the burden of the state and government in order that he may enjoy his domestic happiness in peace.

Hence the training of the man for his calling and station in life must be subordinated to the aim of fitting him to appropriate the pure happiness of home life.

Hence the home is the place where the natural educational process runs its course.

Home! thou school of morals and of the state!

CHRISTOPHER AND ALICE *

Home and School Training. Domestic Education

"That is my chapter, father!" said Alice, when Christopher had read the twelfth chapter of our book;[1] "a pious mother, who herself teaches her children seems to me the finest sight on the earth."

"It is a very different one from a school room, at all events." said Josiah.

Alice. "I did not mean to say that schools are not very good."

Christopher. "Nor would I allow myself to think so."

Josiah. "Well, and it is true, after all, that nothing of what the schoolmaster can say will ever reach the children's hearts in the same way as what their parents teach them; and, generally speaking, I am sure there is not in school-going all the good that people fancy there is."

Christopher. "I am afraid, Josiah, thou art rather straining thy point. We ought to thank God for all the good that there is in the world; and, as for the schools in our country, we can't thank Him enough for them."

Josiah. "Well spoken, master. It is well that there are schools; and God forbid that I should be ungrateful for any good that it has done to us. But, with all this, I think that he must be a fool who, having plenty at home, runs about begging; and that is the very thing which our village folks do, by forgetting all the good lessons which they might teach their children at home, and instead thereof, send them every day to gather up the dry crumbs

* Johann Heinrich Pestalozzi, "Christopher and Alice," *The American Journal of Education*, VII (1859), pp. 665-8. (First published 1782.)

[1] "This chapter represents Gertrude in the midst of her children, teaching them, at the same time that they are engaged in spinning.—B." [Henry Barnard]

which are to be got in our miserable schools. I am sure that is not quite as it ought to be."

Christopher. "Nor is it, perhaps, quite as thou hast put it."

Josiah. "Nay, master! but only look at it in the face, and thou'lt surely see it the same as I do. That which parents can teach their children is always what they stand most in need of in life; and it is a pity that parents should neglect this, by trusting in the words which the schoolmaster makes them get by heart. It is very true, they may be good and wise words, and have an excellent meaning to them; but, after all, they are only words, and coming from the mouth of a stranger, they don't come half as near home as a father's or a mother's words."

Christopher. "I can not see what thou would'st be at, Josiah."

Josiah. "Look, master! The great point in bringing up a child is, that he should be well brought up for his own house; he must learn to know, and handle, and use those things on which his bread and his quiet will depend through life; and it seems to me very plain, that fathers and mothers can teach that much better at home, than any schoolmaster can do it in his school. The schoolmaster, no doubt, tells the children of a great many things which are right and good, but they are never worth as much in his mouth as in the mouth of an upright father, or a pious mother. The schoolmaster, for instance, will tell the child to fear God, and to honor his father and mother, for that such is the word of God; but the child understands little of what he says, and mostly forgets it again before he comes home. But if, at home, his father gives him milk and bread, and his mother denies herself a morsel, that she may give it to him, the child feels and understands that he ought to honor his father and mother, who are so kind to him, and he will not forget his father's words, which tell him that such is the word of God, as easily as the empty word of the schoolmaster. In the same way, if the child is told at school to be merciful and to love his neighbor as himself, he gets the text by heart, and perhaps thinks of it for a few days, till the nice words slip from his memory. But at home he sees a poor neighbor's wife calling in upon his mother, lamenting over her misery, her hunger, and nakedness; he sees her pale countenance, her emaciated and trembling figure, the very image of wretchedness; his heart throbs, his tears flow; he lifts up his eyes full of grief and anxiety to his mother, as if he himself was starving; his mother goes to fetch some refreshments for the poor sufferer, in whose looks the child now reads comfort and reviving hope; his anguish ceases, his tears flow no longer, he approaches her with a smiling face; at last his mother returns, and her gift is received with sobs of gratitude, which draw fresh tears from the child's eye. Here then he learns what it is to be merciful and to love one's neighbor. He learns it without the aid of words, by the real fact; he sees mercy itself, instead of learning words about mercy."

Christopher. "I must own I begin to think thou art not quite mistaken in saying that too much value is put upon the schoolmaster's teaching."

Josiah. "Of course, master! If thou sendest thy sheep up into the mountain, thou reliest upon them being well kept by the shepherd, who is paid for it, and thou dost not think of running about after them thyself; but if thou hast them at home, in thy own stables, thou lookest after them thyself. Now it is just the same thing with the school; only there is this difference, that it is easy to get for the sheep pasture which is infinitely better than the food they have in the stable; but it is not so easy to find a school in which the children are better taught than they might be at home. *The parents' teaching is the kernel of wisdom, and the schoolmaster's business is only to make a husk over it, and there even is a great chance whether it turn out well.*" . . .

Alice ". . . I know this one thing, that I will have my children more about me in future; it seems very natural, indeed, that fathers and mothers should themselves teach their children as much as they possibly can. I think there is a great deal in what Josiah says, and one really shudders, when one comes to reflect what sort of people our village schoolmasters generally are. There are many of them, I know, Christopher, whom thou wouldst not trust with a cow, or a calf, over winter; and it is very true, that one ought to look more one's self after one's children, and not fancy all is well, provided one sends them to school."

WHO IS THE PROPER JUDGE? *

WILLIAM GODWIN TO DR. MATTHEW RAINE, APRIL 12, 1808

Dear Sir,—I am a little shocked at a message I received from you yesterday by Clairmont.

This message is, "That you were the proper judge whether my reasons for detaining him from school were sufficient." To this I cannot agree.

The authority of the tutor is in my opinion derived from that of the parent, and cannot supersede it. I could never consent to lay my reasons for detaining him before you for your approbation. I should, however, be exceedingly sorry to be wanting in any sort of attention or on ceremony. If the meaning of your message is that you would wish to receive a line beforehand, requesting leave for his absence, I will cheerfully comply whenever it is possible, which is not always.—I remain, etc.,

W. Godwin

* C. Kegan Paul, *William Godwin: His Friends and Contemporaries*, Vol. II (Boston: Roberts Brothers, 1876), pp. 166-7.

DR. MATTHEW RAINE TO WILLIAM GODWIN

Charter House, April 12, 1808

Dear Sir,—It may spare you and myself some trouble if, without entering into the accuracy or inaccuracy of the statement of my message by Clairmont, I should explain to you the general rule at this place, relating to attendance upon school business. A rule of this sort I have. I hold it to be indispensably necessary; and bold as the position may be, it is a rule with which I cannot allow parental power or parental caprice to interfere. The rule is this:—That during the time for the performance of school business, no boy is allowed to be absent, except on the score of ill health, or with the leave of a master, previously had. For granting this leave I have ever been accustomed to expect, and never was refused, a sufficient reason in my own judgment, independent of the parent's will.

I have no wish certainly to pry into matters which do not concern me; but I must think that a scholar's absence always concerns a master, and it materially improves the discipline of a school that the master alone should decide on the propriety of a scholar's absence. Nor do I believe this rule to be peculiar to Charter House, but if it were, I feel so little disposition to give it up, that I should rather part with my scholar than relinquish a principle so just, and, so far as I have been concerned, so universally acknowledged. It will not be denied that the mere request of a parent for his child's absence would occasionally be complied with; but I should strongly protest against a frequent repetition of such a request. A man must be everything in his school, or he is nothing; and that parent would seem to me to act the wisest part who should so contrive that his and the schoolmaster's authority would never clash. If this cannot be without inconvenience in this or that case, I am still of the opinion that the individual instance must bend to the general rule. I trust you will believe that I have no wish to perplex you, and that I am very far from seeking to hurt any man's feelings. The point we differ upon may be a point of etiquette, but I have a rule; and, as the venerable Sergeant Hill said, "If I part with my rule I do not know where I shall find another."

I am, dear Sir, your very obedient servant,

Matthew Raine

AN ADDRESS

To the Parents and Guardians of the Children belonging to the Schools under the care of the New York Free-School Society (April 9, 1819).*

Sec. 1. The New York Free Schools, for the instruction of such children as are the objects of a gratuitous education, have been established many years; and the trustees have endeavored to render them useful and promotive of the moral and literary improvement of the scholars, and they still wish to do all in their power to advance the welfare of both children and parent.

Sec. 2. They wish to impress on your minds the importance of this establishment, that you may manifest an increasing concern for its prosperity, seeing that much depends on your cooperation in the support of an institution which is intended to promote not only the good of your children, but their happiness and yours, both here and hereafter.

Sec. 3. It is of great importance that the minds of your children should be early cultivated and moral instruction inculcated, and that, by example, as well as precept, you should use all endeavors to preserve them in innocency.

Sec. 4. As a good education is calculated to lay the foundation of usefulness and respectability, both in civil and religious society, it is your duty to improve every opportunity to promote it.

Sec. 5. This institution holds out much encouragement, and you are bound by every moral obligation to avail yourselves of the advantages which your children may derive from a steady attendance at school, where they may acquire not only school learning to qualify them for business, but be improved in their morals and manners.

Sec. 6. Many of you have not been favored with the privileges your children now enjoy—that of a gratuitous education. Every parent who is solicitous for the welfare of his offspring, but whose circumstances may be such as not to be able to pay the expense, is invited to come forward and place them where they may be instructed in literature, in the paths of virtue, and in the road to happiness.

Sec. 7. The trustees may venture to say, that this institution may be productive of great good to you, and to your children especially, if, on your part, there is a disposition to promote it. We wish your children may be furnished with a good education, and early acquire good habits. As they grow in years, they should be impressed with the importance of industry and frugality. These are the virtues necessary to form useful characters.

* William Oland Bourne, *History of the Public School Society of the City of New York* (New York, William Wood and Company, 1870), pp. 36-9.

Sec. 8. You know that many evils grow out of idleness, and many more out of the improper use of spirituous liquors; that they are ruinous and destructive to morals, and debase the human character below the lowest of all created beings; we therefore earnestly desire you may be watchful and careful in this respect, otherwise in vain may we labor to promote the welfare of your children.

Sec. 9. In domestic life there are many virtues which are requisite in order to promote the comfort and welfare of families. Temperance and economy are indispensable, but without cleanliness, your enjoyments as well as your reputation will be impaired. It is promotive of health, and ought not to be neglected. Parents can, perhaps, scarcely give a greater proof of their care for their children, than by keeping them clean and decent, especially when they are sent to school, where it is expected they will appear with their hands, faces, and heads perfectly clean, and their clothing clean and in good order. The appearance of children exhibits to every observing mind the character of the mother.

Sec. 10. Among other moral and religious duties, that of a due observance of the first day of the week, commonly called Sunday, we consider of importance to yourselves and to your children. Public worship is a duty we owe to our Creator; it is of universal obligation, and you ought to be good examples therein, encouraging your families to the due observance thereof; and believing, as we do, that the establishment of what is called Sunday schools has been a blessing to many, and may prove so to many more, we are desirous you may unite in the support of a plan so well calculated to promote the religious duties of that day, which ought to be appropriated to public worship, retirement, and other duties connected with the improvement of the mind.

Sec. 11. Seeing, next to your own souls, your children and those placed under your care are, or ought to be, the immediate objects of your constant attention and diligent concern, you ought to omit no opportunity to instruct them early in the principles of the Christian religion, in order to bring them, in their youth, to a sense of the unspeakable love and infinite wisdom and power of their Almighty Creator; for good and early impressions on tender minds often prove a lasting means of preserving them in a religious life even to old age. May you, therefore, watch over them for good, and rule over them in the fear of God, maintaining your authority in love; and as very much depends on the care and exemplary conduct of parents, and the judicious management of children by tutors, we cannot too strongly recommend to their serious consideration the importance of the subject, as one deeply interesting to the welfare of the rising generation, and no less connected with the best interests of civil and religious society.

Sec. 12. As the Holy Scriptures, or Bible, with which you ought all to be furnished, contain a full account of things most surely to be believed and

Divine commands most faithfully to be obeyed, and are said to make wise unto salvation through faith which is in Jesus Christ (2 Tim. iii. 15), it is the duty of every Christian to be frequent and diligent in the reading of them in their families, and in privately meditating on those sacred records.

Sec. 13. The trustees of the New York Free School, however desirous they may be to promote the improvement of the scholars in school learning, to qualify and fit them for the common duties of life, cannot view with an eye of indifference the more primary object of an education calculated to form habits of virtue and industry, and to inculcate the general principles of Christianity; for in proportion as you are established in a life of piety and virtue, you will be enabled to bring up your children in the nurture and admonition of the Lord, ever bearing in remembrance that example speaks a louder language than precept.

Sec. 14. It may not be improper to state to you, that the establishment of the New York Free School has been attended with much labor and personal exertions on the part of its friends and patrons; great expense has also accrued, and continues to be the case, where so many buildings are erected and so many teachers employed; and as all this is done in order to promote the good of your children, and to improve their condition, you cannot but feel a weight of obligation to the friends and patrons of so valuable an institution. In speaking of the teachers, it is due to them and their meritorious conduct to say, that they have manifested a zeal and concern for the welfare and improvement of the children placed under their care, and we wish they may be encouraged to persevere in the arduous service assigned them.

Sec. 15. There are divers other things which we could enumerate as connected with the subject of this address; but it cannot be expected, in a communication of this nature, we should embrace every duty or point out minutely every thing which might have a bearing on your religious and moral character; but, before we close, we think it necessary to subjoin the substance of such of the rules of the schools as may in part lay with the parents and guardians to notice and enforce. The trustees therefore call on you to see that these rules are strictly observed by your children:

1. Your children must be in school precisely at 9 o'clock in the morning and 2 o'clock in the afternoon.

2. They ought to be sent to school every day, both morning and afternoon; otherwise they may forget in one day what they learned the day before. Nothing but sickness, or some unavoidable circumstance, should induce you to keep your children at home one day. If they do not attend school regularly, the teacher is to send to you to know the reason; and if they are absent from school six days in a month without sufficient reason, or if they frequently play truant, they are liable to be expelled, and you may find it very difficult to get them into school again. The trustees there-

fore earnestly hope that you will not, by keeping your children at home without cause, or by suffering them to be absent, counteract their endeavors to procure for them a good education.

3. It is necessary that you should see that your children go to school with clean faces and hands, their hair combed and in good order, and their clothes as clean and whole as possible; otherwise they are liable to be punished for your neglect.

4. A morning school is intended to be kept in the summer, to begin at 6 o'clock, and close at 8 o'clock.

5. A library of interesting and useful books has been provided for the use of those children who are forward in their learning; and as they may be indulged at times to take them home for awhile, they may prove a source of pleasure and improvement to both children and parents.

6. If your children behave well, and study their lessons at home, they will be rewarded with tickets; but if they behave badly, and will not study, they must be punished.

7. In order to get a child into the Free School, it is required that application be made at the school on the second day of the week, commonly called Monday, from the hours of 4 to 5 o'clock in the afternoon.

8. No child can be admitted under six years of age.

9. The children of parents who are able to pay for schooling cannot be admitted.

10. It is expected that parents see that their children regularly attend some place of worship.

DE WITT CLINTON, *President.*
JOHN MURRAY, JR., *Vice-President.*
LEONARD BLEECKER, *Treasurer.*
LINDLEY MURRAY, *Secretary.*

MANIFESTO OF THE COMMUNIST PARTY *

Abolition of the family! Even the most radical flare up at this infamous proposal of the Communists.

On what foundation is the present family, the bourgeois family, based? On capital, on private gain. In its completely developed form this family exists only among the bourgeoisie. But this state of things finds its complement in the practical absence of the family among the proletarians, and in public prostitution.

The bourgeois family will vanish as a matter of course when its complement vanishes, and both will vanish with the vanishing of capital.

* Karl Marx and Frederick Engels, *Manifesto of the Communist Party* (Chicago, Charles H. Kerr & Company, n.d.), pp. 36-7. Reprinted by permission.

Do you charge us with wanting to stop the exploitation of children by their parents? To this crime we plead guilty.

But, you will say, we destroy the most hallowed of relations, when we replace home education by social.

And your education! Is not that also social, and determined by the social conditions under which you educate, by the intervention, direct or indirect, of society by means of schools, etc.? The Communists have not invented the intervention of society in education; they do but seek to alter the character of that intervention, and to rescue education from the influence of the ruling class.

The bourgeois clap-trap about the family and education, about the hallowed co-relation of parent and child, becomes all the more disgusting the more, by the action of Modern Industry, all family ties among the proletarians are torn asunder, and their children transformed into simple articles of commerce and instruments of labor.

PRESCHOOL EDUCATION IN RUSSIA *

. . . Less than a week after the Revolution of October 1917, the new People's Commissariat (now Ministry) of Education of the RSFSR created a Directorate of Preschool Education which has functioned ever since. It went on record as considering preschool training to be one of the most important in the system.

The decades since the Revolution of 1917 have brought about changes in the organization and methodology of preschool education (doshkol' noe obrazovanie) in the Soviet Union. The level has now been subdivided into two distinct phases: the nurseries (yasli) or crèches, as they are sometimes called, for children from 6 weeks to 3 years of age; and the kindergartens (detskie sady) for children from 3 to 7 years of age. Each phase includes part-time, summer, and seasonal programs at playgrounds, resorts, and camps in addition to programs in the permanent year-round institutions.

The USSR has become a nation of working mothers, and since the State requires a large number of women in factory and farm work, preschool programs have become an integral part of the national economy. An unusual amount of attention is focused on this component of the Soviet educational system. Nurseries in the Soviet Union are regarded as preschool establishments; their major function is to render child care service. The kindergartens, while providing such service, also carry on educational activity. Since care of babies and toddlers is largely a physical matter, the

* *Education in the USSR* (U.S. Department of Health, Education, and Welfare, Office of Education, Bulletin 1957, No. 14), pp. 39-43.

nurseries are under the jurisdiction of the health ministries of the republics, as are the physical education and medical aspects of the kindergartens. The kindergartens, in other respects, remain a responsibility of the directorate of preschool education in the republic ministries of education.

Often the working mother can find a preschool institution near where she is living or at the economic enterprise where she is employed. If the mother is on night shift she may have her children cared for on a 24-hour basis and take them home only on weekends. Enrollment of children in nurseries and kindergartens is not compulsory. The demand for placement far exceeds available vacancies, particularly in rural areas and small towns where preschool facilities are available only during the summer and at harvest time. The grandmother continues to exercise a primary role in rearing the preschool child. . . .

In 1955 more than 5 million children under 7 years of age were said to have participated in some type of preschool program. Nurseries accommodated 906,000; full-time kindergartens enrolled 1,713,000; seasonal nurseries and kindergartens provided for another 2 million; and summer kindergartens served 565,000. Table 2 . . . indicates the growth of nursery care and full-time kindergarten enrollment.

TABLE 2

ENROLLMENT IN YEAR-ROUND SOVIET NURSERY SCHOOLS AND KINDERGARTENS, BY SPECIFIED YEARS

(Year end; in thousands)

Year	Enrollment in Nursery Schools			Enrollment in Kindergartens		
	Total	Urban	Rural	Total	Urban	Rural
1	2	3	4	5	6	7
1928	62	54	8	130	119	11
1940	859	559	300	1,172	906	266
1950	777	512	265	1,169	958	211
1954	862	589	273	1,577	1,305	272
1955	906	623	283	1,713	1,410	303

. . . Despite required tuition fees, preschool facilities in the USSR are largely State supported. . . . As a general rule, however, the fees paid by parents are expected to cover between 25 and 35 per cent of the annual cost.

Religion and Education

RULES OF A SCHOOL IN ST. AUGUSTINE, FLORIDA, 1786 *

1. In accordance with the devout intentions of his majesty, no one shall be qualified to teach except upon examination and approval of the ecclesiastical and civil superiors of the province and every teacher shall be bound to observe these rules and such other orders and resolutions or any part of them, as the said superiors may see fit to communicate from time to time in the interest of the fullest advancement of the pupils.

. . .

6. As each pupil enters school in the morning and in the afternoon he shall greet with proper courtesy first his teacher and then his fellow pupils. He shall then hang up his hat in the [proper] place and then seat himself in all modesty. After blessing himself in the name of the Blessed Trinity, he shall take up the book or paper with which his study is to begin.

. . .

13. At the beginning of every month there shall be a general examination before the parish priest and the teachers to determine the advancement the pupils may have made during the previous month in writing, reading, arithmetic, christian doctrine, etc., and, as a reward of merit for the advancement shown in the examination, each pupil shall be assigned to a seat or place of preference corresponding to his progress. He shall

---

* Michael J. Curley, *Church and State in the Spanish Floridas, Studies in American Church History*, Vol. XXX (Washington, D. C., Catholic University Press of America, 1940), pp. 78-82.

occupy his place until the next examination when he shall be awarded it again, provided no one excels him in merit. In this latter case he shall descend to occupy the place corresponding to his merit.

14. From pupils studying the alphabet, the syllabary, and reading, the teacher shall hear four lessons a day, two in the morning and two in the afternoon. The teacher shall instruct these pupils at the same time, morning and afternoon, in christian doctrine and in prayers and litanies. . . .

. . .

16. The teacher of the second school shall require his pupils, as they advance, to memorize the tables of arithmetic . . . the teachers may assign in the afternoon to each one according to his capacity, a portion of the historical catechism of Father Flaure, or of some other author, to be memorized at night, thus preventing the pupils from being idle at home.

17. The teachers shall instruct their pupils how to assist at Mass, and every Saturday night and on the eve of the other feasts of the year when there is to be a congregation in the church, they shall name by turns two of their pupils to assist the sacristan in the conduct of divine services.

18. On nights when the Procession of the Rosary leaves the parish church and passes through the streets, the teachers shall attend with their pupils, no exception being allowed and no excuse being valid. The teachers shall take care that the pupils comport themselves with proper modesty and devotion.

19. The teachers shall attend with their pupils the Salve on Saturdays, the Vespers of Sundays, and other principal days, and at all the services of the church when there is preaching of the Gospel.

20. Whenever God may be pleased to call to judgment any of the children the teachers shall go with their pupils in procession to the funeral, and if necessary the remains shall be borne by four of the pupils to the burial place.

21. During each of the Four Ember Seasons of the year, all pupils of seven years and above, shall go to make confession in the presence of their teachers, to which end the teachers shall notify their pupils a day or two beforehand, in order that they may examine their consciences. The teacher shall instruct the pupils in a manner appropriate to their age, how they should prepare themselves, the method they should observe to avoid, by negligence or other culpable reasons, omitting sins that ought to be confessed, and the teachers should inform the pupils also of the necessity of repentence to make the sacrament valid, etc. The teachers shall give these same instructions to the pupils who are of an age to receive the Holy Sacrament of the Eucharist; and in order that everything may be done with system, the pupils shall be divided into three equal divisions and each

teacher shall assign one division of his school for each of the Ember days, in order that by this means the pupils may be attended to with dispatch in the church and sent back promptly to school.

. . .

23. The pupils shall ask with most profound humility that the blessings of their parents accompany them on their way to and from school, and whenever they meet any of their elders in the street, they should salute them with proper courtesy.

24. On leaving school the pupils shall go directly home without loitering, or shouting or committing mischievous pranks in the streets.

25. If any negroes or mulattoes should attend the schools, they shall be placed near the door in seats apart; but in matters of instruction, spiritual and temporal, the teachers shall do to them the same justice as to all the rest.

26. The teachers shall have in their respective schools a copy of these regulations in order that everyone may be promptly informed of their provisions and in order that they may be invariably and duly observed as his majesty desires.

THE SCHOOLS AND RELIGIONS *

It seems hard that a generation which has accumulated not only material wealth, but intellectual riches, to the extent that it is compelled to pull down its barns—its systems of philosophy and doctrine—and build greater, should be lacking in just that grace and sanction of life which ignorant and poor people have possessed as matter of course. But our learnedly self-conscious generation is also mechanical. It has a tool for everything, and almost everything has become for it a tool. Why, then, should we longer suffer from deficiency of religion? We have discovered our lack; let us set the machinery in motion which will supply it. We have mastered the elements of physical well-being; we can make light and heat to order, and can command the means of transportation. Let us now put a similar energy, goodwill, and thoughtfulness into the control of the things of the spiritual life. Having got so far as to search for proper machinery, the next step is easy. Education is the modern universal purveyor, and upon the schools shall rest the responsibility for seeing to it that we recover our threatened religious heritage.

* John Dewey, *Intelligence in the Modern World, John Dewey's Philosophy*, Edited and with an Introduction by Joseph Ratner (New York, The Modern Library, Random House, 1939), pp. 702-15. (Ratner acknowledges reprint permission from Henry Holt and Company in this edition, p. viii.)

I cannot expect that those who are now especially concerned with the maintenance and the spread of conscious and explicit religious instruction (for the time being one must use this question-begging epithet) will recognise their attitude or intention in what I have just said. And it has no application to those who are already committed to special dogmas of religion which are the monopoly of special ecclesiastic institutions. With respect to them, the fight for special agencies and peculiar materials and methods of education in religion is a natural part of their business: just as, however, it is the business of those who do not believe that religion is a monopoly or a protected industry to contend, in the interest both of education and of religion, for keeping the schools free from what they must regard as a false bias. Those who believe that human nature without special divine assistance is lost, who believe that they have in their charge the special channels through which the needed assistance is conveyed, must, naturally, be strenuous in keeping open these channels to the minds of men. But when the arguments for special religious education at special times and places by special means proceed from philosophic sources—from those whose primary premise is denial of any breach between man and the world and God, then a sense of unreality comes over me. The arguments perforce translate themselves ironically. They seem to say that, since religion is a universal function of life, we must particularly safeguard it lest it disappear; that since religion is the consciousness of the spiritual import of experience, we must find mechanical appliances for developing it.

Those who approach religion and education from the side of unconstrained reflection, not from the side of tradition, are of necessity aware of the tremendous transformation of intellectual attitude effected by the systematic denial of the supernatural; they are aware of the changes it imports not merely in special dogma and rites, but in the interpretation of the world, and in the projection of social, and, hence, moral life. It testifies to the current unreality of philosophy (itself probably a product of that forced idealism in which modern thought has taken refuge) that philosophers should seem to think that great intellectual generalizations may be, as it were, plastered over life to label its contents, and not imply profound practical alterations within life itself. In no other way is it easy to account for the attitude of those who are convinced of the final departure of the supernatural interpretation of the world and of man, and who yet think that agencies like the church and the school must not be thoroughly reconstructed before they can be fit organs for nurturing types of religious feeling and thought which are consistent with modern democracy and modern science.

That science has the same spiritual import as supernaturalism; that democracy translates into the same religious attitude as did feudalism; that it is only a matter of slight changes of phraseology, a development of old symbolisms into new shades of meaning—such beliefs testify to that torpor of imagination which is the uniform effect of dogmatic belief. The reconstruction of the Church is a matter which concerns, indeed, the whole community so far as its outcome is concerned; while the responsibility for its initiation belongs primarily to those within the churches. The burden of conducting the development, the reconstruction, of other educational agencies belongs, however, primarily to the community as a whole. With respect to its intellectual aspect, its philosophy, it belongs especially to those who, having become conscious in some degree of the modern ideas of nature, of man and society, are best able to forecast the direction which social changes are taking. It is lucidity, sincerity, and the sense of reality which demand that, until the non-supernatural view is more completely elaborated in all its implications and is more completely in possession of the machinery of education, the schools shall keep hands off and shall do as little as possible.

We need, however, to accept the responsibilities of living in an age marked by the greatest intellectual readjustment history records. There is undoubted loss of joy, of consolation, of some types of strength, and of some sources of inspiration in the change. There is a manifest increase of uncertainty; there is some paralysis of energy, and much excessive application of energy in materialistic directions. Yet nothing is gained by deliberate effort to return to ideas which have become incredible, and to symbols which have been emptied of their content of obvious meaning. Nothing can be gained by moves which will increase confusion and obscurity, which tend to an emotional hypocrisy and to a phrase-mongering or formulae which seem to mean one thing and really import the opposite. Bearing the losses and inconveniences of our time as best we may, it is the part of men to labor persistently and patiently for the clarification and development of the positive creed of life implicit in democracy and in science, and to work for the transformation of all practical instrumentalities of education till they are in harmony with these ideas. Till these ends are further along than we can honestly claim them to be at present, it is better that our schools should do nothing than that they should do wrong things. It is better for them to confine themselves to their obviously urgent tasks than that they should, under the name of spiritual culture, form habits of mind which are at war with the habits of mind congruous with democracy and with science. It is not laziness nor cynicism which calls for this policy; it is honesty, courage, sobriety, and faith.

If one inquires why the American tradition is so strong against any connection of State and Church, why it dreads even the rudiments of religious teaching in state-maintained schools, the immediate answer is not far to seek. The cause was not, mainly, religious indifference, much less hostility to Christianity, although the eighteenth century deism played an important role. The cause lay largely in the diversity and vitality of the various denominations, each fairly sure that, with a fair field and no favor, it could make its own way; and each animated by a jealous fear that, if any connection of State and Church were permitted, some rival denomination would get an unfair advantage. But there was a deeper and by no means wholly unconscious influence at work. The United States became a nation late enough in the history of the world to profit by the growth of that modern (although Greek) thing—the state consciousness. This nation was born under conditions which enabled it to share in and to appropriate the idea that the state life, the vitality of the social whole, is of more importance than the flourishing of any segment or class. So far as church institutions were concerned, the doctrine of popular sovereignty was a reality, not a literary or legal fiction. Upon the economic side, the nation was born too soon to learn the full force of the state idea as against the class idea. Our fathers naively dreamed of the continuation of pioneer conditions and the free opportunity of every individual, and took none of the precautions to maintain the supremacy of the state over that of the class which newer commonwealths are taking. For that lack of foresight we are paying dearly, and are likely to pay more dearly. But the lesson of the two and a half centuries lying between the Protestant revolt and the formation of the nation was well learned as respected the necessity of maintaining the integrity of the state as against all divisive ecclesiastical divisions. Doubtless many of our ancestors would have been somewhat shocked to realize the full logic of their own attitude with respect to the subordination of churches to the state (falsely termed the *separation* of Church and State); but the state idea was inherently of such vitality and constructive force as to carry the practical result, with or without conscious perception of its philosophy. And any general agitation in the United States of the question of religious instruction in the schools could have but one explanation. It would mean that, from economic segregation and unassimilated immigration, the state-consciousness of the country had been sapped by the growth of social factions.

As I recall, some of the Platonic dialogues discuss the question whether virtue can be taught, and all of them contain overtones or reminiscences of the topic. For the discussion led a long way. What is virtue? That is not an altogether easy question; and since to answer it we must know virtue and not merely have opinions about it, it will be well to find out what knowledge is. Moreover, teaching implies learning, and learning is coming to know, or knowledge in process of learning. What, then, is the connection of the becoming of knowledge with the being of knowledge? And since the teaching of virtue means, not getting knowledge "about" virtue, but the conversion of character to the good, what, after all, is the relation between becoming good and that becoming wise which is the result of learning?

Somehow, I am more aware that Plato discusses all these questions than I am certain of any final answer to the question whether virtue may be taught. Yet I seem to recall some hypothetical suggestions for an answer. If, as we have reason to believe, the soul of man is naturally akin to good— if, indeed, it truly *is* only through participation in the good—then may various objects, also in their measure expressions of good, serve to remind the soul of its own or original nature. If these various reminders may be organized into a comprehensive scheme, continuous and continual in operation—if, in other words, there may be found a state organized in righteousness—then may the soul be finally brought to the apprehension of its own being or good; and this coming to know and to be we may term learning. But, if I remember rightly, Plato always classed endeavors to teach virtue apart from an accompanying thorough reorganization of social life and of science as a piece of confused and self-contradictory thinking— as a case, that is, of sophistic.

Have we any reason for taking the present problem of teaching religion to be simpler in conception or easier in execution? The contemporary problem appears, indeed, to be more intricate and difficult. Varied and conflicting as were the views of Plato's Greek contemporaries as to what things should be included and taught under the head of virtues, the question of just what concretely comes under the caption of religion today is as much harder to decide as our social life is more heterogeneous in origin and composition than was the Athenian. We certainly cannot teach religion as an abstract essence. We have got to teach *something* as religion, and that means practically *some* religion. Which? In America, at least, the answer cannot be summarily given even as Christianity in general. Our Jewish fellow citizens not only have the same "hands, organs, dimensions, senses, affections, passions" as the Christians, but, like them, they pay taxes, vote, and serve on school boards. But we should not be very much better off even if it were a question of Christianity alone. *Which* Christianity? Oriental in its origin, it has been since Latinized and Germanized, and there are even those who have dreamed of humanizing it.

The problem of today is more complex as respects also the process of learning, of coming to know. In the day of Plato, art and science, skilled practice and theory, were only beginning to be separated. Just as a man learned shoemaking in process of becoming a shoemaker, so might a man learn virtue in becoming a member of a good state—if such a thing could be found. Today knowledge is something specialised, and learning does not consist in intelligent mastery of an activity, but in acquiring a diversity of information about things, and control over technical methods for instituting symbolic references to things. Knowledge to Plato was the sort of thing that the forefathers of some of us called "getting religion." It was a personal experiencing and a vital realization. But what shall knowledge of religion as an outcome of instruction mean today? Shall it mean the accumulation of information *about* religion? Or are there those who still believe in some magic power resident in memorized words, phrases, and facts of transmuting themselves into personal insight, the development of fundamental mood and the formation of permanent attitudes towards experience?

When we consider knowledge from the side of its method and from the standpoint of what it takes to get something really worthy to be called knowledge, the problem increases in difficulty. As yet, the standpoint of science, its spirit, has not of course leavened very adequately our methods of teaching. From the standpoint of those methods of inquiry and testing which we call science, much, perhaps most, of what passes for knowledge is in reality what Plato called opinion. Our science is still an outward garb more or less awkwardly worn rather than a habit of mind. But none the less the scientific norm of mental activity presses daily closer upon life and upon the schools. We are getting daily further away from the conditions in which one subject more or less taught by dogmatic, catechetical and memoriter methods was of slight consequence. We are becoming aware of the absurdity implied in calling things which happen to be studied and learned in school "knowledge," when they have been acquired by methods frequently at odds with those necessary to give science. Can those who take the philosophic and historic view of religion as a flower and fruition of the human spirit in a congenial atmosphere tolerate the incongruity involved in "teaching" such an intimate and originally vital matter by external and formal methods? And can those who hold that true religion is something externally imported tolerate any other methods? Is it not confusion to seek a reconciliation of two such disparate ideas?

Already the spirit of our schooling is permeated with the feeling that every subject, every topic, every fact, every professed truth must submit to a certain publicity and impartiality. All proffered samples of learning must go to the same assay-room and be subjected to common tests. It is the essence of all dogmatic faiths to hold that any such "show-down" is sacrilegious and perverse. The characteristic of religion, from their point of view, is that it is—intellectually—secret, not public; peculiarly revealed, not generally known; authoritatively declared, not communicated and tested in ordinary ways. What is to be done about this increasing antinomy between the standard for coming to know in other subjects of the school, and coming to know in religous matters? I am far from saying that the antinomy is an inherent one, or that the day may not come when religion will be so thoroughly naturalized in the hearts and minds of men that it can be considered publicly, openly, and by common tests, even among religious people. But it is pertinent to point out that, as long as religion is conceived as it is now conceived by the great majority of professed religionists, there is something self-contradictory in speaking of education in religion in the same sense in which we speak of education in topics where the method of free inquiry has made its way. The "religious" would be the last to be willing that either the history or the content of religion should be taught in this spirit; while those to whom the scientific standpoint is not a merely technical device, but is the embodiment of integrity of mind, must protest against its being taught in any other spirit.

As Plato brought out with reference to the teaching of virtue, there is one other factor in coming to know—the teachers. Plato was quite sure that, whether or no virtue might be taught, it might not be taught by its professed teachers—the sophists. I express my appreciation of Plato rather than my lack of appreciation of the professional teachers of our own day, when I say that if Plato were to return to take part in the current discussion, he would raise questions about those who were to teach religion analogous to those he brought up about the teachers of his own time. It is not that those into whose hands the giving of instruction would fall are so irreligious or so non-religious as to be unfitted for the task. The sophists were doubtless superior rather than inferior in personal virtues to their average neighbor. It is one thing to be fairly or even exceptionally virtuous; it is another thing to command the conditions and the qualifications for successful importation of virtue to others. Where are the experts in religion? and where are the authoritative teachers? There are theologians: do we want theology taught? There are historians, but I fear the day has not come when the history of religion can be taught as history. Here precisely is one of those fields of clarification and criticism where much labor needs to be done, and where the professional religionist is one of the most serious obstacles to reckon with, since a wider and deeper historic knowledge would overthrow his traditional basis.

There are preachers and catechists, but, unless we are committed to some peculiar faith or institution, it is not exhortation or discipline of this sort that constitutes religious instruction. There are psychologists: but is introspection our aim? There remains, indeed, the corps of faithful, more or less well-prepared, hard-working and hard-worked teachers. This brings us to the crux of the whole matter. Is religion a thing so specialized, so technical, so "informational" that, like geography or history or grammar, it may be taught at special hours, times, and places by those who have properly "got it up," and who have been approved as persons of fit character and adequate professional training?

This question of the mode, time, and stuff of specific instruction trenches indeed upon a question in which national temper and tradition count for much. We do not find it feasible or desirable to put upon the regular teachers the burden of teaching a subject which has the nature of religion. The alternative plan of parcelling out pupils among religious teachers drawn from their respective churches and denominations brings us up against exactly the matter which has done most to discredit the churches, and to discredit the cause, not perhaps of religion, but of organized and institutional religion: the multiplication of rival and competing religious bodies, each with its private inspiration and outlook. Our schools, in bringing together those of different nationalities, languages, traditions, and creeds, in assimilating them together upon the basis of what is common and public in endeavor and achievement, are performing an infinitely significant religious work. They are promoting the social unity out of which in the end genuine religious unity must grow. Shall we interfere with this work? Shall we run the risk of undoing it by introducing into education a subject which can be taught only by segregating pupils and turning them over at special hours to separate representatives of rival faiths? This would be deliberately to adopt a scheme which is predicated upon the maintenance of social divisions in just the matter, religion, which is empty and futile save as it expresses the basic unities of life.

We are far, indeed, from having attained an explicit and articulated consciousness of the religious significance of democracy in education, and of education in democracy. But some underlying convictions get ingrained in unconscious habit and find expression in obscure intimation and intense labor, long before they receive consistent theoretic formulation. In such dim, blind, but effective way the American people is conscious that its schools serve best the cause of religion in serving the cause of social unification; and that under certain conditions schools are more religious in substance and in promise without any of the conventional badges and machinery of religious instruction than they could be in cultivating these forms at the expense of a state-consciousness.

We may indeed question whether it is true that in any relative sense this is a peculiarly irreligious age. Absolutely speaking, it doubtless is so; but have superficiality, flippancy, and externality of life been such uniformly absent traits of past ages? Our historic imagination is at best slightly developed. We generalize and idealize the past egregiously. We set up little toys to stand as symbols for long centuries and the complicated lives of countless individuals. And we are still, even those who have nominally surrendered supernatural dogma, largely under the dominion of the ideas of those who have succeeded in identifying religion with the rites, symbols, and emotions associated with these dogmatic beliefs. As we see the latter disappearing, we think we are growing irreligious. For all we know, the integrity of mind which is loosening the hold of these things is potentially much more religious than all that it is displacing. It is increased knowledge of nature which has made supra-nature incredible, or at least difficult of belief. We measure the change from the standpoint of the supranatural and we call it irreligious. Possibly if we measured it from the standpoint of the natural piety it is fostering, the sense of the permanent and inevitable implication of nature and man in a common career and destiny, it would appear as the growth of religion. We take note of the decay of cohesion and influence among the religiously organized bodies of the familiar historic type, and again we conventionally judge religion to be on the decrease. But it may be that their decadence is the fruit of a broader and more catholic principle of human intercourse and association which is too religious to tolerate these pretensions to monopolize truth and to make private possessions of spiritual insight and aspiration.

It may be so; it may be that the symptoms of religious ebb as conventionally interpreted are symptoms of the coming of a fuller and deeper religion. I do not claim to know. But of one thing I am quite sure: our ordinary opinions about the rise and falling off of religion are highly conventional, based mostly upon the acceptance of a standard of religion which is the product of just those things in historic religions which are ceasing to be credible. So far as education is concerned, those who believe in religion as a natural expression of human experience must devote themselves to the development of the ideas of life which lie implicit in our still new science and our still newer democracy. They must interest themselves in the transformation of those institutions which still bear the dogmatic and the feudal stamp (and which do not?) till they are in accord with these ideas. In performing this service, it is their business to do what they can to prevent all public educational agencies from being employed in ways which inevitably impede the recognition of the spiritual import of science and of democracy, and hence of that type of religion which will be the fine flower of the modern spirit's achievement.

ENCYCLICAL LETTER ON CHRISTIAN EDUCATION OF YOUTH *

To Whom Does Education Belong in General?

Education is essentially a social and not a mere individual activity. Now there are three necessary societies distinct from one another and yet harmoniously combined by God, into which man is born: two, namely the family and civil society, belong to the natural order; the third, the Church, to the supernatural order.

In the first place comes the family, instituted directly by God for its peculiar purpose, the generation and formation of offspring; for this reason it has priority of nature and therefore of rights over civil society. Nevertheless, the family is an imperfect society, since it has not in itself all the means for its own complete development; whereas civil society is a perfect society, having in itself all the means for its peculiar end, which is the temporal well-being of the community; and so, in this respect, that is, in view of the common good, it has preëminence over the family, which finds its own suitable temporal perfection precisely in civil society.

The third society, into which man is born when through Baptism he receives the divine life of grace, is the Church; a society of the supernatural order and of universal extent; a perfect society, because it has in itself all the means required for its own end, which is the eternal salvation of mankind; hence it is supreme in its own domain.

Consequently, education which is concerned with man as a whole, individually and socially, in the order of nature and in the order of grace, necessarily belongs to all these three societies, in due proportion, corresponding, according to the disposition of Divine Providence, to the coordination of their respective ends.

In Particular: To the Church

And first of all education belongs preëminently to the Church, by reason of a double title in the supernatural order, conferred exclusively upon her by God Himself; absolutely superior therefore to any other title in the natural order.

The first title is founded upon the express mission and supreme authority to teach given her by her Divine Founder: "All power is given to Me in heaven and in earth. Going therefore, teach ye all nations, baptizing them in the Name of the Father, and of the Son, and of the Holy Ghost, teach-

* Pius XI, "Full Text of Pope's Encyclical" (Christian Education of Youth, January 11, 1930) *Current History,* XXXI (March 1930), pp. 1092-8.

ing them to observe all things whatsoever I have commanded you, and behold I am with you all days, even to the consummation of the world." Upon this magisterial office Christ conferred infallibility, together with the command to teach His doctrine. Hence the Church "was set by her Divine Author as the pillar and ground of truth, in order to teach the divine faith to men, and keep whole and inviolate the deposit confided to her; to direct and fashion men, in all their actions individually and socially, to purity of morals and integrity of life, in accordance with revealed doctrine."

SUPERNATURAL MOTHERHOOD

The second title is the supernatural motherhood, in virtue of which the Church, spotless spouse of Christ, generates, nurtures and educates souls in the divine life of grace, with her Sacraments and her doctrine. With good reason then does St. Augustine maintain: "He has not God for father who refuses to have the Church as mother."

Hence it is that in this proper object of her mission, that is, "in faith and morals, God Himself has made the Church sharer in the divine magisterium and, by a special privilege, granted her immunity from error; hence she is the mistress of men, supreme and absolutely sure, and she has inherent in herself an inviolable right to freedom in teaching." By necessary consequence the Church is independent of any sort of earthly power as well in the origin as in exercise of her mission as educator, not merely in regard to her proper end and object, but also in regard to the means necessary and suitable to attain that end. Hence with regard to every other kind of human learning and instruction, which is the common patrimony of individuals and society, the Church has an independent right to make use of it, and above all to decide what may help or harm Christian education. And this must be so, because the Church as a perfect society has an independent right to the means conducive to its end, and because every form of instruction, no less than every human action, has a necessary connection with man's last end, and therefore cannot be withdrawn from the dictates of the divine law, of which the Church is guardian, interpreter and infallible mistress.

This truth is clearly set forth by Pius X of saintly memory: "Whatever a Christian does even in the order of things of earth, he may not overlook the supernatural; indeed, he must, according to the teaching of Christian wisdom, direct all things towards the supreme good as to his last end; all his actions, besides, in so far as good or evil in the order of morality, that is, in keeping or not with natural and divine law, fall under the judgment and jurisdiction of the Church." . . .

It is worthy of note how a layman, an excellent writer and at the same time a profound and conscientious thinker, has been able to understand well and express exactly this fundamental Catholic doctrine! "The Church does not say that morality belongs purely, in the sense of exclusively, to her; but that it belongs wholly to her. She has never maintained that outside her fold and apart from her teaching, man cannot arrive at any moral truth; she has on the contrary more than once condemned this opinion because it has appeared under more forms than one. She does however say, has said, and will ever say, that because of her institution by Jesus Christ, because of the Holy Ghost sent her in His Name by the Father, she alone possesses what she has had immediately from God and can never lose, the whole of moral truth, *omnem veritatem,* in which all individual moral truths are included, as well those which man may learn by the help of reason, as those which form part of revelation or which may be deduced from it."

EXTENT OF THE RIGHTS OF THE CHURCH

Therefore with full right the Church promotes letters, science, art, in so far as necessary or helpful to Christian education, in addition to her work for the salvation of souls; founding and maintaining schools and institutions adapted to every branch of learning and degree of culture. Nor may even physical culture, as it is called, be considered outside the range of her maternal supervision, for the reason that it also is a means which may help or harm Christian education.

And this work of the Church in every branch of culture is of immense benefit to families and nations which without Christ are lost, as St. Hilary points out correctly: "What can be more fraught with danger for the world than the rejection of Christ?" Nor does it interfere in the least with the regulations of the State, because the Church in her motherly prudence is not unwilling that her schools and institutions for the education of the laity be in keeping with the legitimate dispositions of civil authority; she is in every way ready to cooperate with this authority and to make provision for a mutual understanding, should difficulties arise.

Again it is the inalienable right as well as the indispensable duty of the Church, to watch over the entire education of her children, in all institutions, public or private, not merely in regard to the religious instruction there given, but in regard to every other branch of learning and every regulation in so far as religion and morality are concerned.

Nor should the exercise of this right be considered undue interference, but rather maternal care on the part of the Church in protecting her children from the grave danger of all kinds of doctrinal and moral evil. Moreover this watchfulness of the Church not merely can create no real inconvenience, but must on the contrary confer valuable assistance in the right ordering and well-being of families and of civil society; for it keeps far away from youth the moral poison which at that inexperienced and changeable age more easily penetrates the mind and more rapidly spreads its baneful effects. For it is true, as Leo XIII has wisely pointed out, that without proper religious and moral instruction "every form of intellectual culture will be injurious; for young people not accustomed to respect God, will be unable to bear the restraint of a virtuous life, and never having learned to deny themselves anything, they will easily be incited to disturb the public order."

The extent of the Church's mission in the field of education is such as to embrace every nation, without exception, according to the command of Christ: "Teach ye all nations;" and there is no power on earth that may lawfully oppose her or stand in her way. In the first place, it extends over all the Faithful, of whom she has anxious care as a tender mother. For these she has throughout the centuries created and conducted an immense number of schools and institutions in every branch of learning. As we said on a recent occasion: "Right back in the far-off middle ages when there were so many (some have even said too many) monasteries, convents, churches, collegiate churches, Cathedral chapters, etc., there was attached to each a home of study, of teaching, of Christian education. To these we must add all the universities, spread over every country and always by the initiative and under the protection of the Holy See and the Church. That grand spectacle, which today we see better, as it is nearer to us and more imposing because of the conditions of the age, was the spectacle of all times; and they who study and compare historical events remain astounded at what the Church has been able to do in this matter, and marvel at the manner in which she has succeeded in fulfilling her God-given mission to educate generations of men to a Christian life, producing everywhere a magnificent harvest of fruitful results. But if we wonder that the Church in all times has been able to gather about her and educate hundreds, thousands, millions of students, no less wonderful is it to bear in mind what she has done not only in the field of education, but in that also of true and genuine erudition. For, if so many treasures of culture, civilization and literature have escaped destruction, this is due to the action by which the Church, even in times long past and uncivilized, has shed so bright a light in the domain of letters, of philosophy, of art, and in a special manner of architecture."

All this the Church has been able to do because her mission to educate extends equally to those outside the fold, seeing that all men are called to enter the kingdom of God and reach eternal salvation. Just as today when her Missions scatter schools by the thousand in districts and countries not yet Christian, from the banks of the Ganges to the Yellow River and the great islands and archipelagos of the Pacific Ocean, from the Dark Continent to the Land of Fire and to frozen Alaska, so in every age the

Church by her missionaries has educated to Christian life and to civilization the various peoples which now constitute the Christian nations of the civilized world.

Hence it is evident that both by right and in fact the mission to educate belongs pre-eminently to the Church, and that no one free from prejudice can have a reasonable motive for opposing or impeding the Church in this her work, of which the world today enjoys the precious advantages.

Harmony Between the Rights of the Church and Those of the Family and State

This is the more true because the rights of the family and of the State, even the rights of individuals regarding a just liberty in the pursuit of science, of methods of science and all sorts of profane culture, not only are not opposed to this pre-eminence of the Church, but are in complete harmony with it. The fundamental reason for this harmony is that the supernatural order, to which the Church owes her rights, not only does not in the least destroy the natural order, to which pertain the other rights mentioned, but elevates the natural and perfects it, each affording mutual aid to the other, and completing it in a manner proportioned to its respective nature and dignity. The reason is because both come from God, Who cannot contradict Himself: "The works of God are perfect and all His ways are judgments."

This becomes clearer when we consider more closely and in detail the mission of education proper to the family and to the State.

To the Family

In the first place the Church's mission of education is in wonderful agreement with that of the family, for both proceed from God, and in a remarkably similar manner. God directly communicates to the family, in the natural order, fecundity, which is the principle of education to life, together with authority, the principle of order.

The Angelic Doctor with his wonted clearness of thought and precision of style, says; "The father according to the flesh has in a particular way a share in that principle which in a manner universal is found in God. . . . The father is the principle of generation, of education and discipline and of everything that bears upon the perfecting of human life."

The family therefore holds directly from the Creator the mission and hence the right to educate the offspring, a right inalienable because inseparably joined to the strict obligation, a right anterior to any right whatever of civil society and of the State, and therefore inviolable on the part of any power on earth.

That this right is inviolable St. Thomas proves as follows: "The child is naturally something of the father . . . so by natural right the child, before reaching the use of reason, is under the father's care. Hence it would be contrary to natural justice if the child, before the use of reason, were removed from the care of its parents, or if any disposition were made concerning him against the will of the parents." And as this duty on the part of the parents continues up to the time when the child is in a position to provide for itself, this same inviolable parental right of education also endures. "Nature intends not merely the generation of the offspring, but also its development and advance to the perfection of man considered as man, that is, to the state of virtue," says the same St. Thomas.

The wisdom of the Church in this matter is expressed with precision and clearness in the Codex of Canon Law, canon 1113: "Parents are under a grave obligation to see to the religious and moral education of their children, as well as to their physical and civic training, as far as they can, and moreover to provide for their temporal well-being."

On this point the common sense of mankind is in such complete accord, that they would be in open contradiction with it who dared maintain that the children belong to the State before they belong to the family, and that the State has an absolute right over their education. Untenable is the reason they adduce, namely that man is born a citizen and hence belongs primarily to the State, not bearing in mind that before being a citizen man must exist; and existence does not come from the State, but from the parents, as Leo XIII wisely declared: "The children are something of the father, and as it were an extension of the person of the father; and, to be perfectly accurate, they enter into and become part of civil society, not directly by themselves, but through the family in which they were born." "And therefore," says the same Leo XIII, "the father's power is of such a nature that it cannot be destroyed or absorbed by the State; for it has the same origin as human life itself."

It does not, however, follow from this that the parents' right to educate their children is absolute and despotic; for it is necessarily subordinated to the last end and to natural and divine law, as Leo XIII declares in another memorable encyclical, where he thus sums up the rights and duties of parents: "By nature parents have a right to the training of their children, but with this added duty that the education and instruction of the child be in accord with the end for which by God's blessing it was begotten. Therefore it is the duty of parents to make every effort to prevent any invasion of their rights in this matter, and to make absolutely sure that the education of their children remains under their own control in keeping with their Christian duty, and above all to refuse to send them to those schools in which there is danger of imbibing the deadly poison of impiety."

It must be borne in mind also that the obligation of the family to bring up children, includes not only religious and moral education, but physical and civic education as well, principally in so far as it touches upon religion and morality.

This incontestable right of the family has at various times been recognized by nations anxious to respect the natural law in their civil enactments. Thus, to give one recent example, the Supreme Court of the United States of North America, in a decision on an important controversy, declared that it is not in the competence of the State to fix any uniform standard of education by forcing children to receive instruction exclusively in public schools, and it bases its decision on the natural law: the child is not the mere creature of the State; those who nurture him and direct his destiny have the right coupled with the high duty, to educate him and prepare him for the fulfillment of his obligations. . . .

TUTELAGE OF THE CHURCH

History bears witness how, particularly in modern times, the State has violated and does violate rights conferred by God on the family. At the same time it shows magnificently how the Church has ever protected and defended these rights, a fact proved by the special confidence which parents have in Catholic schools. As We pointed out recently in Our letter to the Cardinal Secretary of State: "The family has instinctively understood this to be so, and from the earliest days of Christianity down to our own times, fathers and mothers, even those of little or no faith, have been sending or bringing their children in millions to places of education under the direction of the Church."

It is paternal instinct, given by God, that thus turns with confidence to the Church, certain of finding in her the protection of family rights, thereby illustrating that harmony with which God has ordered all things. The Church is indeed conscious of her divine mission to all mankind, and of the obligation which all men have to practise the one true religion; and therefore she never tires of defending her right, and of reminding parents of their duty, to have all Catholic-born children baptized and brought up as Christians. On the other hand so jealous is she of the family's inviolable natural right to educate the children, that she never consents, save under peculiar circumstances and with special cautions, to baptize the children of infidels, or provide for their education against the will of the parents, till such time as the children can choose for themselves and freely embrace the faith.

We have therefore two facts of supreme importance, as We said in Our discourse cited above: The Church placing at the disposal of families her office of mistress and educator, and the families eager to profit by the offer, and entrusting their children to the Church in hundreds and thousands.

These two facts recall and proclaim a striking truth of the greatest significance in the moral and social order. They declare that the mission of education regards before all, above all, primarily the Church and the family, and this by natural and divine law, and that therefore it cannot be slighted, cannot be evaded, cannot be supplanted.

TO THE STATE

From such priority of rights on the part of the Church and of the family in the field of education, most important advantages, as we have seen, accrue to the whole of society. Moreover in accordance with the divinely established order of things, no damage can follow from it to the true and just rights of the State in regard to the education of its citizens.

These rights have been conferred upon civil society by the Author of nature Himself, not by title of fatherhood, as in the case of the Church and of the family, but in virtue of the authority which it possesses to promote the common temporal welfare, which is precisely the purpose of its existence. Consequently education cannot pertain to civil society in the same way in which it pertains to the Church and to the family, but in a different way corresponding to its own particular end and object.

Now this end and object, the common welfare in the temporal order, consists in that peace and security in which families and individual citizens have the free exercise of their rights, and at the same time enjoy the greatest spiritual and temporal prosperity possible in this life, by the mutual union and coordination of the work of all. The function therefore of the civil authority residing in the State is twofold, to protect and to foster, but by no means to absorb the family and the individual, or to substitute itself for them.

Accordingly in the matter of education, it is the right, or to speak more correctly, it is the duty of the State to protect in its legislation, the prior rights, already described, of the family as regards the Christian education of its offspring, and consequently also to respect the supernatural rights of the Church in this same realm of Christian education.

It also belongs to the State to protect the rights of the child itself when the parents are found wanting either physically or morally in this respect, whether by default, incapacity, or misconduct, since, as has been shown, their right to educate is not an absolute and despotic one, but dependent on the natural and divine law, and therefore subject alike to the authority and jurisdiction of the Church, and to the vigilance and administrative care of the State in view of the common good. Besides, the family is not a perfect society, that is, it has not in itself all the means necessary for its full development. In such cases, exceptional no doubt, the State does not put itself in the place of the family, but merely supplies deficiencies, and provides suitable means, always in conformity with the natural rights of the child and the supernatural rights of the Church.

In general then it is the right and duty of the State to protect, according to the rules of right reason and faith, the moral and religious education of youth, by removing public impediments that stand in the way.

In the first place it pertains to the State, in view of the common good, to promote in various ways the education and instruction of youth. It should begin by encouraging and assisting, of its own accord, the initiative and activity of the Church and the family, whose successes in this field have been clearly demonstrated by history and experience. It should moreover supplement their work whenever this falls short of what is necessary, even by means of its own schools and institutions. For the State more than any other society is provided with the means put at its disposal for the needs of all, and it is only right that it use these means to the advantage of those who have contributed them.

Over and above this, the State can exact, and take measures to secure that all its citizens have the necessary knowledge of their civic and political duties, and a certain degree of physical, intellectual and moral culture, which, considering the conditions of our times, is really necessary for the common good.

However it is clear that in all these ways of promoting education and instruction, both public and private, the State should respect the inherent rights of the Church and of the family concerning Christian education, and moreover have regard for distributive justice. Accordingly, unjust and unlawful is any monopoly, educational or scholastic, which, physically or morally, forces families to make use of government schools, contrary to the dictates of their Christian conscience, or contrary even to their legitimate preferences.

This does not prevent the State from making due provision for the right administration of public affairs and for the protection of its peace, within or without the realm. These are things which directly concern the public good and call for special aptitudes and special preparation. The State may therefore reserve to itself the establishment and direction of schools intended to prepare for certain civic duties and especially for military service, provided it be careful not to injure the rights of the Church or of the family in what pertains to them. It is well to repeat this warning here; for in these days there is spreading a spirit of nationalism which is falsely exaggerated, as well as dangerous to true peace and prosperity. Under its influence various excesses are committed in giving a military turn to the so-called physical training of boys (sometimes even of girls, contrary to the very instincts of human nature); or again in usurping unreasonably on Sunday, the time which should be devoted to religious duties and to family life at home.

It is not our intention however to condemn what is good in the spirit of discipline and legitimate bravery promoted by these methods: We condemn only what is excessive, as for example violence, which must not be confounded with courage nor with the noble sentiment of military valor in defense of country and public order; or again exaltation of athleticism, which even in classic pagan times marked the decline and downfall of genuine physical training.

In general also it belongs to civil society and the State to provide what may be called civic education, not only for its youth, but for all ages and classes. This consists in the practise of presenting publicly to groups of individuals information having an intellectual, imaginative and emotional appeal, calculated to draw their wills to what is upright and honest, and to urge its practise by a sort of moral compulsion, positively by disseminating such knowledge, and negatively by suppressing what is opposed to it. This civic education, so wide and varied in itself as to include almost every activity of the State intended for the public good, ought also to be regulated by the norms of rectitude, and therefore cannot conflict with the doctrines of the Church which is the divinely appointed teacher of these norms.

RELATION BETWEEN CHURCH AND STATE

All that we have said so far regarding the activity of the State in educational matters, rests on the solid and immovable foundation of the Catholic doctrine of The Christian Constitution of States set forth in such masterly fashion by Our Predecessor Leo XIII, notably in the Encyclicals *Immortale Dei* and *Sapientiae Christianae*. He writes as follows: "God has divided the government of the human race between two authorities, ecclesiastical and civil, establishing one over things divine, the other over things human. Both are supreme, each in its own domain; each has its own fixed boundaries which limit its activities. These boundaries are determined by the peculiar nature and the proximate end of each, and describe as it were a sphere within which, with exclusive right, each may develop its influence. As however the same subjects are under the two authorities, it may happen that the same matter, though from a different point of view, may come under the competence and jurisdiction of each of them. It follows that Divine Providence, whence both authorities have their origin, must have traced with due order the proper line of action for each. The powers that are, are ordained of God."

Now the education of youth is precisely one of those matters that belong both to the Church and to the State, "though in different ways," as explained above. "Therefore," continues Leo XIII, "between the two powers there must reign a well ordered harmony. Not without reason may this mutual agreement be compared to the union of body and soul in man. Its nature and extent can only be determined by considering, as we have said, the nature of each of the two powers, and in particular the excellence and nobility of the respective ends. One is committed directly and specifically the charge of what is helpful in worldly matters; while the other is to concern itself with the things that pertain to heaven and eternity. Everything therefore in human affairs that is in any way sacred, or has reference to the salvation of souls and the worship of God, whether by its nature or by its end, is subject to the jurisdiction and discipline of the Church. Whatever else is comprised in the civil and political order, rightly comes under the authority of the State; for Christ commanded us to give to Caesar the things that are Caesar's, and to God the things that are God's."

Whoever refuses to admit these principles, and hence to apply them to education, must necessarily deny that Christ has founded His Church for the eternal salvation of mankind, and maintain instead that civil society and the State are not subject to God and to His law, natural and divine. Such a doctrine is manifestly impious, contrary to right reason, and, especially in this matter of education, extremely harmful to the proper training of youth, and disastrous as well for civil society as for the well-being of all mankind. On the other hand from the application of these principles, there inevitably result immense advantages for the right formation of citizens. This is abundantly proved by the history of every age. Tertullian in his *Apologeticus* could throw down a challenge to the enemies of the Church in the early days of Christianity, just as St. Augustine did in his; and we today can repeat with him, "Let those who declare the teaching of Christ to be opposed to the welfare of the State, furnish us with an army of soldiers such as Christ says soldiers ought to be; let them give us subjects, husbands, wives, parents, children, masters, servants, kings, judges, taxpayers, and taxgatherers who live up to the teachings of Christ; and then let them dare assert that Christian doctrine is harmful to the State. Rather let them not hesitate one moment to acclaim that doctrine, rightly observed, the greatest safeguard of the State." . . .

While treating of education, it is not out of place to show here how an ecclesiastical writer, who flourished in more recent times, during the Renaissance, the holy and learned Cardinal Silvio Antoniano, to whom the cause of Christian education is greatly indebted, has set forth most clearly this well established point of Catholic doctrine. He had been a disciple of that wonderful educator of youth, St. Philip Neri; he was teacher and Latin secretary to St. Charles Borromeo, and it was at the latter's suggestion and under his inspiration that he wrote his splendid treatise on *The Christian Education of Youth*. In it he argues as follows:

Necessity and Advantages of Mutual Agreement

"The more closely the temporal power of a nation aligns itself with the spiritual, and the more it fosters and promotes the latter, by so much the more it contributes to the conservation of the commonwealth. For it is the aim of the ecclesiastical authority by the use of spiritual means, to form good Christians in accordance with its own particular end and object; and in doing this it helps at the same time to form good citizens, and prepares them to meet their obligations as members of a civil society. This follows of necessity because in the City of God, the Holy Roman Catholic Church, a good citizen and an upright man are absolutely one and the same thing. How grave therefore is the error of those who separate things so closely united, and who think that they can produce good citizens by ways and methods other than those which make for the formation of good Christians. For, let human prudence say what it likes and reason as it pleases, it is impossible to produce true temporal peace and tranquillity by things repugnant or opposed to the peace and happiness of eternity."

What is true of the State, is true also of science, scientific methods and scientific research; they have nothing to fear from the full and perfect mandate which the Church holds in the field of education. Our Catholic institutions, whatever their grade in the educational and scientific world, have no need of apology. The esteem they enjoy, the praise they receive, the learned works which they promote and produce in such abundance, and above all, the men, fully and splendidly equipped, whom they provide for the magistracy, for the professions, for the teaching career, in fact for every walk of life, more than sufficiently testify in their favor.

These facts moreover present a most striking confirmation of the Catholic doctrine defined by the Vatican Council: "Not only is it impossible for faith and reason to be at variance with each other, they are on the contrary of mutual help. For while right reason establishes the foundations of Faith, and, by the help of its light, develops a knowledge of the things of God, Faith on the other hand frees and preserves reason from error and enriches it with varied knowledge. The Church therefore, far from hindering the pursuit of the arts and sciences, fosters and promotes them in many ways. For she is neither ignorant nor unappreciative of the many advantages which flow from them to mankind. On the contrary she admits that just as they come from God, Lord of all knowledge, so too if rightly used, with the help of His grace they lead to God. Nor does she prevent sciences, each in its own sphere, from making use of principles and methods of their own. Only while acknowledging the freedom due to them, she takes every precaution to prevent them from falling into error by opposition to divine doctrine, or from overstepping their proper limits, and thus invading and disturbing the domain of Faith."

This norm of a just freedom in things scientific, serves also as an inviolable norm of a just freedom in things didactic, or for rightly understood liberty in teaching; it should be observed therefore in what ever instruction is imparted to others. Its obligation is all the more binding in justice when there is question of instructing youth. For in this work the teacher, whether public or private, has no absolute right of his own, but only such as has been communicated to him by others. Besides every Christian child or youth has a strict right to instruction in harmony with the teaching of the Church, the pillar and ground of truth. And whoever disturbs the pupil's Faith in any way, does him grave wrong, inasmuch as he abuses the trust which children place in their teachers, and takes unfair advantage of their inexperience and of their natural craving for unrestrained liberty, at once illusory and false. . . .

THE RELEASED TIME DECISION, 1952 *

(Mr. Justice Douglas delivered the opinion of the Court.)

New York City has a program which permits its public schools to release students during the school day so that they may leave the school buildings and school grounds and go to religious centers for religious instruction or devotional exercises. A student is released on written request of his parents. Those not released stay in the classrooms. The churches make weekly reports to the schools, sending a list of children who have been released from public school but who have not reported for religious instruction.

This "released time" program involves neither religious instruction in public school classrooms nor the expenditure of public funds. All costs, including the application blanks, are paid by the religious organizations. The case is therefore unlike *McCollum* v. *Board of Education,* 333 U.S. 203, which involved a "released time" program from Illinois. In that case the classrooms were turned over to religious instructors. We accordingly held that the program violated the First Amendment which (by reason of the Fourteenth Amendment) prohibits the states from establishing religion or prohibiting its free exercise. . . .

It takes obtuse reasoning to inject any issue of the "free exercise" of religion into the present case. No one is forced to go to the religious classroom and no religious exercise or instruction is brought to the classrooms of the public schools. A student need not take religious instruction. He is

* *Zorach v. Clausen,* 343 U.S. 306 (1952).

left to his own desires as to the manner or time of his religious devotions, if any.

There is a suggestion that the system involves the use of coercion to get public school students into religious classrooms. There is no evidence in the record before us that supports that conclusion. The present record indeed tells us that the school authorities are neutral in this regard and do no more than release students whose parents so request. If in fact coercion were used, if it were established that any one or more teachers were using their office to persuade or force students to take the religious instruction, a wholly different case would be presented. Hence we put aside that claim of coercion both as respects the "free exercise" of religion and "an establishment of religion" within the meaning of the First Amendment.

We are a religious people whose institutions presuppose a Supreme Being. We guarantee the freedom to worship as one chooses. We make room for as wide a variety of beliefs and creeds as the spiritual needs of man deem necessary. We sponsor an attitude on the part of government that shows no partiality to any one group and that lets each flourish according to the zeal of its adherents and the appeal of its dogma. When the state encourages religious instruction or cooperates with religious authorities by adjusting the schedule of public events to sectarian needs, it follows the best of our traditions. For it then respects the religious nature of our people and accommodates the public service to their spiritual needs. To hold that it may not would be to find in the Constitution a requirement that the government show a callous indifference to religious groups. That would be preferring those who believe in no religion over those who do believe. Government may not finance religious groups nor undertake religious instruction nor blend secular and sectarian education nor use secular institutions to force one or some religion on any person. But we find no constitutional requirement which makes it necessary for government to be hostile to religion and to throw its weight against efforts to widen the effective scope of religious influence. The government must be neutral when it comes to competition between sects. It may not thrust any sect on any person. It may not make a religious observance compulsory. It may not coerce anyone to attend church, to observe a religious holiday, or to take religious instruction. But it can close its doors or suspend its operations as to those who want to repair to their religious sanctuary for worship or instruction. No more than that is undertaken here.

In the *McCollum* case the classrooms were used for religious instruction and the force of the public school was used to promote that instruction. Here, as we have said, the public schools do no more than accommodate their schedules to a program of outside religious instruction. We follow the *McCollum* case. But we cannot expand it to cover the present released time program unless separation of Church and State means that public institutions can make no adjustments of their schedules to accommodate the religious needs of the people. We cannot read into the Bill of Rights such a philosophy of hostility to religion.

Affirmed.

MR. JUSTICE BLACK, dissenting

Illinois ex rel. McCollum v. Board of Education, 333 U.S. 203, held invalid as an "establishment of religion" an Illinois system under which school children, compelled by law to go to public schools, were freed from some hours of required school work on condition that they attend special religious classes held in the school buildings. Although the classes were taught by sectarian teachers neither employed nor paid by the state, the state did use its power to further the program by releasing some of the children from regular class work, insisting that those released attend the religious classes, and requiring that those who remained behind do some kind of academic work while the others received their religious training. We said this about the Illinois system:

> Pupils compelled by law to go to school for secular education are released in part from their legal duty upon the condition that they attend the religious classes. This is beyond all question a utilization of the tax-established and tax-supported public school system to aid religious groups to spread their faith. And it falls squarely under the ban of the First Amendment. . . . *McCollum v. Board of Education, supra,* at pp. 209-10.

I see no significant difference between the invalid Illinois system and that of New York here sustained. Except for the use of the school buildings in Illinois, there is no difference between the systems which I consider even worthy of mention. In the New York program, as in that of Illinois, the school authorities release some of the children on the condition that they attend the religious classes, get reports on whether they attend, and hold the other children in the school building until the religious hour is over. As we attempted to make categorically clear, the *McCollum* decision would have been the same if the religious classes had not been held in the school buildings. We said:

> "Here *not only* are the State's tax-supported public school buildings used for the dissemination of religious doctrines. The State *also* affords sectarian groups an invaluable aid in that it helps to provide pupils for their religious classes through use of the State's compulsory public school machinery. *This* is not separation of Church and State." (Emphasis supplied.) *McCollum v. Board of Education, supra,* at p. 212.

Religion and Education   533

McCollum thus held that Illinois could not constitutionally manipulate the compelled classroom hours of its compulsory school machinery so as to channel children into sectarian classes. Yet that is exactly what the Court holds New York can do.

Here the sole question is whether New York can use its compulsory education laws to help religious sects get attendants presumably too unenthusiastic to go unless moved to do so by the pressure of this state machinery. That this is the plan, purpose, design and consequence of the New York program cannot be denied. The state thus makes religious sects beneficiaries of its power to compel children to attend secular schools. Any use of such coercive power by the state to help or hinder some religious sects or to prefer all religious sects over nonbelievers or vice versa is just what I think the First Amendment forbids. In considering whether a state has entered this forbidden field the question is not whether it has entered too far but whether it has entered at all. New York is manipulating its compulsory education laws to help religious sects get pupils. This is not separation but combination of Church and State.

The Court's validation of the New York system rests in part on its statement that Americans are "a religious people whose institutions presuppose a Supreme Being." This was at least as true when the First Amendment was adopted; and it was just as true when eight Justices of this Court invalidated the released time system in *McCollum* on the premise that a state can no more "aid all religions" than it can aid one. It was precisely because Eighteenth Century Americans were a religious people divided into many fighting sects that we were given the constitutional mandate to keep Church and State completely separate. Colonial history had already shown that, here as elsewhere, zealous sectarians entrusted with governmental power to further their causes would sometimes torture, maim and kill those they branded "heretics," "atheists" or "agnostics." The First Amendment was therefore to insure that no one powerful sect or combination of sects could use political or governmental power to punish dissenters whom they could not convert to their faith. Now as then, it is only by wholly isolating the state from the religious sphere and compelling it to be completely neutral, that the freedom of each and every denomination and of all nonbelievers can be maintained. It is this neutrality the Court abandons today when it treats New York's coercive system as a program which *merely* "encourages religious instruction or cooperates with religious authorities." The abandonment is all the more dangerous to liberty because of the Court's legal exaltation of the orthodox and its derogation of unbelievers.

Under our system of religious freedom, people have gone to their religious sanctuaries not because they feared the law but because they loved their God. The choice of all has been as free as the choice of those who answered the call to worship moved only by the music of the old Sunday morning church bells. The spiritual mind of man has thus been free to believe, disbelieve, or doubt, without repression, great or small, by the heavy hand of government. Statutes authorizing such repression have been stricken. Before today, our judicial opinions have refrained from drawing invidious distinctions between those who believe in no religion and those who do believe. The First Amendment has lost much if the religious follower and the atheist are no longer to be judically regarded as entitled to equal justice under law.

State help to religion injects political and party prejudices into a holy field. It too often substitutes force for prayer, hate for love, and persecution for persuasion. Government should not be allowed, under cover of the soft euphemism of "co-operation," to steal into the sacred area of religious choice.

Communications and Education

ON THE STORIES CHILDREN HEAR *

You know, I said, that we begin by telling children stories which, though not wholly destitute of truth, are in the main fictitious; and these stories are told them when they are not of an age to learn gymnastics.

Very true.

That was my meaning when I said that we must teach music before gymnastics.

Quite right, he said.

You know also that the beginning is the most important part of any work, especially in the case of a young and tender thing; for that is the time at which the character is being formed and the desired impression is more readily taken.

Quite true.

And shall we just carelessly allow children to hear any casual tales which may be devised by casual persons, and to receive into their minds ideas for the most part the very opposite of those which we should wish them to have when they are grown up?

We cannot.

Then the first thing will be to establish a censorship of the writers of fiction, and let the censors receive any tale of fiction which is good, and reject the bad; and we will desire mothers and nurses to tell their children the authorised ones only. Let them fashion the mind with such tales, even

---

* Plato, *The Republic,* Book II, from *The Dialogues of Plato,* translated by Benjamin Jowett (New York: Oxford University Press, 1953), pp. 640-42, 647f. Reprinted by permission. (Fourth century B.C.)

more fondly than they mould the body with their hands; but most of those which are now in use must be discarded.

Of what tales are you speaking? he said.

You may find a model of the lesser in the greater, I said; for they are necessarily of the same type, and there is the same spirit in both of them.

Very likely, he replied; but I do not as yet know what you would term the greater.

Those, I said, which are narrated by Homer and Hesiod, and the rest of the poets, who have ever been the great story-tellers of mankind.

But which stories do you mean, he said; and what fault do you find with them?

A fault which is most serious, I said; the fault of telling a lie, and, what is more, a bad lie.

But when is this fault committed?

Whenever an erroneous representation is made of the nature of gods and heroes,—as when a painter paints a portrait not having the shadow of a likeness to the original.

Yes, he said, that sort of thing is certainly very blameable; but what are the stories which you mean?

First of all, I said, there was that greatest of all lies, in high places, which the poet told about Uranus, and which was a bad lie too,—I mean what Hesiod says that Uranus did, and how Cronus retaliated on him.[1] The doings of Cronus, and the sufferings which in turn his son inflicted upon him, even if they were true, ought certainly not to be lightly told to young and thoughtless persons; if possible, they had better be buried in silence. But if there is an absolute necessity for their mention, a chosen few might hear them in a mystery, and they should sacrifice not a common [Eleusinian] pig, but some huge and unprocurable victim; and then the number of the hearers will be very few indeed.

Why, yes, said he, those stories are extremely objectionable.

Yes, Adeimantus, they are stories not to be repeated in our State; the young man should not be told that in committing the worst of crimes he is far from doing anything outrageous; and that even if he chastises his father when he does wrong, in whatever manner, he will only be following the example of the first and greatest among the gods.

I entirely agree with you, he said; in my opinion those stories are quite unfit to be repeated.

Neither, if we mean our future guardians to regard the habit of quarrelling among themselves as of all things the basest, should any word be said to them of the wars in heaven, and of the plots and fightings of the gods against one another, for they are not true. No, we shall never mention

[1] Hesiod, *Theogony*, 154, 459.

the battles of the giants, or let them be embroidered on garments; and we shall be silent about the innumerable other quarrels of gods and heroes with their friends and relatives. If they would only believe us we would tell them that quarrelling is unholy, and that never up to this time has there been any quarrel between citizens; this is what old men and old women should begin by telling children; and when they grow up, the poets also should be told to compose for them in a similar spirit. But the narrative of Hephaestus binding Here his mother, or how on another occasion Zeus sent him flying for taking her part when she was being beaten, and all the battles of the gods in Homer—these tales must not be admitted into our State, whether they are supposed to have an allegorical meaning or not. For a young person cannot judge what is allegorical and what is literal; anything that he receives into his mind at that age is likely to become indelible and unalterable; and therefore it is most important that the tales which the young first hear should be models of virtuous thoughts. . . .

Then, although we are admirers of Homer, we do not admire the lying dream which Zeus sends to Agamemnon; neither will we praise the verses of Aeschylus in which Thetis says that Apollo at her nuptials

> Was celebrating in song her fair progeny whose days were to be long, and to know no sickness. And when he had spoken of my lot as in all things blessed of heaven he raised a note of triumph and cheered my soul. And I thought that the word of Phoebus, being divine and full of prophecy, would not fail. And now he himself who uttered the strain, he who was present at the banquet, and who said this—he it is who has slain my son.[2]

These are the kind of sentiments about the gods which will arouse our anger; and he who utters them shall be refused a chorus; neither shall we allow teachers to make use of them in the instruction of the young, meaning, as we do, that our guardians, as far as men can be, should be true worshippers of the gods and like them.

I entirely agree, he said, in these principles, and promise to make them my laws.

STORYTELLERS AS TUTORS [*]

A. I like Superman better than the others because they can't do everything Superman can do. Batman can't fly and that is very important.

Q. Would you like to be able to fly?

[2] From a lost play.
[*] David Riesman et al., *The Lonely Crowd* (New Haven: Yale University Press, 1950), pp. 84-111.

A. I would like to be able to fly if everybody else did, but otherwise it would be kind of conspicuous.

From an interview with a twelve-year-old girl.[1]

. . .

Our interest in this chapter will not be in the commercial purveyors of language and imagery or the storytellers themselves but in the effects on the child audience. And of course these effects cannot be considered in isolation from the constellation of parents, teachers, and peer-groupers who operate on the assembly line of character. If we find, for instance, a child who seems more affected by print than by people, it may be because people are so overwhelming for him that he must take refuge in print. Furthermore, cultures differ very much in the perceptions they stress in teaching the child to differentiate among images and to differentiate among people. But in general it seems fair to say that the storytellers (or more technically the mass media of communication) are indispensable agents of socialization. They picture the world for the child and thus give both form and limits to his memory and imagination.[2]

. . .

Societies in the phase of incipient population decline can afford, can technically provide, and have both the time and the need to receive a bounteous flow of imagery from urban centers of distribution. Industrialism and mass literacy seem to go together. These same societies, moreover, rely more heavily than their predecessors on character-forming agencies outside the home. Hence, as we would expect, the storytellers of the mass media play a great role among other-directed children. We can see what has changed in recent generations only by comparing today's experience with that of children in societies depending on tradition-direction and inner-direction.

I. SONG AND STORY IN THE STAGE OF TRADITION-DIRECTION

The society which depends for conformity on tradition-direction uses as part of its stock in trade its oral traditions, its myths, legends, and songs. These are transmitted by the same family members who play an active part in all the other phases of socializing the young.

---

[1] Katherine M. Wolfe and Marjorie Fiske, "The Children Talk About Comics," *Communications Research 1948-1949,* ed. Paul F. Lazarsfeld and Frank Stanton (New York, Harper, 1949), pp. 26-7.

[2] See the remarkable discussion by Ernest Schachtel, "On Memory and Childhood Amnesia," *Psychiatry,* X (1947), 1; see also Evelyn T. Riesman, "Childhood Memory in the Painting of Joan Miro," *ETC,* VI (1949), 160.

CHIMNEY-CORNER MEDIA

When we find a society in which stories are transmitted by word of mouth, we put our finger on one of the very indexes by which we know it as a society depending on tradition-direction. In terms of the technique of transmission, the important thing is that the story or fable is told orally, not in print. In terms of the storytelling situation, the important thing is that the story is told, ordinarily, by a family member or by a professional or semiprofessional closely connected with the extended family group. In both cases the result is that the story is modulated for, and built into, the web of values that the storyteller also controls and relates himself to in active ways. One way of expressing this is to say that storytelling is like a handicraft industry: each telling is different from the other, and each is tailored to the taste and disposition of the audience.

These factors are all-important in their effect on audiences. Since the physical and social distance between the teller and listener is slight, the listener is to some extent a participant in the telling. A child can correct the teller or criticize the theme or elaborate the narrative—though more often he is probably confined to asking questions. This means that the listener even as a child, is in a position to find and develop his own likings. . . .

It is not surprising that songs and stories rendered in face-to-face performance among relatives and friends are often baldly cautionary tales; they tell what happens to those who disobey the community or the supernatural authorities. Or they illustrate by reference to the illustrious what kind of person one ought to be in the culture in terms of such traits as bravery and endurance. A surprising number of tales, however, in many cultures depending on tradition-direction are not cautionary in this direct sense. As in the Bible, some tales recount rebellions, successful or tragic, against the powers that be—though in many cases the theme of rebellion is disguised.

TALES OF NORM AND "ABNORM"

As we move over to the consideration of content, we can take the rebellious note struck in these tales to indicate that even in a society depending on tradition-direction there still remain strivings which are not completely socialized. By and large, people accept the harness of their culture, and it is hard for them to conceive of another make of harness. But they are not unaware of constraint, and their stories, as frequently their dreams, are the refuge and succor of this awareness and help to make it possible to go on with ordinary life. The communal load of shame or anxiety is reduced by the common "confession," the common release which the myth permits. There is in these myths, then, a good deal of "realism" about stubborn, unsocialized human nature—this is precisely why they can appeal to us across the centuries and across the cultural boundaries. They show people to be more fierce, more jealous, more rebellious than appears on the surface.

Why is this so? It appears that if people were only "adjusted"—if they never had even a thought which transcended the cultural prohibitions—life would have so little savor as to endanger the culture itself. Cultures depending upon tradition-direction usually manage to institutionalize a degree of rebellion not only for their deviants but for everybody. Sometimes this is done on a life-cycle basis. Thus some cultures permit, even encourage, sauciness from children only to clamp down on the adult; others allow the older women a bawdiness denied the younger ones. Sometimes there are special days—feast days—when bars are down.

Now when the aperture for rebellion lies in the realm of culturally approved fantasy, the socializing function of the tales and stories which are the predecessors of the mass media is clearly a dual one. The elders use the stories to tell the young: you must be like so-and-so if you are to be admired and to live up to the noble traditions of the group. But the young are also told—sometimes in the very same message—that there have been people like so-and-so who broke the rules, who did many worse things than you ever did, and perhaps ever dreamed of, and whether he lived to tell the tale or not, he did live and we speak of him.

This very ambivalence of the stories helps the young to integrate their forbidden impulses by recognizing them as part of their legacy as human beings. Stories make it possible for the face-to-face group which is charged with socialization of the young to draw on a cultural warehouse that provides models for behavior not to be found completely in any given face-to-face group. In this tradition-directed form of "popular culture" stories make it possible to form an underground connection, via myth, between repressed sectors of the adults and sectors of the young. Finally, they make it possible to hold the young to both more and less than what they see around them, either of approved behavior or of behavior which, while disapproved, is still done.

. . .

II. The Socializing Functions of Print in the Stage of Inner-Direction

When societies enter the phase of transitional growth of population, formal schooling increases, in part to train people for the new, more specialized tasks of industry and agriculture, in part to absorb the young who are no longer needed on farms and whose schooling can be supported by the greater productivity of the society. Of course, these young people learn to read. But the excitement and novelty of literacy in this period affect old as well as young. There is a hunger for the press and for books. . . .

In the United States, as in other countries of incipient population decline, this hunger has abated; indeed, it has been succeeded for many by a kind of satiety with serious print, coupled with insatiability for the amusements and agenda of popular culture. To remind ourselves of the older pattern we need only look at countries such as Mexico and Russia, now undergoing industrialization, where the old are avid for print and the young admired for learning. Some of this we can still see among the largely self-educated Negroes of the deep South who live among our surviving stratum of white and black illiterates.

How this development aided the shift from tradition-direction to inner-direction can be vividly traced in Thomas and Znanieki's *Polish Peasant*.[3] These writers describe the way in which the Polish rural press helped to restructure attitudes and values among the peasantry at the turn of the last century. They show that an individual peasant who learned to read at that time did not merely acquire a skill with little impact on his character; rather he made a decisive break with the primary group, with tradition-direction. The press picked him up at this turning point and supported his uncertain steps away from the primary group by criticizing the values of that group and by giving him a sense of having allies, albeit anonymous ones, in this move.

In this way the press helped link the newly individuated person to the newly forming society. The Polish press also supported very specific "character-building" measures, such as temperance and thrift, and fostered scientific farming as the American agricultural extension services have done; science was viewed as a kind of inner-directed morality as against the superstition of the remaining, tradition-directed peasantry. These attitudes, expounded in newspaper nonfiction, were reinforced in newspaper and periodical "edifying" fiction.

In these ways the local reader could escape into print from the criticisms of his neighbors and could test his inner-direction against the models given in the press. . . .

The tradition-directed person has not only a traditional standard of living but a traditional standard of how hard and long he works; and print serves, along with other agencies of socialization, to destroy both of these standards. The inner-directed man, open to "reason" via print, often develops a character structure which drives him to work longer hours and to live on lower budgets of leisure and laxity than would have been deemed possible before. He can be driven because he is ready to drive himself.

[3] W. I. Thomas and Florian Znaniecki, *The Polish Peasant in Europe and America* (New York, Knopf, 1927), II, 1367-96.

The skeptic may ask how can words, especially printed words, mold character? We might ask him in turn whether he has ever been frightened reading a detective story or excited reading a love story. Words not only affect us temporarily; they change us, they socialize or unsocialize us. Doubtless the printing press alone cannot completely assure any particular form of social coercion—and of course not all children, even in the inner-directed middle class, were readers. But print can powerfully rationalize the models which tell people what they ought to be like. Reaching children directly as well as through their parents and teachers, it can take the process of socialization out of the communal chimney corner of the era depending on tradition-direction and penetrate into the private bedrooms and libraries of the rising middle class: the child is allowed to gird himself for the battle of life in the small circle of light cast by his reading lamp or candle.

. . .

The general relation between teller and reader becomes a special case in situations in which the child is the reader. By teaching children to read, a gain is made in the efficiency of the socialization process. The supervising adult cannot be present all the time; but when he is not there, or is unimpressive, the written words and their accompanying illustration speak for him. The child, no longer a listener at the adult's knee, begins to take a more active part in the process of forming his own character by his selection among possible readings and possible interpretations of what is read. In his choice among socializing agencies in the mass communications field, he is soon engaged in inner-directed activity. While in one respect he is socialized from outside, in another he calculated his social possibilities himself as he reads. He begins to make more use of the increase in the number of possible relationships between himself and the storytellers following the change from word of mouth to print.

MODELS IN PRINT

With this image of the print-influenced child in mind, we can turn to examine the homiletic themes which, in the period dependent on inner-direction, unite the otherwise disparate media of the Protestant and Catholic lands. One main purpose of print is to teach the child something about the variety of adult roles he may enter upon and to permit him to "try on" these roles in fantasy. Life during the period of transitional population growth differs from earlier epochs in that the adult engages in activities which the growing child no longer sees nor understands. This is why he needs not only the rich vicariousness of print but also a mode of internal direction other than tradition to guide him in unaccustomed places and situations. Both the printed media and other forms of popular culture meet this need by adding their own spurs to the parents' admonitions on behalf of ambition as well as by offering more specific guidance about the variety of new paths to success.

These new paths, in both northern and southern lands after the Renaissance, are conceived and described in adult terms. For in the earlier stages of population growth adult life is not long, on the average; the age difference—and perhaps the difference in maturity—between the literate child and the full-grown adult is less than in the period of incipient decline of population. Moreover, while the distribution of imagery and print becomes wider and cheaper than ever before, there are still many people excluded by poverty from the storyteller's market; some of these are also the overworked young. In such a society the adult stories and adult styles of narrative are often made to do for children. Even when the trick, later so prevalent, of using the child's own language, gets started, the storyteller works on the notion that he can more successfully instill *adult* ideas if he uses the language of children.

Among the earliest signposts erected on the printed path to success, aside from the indirect guides of catechism and religious teaching, were the great authorities on etiquette. A volume like Castiglione's *The Courtier*, for example, was meant for adults; but there was nothing else on the subject for the near-adult to read. At the same time people were willing to assume, as Lord Chesterfield did, that the young man was ready in his teens to operate successfully in situations requiring etiquette. In the Protestant lands and classes however, after 1600 or so, the purpose of print is concerned more and more directly with how to succeed not in love or war but in business. Then follows the commercial inspirational literature that reached a sort of climax in Victorian England with the success biographies written by Samuel Smiles—and in the United States with the Horatio Alger books, which come closer to being slanted for the teen-age market.

The variety of such books is great, but it is not unfair to refer their pattern to such an exemplar as Franklin's *Poor Richard's Almanack*. It is the more useful to us because it happens to be the text selected by Max Weber as a typical self-inspirational document of the period of the Protestant ethic. The same themes appear in earlier works, such as *Pilgrim's Progress* or *Robinson Crusoe*, which on the surface do not seem to be concerned with proper conduct for would-be enterprisers. Yet in the first we can trace the motive of social election and salvation which can so easily become secularized, while in the second the motive of economic self-sufficiency is expressed in its classical paradigm. Both works aim to fire the ambition and élan, spiritual and adventurous, of inner-directed youth.

This documentary style is the literary index of an era increasingly dependent on inner-direction. There is leisure in such an era for fiction—but little for fantasy. Defoe may be taken as archetypical. He used a variety of techniques, such as first person narration, elaborate descriptions of food, clothing, and shelter, diary-like accounts of money transactions, and collaborative witnesses, to provide a realistic setting for his wildly adventurous tales. In this respect he is certainly the ancestor of the comic book, which excels in exploiting realism of detail as a distraction to hide improbability of situation. . . .

Biography also allows children, in a society dependent on inner-direction, to move away from family and into a rationalized world—cooperating in this way with the parental installation of internal, self-piloting processes. Consider, for instance, the George Washington myth. Not only are little boys told in the era of inner-direction that they may grow up to be president but they are given scales by which to measure and discipline themselves for the job during boyhood. If they do not tell lies, if they work hard, and so on—if, that is, they act in their boyhoods as the legendary Washington acted in his—then they may succeed to his adult role. The role, moreover, by its very nature, is a continuing one; somebody is always president; thus its heroes do not have the once-for-all quality of those in the myths and legends of the earlier era. In fantasy the little boy not only identifies with young Washington in the French and Indian wars but also with the adult role of president—either role will take him far from home, socially and geographically.

What the story of George Washington was for the white child the story of Booker Washington was for the black. The latter's whole effort was to turn the Negro away from dependence on tradition-direction toward dependence on inner-direction. With the role of the freedman as yet undetermined, he placed enormous emphasis on character building to enable the Negro to assume any role once he was established as a middle-class, respectable American. One of his books addressed to Negroes was called *Character Building;* and *The Negro Worker,* a journal published at Tuskegee, with its strong emphasis on thrift, diligence, and manners, is one of the laggard remnants (of course, under violent attack from northern urban Negroes) of a vast literature concerned not with improving "personality" but with improving "character."

THE OVERSTEERED CHILD

There is, however, a danger for the child in such pious biographical portraits of exemplary persons and roles because of the very fact that he can read in isolation, without the intervention either of adults or peers; he can be "oversteered." This is not so much the danger of being driven by one's character so that one is easily exploited by industrialism, but rather the danger of being set on a course one cannot realistically follow. The inner-directed child, trying to shape his character according to the ideals presented in print, does not see these models, any more than he sees his parents, in a state of undress. There is none of the familiarity with the hero, even the gods in the guise of heroes, to be found in the orally mediated myths of the society depending on tradition-direction. Thus, Washington or Cromwell, Garibaldi or Bismarck, Edison or Ford, take on some of the awesomeness of the Calvinist God. The result for many is a dreadful insecurity as to whether they live up to their exalted models. The insecurity not even the parents (when they do not themselves make matters worse by trying to be such models) can easily assuage.

Nevertheless, this unmitigated pressure for inner-directed activity in pursuit of goodness and fame succeeded, as we know, in producing in many cases an "adjusted" person because social conditions rewarded inhibitions and solaced insecurities. In other cases, however, the gap between the demand for inner-direction and the capacity for it became too great and the individual broke down—the revival meeting represents, at one class level, the emotional pressures of such a conflict. While the parents alone, with their demands on all the children, were often responsible for children's emotional collapse, the storytellers tended to reinforce the social pressures even where the adults might have been more lenient.

The discussion has emphasized but cannot, indeed, emphasize too much the significance of putting some of the task of socializing the child onto other than the face-to-face adults. Just as the whipping Kachinas of the Hopi Indians can tailor their punishing or initiatory blows to a particularly sensitive child, so the adults in the era of tradition-direction can see to it that the bite of the story is not too grim for any in the audience. The child in the inner-directed era, however, leaves home both to go to school and to go to books and other mass-media products; and here such mediation is no longer possible.

Moreover, the child in a period of rising literacy is much more likely than his parents to be able to read. Thus, while some children learn from books and plays how to act in a career which will be different from that of their parents—or indeed that it is possible to have such a career—other children, less able to conform in the characterologically prescribed ways, less self-disciplined and systematic, for instance, learn from precisely the same media how lost they are. . . .

Yet it is my impression that the stream of print is seldom without alleviating tendencies, even in the theocratic regimes. Almost always there is an underground of a more picaresque sort in which the growing boy at least can take some refuge. To be sure, the power of the parents in an era dependent on inner-direction may keep out such literature, as the pastors in puritan countries might also keep it out of the community. But they can hardly destroy, even in the worst case, the refuge of print itself—and we must not forget that the great reading-hour storehouse of the era depending on inner-direction is the Bible and that the Bible is not one book but many, with an inexhaustible variety of messages.

On the whole, therefore, the influence of the storytellers in the era of inner-direction is probably a liberating one. Print encourages and permits the child to free himself from his family and primary group; and he learns to criticize what he leaves behind, as did the self-emancipating readers of the Polish peasant press. It opens up to him a whole range of models—the "five-foot wardrobe" from which he can try on new roles. . . .

III. THE MASS MEDIA IN THE STAGE OF OTHER-DIRECTION

I have assumed that the mass media today—radio, movies, records, comics, books, and magazines for children—play a greater role in shaping character than was the case in previous epochs. Certainly these agencies are more centralized and reach more people more of the time than ever before. . . .

THE CHILD MARKET

. . . In America middle-class children have allowances of their own at four or five; they have, as opinion leaders in the home, some say in the family budget. The allowances are expected to be spent, whereas in the earlier era they were often used as cudgels of thrift. Moreover, the monopolistic competition characteristic of this era can afford, and is interested in, building up in the child habits of consumption he will employ as an adult. . . .

The children are more heavily cultivated in their own terms than ever before. But while the educator in earlier eras might use the child's language to put across an adult message, today the child's language may be used to put across the advertiser's and storyteller's idea of what children are like. No longer is it thought to be the child's job to learn the adult world as the adult sees it; for one thing, the world as the adult sees it today is perhaps a more complicated one.[4] Instead, the mass media ask the child to see the world as "the" child—that is, the *other* child—sees it. This is partly, but only partly, the result of the technical advances that make it possible for the movies to create the child world of Margaret O'Brien and

---

[4] Certainly the adult literature is more complicated and/or more salacious on its top levels, as compared with the earlier era when both child and adult could read Mark Twain even at his most bitter, Dickens even at his most crude, H. G. Wells even at his most involved.

her compeers, for the radio to have its array of Hardys, Aldriches, and other juveniles, and for advertising and cover art to make use of professional child models. The media have created a picture of what boyhood and girlhood are like (as during the war they created the picture of the GI, again using the considerably edited language of the soldier) and they force children either to accept or aggressively to resist this picture of themselves.

The child begins to be bombarded by radio and comics from the moment he can listen and just barely read. The bombardment—with of course inevitable over- and undershots—hits specifically at very narrow age grades. For example, there seems to be for many children a regular gradation of comic-reading stages: from the animal stories like *Bugs Bunny* to invincible heroes like *Superman,* and from there to heroes like *Batman* who, human in make-up, are vulnerable, though of course they always win. The authors of "The Children Talk About Comics" find that the children themselves are aware of the progression, aware of those laggards who still read romper media when they should have graduated to blue jeans. . . .

To be sure, the change from the preceding era of inner-direction in America is not abrupt; such changes never are. Formerly the mass media catered to the child market in at least three fields: school texts or homilies, magazines designed for children, and penny dreadfuls. But their appraisal of the market was amateurish in comparison with market research today. Moreover, they aimed generally to spur work drives and role experiments in the mobile, rather than to effect any socialization of taste. The English boys' weeklies, as Orwell describes them,[5] usually opposed liquor and tobacco—as did the clergyman authors of school and church readers. Such admonitions remind us of the "crime doesn't pay" lesson of the comics, a façade for messages of more importance. The boys' weeklies and their American counterparts were involved with training the young for the frontiers of production (including warfare), and as an incident of that training the embryo athlete might eschew smoke and drink. The comparable media today train the young for the frontiers of consumption—to tell the difference between Pepsi-Cola and Coca-Cola, as later between Old Golds and Chesterfields.

We may mark the change by citing an old nursery rhyme:

>This little pig went to market;
>This little pig stayed at home.
>This little pig had roast beef;
>This little pig had none.
>This little pig went wee-wee-wee
>All the way home.

[5] George Orwell, *Dickens, Dali & Others* (New York, Reynal & Hitchcock, 1946), p. 76.

The rhyme may be taken as a paradigm of individuation and unsocialized behavior among children of an earlier era. Today, however, all little pigs go to market; none stay home; all have roast beef, if any do; and all say "we-we."

WINNER TAKE ALL?

Yet perhaps the most important change is the shift in the situation in which listening and reading occur. In contrast with the lone reader of the era of inner-direction, we have the group of kids today, lying on the bed or floor, reading and trading comics and preferences among comics, or listening jointly to "The Lone Ranger." When reading and listening are not communal in fact, they are apt to be so in feeling: one is always conscious of the brooding omnipresence of the peer-group. Thus the Superman fan quoted at the head of the chapter cannot allow herself to identify with Superman—the others would think her foolish—while they would not think her foolish for believing that flying is very important.

In a society dependent on tradition-direction children are, as we have seen, introduced to stories by adult storytellers. The latter do not feel themselves to be in critical competition with the young. Hence they can encourage, or at least patronize, children's unsophisticated reactions of alarm or excitement at the tales they are told—and, later on, encourage the youngster's own tall talk and tale embroidery. But the peer-groupers who read or listen together without the protective presence of adults are in no such cozy relation of "listen my children and you shall hear. . . ." They cannot afford to let go—to fly.

One correlate is that the comic book differs from the fairy tale in several important respects. In the fairy tale the protagonist is frequently an underdog figure, a younger child, an ugly duckling, a commoner, while the villain is frequently an authority figure, a king, a giant, a stepmother. In the comics the protagonist is apt to be an invulnerable or near-invulnerable adult who is equipped, if not with supernatural powers, at least with two guns and a tall, terrific physique. Magical aid comes to the underdog—who remains a peripheral character—only through the mediation of this figure. Thus, whereas Jack of *Jack and the Beanstalk* gains magical assistance chiefly through his own daring, curiosity, and luck, a comic-book Jack would gain magical assistance chiefly through an all-powerful helper. While vaguely similar themes may be found in the stories of Robin Hood and Sir Galahad, the comics show a quantitative increase in the role of the more or less invulnerable authority-hero.

The relative change in this pattern [6] is not the "fault" of the comics.

---

[6] Here, too, the abruptness of the change from inner-direction should not be exaggerated. Eliot Freidson, a graduate student in sociology at the University of Chicago,

These merely play into a style of reception that is fitted to peer-group reading. Indeed—and this is both the conclusion of "The Children Talk About Comics" and of my own observations—if other-directed child comic fans read or hear stories that are not comics they will read them as if they were comics. They will tend to focus on who won and to miss the internal complexities of the tale, of a moral sort or otherwise. If one asks them, then, how they distinguish the "good guys" from the "bad guys" in the mass media, it usually boils down to the fact that the former always win; they are good guys by definition.

But of course the child wants to anticipate the result and so looks for external clues which will help him pick the winner. In the comics this is no problem: the good guys *look it,* being square-jawed, clear-eyed, tall men; the bad guys also look it, being, for reasons of piety, of no recognizable ethnic group but rather of a generally messy southern European frame—oafish and unshaven or cadaverous and over-smooth. But in movies (and in some comics with slinky beauties in them) this identification is not easy: the very types that are good guys in most comics may turn out to be villains after all. A striking example I have observed is the bafflement of several comic fans at the movie portrayal of the Countess de Winter (Lana Turner) in *The Three Musketeers.* If she looked so nice, how could she be so mean?

Thus we come to a paradox. The other-directed child is trained to be sensitive to interpersonal relations, and often he understands these with a sophistication few adults had in the era of inner-direction. Yet he is strikingly insensitive to problems of character as presented by his favorite storytellers; he tends to race through the story for its ending, or to read the ending first, and to miss just those problems of personal development that are not telltale clues to the outcome. . . .

It is not . . . the storytellers per se who teach children an emphasis on who wins—an emphasis also found in fairy tales and the Frank Merriwell books. The dime novels and melodramas of the period dependent on inner-direction also emphasized winning; hence it is important to see the precise differences introduced by the contemporary media as well as by the changed focus of the readers.

At the outset it seems helpful to distinguish between the inculcation of ambition and of antagonistic cooperation. "Ambition" I define as an indoctrination of goals in the period of inner-direction; it is a striving for fame or for goodness but always for clear goals: to get the job, to win the battle, to build the bridge. Competition in the era depending on inner-direction is

studying the ability of young children to remember stories, found them much more apt to recall a few traditional fairy tales like *Goldilocks* or *The Three Little Pigs* than either Golden Books or comics or movies. "Myth and the Child: An Aspect of Socialization" (Master's thesis, University of Chicago, 1949).

frequently ruthless, but at the same time people are in no doubt as to their place in the race—and that there is a race. If they feel guilt it is when they fail, not when they succeed. By contrast, "antagonistic cooperation" may be defined as an inculcated striving among the groups affected by other-direction. Here the important thing is not the goal but the relationship to the "others"; not one's own victory but the others' failure. In this new-style competition people are often in doubt whether there is a race at all, and if so, what its goals are. Since they are supposed to be cooperative rather than rivalrous, they may well feel guilt about success.[7]

The heroes of boys' literature of the older period were ambitious. They had goals. And the reader identified with them and tried to emulate them, at least in fantasy. Though these heroes might fight Indians or swim icy rivers or detect crime, they were not so remote from the reader as to make identification difficult. These heroes, like the modern ones, always won; but the reader was encouraged to be concerned not only with the final victorious outcome but with the inner struggles that preceded it and made it possible. The virtue which brought victory was frequently an ability to control the self, for instance, to be brave.

While it is often assumed that the comic strip simply continues this older pattern, this is not generally true. For many reasons the child reader does not identify himself with the comic-strip hero so frequently. For one thing, many children prefer the comics where the hero is not man but Superman or Plastic Man—possessing powers that are obviously unique. No correspondence course with Lionel Strongfort will turn one, even in the wildest flight of fantasy, into Superman. What is more important, the realism of petty detail which has reached a fine art in the comics, the radio, and the movies inhibits identification. This realism, with its color effects and sound effects, exceeds by far what Defoe and his direct successors could accomplish. The characters in much fiction of the era dependent on inner-direction are props—stereotypes of the sort indicated in the preceding section. In Jules Verne, for instance, it is the adventures, the mechanical details, not the characters, that are sharply delineated; the latter are loose-fitting uniforms into which many boys could fit themselves. The imaginative, tenebrous illustrations of an artist like Howard Pyle also left openings for identification by the reader who wanted to picture himself as the hero.

Little of this looseness of fit remains for the imagination of the modern reader or listener to fill in. Though comic-strip and comic-book characterization is, if anything, less sharp, externals are pinned down conclusively: every detail of costuming and speech is given. This is the more necessary because, with so many mass-media heroes competing for attention, their

[7] Cf. Karen Horney, *The Neurotic Personality of Our Time* (New York, W. W. Norton, 1937), pp. 192-3.

portrayers must engage in marginal differentiation in search of their trademark. Bodies by Milton Caniff must be as instantly recognizable as bodies by Fisher.

There is paradox in the reception of this realism. On the one hand, every additional brush stroke of the comic-strip artist rules out identifications for millions; the small-breasted girl, for example, may find only disapproval for herself in the comics. On the other hand, the same realism is one source of the fear of being conspicuous in our little Supergirl cited at the chapter head. If she were Superman, she would be instantly recognizable. She would lack the privacy of narcissism permitted the reader of an earlier day who could gloat over the fact that he was M. Vidocq or Sherlock Holmes—only nobody knew it.[8]

These generalizations need not be pushed too far. There are children—at least one has heard of them—who identify with Superman, or more easily, with Terry or the Saint. Nor is it out of the question to identify, at the same time, on one level of consciousness with the hero and on another level with the person he rescues. And while the heroes of the comics are ageless, having discovered the secret of eternal youth, the growing child can move from one hero to another who better fits his own changing needs and aspirations. These counter-tendencies are encouraged by the gadgetry —Superman cloaks, box-top items, and so on—that relates children to their radio, movie, and comic-book heroes. But it would be a mistake to assume that each wearer of a Superman cloak identifies with Superman; he may only be a fan, wearing his hero's colors.

Perhaps it is also significant that the comic book compresses into a few minutes' reading time a sequence which, in the earlier era, was dragged out in many pages of print. Think of the Count of Monte Cristo's years in jail, his suffering, his incredible patience, and the industry and study of the abbé's teaching; both his gain and his vengeance are moralized by these prolongations, and he is an old man when, after many chapters, he wins. By contrast, the comic-book or radio-drama hero wins almost effortlessly; the very curtailment of the telling time itself makes this more apparent. To be sure, like his movie counterpart, this hero does frequently get beaten

[8] One additional dimension here is that the child literature of today, though written by specialists on the child market, often reaches, as in the case of the comics, millions of more or less childish adults. There are no magazines left, such as *The American Boy* or *St. Nicholas*, which the young boy can read without sharing his readership with adults—for which he can even write, occasionally, as we are reminded by Henry Steele Commager's fine *St. Nicholas Anthology*. (A similar lack of sharp cleavage between child and adult life may be seen in the fact that it is no longer a decisive step for a boy to put on long pants or for a girl to put up her hair. With clothes as with books, when and in what doses to "put away childish things" becomes a matter for the peer-group to decide, within the limits of marginal differentiation.)

up, but this adds to excitement, not to morality or inner change, and helps justify an even worse beating administered to the "crooks."

Still another aspect of this change is worth looking at. If one does not identify with the winner but is at the very same time preoccupied with the process of winning itself, as the very handle by which one grasps a story, one is prepared for the role of consumer of others' winnings. One is prepared, that is, for the adult role of betting on the right horse, with no interest in the jockey or horse or knowledge of what it takes to be either. The content of the identification is impoverished to the point where virtually the only bond between reader and hero is the fact of the hero's winning. The spectator—the same holds for a quiz game, a sport contest, and, as we shall see, a political contest—wants to become involved with the winner simply in order to make the contest meaningful: his hope of victory makes the event exciting, while the game or contest or story is not appreciated for its own sake.

The victory of the hero, then, is only ostensibly a moral one. To be sure, vestiges of older moralities hang on, often as conventions enforced by censorship or the fear of it. But morality in the sense of a literary character's development, rather than morality in the sense of being on the "right" side, is not depicted. Consequently, morality is an inference from winning. Just as in a whodunit all appear guilty until they are retroactively cleared by finding the real killer, so the victory of the hero retroactively justifies his deeds and misdeeds. "Winner take all" becomes a tautology.

TOOTLE: A MODERN CAUTIONARY TALE

I have spoken as if the comic books, the cheapest and most widespread media, are the chief evidences of the pattern I am describing. It could be easily assumed that, in a home barricaded against the comic books, these patterns of readership would obtain no entrance. On the contrary, however, at least some of the important elements in the pattern are refined, disguised, and introduced into the socializing and informative books of the noncomic variety which are customarily purchased for their children by the middle and upper middle class. Furthermore, a whole range of these media teaches children the lesson given parents and teachers in many recent works on child development. The slant of that lesson is suggested by a passage from a book in use by teachers and PTA groups:

> The usual and desirable developmental picture is one of increasing self-control on the part of the individual children, of increasingly smooth social or play technics, and of an emergence at adolescence or early adulthood of higher forms of cooperation. The adolescent should have learned better "to take it" in group activity, should have developed an

Communications and Education 553

improved, though not yet perfect, self-control, and should have real insight into the needs and wishes of others.[9]

Tootle the Engine (text by Gertrude Crampton, pictures by Tibor Gergely) is a popular and in many ways charming volume in the "Little Golden Books" series—a series for children with a circulation of well over two million, an audience which includes, it seems, all classes of children. It is a cautionary tale even though it appears to be simply one of the many books about anthropomorphic vehicles—trucks, fire engines, taxicabs, tugboats, and so on—that are supposed to give a child a picture of real life. Tootle is a young engine who goes to engine school, where two main lessons are taught: stop at a red flag and "always stay on the track no matter what." Diligence in the lessons will result in the young engine's growing up to be a big streamliner. Tootle is obedient for a while and then one day discovers the delight of going off the tracks and finding flowers in the field. This violation of the rules cannot, however, be kept secret; there are telltale traces in the cowcatcher. Nevertheless, Tootle's play becomes more and more of a craving, and despite warnings he continues to go off the tracks and wander in the field. Finally the engine schoolmaster is desperate. He consults the mayor of the little town of Engineville, in which the school is located, the mayor calls a town meeting, and Tootle's failings are discussed—of course Tootle knows nothing of this. The meeting decides on a course of action, and the next time Tootle goes out for a spin alone and goes off the track he runs right into a red flag and halts. He turns in another direction only to encounter another red flag; still another—the result is the same. He turns and twists but can find no spot of grass in which a red flag does not spring up, for all the citizens of the town have cooperated in this lesson.

Chastened and bewildered he looks toward the track, where the inviting green flag of his teacher gives him the signal to return. Confused by conditioned reflexes to stop signs, he is only too glad to use the track and tears happily up and down. He promises that he will never leave the track again, and he returns to the roundhouse to be rewarded by the cheers of the teachers and the citizenry and the assurance that he will indeed grow up to be a streamliner.

The story is an appropriate one for bringing up children in an other-directed mode of conformity. They learn it is bad to go off the tracks and play with flowers and that, in the long run, there is not only success and approval but even freedom to be found in following the green lights. The moral is a very different one from that of *Little Red Riding Hood*. She, too, gets off the track on her trip to the grandmother; she is taught by a wolf

[9] M. E. Breckenridge and E. L. Vincent, *Child Development* (Philadelphia, W. B. Saunders, 1943), p. 456.

about the beauties of nature—a hardly veiled symbol for sex. Then, to be sure, she is eaten—a terrifying fate—but the tables are eventually turned, and she and grandmother both are taken from the wolf's belly by the handsome woodchopper. The story, though it may be read as a cautionary tale, deals with real human passions, sexual and aggressive; it certainly does not present the rewards of virtue in any unambiguous form or show the adult world in any wholly benevolent light. It is, therefore, essentially realistic, underneath the cover of fantasy, or, more accurately, owing to the *quality* of the fantasy.

There is, perhaps, a streak of similar realism in *Tootle*. There the adults play the role we have described earlier: they manipulate the child into conformity with the peer-group and then reward him for the behavior for which they have already set the stage. Moreover, the citizens of Engineville are tolerant of Tootle: they understand and do not get indignant. And while they gang up on him with red flags they do so for his benefit, and they reward him for his obedience as if they had played no hand in bringing it about. The whole story, in fact, might have been written by a student of learning theory, so palpably does it deal in terms of conditioned responses.

Yet with all that, there is something overvarnished in this tale. The adult world (the teachers) is *not* that benevolent, the citizenry (the peer-group) *not* that participative and cooperative, the signals are *not* that clear, nor the rewards of being a streamliner that great or that certain. Nevertheless, the child may be impressed because it is all so nice—there is none of the grimness of Red Riding Hood. There is, therefore, a swindle about the whole thing—a fake like that the citizens put on for Tootle's benefit. At the end Tootle has forgotten that he ever did like flowers anyway—how childish they are in comparison with the great big grown-up world of engines, signals, tracks, and meetings!

While the antagonistic and rebellious elements may be veiled in a folk tale, the children who read *Tootle* or have it read to them are manipulated away from rebellion and taught the lesson of obedience to signals. Strikingly enough, moreover, the story also bears on the presumptive topic of peer-group cooperation: the exercise of consumption preferences. Those middle-class children who read the tale are not going to grow up to be railroad engineers; that is a craft followed by more inner-directed types from the working class. But while neither *Tootle* nor its readers are concerned about what it really means to be an engineer, the book does confirm one of the consumption preferences of the other-directed: big streamliners—if one cannot go by plane—are better than old coal-burning engines.¹⁰ To be sure, *Tootle* has something to teach about train lore. It indicates that there are tracks, signals, roundhouses, just as fairy tales indicate that there are forests, woodchoppers, wolves. On the whole, however, children are attuned to the magic of travel, of communications, not in an adventurous way but in what educators are pleased to call a "realistic" one.

We return, finally, to the theme of winning dealt with in the preceding section. Tootle does, after all, win; with his winning ways he will grow up to be a big streamliner. The reader's identification with the consumption of others' winnings is, therefore, not betrayed. But it is not made clear in the story what happens to Tootle's schoolmates in engine school: do they *all* grow up to be streamliners, too? The peer-group relations of Tootle, either to the other engines or the other citizens of Engineville, are entirely amiable, and Tootle's winning does not mean that others fail. It is akin to the "benevolent conspiracy" of progressive parents and teachers who see to it that every child is a leader and that no one is left out, or conspicuous, thus reinforcing the tendencies toward antagonistic cooperation of the peer-group itself. Who can be sure that Tootle would want to be a streamliner if others were not to be streamliners too?

---

¹⁰ This preference is so strong that it influences directorates of railroads in coal-mining territory, concerned not only with public relations but with their own feeling for their road. A fine study could be made of railroad management's belated conversion to glamour, and the influence on this of the development of a new generation of consumers—more eager to be told that their conveyance is up to date than to be comfortable—or, more accurately, eager to be *told* they are comfortable.

Education and the Social Order

OF THE USE WHICH THE AMERICANS MAKE OF PUBLIC ASSOCIATIONS IN CIVIL LIFE *

... Americans of all ages, all conditions, and all dispositions constantly form associations. They have not only commercial and manufacturing companies, in which all take part, but associations of a thousand other kinds—religious, moral, serious, futile, extensive or restricted, enormous or diminutive. The Americans make associations to give entertainments, to found establishments for education, to build inns, to construct churches, to diffuse books, to send missionaries to the antipodes; and in this manner they found hospitals, prisons, and schools. If it is proposed to advance some truth or to foster some feeling by the encouragement of a great example, they form a society. Wherever at the head of some new undertaking you see the government in France, or a man of rank in England, in the United States you will be sure to find an association. . . .

When the members of an aristocratic community adopt a new opinion or conceive a new sentiment, they give it a station, as it were, beside themselves, upon the lofty platform where they stand; and opinions or sentiments so conspicuous to the eyes of the multitude are easily introduced into the minds or hearts of all around. In democratic countries the governing power alone is naturally in a condition to act in this manner; but it is easy to see that its action is always inadequate, and often dangerous. A government can no more be competent to keep alive and to renew the circulation of

* Alexis de Tocqueville, *Democracy in America,* Henry Reeve, ed. (New York: P. F. Collier and Son, 1900), Vol. II, pp. 114-22. (First published 1835-40.)

opinions and feelings amongst a great people than to manage all the speculations of productive industry. No sooner does a government attempt to go beyond its political sphere and to enter upon this new track than it exercises, even unintentionally, an insupportable tyranny; for a government can only dictate strict rules, the opinions which it favors are rigidly enforced, and it is never easy to discriminate between its advice and its commands. . . . Government therefore should not be the only active powers: associations ought, in democratic nations, to stand in lieu of those powerful private individuals whom the equality of conditions has swept away.

As soon as several of the inhabitants of the United States have taken up an opinion or a feeling which they wish to promote in the world, they look out for mutual assistance; and as soon as they have found each other out, they combine. From that moment they are no longer isolated men, but a power seen from afar, whose actions serve for an example and whose language is listened to. The first time I heard in the United States that 100,000 men had bound themselves publicly to abstain from spirituous liquors, it appeared to me more like a joke than a serious engagement; and I did not at once perceive why these temperate citizens could not content themselves with drinking water by their own firesides. I at last understood that 100,000 Americans, alarmed by the progress of drunkenness around them, had made up their minds to patronize temperance. They acted just in the same way as a man of high rank who should dress very plainly in order to inspire the humbler orders with a contempt of luxury. It is probable that if these 100,000 men had lived in France, each of them would singly have memorialized the government to watch the public houses all over the kingdom.

Nothing, in my opinion, is more deserving of our attention than the intellectual and moral associations of America. The political and industrial associations of that country strike us forcibly; but the others elude our observation, or if we discover them we understand them imperfectly because we have hardly ever seen anything of the kind. It must, however, be acknowledged that they are as necessary to the American people as the former, and perhaps more so. In democratic countries the science of association is the mother of science; the progress of all the rest depends upon the progress it has made.

Amongst the laws which rule human societies there is one which seems to be more precise and clear than all others. If men are to remain civilized, or to become so, the art of associating together must grow and improve in the same ratio in which the equality of conditions is increased.

THE ORGANIZATION MAN AND HIS SCHOOLS *

... America has paid much attention to the economic and political consequences of big organization—the concentration of power in large corporations, for example, the political power of the civil-service bureaucracies, the possible emergence of a managerial hierarchy that might dominate the rest of us. These are proper concerns, but no less important is the principle impact that organization life has had on the individuals within it. A collision has been taking place—indeed, hundreds of thousands of them, and in the aggregate they have been producing what I believe is a major shift in American ideology.

Officially, we are a people who hold to the Protestant Ethic. Because of the denominational implications of the term many would deny its relevance to them, but let them eulogize the American Dream, however, and they virtually define the Protestant Ethic. Whatever the embroidery, there is almost always the thought that pursuit of individual salvation through hard work, thrift, and competitive struggle is the heart of the American achievement.

But the harsh facts of organization life simply do not jibe with these precepts. This conflict is certainly not a peculiarly American development. In their own countries such Europeans as Max Weber and Durkheim many years ago foretold the change, and though Europeans now like to see their troubles as an American export, the problems they speak of stem from a bureaucratization of society that has affected every Western country.

It is in America, however, that the contrast between the old ethic and current reality has been most apparent—and most poignant. Of all peoples it is we who have led in the public worship of individualism. One hundred years ago De Tocqueville was noting that though our special genius—and failing—lay in co-operative action, we talked more than others of personal independence and freedom. We kept on, and as late as the twenties, when big organization was long since a fact, affirmed the old faith as if nothing had really changed at all.

Today many still try, and it is the members of the kind of organization most responsible for the change, the corporation, who try the hardest. It is the corporation man whose institutional ads protest so much that Americans speak up in town meeting, that Americans are the best inventors because Americans don't care that other people scoff, that Americans are the best soldiers because they have so much initiative and native ingenuity,

* William H. Whyte, Jr., *The Organization Man* (New York, Simon and Schuster, 1956), pp. 4-6, 7-9, 382, 383-5, 386-8, 392. Copyright 1956 by William H. Whyte, Jr. Reprinted by permission of the publishers.

that the boy selling papers on the street corner is the prototype of our business society. Collectivism? He abhors it, and when he makes his ritualistic attack on Welfare Statism, it is in terms of a Protestant Ethic undefiled by change—the sacredness of property, the enervating effect of security, the virtues of thrift, of hard work and independence. Thanks be, he says, that there are some people left—e.g., businessmen—to defend the American Dream.

He is not being hypocritical, only compulsive. He honestly wants to believe he follows the tenets he extols, and if he extols them so frequently it is, perhaps, to shut out a nagging suspicion that he, too, the last defender of the faith, is no longer pure. Only by using the language of individualism to describe the collective can he stave off the thought that he himself is in a collective as pervading as any ever dreamed of by the reformers, the intellectuals, and the utopian visionaries he so regularly warns against.

The older generation may still convince themselves; the younger generation does not. When a young man says that to make a living these days you must do what somebody else wants you to do, he states it not only as a fact of life that must be accepted but as an inherently good proposition. If the American Dream deprecates this for him, it is the American Dream that is going to have to give, whatever its more elderly guardians may think. People grow restive with a mythology that is too distant from the way things actually are, and as more and more lives have been encompassed by the organization way of life, the pressures for an accompanying ideological shift have been mounting. The pressures of the group, the frustrations of individual creativity, the anonymity of achievement: are these defects to struggle against—or are they virtues in disguise? The organization man seeks a redefinition of his place on earth—a faith that will satisfy him that what he must endure has a deeper meaning than appears on the surface. He needs, in short, something that will do for him what the Protestant Ethic did once. And slowly, almost imperceptibly, a body of thought has been coalescing that does that.

I am going to call it a Social Ethic. With reason it could be called an organization ethic, or a bureaucratic ethic; more than anything else it rationalizes the organization's demands for fealty and gives those who offer it wholeheartedly a sense of dedication in doing so—*in extremis,* you might say, it converts what would seem in other times a bill of no rights into a restatement of individualism.

But there is a real moral imperative behind it, and whether one inclines to its beliefs or not he must acknowledge that this moral basis, not mere expediency, is the source of its power. Nor is it simply an opiate for those who must work in big organizations. The search for a secular faith that it represents can be found throughout our society. . . .

Let me now define my terms. By Social Ethic I mean that contemporary body of thought which makes morally legitimate the pressures of society against the individual. Its major propositions are three: a belief in the group as the source of creativity; a belief in "belongingness" as the ultimate need of the individual; and a belief in the application of science to achieve the belongingness.

In subsequent chapters I will explore these ideas more thoroughly, but for the moment I think the gist can be paraphrased thus: Man exists as a unit of society. Of himself, he is isolated, meaningless; only as he collaborates with others does he become worth while, for by sublimating himself in the group, he helps produce a whole that is greater than the sum of its parts. There should be, then, no conflict between man and society. What we think are conflicts are misunderstandings, breakdowns in communication. By applying the methods of science to human relations we can eliminate these obstacles to consensus and create an equilibrium in which society's needs and the needs of the individual are one and the same.

Essentially, it is a utopian faith. Superficially, it seems dedicated to the practical problems of organization life, and its proponents often use the word *hard* (versus *soft*) to describe their approach. But it is the long-range promise that animates its followers, for it relates techniques to the vision of a finite, achievable harmony. It is quite reminiscent of the beliefs of utopian communities of the 1840s. As in the Owen communities, there is the same idea that man's character is decided, almost irretrievably, by his environment. As in the Fourier communities, there is the same faith that there need be no conflict between the individual's aspirations and the community's wishes, because it is the natural order of things that the two be synonymous.

Like the utopian communities, it interprets society in a fairly narrow, immediate sense. One can believe man has a social obligation and that the individual must ultimately contribute to the community without believing that group harmony is the test of it. In the Social Ethic I am describing, however, man's obligation is in the here and now; his duty is not so much to the community in a broad sense but to the actual, physical one about him, and the idea that in isolation from it—or active rebellion against it— he might eventually discharge the greater service is little considered. In practice, those who most eagerly subscribe to the Social Ethic worry very little over the long-range problems of society. It is not that they don't care but rather that they tend to assume that the ends of organization and morality coincide, and on such matters as social welfare they give their proxy to the organization.

It is possible that I am attaching too much weight to what, after all, is something of a mythology. Those more sanguine than I have argued that this faith is betrayed by reality in some key respects and that because it cannot long hide from organization man that life is still essentially competitive the faith must fall of its own weight. They also maintain that the Social Ethic is only one trend in a society which is a prolific breeder of counter-trends. The farther the pendulum swings, they believe, the more it must eventually swing back.

I am not persuaded. We are indeed a flexible people, but society is not a clock and to stake so much on counter-trends is to put a rather heavy burden on providence. Let me get ahead of my story a bit with two examples of trend vs. counter-trend. One is the long-term swing to the highly vocational business-administration courses. Each year for seven years I have collected all the speeches by businessmen, educators, and others on the subject, and invariably each year the gist of them is that this particular pendulum has swung much too far and that there will shortly be a reversal. Similarly sanguine, many academic people have been announcing that they discern the beginnings of a popular swing back to the humanities. Another index is the growth of personality testing. Regularly year after year many social scientists have assured me that this bowdlerization of psychology is a contemporary aberration soon to be laughed out of court.

Meanwhile, the organization world grinds on. Each year the number of business-administration majors has increased over the last year—until, in 1954, they together made up the largest single field of undergraduate instruction outside of the field of education itself. Personality testing? Again, each year the number of people subjected to it has grown, and the criticism has served mainly to make organizations more adept in sugar-coating their purpose. No one can say whether these trends will continue to outpace the counter-trends, but neither can we trust that an equilibrium-minded providence will see to it that excesses will cancel each other out. Counter-trends there are. There always have been, and in the sweep of ideas ineffectual many have proved to be.

It is also true that the Social Ethic is something of a mythology, and there is a great difference between mythology and practice. An individualism as stringent, as selfish as that often preached in the name of the Protestant Ethic would never have been tolerated, and in reality our predecessors co-operated with one another far more skillfully than nineteenth-century oratory would suggest. Something of the obverse is true of the Social Ethic; so complete a denial of individual will won't work either, and even the most willing believers in the group harbor some secret misgivings, some latent antagonism toward the pressures they seek to deify.

But the Social Ethic is no less powerful for that, and though it can never produce the peace of mind it seems to offer, it will help shape the nature of the quest in the years to come. The old dogma of individualism betrayed reality too, yet few would argue, I dare say, that it was not an immensely powerful influence in the time of its dominance. So I argue of the Social Ethic; call it mythology, if you will, but it is becoming the dominant one. . . .

The organization man's emphasis on the group, I have been maintaining, is not a temporary phenomenon dictated by external necessity; it is a response to what he feels is a moral imperative, and more and more he is openly articulating it. I have looked at the church in this perspective; now I would like to turn to the schools. Like the churches they had to be built from scratch, and in building them the young parents had to declare themselves. Their children will be transients too, and the pressures of the organization life ahead for them will be, if anything, more intense. What, then, should be emphasized? In helping shape the curriculum, parents are at once giving a guide and revealing themselves. . . .

Like their parents, in short, the children already have a high degree of social skill, and the environment itself will further intensify this in them. This being the case, it could be argued, there is no necessity for the school to duplicate, and thus they are all the more free to concentrate on the other, more inward, aspects. But neither the parents nor the schools feel this way. From the beginning the curriculum has borne down very heavily on the pragmatic and the social, and the concept of adjustment has been dominant.

The first superintendent [at Park Forest] left, with a well-earned sigh of relief, to be a professor at the Harvard Graduate School of Education. What curriculum changes have ensued, however, have not been major. Anderson's successor, Superintendent Gerald Smith, has talked of introducing the "Fourth R, Responsibility," but this seems largely another way of describing the established policy. The disciplining vehicle, Smith explains, is the group. The teacher strives not to discipline the child directly but to influence all the children's attitudes so that as a group they recognize correct behavior. If a child falls out of line, he does not have to be subjected to authoritarian strictures of elders; he senses the disapproval of the group and, in that way, the school believes, learns to discipline himself as much as possible.

The child who tends to be withdrawn is given special attention. "Johnny wasn't doing so well at school," one mother told me. "The teacher explained to me that he was doing fine on his lessons but that his social adjustment was not as good as it might be. He would pick just one or two friends to play with, and sometimes he was happy to remain by himself." There are many such instances, and, save for a few odd parents, most are grateful that the schools work so hard to offset tendencies to introversion and other suburban abnormalities.

Park Forest schools are not extreme in this respect, and more Park

Education and the Social Order

Foresters are anxious that the curriculum be recognized as middle of the road. But they do agree that there is a noticeable permissive atmosphere. They point out, for example, that the schools follow a method by which the student group is encouraged to take a strong hand in the planning of what they are to be taught. The children are not exactly put in charge, but the teacher makes a point of asking them what it is they would like to know about a particular subject, rather than unilaterally giving them what she thinks they ought to learn. As Superintendent Smith explained it: "If the topic under discussion is India, the children are asked what they would like to know about that country. Queries might range from elephants to the mysteries of bathing in the Ganges. By the time juvenile curiosities are satisfied, the children have a reasonable knowledge of India's terrain, vegetation, animal life, religions, caste systems, and politics."

The schools are similarly flexible in grading. To use fixed standards of performance, the authorities feel, would strait-jacket the child. As a consequence, the primaries, as in many other schools, are ungraded, and in later classes formal reports of the A-B-C-D-F or percentage type have been discarded. "It is obviously impossible," curriculum consultant Lucille Thimblin explains, "for a teacher to reduce the many-sided aspects of a pupil's development to an accurate numerical value." Under the old method, she says, a bright pupil who has made little effort might get the highest mark while another child who works hard might fail to get a respectable mark. The school could get around this by simply using the two terms "satisfactory" and "unsatisfactory" and this would be helpful, Mrs. Thimblin points out, in that "this type of report does reduce the competition for scholastic leadership." Unfortunately, however, while it would make for better adjustment, "it is very likely also to reduce some pupils' incentive to do better work." The solution: a check list to supplement parent-teacher conferences. In this the student's academic progress is rated on the basis of his individual capabilities rather than against an arbitrary norm. He is also rated in terms of his social group and whether or not he meets the standards attainable for every member of the group. . . .

It is in the high school, however, that the new suburbia's philosophy gets its most significant expression. The philosophy is by no means unique to Park Forest. High-school superintendent Eric Baber speaks very much like many superintendents elsewhere, and his writings do not show unorthodoxy but, rather, a deep grasp of contemporary educational literature. What makes Park Forest's high school unique is that, where in traditional communities what has been called the "life adjustment" curriculum has been introduced a bit at a time, at Park Forest it has been the foundation. The new $1,600,000 "learning laboratory" is not only one of the most modern in the country; in spirit as well as brick it is the embodiment of the suburban temper.

Five years ago, when the school was still in the planning stage, Baber told parents that the trouble with U.S. education is that it is concentrated far too much on the intellectual aspect of education. Even teachers' colleges, he observed sadly, still require plane geometry for admission. Except for a small coterie, he asked, of what value to most people are the traditional academic disciplines? "The so-called 'bright student' is often one of the dumbest or least apt when he gets away from his textbooks and memory work," Baber told a teachers' workshop. "This is evidenced by the fact that many $20,000-to-$100,000-a-year jobs in business, sales, sports, radio . . . are held by persons with I.Q.s of less than ninety."

Baber is not actually against intelligence. He believes it should be channeled toward real-life, vocational needs more than to the academic requirements of the colleges. Since Park Forest, unlike many towns, is predominantly college-educated, most students will be going on to college anyway; thus the "two-school," vocational versus academic problems might not seem particularly pertinent. A large share of the school plant nevertheless was designed with great attention to the vocational, and so was the curriculum.

Of the total of seventy subjects originally offered, only one half were in traditional academic subjects—and the latter, furthermore, were by no means ivory tower. Of seven offerings in English available to juniors and seniors, the one devoted to grammar, rhetoric, and composition was a one-semester "refresher course . . . for students who feel the need for additional preparation." Of more appeal to teen-agers would be the full-year courses in journalism and in speech (for which, in the "communication laboratory," facilities are available for practical things like radio and TV debating).

The seventy formal subject offerings by no means exhausted the life-adjustment curriculum. Baber felt that the schools must assume more responsibility for the *total* growth of the child. Conceivably, this could be left to other agencies—to the family, or the church, or society itself, for example. Nevertheless, through such media as courses in family group living (twelfth-grade elective) and "doing" sessions in actual situations, the school tackled it. . . .

It is possible, if not very probable, that there will be shifts in the future. Significantly, the few critics are from what is regarded as the progressive element in Park Forest, and they are poles apart from the right-wing reactionaries who have muddied the issue in some communities. But they remain very much a minority, and at present writing it must be concluded that the philosophy of the elementary and high schools is a fair reflection of the community. If any debate has developed, it is because Baber has been so eminently fair in making his position explicit.

The majority do not see any basic philosophic differences. Differences of degree, yes—they don't want the school to be *too* progressive, *too* practical—but on the basic concept of social utility they have no argument to make. If one wishes to quarrel with the philosophy, he must address himself to the people themselves. The educators may be in the vanguard, but they are going with, not against, the grain of their society.

For what is it that the parents want most emphasized by the school? At Park Forest they were asked just such a question, and when they wrote the answer in their own words, one note was found more often than any other. The primary job of the high school, they wrote, should be to teach students how to be citizens and how to get along with other people.

THE SCHOOL AND THE COMMUNITY *

One who thinks about the relation of the school to the community which supports it will soon come upon questions of public policy which it would take an Einsteinian grasp of the calculus of felicity to answer. Difficulty arises because the aims of the school and the community are often divergent. It is very well to say that the school should serve the community, but it is difficult to decide what opinion should govern when school and community differ. The lights of the school authorities are often better than those of the community in general. School men have given some study to their own problems, and could reasonably be expected to know more about them than outsiders do. Yet the community is often wiser than the school, because the community is whole and the school is fragmentary. The school, as a fragment of the common life, is a prey to institutionalism. Institutionalism causes the school to forget its purpose; it makes the school give education for education and teaching for teaching, perhaps for teachers; in short, it makes an end of what is logically only a means to an end. This vice the community escapes because the community is whole, because it is not simply a place where teachers teach and children learn. The community is whole because whole men live in it. And the community is sometimes wise with a knowledge of the complete life that surpasses the knowledge of the schools. It becomes, then, one of the important questions of public policy as to how far the community should determine the policy of the school and how far the school should be self-determining. We have not yet the formula.

A complication of a different order arises from the fact that communities

* Willard Waller, *The Sociology of Teaching* (New York, John Wiley and Sons, 1932), pp. 33-5.

in general, perhaps especially American communities, have chosen to use the schools as repositories for certain ideals. The ideals which are supposed to have their stronghold in the schools are of several different sorts. The belief is abroad that young people ought to be trained to think the world a little more beautiful and much more just than it is, as they ought to think men more honest and women more virtuous than they are. A high-school student must learn that honesty is always the best policy; perhaps his father secretly believes that he knows better; perhaps the boy himself may be learning something quite different in the world of business, but it does the boy no harm to start with that assumption. We can teach him enough honesty to keep him out of jail all his life; later he can make such amendments to our principles as seem necessary to him. All must learn that the United States is the greatest and best of all the nations of history, unequalled in wealth or virtue since time began. Perhaps it does no harm for students to think that the world is getting better and better, though this is a very dangerous doctrine if one thinks about it very long.

Among these ideals are those moral principles which the majority of adults more or less frankly disavow for themselves but want others to practice; they are ideals for the helpless, ideals for children and for teachers. There are other ideals which are nearly out of print, because people do not believe in them any more. Though most adults have left such ideals behind, they are not willing to discard them finally. The school must keep them alive. The school must serve as a museum of virtue.

We have in our culture a highly developed system of idealism for the young. The young have not yet come into contact with a world that might soil them, and we do what we can to keep the young unsullied. There are certain things that are not for the ears of the young. There are certain facts about human nature that they must not learn. There are certain bits of reality that they must not touch. There are certain facts of history that we think it best not to teach them. There is an idealized world view that it is thought best to pass on to adolescents. The notion that it is not proper to tell the whole truth is often carried over into college teaching, and it affects materially the point of view of many university professors. There is just enough apparent wisdom in the policy of hiding difficult facts from the young to justify it in the popular mind as a general policy. For it is often argued that character training must begin by the inculcation of an impossible virtue, in order that the individual may have a surplus of virtue to trade upon. The world, of course, is thoroughly committed to the policy of not telling the whole truth to youngsters, to the policy of telling them falsehoods which will make the world more attractive or themselves more tractable and virtuous.

The conventional belief, as we have noted, is that the young must be shielded from contact with the unpleasant and amoral aspects of the universe and that they must be kept in an ultra-conservative environment. These ideals may be justified by the fact that they prevent the demoralization of the young; as to that we have preferred to keep an open mind. But it is certain that the necessity of serving as the repository for these ideals limits the larger utility of the school. For if it is the purpose of education to prepare for life in the world, then the school must give its students that world in order that they may get themselves ready for living in it. Actually it cannot give students the world, but only an imitation or a representation of the world; in any case, it should be an accurate imitation or a faithful representation if the training which the student receives in school is to have any validity. The less the discontinuity between the life of the school and the life of the world outside, the better will be the training for life which the school gives to its students. Any ideal which cuts down the ability of the school to reproduce reality interferes with its real function of preparing students for life. The utility of such ideals may even be disputed from the moral point of view; the argument against them is the good one that the individual upon whom we have foisted off a too idealistic world view will be more readily disorganized by contact with a far from perfect world than will an individual who has already had some experience of the world; it is the old principle of inoculation. In almost any case, if a school man believes in the policy of training young persons to be virtuous by not telling them the truth, he sets very definite limits to his own continuing influence upon those who come in contact with him. There is reason for the bitter jest that a school teacher is a man hired to tell lies to little boys. . . .

ENGLISH AND RUSSIAN EDUCATION CONTRASTED *

Education in the United Kingdom and education in the U.S.S.R. are, in many ways, poles apart. Nor is this surprising since English education is a thousand years old and Russian education, though it cannot ignore its ancestry, is a brainchild of the last forty years, created *de novo* as the central part of a vast Platonic plan. English education is like a coral reef raising itself year by year with life as the seafloor sinks; Russian education is like a new volcanic island which appeared overnight. . . .

* C. H. Dobinson, "English and Russian Education Contrasted," *The Educational Forum* 22:401-10, May 1958. Copyright 1958 by Kappa Delta Pi. Reprinted by permission.

These similes, though a little extravagant, are intended to emphasize the contrast between the slow evolution and adjustment of the English school and university system and the creation of a system which is based on a great explosive idea and which changes with sudden giant movements.

It is inevitable that the system which is based on an idea is a logical system conforming to the deductions which follow from the premises. It is equally inevitable that the system which has developed by evolution may be as illogical in its shape as the giraffe, but it will be the result of struggle with the real world. To the Russian politician human nature is infinitely plastic and improvable: to the average Englishman human nature is extremely stable, the "old Adam" ineradicable and heredity extremely significant. Probably the truth lies between the two points of view. Certainly the Russians, like the Americans, have demonstrated that education, even if it cannot do everything, can do a great deal more to a nation than Englishmen, even today, believe. In forty years Russian education, starting from scratch, has transformed a congeries of ethnic groups, most of which were ignorant, half-starved, superstitious and primitive, into a federation of peoples disposing of vast resources of agricultural and industrial production and living lives which are healthy and to a considerable extent, intellectual.

This has not been achieved either by evolution or by persuasion but by force and control. Indeed the word *control* is, in many respects, the keynote of the Russian educational system. From the very top level, at which the decisions of the Central Praesidium formulate the policy of education of all the constituent republics, down to the humblest teacher in the seven-year primary school, there is an iron strand of control. There are nations that still have, or have had, a similar centralized system, but in England nothing of the kind has ever existed. The keynote of all English education is the word "freedom." Indeed, so great is the degree of freedom that most visitors from abroad are puzzled and nonplussed. The results of freedom may seem to them to be chaos and the average Englishman an eleutheromaniac. Certainly there is no teacher in the world who is as free, or who has ever been as free, as the English teacher of today. Inside his classroom and within the confines of his subject or group of subjects, he may, in effect, teach what he likes and how he likes. Headmasters and inspectors may approve or disapprove, but provided that he does not use his position for political or religious propaganda, or behave towards his pupils in any unprofessional way, the teacher in his classroom is king of his castle and he would sooner not teach than have it otherwise.

No officer of the Ministry of Education, no inspector of his employer, the local education authority, lays down for him the syllabus of work that he

Education and the Social Order

must teach: that is a matter for him to decide in collaboration with the colleagues who share the same field of studies.

Since all other differences between education in England and in the U.S.S.R. are insignificant in comparison with this fundamental difference between freedom and control, let us consider, in detail, a quotation from a Russian educational newspaper; an extract [1] which takes us to the very heart of this great conflict in basic educational principle. Since this passage deals with the Russian school examination system, it should be explained that:

(a) in subjects where it is appropriate the examination is wholly or mainly oral;

(b) the questions are drawn at random by the candidate from a series constructed or approved by the Ministry of the Republic concerned;

(c) the marking is on a scale from 1 to 5 in which the highest mark 5, "excellent," is awarded only to a small proportion of the candidates;

(d) the examination is administered by the principal of the school assisted by external assessors appointed by the Ministry of Education of the Republic.

"The examinations went best in Boys' School No. 1 in Perov (master, Comrade Ya. G. Chernov). For example, in the first group of the ninth form there were 6 boys with a mark, for the year, of 5, two with 4, and three with 3. In the tenth form, too, more than half the pupils received the mark 5. The examination results in the tenth form of School No. 1 in Klyazma (master, Comrade M. P. Barinov) were also quite good.

"There are, however, forms where pupils showed an unsatisfactory and even poor knowledge, such as form 9b in School No. 1 in Klyazma (mistress, Comrade A. F. Ivanovskaya) and the tenth form in Perov Girls' School No. 6 (mistress, Comrade R. V. Metelitsa). Here are some of the answers:

"A tenth form girl in Perov School No. 6, whose mark for the year was 3, answered ticket No. 34 (questions on the five-year plans). Her account of the results of the first five-year plan was short and poor. It amounted mainly to an account of constructions. In her reply she left out the main point, i.e., a definition of the tasks of the five-year plan and a description of the struggle for its fulfilment. Thus she did not even mention that as a result of the first five-year plan the foundations for a socialist economy were laid, and that on the whole technical reconstruction was achieved and the Kulak class eliminated.

"A ninth form boy from School No. 1 in Klyazma, whose mark for the

[1] From "Soviet Studies," April 1951. Blackwell, Oxford, an article "On the Results of School Examinations in Modern History."

year was 3, gave a fluent but empty answer to a question (ticket No. 21) on the rise of scientific communism. To an additional question on the basic content of Marx's teaching he did not answer at all. . . . The two mistresses, Comrades Melelitsa and Ivanovskaya, explained their pupils' poor knowledge by weak preparation of the forms. However, the main cause is another: both teachers were liberal in their marking and set low standards for the pupils. Comrade Ivanovskaya did not give a single 2 mark in one term. She failed none of her pupils and many had even a 4 or a 5 mark. But in the examinations many of them received marks lower than their average for the year. The examination results showed one 5, seven 3's, and three 2's. . . .

"The examinations gave an extremely clear confirmation of the fact that the systematic work of the teacher on himself, his theoretical preparation, the creativeness of his mind and his efforts to perfect his method play a decisive part in raising the ideo-political standard of teaching. This comes out clearly in those parts of the curriculum which are not covered by the textbook. . . ."

First, we should note that, while most English boys and girls who have stayed at school to the age of sixteen are also presented for an external examination in a wide range of subjects, there is no examination which is either set or in any way assessed or controlled by the Ministry of Education. Instead there are nine different examining bodies for the General Certificate of Education and eight of these are regulated by boards centered upon either one university or upon several universities. The Boards are composed not only of representatives of the universities but also of teachers' organizations and other educational interests. It is for the headmaster or headmistress of the secondary school, in consultation with his colleagues and his board of governors, to decide which examining board shall be used by the school; sometimes more than one examining board is utilized, since not all boards offer exactly the same range of subjects. Even subjects which are offered by all, e.g., elementary mathematics, chemistry, French, geography, history, have syllabuses which differ slightly and there also may be a somewhat different approach in the questions set on the same topic. In addition schools are encouraged to submit a syllabus of their own, of corresponding standard, if, for any reason, they wish to introduce different factual material into a subject. They may even ask to introduce a new subject, though, since a great range of subjects is available, this last variation from the normal is rare. . . .

We should note particularly that history, a subject which so readily lends itself to partisan treatment, is not a compulsory subject for the G.C.E. examination for English boys and girls. Though all will study some history at some stage of their school career, by the age of 16 many will have "dropped" it in favor of an alternative subject such as geography, physics, Greek or German. Even those who prepare for examination in history at "O" level will, according to the wish of their history teacher, be entered for such alternatives as "British Empire History," "Foreign History," "British or Foreign History" or "British History"; in this last only one out of five periods, e.g., 1066 to 1485 or 1815 to 1931, is studied in detail.

There is, therefore, no opportunity for English boys and girls as a whole to be given, as in the U.S.S.R., a common grounding in an ideo-political approach to history. That is not to say that history as taught in English schools is completely objective; just as every age tends to produce its own interpretation of various aspects of history, so every nation-state inevitably tends to produce its own version of things gone by, despite the efforts of all the best historians and teachers of history to get as near as possible to what appears to be the truth. . . .

In the teaching of history, then, the educational practices in the U.S.S.R. and in the United Kingdom, are as different as they could possibly be. Still more astonishing to Russian eyes is the freedom given to English teachers, in history and in every other subject, to choose and to change their textbooks, so far as school funds permit. This means, of course, that the minority of history teachers, who wish to present the subject from a given point of view can generally find books that meet their need. The stories of Henry VIII's destruction of the monasteries and the burning of bishops in the reign of "Bloody Mary" are told somewhat differently in Protestant and in Roman Catholic schools. . . .

And here we note, in passing, that in England and Wales aid from public funds is given to many schools which are openly denominational in their outlook, the schools of the Church of England and of the Roman Catholic Church forming the majority of the schools thus aided.

But whatever the nature of the answers served up by pupils in history examinations (which are entirely "written" examinations; only examinations in modern languages having an oral section) no teacher can subsequently be publicly pilloried in the press, educational or otherwise. A series of poor results in a class is first and foremost a matter for the head of the school to discuss with the teacher concerned. . . . But that the criticisms of an inspector—or of any other school official for that matter—should be given publicity; still worse, given printed publicity, that is something which English educational tradition renders utterly impossible.

. . .

So, from the Russian point of view the English teacher is in a ridiculously privileged position and even the system itself is absurd since it serves to promote not uniformity of thought on the ideo-political plane, but infinite variety of opinion. . . . because of the way in which education and the better social habits have been filtering downwards through the past two centuries there is slow but steady movement towards a homogeneous classless society. In the U.S.S.R. such a society was established by Bolshevist decree and a uniform educational system, the same for everybody at the primary level, was provided to perpetuate equality of initial opportunity. In England, however, at every level below the university, there exist different types of educational establishment some of which have definite class affiliations and serve, to some extent, to perpetuate vertical cleavages in society. Many middle-class parents wish to protect their small children from the infection of bad speech, badly-produced voices, bad habits and disease to which they may be exposed in the large classes of the local primary school. Obviously such conditions vary greatly with the locality in which the school is situated, primary schools in the more central parts of large industrial cities being, from these points of view, fairly undesirable. So private nursery schools, kindergartens and primary schools exist in considerable numbers though since these schools are small the proportion of the total population of that age which attend them is small—about 3% in 1957. . . .

The number of boys and girls between the ages of thirteen and eighteen who are attending Independent Schools is nearly 8% of the total attending full time school between these ages. In addition there are 4% of the same group in attendance at Direct Grant Schools, which share the honored position of the Independent Schools in being free from any control by the local education authority. These schools do, however, receive assistance from public funds, this assistance coming direct from the Ministry of Education on a *per capita* basis. From the Russian point of view, and from the point of view of many Labor voters in England, both these types of school are pernicious anachronisms, even though between 25% and 50% of the places in Direct Grant Schools must be free places, awarded on merit at entry examination . . . these Independent and Direct Grant Schools, as a result of their freedom, are able not only to experiment, but also to set higher standards in staffing and in equipment—standards which tend gradually to improve the practice of the L.E.A. schools. So this English contrast with the Russian system of uniformity of secondary schools is likely to remain, whatever political party may be in power.

. . .

Education and the Social Order

But what may appear, superficially, to be a much more serious contrast in practice between England and the U.S.S.R. is the English system of selection for secondary education. Based on the assumption that children are not born equal, certainly not intellectually equal, this system seeks, largely by a series of tests at the age of eleven together with examination of cumulative records, to direct the boys and girls along different lines of secondary education. The clearest statement of this plan was that given by the now-discredited Norwood Report of 1943 which predicated the existence of three distinct types of children, each type admirably adapted to one or other of the three types of state-aided secondary schools then in existence—the secondary grammar school which might lead to the university, the secondary technical school which might lead to the technical college and the secondary modern school which led to the present-day equivalents to hewing wood and drawing water. . . . This ridiculous doctrine, unsubstantiated by any psychological or other evidence has left its mark on the English secondary school system which, by and large, contrasts vividly with the system of comprehensive secondary schools in the U.S.S.R.

After the Bolshevist revolution the first need had been to establish seven years of compulsory primary education for all from eight to fifteen years of age, though in rural parts many children for some years continued to leave school at twelve years. The second stage was a vast development of technical education which, beginning with the training of semi-skilled workers rapidly pushed on to train hundreds of thousands of skilled workers and technicians and finally of technologists. This edifice of technical education rose with astounding speed each story being built firmly upon the one below, and the bottom story spreading year by year over more ground, then developing a second floor and so on. As early as 1937 it was possible in the largest cities to encourage a substantial proportion of the most able boys and girls to remain at school to the age of eighteen for admission to the universities and institutes of technology and to talk of ten years of compulsory schooling for all. The attack by Hitler in 1941 pushed this plan aside for a while and lowered the age of school entry to seven years, thus releasing boys and girls from school at fourteen years instead of fifteen. This made it possible for them to be sent to labor-reserve schools (often residential) where they received low-grade technical education and training within industry as part of the great drive for production of war material. The more gifted boys and girls, however, were encouraged either to enter *technicums* where they had a four-year course making them into highly skilled technicians, or to stay at school to the age of seventeen so as to proceed to university and kindred studies mainly scientific and technological.

With the end of the war the old concept of ten years' schooling for all was revived (in 1951). This raising of the school-leaving age to seventeen means, of course, that no longer are the least able boys and girls going to find their way to labor-reserve schools, nor can the *technicums* recruit at the age of fourteen or fifteen, leaving only the boys and girls most academically gifted to continue at school to the age of seventeen. In short we now see the Russians, with a theory that all children are born equal, facing in their schools, in the age range fourteen to seventeen, the very obvious fact that they are *not* equal. Hitherto shortage of places, the needs of a changing economy and the exigencies of war had, to a large extent, avoided any large scale facing of the fact that differences in mental endowment, which are marked even in primary school, are even more disconcerting to the teacher in the secondary school.

It is not surprising, therefore, that since 1951 there has been an all-out campaign for the "polytechnicization" of the secondary school. The subject is worthy of an article to itself and is difficult to summarize in a few sentences. But the essential feature is the interpenetration of industry and school, or agriculture and school, according to the location of the school. As a result the formalism of book-learning will be sweetened, especially for the less able pupils, by practical work which stands in immediate relationship to production. This fulfils the demand of adolescents everywhere that school-work during the years of puberty should have a clear relationship to adult life. In short, polytechnicization in the comprehensive secondary school in the U.S.S.R. is comparable, in many ways, with the pre-vocational work which is being introduced more and more into English secondary education for the same reason. . . .

Finally, as heretofore, the most able of all will proceed to the universities and to the technical institutes. The proportion of the year-group which in Russia is considered fit for higher education is considerably larger than in England. Can the reason be that Russian children, on the whole, are more intelligent than English children? This is possible since the taxation system in England for the past fifty years has been unquestionably dysgenic. But a more likely explanation is that the English selection system, originating at the turn of the century as a scholarship scheme intended for only the very brightest children of the working classes, is entirely responsible for the present relative paucity of candidates for higher education. There is now abundant evidence that boys and girls who have subsequently developed high ability failed to gain entrance to secondary grammar or secondary technical schools (these latter are very few indeed, anyhow). As a consequence the pupils were, or are, restricted to education in a secondary modern school, where, in general, no homework is set and where, by and large, the intellectual standards do less than justice to the more able pupils. As a consequence many local education authorities in England are building comprehensive secondary schools or bilateral schools where a broad range of abilities is catered to and several pre-vocational options are provided. In such areas it is being found that many boys and girls who would probably have left a secondary modern school at the end of compulsory schooling, i.e., at the age of fifteen years, are now staying at school to the age of sixteen or seventeen and so increasing the demand for education at technical colleges and universities. Similarly at Secondary Modern Schools where pre-vocational courses and/or General Certificate courses are provided pupils tend to stay at school beyond the age of fifteen. Thus, slowly and very irregularly, as befits a system which is almost unplanned and develops from the grass roots, English school boys and school girls are, in effect, raising the school-leaving age nearer to that which is being established by decree in the U.S.S.R.

. . .

What is lacking, however, is the willingness on the part of the nation as a whole, or at least of the majority of its present representatives in Parliament, to provide the necessary funds for the educational expansion which ought to take place, not least at the university level. Admittedly taxation is still extremely high in England, but even so, education seems to be low in the order of priority for claims upon the nation's purse. There is a tendency for the needs of the present, or the wooing of the electorate, to overshadow the needs of the future. But in Russia the proportion of the national income which is devoted to the various aspects of education is far higher and the comforts of the present are almost always sacrificed in order that the needs of the future may be fully met. . . .

Schooling in the U.S.S.R. makes demands upon the pupils whatever their intellectual endowment; in England, until recently, only the best pupils have been encouraged to work to capacity.

Whether the present rather feverish pulse of activity in the U.S.S.R. can be maintained without the present system of inducements and pressures is another question. At present it is assisted by an utterly false picture of the non-Russian world and by fears of encirclement and of attack. When these fears can be shown to be groundless, and when the Dickensian England of which Russian children read in school is found by the Russian people to be no longer in existence, then they will have less motivation for the strenuous, drab and rather deprived existence which they lead at present. They will expect less crowded conditions of living in their meagre apartments, more goods in the shops, more color in their clothes and, we hope, more collaboration and interchange in educational and cultural fields with England and other countries of the West.

In actual fact during the last five or six years there has been quite a lot of important educational visiting between England and the U.S.S.R. from university levels downwards. And at the time when this article was being written there were in England, on a six-week visit, fifty young men and women of about twenty-two years of age who were in their last year of preparation for teaching at the senior high school level. These young people, slightly more than half of whom were women, were staying in twos in residential teacher-training colleges. As all were training to be specialists in the teaching of English, there were no linguistic difficulties, and, especially towards the end of the stay, there were friendly, though frank, comparisons. For instance, some of the young Russians asked why, in this stage of the development of the world, English teachers-in-training are not compelled to continue the study of at least one modern language. They further asked why there is almost no Russian being taught in English schools or teacher-training colleges.

The explanation, of course, is the same as that offered for almost every feature of English education—it is just the way that English education grew up. France is our nearest neighbor, so French is the main language studied in schools with German a very long way behind and Spanish a vast distance behind that. But the young Russian critics are as justified as English student critics are of some weaknesses that they in their turn notice in Russian education.

Such educational interchanges as these can do nothing but good and the British Foreign Secretary, Mr. Selwyn Lloyd, has recently stressed that such cultural interchanges on a vastly greater scale, between the United Kingdom and the U.S.S.R., are essential as preliminaries to the establishment of lasting political understanding.

THE CONSCIENCE OF SOCIETY *

There is a wonderful passage in Plato's *Republic* where Socrates, well aware of the mutterings against him that were to culminate in the judgment of death passed upon him, discusses with his friend Adimentes the relations of teacher and pupils and of society and children.

"Do you hold the popular belief," he asks, "that here and there certain young men are demoralized by the private instructions of some individual Sophist? Does that sort of influence amount to much? Is not the public it-

---

* Henry Steele Commager in *Education for American Freedom* (Washington. D. C., Association for Supervision and Curriculum Development, 1954), pp. 1-15.

self the greatest of all Sophists, training up young and old, men and women alike into the most accomplished specimens of the character it desires to produce?"

"When is this accomplished?" asks Adimentes.

"Whenever the populace crowds together at any public gathering in the assembly, the law courts, the theater or the camp, and sits there clamoring approval or disapproval, both alike excessive, of whatever is being said or done, booing and clapping until the rocks ring and the whole place redoubles the noise of their applause and outcries. In such a scene what do you suppose will be the young man's state of mind? What sort of private instruction will have given him the strength to hold out against the force of such a torrent or will save him from being swept away down the stream until he accepts all their notions of right and wrong, does as they do, and comes to be just as they are?"

The young, Socrates pointed out 2,000 years ago, are the creatures of the environment which society creates for them. They reflect what they see, they echo what they hear. Their standards are formed by the standards of the society in which they live. If they should try to resist this torrent, society, as Socrates pointed out, will compel them to conform. What was true in Periclean Athens is even more true in a democracy. Our own schools, needless to say, neither are nor ought to be exempt from the pressures of opinion, from the standards and values of the society in which they exist, in which they are to serve.

Yet all of us know, too, the schools are not merely the mirrors of society, not merely reflections and echoes, not merely passive objects on which the very pressures of society work. Schools are in their own right makers and molders. In a democracy, in a homogeneous society, relations of school and society are harmonious. But it is not the function of schools merely to reflect, or to react, or to adjust to environment. It is not even the function of schools merely to achieve harmony. It is their function to improve and to create.

PRIMARY RESPONSIBILITIES OF DEMOCRACY'S SCHOOLS

Schools are not the only instruments of society, nor are they only the instruments of society. They are in one sense the conscience of society. Now, ordinarily, there is no conflict here. In a healthy society the schools serve the same interests and sustain the same values as do all other institutions, such as the church, or the press, or government itself. It follows that where the school seems to be out of harmony with society, where it works or appears to work at cross purposes with other instruments that form opinion, something is very much out of joint. Our own experience—it is well to keep in mind that it is a longer experience than any other people have—our own experience suggests that schools can and do serve well the interests of democracy and serve those interests best when they are themselves most democratic. That they serve well the interests of freedom and serve those interests best when they are themselves free. Our experience is that school and society flourished together harmoniously, and interacted with each other to produce that civilization which we now have.

Upon our schools we placed responsibilities heavier than those which schools in other countries had to bear. We required not only that they perform the familiar task of educating the young, but that they undertake mass education such as had not heretofore been attempted in the western world. We required, in addition, that they create and foster national unity, that they Americanize hundreds of thousands of children of foreign language background and culture, that they inculcate and develop democracy and equality, helping in the great, the unprecedented task of leveling the barriers of class and caste and religion, of language and religion.

These tasks the schools performed and, on the whole, well. With the solution—the partial solution at least—of older problems, has come not peace and serenity, but responsibility for a host of new problems that rush in on us like a torrent.

How then are we to prepare the next generation, the generations thereafter—for this is a continuous chain, each one linked to past and to future —help prepare them for the old familiar but ever new tasks, help prepare them to be Pilgrims and launch their own Mayflower? We must train them to keep the nation secure and intact, to protect its resources and to develop them, to cherish true Americanism and true loyalty—something very different from the shoddy behavior that masquerades so impudently as Americanism and loyalty in some quarters today. We must prepare the new generation for the new duties and new responsibilities that have come to us and will remain with us as a world power.

But there is nothing more misleading than to suppose that elementary and secondary schools can address themselves directly to these responsibilities. That they should prepare directly for the world of science, let us say, of atomic physics or for the world of international duties by training physicists, or by training for the international civil service. In education, certainly in elementary and secondary education, a straight line is not the shortest distance between two points. We cannot prepare the young for the duties of democracy in the way that we train them for automobile driving, or cooking, or typewriting, but we can expect that schools will function as they did in the 19th century, function to help fit young people to live in the new world. We cannot train them in all these specific skills they will need, but we can train them in philosophy or, if that is too formidable a word, in the right attitudes and duties and in the development of character.

Let us keep ever in mind that we can do this only in a favorable climate. Neither schools nor young people can run counter to what Plato calls the torrent of opinion. They cannot divorce themselves from their society and they should not. They must operate in a friendly and a favorable climate. They must fit in as part of the many-sided institution that makes for freedom and for responsibility. Almost all of us ask too much of our schools and too little of ourselves. The school can help, but it can help only if its own practices and teachings blend with those of society, of the home, of the economy, of all other instruments of communication. As President Harold Taylor of Sarah Lawrence College has recently written: "There are many things learned which are not taught and some which cannot be unlearned. Children catch their values through the atmosphere and are infected by courage or by cynicism, by love and hate, by generosity and meanness, by snobbery and kindness, by selfishness and unselfishness. The formal part of most college programs"—and he was writing chiefly of colleges—"has very little to do with such values and the life on the campus very much. Students are on the whole tolerant and liberal and wish to do what is expected of them in the matter of their attitudes, and they will fit themselves to the actual situation which the college arranges for them. Since liberal education is intentionally designed to liberalize and humanize each generation of young, it is essential that the social situation be congenial to these attitudes."

To Raise the General Intellectual Level

What then are some of the standards that society must maintain and inculcate if our schools are to perform the tasks we call upon them to perform? One of the essential tasks that our schools must perform is that of raising the general intellectual level—of encouraging brains. And this for the elementary reason that in the kind of world in which we now find ourselves we need brains. We need the expert, we need the intelligent public servant, the intelligent scientist, the intelligent social scientist, we need the poet and the philosopher. We can no longer be content with mediocrity, we can no longer go along with the second rate or leveling down intellectually when we level up socially and economically. Our schools must put a premium on intelligence. There is nothing undemocratic about this, needless to say; to develop an intellectual elite is no more undemocratic than to develop an athletic elite, or journalistic elite, or radio and television elite. We must learn to take brains in our stride as we take expertness on the football field and basketball floor, or the stage or the news room, or, we will all agree, in the symphony orchestra, in our stride. Let us then establish the category of brains on the same basis as we have established other categories. But it is not as simple as this. The schools cannot of themselves put a premium on brains if society does not put a premium on brains. And what is the attitude of society towards the intellectual? What do boys and girls learn at home, or in the newspapers—the comic strips perhaps—or over the radio, or on television? They learn in many places and many ways that intellectuals are at a minimum silly and at most dangerous. They learn that professors, for example, are invariably absent-minded and woolly, and that the expert is never as wise as the practical man. They learn that the term "Brain Trust" was one of contempt. When they grow old enough to concern themselves with practical questions, they learn that the teacher, the librarian, the scholar, are the lowest paid of professional workers—or perhaps of all workers. I do not suggest that the intellectual and the artist should expect handsome monetary rewards—certainly not rewards comparable to those we shower on the men and women who entertain us or who sell us tooth-paste or automobiles, but I do suggest that before we demand that our schools exalt the intellectual we compare our popular attitude towards the intellectual with that of the English or the French, the Swedes or the Danes, and that we do not ask the impossible of our schools.

The problem of the place of brains in our society is peculiarly urgent at the present time because we are witnessing not only a characteristic and traditional suspicion of the expert, but a wave of irrationalism that is without parallel in our past history. It is an irrationalism which threatens not only the intellectual, the scholar, the scientist and the artist, but threatens ultimately the whole educational system of the country. Irrationalism has engulfed ancient nations of the Old World, and contributed to their destruction—witness the terrible example of Nazi Germany—and we would do well to beware its ravages here.

To Inculcate Respect for Law and for Others' Interests

Another thing that we ask of our schools—ask rather stridently these days—is that they inculcate in the young a respect for law and for the interests of others—in short, discipline. The younger generation is, we assure each other anxiously, peculiarly undisciplined, and for this breakdown of discipline we tend to hold the schools responsible, or at least in part responsible. No one can, I think, reject the indictment. The younger generation is singularly undisciplined. But so, it is scarcely necessary to observe, is the older generation.

We cannot require or expect that schools teach discipline if society rejects and flouts it. What is the lesson that boys and girls learn—at home, on the roads, at the films, from the radio and the television, in the newspapers and magazines and comics—from almost every activity and institution? It is not the lesson of discipline, but the opposite. Our newspaper press gives us every day and in every city an object lesson in extravagance, sensationalism and disorder. Those hundreds of millions of so-called "comics" which we permit to circulate under the specious claim of freedom of the press but actually for business reasons, teach their daily lessons of violence, corruption and perversion. Our conduct at athletic contests—and I am referring rather to the adults than to the children—is all too often disorderly conduct. No one can walk through the streets of mid-town Manhattan without seeing overwhelming evidence of lawlessness and disorder in the nonobservance of parking and traffic regulations, and I suspect the situation is the same in other cities. We are not disciplined on the highways, not disciplined in conduct or in language. Our advertising, with its emphasis on exaggeration, on sensationalism, on the irrelevant and the salacious, is undisciplined. We are undisciplined, many of us, in our drinking habits, our eating habits, our playing habits. It would be a bold critic who would assert that our moving pictures taught discipline, that our radio dramas and soap operas inculcated discipline, that the necessity and dignity of discipline was the moral to be drawn from our television.

To Encourage a Habit of Enterprise

What else do we ask of our schools? We ask, do we not, that they put a premium on enterprise, particularly on private enterprise, that they inculcate in the young a habit of enterprise and an appreciation of it? What is the social climate here—the climate of enterprise? It is, I think, a misty and foggy one. For what is that private enterprise that our society appears to cherish, enterprise that it exalts in every advertisement, every radio broadcast, every editorial pronouncement, every manifesto of business organizations, of political parties? It is, of course, private enterprise in the economic realm. Valuable as such enterprise is—and who can doubt the role that it has played in our history?—it is, after all, secondary. The important enterprise, and in the long run the only important private enterprise, is private enterprise in the realm of ideas—private enterprise in the intellectual and in the spiritual realm. If our nation is to prosper and to progress, we must, at all cost, encourage private enterprise in these realms for enterprise here is antecedent to all other enterprise. I need scarcely remark that we are not doing this. On the contrary, we appear to be engaged in a major effort to frustrate enterprise in the intellectual and spiritual arena. Here is one of the paradoxes of your time, though by no means the only one, that we seem to think that we can have alert and lively minds, ingenious and experimental minds in the realms of the economy but conformist and acquiescent and apathetic minds in the realms of politics, or in the realms of art or science. You cannot divide up the mind in this fashion. You cannot have it lively on Monday, Wednesday and Friday, and dull on Tuesday, Thursday and Saturday. A society that encourages enterprise in the economic realm but discourages it in the intellectual and moral realms will soon discover that without bold and original thought and without criticism there can be no progress in any area, including the economic and the social.

We cannot expect our schools to inculcate the virtues of private enterprise if we do not allow intellectual enterprise to flourish even in the schools. We cannot expect our schools to train young men and women to think imaginatively and audaciously if we intimidate and punish imaginative and audacious thinking. We cannot expect to turn out those music makers and dreamers of dreams who make for progress in every generation, progress even in the realm of science and invention and mechanics, if we penalize thinking that does not conform to our dull notions of what safe thinking ought to be. Nor can we expect our school teachers and administrators to furnish examples of enterprise if we continue to discourage and harass those who show originality and enterprise. The discouragement of enterprise extends even to the young, and evidence is persuasive that students in colleges are increasingly taking refuge in prudence and caution—shabby virtues both of them, in the young. Many of the most articulate elements in our society would have teachers adopt the advice of Professor Worldly Wisdom in Butler's Erewhon:

"It is not our business to help students to think for themselves. Surely that is the very last thing which one who wishes them well should encourage them to do. Our duty is to ensure that they shall think as we do, or at any rate, as we hold it expedient to say that we do."

We must restore to our colleges and universities that atmosphere which Judge Learned Hand recalls and celebrates in the Harvard of half a century ago—and which still permeates that great institution:

"You gathered it unwittingly from uncorrupted and incorruptible masters, it was in the air—you did not need to affirm or proclaim it—you would have felt ashamed to demonstrate the obvious. You came to know that you could hold no certain title to beliefs that you had not won. Best of all, you were in the company of those who thought that the noblest of man's works was the pursuit of truth, who valued the goal so highly they were never quite convinced that the goal they had reached was the goal they were after, who believed that man's highest courage was to bet his all on what was no more than the best guess he could make, who asked no warranties and distrusted all such, who faced the puzzle of life without any readymade answers."

What else must we ask of our schools if we would be sure of a generation competent to the great tasks before it? We must ask that they encourage the young to respect the mind and things of the mind and the spirit, inculcate discipline and self-respect, and encourage free enterprise in ideas.

TO FOSTER EXPERIMENTATION

And in the fourth place we must ask that they encourage experimentation, for without experimentation there can be no progress and there can be no safety. Ours is peculiarly an experimental system. America itself the greatest of experiments, American nationalism, American republicanism, American constitutionalism, American democracy. The American system was set up on an experimental basis with this Federal system, with its provisions for experimental laboratories in every state. The American economy and the American educational system, even the American churches and American philosophy, have been peculiarly experimental in character.

Our schools and our societies must then encourage the open mind, because that is the traditional American habit of mind. And because only by the persistence of that habit of mind can we have any expectation of meeting new problems or working out solutions to old ones. We must encourage experimentation in science, because if we create a climate of opinion in which scientists fear to be experimental, or bold, or original— a Fort Monmouth climate—or if we require that they work only on approved projects, or if we intimidate them and harass them, we will end up with scientists who are incompetent and scientific knowledge that is inadequate. This is what happened, needless to say, in Nazi Germany, and it is one of the reasons that Germany lost the war.

We must encourage experimentation in politics because only if we realize that politics is not a closed but an open system, that there is room not only for improvement in the machinery but for new machinery and new principles, can we hope to adapt the existing political system to the problems we have to solve. We must try to be as bold and as experimental as the Founding Fathers; we must keep in mind Jefferson's warning against the spirit that fears and opposes "all change, stigmatizing it under the name of *innovation,* and not considering that all improvement is innovation, and that without innovation we should still have been inhabitants of the forest, brutes among brutes. Patience, pressure, as unremitting as gravity itself, can alone urge man on to the happiness of which he is capable."

If we close the avenues of political experimentation, either by imposing intellectual conformity on the civil service or by discouraging independence in our foreign service, or by such tightening up of the Constitution as is implicit in the unlamented Bricker Amendment, we will find that our political machinery will grind to a halt. Experience should teach us to leave to such countries as Germany, Italy, Spain and Russia and their imitators the self-indulgence of closed political systems.

We must encourage experimentation in the economy, because the heavy responsibilities that have come to us as economic leader of the Western World require that we keep our minds as we keep our machinery—flexible and resourceful. We must realize that if we equate the American system with private enterprise, and private enterprise with hostility to TVA or Federal Housing programs, or even to socialized medicine, we will saddle private enterprise with a very heavy burden and expose the American system to grave misunderstanding abroad, as we have already done. Here again we must not ask of the schools impossible things. We must not ask them to produce open-minded and experimental young men and women if the climate of public opinion is hostile to open-mindedness and experimentation. If we wish to assure that the next generation is indeed experimental, we must do more than pay lip service to the ideals of heterodoxy—we must put a premium on heterodoxy. We must reward nonconformity; we must create a climate of opinion in which the young naturally challenge the assumptions of the old, as well they might, and naturally embark on new enterprises, which they must, and use new efforts to achieve new goals. We must take this for granted in intellectual and social realms as well as in economic and scientific.

One of the gravest dangers which confront us today is the temptation to reject our tradition of experimentation, our tradition of taking risks, of gambling on the intelligence and the virtue of the American people. It is not difficult to understand the yearning for security that has swept over us in recent years, but if we suppose that we can achieve security by resort to the traditional and the dogmatic and the absolute, we gravely delude ourselves. If we suppose that we can exact guarantees from history and from God, we delude ourselves. We must avoid the habit—an infectious one—of exacting guarantees against all conceivable misadventures. We want guarantees that all our teachers in schools and all our professors in colleges and universities conform to our notions of Americanism, forgetting that those societies like Nazi Germany and Communist Russia that enforce conformity on educators make irremediable mistakes and those societies like the English and the Scandinavian and the Swiss and our own, which protect the freedom of the scholar and the student, survive and flourish. We want guarantees that our children will not be exposed to dangerous ideas, forgetting that all ideas are dangerous, and that only by familiarity with ideas can children ever learn to distinguish between the true and the false. We want guarantees that every immigrant is pure in character, and in mind, and in morals, and we subject every potential immigrant to most rigorous examination on these counts, forgetting that all of us are immigrants or the descendants of immigrants, and that neither the Puritans nor the Pilgrims with their long records of lawlessness could have received visas to come to America today. We want guarantees that all our organizations are patriotic and loyal in membership and purpose, forgetting that very few of the organizations that carried through the major reforms of history from the Puritan Church and the revolutionary Committees of Correspondence to the Populist party or the Committee to Aid the Allies in recent years, could pass the current tests. We want guarantees that no power granted in our Constitution can ever be abused, and distinguished statesmen point with alarm to certain potential abuses in the Constitution, forgetting that every power granted in the Constitution is subject to abuse, including the legislative and—most emphatically—the investigative.

Does all this mean that we are losing confidence not only in ourselves, but in the next generation? If so we can scarcely expect that the next generation will have confidence in itself—or gratitude to us! Does it mean that we are forgetting what we have heretofore known, almost instinctively, that each generation must validate old truth and discover new truth for itself—and that each new generation is just as capable of doing this as were past generations, or will be if we keep the channels of ideas open? Does it mean that we have forgotten that noble concept implicit in Isaac Newton's description of himself as a child sitting on the beach playing with sand pebbles while all about him stretched the great ocean of truth?

To Develop the Habit of Cooperation

Fifth, our schools should inculcate and encourage and develop the habit of cooperation, the habit of joining, the habit, if you will, of voluntary association. This they do almost inevitably for every school contains a dozen or a score of student organizations—societies, clubs, cooperative ventures of one kind or another. And the schools are, themselves, the special concern of what is perhaps the largest of voluntary organizations, outside one or two churches and a couple of political parties—the Parent-Teacher Association. Americans take naturally to joining—we are joiners by instinct and by habit—and it is well that this is so, for it is this way that our democracy has chiefly functioned: through private associations like churches, parties, unions, professional groups, reform societies, fraternal orders, and so forth. It is through such associations that our democracy must continue to function, and to flourish.

But the habit of voluntary association will not flourish if society becomes afraid of such association. It will not flourish if voluntary associations are to be suspect. It will not flourish if men and women have to be careful what they join because some, somewhere, somehow, might think their organization radical or subversive. De Tocqueville observed wisely, over a century ago, that "When some kinds of associations are prohibited and others are allowed, it is difficult to distinguish the former from the latter beforehand. In this state of doubt men abstain from them altogether, and a sort of public opinion passes current, that tends to cause any association whatsoever to be regarded as a bold and almost an illicit enterprise. It is therefore chimerical to suppose that the spirit of association, when it is repressed on some one point will nevertheless display the same vigor on all others, and that if men be allowed to prosecute certain undertakings in common, that is quite enough for them eagerly to set about them. . . . It is in vain that you will leave them entirely free to prosecute their business on joint-stock account; they will hardly care to avail themselves of the rights you have granted to them, and after having exhausted your strength in vain efforts to put down prohibited associations, you will be surprised that you cannot persuade men to form the associations you encourage."

As yet the fear of association has not reached down into the schools, but that it pervades the air on many a campus is inescapably clear. It may in time pervade the whole educational scene, the whole school system. Already we are witnessing efforts to require loyalty oaths from officials of Parent-Teacher Associations; if this is required there is logically no reason why the thing should not be carried to its ultimate conclusion, and loyalty oaths be required of all parents, and of all prospective parents. Let us beware lest we adopt positions that in the end discourage the very practice of private voluntary association. If that happens, we will have dealt the most serious of all blows to freedom and democracy in America.

To Encourage Pluralism

Sixth, our schools must encourage pluralism—it is a practice (I was about to say a virtue) closely related to the practices of enterprise and association. They must do this because ours is a pluralistic society, and because only through pluralism, through diversity and variety, can we hope to avoid the dangers of overcentralization, of uniformity, of the monolithic state. We have avoided this danger in part because the American system, beyond that of most others, is a pluralistic system. How, indeed, could it be otherwise in the light of our history? Our people are drawn from every race and every land, they worship God in the greatest variety of churches, and we have chosen a Federal system rather than a Unitary system of government. Given a nation as large as any other continent and with as many sectional and racial and religious and class interests as any continent, how else could we achieve unity but by leaving room for these groups and interests to balance each other out? Those wise men, Jefferson and John Adams and Benjamin Franklin, wrought better even than they knew, when they chose as the motto for this nation "E Pluribus Unum." Unity in diversity and diversity in unity—this has been the secret of

American unity, the encouragement of pluralism. The unity has grown from within—not been superimposed from without. It is well for us to keep in mind as we insist upon unity and conformity that those nations that have required and imposed conformity have broken apart and those nations like America and Britain, that have left room for diversity, have held together and have achieved unity in their own way.

Here again the times are not propitious. Our schools cannot encourage pluralism if our society discourages it. The climate of opinion in America is not propitious to diversity, it is one that calls rather stridently for superficial unity. From every side the pressure for conformity has become all but irresistible. The young, as every teacher knows, are natural conformists. All the dominant forces in our society are conformist forces—the radio, the movies, advertising, all the most powerful pressures create and maintain a monolithic culture. The very physical organization of our society makes for conformity and uniformity. Trains and automobiles, the regimentation of industry and the regimentation of business, the social organization of society all make for conformity. Much of the political organization of our society makes for conformity and for uniformity—pressure for colorless acquiescence in the civil service, in the Army and Navy, the standards involved in getting and keeping government jobs, or getting and keeping passports.

But at its peril our society must encourage diversity. Confronted by massive and pervasive pressures for uniformity, the teacher, the school administrator, the intellectual must address himself energetically and consciously to creating an atmosphere in which nonconformity and diversity and pluralism will have a chance.

To Cherish Freedom

Seventh, our schools must encourage freedom, and they can do this only in an atmosphere of freedom. They do not function today in an atmosphere of complete freedom. They function in an atmosphere clouded by fear. Teachers are distracted by loyalty oaths, by incessant investigations into orthodoxy, by supervision of what they read, of what they join, of what they say, and of what they think. Scholars are distracted by official and unofficial self-appointed censors who require their investigations and even their findings to conform to vulgar notions of loyalty or Americanism. Students—and this is perhaps the ultimate indignity—students are harassed and intimidated, induced to avoid controversy, to avoid joining, to avoid political activities, to suppress all their natural instincts of benevolence and liberalism and inquisitiveness and adopt the virtues of prudence and caution and conformity.

In this kind of atmosphere our schools cannot perform the grand purpose which they alone are capable of performing. It is not only the schools that will suffer, it is not only the teachers and scholars and librarians who will suffer, it is needless to say that the Commonwealth may suffer irreparable harm, for without freedom there can be neither security nor progress nor future freedom. If out of timidity, out of fear, out of suspicion, out of envy or hatred we start hacking away at our freedoms, freedom for the scientist, the scholar, the teacher, the student, we will in the end forfeit both security and progress. If the Commonwealth which we all cherish is to survive and prosper, we must encourage freedom in every realm—and above all the intellectual. If by silence in inquiry and criticism, if by training up a generation incapable of exercising freedom, or even knowing it, we fall into error here, the whole of civilization as we know it may go down into the abyss of defeat and destruction.

If our schools are to serve us in the future as they have served us in the past, they must inspire in the young the habit and the practice of freedom. They cannot do this unless they themselves practice freedom. They cannot raise up a generation dedicated to freedom if that generation learns by newspaper headlines, by radio broadcasts, from the arrogant speeches of Congressmen and the reckless acts of legislators, and the avengeful or misguided vendettas of patriotic and filiopietistic societies that freedom is dangerous and a thing of little worth. For it is useless to suppose that the moral of the current crusade is going to be lost on the young—they are brighter than we think. It is useless to suppose that we can stain and tarnish the spirit of freedom, yet have it emerge somehow bright and gleaming in the next generation. As Mr. Hutchins has somewhere said, "It is not necessary to burn the books, just let them go unread for one generation." Let us remember when we indulge a passion for reporting dangerous books or dangerous associations to the FBI, when we identify opposition to segregation or to the hydrogen bomb with subversion, let us remember the sober warning of William James that we cannot indulge in this kind of recklessness without doing ourselves irreparable harm. "We are spinning our own fates," he wrote—and he was a psychologist before he was a philosopher. "We are spinning our own fates—good or evil—and never to be undone. Every small stroke of virtue or of vice leaves its never so little scar." The drunken Rip Van Winkle in Jefferson's play excuses himself for every fresh dereliction by saying "I won't count it this time." Well, he may not count it, and a kind Heaven may not count it, but it is being counted nonetheless. Down among the nerve cells and the fibres the molecules are counting it, registering and storing it up to be used against him when the next temptation comes. Nothing we ever do in strict scientific literalness, is ever wiped out; and nothing we ever do in history, and nothing we ever do in morality, is ever wholly wiped out.

To Preserve and Protect the Community of Learning

There is another demand that we make—and should make—upon our schools, and especially upon colleges, universities, libraries, foundations, all of those institutions that come under the vague category of "higher learning." It is that they help to preserve and protect and advance the great community of learning—that community which knows no national or racial or religious boundary lines. Almost all scholars subscribe to the principle that science, scholarship, poetry, music—these products of the human mind and spirit—are not the possessions of a single people or nation, but of all peoples, and that if they are jealously preserved, they will dry up and wilt away. Yet here again there is something like a conspiracy to force scholarship into national molds. From all sides, but particularly from the political, come pressures to study along national lines. While one bureau of our government does notably foster internationalism in scholarship (I have reference to work of the Fulbright Commission of cooperation with UNESCO), others put impediments in the way of the exchange of ideas and of persons. Indeed there are some persons in high position who appear to think that dangerous thought can be stopped by refusing passports to the thinkers; they should keep in mind those words of Homer, 2500 years ago, that "words, winged words, they fly around the earth."

To Instil Faith

There is one final quality which our schools should encourage, which our society must encourage. It is one which, in a sense, is antecedent to and embraces all the others. It is the quality of faith—faith in our country, faith in our government, faith in each other, faith in our institutions, in our schools, faith above all in the next generation. But our schools cannot supply faith if we have lost it; they cannot instil faith if we repudiate it.

Within the last decade, within the last four or five years, many among us have given way to fear and suspicion and envy. That we should do this at a time when we had won such victory as shall wear sheer triumph out, at a time when we had achieved the highest standard of living known to man, the widest diffusion of enlightenment, the greatest degree of unity, world leadership—that at this juncture in our history we should have given in to fear and suspicion, to hatred even, will forever remain a puzzle and a wonder to the historian. It is well to remember that no great constructive program was ever based on fear. We have created an atmosphere of corrosive suspicion and no gentle people can be reared in an atmosphere of suspicion. We have substituted the vocabulary of passion for the vocabulary of reason, and no great sound policies can be formulated in this language. We have all but convinced ourselves—and others too—that our society is torn by dissension, wracked by disloyalty, convulsed by treason

—and if we ever come to believe that we will forfeit two hundred years of unity.

As Judge Hand said in that eloquent plea for a return to traditional habits that he made two years ago: "I believe that that community is already in process of dissolution where each man begins to eye his neighbor as a possible enemy; where nonconformity with the accepted creed, political as well as religious, is a mark of disaffection; where denunciation without specification of backing takes the place of evidence; where orthodoxy chokes freedom of dissent; where faith in the eventual supremacy of reason has become so timid that we dare not enter our convictions in the open lists to win or lose. Such fears as these are a solvent which can eat out the cement that binds the stones together and they may in the end subject us to a despotism as evil as any that we dread; they can be allayed only insofar as we refuse to proceed on suspicion, and trust one another until we have tangible grounds for misgiving." [1]

Is it not clear that if we continue in the paths so many of us are now following we will find ourselves in the end in some dark labyrinth of fear and ignorance instead of out on a high plateau of confidence and faith whence we can view the promised land of peace and of freedom? As there is no ruin like self-ruin and no prison like that we build for ourselves, so there is no peace, no prosperity and no security without freedom and without faith. This our forefathers knew, and they addressed themselves to the great task of building a Commonwealth which was to be the model for all others, the object of pride and love for those who lived under its benign laws. In that Commonwealth the public schools played a part of absolutely essential importance.

It is unworthy of us of this generation to impose upon schools a burden greater than they can bear. It is incumbent upon us to establish standards which may prove worthy of the emulation of the young, which may inspire them to greatness. We can provide our schools with the climate that will make greatness only if we ourselves show ourselves fit for greatness. If we exalt reason, enterprise, discipline, imagination, boldness, tolerance, pluralism, freedom and faith we may be sure that the schools will inculcate these things, and that the next generation will prize these things.

Almost 200 years ago a great English judge, Mansfield, forever disposed of slavery in that Kingdom with the words, "England is too pure an air for slaves to breathe." We in America must keep our air too pure for men of violence, men of hatred, men of fear, men of little faith; we must keep an atmosphere in which the next generation can grow healthy and virtuous— the atmosphere of freedom.

[1] Learned Hand, "The Future of Wisdom in America," *The Saturday Review,* 35: 9-10, 55-6, November 22, 1952.